Business economics:
A contemporary approach

Business economics:
A contemporary approach

Peter Earl & Tim Wakeley

The **McGraw·Hill** Companies

London Boston Burr Ridge, IL Dubuque, IA Madison, WI New York San Francisco
St. Louis Bangkok Bogotá Caracas Kuala Lumpur Lisbon Madrid Mexico City
Milan Montreal New Delhi Santiago Seoul Singapore Sydney Taipei Toronto

Business Economics: A Contemporary Approach
Peter Earl & Tim Wakeley
ISBN 0-07-7103920

 **Education**

Published by McGraw-Hill Education
Shoppenhangers Road
Maidenhead
Berkshire
SL6 2QL
Telephone: 44 (0) 1628 502 500
Fax: 44 (0) 1628 770 224
Website: www.mcgraw-hill.co.uk

British Library Cataloguing in Publication Data
A catalogue record for this book is available from the British Library

Library of Congress Cataloguing in Publication Data
The Library of Congress data for this book has been applied for from the Library of
Congress

Acquisitions Editor: Kirsty Reade
Development Editors: Emily Jefferson and Catriona Watson
Marketing Director: Petra Skytte
Senior Production Editor: Eleanor Hayes

Text Design by Pantek Arts Ltd, Maidstone Kent
Cover design by Ego Creative Ltd
Printed and bound in Great Britain by Ashford Colour Press Ltd

Dedication

We would like to dedicate this book to the following scholars, or to their memory. They have inspired us to seek a deeper understanding of how the world really works. It is because of their efforts that contemporary economics is something more than an esoteric science.

Philip Andrews
Alfred Chandler
Richard Cyert
Jack Downie
Neil Kay
Richard Langlois
Brian Loasby
James March
Alfred Marshall
Richard Nelson
Edith Penrose
Jason Potts
George Richardson
Joseph Schumpeter
George Shackle
Herbert Simon
Sidney Winter

Brief Table of Contents

Detailed Table of Contents

Preface

Once upon a time if you wanted to learn about business you would have been advised to study economics. It used to be pretty much your only option. Nowadays you will probably choose instead to study business administration or business studies and your only exposure to economics is likely to be a compulsory unit called 'Business Economics'. It is compulsory because it is seen as an essential foundation stone for the rest of your business education, so the content of this unit had better give you the opportunity to learn some useful stuff! That's exactly what this book aims to do.

Business economics in relation to other business disciplines

If you were free to choose, would business economics really be the sort of subject you would choose as part of your training in business? We think the answer is a definite 'Yes', because we also have experience of working in other business disciplines. This experience has led us to believe that if you can develop an 'economic way of thinking', you will be far better able to appreciate the issues that are dealt with in business disciplines such as accounting, marketing and strategic management.

In fact, these other business disciplines owe a great deal to economics. For example:

- Cost concepts in accountancy grew out of work by economists at the University of Chicago and the London School of Economics in the 1920s and 1930s (the current state of economists' thinking in this area of costs is explored in Chapters 5 and 6).

- Marketing as a field of academic research grew out of economics in the early twentieth century and the '4Ps of marketing management' (price, product, place and promotion) come straight from economics, namely from the theory of monopolistic competition (which is considered in Chapter 7).

- Modern work in strategic management theory draws heavily on economists' writings on industrial organization, which are considered in Chapters 8, 9, 10 and 11.

Why use this book rather than another business economics text?

From the outset, this book was designed to offer a very different approach to business economics from that presented in existing texts. This is because the authors, the publisher and many lecturers believe that you will be better served by a complete rethink of what a business economics text covers and how the ideas in it are presented. As a result this book offers a pluralistic approach to economics. What does this mean?

A typical textbook looks at business economics in terms of just *one* brand of economic theory and presents it as a definitive, finished product. This theory is typically called mainstream (or neoclassical) economics and it is what virtually all Western economists learn in their first few years of study (hence its 'mainstream' tag). The mainstream approach dates from the 1870s but the version employed today is largely due to the independent reworking of it in the 1930s and 1940s by Nobel Laureates Sir John Hicks in the UK and Paul Samuelson in the USA. It lends itself readily to translation into mathematical form, and thereby into numerical exercises that have definite answers. By contrast:

> A scientist who practises pluralism considers which problems are worth investigating and how to make sense of them in terms of more than one theoretical perspective and does not claim that any one perspective is definitive.

As pluralists, then, we will be offering you not just a taste of mainstream economics but also of non-mainstream approaches. We have grouped the non-mainstream approaches under the title 'heterodox economics' (contributions to heterodox economics come from the related approaches of behavioural economics, institutional economics, evolutionary economics and post-Keynesian economics).

Adopting a pluralistic approach is more intellectually honest than adopting a mainstream-only approach because it does not conceal the existence of alternative points of view. Nor does it fail to confront difficulties in one point of view that have led some economists to construct different ways of making sense of the world of business. With a variety of perspectives at your disposal, you should have a better chance of offering good advice when you get involved with real business decisions. You should at least be able to avoid coming to simplistic conclusions and be well equipped to challenge colleagues who offer them. But, as with everything in economics, this advantage comes at a cost. In this case, the cost is that it initially requires a bit more effort and can seem rather daunting.

Pluralistic thinking tends to be unsettling partly because we live in a world where engineers seem to create definite outcomes in the form of machines and appliances that work with a particular degree of reliability, and where managers are expected to be able to quantify everything. Most buildings don't fall down, and most large companies don't go broke. This probably gives the impression that a science such as economics, which has been around for a couple of centuries or more, should likewise be able to come up with black-and-white answers to economic problems. Here, by contrast, we are promising shades of grey: in other words, a world in which the best way to solve the problems of businesses will often appear to be debatable. It may take you a while to get used to this but the effort will be well worthwhile, because the real world of business – including the quality of engineers' designs and the numbers that managers work with – is *not* normally a world of black and white.

A good way to start coming to terms with this is to recognize that in other parts of everyday life things are, on a closer examination, not so black and white either. Despite this, and despite often having no formal education in the area in question, we do manage to develop an ability to argue about things, such as the quality of a politician's or sporting referee's decision, whether or not a film review was unfair or whether a friend has made a wise career move.

If you see the process of studying business economics as entailing gathering tools for arguing about practical problems, and honing up your skills in using them, and if you recognize that you are already quite relaxed about arguing about other debatable areas, then you should find you can proceed with confidence into this book. You should not feel worried that sometimes you may want to use ideas from one variety of economics to look at a problem, whilst at other times you would prefer to use other perspectives: it is a matter of 'horses for courses', of developing an eye for a suitable tool for the job at hand. Just be sure to reflect on whether your alternative tools give you grounds for being careful not to claim too much for the results you get with the tool you favour in the context in question.

The fact that your instructors have chosen to recommend this text should also inspire confidence that you will be able to handle the challenge of pluralism. Their recommendation is a sign of how seriously they take the pursuit of knowledge about business economics. Instead of resting easily with sets of notes used many times before and problems that have definite answers, they too are working that bit harder on your behalf. They are happy to do so in many cases because they know that the mainstream approach to economics is of limited use when it comes to dealing with many business problems.

Despite its limited use we do cover the essence of mainstream economics. We cover mainstream economics for three reasons:

♦ because at times it provides a useful starting point, so long as we keep an eye out for its limitations;

- so that you will know what others are studying;
- so that you will be able to cope with elective courses in other areas of economics where the traditional view dominates.

The organization of the book

The way we have organized the material in this book was inspired by the work of three great scholars who focused on the process of doing business:

(i)   Alfred Marshall, who taught economics at Cambridge University at the end of the nineteenth century.

(ii)   Joseph Schumpeter, originally from Austria, who taught at Harvard University in the middle of the twentieth century.

(iii)   Harvard University's Alfred Chandler, the most influential business historian of the past four decades.

Marshall was fascinated by the problems that new firms had in securing footholds in their markets, and by the problems that established firms had in remaining innovative and adaptable. Writing shortly after Charles Darwin's *The Origin of Species*, Marshall likened the competitive struggle of firms in an industry to plants competing in a forest ecosystem.

Schumpeter saw little hope for managers ever to be able to get a peaceful life. This was because he thought the essence of competition between firms was innovation, which meant that an innovation introduced by one rival would require the others to try and hit back with something even better. He called this the process of 'creative destruction' and also noted that entire industries could sometimes be thrown into turmoil by one innovation leading to many others related to it.

Whilst Marshall's vision seems to have been inspired by the rise and fall of family businesses of a relatively small scale, Chandler sought to document and make sense of the development of giant corporations from around 1870 onwards. These organizations, run by salaried managers rather than their shareholders, pioneered strategic decision making and worked out solutions to new kinds of problems, such as those of internal organizational design, long before academic theorists had much to say about them. Along the way, these firms developed new capabilities, both managerial and operational, that helped them expand both their scale and diversity of operations, and helped them to keep lobbing new competitive bombshells at their opponents.

As a result of the influence of these three great scholars this book has an unfolding plot. It is structured around the changing sets of problems that decision makers need to be able to solve at different points in time in order to:

(i)   get a firm started;

(ii) keep the firm in business in the face of growing competitive rivalry;

(iii) if they so desire, grow the firm into a much larger operation;

(iv) rejuvenate the firm in the face of declining demand.

In terms of specific content, Chapters 1 and 2 are essential grounding. In Chapter 1 we take you through some preliminary ideas that are essential for you to begin to see the world through the eyes of a pluralist business economist. In Chapter 2 we discuss markets and their limits and along the way introduce you to the idea of economic model building. Once again this is fundamental material.

Firms are created by entrepreneurs, so in Chapter 3 we take a good look at what entrepreneurs do and provide you with insights into what it really means to be an entrepreneur. We begin here with a detailed story of the early days of one of the world's most famous entrepreneurs – Sir Richard Branson. Despite the rather obvious importance of entrepreneurs in the economy you might be surprised to learn that it is unusual for an economics textbook to dedicate an entire chapter to them.

In Chapter 4 we examine how potential customers make their purchasing decisions. If an entrepreneur has had a business idea he or she will have to gain an insight into what makes customers 'tick'. It is usual in mainstream economics to paint a rather one-dimensional picture of customers, but here we explore their motivations and their decision-making processes in greater detail than a standard business economics text would bother to do. Like Chapter 3, this is an atypical chapter, but the material we cover here should be of more practical use to you than the typical mainstream economic analysis of the consumer.

Chapters 5 and 6 are complements in which we examine the kinds of knowledge and resources an entrepreneur needs to have access to in order to set up a business enterprise and the implications his or her choices have for the costs the firm will incur. We begin Chapter 5 with a detailed look at the story of the British entrepreneur James Dyson as a way of grounding the discussion that follows in a real world scenario. We hope that this will help you to see the kinds of problems real world entrepreneurs face in regard to their production decisions and their associated costs and also help you to see the limitations of a purely mainstream approach.

In Chapter 7 the mainstream approach is used to good effect to tell some simple stories about the kinds of things that need to be taken into account when the entrepreneur is trying to decide on a price for the firm's product. We also look at the heterodox approach which outlines the practicalities of the pricing problem that are glossed over in the mainstream approach. This chapter marks something of a turning point in the book because subsequent chapters feature much less mainstream economics.

Chapter 8 deals with the problem of competitive rivalry: before committing resources and taking the plunge into the market an entrepreneur will need to think seriously about how long the window of opportunity for making healthy profits will be open. Here we introduce the evolutionary theory of the firm and industry to gain deeper insights into how firms can earn persistent profits in a dynamic setting.

Having thought about the things covered in Chapters 4 through to 8 the entrepreneur will be in a good position to put together a business plan in order to seek funding for the new enterprise. This is the subject of Chapter 9. In Chapter 10 we examine how an established firm can grow (if the entrepreneur wishes it to) and in Chapter 11 we consider what an entrepreneur or management team can do in order to stave off decline in one or more of its lines of business, or alternatively how it can exit from a declining market.

In Chapter 12 we change emphasis from the more microeconomic focus of previous chapters by turning your attention to macroeconomics. Here we introduce you to a baseline macroeconomic model that you can use to understand big issues such as unemployment and inflation and to derive the likely implications for the firm. In Chapter 13 we explore some of the controversies that have cropped up in macroeconomics and, finally, in Chapter 14 we consider international trade, exchange rates and globalization and once again look at implications for the firm.

How to use this book

As befits an introductory text, we have tried to break up the economic ideas covered in this book into bite-sized chunks with simple chains of links in explanations of how they work. However, it is in the nature of economics, as a subtle subject that deals with complex systems of interrelationships, that sometimes a point-by-point explanation is not possible and, instead, it is necessary to grasp a set of connected points as a whole all at once. Because of this, you should not presume that you will be able to 'get' everything first time around. Some portions, be they sentences, paragraphs or entire sections, may require several attempts before they become clear.

The pluralistic approach is another complicating factor that will sometimes necessitate dwelling on a particular piece of the text, for sometimes you may find it possible to see one perspective on an issue but be totally unable to 'get' another one that is being presented. (The point here is the same as that illustrated by some famous ambiguous diagrams developed in cognitive psychology, such as a rabbit that can also be seen as a duck, or a picture of a wrinkled elderly woman that can also be seen as a beautiful young woman: many people can see one immediately but can only see the other interpretation if it is carefully explained to them, and it is hard to keep both in mind at the same time.)

An inability to 'get it' is not something that only afflicts students: many debates in economics persist because established ways of looking at the world get in the way of seeing another theorist's point of view. Often it is useful to get another person's point of view in such a situation, so don't be afraid to discuss with your lecturers or tutors any hurdles that you can't jump yourself.

Don't feel that asking for help is a sign of failure if you have had a serious go at cracking the problem yourself. After all, if teaching materials could be guaranteed to be completely transparent to students, there would be little need for the alternative perspective offered by the lecturer who has chosen to adopt a particular text. Teaching staff would far rather deal with important puzzles at an early stage, rather than try to pick up the pieces close to exam time after you have gone for weeks without having grasped basic points. We also strongly recommend that you form a study group with two or three others to help share ideas about possible interpretations of theory materials and coursework questions.

At the end of each chapter we provide 'recommended additional reading sources', normally including some brief notes on what particular readings have to offer. We do not expect that you will have the time to follow up most of these but we expect that from time to time you will be intrigued by particular ideas or will have an assignment that requires deeper knowledge of particular ideas. If so, these listings should make it easy to find out more. Like a conventional text in this Internet age, this book has its own website of materials to help you grasp the ideas it covers and get proficient in applying them. We hope you will enjoy using the materials there and find them useful.

Finally, we offer what may seem an unlikely piece of advice yet one that we think is very valuable: if you are trying to tackle questions about particular business problems or industries using theory from this book, don't initially try to gather a lot of information about the particular business or industry. Many students tackle case study problems by 'researching' them to find 'the' answer, only to end up scoring quite mediocre grades. The problem here lies in the difference between information and knowledge (which we discuss in Chapter 1). If you have a lot of information about what is actually going on, it is likely to get in the way of you using your knowledge of economic theory to predict what is likely to be going on. If you have a lot of information you are likely to write answers that involve using commonsense to organize this information without analysing it using economic theory. By contrast, if you have no information from research, all you can do is to try to use your knowledge of economic theory to tell a story about how things are likely to be under various assumptions. If you do this, you are doing economic analysis.

Peter Earl and Tim Wakeley

Acknowledgements

Writing a textbook is a lonely business, but along the way there have been numerous people who have provided us with help and encouragement (sometimes unwittingly!). We would especially like to mention: Stephen Brammer; Mark Grimmer; Eleanor Morgan; Andrew Millington; Paul Osborne; Julian Partridge; Jason Potts; Jennifer and Mike Wakeley. Also, the members of the University of Queensland's undergraduate and MBA business economics classes, and the students on the various business economics courses at the University of Bath, many of whom provided us with helpful feedback on draft chapters.

In addition, the book's final content has been shaped by the insightful comments received from reviewers of draft versions of the material and it is much better for it. Thank you to:

Steve Bradley – University of Lancaster
Martin Carter – University of Leeds
Douglas Chalmers – Glasgow Caledonian University
Roger Fitzer – University of Surrey
Frederick Hay – University of Glasgow
Geoffrey Hodgson – University of Hertfordshire
Debra Johnson – University of Hull
Gerald Steele – University of Lancaster
Harjinder Virdee – Southampton Institute
Pam Whisker – University of Plymouth
David Williams – Nottingham Trent University

Thanks also go to the team at McGraw-Hill – Kirsty Reade, Emily Jefferson, Eleanor Hayes and Catriona Watson.

Peter Earl and Tim Wakeley

Guided Tour

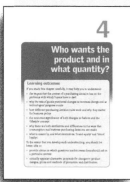

Learning outcomes

Each chapter opens with a set of learning outcomes identifying the key concepts that will be covered within the chapter.

Introduction

An Introduction sets the scene for the reader and introduces them to the issues that will be addressed in the chapter.

Important concepts/ideas

These are highlighted throughout each chapter and provide key points for ease of reference.

Illustrative boxes

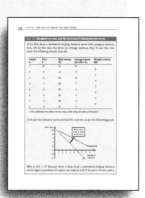

Extensions and applications are placed in boxes throughout the text in order to help students appreciate better the practical significance of the adjacent models and theoretical discussions.

Figures and tables

Each chapter provides a number of figures and tables to help you to visualize the various economic models, and to illustrate and summarize important concepts.

End of chapter summary

This briefly reviews and reinforces the main topics the authors have introduced in each chapter to ensure that students have acquired a solid understanding of the ideas covered.

Some questions to consider

End of chapter questions encourage students to review and apply the knowledge acquired from each chapter. The exercises range from short answer to longer essay-style questions offering a range of assessments for test and exam practice.

Recommended additional reading sources

A list of sources appears at the end of each chapter, pointing students towards books and articles that can explore the ideas in the chapter in further depth. The authors provide a brief synopsis of each suggested reading.

Technology to enhance learning and teaching

Online Learning Centre (OLC)

After completing each chapter, log on to the supporting Online Learning Centre website. Take advantage of the study tools offered to reinforce the material you have read in the text, and to develop your knowledge of marketing in a fun and effective way.

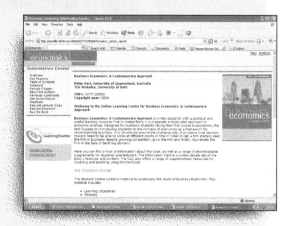

Resources for students include:

- Chapter by Chapter Learning Objectives
- Chapter by Chapter Self Tests
- Chapter by Chapter Crosswords

- Solutions to Review Questions
- Useful Web Links
- Glossary
- Specimen Exam Papers

Also available for lecturers:

- Lecture Outlines
- PowerPoint Slides
- Artwork from the Textbook

- Futher Reading
- Testbank

For lecturers:
Primis Content Centre

If you need to supplement your course with additional cases or content, create a personalized e-book for your students.
Visit **www.primiscontentcenter.com** or e-mail **primis euro@mcgraw-hill.com** for more information.

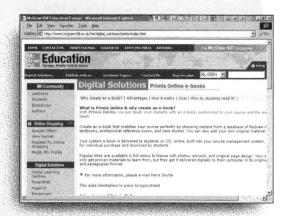

Study Skills

We publish guides to help you study, research, pass exams and write essays, all the way through your university studies.

Visit **www.openup.co.uk/ss/** to see the full selection and get £2 discount by entering promotional code **study** when buying online!

Computing Skills

If you'd like to brush up on your computing skills, we have a range of titles covering MS Office applications such as Word, Excel, PowerPoint, Access and more.

Get a £2 discount off these titles by entering the promotional code **app** when ordering online at **www.mcgraw-hill.co.uk/app**

Visit **www.mcgraw-hill.co.uk/textbooks/earlandwakeley** today

1

Introduction

Learning outcomes

If you study this chapter carefully, it may help you to understand:

- the nature of 'the economic problem' and what is meant by opportunity cost

- that economic analysis requires skill in knowing which questions to *ask* about the situation being analysed, not just ability to provide answers

- the differences between a variety of problems of information and knowledge that complicate the process of business decision making.

To the extent that you develop such understanding, you should be better able to:

- develop a willingness to embrace tasks that involve open-ended problems rather than ones that are 'black and white' with well-defined solutions

- enjoy studying business economics.

1.1 Introduction

In this chapter we are going to introduce you to some fundamental concepts that will crop up throughout the rest of the book. In writing it we have assumed that you have read the Preface to the book and so are familiar with the idea that we adopt a **pluralistic perspective**. If you have not yet read the Preface, please do so now. If you find that you are becoming confused by discussions in later chapters you might find it useful to revisit the material in this chapter in order to 'get back to basics'.

1.2 The economic problem

Economics is normally defined as **the study of how decision makers choose to allocate resources** between alternative uses. The resources in question can take a variety of forms:

- **Financial resources:** cash, bank deposits, loans and securities that might be sold to raise money.

- **Physical resources:** land, buildings, durable goods such as machines and appliances, tools and furniture, and perishable products such as food.

- **Human resources:** the decision maker's own time and skills, and those of other people whose efforts can be called upon by the decision maker.

Most resources are only available in limited quantities at any point in time: in other words they are **scarce**. The 'economic problem' centres on how to allocate these scarce resources in ways that do not leave a trail of missed opportunities for doing something better with them. For example, consumers have to choose between work and leisure, and between using their pay to rent or buy a home, to spend it on goods and services, or to save some of it in order to spend it at some point in the future. Likewise, governments have to choose between spending more on defence or more on education, social welfare, better roads and so on. In the process of using resources learning may occur, not merely when resources are devoted to education but also in the process of consumption and in organizations. The choices of how to use scarce resources today may thus affect the resources available to allocate in future (since the pool of skills available may change), and what people want to do with them.

Among the kinds of resource allocation decisions that people involved in business have to wrestle with are the following:

- Shall I work for someone as an employee, or shall I start a business and be my own boss?

- What shall we make?

- What production method shall we use – for example, shall we use human inputs or replace them with machines?

- How many units of each of our product lines should we produce and when should we stop producing something altogether?

- Should we set up a factory overseas?

- Should we make our own inputs or should we concentrate on assembling inputs purchased from other businesses?

- Should we market and distribute our product ourselves, or should we get another firm to do this on our behalf?

- Should we spend more on research and development rather than on marketing?

- Should we expand the size of our business by building a brand-new factory or by taking over an existing business?

Ways of addressing all of these **problems of choice** – and many more – are the domain of business economics. The economic analysis of choice begins with a very simple proposition: **everything has an opportunity cost**. In terms of every-day speech, this proposition is captured by the expression 'you can't have your cake and eat it'.

> The opportunity cost of doing something is the value you place on what you would have done if you had not been able to do what you actually chose to do.

If you have a piece of cake, it can either be sitting on a plate uneaten, or it can be inside you because you have eaten it; it cannot, in its entirety, simultaneously be both on the plate and inside your stomach. Where it is results from your choice.

Now suppose that, although you would rather eat the cake right now than leave it on the plate, you instead choose to give it to a friend: if so, the cost of the gift of cake is the value you would have derived if you had consumed it yourself right now. So, even if you did not have to buy the cake, the act of giving it to someone else has a cost. If you baked the cake yourself to give to your friend, then there is an additional opportunity cost to the gift: the time you spent bak-ing the cake could have been used to do something else, such as spend some time at the gym, or bake something else. Even from the cake recipient's stand-point, the cake has a cost: if they eat it, it gets in the way of eating something else at that time; if they choose to defer eating it, storage space is required. To put it another way, 'there's no such thing as a free lunch', *even when the gift carries no return obligations.*

Opportunity costs exist in the minds of those who incur them; they cannot be observed directly. If we cannot ask decision makers about how they see their opportunity costs in a particular context, economic theory may provide us with clues as to how they may be thinking. What determines a choice is how opportunity costs are seen at the time of choosing, but with hindsight they may look very different: we suffer regret when we realize just how much we gave up to get what we got, or we rejoice because we are surprised at how much we got and can now see how bad things would have been had we chosen the option we had judged was the next best thing.

So, the **hallmark of the economist is a focus on opportunity costs**, on different ways of doing things with a given set of resources. This involves being adept at lateral thinking as a means of expanding the menu of possibilities and it is not something that you will find yourself doing automatically in your first couple of weeks' studying business economics. But once you get there, you should find it easier to achieve high grades in other business subjects and you should gradually become able to analyse all manner of everyday situations and business problems in ways that are not available to the 'person in the street'.

As a student of business economics you will be developing skills that lead you automatically to ask:

- What does economic theory lead me to expect in this situation?

- Is there another way things could be, or could have been, done, or different ways of using resources?

- What does economic theory predict would be the likely costs and benefits of these alternatives?

In other words, how you see costs and benefits of particular actions will be shaped by your knowledge of economic theory; you will take nothing at face value; and you will develop a better understanding of the facts presented to you by questioning everything, even in situations where a firm is clearly being very successful.

1.3   An example of the 'economic way of thinking'

Let us take a simple example of how this superior question-asking ability of the business economist leads to an awareness of issues that the untrained eye might not notice. Our example is chosen quite deliberately to seem a long way from familiar territory for most readers and to have as its subject something that at first sight does not appear to be a 'business' issue.

Suppose you and a friend are backpacking around Australia after graduating and your friend is taken ill and ends up in the publicly funded Royal Brisbane Hospital. As a business economist in a foreign land, consider what you might think when, during a visit to your sick friend, someone comes around with a clipboard and cashbox and asks your friend if they would like to pay a particular sum to have the television above their bed connected for the next day or two and, if so, whether they would like to pay an extra daily sum to have access to the Foxtel cable television network as well.

A background in mainstream economics might lead you to consider how the number of days of television access requested by patients might vary depending on differences in prices that were charged, and which would be the most profitable price to charge given the costs associated with providing the service. This would lend itself very nicely to mathematical analysis if the relevant numbers were available. However, the kind of wide-ranging way of thinking that we are encouraging you to adopt ought to lead you to wonder about additional questions, such as:

- Who, apart from Foxtel, is making money from the television rental service – the hospital or some private company, or both?

- Would it be better for the hospital to own the televisions and cabling, and merely allow a private contractor to run the service?

- If a private contractor is involved, what kind of contract underlies the deal with the hospital – for example, how long a period does it cover, and is there some flat fee/daily royalty payment to the hospital? What sorts of arrangement would make the most sense from the point of view of the hospital and the contractor, and which would both find satisfactory?

- Should the hospital include some kind of price regulation in such dealings, given that the patients are dealing with a monopoly supplier and may not even be in a fit state to make rational decisions?

- Would it be a good idea to have the television hardware set up so patients can choose between rival providers of viewing access and cable channels?

- Might it not be less wasteful to have patients nominate their television preferences on the same form as they nominate their meal preferences, and to present them with a single bill at the time of leaving the hospital?

- Why not simply provide patients with free access to free-to-air television as part of the general range of services provided by the hospital at no specific charge, as part of the process of aiding the patients' speedy recoveries? And so on...

This example brings out two themes that you should keep in mind as you study business economics. The first is that the task of **managing** an organization basically entails **economizing**. This means trying to work out ways of improving a person's or an organization's well-being without wasting resources that are limited in supply and that can be employed in diverse ways and by different organizations. The example concerns decisions about strategic management – the range of activities the hospital is going to be involved with, and how it will be involved with them. However, managers wrestle with problems of allocating scarce resources at every turn, whether they are involved in forward planning or in solving unexpected problems, such as breakdowns, disruptions to supply, sudden changes in the business climate or product defects.

The second thing to note about the example is that it implies that expertise in business economics is relevant for those involved in **not-for-profit organizations**, such as public hospitals, every bit as much as for managers of a corporation such as General Motors or IBM. If we think further about the resource allocation problem faced by hospital administrators the issues that arise are basically the same as those faced by, say, a car manufacturer:

- Would it make sense to close down small regional hospitals and consolidate care in larger hospitals in major cities where specialist staff and equipment can be employed to full capacity? (Should manufacturing operations be consolidated into fewer, larger factories?)

- How many hip replacements should be sacrificed to do a heart transplant? (Would it be better to spend limited investment funds on improvements in engines or interiors?)

- Will better quality hospital food and cleaning services be available, and at lower prices, if these inputs are provided by independent contractors? (Should fuel injection systems be made in-house or purchased from another firm?)

So, although we might be somewhat nervous about hospitals hiring former car-industry executives for senior management positions, a requirement that medical staff should study for business economics or MBA degrees if they wish to become hospital administrators should not be seen necessarily as a sign that patients will be treated in a dehumanizing manner.

1.4 Problems of information and imperfect knowledge faced by decision makers

[T]here are known knowns; there are things we know we know. We also know there are known unknowns; that is to say we know there are some things we do not know. But there are also unknown unknowns – the ones we don't know we don't know.

US Defense Secretary, Donald Rumsfeld (2003)

Associated with our adoption of a pluralistic approach to business economics is an emphasis on how resource allocation is affected by problems of too much or too little **information** and **imperfect knowledge**. The resource allocation problem is not a problem merely because the supply of resources is limited. It is also a problem because decision makers often find it difficult to work out what to do with the scarce resources. This means they run the risk that they will waste them, with the result that they, or the people for whom they are working, end up being worse off than if it had been obvious what the consequences of making particular choices would be. Resources are difficult to allocate because decision makers suffer from a number of limitations in respect of information and knowledge. Because of this, it is often unwise to try, as a typical mainstream introduction to economics does, to reduce the resource allocation problem to a series of well-defined issues that assume problems of information and knowledge do not exist (you will see examples of the mainstream approach, which makes extensive use of graphical analysis, later in the book).

If this seems like bad news in terms of economics looking more complicated if it attempts to get to grips with problems of information and imperfect knowledge, the good news is that economics becomes a much more exciting and engaging subject once these problems are recognized. In particular, the decisions of entrepreneurs and business strategists can often seem quite heroic because, at the time of choice, the quality of the decision cannot be known and there is scope for things to turn out spectacularly well or go horribly wrong.

Let us now consider the forms these problems of information and knowledge take, as a foundation for the rest of the book. First, though, we must comment on the **distinction between information and knowledge** since these are terms that are often used interchangeably. We see knowledge as having a slightly different meaning from information and normally use knowledge in relation to an individual's **capabilities or understanding**, picked up from **experience** and shaped by the way the person looks at the world. A person can be given a piece of information and have no idea of its significance unless given many other pieces of information that enable it to be interpreted in context. **The person with**

knowledge has a way of linking pieces of information together to extract meaning from them or to be able to do something with them. Put it another way, you might see this book as containing a lot of information about business economics, but reading the book does not guarantee you will end up with a functional knowledge of business economics; such knowledge depends on what *you* make of the information we present here and the capacity *you* develop for using this interpretation to take business puzzles to pieces and suggest solutions to them.

1.4.1 Varieties of problems of information and knowledge

The definitions presented below deserve careful attention, for the terms that we differentiate are often muddled together in everyday speech. The examples that accompany them should help you further to see the rich array of problems that come under the broad 'information and knowledge' heading.

Risk

> A situation is said to be risky when the decision maker does not know what is actually going to happen at a particular point in time but does know the probability that a particular thing will happen – in other words, that it will happen with a particular frequency in a particular number of periods, or in a particular population.

For example, an insurance company does not know whether houses in a particular area will be flooded in a particular year, but it might expect the locality to be flooded once a century. Likewise, it may not know precisely which drivers in a particular risk category will have a crash resulting in a claim of a particular amount in the next year, but it typically does have a very good idea about the percentage that will do so. From this standpoint, insurance normally is not a particularly heroic kind of business.

Uncertainty

Many economists treat uncertainty and risk as if they mean the same thing. In this book, however, they mean very different things.

> Decision makers are uncertain when they are aware that they do not know what will happen in a particular situation or what could happen, or are aware that they do not know, or are unable to calculate relevant probabilities or that these are not relevant since they only get one chance to achieve a particular outcome.

An obvious example of an uncertain event is a third World War: such a war never materialized during the Cold War era despite many people worrying about it as a possibility. It might never occur at some point in the future; but then again, it might happen one day. We simply do no know whether such an event will occur and hence it is completely inappropriate to see it in terms of risk. Likewise, it does not make much sense to say 'I have a one in a hundred chance of getting this job' if you know that 99 other people have also applied: you either get the job or you do not. In any case, prospective job applicants often have little idea how many other applicants there will be. Even if the selection criteria for a job have been spelt out to potential applicants, those who apply may be unclear just how problematic it might be to fail to meet particular 'desirable' or 'essential' criteria, or how they will be seen in respect of them. Perhaps none of the applicants will have what is required, but how can any would-be applicant know?

The business of insurance becomes much more heroic when the business environment suddenly changes so that established probabilities are questioned and nasty surprises suddenly seem possible. This happened in the UK car insurance market in the late 1980s/early 1990s when thieves unexpectedly started taking large four-wheel drive vehicles for use as ram-raiding tools and there was a great increase in the theft of high-performance cars for joy-riding purposes. The insurance companies found it very hard to know whether these were temporary phenomena, or even whether they had yet seen the worst of what they should come to expect on a regular basis. Their lack of willingness to make heroic guesses led to some brands of vehicle becoming virtually uninsurable.

Ongoing debates about genetically modified foods and climate change are driven by uncertainty. The anti-genetic modification lobby worry about unspecified mutations and side-effects from consuming genetically engineered foods, while scientists with different models of climate change argue about whether we are definitely experiencing a new climatic trend and what is necessary in terms of reduced greenhouse gas emissions to stabilize temperatures. Sceptics deny the existence of these problems but cannot demonstrate this definitively. It is crucial to avoid errors here, since if the sceptics are wrong, some of the damage may be not be reversible for many generations, or not at all.

Ignorance

Confucius posed the question, 'Shall I tell you what knowledge is?' He answered, 'It is to know both what one knows and what one does not know.' In a state of ignorance, by contrast, as Donald Rumsfeld famously put it more recently, decision makers may have some 'unknown unknowns':

Ignorance is a lack of awareness of the limits to one's knowledge.

For example, consider the role of ignorance in determining a person's disappointment with a change of jobs. At the time of choosing to accept the job, the person might have worried about a number of issues only to find in the event that these worries were unfounded. However, there could have been nasty surprises due to things that they did not even consider at the time of the choice or in respect of which they perceived no uncertainty but which proved to be very different from their expectations (as in, 'I had no idea that ...'). The worries were caused by uncertainty, the nasty surprises by ignorance.

Although ignorance is often a cause of regret, its potential positive role as a source of rejoicing should not be ignored. Indeed, **it is possible that partial ignorance is an essential ingredient in bold decisions in the business world**: if entrepreneurs thought really carefully about the sheer range of things that could go wrong with their ventures, many of them might have decided against investing in particular schemes that actually proved to be successful.

If decisions are often made in a state of ignorance, then improved resource allocation may depend on developing a capacity to make the best of a situation, such as building **flexibility** into one's plans and ways of thinking. Flexibility comes, of course, at a cost and to know whether the cost is worth incurring decision makers need to have an idea of their potential fallibility in broad terms even if they cannot develop a capacity for uncovering specific kinds of uncertainty at the time decisions are being made.

Information asymmetry/information impactedness

A situation of information asymmetry is said to exist if parties to a deal differ in the amount of relevant information that they possess.

In many cases, this is a result of some people strategically 'keeping their cards close to their chest' rather than sharing information with those who need it. A person who is selling something may know more about it, from personal experience of using it, than the prospective buyer does, though sometimes it is the buyer who has a better idea of the nature of the product due to expertise in the particular market compared with the ignorance of the seller. Sometimes, a problem of asymmetric information can be resolved if the information-deficient party incurs costs of buying information from a third party, as when a person gets the Automobile Association (the AA) to inspect a car they are considering buying. But sometimes, like an impacted wisdom tooth, relevant information may be very hard to get at.

A state of information impactedness exists where one party to a deal judges that the other has relevant information which cannot be uncovered without a significant cost being incurred, or which cannot be uncovered at all.

For example, even the AA's mechanics may fail to discover problems in a used car, such as those that are of an intermittent nature or are only evident if the vehicle runs for a significant period of time.

Closely related to information impactedness is the notion of **opportunism**, which brings us close to the territory of **business ethics**, namely the study of the kinds of business behaviour that are morally appropriate in particular circumstances.

> Opportunism is the guileful, self-serving exploitation of an information advantage.

Opportunism is not just the preserve of some used-car sales people, or officials in firms such as Enron or Worldcom that for a time manage to use 'creative accounting' to keep their firms from appearing insolvent. It also occurs when workers perform below the maximum rate they would deliver if they were being monitored more closely, or when someone knowingly tries to pass to others the blame for a problem that has come about due to their own sloppiness or incompetence.

Information overload

While the absence or inaccessibility of information that could be relevant to choice may make decisions problematic or cause regret, decisions can also prove difficult because seemingly relevant information is very easy to come by. Compared with super-computers, **human beings can only process information slowly**: in most situations we can do the equivalent of answering no more than about ten 'yes' or 'no' questions in a second. (Skilled musicians and typists can identify notes or letters rather faster than this by seeing groups of them in chunked form.) Added to this is the limiting factor known, after cognitive psychologist George Miller, as **Miller's Rule:** we can only keep in mind 7 ± 2 things at once.

> Information overload is the term used to describe situations in which decision makers have access to so much information that they cannot reach a decision at all, or can only reach a decision by consciously or unconsciously discarding some of the information and focusing on the rest.

With many decisions, such as the task of buying a car or a house, or deciding which worker to hire from a thick pile of applications, we tend to face more than 'about seven' options and each option tends to have multiple dimensions, so we are likely to suffer from information overload. In principle, shopping via the Internet enables us to avoid missing opportunities due to ignorance, but it opens up massive scope for information overload as we try to keep in mind all the things that we discover to be available.

Tacit knowledge

One person's ability to make a decision or undertake a task may be hampered by the limited ability of someone else to spell out something of relevance to that task. The person may know what they want, or how to do something to a high standard, but have trouble putting it into words ('It's sort of like...'). If so, we say that there is a problem of tacit knowledge.

> Tacit knowledge is knowledge that a person may be willing to share with others but which they cannot articulate in a manner that accurately conveys it in a manner that other parties can grasp. This includes situations in which people are able to perform a particular task but do not know how they do so.

Many things require a 'knack' and even if we have it, we don't always know what it entails; we just perform the task automatically, without even thinking. Teachers face the tacit knowledge problem frequently, whether they are trying to teach a subject such as business economics or rocket science, or are merely trying to show someone how to ride a bicycle, play a musical instrument or swim.

In business, tacit knowledge can be an issue in terms of marketing communications (getting across a message about the nature of the product or understanding what customers want), transferring established technology to new branches of a firm, or in licensing technology to another organization, and getting the best out of workers who have recently joined a business. Often, the tacit knowledge problem can only be overcome by working alongside the mentor who has the expertise (**'learning-by-doing'**), or spending time getting to know a client's situation to find out their needs.

Bounded rationality versus global rationality

Taken together, these problems of information and knowledge lead to a view of decision makers as acting with what Herbert Simon, winner of the 1978 Nobel Prize in economics, called **bounded rationality**.

> A person is said to be acting in a boundedly rational manner when they are acting purposively and trying to make good decisions despite the fact that it is impossible for them to know what the best decision would be in the circumstances because they are not clear what their circumstances are or what the problem they face really is.

From the standpoint of much of the heterodox economics used in this book, it seems reasonable to see the idea of economizing as being about what Herbert Simon called '**satisficing**' behaviour – in other words, it is about how people try to find **satisfactory** solutions to perceived problems and meet particular **performance targets**. If a target seems to be impossible to meet, then from this standpoint it seems perfectly reasonable to lower it. On the other hand, if targets seem to be easy to meet, then it seems to make sense to set them a bit higher, using a simple rule as the means of judging when and how much to change them.

Mainstream economists, by contrast, prefer to characterize economic problems as if decision makers can formulate and solve them in an optimal manner – in other words, as if decision makers can see the whole picture and are 'globally rational'.

> Global rationality is said to prevail in situations where decision makers face well-defined problems (certain or, at worse, risky in the sense of having known probabilities), with a well-defined set of possible solutions, and can identify these problems at the right time and work out the best thing to do in respect of whatever their goal happens to be.

Given the list of problems of information and knowledge that has just been presented, this may seem rather unlikely in reality.

Few of the economists who assume optimizing behaviour and global rationality would deny the challenges that decision makers have to deal with when allocating resources. Rather, the conventional wisdom is based on a 'survival of the fittest' idea. Skilled decision makers who set out to maximize profits or those who happen, purely by chance, to maximize profits will drive out of business those who merely set themselves workable targets and adjust those targets up or down in the light of what seems to be possible. In other words, in the jungle of the market, optimal behaviour drives out satisficing behaviour.

Behavioural and evolutionary economists do not accept this line of thinking. They point out that to survive in a competitive arena one does not have to perform at the highest possible level. All one has to do is to match current **performance standards** on average and be able to keep raising one's standard as rivals raise theirs. (Note that to be a world champion runner it is not necessary to run as fast as is humanly possible, merely to run faster than all the others who choose to compete at that time.) Indeed, if decision makers try to cope in the face of problems of information and knowledge by applying simple 'rules of thumb' or following conventions so long as these deliver acceptable outcomes, they might even do better in some situations than they would if they tried to address a problem by unravelling it in all its complexity. If the decision-making environment is changing rapidly, a business that can take **adequate decisions** quickly might outperform businesses that spend a lot of time gathering information and arguing over the best course of action to take, for by the time the latter have worked out the ideal course of action, the situation will have changed.

1.4.2 Factors that generate problems of information and knowledge

Arguments amongst economists about whether to assume optimization/global rationality or satisficing/bounded rationality are essentially about how to do economics best/get by in doing economics, given the complexity of the subject matter. (Note the irony here in relation to the mainstream position!) The mainstream perspective keeps economic analysis relatively simple by assuming that most of the time the situations that decision makers face are straightforward enough to be seen as if they are well defined. The heterodox perspective takes seriously real world complications such as:

- uncertainty about the timing and extent of technical progress in the future;
- the sheer variety of products available;
- uncertainty about which technology will become the dominant system;
- exchange rate uncertainty;
- uncertainty about government policy, actions of terrorists, lobby groups, etc.;
- the need to make predictions about the actions of competitors whose pricing or capacity expansion choices will affect the profitability of the firm's market;
- the need to predict the reliability, loyalty and pricing of supply-chain participants, whose behaviour will affect a firm's costs and sales;
- problems in predicting the climate, earthquakes and other states of nature, and discoveries of stocks of natural resources;
- uncertainty about the direction and timing of changes in fashion;
- uncertainty about how fast consumers and employees can learn;
- uncertainty about how much should be spent on advertising and on research and development, given that the payoffs to these areas are inherently hard to assess;
- uncertainty faced by workers regarding how hard is it necessary to work to keep one's job or win promotion;
- quality uncertainty: the problem of judging if one is being sold a 'lemon';
- the principal–agent problem, of knowing whether someone acting as agent is doing what they have been asked to do/acting in the interest of the person for whom they are acting;
- uncertainty about relative prices and the future rate of inflation;
- uncertainty about where the good deals are to be found in terms of price right now;

+ uncertainty about the confidence of other firms and consumers and hence their willingness to spend.

This is a formidable list, and as this book unfolds you will see that it accounts for many kinds of economic behaviour and modes of organization that are prone to be neglected in purely mainstream approaches to economics. Indeed, in his 1984 book *The Emergent Firm*, economics professor Neil Kay has gone so far as to suggest that very little is left of the firm if we strip away functions of firms that would not be needed in a world with no information and knowledge problems. Out go:

+ marketing;

+ finance (accounting information systems, auditing, etc.);

+ research and development;

+ all workers except for direct labour;

+ any differences between workers in terms of their skills and experience;

+ internal organizational structures;

+ head office, except for the entrepreneur who hires factors of production and decides what to produce, how to produce it and what price to charge for it;

+ all non-profit maximizing behaviour.

All that remains is the entrepreneur, capital and homogeneous labour – which are the elements of traditional approaches to production theory (see Chapter 5). Kay, by contrast, prefers not to lose touch with reality and asks his readers to accept his suggestion that: 'Economics is about the role of information in resource allocation. All economic problems are reducible to problems of information. In the absence of information problems there is no economic problem.' (Kay, 1984: 1)

1.5 Summary

This chapter is an important foundation stone for the material we will be covering in the rest of the book. A central concept is the idea that all choices can be seen in terms of their opportunity costs. Another central concept that we will reiterate throughout the chapters that follow is that human decision makers are boundedly rational. Very often we will begin a chapter by looking at problems as if bounded rationality was not an issue, but then we will modify our analysis to see what impact the introduction of problems of information and knowledge have on our understanding of the topics under discussion.

1.6 Some questions to consider

1. Examine the resource allocation problems faced by senior managers in the police service. What kinds of choices do they have to make, and what aspects of the police 'business' make these decisions difficult to take? (As part of preparing for this, you might find it useful to watch a television programme such as *The Bill* and reflect on the economic aspects of the drama.)

2. Economists formally define 'opportunity costs' in subjective terms, as the next best thing a person imagined doing if they couldn't do what they actually did. This makes them difficult to observe. Even so, economists may be able to help people take better decisions by advising them on what their opportunity costs might be. If someone asked you for advice on how to work out the 'cost' of owning/running a particular car, what advice would you give? How would your advice differ if you were giving it to people of different ages?

3. Explain how you would make use of the opportunity cost concept in the following contexts, and as you do so note what makes it difficult to assess the relevant opportunity costs:

   (a) As a manager considering how to deal with underperforming staff and when considering what to do when key personnel announce their intention to resign after being offered a better deal elsewhere.

   (b) As a marketing manager designing a marketing strategy.

   (c) As a homeowner trying to decide whether to do a kitchen upgrade and install double-glazing.

   (d) As a health service administrator advising a new Minister of Health on the essence of resource allocation problems in the healthcare area.

1.7 Recommended additional reading sources

The limitations of the 'survival of the fittest' justification for assuming optimizing behaviour were originally explored in Armen A. Alchian (1950) 'Uncertainty, evolution and economic theory', *Journal of Political Economy*, **57**, pp. 211–21. The strange story of how Alchian's article was used to justify the mainstream perspective instead is told in Neil M. Kay (1995) 'Alchian and "the Alchian thesis"', *Journal of Economic Methodology*, **2**(2), December, pp. 281–6. Kay's paper is a warning about the need to check original sources rather than relying upon second-hand information.

For a perceptive and very readable examination of the importance of problems of information and knowledge in the economics of industrial organization, see Neil M. Kay (1984) *The Emergent Firm*, London, Macmillan. The chapter 'Entrepreneurial Salome' is particularly recommended at this stage.

If you are also studying marketing then you may find it interesting to take a look at John O'Shaughnessy (1984) *Competitive Marketing: A Strategic Approach*, Boston, MA, Allen & Unwin. It is a thoughtful, frank account of why marketing is (like business economics) a subtle subject with no easy answers, in contrast to the impression given by better-known texts.

2

Markets and models

Learning outcomes

If you study this chapter carefully, it may help you to understand:

- why resource allocation sometimes takes place inside organizations and sometimes involves interaction between organizations (and individuals) in markets

- what is meant by 'comparative advantage' and how it leads people and firms to specialize

- what is meant by economic co-ordination and why specialization can lead to co-ordination problems

- how the 'invisible hand' of the price mechanism guides the allocation of resources

- what is meant by an 'economic model'

- the difference between a '(force-)field' view of the economy and a 'complex systems' view

- what is meant by a 'market', the social role that markets play and why government regulation of markets is sometimes necessary

- why firms exist.

To the extent that you develop such understanding, you should be better able to engage in discussions about:

- the assumptions used in economic models

- the need for state intervention in markets and the benefits of market deregulation.

2.1 Introduction

As you know, this is primarily a book about the economics of setting up and running a firm, but before we can proceed with our analysis in subsequent chapters we need to **solve a puzzle: 'Given that setting up and running a business is a process fraught with difficulties, why do people with ideas for making money bother to set up firms to put those ideas into practice?'**

Most of us avoid the difficulties of building a firm by working for a business or organization that someone else has set up. People with ideas for profit-making ventures can, and sometimes do, *sell* them to other people or to other businesses. Many firms are started by people 'jumping ship' from their employers and trying to capture rewards from their ability to see profit opportunities; they can use their experience as a basis for creating their businesses and may even turn into major competitors of their former employers. But despite the scope for doing this, much new business activity results from people employed within established businesses having ideas that are then implemented by those businesses. In the latter cases, the firms may grow but those who had the ideas may not receive any particular reward except, perhaps, promotion: for them, thinking of how the firm that employs them might expand its scope may be one of the things they are paid to do as, say, 'business strategists'.

To understand how business ideas get put into practice and why new firms get set up, it is necessary to recognize that **firms operate in the context of markets** and involve an alternative way of allocating resources to that provided in markets. Inside a firm, a **hierarchy of managers** allocates resources by asking/requesting/ordering more junior managers and other employees to perform particular tasks in conjunction with particular items of equipment and goods and services purchased from other businesses. Though many of these requests are nowadays given by internal memos and via email, this method of determining how resources are used is essentially a **voice mechanism** in which instructions flowing down the hierarchy from person to person are the outcome of a process of planning how the resources should be used. In a market, by contrast, it is how buyers and sellers respond to changing patterns of relative prices that determines who ends up using resources and the purposes for which they get used. Hence economists typically speak of the **price mechanism** when discussing how markets work.

The dividing line between firms and markets and voice and price mechanisms for allocating resources is actually a bit fuzzier than this. For example, when consumers complain in an effort to improve the deal they get, we have the voice mechanism working in a market; in such a situation they are not simply taking their money elsewhere to get better value. Markets also exist, to a degree, inside organizations, as when different branches of a multinational corporation bid against each other to supply another branch of the firm with a particular input.

Recognition that the price mechanism can be used instead of the voice mechanism for allocating resources leads to a variation on our opening question: 'Even if people with ideas for ways of making money don't simply sell them to others, why do they bother to create firms as vehicles for getting them implemented rather than seeking to get this done by doing deals in markets?' After all, if they adopt the latter approach they avoid having to pay managers for allocating resources.

With some products, such as bicycles and Windows-based personal computers, what actually happens is rather close to the market situation: many bicycle and PC manufacturers don't really manufacture most of what they sell. Instead, they assemble components bought from firms that specialize in making hard disk drives, motherboards, pedals, tyres and so on. A typical bicycle firm nowadays makes only the frames of its bicycles, while many PC makers even buy their equivalent of a frame – the computer's casing – from another business.

In many other product areas, resource allocation involves a much bigger role for managers relative to the market: for example, Rupert Murdoch's News Corporation controls a vast web of print and electronic media companies, film studios and so on. Indeed, the growing reach of Murdoch's empire and other gigantic firms, whose turnovers exceed those of many national economies, suggests that the benefits of non-market systems of resource allocation can be considerable in some contexts.

We will be addressing the question of why businesses take such different forms much later in this book, during Chapters 9 and 10. But we need to understand the nature of markets in terms of what they are, how they work, and limits on how well they work, right now, and not merely to answer the question with which this chapter began. Otherwise, it will be difficult in Chapter 3 to get to grips with what economists have had to say about entrepreneurs, the people who start and shape businesses. The present chapter thus explores these questions. In doing so, it uncovers some major differences between the ways that the different brands of economics view markets. For this reason, it seems a good place to explore the general nature of economic model building, using the modelling of markets as a case study of how economists can end up with very different models of a particular feature of the world in which we live. First, though, we consider a point that is shared by economists in general, the idea that markets come into existence because people see gains from **specializing** in what they do and then **trading** with each other.

2.2 Specialization

The person in the street may have no training in economic theory but often has good economic intuition, as with the idea that 'you can't have your cake and eat it'. Another example of this economic intuition is the maxim: 'If you need to get something special done, call in a specialist.' This familiar piece of advice is consistent with the economist's notion of '**comparative advantage**', which is in turn an application of the idea of **opportunity cost**. However, the person in the street may often be thinking in terms of what the economist would call '**absolute advantage**' when discussing why differences in skills mean that it makes sense to specialize and engage in trade. It is vital that you take the time to see the difference here, for without an appreciation of it there will be difficulty in understanding why a person, or a firm, that is better than other parties at doing a multitude of things may still find that it makes sense to specialize and trade with the others.

First, we will illustrate the concept of absolute advantage. Suppose that an accountant can unblock a drain in four hours and do the accounts of a plumber in two hours, and a plumber can unblock a drain in one hour but takes three hours to do her accounts. If so, it will probably pay for them both to stick to their respective professions. By not taking up time unblocking his drain, the accountant can do the accounts of two plumbers, and a plumber can unblock three drains in the time freed up by getting an accountant in to do her accounts. If they do not specialize, then in four hours' time the accountant will have just finished unblocking his drain and the plumber will have unblocked one drain as well as having done her accounts. If they specialize, then in four hours the accountant can complete a second accounting task and the plumber can unblock four drains. The gain from trade and specialization is thus the ability to produce in the four hours one extra lot of accounting services and two more unblocked drains.

The economist's more sophisticated 'comparative advantage' basis for specialization focuses not on absolute differences in ability to undertake a particular task, but relative differences in ability to perform different tasks. To illustrate this, let us change the numbers in the example such that the plumber is better than the accountant at both unblocking drains and doing accounts. The accountant's situation is as before, but now the plumber can unblock drains in one hour and do accounts in an hour and a half. If they both continue to specialize in their respective trades, then in four hours' time the plumber will have unblocked four drains and the accountant will have completed two accounting tasks. If they do not trade with each other, then in four hours' time the accountant will have just finished unblocking his drain and the plumber will have done her accounts but only be halfway through unblocking a third drain. Failure to specialize reduces output in the four-hour period by half an unblocked drain and one accounting task. In short, if everyone specializes in the things they are relatively good at doing and then exchanges the output for things that other specialists have produced, everyone could be better off than if they operated as generalists.

The comparative advantage story of the gains from trade is based on several major **assumptions**:

- There is **full employment** – in other words, there is sufficient demand for the services of both the plumber and the accountant to keep them both working as specialists for as long as they wish each week.

- **Relative capabilities are fixed**. In practice, relative capabilities can be changed via education, having more practice and so on. Just imagine what would have happened if Japanese business had continued to specialize where it had a comparative advantage a century ago, rather than setting out to learn how to make advanced industrial products that it could have imported from Europe and the USA. In the short run, Japanese attempts to make such products came at the cost of poor productivity and low quality (as the comparative advantage analysis would lead us to expect), but in the long run Japanese firms were able to match or get ahead of those in the West.

- People will always attempt to make the most of potential gains from trade. Sometimes, however, they may have reasons for foregoing such gains. For example, they may derive a sense of achievement from doing a particular task themselves, not merely from the end result – 'It took me ages, but, hey, *I* did it!' – and in a world of change may recognize the **strategic advantages of being multi-skilled**, of not 'putting all their eggs in the one basket'.

- There are no **evaluation costs** or **monitoring costs** – in other words, no costs of making sure that the specialist is able to do the job and actually does do it. The numbers in these kinds of examples would look very different if customers found it necessary to take time to give the specialist access to the relevant site or documents and then had to keep an eye on the specialist to make sure the work got done.

To the extent these assumptions seem unrealistic, we may wonder how far the comparative advantage analysis of specialization is giving us the right answer for the wrong reasons. But, even if we do that, there is no getting away from the fact that many people and businesses do choose to specialize rather than try to be self-sufficient in all areas where they need to get things done.

2.3 Scope for failures in economic co-ordination

Specialization brings potential for people to be better off than if they adopt a 'do-it-yourself' approach to life. However, because it involves social interaction in the presence of problems of information and knowledge, it also brings the risk of **co-ordination failures** such as the following:

- Buyers cannot find what they want, when they want it, at a price they are prepared to pay, even though this price is greater than or equal to the cost to society of producing it.

- Communication failures lead to the delivery of the wrong goods, or of **system components** that do not fit together.

- Breakdown or late delivery in the **supply chain** disrupts the flow of production elsewhere.

- There are so many suppliers in a market that 'normal' rates of return cannot be achieved.

- Uncertainty about **product standards** leads buyers to hold back until an industry standard is established.

- Organizations fail to improve their operations due to failures in **feedback mechanisms**, as in cases where customers simply stop buying and take their business elsewhere, rather than voicing complaints about particular shortcomings of the firm in terms of price or product standards.

A self-sufficient individual living as a recluse does not have to worry about the problems just listed. By contrast, **craft workers**, who produce things from start to finish, have to worry about selling their output to someone else – but otherwise they can 'be their own boss' and not have to worry about fitting in with others. The craft worker can perform some stages in a production process in a leisurely manner on some days but not others, or not work at all some days and work long hours on other days, as he or she chooses; there is no need to keep an eye on the clock and the pace of production.

The co-ordination issue impinges much more on the lives of employees working in a factory. They cannot work effectively if others do not provide inputs of particular goods and services at the right time, and if they fail to perform as their managers expect, then other employees further down the production line will be unable to perform their own roles in the production chain.

Clocking on and keeping an eye on the clock and output requirements made life much more stressful for workers in the factory systems that emerged in the Industrial Revolution, but without such discipline and a steady work pace, production costs would have been much higher, with higher inventories needing to be carried as buffers to enable production to keep going when some workers were running behind or were absent.

Figures 2.1 and 2.2 (inspired by Axel Leijonhufvud, 1986) may help clarify the significance of specialization for the management of supply. In both cases, production entails four stages and four workers. In Figure 2.1, each worker makes the entire product, but paces the production process differently; different workers may opt to work very different working hours. In Figure 2.2, by contrast, each worker performs only one of the stages, according to who can perform which task most efficiently: Dick just does cutting, Tina just does machining, Harry just does polishing and Sue just does painting. For all the workers to be fully employed, they must be able to pass their output on to the next worker just when it is finished and at the same time receive the inputs on which they need to work.

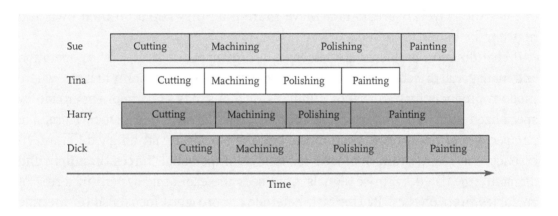

Figure 2.1 Crafts production

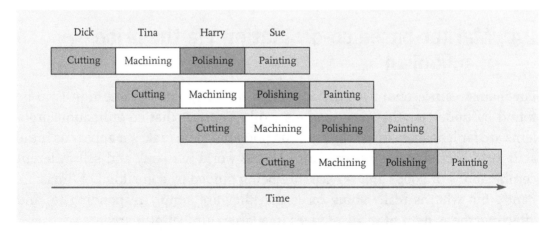

Figure 2.2 Factory production

Clearly, a factory in which people did as they wished, when they wished, could be completely chaotic. But at least if the factory were quite compact, each worker might get some sense of the consequences of his or her actions for the performance of the enterprise as a whole. They would also be able to **communicate** readily with each other and work out ways of **co-operating** to achieve mutually beneficial outcomes. Within a larger business, the co-ordination problem tends to be resolved more by a **hierarchical management system** in which managers (planners) tell workers (doers) what needs to be done. Being a member of a sizable organization in the long term means being generally willing to do what the boss asks. To the extent that workers forego the chance to be their own boss and accede to someone else's demands they must be enjoying some benefit associated with the improved co-ordination that bosses bring, despite the bosses absorbing some of the value that the organization generates. In an important sense, the boss is rather like the coach of a sporting team – someone who enables the players/workers to achieve more than they could on their own and hence to be better rewarded.

If co-ordination problems are lessened in organizations largely by co-operation and managerial direction, how are they kept in check in the economy at large, where modern products may consist of hundreds or thousands of components made by specialized suppliers and possibly sourced from all over the globe? Here, the perspectives of mainstream economists and their rivals are strikingly different. In essence, the mainstream approach focuses on impersonal '**forces of supply and demand**', mediated by '**price signals**', and sees the economic system in terms of analogies from physics. By contrast, heterodox approaches focus also on the role played by **relationships** and **social institutions** and have a vision that, if it resembles any of the physical sciences, looks rather more like chemistry or ecology.

2.4 Market-based co-ordination via the price mechanism

For mainstream economists, the answer to the co-ordination question is to be found by understanding how markets work. The fact that co-ordination problems are far less acute than they have the potential to be makes it appear as if the actions of over six billion people around the world who buy and sell different combinations of goods and services are being guided by some kind of 'invisible hand'. But what is really going on is that they are simply responding to, and affecting, the pattern of relative prices in a large number of markets.

2.4.1 The mainstream view of 'a market'

The standard definition of a market is a place where buyers and sellers of goods and services meet in order to trade with each other.

Note that this definition interprets the word 'place' in a very general way. It does not necessarily refer to a specific or identifiable geographical location. The most obvious examples of this lack of geographical location are provided by the virtual markets for a variety of goods and services located on the Internet. If you order a book from Amazon.com you will conduct your trade in a market located in 'cyberspace'.

2.4.2 How markets work

How does a market work? This short question has a long answer, so we will develop it gradually. A market for a specific good or service can be thought of as consisting of two sides. On the one side of the market are people we will call **buyers** or **consumers** who have wants or needs. Some of these will be procurement officers of firms and other organizations who need to obtain goods and services used in the production of other goods and services. On the other side of the market are people who we will call **suppliers** who offer goods and services for sale. When the goods and services offered for sale by suppliers coincide with the wants and needs of consumers the two sides will wish to **trade** with each other.

Trading involves an **exchange** between the members of each side. Purchasers give the suppliers a money payment in return for taking over ownership and custody of the particular good or service being traded. To help with our explanation we will consider in some detail the hypothetical example of buying a lunchtime hot dog from a street vendor. It may be helpful to imagine yourself in the role of the hot dog consumer.

When you buy a lunchtime hot dog from a street vendor you give the vendor cash and, in return, the vendor gives you ownership and custody of a hot dog. The amount of cash you give in exchange for the hot dog is called its **price**. (This may seem to be stating the obvious but we bring in the notion of price in this way to try to preclude confusion between price and cost. It would be incorrect, in economic terms, to say that the amount of cash handed over is the cost of the hot dog, since if you had been unable to buy the hot dog, 'whatever else you would have done with the money' is the opportunity cost of the hot dog. You might have bought something else, or decided to forego lunch altogether and hang on to your money for the moment. The best alternative is the 'opportunity cost' of the hot dog to you.) The price you will pay for the hot dog depends upon a number of factors.

If we assume that you are happy with the quality of the hot dogs being offered for sale (maybe because you have purchased one from this vendor before, or a friend has recommended her to you, or the vendor has let you taste a sample), then, from your perspective as a potential consumer, one of the prime considerations for buying a hot dog will be whether it is worth the vendor's asking price. In other words, does the hot dog represent good value for money to you? In order to decide whether or not something is good value for money you can ask yourself the question, 'What is the highest amount I am prepared to pay for this good or service?' So, if you are prepared to pay a maximum of £3.00 for the hot dog but the vendor is selling the hot dog for less than this, say £2.50, then it represents good value for money to you and you will be willing to buy it. Note, however, that when the hot dog vendor set the asking price she had no idea that you would have been willing to pay up to £3.00 for the hot dog. The valuation you have formed in your head is said to be **subjective** because it is based upon your own feelings, tastes and opinions (see Chapter 4 for a more extensive discussion of tastes).

It is reasonable to assume that you are not the only hungry person at lunchtime, so the hot dog vendor might expect to serve more than one customer. Other potential consumers will be asking themselves the same subjective value-for-money question that you have asked yourself, but because we are all different from each other some of these potential consumers may place a lower value on the hot dog than the asking price and, as a result, they will choose not to buy from the vendor. On the other hand, others may share your valuation of the vendor's wares or even value them more highly and so choose to purchase a hot dog for lunch at a price of £2.50.

The problem for the hot dog vendor is to set an asking price that allows her to attract a sufficient number of consumers to make being in the hot dog business worthwhile. Given that the hot dog vendor cannot have direct access to the subjective valuations of potential consumers she can only arrive at a suitable asking price by a process of trial-and-error price setting in the market. For example, if she sets a price that is too high, sales will be low and the vendor will have to reduce her price in the hope of attracting more consumers to her stand. Alternatively, if the vendor finds herself swamped by orders and is unable to provide every consumer who wants one with a hot dog, the asking price may be too low. In this case an increase in the asking price should lead to some of the consumers deciding not to have a hot dog for lunch.

Summary so far:

♦ When setting asking prices the vendor responds to a signal from the market.

♦ The signal to which the vendor responds is the number of units sold.

♦ The number of units sold reflects the collective decisions of consumers about whether or not to purchase hot dogs at the current asking price.

♦ Each individual consumer bases their own decision upon a comparison between their subjective valuation of the hot dog and the actual current asking price.

You should note here that the vendor acts upon **observable data**, namely, the number of units sold. While it would be nice to know precisely what subjective value each potential consumer places upon the hot dogs being offered, the collection of such data would be extremely time consuming. It may also be impossible, for the simple reason that potential consumers may be unwilling to reveal this data directly or honestly. We can conclude, therefore, that the collective data fed back from the market to the vendor is a very important source of **information**. Obtaining reliable information is crucial to the success of any business because without it decisions are very hard to make.

Our explanation of prices up to this point has been kept relatively simple by the **implicit assumption** that you, and other potential consumers, go to the same vendor when you want a hot dog lunch. If we include now the possibility that the hot dog vendor has several rivals who sell hot dogs of similar quality it means that the potential consumers of lunchtime hot dogs will have a **choice** of vendors. In this case, in order to get the best deal on a hot dog, the sensible consumer will **search** through the vendors in the **local area** in order to find the lowest asking price. The consumer will then compare the lowest asking price to his or her subjective valuation of a hot dog and choose whether or not to make a purchase.

At this point you may well be thinking that the addition of rival vendors to the story makes the original vendor's pricing problem a little more complex and, to a certain extent, you are correct. This is because now the original vendor may lose sales to lower-priced rivals, even if her asking price is less than the subjective valuation of hot dogs held by a significant number of potential consumers. For example, if your own search reveals a rival who is asking £2.00 for a hot dog of equal quality to your original vendor (whom you will recall is asking £2.50), you would be sensible to buy your lunch from the rival's stand because you will save money.

Does this wider choice for consumers change the basic way the original vendor makes use of the market to obtain information about the price consumers are willing to pay for her hot dogs? The answer is 'no', because the vendor can still use a process of trial-and-error pricing and respond to the number of units she actually sells at a particular price by adjusting the asking price downwards in order to sell more hot dogs, or upwards in order to sell less. There is no reason to change this trial-and-error approach even in this more complicated market that contains rival vendors. In other words, the market **signal** (the number of units sold at a particular price) is as useful in a world with rivals as it is in a world without rivals. Put another way, **the market is like a scientist's laboratory**, because every exchange with consumers can be thought of as part of a **process of discovery** that will give rise to new data.

If you compare this story to your own fast-food buying experiences you will probably be puzzled by the fact that price changes you have observed in the fast-food outlets in your local area occur relatively infrequently. So, how can we reconcile the story of apparently continual price adjustment being told here with the facts as we know them from our observations of the real world? Put slightly differently: does the process of price adjustment by individual vendors mean that consumers will face continually changing hot dog prices and therefore have to keep buying their lunch from different vendors every day or will the going price for a hot dog settle down to a stable level? In order to help us arrive at an answer to this question we will construct a **model** of the hypothetical hot dog market to see where the process of trial-and-error adjustment of prices leads us.

> A model is nothing more than a simplified description of something, an approximation to the more complex aspect of the world it represents.

The model that we construct attempts to present a simple picture of how mainstream economists would see this sort of market. As you work through the explanation of the model outlined in Section 2.5 below you will probably want to ask several questions because of the assumptions we have made. This is good – we would encourage you to develop a critical approach to things that you read – but do not let your questions stop you reading through to the end of the section. Instead, note your questions down and compare them with our discussion of the model in Section 2.6.

2.5 A mainstream model of the hot dog market

We will keep things simple by making the following assumptions:

(i) There are four hot dog vendors, who we will label V1, V2, V3 and V4, who compete with each other for business in the local area. Each vendor supplies an identical hot dog to its rivals.

(ii) The cost to each vendor of making a hot dog is £1.50.

(iii) There are 14 potential customers in the local area. We will identify each customer by assigning him or her a letter, A through to N. Each customer's subjective value of a hot dog is listed in Table 2.1. Note that the hot dog vendors do not have direct access to the information contained in Table 2.1.

(iv) Trade takes place on a daily basis and each vendor decides on the current day's asking price in response to the number of units sold on the previous day.

(v) Each consumer searches his or her local area thoroughly every day and buys a hot dog from the vendor who has the lowest asking price on the day, but only if this asking price is less than or equal to their subjective valuation. If two or more dealers share the lowest asking price consumers will be shared equally between them.

We can use this model to analyse typical decisions that each vendor will make on each day of trading.

Day 1 To get things started we will let each vendor set an asking price that is arbitrary because they currently have no information about the market upon which to act. Let us say the following asking prices per hot dog are posted:

$$V1 = £2.20; V2 = £2.30; V3 = £1.90; V4 = £2.00$$

Table 2.1 Consumers' subjective evaluations of a hot dog

Consumer	Subjective value (£)
A	2.60
B	2.50
C	2.40
D	2.30
E	2.20
F	2.10
G	2.00
H	1.90
I	1.80
J	1.70
K	1.60
L	1.50
M	1.40
N	1.30

When the consumers search for their lunchtime hot dogs they will discover that vendor V3 has the lowest asking price. Given the distribution of subjective values in Table 2.1 we will expect customers A through to H to purchase a hot dog from V3. Customers I through to N will not buy a hot dog. Vendors V1, V2 and V4 will not sell any hot dogs.

Day 2 Clearly vendors V1, V2 and V4 will set a different asking price today in an attempt to attract some customers. V3 has no real need to set a different price although she could lower her price in order to try to increase the number of consumers visiting her stand. Also, V3 will probably have talked with her customers and found out that V1, V2 and V4 were charging higher prices yesterday and are therefore likely to reduce prices today. Similarly, V1, V2 and V4 may well have learned what price V3 was charging yesterday and will take this as a starting point for their decision today. Note that there is no unique answer to the pricing problem for each vendor at this stage so let us see what happens when each charges the following prices:

$$V1 = £1.70; V2 = £1.60; V3 = £1.80; V4 = £1.50$$

When consumers search the local area today they will discover that V4 has the lowest asking price, so V1, V2 and V3 will sell no hot dogs. V4 is asking a price that attracts customers A through L, so he will sell 12 hot dogs.

Day 3 V1, V2 and V3 will have to reduce their asking prices today if they wish to sell some hot dogs. V4, however, will be quite happy with a price of £1.50 even though a further price cut will probably tempt more consumers to buy a hot dog. You should note, however, that V4 has no incentive to carry out a further price cut, because if he did this every hot dog would be sold at a loss. If we assume that V1, V2 and V3 have somehow discovered the price being charged by V4 yesterday they will be able to work out that their only choice now is to ask a price of £1.50 also. Just like V4, none of the others has an incentive to reduce prices below £1.50 because nobody wants to sell hot dogs at a loss.

Today then, V1 = V2 = V3 = V4 = £1.50. At a price of £1.50 each firm takes an equal share of the market (three consumers each) and none of them has an incentive to adjust their prices up or down in the days that follow. A price reduction by any vendor will lead to losses while price increases will lead to zero sales. The process of market competition has given rise to a stable market price.

2.6 Further discussion of the hot dog model

We have just introduced you to your first economic model. Business economists use many models to help them understand things better so it is important that you learn how to use models properly too. Many people find this aspect of business economics difficult to understand, but our discussions with students over the years have revealed to us that this is mainly because they find it very hard to believe that an 'unrealistic' model can provide us with meaningful insights about the real world of business. This problem arises because when we look at the world around us we see that it is a fairly complicated place and this leads some people to ask, 'Shouldn't economists' models describe this world in detail?' Let's use the hot dog model to explore this question.

The claim we have made for our hot dog model is that it illustrates how interactions between consumers and suppliers in a market will give rise to a stable price. We have arrived at this conclusion by telling a very simple story devoid of intricate details. For example, we have:

- labelled consumers with letters from the alphabet rather than identified them with real people who have particular names and particular jobs or careers;

- failed to name the hot dog vendors and provided no details about their reasons for being in the hot dog business;

- not stated which town or city the consumers and vendors live in.

Ask yourself, 'Would the inclusion of these details make the story about how a stable price came about more believable?' The answer is 'No'; the inclusion of these descriptive details would add nothing useful to our analysis, in fact they would probably clutter it up and make it more difficult to concentrate on the issue under investigation.

When building models the skill you must master is to include only those details about the problem under investigation that are relevant. Put another way, if you build a model of something, you should look at it when you have finished and ask if you could cut away any element of the model without destroying the essence of the story you are telling. This practice is known as applying **Ockham's razor** (also called Occam's razor) after a fourteenth-century English philosopher called William of Ockham.

Ockham stated that if it is not necessary to introduce complexities into arguments then you should not do so. In other words, Ockham's razor is a logical tool to help you cut the fat from your models and arguments. This means that we should not seek to build models that are realistic in the sense that they are full descriptions of the real world, but instead we should try to build models that capture the **relevant features** of the real world. This brings us to a discussion about the role of simplifying assumptions in our models.

When we built the model of the hot dog market we listed several assumptions that helped us to define the model. In particular we made assumptions about how the human actors (the consumers and the suppliers) in the model would behave. Recall that the actors in the model spend time and effort gathering information and base their decisions about what to do upon this information. Given that we have built the model to provide us with some insights into the consequences of interactions between real world consumers and real world suppliers in real world markets, we must ask ourselves if the assumptions we have made are sensible.

We discuss the particular assumptions of our hypothetical hot dog market in greater detail below, but you should bear in mind that the single most important test of relevance for our model is whether the modelled human beings are behaving in a manner that is consistent with what we know about the characteristics of real human beings. The other assumptions such as the cost of producing a hot dog, the number of consumers in the market and the number of hot dog vendors are important too, but only because they help to explain the features of the environment within which the modelled actors make their decisions.

Clearly, the results of the model we have built and the conclusions we derive from it will depend crucially upon the assumptions we have made, so if we find that some of the assumptions are not very sensible we may well be right to worry about the usefulness and relevance of the model. This point is very important more generally because business economics is a **normative** subject. This means that we study business economics in order to work out how we *should* act when we manage businesses of our own, or when we offer consulting advice to other business managers. So, if we have based our understanding of how a market works on a model of a market which has questionable relevance to a real world market of interest then any action we take when we use this particular real world market, or advice we offer to others when they use this real world market, is likely to be badly flawed.

You should note that when you use a model to help you understand some aspect of the real world you are said to be **applying** it, and it is highly unlikely that a single model can be applied to all real world cases. For example, we are not claiming that our simple model of the hot dog market can be applied to the market for motorcycles in the UK, although it may provide us with a useful starting point. In different applications you will almost certainly have to modify a basic version of the model to make it more relevant to the specific case you are looking at. Don't worry – we'll be giving you plenty of examples and practise at applying models as you work through the book.

Let's examine the assumptions of the hot dog market model in turn to see if they seem to be sensible. We will start with assumption (v) because it describes how the consumers in the model behave and then we will work through the other assumptions in reverse order.

Assumption (v) states that consumers **search** their local area on a daily basis in order to find out which of the hot dog vendors has the lowest price. The first question we might ask here is why consumers are searching their local area. The answer is to get hold of information so that they can make a decision. A possible alternative to this assumption could be to state that consumers are simply given this information. This would seem to be an unreasonable assumption to make in the context of the hot dog market because it would mean we have to either add another actor to our story (someone who spends their time giving out information) or, alternatively, postulate that human beings have some kind of all-seeing psychic connection to the vendors and, as a result, receive automatic updates of their respective asking prices. So, the statement that consumers search for suitable information seems to make sense. However, we have provided no details about how these consumers make their searches. Do they walk to each vendor in turn, take a bus, look up the information on a suitable website, ask their friends, or phone the vendors? It does not really matter which of these methods is used for the purposes of our example here because we are building a model to examine the consequences of search behaviour, not the actual detail of the search behaviour itself. It would only matter if we were building a model to explore the implications of different kinds of consumer search behaviour. We will be doing this in a later chapter, but here we can apply Ockham's razor to good effect.

The final point to note about assumption (v) is our statement that consumers search their local area. We do not define the boundaries of this local area explicitly, nor do we need to; the statement is there to indicate that consumers do not carry out searches over a large area when they decide they would like a hot dog. For example, if you were an office worker in the centre of London and were looking for a lunchtime hot dog you would probably not devote too much time and energy to your search activity and as a result would not search the whole of London, nor would you make a 150-mile road trip to Manchester on the off chance that the asking price for a hot dog may be lower there! The general idea of locality is important because it defines the extent of consumers' search areas and this in turn helps us to identify the boundaries of markets. We will show you later in the book how different types of goods and services have different sized localities and how some of these can be global in scale.

Assumption (iv) states that trade takes place on a daily basis, with each vendor choosing the current day's asking price based upon information revealed from yesterday's market experience. This assumption introduces us explicitly to the concept of **time** in economic models. Taking account of the passage of time is important, because when a hot dog vendor chooses a price his action will have effects in the market that will lead to consequences for the vendor, the vendor's rivals and consumers. These consequences will only become apparent as time passes.

This means that when we examine markets it is important to ask how long it will take for the consequences of specific actions to become apparent. In the example here, we have arbitrarily decided that each vendor makes a decision on a daily basis, but we might just as easily have decided to model the market for hot dogs by assuming that each vendor makes a new pricing decision every hour. For example, if a vendor sets a price and after one hour has sold no hot dogs then this vendor may well decide to reduce the asking price at the end of this hour. In other words, the vendor may respond to the signal he has received from the market in a much shorter time period than the one we have used in our example. The other vendors may act in a similar fashion. We have predicted above that the process of competition will lead to stable prices by day 3, so what does this new story, where vendors' decisions are made hourly, lead us to conclude? Well, the same process of price adjustment will hold true, only now the stable price of £1.50 may be reached sooner because vendors are responding more frequently to market signals.

By changing assumption (iv) we do not alter the final outcome of the model and we do not change the basic story of vendors responding to signals from the market. This means that for our current purpose, which you will recall is to explain the basic elements of the market process, the units of time that define the vendors' decision period can remain arbitrary and we can accept that assumption (iv) is reasonable. So, when we look at a real world market does taking account of the passage of time really matter? The answer to this question could only ever be 'no' if all we were interested in was the end result of the competitive market process described here. But this is not all that we are interested in. **Real world business activity takes place in real time** and it is important for us to understand that, for various reasons, not all markets in the real world reach stable prices as quickly as the hypothetical hot dog market we have been discussing here. This means that we should always try to understand the timing of the events taking place in any market, as well as understanding where the series of events is likely to take us. It is particularly important because the usual aim of people who run businesses is to make as much profit as possible and the **window of opportunity** they have to do this in may be only brief and occur before a situation of stable prices has come about. We will return to this issue several times in the book.

Assumption (iii) states that there are 14 potential consumers of hot dogs. Assuming that only 14 potential consumers exist is, of course, a teacher's technique to help make our job of explaining things to you as easy as possible. In the real world if only 14 potential consumers existed for hot dogs it is highly unlikely that anyone would bother to become a hot dog vendor! We could have stated that 14 000 potential consumers of hot dogs existed in the local area with 1000 of these sharing consumer A's subjective value, another 1000 sharing B's subjective value and so on, but at the end of the day we would still tell the same story about how prices converge to the stable level because the underlying **principles** of market adjustment discussed above would still be the same. This is not to say that the number of consumers in a market does not matter generally but, *for our current purpose*, we have used Ockham's razor to trim away superfluous complexity.

We have also applied Ockham's razor judiciously to assumptions (ii) and (i) for exactly the same reasons that we have applied it to assumption (iii). We could modify assumption (ii), for example, by assuming that each vendor has a different cost of production from its rivals, or we could have assumed that a vendor who sells more than two hot dogs enjoys some cost savings on production of the third and fourth hot dogs and above. Alternatively we could have assumed that each firm produces a given number of hot dogs at the start of the day and any that remain unsold have to be stored until the following day at some cost. We could modify assumption (i), for example, by assuming there are more than four vendors, or we could assume that new vendors enter the industry on day 2, or that one vendor offers a higher quality hot dog than the others. All of these modified assumptions are reasonable, but once again *for our purposes* they add unnecessary complications to the model.

Where we might want to worry about the assumption that there are only four hot dog suppliers is if questions get asked about whether we are making any further assumptions that are not explicitly stated. For example, we have said nothing about the possibility that the hot dog sellers might collude to try to push up the market price, yet **collusion** might be argued to be more likely if there are only a few suppliers who need to get together to work out a joint strategy and keep an eye on each other to ensure it is followed. So perhaps we have been implicitly assuming that collusion is illegal (as it normally is) and the hot dog vendors are all law-abiding.

Other charges that we have been making implicit assumptions might also be raised. If one vendor were wealthier than the others, she might have the resources to drive the others out of the market by setting a price below £1.50. The others might take a while to go (to know how long, we would need to introduce assumptions about their expectations regarding the duration of this vendor's strategy, their wealth and opportunity costs). Even so, such a **predatory pricing** strategy might be worthwhile if the subsequent increase in profits exceeded the value of wealth sacrificed whilst selling hot dogs below their production cost. Perhaps we are implicitly assuming that the four vendors have equal wealth, or that predatory pricing is illegal, as it often is (cf. the battle between Virgin Atlantic and British Airways), or that ethical concerns get in the way of such behaviour.

In this section we have discussed the model of our hypothetical hot dog market in some detail and we have shown that competition between hot dog vendors for the patronage of consumers leads to the emergence of a stable price. Economists usually refer to this stable price as the **equilibrium market price** to reflect the notion that once it has been reached it will not change unless the specification of the market changes in some way.

An equilibrium market price is obtained when the process of competition between suppliers leads to a situation where nobody has an incentive to change their current behaviour. As you saw, at a price of £1.50 none of the hot dog suppliers has an incentive to cut prices any further because each hot dog costs them £1.50 to produce. Likewise, none of the hot dog suppliers has an incentive to increase their asking price above the equilibrium price because consumers will not buy a hot dog from a more expensive supplier when alternative suppliers are offering hot dogs for sale at lower asking prices.

We hope you will agree that the story we have told about price adjustment in the hot dog market makes sense and does not seem excessively unrealistic. We have populated the model with representative human actors who make decisions on the basis of information they have gathered from their environment; consumers actively search for information about asking prices among rival vendors, while vendors choose asking prices as a result of previous sales figures. If you were a consumer and you wanted to buy a good or service you would also have to carry out some kind of search to discover prices being charged by rival suppliers, and if you were a vendor you would be keen to learn how sales of your product were affected by your asking price, so we can claim that our model captures important aspects of the behaviour of real consumers and real suppliers. It is still a very basic model, but its specification has been sufficient to enable us to tell a story about price movements.

You have now reached the stage where you can begin to apply the lessons you have learned from the hypothetical model to real world markets. Applying economic models is not a question of following a set of predetermined easy steps; in fact, it is something of an art that requires you to exercise your judgement. That said, the more often you do it the more skilled you will become and many of the lessons you will learn in the following section apply equally to applying other models to which we will introduce you later in the book.

2.7 The art of applying a model

To help you learn how to apply economic models we will use a mini-case study. Table 2.2 lists some real world price data. The data are for a specific model of hand-held global positioning system (GPS) – the *Garmin GPS III+*. These data were collected from various UK-based Internet retail sites on Tuesday 14 January 2003 in an exercise that took about ten minutes to complete. Additional information of note is that the *Garmin GPS III+* is a navigational aid that had been available for well over two years at this date. It has been the subject of detailed consumer reports and has always been favourably reviewed, which has helped it to become a very popular product; it is now a well-established instrument with a variety of outdoor enthusiasts including hikers, mountaineers, mountain bikers, yachtspeople, paraglider pilots, skiers, rally drivers and the like. A comprehensive list of monthly magazine publications exists to offer advice and inform these leisure pursuits. A more advanced GPS, the *Garmin GPS V*, has been introduced recently. This instrument features a number of significant enhancements over the *GPS III+* and its retail price in early 2003 reflected this, being on average almost twice that of the *GPS III+*.

Our aim here is to see whether our economic model of the market helps us explain the prices recorded in Table 2.2. This means we are required to tell a convincing story about how retailers of the *GPS III+* have arrived at their respective asking prices. We can begin building our story by simply inspecting the data and

Table 2.2 Asking prices for a Garmin GPS III+, 14 January 2003

Supplier's web address	Supplier's asking price
www.offroadstore.co.uk	£290.23
www.gpsw.co.uk	£292.54
www.navcity.co.uk	£292.54
www.outdoorgear.co.uk	£305.95
www.askdirect.co.uk	£314.00
www.mailspeedmarine.co.uk	£334.00
www.southernmarine.co.uk	£363.32
www.expansys.com	£370.39
www.ultimatedesign.co.uk	£390.00
www.harwoods-yacht-chandlers.co.uk	£429.95

making a rather obvious, but nevertheless important, observation: the market for the *GPS III+* does not appear to have achieved an equilibrium price. Does this mean that our understanding of how markets work that we developed earlier is wrong and should be ignored? To help us address this question let's review the facts as we know them:

(i) Asking prices vary between a lowest price of £290.23 and a highest price of £429.95. The lowest asking price is only two-thirds of the highest asking price.

(ii) The comparative price information collected in Table 2.2 can be obtained quickly and easily by anybody who has access to the Internet.

(iii) The *GPS III+* has been available for over two years so we might reasonably assume that the market is well established. Furthermore the product has been reviewed favourably in a multitude of leisure magazines.

(iv) A superior model, the *GPS V*, has been introduced recently.

Clearly, we are going to have to take account of these facts if we are to construct a believable story – that is, an explanation in which we can have confidence. One interpretation of fact (i), the large difference in asking prices for the *GPS III+*, is that consumers are failing to provide a competitive environment for suppliers, due to factors such as the following:

◆ Buyers are not behaving sensibly.

◆ Buyers are simply too lazy to search for a short time on the Internet.

◆ Buyers do not have personal access to the Internet and do not believe it to be worthwhile to use publicly-available Internet access.

◆ Buyers do not search via the Internet because they do not have the computer skills required.

If many consumers were, for such reasons, poorly informed about where the best deals were to be had, some suppliers might decide that it is worth trying to charge prices well in excess of the ex-factory price that they pay Garmin for stocks of the *GPS III+*. Such suppliers might judge that the excess profits obtained on those sales that were thereby achieved could be greater than the profits foregone by not selling to those consumers who were well informed. From this standpoint, the model does not look like one we should apply to this market.

A mainstream economist might nonetheless attempt to dispute such an interpretation of the failure of a single price to emerge for the *GPS III+* on the basis that information about relative prices is quite straightforward to obtain. Those who do not have access to the Internet might well have friends that do, and may well have an idea of what prices to expect from seeing advertisements and reviews in consumer magazines – after all, fact (iii) suggests that consumers are very well informed about the features and capabilities of the *GPS III+* because leisure activities are strongly supported by magazine publications that exist primarily to inform leisure activity enthusiasts about all aspects of their chosen pursuit, including performance assessments of salient gadgets.

If such a defence were in order, perhaps fact (iv) holds the key to our mystery. A new model of GPS has been launched recently and it is better in several respects to the *GPS III+* albeit for a greater price. We can look at this fact from each of the two sides of the market.

On the demand side, a mainstream economist might reason that if consumers of GPS gadgets are on the whole a well-informed bunch, it is reasonable to propose that when a new, improved version of a gadget becomes available they would rather purchase this than the older model if the better specification seems worth the extra outlay. On the supply side, retailers will notice sales of *GPS III+* falling off, so we might expect to see them reduce their asking prices in the hope that the now reduced priced older gadget still passes the value-for-money test for a significant number of consumers.

Now, if this story is true it might mean that the market for the *GPS III+* was not in equilibrium when the prices listed in Table 2.2 were recorded. The price differentials between the listed retailers may therefore simply reflect that some have responded to the introduction of the *GPS V* more quickly than others and in the fullness of time the laggards (i.e. the higher priced retailers) may well bring their prices into line with the lower priced retailers. The latter are likely to do this if they find that they are holding unsold stocks of the *GPS III+* for longer than they were expecting. From the standpoint of the model, the market for the *GPS III+* would be predicted to be in equilibrium prior to the introduction of the *GPS V*. This is something we could test if we could obtain pricing data for several dates prior to the introduction of the *GPS V*, to see if there was a corresponding greater equality in prices between the retailers than that displayed in Table 2.2. The model would also lead us to expect that, after the new gadget has been on sale for a while, the prices asked for it by retailers should not display the kind of dispersion evident in Table 2.2. If significant price differentials are revealed we may have a more complicated story on our hands than we originally might have expected.

What actually happens in the latter case is revealed in Table 2.3, compiled by a search on 10 May 2004. Two sites did not list the *Garmin GPS V*, but the results for the rest are very interesting and not particularly good news for the mainstream model.

Table 2.3 Asking prices for a Garmin GPS V Deluxe, 10 May 2004

Supplier's web address	Supplier's asking price and ratio of its *GPS V* price to its *GPS III+* price	
www.offroadstore.co.uk	£399.00	1.38
www.gpsw.co.uk	£361.95	1.24
www.navcity.co.uk	£359.95	1.23
www.outdoorgear.co.uk	£442.95	1.45
www.askdirect.co.uk	£299 ('reduced from £409') 0.95 (pre-reduction: 1.30)	
www.mailspeedmarine.co.uk	Product not listed	
www.southernmarine.co.uk	£433.60	1.19
www.expansys.com	£360.45	0.97
www.ultimatedesign.co.uk	Product not listed	
www.harwoods-yacht-chandlers.co.uk	£539.95	1.25

Although no single pattern is evident, two features at least stand out when we compare Tables 2.2 and 2.3. One is that Harwoods Yacht Chandlers, the last firm listed, is the most expensive in both cases: 48 per cent more for the *GPS III+* and 80 per cent more for the *GPS V Deluxe* compared with the cheapest quotations. It is interesting also to note that if the ASK Direct price had not been drastically marked down, the Harwoods price is 50 per cent higher than the most common price (i.e. roughly £360) – almost exactly the same margin more than on the most common price of the older product. The second thing that stands out is that four of the suppliers (of which Harwoods is one) have ratios of around 1.20–1.25 between their *GPS V* and *GPS III+* prices. One possible interpretation of this is that these suppliers are using some kind of simple **mark-up rule for pricing** these products: it could well be that the price they were paying Garmin in May 2004 for the *GPS V* is about 20–25 per cent more than they paid for the *GPS III+* in January 2003, and the reason their prices are different is that they each use a different mark-up rule. It appears that The Offroad Store, the firm that was previously the cheapest, is now experimenting with a higher price, whereas Expansys is being less ambitious than before and is charging a price that matches the most commonly quoted price almost exactly. The ASK Direct price, once about 10 per cent above the most popular price, has been cut drastically to make it the best deal, but this might be more in the nature of a 'special offer' than something that the firm expects to maintain. Overall, the messages are mixed: perhaps we should infer that if the market worked as in our model equilibrium prices of the *GPS III+* and *GPS V Deluxe* would be £290 and £360, respectively, and there are two suppliers that consistently charge prices that are higher by similar amounts. Instead of using the mainstream model in this context, perhaps we would be wiser to apply the heterodox perspective. The latter both questions how well informed the consumer will be and suggests that prices are often set with the aid of simple mark-up rules (see Chapter 7). It might be a better framework for interpreting what is going on in this market, as least in respect of some of the firms.

2.8 The mainstream view of economic systems

Mainstream economists work at two levels of analysis when theorizing about how economies work: at the level of the market **(partial equilibrium analysis)** and at the level of the economy as a whole **(general equilibrium analysis)**. Our mainstream-style model of the hot dog market is an example of partial equilibrium analysis. Though simplified, the story we told was rather more complicated than the basic vision of how markets work that underlies mainstream economics. This vision can be encapsulated in a **supply and demand diagram** such as Figure 2.3.

It is important to be completely clear about what the supply and demand curves on such diagrams represent.

> A supply curve shows how much of the product in question suppliers will be
> prepared to offer for sale if they expect to be able to get particular prices for
> it in the product's market.

The supply curve in Figure 2.3 is assumed to be upward sloping on the basis that if more is to be produced, a better deal will have to be offered to lure additional resources away from other uses. This may not be a good assumption if there is

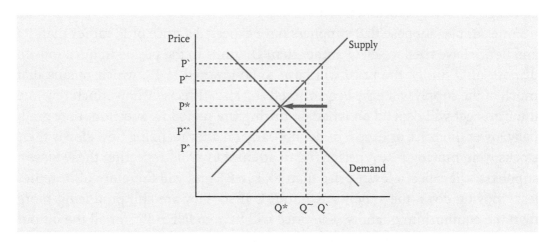

Figure 2.3 Convergence to equilibrium in a market

unemployment or firms are working with spare capacity. A supply curve's position is fixed so long as *ceteris paribus* (other things being equal) holds – i.e. as long as nothing but the price of the product in question can be changed. If any other factor affecting supply changes, then a supply curve may shift to the left or the right. For example, adverse climatic conditions may cause a decline in output of a crop used as an input in production, thereby shifting the supply curve to the left. Conversely, improvements in technological knowledge may make it possible to produce the product more cheaply, thereby shifting the supply curve to the right.

> A demand curve shows the relationship between the price of the product in question and the number of units that can be sold in the period in question.

The demand curve in Figure 2.3 is drawn sloping downwards to the right on the presumption that in order to get people to buy more of the product, a better deal will have to be offered. As with the supply curve, it is drawn assuming *ceteris paribus*, other things being equal. A rise in consumer incomes could cause the curve to shift to the right (if the product is a luxury), whereas a fall in price of rival products or adverse news about the product could cause a leftward shift in the demand curve.

At price P* and quantity Q*, where the supply curve and the demand curve intersect, the amount that customers are prepared to buy and the amount that suppliers are willing to offer for sale are equal. If this is the actual price and quantity, then co-ordination has been achieved and the market is in equilibrium, since neither the buyers nor the sellers have an incentive to change what they are doing. Central to the mainstream perspective is a belief that, if a market is not initially in equilibrium, the way that people respond to losses or above-normal profits caused by a co-ordination failure will sooner or later cause the market to converge to the equilibrium point.

For example, suppose that suppliers have expected a price of P` rather than P* and hence have tried to sell Q` rather than Q* units in the period in question. To dispose of Q` units, the price will have to be lowered to P^, which means that much of the supply will have been offered at a loss. (Precisely how much revenue the firms get will depend on whether, during the period in question, they gradually lower the price or drop it suddenly early on after realizing how slowly their stocks were moving.) Next period, in an attempt to avoid repeating these losses, suppliers will expect a lower price than P`, say P~, and will therefore offer rather less, moving down the supply curve to Q~. If so, they are still producing more than the equilibrium quantity. The price will have to fall to P^^ for all the output to be sold. The continuing loss is an incentive to cut output further and eventually they will stumble upon the P*, Q* combination, rather as if they had been guided there by some kind of 'invisible hand'. Conversely, if initially too little is supplied, the fat profits that ensue will provide an incentive to expand production somewhat and again the market will move towards equilibrium – where the price that the marginal buyer (the least-willing buyer) is prepared to pay is the same as the price required to make suppliers willing to offer that extra unit of output. In short, although there may be problems of information and knowledge that result in temporary co-ordination failures in a market, profits and losses provide incentives to adjust production and correct errors in choices of output. Markets, it would appear, tend towards stable equilibrium positions.

A general equilibrium perspective takes into account the **interconnections** between markets and dispenses with the 'all other things being equal' assumption in respect of relative prices and incomes. In its most basic form it simply takes the following three things as fixed for the time period under consideration:

- The set of **technological possibilities** limiting the relationship between possible combinations of inputs and outputs.

- Consumer **tastes** and information about how products relate to those tastes.

- The physical and financial assets and individual **capabilities** that market participants have at the start of the period.

Given these three kinds of data, and assuming that tastes and technology imply downward-sloping demand curves and upward-sloping supply curves, then a set of equilibrium price/quantity pairings may exist that would ensure simultaneous equilibrium in all markets for outputs and for supplies of inputs, including labour services.

The task of finding a state of general equilibrium is much more demanding for the price mechanism than is the attainment of equilibrium in a single market. Suppose there has been under-supply and big profits in one market. If resources are moved into that market they might come from markets that were previously in equilibrium but not able to offer the abnormally high returns of the market into which they are being moved. Meanwhile, those who, say, earn overtime payments for producing more of the product whose supply is being expanded may then spend their extra income on luxury products and cease demanding goods of lower quality, thereby disturbing equilibrium situations in the latter markets. Adjustments in the latter might disturb yet other markets and so on. The common presumption is that the responses to changing relative prices, profits and losses in the economic system will eventually sort it all out, even though the most sophisticated of general equilibrium researchers have been careful to point out that this can only be assumed under very restrictive conditions.

Now, if everyday experience suggests that the economy operates typically in a reasonably orderly manner, one thing that it might seem logical to assume is that the economic system is organized in something approaching a **modular form**, such that adjustments and imbalances in one market have ripple effects for only a select set of other markets. Mainstream economists take a different logic, however, one that reflects a vision of markets and the price mechanism as a giant machine crunching out solutions to a huge set of simultaneous supply and demand equations. When they think formally about how the 'forces of supply and demand' work in the economy as a whole they do so by characterizing the economic system as if it is what physicists and mathematicians call a 'field'.

A field is a system in which everything is connected to everything else.

In this setting, the idea of a 'field' is exactly the same as a gravitational field in astronomy. If adjustments take place in a number of markets in a particular period, the theory proceeds as if every pair of markets is directly linked, rather than coming about via a particular set of ripple effects going from market A to market B to market C and so on. So, just as distant Pluto might exert a small but direct pull on Earth, and vice versa, with both planets also interacting directly with the orbit of Jupiter, etc., so a mainstream economist is prepared to imagine prices and quantities of, say, yak milk in Tibet as being affected by, and affecting, to some degree the prices and quantities of hang-gliders sold in Wales, handguns sold in Texas and so on.

To tell a coherent story of how the 'everything affects everything else' force-field view might operate in the world of business, it seems necessary to assume that:

- *any* buyer is free to interact with *any* seller;

- even if in reality different types of goods are not *seen* as direct substitutes in a physical sense (would you use a tube of toothpaste as a substitute for a tube of moisturiser, or vice versa?), in practice all goods are indeed substitutes in an economics sense (a rise in the price of moisturisers may lead a consumer to economize on spending elsewhere to keep using it, which may include switching to a cheaper brand of toothpaste; or consumers might cut consumption of moisturiser and spend more elsewhere, including spending more on toothpaste);

- markets are very easy for producers to enter and exit;

- buyers and sellers can very easily obtain information about what is available, its location, price and quality;

- buyers and sellers have no compunction about switching to other sellers and buyers if they perceive a better deal.

This might seem an unrealistic set of requirements at first glance but for the past two decades policymakers following the advice of mainstream pro-market economists have been changing the rules of the economic game to make the real economy much more like this theoretical ideal.

The **deregulation** of markets and removal of barriers to trade between countries, coupled with the rise of the Internet, have greatly increased awareness in business that competition can come from anywhere on the planet. Consumers can bypass traditional sources of supply and distribution systems and obtain products more cheaply by using their credit cards to make email orders from distant lands. Global financial markets never close and events in a relatively small economy such as Thailand may generate repercussions in much larger economies all around the world, as happened in the Asian economic crisis of 1997. Workers may be internationally mobile, but jobs in developed nations can suddenly evaporate as production is switched to emerging low-wage economies.

While this **globalization** of markets may seem very much a contemporary phenomenon, it can be seen as a return to what was happening between about 1870 and 1914, before the rise of interventionist government policies and protectionist approaches to trade in the face of high unemployment. During that period, the invention of the telegraph and telephone linked together markets all around the world, and millions of people migrated freely. And it was in precisely this period that the core ideas of mainstream economics were developed. Even in the era of trade barriers and market regulation, some parts of the world economy continued to operate in terms of a global free-for-all, with very strong competitive pressures. Tramp steamers, for example, could be readily purchased secondhand, were inherently mobile and capable of being registered under flags of convenience and, if the potential profits were attractive, could sail between any pair of ports where cargos were to be found.

2.9 The heterodox view of economic systems and co-ordination

Challenges to the mainstream view of economic systems come from many different schools of economic thought, but they implicitly **share a common central theme**, namely, that if we are to make sense of how the economy works we need to focus on **patterns of connections between elements** of the economy seen as a complex system.

A complex system is a system in which the network of connections between its component parts is incomplete.

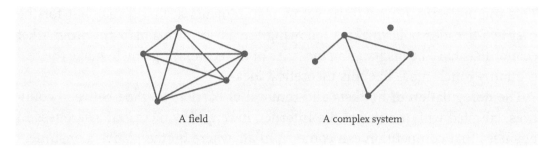

A field   A complex system

Figure 2.4 A field and a complex system

From this standpoint, the 'field' view of an economy is not really portraying it as a system, since if everything is connected to everything else the whole has no structure. The heterodox viewpoint is much more like chemistry than the Newtonian physics that mainstream economists seek to emulate. Chemists are essentially interested in molecular and crystalline structures – note, for example, how graphite and diamonds are both made of carbon but differ in the way the carbon atoms are organized and hence have very different properties – and in how certain kinds of elements react with each other. Likewise, the heterodox economist believes that **structures matter for determining how well markets operate and how firms and consumers survive, grow and evolve**. Figure 2.4 contrasts field and complex systems in graphical terms.

Heterodox economists apply the complex systems idea at a variety of levels. The economy as a whole can be seen as a **complex system of partially interconnected elements**. These elements are themselves complex systems, made up of complex systems:

◆ Firms and **networks** of related firms (as we emphasize in Chapters 9 and 10).

◆ Consumers with both **lifestyles** of interlocking consumption activities and networks of **social relationships** with other consumers.

◆ Products that involve **multiple technologies** or ingredients that have to be assembled in particular ways for the products to function properly.

Heterodox economists think in terms of a very different set of ideas that account for, or are a consequence of, this partial connectivity:

◆ Problems of knowledge – and costs of marketing – limit the set of parties with whom any buyer or seller might try to deal.

◆ People are not always willing to make trade-offs even in the event of large changes in relative prices. In some parts of their lives, rather as in university degree regulations, they may impose structures involving **priorities** or

prerequisites. In other words, whether or not something 'fits' may be the crucial requirement, and a poor fit may not be compensated for by being offered more in some other respect, such as a cheaper price.

◆ A lack of knowledge/**specific capabilities** may make markets difficult to enter; knowledge problems may make markets difficult to exit, too, by making assets hard to dispose of for anything like their initial prices.

◆ Difficulties in obtaining information in markets may lead to **brand loyalty** and **brand equity** – buyers do not set out to fill in all the gaps in their knowledge and instead stick with particular familiar brands even if these have premium prices.

◆ Since buyers and sellers both benefit from getting to know each other, trade is often based on stable **relationships**.

◆ It may be unwise to focus on individual product markets as buyers may be thinking of where they can get the best value in terms of an entire **bundle** of related products. (This might help to account for some of the dispersion we saw in the pricing of GPS products. The retailers of these systems were selling different mixes of products for different parts of the outdoor leisure market and hence might not all see themselves as rivals. Neither might the consumers categorize yacht chandlers as competing with off-road accessory suppliers. Hence they might not bother to compare their prices, even though both sell GPS products.)

◆ History matters. Economic processes are **path dependent**: the set of possibilities open to decision makers today, and the perceived pros and cons associated with each of them, is shaped by previous decisions that lock the economy into particular ways of doing things (for example, Microsoft Windows computer operating systems and VHS video systems).

◆ Economic systems may evolve at times in a discontinuous manner, whilst at other times changing slowly as if moving down a well-defined pathway.

◆ The structure of connections may affect the ability of the system to adapt to change and its resilience when subjected to shocks that disrupt particular connections.

◆ It may be counter-productive to make the system more like the mainstream economist's ideal.

Heterodox economists thus tend to highlight rather different features of the real world economy than those emphasized by mainstream writers. For example, if thinking about the shipping industry a heterodox economist would tend to emphasize not the tramp steamer part of it but, rather, that: (a) certain nations (such as Greece and Norway) have a disproportionate representation in terms of ship ownership; (b) shipping companies tend to operate fleets of vessels; (c) cargo transportation is nowadays based around a technology standard, namely, the container system; (d) after reliable steam power was applied to ships in place of wind-dependent sails, regular timetabled 'liner' routes emerged, linking particular pairs of ports; and so on. Moreover, whilst they do not dispute the facts suggesting trends towards globalization of markets and the increasingly interconnected nature of modern financial systems in different countries, heterodox economists see an ongoing role for networks of partial connections in the modern economy:

- There is still a place for physical financial centres in a world of virtual financial markets, since mixing with people face-to-face enables better access to hints of possible deals of significance, and enables those engaged in deal making to pick up nuances regarding the quality of information disclosure and bargaining strategies of their trading partners.

- The wider the range of financial possibilities that are open to us, the more we may need to build up relationships with investment advisors who understand our needs and whom we can trust.

- Despite the power of Internet search engines for uncovering what is available and exposing any differences in price and quality of rival suppliers' offerings, the sheer range of businesses with whom we might deal is potentially overwhelming and we cope by bookmarking trusted websites and navigating the World Wide Web via specific linkages between websites.

More generally, the heterodox way of approaching economics looks at factors other than adjustments of relative prices as means of achieving economic co-ordination. The mainstream picture concentrates essentially on error correction, ignoring how the structure of the economic system might limit co-ordination failures in the first place. For this reason, heterodox economists do not rule out the possibility that in some contexts markets may be inferior to systems based on **planning**. The **pursuit curve** story illustrated in Figure 2.5 is a thought-provoking parable on this theme, from Maurice Dobb (1967), one of the great socialist economists of the last century.

In Dobb's tale, a dog sees its owner cycling in the distance and starts running towards him, not realizing that he is going in a different direction. After a while the dog notices that she is no longer on course for her owner and changes track. The trouble is, her owner still has not seen her and keeps going. More time passes and the dog once again realizes she is no longer on track. And so the process is

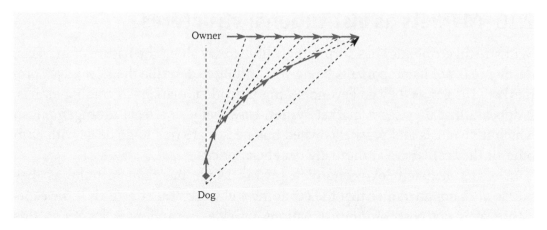

Figure 2.5 The pursuit curve: error correction versus planning

repeated. If only the dog were able to assess her master's speed and direction of movement properly, she could take the bold step of calculating the best path to take to get to where he *will* get to if she takes the quickest path to meet him (as shown by the long, straight, dashed arrow). It should be noted that Dobb warns that the parable should not be taken too far: planners may actually want to take the economy in a different direction rather than to where the price mechanism might eventually take it.

Dogmatic opposition from mainstream economists means that economic planning is out of fashion at the level of the economy as a whole in many countries. These economists often fail to recognize that **planning is actually the means by which much resource allocation is done, in conjunction with face-to-face co-operation, within businesses** as they compete in markets. At the **inter-firm level**, too, there is a substantial element of informal planning of various kinds, such as the use of **co-operative relationships, interlocking company directorships and hierarchical relationships between major contractors and subcontractors** to ensure that projects get completed without major cost overruns. Competitive price tenders may determine which firms win particular supply contracts, but prior relationships will count if several contractors are otherwise equally attractive. The **voice mechanism** may then play a major role in the implementation process for dealing with surprises and filling in details not fully spelt out at the time the deals were done.

In later chapters of this book we will explore these essential features of the business world in some detail. For the present, we will end our analysis of markets by presenting a **heterodox view** of the nature of **markets as devices that make transactions easier to do in a world of problems of information and knowledge.**

2.10 Markets as institutional structures

Mainstream economics has surprisingly little to say about the nature of markets, despite many of its proponents being very willing to describe themselves as 'pro-market'. Insofar as they go beyond seeing individual markets as trading arenas, it appears that they see a market system essentially as a legal arrangement in which individuals and privately owned businesses are free to do deals with each other if they can arrive at mutually beneficial prices.

In terms of heterodox economics, giving people the right to trade as they please does not guarantee that the economy will work very effectively – the experience of many post-communist nations provides a cautionary lesson in this respect. A free-enterprise system has a much better chance of avoiding co-ordination failures and wasted opportunities for mutual benefit if its markets have evolved to be markets in the following sense:

> A market is defined in heterodox economics as a system of social institutions that help buyers and sellers reduce transaction costs.

A market of this kind reduces transaction costs in the sense that it enables buyers and sellers to:

- **find each other** easily and make price comparisons;
- **judge effectively** whether trade is likely to be mutually beneficial in terms of product quality, safety and standards of service;
- **co-ordinate the fit** between products (via standard sizes, measurement systems, physical interfaces, etc.);
- **obtain redress** in the event that a deal results in an unsatisfactory outcome, such as a dispute between the buyer and seller over what has been delivered, the failure of the buyers to make payment, or the failure of the good or service to be delivered in whole or part due to the financial collapse of the supplier.

> Institutions are features of everyday life that have been around for some time and are widely known and taken for granted in social interaction; more formally, they are systems of embedded social rules.

Market institutions include:

- Trade associations, that, for example, co-ordinate standards of service offered by members and monitor them, or operate insurance funds to guard against customers suffering losses in the event of a member going out of business (as with an association of travel agents).
- Yellow Pages and other business directories.

- Tendencies of suppliers to stay in the same line of business for long periods and to try to make a name for themselves there.

- Conventions used in setting prices, such as holding prices steady in the face of fluctuating demand (except for well-known 'sale' periods, such as the New Year).

- Districts or particular roads known for groupings of particular kinds of firms, such as Silicon Valley, Hollywood, Madison Avenue, Broadway, the City of London, Fleet Street or Soho. These are known in the modern literature as 'Marshallian business districts' after Alfred Marshall, who drew attention to them over a century ago.

- Trade fairs, business conferences/conventions and exhibitions that enable rival suppliers and would-be customers to mingle with each other and gather intelligence about where the market may be heading.

- Trade press and other regular, well-known advertising forums.

- Websites that provide information on product reliability, specifications and prices (e.g. www.jdpower.com or www.redbook.com.au).

- Experienced consumers, known for their expertise and willingness to share it.

- Voluntary codes of practice under which suppliers are widely known to be operating.

- Product standards for size, physical connections and functional compatibility (for example, imperial/metric doors and tools, 240 volt/50hz power supplies, ISO 9000, BSI Woolmark, DIN and Phono cables).

- Statutory requirements, such as product safety and environmental protection legislation, or requirements that suppliers should be licensed and subject to periodic monitoring by a regulatory authority.

- The presence of anti-monopoly bodies (such as the Competition Commission in the UK) and consumer watchdog groups (such as the Consumers' Association) and their reputations (or lack of them) for stepping in when customer interests are threatened by suppliers' policies.

- Laws and legal institutions, including bodies such as small claims courts.

A moment's reflection on the process of buying or selling a used car, having an evening out or getting a plumber to fix a burst pipe should indicate how much we may miss the point about how the economy works if we focus too much on changes in relative prices and ignore the vital role such institutions play in enabling transactions to be organized with little fuss. Statutory intervention is not always an important part of a market, for firms that aim to be long-term suppliers may recognize that it makes sense to set up trade associations and assign them powers of accreditation and exclusion from membership, for this will enable customers to choose suppliers with more confidence. Paradoxically, the need for state regulation is often just as great when markets fit the mainstream ideal of being very easy to enter, as it is when markets are dominated by just a handful of suppliers and entry by others is difficult. There is a simple reason why unregulated easy-entry markets may be dangerous for customers: too many firms may try to operate in them, which makes it very hard for them to make any money and leads some to take devious steps to cut costs.

It is important to understand that **not all exchanges take place in markets**. For example, if you sell an old computer to your neighbour as a result of a chance conversation over the garden fence, this is a one-off case of **bilateral exchange**; it is quite different from selling it at a widely known venue for 'car boot sales' or after placing a small advertisement in the local paper's 'computers' section. You might also engage in **relational exchange** with your neighbour, such as minding each other's homes when one of you is away on holiday; once again, no market is involved. It might also be tempting to say that unique commodities cannot be the subjects of market exchange. However, we make sense of the world by pigeon-holing things in terms of their likenesses and differences with other things; hence even a unique product may be capable of appraisal by a known expert in the area into which it seems to fit and be advertised in the regular media used in that area, even if it only changes hands very occasionally.

2.11 The firm as an answer to market failure

Although markets of the kind just described make it much easier for buyers and sellers to do mutually beneficial deals, compared with how things would be in a world without them, they are not always the best means for changing the allocation of resources. They reduce transaction costs but they do not eliminate them altogether, leaving plenty of scope for certain kinds of market-based changes in resource allocation to work out badly or be impossible to arrange at all. Economists owe their awareness of the costs of using markets to Ronald Coase, winner of the 1991 Nobel Prize in economics. In 1937, very early in his academic career, Coase wrote a classic article that used the presence of such costs to help explain why firms exist. Coase's analysis centred on the possibility that what we call **voice and planning mechanisms inside firms** might be a cheaper means than markets and the price mechanism for allocating resources. His article is really about what limits the size of a firm that already exists and thereby stops more and more things that might be the subject of market transactions from being conducted on the basis of directives inside firms.

However, his basic insight that **problems with markets provide a rationale for firms** seems to offer a good way to answer the question that we posed at the start of this chapter, namely, why do people bother to set up firms as a means of making money?

For many who decide to start a business as an alternative to being employed by someone else, the reason may not be a vision that they will make a fortune through a unique entrepreneurial insight. Rather, it may be simply that, as far as they are concerned, the labour market is failing them. Becoming one's own boss is a way of avoiding or escaping from:

♦ long-term unemployment due to one's skills no longer being in demand;

♦ having repeatedly to find a new job at the end of a temporary contract or because employers keep cutting back on staff;

♦ having to fit in with the working hours demanded by employers, which may be incompatible with, say, family commitments;

♦ feelings of alienation that come from being bossed around or being a tiny cog in a giant machine, with little control over one's pace of work;

♦ missing out on the tax and financial advantages of running a business rather than being an employee, including scope for illegal tax evasion by accepting payment from customers in cash, or access to preferential leasing deals on cars and scope for claiming expenses against income tax.

Many of those who start businesses for these kinds of reasons may lack entrepreneurial abilities in terms of seeing scope for a new business. If so, it is still possible for them to get started by buying a business idea from someone else in ready-to-go form. This is the essence of owning a franchise, which is how, for example, many McDonald's outlets come into existence.

Although, as the McDonald's franchise example indicates, it is possible to develop a business idea and sell it to others, people with ideas for business ventures often conclude that the only way to get them up and running is to do it themselves by starting a firm. A person with what seems a potentially lucrative idea may run into the following problems in the market for ideas if they try to get someone else to put it into practice:

♦ Their current employers do not share their vision and will not put it into practice even if they are not demanding a slice of the returns that it generates.

♦ They believe the idea is worth far more to their current employers than any extra remuneration that they would receive as a consequence of suggesting it.

♦ They are wary of trying to sell it to someone else or to an existing business because of the risk of not being able to capture the value of what is, at the moment, this person's own **intellectual property**. The market for ideas has a basic problem, raised by Nobel Prize-winning economist Kenneth Arrow and known as the **Arrow Paradox**:

> The Arrow Paradox states that for someone to know whether an idea is worth paying for, the seller must give them information about it, but once the information has been provided for inspection, they have got access to it without having to pay for it and as a result they may be able go and use it 'for free'.

This is the problem that retailers of consumer magazines face: if we browse at length in a magazine store, we can get the specific information we are looking for and then leave the store without buying the magazine; yet if magazines are displayed in sealed wrapping, how can we know whether the magazine will be worth buying? A person who has a potentially lucrative idea can try to protect it via the patent system or by doing whatever is required by copyright law to claim ownership of it prior to presenting it to companies that might be interested in buying it. However, even this may not be enough protection, for the firms they approach may be able to design a variation on it that does not breach their patent or copyright after turning the proposal down. Such firms may even be able to get their near-pirate version into production before the original. (As you will see in Section 5.2, precisely these issues arose early in the story of the Dyson Dual Cyclone vacuum cleaner.)

- They may be unable to find a buyer for their idea. Those whom they approach may be genuinely pessimistic about the likely volume of demand or the scale of development costs required to turn the concept into a production-ready reality.

- Quite apart from the financial side, they may simply be interested in seeing their idea turned into a production reality and fear that this will not happen if the only parties interested in buying it have an interest in suppressing it because it threatens to render their existing investments obsolete. Of course, devious behaviour by such a purchaser could also have major financial implications: if they sold the firm a licence to use their idea with a per-unit royalty payment on sales of the product embodying it, they might simply receive a lump sum and no subsequent royalty earnings. At the very least, they would be wise to devise a licensing deal of finite duration or one with clauses under which it would expire if not put into operation within a particular period. Such complexities in the deal could entail major legal bills with still no guarantee that production will ever occur.

♦ If the idea is not completely spelt out in a contract by which it is sold (for example, due to problems of **tacit knowledge**), there is a risk that the party to whom it might be sold will not implement it in the manner that they envisage. This could happen due to **opportunism** by the purchaser or simply because, despite the 'best will in the world', the purchaser of the idea doesn't quite 'get' it. Once again, if the person with the idea values being able to see it implemented for its own sake and not in, say, a 'dumbed down/Hollywood' version, this may be a major stumbling block. Implementation in an edited form might also be bad for financial returns if these are based on royalty payments and sales suffer due to the production version not matching the person's original vision. Those who sell their ideas purely in the hope of making money from them need to be confident that those to whom they entrust scope for making changes to improve earnings know the product's market better than they do.

Those who start their own businesses may avoid such problems but, as you will now be recognizing, everything has its cost and they may find they have jumped out of the frying pan and into the fire, facing a host of other problems that need answers. In the chapters that follow we first explore the nature of entrepreneurship and then examine the questions that an entrepreneur will need to address in trying to create an enduring business.

2.12 Summary

In this chapter we have attempted to give a flavour of how mainstream and heterodox economists think about markets and the nature of economic systems in which decision makers participate as buyers and sellers in order to reap benefits from specializing rather than trying to be self-sufficient. We pointed out that the use of managerial hierarchies inside firms as a means of allocating resources is an alternative to letting market prices reconcile the different demand and supply offers of buyers and sellers and we emphasized the information problems that market participants often face. In the mainstream view, these problems are not emphasized because of presumptions about the error-correcting capabilities of the price mechanism – the way that people will change what they buy or sell as relative prices and profit opportunities change. In the heterodox view, these problems are often made less acute by the evolution of market institutions. Even so, as we emphasized in Chapter 1, problems of information and knowledge still overshadow many

2.12 **Summary** (continued)

economic decisions, making the action of choosing very much a heroic leap in the dark in some contexts. **Sometimes, to get around difficulties they have experienced in making acceptable deals in markets for labour and for ideas, people start their own businesses.**

2.13 Some questions to consider

1. Examine the problems that unregulated market forces might have in co-ordinating supply and demand in a rapidly growing tourist centre. How might the local government authorities seek to reduce these difficulties? What kinds of market institutions might evolve to reduce them?

2. How would you explain the fact that, in many countries, the taxi market (a) is dominated by fleets of branded cabs rather than independent owner-operator cabs, and (b) is often subject to government regulation?

3. Why are international, multi-branch/franchised restaurants dominant in the supply of hamburgers and pizzas, whereas Chinese restaurants tend to be one-off and owner-operated?

4. Introduction agencies serve a similar role to banks and real estate agents in the sense that they are market intermediaries that bring together people who have got something to offer with other people who want something. Yet whereas banking and real estate are dominated by multi-branch, nationally known business organizations, introduction agencies remain small-scale and unfamiliar to the general public. How would you explain this contrast? Do you think the rise of the Internet will cause the situation to change?

5. Why do prices of agricultural and mineral products tend to be less stable than the prices of manufactured products?

6. Examine the potential for supply and demand mismatches in the market for tertiary education services in both the short run and the long run, and the consequences of such mismatches for the broader community. As you answer, keep in mind that such mismatches can be in terms of the quality of education services and not just their quantity, so be sure to consider how education markets develop to handle the quality issue.

2.14 Recommended additional reading sources

If you wish to read more about how economists build models and argue about the worth of these models as contributions to knowledge, see Mark Blaug (1980) *The Methodology of Economics: Or How Economists Explain* (1st edn), Cambridge, Cambridge University Press. For a more controversial and engaging perspective, see the best-seller by heterodox economic model builder Paul Ormerod (1994) *The Death of Economics*, London, Faber & Faber (especially part I). For an excellent set of key readings, see Bruce Caldwell (ed.) (1984) *Appraisal and Criticism in Economics*, London, Allen & Unwin; however, if you have never read on the philosophy of science before, then it would be wise to begin with a short book by John Pheby (1988) *Methodology and Economics: A Critical Introduction*, London, Macmillan.

Albert Hirschman (1970) *Exit, Voice and Loyalty: Responses to Decline in Firms, Organizations and States*, New York, Norton. This short book explores adjustment problems in economic systems and highlights the importance of complaints ('voice') as feedback for improving resource allocation decisions, compared with the economist's usual focus on dissatisfied buyers simply taking their business elsewhere ('exit'). Hirschman also emphasizes how customer loyalty provides firms with some slack, enabling them to stay in business whilst trying to restore their relative competitive standing.

Karl Sabbagh (1989) *Skyscraper: The Making of a Building*, London, Macmillan/Channel 4. This book is based on a television documentary series about the construction of Worldwide Plaza in New York and provides an excellent picture of the co-ordination problems involved in a project of this kind. It provided the basis for a case study by Peter Earl (1996) 'Contracts, co-ordination and the construction industry' in his edited volume *Management, Marketing and the Competitive Process*, Cheltenham, Edward Elgar, pp. 149–71.

Figures 2.1 and 2.2 were inspired by Axel Leijonhufvud (1986) 'Capitalism and the factory system', in Richard Langlois (ed.) *Economics as a Process: Essays in the New Institutional Economics*, New York, Cambridge University Press.

The work of George Richardson provides perceptive reflections on how different methods of resource allocation work, and how co-operation is a vital part of a modern competitive economy. At this stage, the most relevant of his works to look at are two of his articles: 'Planning versus competition' (from *Soviet Studies*, 1971, **22**, pp. 433–47) and 'The organization of industry' (*Economic Journal*, 1972, **82**, pp. 883–96). Both of these are reprinted in the 1990 edition of his book *Information* *and Investment*, Oxford, Oxford University Press. Richardson's other work focuses on problems with the mainstream supply and demand story that we have not revealed in this chapter; they are raised in Chapter 9.

For an interesting discussion of some markets in which consumers do not seem as willing to switch between suppliers as mainstream economists often presume, see Michael Waterson (2003) 'The role of consumers in competition and competition policy', *International Journal of Industrial Organisation*, **21**, pp. 129–50.

For an information-centred reflection on problems with attempts to replace socialist systems with markets in the former Soviet Union, see the work of 2001 Nobel Prize winner Joseph Sitglitz (1994) *Whither Socialism?* Cambridge, MA and London, MIT Press.

Jason Potts (2000) *The New Evolutionary Microeconomics: Complexity, Competence and Adaptive Behaviour*, Cheltenham, Edward Elgar. If you are interested in exploring the 'field' versus 'complex system' contrast between mainstream and heterodox economics, then this acclaimed book is the one to read, though it is probably best first to read Tim Wakeley's review of it in the *Journal of Economic Psychology*, 2002, **23**, 2, pp. 279–86.

Thomas Friedman (1999) *The Lexus and the Olive Tree*, New York, Farrar, Giroux and Strauss; or John Micklethwait and Adrian Wooldridge (2000) *A Future Perfect: The Challenge and Hidden Promise of Globalization*, New York, Times Books. These are two of the best-sellers amongst the recent wave of books on globalization. Though at times lacking in critical insight, they both certainly give a good sense of the interconnectedness of the modern global economy, the vision of free-market thinkers and the importance of institutions in making markets work effectively.

The 'pursuit curve' story depicted in Figure 2.5 is adapted from pp. 87–8 of Maurice H. Dobb (1967) *Papers on Capitalism, Development and Planning*, London, Routledge & Kegan Paul.

The role of costs of using markets in explaining the rationale of firms is explored in Ronald Coase (1937) 'The nature of the firm', *Economica*, **4**, pp. 386–405.

Geoffrey M. Hodgson (1988) *Economics and Institutions*, Oxford, Polity Press. Chapter 8 of this book is particularly significant for its discussion of the role and nature of markets. Our discussion of why firms get created is partly inspired by one of Hodgson's more recent works: 'Opportunism is not the only reason why firms exist: Why an explanatory emphasis on opportunism may mislead management strategy', *Industrial and Corporate Change*, 2004, **13**, 2, pp. 401–18.

3

What do entrepreneurs do?

Learning outcomes

If you study this chapter carefully, it may help you to understand:

- the personal and cognitive qualities that can help an entrepreneur to succeed in business

- why the entrepreneur has a rather limited role in mainstream economics

- what is meant by 'X-inefficiency', and the role of the entrepreneur in combating it by getting staff to work harder or smarter

- why some economists see entrepreneurs as people who help steer the economy towards equilibrium, while other economists see entrepreneurs as disruptive agents of change

- the kinds of mental connections that successful entrepreneurs are particularly skilled at making.

To the extent that you develop such understanding, you should be better able to develop a more complete picture of the nature and role of entrepreneurship than the populist understanding by drawing together the different theories discussed here.

Woolworths, the pyramids and the Internet have one thing in common: they started out as nothing but an idea.

Guy Claxton (2001)

3.1 Introduction

Without doubt the entrepreneur holds a special place in the collective consciousness of society; indeed some entrepreneurs have achieved fame or notoriety that is on a par with Hollywood superstars. The business exploits of a number of high profile entrepreneurs such as Richard Branson (Virgin), Anita Roddick (The Body Shop), James Dyson (Dyson) and Stelios Haji-Ioannu (EasyJet) are reported regularly in the media. These people, and others like them, are famous because they are successful in business.

But what does an entrepreneur do? In this chapter we look beyond the populist conception of the entrepreneur and introduce a more rigorous analysis of this key actor on the economic stage. In particular we are interested here in identifying the **economic role of the entrepreneur**, because entrepreneurship lies at the **heart of business economics** and a better understanding of it will provide us with important clues about the sources of business success and failure. These are big issues.

It will probably not have escaped your attention that we have started our discussion of the entrepreneur on the assumption that we all know one when we see one. It is not straightforward to define who or what an entrepreneur is, but by the end of this chapter you should be able to construct your own definition based upon the functions and activities that we identify as being entrepreneurial. To help us get started, we will take a look at the story of Richard Branson. We will then move on to examine what economists have said about entrepreneurship.

3.2 An entrepreneur's story: the early years of Sir Richard Branson

Sir Richard Branson is a household name but this hasn't always been the case, so, rather than focusing upon his most recent exploits, we will take a look at his early years because these provide us with important clues about the activities of entrepreneurs more generally. It is useful also because it suggests that certain personal qualities can help turn an original entrepreneurial vision into a successful reality.

The start of the path which leads to the multi-business Virgin empire of today can be found back in Branson's schooldays when he first thought of producing a national magazine dealing with issues relating to youth culture. This magazine, *Student*, was originally conceived in 1966 when Branson was just 15 years old. The initial spur to create the magazine came from Branson's belief that various school activities such as corporal punishment, games, chapel and the school meal system were either organized inefficiently or were simply wrong, and the creation of an alternative school magazine would provide a forum to air these radical views. It did not take long, however, for this simple idea to metamorphose into a plan to create an interschool magazine and then for this idea to expand into a plan to create a magazine aimed at technical college and university students with a nationwide market. It should be noted that this transition of ideas took place at a conceptual level; *Student* was very much a concept inside Branson's **imagination**.

After much effort and **persistence** on the part of Branson and his friend Jonny Gems the magazine was launched some two years later in 1968. In the intervening period Branson had devoted a significant amount of time and energy to the task of **persuading** commercial organizations to take out advertising space in the magazine and also to persuading politicians and celebrities either to write for the magazine (for nothing) or to agree to be interviewed. In Branson's own words, 'I had the ability to persuade them to say yes, and the obstinacy never to accept no for an answer.' We might add also that he displayed a lot of self-confidence for a school boy.

Interestingly, while the label 'entrepreneur' seems to be a natural one to apply to Branson, he claims that he became one largely by default as a result of taking care of the business side of *Student* while Gems took care of the editorial side of the magazine. The motivation behind the magazine was **creative** rather than money-making, which was seen simply as a necessary activity to keep the magazine alive. Later on Branson claims to have realized that business 'could be a creative enterprise in itself'. He outlines his philosophy of business in the following terms: 'Above all, you want to create something you are proud of … I can honestly say that I have never gone into any business purely to make money. … A business has to be involving; it has to be fun, and it has to exercise your creative instincts.' Despite this claim, Branson realized that the now-established magazine was not making sufficient money to survive and this prompted him to explore ways in which he could develop the *Student* name into a travel company, an accommodation agency and an advisory centre among other things.

The *Student* offices and the advisory centre exposed Branson to a variety of young people and it was this that revealed to him how important popular music was in youth culture: 'One thing I knew from everyone who came in to chat or work for us was that they spent a good deal of time listening to music and a good deal of money buying records.' This struck him as a **business opportunity** and, aided by the recent outlawing of resale price maintenance (RPM), he conceived of a discount mail-order record distribution business. Virgin Mail Order Records came into existence in 1970 with its first advertisement appearing in what turned out to be the last ever edition of *Student*. The business, which Branson shared on a 60:40 basis with his childhood friend Nik Powell, proved to be a great success; people were attracted by the fact that they could buy records from Virgin for a significantly lower price than that being charged by the two record-retailing giants WH Smith and John Menzies who, despite the abolition of RPM on the part of manufacturers, seemed content to maintain the status quo rather than engage in price competition. Branson had **perceived a business opportunity and taken advantage of an attractive pricing situation**.

Throughout 1970 Virgin Mail Order Records thrived, but then potential disaster loomed in the form of a prolonged strike by Post Office workers in January 1971. With the postal system not working, money and orders stopped coming into the business, and records could not be sent out to customers. Given that the margins on the business were so small and the business was far from cash rich something had to be done, and quickly, to save the enterprise.

In response to this crisis Branson demonstrated a very important trait – **adaptability**. The solution he arrived at was to open a shop, in other words provide an **alternative distribution channel** to customers. WH Smith and John Menzies were still sitting on their laurels to the point of displaying complete apathy towards the music-buying youth, so Branson created the first Virgin Record Shop above a shoe shop on Oxford Street in London. The ethos of the shop was based upon Branson's belief that: 'People take music far more seriously than many other things in life. It is part of the way they define themselves, like the cars they drive, the films they watch, and the clothes they wear.' Consequently, customers were encouraged to lounge around on beanbags listening to music and discussing their potential purchases with interested shop staff. Once again Branson's **negotiating skills** came to the fore as he persuaded the shoe shop owner to let them use the upstairs as a record shop rent-free. The whole process of saving the Virgin record business, from inception to execution, took about one week.

On the back of a concerted localized advertising campaign consisting of leaflet distribution in Oxford Street the shop took off and as time passed the sales staff began to report that the same people were coming back to the shop on a regular basis; it became clear that a loyal customer base was developing and with it so was the Virgin **reputation**. Key to the establishment of the reputation was Branson's cousin Simon Draper who had an acutely developed sense of taste about modern music. Draper was adept at using his knowledge of music to **predict** which bands' records would sell **well before the bands had become successful.** His reward was to be employed as chief record buyer on the standard Virgin wage of £20 per week.

Complementary to Draper was John Varnom, who had a talent for record promotion and advertising. Branson, however, was not content; retail margins were small, particularly given the discounted prices being charged for records, so he sought out business opportunities that might offer a bigger margin. He saw that the people who were making serious money in the record industry were the record companies.

Branson had heard that recording studios were a very formal place with rather strict scheduling from the early morning onwards. This seemed to be their weakness. Just like the contemporary record retailers, the recording studios did not seem to be run in such a way that they catered sufficiently to the needs of their customers – the bands who used them. As Branson observed: 'The idea of the Rolling Stones having to record "Brown Sugar" straight after finishing their bowls of cornflakes struck me as ridiculous. I imagined that the best environment for making records would be a big, comfortable house in the country where a band could come and stay for weeks at a time and record whenever they felt like it, probably in the evening.' As a result of this belief, Branson began to search for a big country house that would be suitable for conversion to a recording studio. Having located a suitable manor house in Oxfordshire a mortgage was arranged and all hands were drafted in to convert it into a recording studio. Instrumental in this process was the Virgin employee Tom Newman who had the knowledge required to create a recording studio that was as least as good as the major London studios. Branson meanwhile continued utilizing his skills of persuasion to attract bands to the Manor recording studios, which became fully operational in early 1972.

Increasing the number of record shops was also on the agenda throughout the tail end of 1971 and all of 1972. By the end of 1972 14 shops had been opened across the UK on a cleverly designed schedule (one a month), where Branson used his negotiating skills to ensure that minimum rent was payable and that each shop had a three-month rent-free period after the initial opening. In this way revenue from successful openings could be used to pay the rent of earlier shops as it fell due and the losses from a failed shop could be minimized.

In essence, Branson's approach here revealed that he was prepared to **experiment in the market place** but he always ensured that the downside of any risky venture was minimized. As he said: '... when we opened we knew that the record sales in the first three months would help pay for the rent on the previous shop that we had opened. The sales also demonstrated, without committing to a huge overhead, whether the site we had chosen attracted enough people off the streets to make the shop viable.'

With the Manor recording studios in place and the string of shops Branson further expanded the reach of the Virgin business in 1973 by starting a record label. Here he used Simon Draper's expertise once more by appointing him as the talent scout and gave him a significant incentive to do the job well: 20 per cent of the company called Virgin Music.

Once again, Branson demonstrated his willingness to take risks. It was usual for newly established record labels to license their records out to other companies who took responsibility for manufacture, distribution and, crucially, promotion while offering an upfront payment and a royalty stream from successful albums. Of course this meant that the other company got most of the upside from successful records since they kept the majority of the profits. Instead Branson was confident that they should simply pay another record company to manufacture and distribute their records while Virgin Music took on the job of promotion (the costly part of the business), and therefore carried the risk but also had the opportunity to enjoy larger profits if their signings were successful. This meant that Draper's role would be crucial, because his signing decisions would be exposed to the harshest of tests and Virgin Music would stand or fall on the quality of his choices.

Virgin Music's first signing was the then-unknown Mike Oldfield, but everyone who heard the early recordings of what eventually became the record *Tubular Bells* was certain that the company had something unique to promote and sure enough as Branson puts it: 'Our gamble that we could promote it ourselves made us our first fortune.' *Tubular Bells* was a runaway success and by the end of 1973 Virgin consisted of three mutually compatible businesses: a recording studio, a record label and a retail network.

Lessons from the Richard Branson story

This story of Richard Branson's early years as an entrepreneur contains several clues about the role of entrepreneurs in general and also the personal qualities that help generate success. It is an interesting exercise to re-read the brief account we have written above to see if you can identify key words or phrases that seem to describe what entrepreneurs do. Such a list may contain the following:

- take risks

- make decisions about entering markets

- exercise foresight, exercise creativity

- employ other people

- persuade

- sell, make things happen

- create companies

- perceive business opportunities

- manage the workforce.

This list is far from complete and we would encourage you to construct your own, but it does serve to illustrate some of the things that people like Richard Branson do that lead us to the unanimous view that he is indeed an entrepreneur as opposed to the apparently more mundane and common business administrator. Of course lists of descriptive phrases are no substitute for deeper analysis, so with this in mind we will turn our attention to the work of economists who have attempted to construct rigorous theories of the entrepreneur.

3.3 Six perspectives on the economics of the entrepreneur

When it comes to analysing what entrepreneurs do economists have developed several perspectives. If you have read Chapter 1 this probably won't surprise you! The **aim of economists** has been to analyse **what it is that entrepreneurs do that distinguishes them from other economic actors** and consequently to assess the relative importance of their role in the economy. It might seem obvious to the casual observer that entrepreneurs perform a crucial task in the process of wealth generation in the economy, but the detail of how they achieve this needs to be understood. From the perspective of the individual with aspirations to become an entrepreneur the theories provide a host of valuable practical insights about the nature of the role and the type and breadth of issues that entrepreneurs need to consider and deal with.

In order to keep our discussion manageable we will build up our picture of the entrepreneur in gradual stages by addressing each of the major perspectives in turn. You will see that each perspective has something useful to contribute to a more complete understanding of the entrepreneurial function. You will discover also that many of the topics we discuss here have implications that go beyond the study of entrepreneurship *per se*.

3.3.1 The mainstream perspective on the entrepreneur

The mainstream treatment of the entrepreneur is intimately bound up with the mainstream theory of the firm. Essentially the theory of the firm examines how scarce factors of production, which fall into one of three broad categories – land, labour and capital – should best be used in the production of goods and services for society. Within this framework, the entrepreneur is identified as the **fourth factor of production**.

In contrast to heterodox economists' focus on problems of information and knowledge, mainstream economics presumes that people are always looking out for, readily perceive and act upon opportunities for improving their positions as much as possible. One implication of this presumption is that everybody has what it takes to be an entrepreneur. In other words, mainstream theory treats entrepreneurs as if they were a resource with an infinite supply. If something is in infinite supply economists tend not to pay much attention to it because economics focuses on how best to use scarce resources. It is partly for this reason that mainstream economics has not developed a specific theory of the entrepreneur. This is not to say that entrepreneurs have no part to play in the mainstream theory of the firm, it is just that their role is trivialized.

In the mainstream theory entrepreneurs are the founders, the owners and the managers of the firm all rolled into one and are responsible for organizing the other factors of production so that the firm can produce a good or service to sell to customers. They reside in a world where economic agents have full information about:

- the availability of factor inputs;
- the quality of factor inputs;
- the variety of ways in which factor inputs can be combined; and
- buyers' demand for the firm's product.

As a result, the practical questions that would face and challenge a boundedly rational real world entrepreneur, such as those faced by Richard Branson, effectively become automatic choices.

In particular, two things are glossed over by the theory of the firm. The first is the question of how the business opportunity which led to the founding of the firm was recognized in the first place; here mainstream economics simply assumes that business opportunities will be automatically recognized and acted upon. The second is how entrepreneurs decide on the best way to organize and use the productive resources under their control. The assumption here is that if two entrepreneurs had access to the same quantity and quality of factor inputs, then we should expect both entrepreneurs to utilize and organize these factors in an identical way within their respective firms. In other words, the rival firms would not only be as efficient as each other, but each firm would also be expected to operate at optimum efficiency.

We should point out that anybody who understands how the mainstream theory of the firm evolved appreciates that it was never intended to be a platform from which advice could be offered to entrepreneurs and business managers in the first place. It is instead a small part of a much bigger theory about how competitive markets work (we discuss this in Chapters 2 and 7). It is worth noting, however, that, despite this, it has been used in the field of strategic management to offer advice to firms as they seek to gain a competitive edge (often called **competitive advantage**) over their rivals, and this has had important implications for actual business decisions and behaviour. Because the theory expects that any two entrepreneurs will make identical and optimal decisions for any given bundle of factor inputs, it follows that a firm can only obtain an edge over its rivals if it has ownership/access to factors of production that are not available to its rivals for some reason. In other words, competitive advantage derives from the ownership of unique physical assets rather than unique **intellectual assets** such as the **knowledge** and the **imagination** of the entrepreneur.

Casual empirical observation suggests that this view of the source of competitive advantage is incomplete because the variable quality of decisions made by real world entrepreneurs seems quite clearly to make a difference to the success or failure of firms. One economist who has taken this point seriously is Harvey Leibenstein, who suggested that firms would not necessarily use resources as efficiently as the mainstream theory of the firm implies. In doing so, Leibenstein opened up an important role for the entrepreneur in economic theory.

3.3.2 The entrepreneur and the inefficient firm

Leibenstein coined the phrase 'X-inefficiency' to describe the key feature of his theory of the inefficient firm.

> X-inefficiency is defined as a state where the firm is underutilizing its resources for some reason and as a result its costs per unit of output are higher than they need to be.

In other words, an X-inefficient firm is not fulfilling its productive potential. This opens up scope for it to obtain an improvement in its position, as it were, 'for free'.

One of the principal reasons why the firm may not be fulfilling its potential is the nature of labour employment contracts. **Labour employment contracts are incomplete:** while a typical employment contract describes the hours of work for which the employee will be rewarded it cannot specify the **level of effort** that the employee will put into the job. Consequently the effort level of employees is a discretionary variable (in other words, it is up to the individual) and there is scope for the productivity of the labour force to be less than its inherent potential.

It should be noted at this point that managers, as employees of the firm, are also a part of the labour force hired by the entrepreneur. This means that a crucial role for the entrepreneur is to hire 'good' managers who are able to motivate the workforce to produce effort at or close to its maximum potential. Of course the entrepreneur has no unique way of knowing if a manager is putting in maximum effort although various options can be used to try to bring this about. One option is to offer profit-sharing incentives (this could also be offered to the non-managerial workforce) but getting the balance right here is something of an art – the more of the profit that is offered to others the less will be left for the entrepreneur. Richard Branson seems to have surmounted this problem by recruiting friends (Nik Powell) and relations (Simon Draper) and more generally by creating an ethos of joint ownership, if not actual joint ownership. The fundamental message from this analysis is that entrepreneurs have to possess the skill to **motivate and inspire effort in others**.

A further implication of the X-inefficiency approach is that **entrepreneurs should be aware of inefficiencies in rival firms** because such inefficiency offers scope for a better-run operation to be competitively superior. One could argue that in 1970 WH Smith and John Menzies were inefficient in the sense that their sales staff were apathetic towards the record-buying customer and Richard Branson was fully aware of this. Also, having chosen not to respond to the abolition of RPM, the price of records from Smiths and Menzies was high. Virgin Mail Order and, more importantly, the Virgin record shops were a creative response to the inefficiency displayed by the two retail giants.

Awareness of business opportunities is a feature of the entrepreneur that has been discussed in great detail by a group of non-mainstream economists who are known collectively as the Austrian school. Friedrich von Hayek and Israel Kirzner exemplify this approach.

3.3.3 The Austrian perspective on the entrepreneur

The Austrian analysis of the entrepreneur is intimately associated with the quest for a deeper understanding of how markets work. You will recall that in Chapter 2 we introduced the notions of partial equilibrium analysis and the supply and demand diagram (Figure 2.3), and we outlined the mainstream view that markets tend towards stable equilibrium positions. Austrian economists take as their point of departure the notion that **market equilibrium is the end result of the economic process** and as such it is a relatively uninteresting phenomenon. The implication of their view is that economists ought to devote most of their time and energy to developing a deeper understanding of the disequilibrium processes that generate eventual equilibrium outcomes. It is only when a market is in disequilibrium that active decisions are being taken by suppliers and demanders. The Austrian theory of the entrepreneur is developed in this disequilibrium context.

If a market is in equilibrium it implies that entrepreneurs and their customers have arrived at a state of the world where neither group has any incentive to change their trading behaviour. From an entrepreneur's perspective this means that no further profit opportunities remain to be exploited in the market.

Hayek describes the equilibrium state as one where everyone has full information about potential trading opportunities and where everyone has acted optimally in the light of this information. Disequilibrium behaviour is therefore exemplified firstly by the acquisition of useful knowledge and, secondly, by its communication. For example, an entrepreneur may have acquired some useful knowledge that allows a particular good to be obtained at a lower cost than is being achieved by rival entrepreneurs, but unless this fact is communicated to customers (in the form of lower asking prices) they are unlikely to switch their custom away from the low-cost entrepreneur's rivals.

For Hayek the **disequilibrium market process** can usefully be described as a **process of discovery**. For example, the entrepreneur discovers if asking prices and product quality are appropriate while customers discover who is able to supply them with goods of acceptable quality at prices that offer them value for money. Virgin Mail Order Records provides a poignant example of this.

Kirzner picks up Hayek's theme and points out that **disequilibrium situations can arise because of interspatial (geographical) differences** between suppliers and demanders. For example, for much of the 1990s the most popular Japanese motorcycles were available to the motorcycle riding public in continental Europe and other countries of the world for prices that were considerably lower than those paid by UK customers. Awareness of this led a few enterprising UK-based motorcycle retailers to purchase motorcycles from these markets rather than through official manufacturer's channels and this led to a burgeoning growth in so-called parallel imports into the UK. The upshot of this was that official imports were dramatically reduced in price. This process of buying cheap and selling on is generally given the name **arbitrage**. According to Kirzner anyone who partakes in this practice is an entrepreneur. In fact the key characteristic of the entrepreneur for Kirzner is **alertness** to such potential sources of profit.

Another source of disequilibrium arises because of **intertemporal differences between supply and demand**. The entrepreneur who is alert to this situation undertakes to obtain or produce goods or services in advance of buyers demanding the product. In its extreme form the entrepreneur may have no idea what demand for the product will be. In this situation the entrepreneur must necessarily exercise some kind of **foresight** (which may be based upon gut instinct or an educated guess) and as a result take something of a gamble in much the same way that Richard Branson did on Mike Oldfield's album *Tubular Bells*. As we have discussed in Chapter 1, the entrepreneur in this situation takes a truly heroic decision in the sense that he or she faces **uncertainty** rather than calculable risk.

It will be clear from the discussion of Hayek's and Kirzner's ideas that Austrian economics is concerned with explaining movements towards equilibrium in markets that already exist as a result of the actions of individuals who are alert to profit opportunities. This view contrasts that of Joseph Schumpeter who constructed an entire theory of economic development around the contention that the entrepreneur is a destroyer of equilibrium situations.

3.3.4 Schumpeter on the entrepreneur as innovator

Schumpeter is very clear about what entrepreneurs do. In essence they are the **primary agents of economic development and change** and they think up ways of **putting scarce resources to new uses**. They do this by carrying out one or more of five broad activities:

- Introducing new goods or a new quality of good.
- Introducing new ways of producing goods.
- Opening up new markets (usually overseas).
- Discovering new sources of supply of raw materials or partly-manufactured goods.
- Reorganizing the structure of an industry (for example, by creating a monopoly or breaking up a monopoly situation).

Each of these activities is an example of **innovation**.

Schumpeter is very precise about the meaning of innovation. In particular he is very careful to distinguish between **invention** and **imitation**. Invention is an activity which can be thought of as more in the realm of the creation of scientific knowledge than business, although this is not necessarily the case, and it provides a possible source of raw material upon which entrepreneurial individuals can draw as they seek out business opportunities (one might think of the scientific knowledge that underpins everyday commercial products such as the light bulb, the motor car and the aeroplane). Innovation, on the other hand, refers to the **very first commercial application** of what up to that point has remained non-commercialized knowledge, and the first person to do this is called the entrepreneur.

Schumpeter points out that 'to produce means to combine materials and forces within our reach' and that the same materials may well be used in different ways. He describes these potential alternatives as new combinations and identifies **the entrepreneur's role as the discovery and commercialization of new combinations**.

The second person in the market is not an entrepreneur on Schumpeter's definition because the first person has already shown the way. The second and subsequent entrants/adopters are simply imitators.

Schumpeter's discussion also points out that particular people should only be described as entrepreneurs at the point when they first introduce their innovation. The subsequent activity of running and managing the resulting business is not entrepreneurship in Schumpeter's view – it is instead the more routine job of business administration. However, Schumpeter also points out that an entrepreneur does not necessarily have to be a business proprietor; it is quite plausible within his definition of entrepreneurship for a manager employed by a firm to carry out an entrepreneurial act and, in fact, given the prevalence of large corporations within the developed economies of the world, this implies that continued business success may well depend upon the development of entrepreneurially inclined executives. This phenomenon is known as **intrapreneurship**.

Schumpeter draws a clear distinction between entrepreneurs and capitalists. Capitalists are the providers of finance; they lend money to entrepreneurs and as such Schumpeter is adamant that entrepreneurs do not bear the financial risks associated with their novel actions. This is a point of contention and one that we explore further in Section 9.2. The problem with Schumpeter's view is that by definition the outcome of innovative activity is uncertain and it may be very difficult to persuade third parties to invest in unproven activities. Be that as it may, his fundamental point is that the act of providing credit to finance innovation is not, in his view, how we can recognize who is and who is not an entrepreneur. This is important in Schumpeter's theory of economic development because, among other reasons, it allows him to analyse the existence of entrepreneurship in economic systems other than capitalism.

The most significant and coherent analysis of entrepreneurship in economics apart from that of Schumpeter is arguably that provided by the British economist Mark Casson. Casson's theory of the entrepreneur was first articulated in 1982 and, like Schumpeter's, is part of a bigger theory of how economies work and analyses the role played by the entrepreneur in the co-ordination of scarce resources in a world where information and knowledge are imperfect. (Before proceeding further you may like to re-read Section 2.3 where we discuss the problem of economic co-ordination.)

3.3.5 The entrepreneur as a specialist in co-ordination

Casson begins his detailed analysis with a very precise definition: '**an entrepreneur is someone who specializes in taking judgemental decisions about the co-ordination of scarce resources.**' Three key points arise out of this definition. The first point is that entrepreneurs are **specialists** at what they do. From an economics perspective when somebody specializes in an activity they do so because they have a comparative advantage. We have pointed out in Section 2.2 that the economic theory of comparative advantage implies that relative capabilities are fixed and we have suggested that this assumption ignores the effects of education, training and practise which will allow people to improve their capabilities as time passes. However, this observation does not pose a problem for Casson because he argues that the core capabilities of entrepreneurs (which are the source of their comparative advantage) are very difficult or impossible to learn – in fact he argues that some of these capabilities are more or less innate. Furthermore, he suggests that these innate capabilities are unevenly distributed throughout the population and that they are scarce.

In order to pinpoint which core capabilities are identified exclusively with Casson's decision-making entrepreneur we first have to understand a little bit of detail about how decisions are made generally. Table 3.1 summarizes the typical stages in decision making and the correspondent qualities (capabilities) that are required by the decision maker.

Of the qualities listed in the right-hand column of Table 3.1 Casson identifies **two as essential** for the successful entrepreneur, namely, **imagination** and **foresight**. Imagination is needed to see alternative ways of using resources – it might also be called vision. Foresight is a complement to imagination and entrepreneurs especially need it because there may well be a shortage of suitable data to collect as a result of the novelty of the alternatives conjured up at the imagination stage. If possessed on their own these qualities will not make a successful entrepreneur; ideally the entrepreneur should possess all of the qualities

Table 3.1 **Decision-making activities and the qualities they require**	
Activities	**Qualities**
First stage: formulation of the decision problem	
Specification of the objective	Self-knowledge (or knowledge of the principal's objectives)
Specification of the options	Imagination
Specification of the constraints	Practical knowledge
Derivation of the decision rule	Analytical ability
Second stage: generating the data	
Data collection	Search skill
Data estimation	Foresight
Third stage: execution of the decision	
Application of the data to the decision rule	Computational skill
Initiation of the implementation process	Communication skill (in formulating instructions)

(Source: Mark Casson (1982) *The Entrepreneur*, Oxford, Blackwell Publishing, p. 29)

(i.e. be a generalist). However, Casson argues that the nature of the other qualities means that they are perhaps less difficult to hire in than the two essential ones. It may therefore be possible to employ other people who possess the requisite 'missing' qualities (recall that Richard Branson relied heavily on Simon Draper's specialized music knowledge). He does not suggest that this task is an easy one because of difficulties with identifying these qualities in people. Furthermore, if the 'hiring in' route is followed, the successful entrepreneur will need to possess two extra qualities that do not appear in Table 3.1. These are **delegation skills** and **organizational skills.**

The second important point highlighted by Casson's definition is the **judgemental nature of the decisions** that the entrepreneur makes. Judgemental decisions are those for which there are no objective criteria to guide the decision maker's choice. In other words, if two different people were asked to make a decision to recommend a particular course of action and no objective data or solution concept were available, they would have to exercise their respective judgements and in so doing they would, in all likelihood, arrive at two different recommendations. On the other hand, if the same two people were asked to 'recommend' an answer to the mathematical question, 'what is 10 + 10?' they would be able to apply an objective decision rule and both would arrive at the same answer. In short, judgemental decisions involve different perceptions of problems and issues, different interpretations and possibly access to different information.

Typically an entrepreneur can be thought of as someone who judges situations and opportunities differently from the majority of other people – in essence, it is this difference of opinion that allows the entrepreneur to act when others will not do so. This brings us on to the third important point highlighted in Casson's definition: when an entrepreneur co-ordinates scarce resources he or she essentially **reallocates them to alternative uses.** In other words, Casson's approach is consistent with the Austrian and Schumpeterian notion that the entrepreneur is an agent of change. Unlike Schumpeter, however, Casson is very clear that **entrepreneurship is an ongoing function** rather than a one-off act of innovation. His argument in support of this contention is that entrepreneurs essentially spend most of their time looking out for new information that makes the current allocation of resources appear to be inefficient.

Casson goes on to develop the implications of his definition in some detail. At the risk of oversimplifying his argument, we can say that he makes the point that in order to execute a reallocation of scarce resources, that is to carry out the role of co-ordination, the entrepreneur must have control over these resources. In a capitalist system this is achieved by taking on ownership of the relevant resources, in other words the entrepreneur has to buy or hire them. This observation is compatible with a number of activities, including:

- starting up a new firm;
- taking over an inefficient established firm; and
- acting as an arbitrageur.

For an example of the second of these activities of entrepreneurship, see Box 3.1 on Victor Kiam and Remington Inc.

Box 3.1 The entrepreneur in action – Victor Kiam and Remington Inc.

'You can make big money buying trouble.'
(Alan Burak, President of Helena Rubinstein)

Virtually everyone who remembers the 1980s and 1990s in the UK and USA will also remember Victor Kiam – he became famous as the man who coined the catchline, 'I liked the shaver so much I bought the company,' in his TV advertisements for the Remington shaver. Kiam was an entrepreneur with an eye for a new business opportunity and a knack for selling.

Box 3.1 (continued)

Kiam began his business career as a management trainee with Lever Brothers after graduating from Harvard Business School in 1951. He stayed with the company until 1955 when he joined Playtex. He moved rapidly up the corporate ladder and when he left in 1968 he had made it to executive vice-president of International Latex. After leaving Playtex Kiam was not sure what to do next so he took advice from the director of a New York headhunting company who suggested that he either start his own company or buy an existing company to run. Kiam claims that this advice changed his life because it gave him the push he needed to go down the entrepreneurial road. Shortly after taking this advice he used sales of shares he had acquired in Playtex to buy a stake in the struggling Benrus Corp. (watches and jewellery) and he used his marketing skills to help turn it around. In 1976 Kiam learned from a colleague that the electric shaver company Remington was up for sale, but he thought little of it because he knew nothing about the shaver business. Then one Saturday in 1978 Kiam was reading *Business Week*, as was his usual ritual, when he spotted a business opportunity wrapped up in the words of an interview with J.P. Lyet, the chairman of Sperry Corp. (of which Remington was one division): 'We'd rather sell one computer installation than 100,000 Remington shavers.' Kiam wondered why the head of Sperry would denigrate one of his own products and took his attitude as an indication that something was not right at Remington.

Kiam wasted no time; he obtained the company's financial records first thing on Monday morning and began the process of learning about its operations. At the time, Remington produced a variety of products for different countries (such as watches for Mexico, steam irons for Italy) and only its electric shaver was common across all of them. He confined his study to the shaver business. Having never used an electric shaver he obtained a Remington to try the product for himself. After his first electric shave he was impressed with the closeness and comfort, so he purchased the products of rival companies and tested them against the Remington over the course of a week by shaving one half of his face with the Remington and the other half with a variety of rival shavers. He remained impressed; in fact, in his opinion, the Remington was easily a superior product. He augmented his personal research by telephoning retailers whose acquaintance he had made while running Benrus; many of these had stocked Benrus's watches and they also stocked shavers. Without mentioning his interest in Remington he asked them to tell him anything they could about the shaver business. The general

Box 3.1 (continued)

consensus was that Remington had the best product but the clear market leader in the USA was Norelco with a 70 per cent market share. Kiam concluded that Remington management didn't seem to know how to sell their product: 'I knew the product was a winner. With the right management and improved marketing, the company could be turned around.' Kiam bought the company in a leveraged buyout deal (a purchase largely based on debt) for $25 million in December 1978. The problems he identified at Remington were:

- Overemphasis on creative product design leading to new lines of shavers every six months. Kiam believed the principal reason for this was that the company was run by engineers. This led to retailers being alienated because every six months they would find themselves carrying obsolete stock. Norelco never changed its design and it outsold Remington by a ratio of 5 to 1.

- The latest Remington shavers were frequently out of stock because the company did not have an efficient distribution policy.

- Pricing followed a 'me too' strategy; every time a rival increased their price so did Remington.

- The company culture was too hierarchical and the workforce not sufficiently motivated.

- The company did not focus its efforts on its best product (the shaver).

Kiam dealt with each of these issues systematically:

- He pulled Remington out of all non-shaver-related business and as a result trimmed down the management team.

- He put the engineers to work on designing a no-frills shaver based around the fact that they already had the most powerful motor on the market – the result was a shaver which still retained performance but which retailed for $19.95 compared to the next lowest priced rival's retail price of $34.95.

- He set about eradicating the gap between blue collar workers and white collar managers and made everyone part of a profit-sharing plan: 'As far as I was concerned, we were all labour and we were all working for Remington.'

- He improved the marketing of the shaver by emphasizing the superiority of its functionality (its unique selling point); the first TV advertisement used the catchline: 'Shaves as close as a blade or your money back.'

> **Box 3.1** (continued)
>
> - He improved distribution. Initially, he raised the profile of Remington with retailers by sending out a team to paint a picture of what was going on internally and to restore confidence in Remington in the retailers' eyes. Central to this was explaining that the new lines were going to be stable and orders would be shipped in 24 hours. At the time a recession was biting so the new low price helped too.
>
> Kiam's approach worked wonderfully and half a million shavers were sold in the first year with significant market share taken from rivals. Kiam achieved this when other people were sceptical about the business opportunity tied up in Remington. His perspective on this was that entrepreneurs who see an opportunity to turn the fortunes of a company around are like firemen: 'they are running into a situation when everyone else is trying to leave.'

Casson augments his theory with an analysis of the crucial role played by the entrepreneur in the setting up of markets. Essentially he develops the theory that **entrepreneurs are market makers** and in so doing provides important insights into the nature of this important **institution**. Casson's insights have particular resonance for the nascent entrepreneur because they provide a good deal of practical advice about the obstacles to trade. In fact his market-making theory suggests that an entrepreneur may need to develop or have access to qualities in addition to those associated with decision making.

The purpose of a market is to allow buyers and sellers to trade with each other. Mainstream economics assumes that markets spontaneously arise and that they are costless to use, but Casson points out that markets do not simply appear out of the ether but are constructed by human action, in particular by entrepreneurs. There are six main obstacles to trade and each arises because of a lack of information. Overcoming each of the six obstacles in turn can be thought of as taking the steps required to allow a successful trade to take place or, as Casson puts it, each step is designed to take transactors from a state of mutual isolation towards the successful completion of a trade. The **six obstacles to trade** are:

(i)   The need for the potential buyer and seller to find each other.

(ii) The need for each party to communicate reciprocal wants.

(iii) The need to negotiate a price.

(iv) The need to exchange custody of the goods in return for payment.

(v) The need to screen for quality of the goods (in other words, are the goods up to the promised specification?).

(vi) The need to be able to enforce compensation if the goods are revealed not to be of the promised specification.

We have discussed some of the institutions that help to overcome these obstacles in Chapter 2 so we will not discuss them further here. But Casson's chief point is that if entrepreneurs wish to sell their goods then they have to take the initiative in constructing mechanisms to overcome these obstacles to trade – customers have little or no role to play here – and, as a result, the costs of setting up a market are borne by the entrepreneur in the first instance. Furthermore, these are **sunk costs** that typically have to be **made in advance of any trading activity** and which continue to be incurred ahead of the receipt of sales revenue.

> Sunk costs are defined as opportunity costs that cannot be recovered by selling the enterprise to someone else or by liquidating its assets – either because they involve assets whose market value is below their purchase price, or because they involve committing resources to intangible activities.

These sunk costs include resources devoted to product development and copyrighting, highly specific tooling and other equipment, signs, logos and other marketing expenses, and the foregone use of the entrepreneur's time from alternative activities. They make the entrepreneur vulnerable, given the uncertainties associated with subsequent revenue.

The strong implication of this perspective is that entrepreneurs need to possess or to acquire excellent **bargaining skills** if they are to recover upfront investments and correspondingly make a **profit** from their superior ability at making judgemental decisions.

> Profits that accrue to the entrepreneur are commonly defined in economics as a residual income left over after the entrepreneur has paid the costs of the other factors.

Casson, however, does not see **entrepreneurial profit** as a residual but instead as **earned income** since entrepreneurs have to perform their function actively rather than sit back and let the other factors of production do all of the work.

3.3.6 Empirical analysis of the entrepreneur

With the exception of the mainstream perspective it will be clear that the economic perspectives on entrepreneurship outlined above share the common precept that entrepreneurial raw material is a scarce resource. Casson makes a particularly strong case for this argument, but does empirical research support this view?

All empirical research is subject to problems and limitations and empirical investigations of entrepreneurship are no exception. One of the biggest problems with empirical work on entrepreneurship is getting hold of representative data. Most researchers simplify this task by assuming that entrepreneurs operate through the creation of new (small) firms. We have deliberately avoided placing the entrepreneur within this context in our discussions above and indeed the case of Victor Kiam illustrates the danger of the assumption that entrepreneurs only operate through small and medium sized enterprises (SMEs). The small firm sector is nonetheless an important element of many Western economies and, despite the limitations of the perspective, it can provide some useful insights.

David Deakins and Mark Freel (2003), for example, provide data for the UK which indicate that the smallest SMEs (defined as those employing no more than nine people) increased in number from 1 597 000 in 1979 to 3 490 000 in 1999. This suggests that an increasing number of individuals decided to become entrepreneurs in this period but even so, if we assume that these small firms are run by a single owner-entrepreneur, in a population of approximately 60 million people the proportion of entrepreneurs is just 6 per cent. This would seem to confirm the economist's view that entrepreneurs are a scarce resource in the general population. Of course our analysis here is highly simplified and it is difficult to know how to interpret such crude data manipulation.

Data that report the number of existing businesses do not capture the true extent of entrepreneurial talent because some people who possess it may choose to exercise it in contexts other than the small firm environment, or they may not exercise it at all because of the opportunity cost of doing so. To give some perspective to the smallest firm calculation, in the next size category, those firms that employ 10–19 people, numbers drop off dramatically to 109 000 in 1999. If we assume that all of these firms are run by an entrepreneur, this does little to change our conclusion that entrepreneurs are relatively scarce in the UK economy.

Frédéric Delmar and Per Davidsson (2000) conduct a more sophisticated study of population involvement in the small business sector for Sweden and compare it to figures from the USA. Rather than record the actual number of supposedly entrepreneurial firms in any category, this study surveys people who are nascent entrepreneurs in the sense that they may not yet have actually started the business. These data are not comparable with our simplified UK analysis but they do reinforce the notion that entrepreneurship is a relatively scarce resource. For example, only 2 per cent of the Swedish population aged between 18 and 70 were trying to start an independent business at the time of the survey in 1998. This compares to a figure of 3.8 per cent in the USA in 1996.

The issue of scarcity aside, our discussions above indicate clearly that providing an answer to the question, 'what is an entrepreneur?' is far from straightforward. It should be clear also that this is because entrepreneurship is not easily identified with a single function. At the risk of oversimplifying the issue it is probably fair to say that the Austrian perspective attempts to identify entrepreneurship with a single function, alertness to opportunities for arbitrage, while Schumpeter makes a similar attempt but equates entrepreneurship with innovation. Both of these functions are entrepreneurial. In contrast, Casson's theory of the entrepreneur is more general and treats the role as multifunctional. Also, it has the virtue of being able to incorporate the Austrian and Schumpeterian perspectives while extending Leibenstein's perspective that the role of the entrepreneur is to seek out and rectify inefficient resource allocation. Casson's explicit treatment of judgemental decision making paints a picture of the entrepreneur as a sophisticated multi-talented individual, while his treatment of market making grounds his theory in the practical business of everyday trade. In consequence it is a more inclusive and detailed theory of the entrepreneur than the narrower formulations that precede it. This said, Casson does not explore the economic psychology of the entrepreneur in any detail and as a result his theory is incomplete. With this in mind we now introduce a further complementary theory of the entrepreneur, which takes as its point of departure the notion that every business opportunity begins life as an idea. This interpretation of the entrepreneur builds upon the discussion we introduced in Chapter 2 which suggests that the economy can usefully be viewed as a complex system of partially interconnected elements. In an economy where connections are incomplete (which implies that all possible combinations of resources have yet to be perceived), the task of the entrepreneur can be thought of as constructing as yet unrealized connections.

3.3.7   A new departure – the entrepreneur as a constructor of connections

The theory of the entrepreneur as a constructor of connections takes as given the notion articulated by Kirzner, Schumpeter, Leibenstein and Casson that entrepreneurial individuals spend much of their time looking out for profit opportunities. The perspective takes its cue from the work of the philosopher-economist George Shackle who proposed that most thoughts, including new ideas, are based upon a limited set of elements that are capable of being combined in new ways. A non-economic but nonetheless vivid example of this is the 26 letters of the alphabet that can be formed into new words. The implication of

Shackle's proposition is that profit opportunities are constructed initially as possibilities in the minds of entrepreneurs and this means recognizing connections between hitherto unconnected elements. The fundamental insight of this perspective is that **profit opportunities are not things that lie around waiting to be found; the entrepreneur has to construct them actively**. In order to illustrate the implications of the connectionist view we will discuss an array of examples.

Consider the case of an academic publisher as an entrepreneur. When the publisher receives an unsolicited book proposal the would-be author is, in effect, saying, 'I construe this as a profit opportunity', but whether or not it becomes one in the eye of the entrepreneur depends on the prospective net revenue stream that the latter assigns to it. If the publisher sends it out to academic referees, their construction of it as a profit opportunity may be rather different because they lack the publisher's knowledge of how similar books have turned out in terms of costs and revenues. Likewise, different publishers, with different pools of experience and different ways of forming conjectures, may differ over whether or not it could be profitable to take on a particular book. The point here is that it is not awareness of the possible business activity *per se* that makes it a profit opportunity but the **awareness of the activity combined with the imagined net revenue stream** the publisher attaches to it. Clearly, people who can call upon different sets of elements will differ in the new ideas that they can construct and therefore the business opportunities they perceive.

Entrepreneurs may not only differ from the general public in terms of the mental ingredients they employ and their tendencies to **experiment mentally** with making new combinations. They may also be more willing to take risks because they do not construe hazards that the rest of the population sees – either due to not thinking in terms of particular dimensions, or because they have extra thought dimensions in certain areas that lead them to construe wider opportunities than the general public for gain and for managing problems.

If entrepreneurs are to survive in business – in other words, if they are going to make successful connections – they will need to possess some understanding of how their potential customers make mental connections. Sales will not be achieved if the package on offer does not match up with the requirements of many of those in the target market. Knowing what will appeal to particular consumers requires an appreciation of the contexts in which choices are being made, which are themselves a reflection of the thought systems that customers use. As a consequence of employing their individual ways of looking at the world, consumers end up having lives that are based around linked sets of activities and products that comprise their 'lifestyle' (see also Section 4.6). For many consumers, it would be hard to imagine living without certain components of the set that makes up their own lifestyle and yet they would not even dream of consuming many of the goods that lie outside of these sets but which fall within the lifestyles of others. In principle, to understand the 'fabric' of particular individuals' lives, it appears that the entrepreneur may need to trade with them repeatedly. Fortunately for entrepreneurs, however, people can often be lumped approximately into particular lifestyle stereotypes – such as 'greenie', 'yuppie', 'double income, no kids' – on the basis of relatively limited market research.

The existence of consumer lifestyles means that patterns of substitution between rival brands of particular kinds of product depend on their linkages with other kinds of products. For example, consider the adoption of automatic washing machines in Britain in the 1970s in place of twin-tub designs. British suppliers were bemused by the loss of market share to Italian products. The latter offered inferior drying abilities compared with more expensive local machines that had been designed to cope with the inclement British weather. The change in market share arose not because of the price difference *per se* but in association with the adoption of central heating systems that made it far easier to finish the drying process indoors if necessary. British manufacturers did not see this connection and had made their automatic machines so that they offered spin speeds equivalent to the outgoing twin-tubs, with all that this entailed in terms of extra costs of production.

Due to the complexities of household consumption systems, one change of lifestyle can have all manner of market implications. Continuing the previous example, we might also note that the demand for automatic washing machines itself would have been associated with the growth in households where both spouses went out to work and hence required the convenience of machines that could perform the entire wash/spin cycle on their own, for example, during the night. Dual income households, in turn, were better able to afford central heating and double-glazing systems. However, they often could not function without a child-minding infrastructure (children's television included!) and convenience foods. Because they were unable to be at home to deal with tradespeople during business hours, they would often spend weekends engaged in do-it-yourself work. They would demand reliability as a key requirement of their appliances and provided a fertile market for home security systems – and so on.

The successful entrepreneur may not only need to understand how potential customers make mental connections, and the connections that make up their lifestyles. There is money also to be made by seeing marketing links between products and possible tie-in products based on a common brand. Shrewd thinking in terms of connections has led to the assembly of modern mass-media/entertainment operations whose magazines promote television programmes, and vice versa, and both promote particular kinds of merchandise (such as movies and recorded music) produced elsewhere in the corporate empire. Failing that, the media contents can be connected to products of particular advertising sponsors (as with travel and home-improvement programmes) or devised to be ripe for commanding product placement fees. Similarly, a highly successful children's novel is no longer merely a book competing in no particular manner with other books and other ways of spending money. Now it is a book which may be connected to a movie (with soundtrack CD and subsequent video and DVD release), PC and PlayStation games, displays or rides at theme-parks, a wide range of toys and artefacts, with licensed brand extensions even to clothing, bedding, food, toothpaste and so on.

From the Shackle perspective, the creation of new products does not entail the creation of something from scratch but new connections between existing ideas, capabilities and technologies. An informal examination of the catalogues of modern consumer electronics firms such as Sony will reveal that innovation tends to entail new combinations of a multiplicity of technologies. Each new product feature, such as a PlayStation II's capacity to read DVDs, or electronic stability systems in cars, builds upon existing technologies, and the products of supposedly 'different' industries may end up as elements of other products – as with the incorporation of audio-visual entertainment systems in cars. Some technologies, such as LCD systems, soft touch keypads and memory chips, may be added to an astonishing variety of products, and their growing ubiquity makes it easier to apply them in yet more applications, as users can employ the same skills in all manner of different contexts. All it requires is that an entrepreneur dreams up the possible connections or is prepared to provide financial backing to an inventor who sees them sooner.

3.4 Summary

Our aim in this chapter has been to introduce you to the economics of the entrepreneur with a view to helping you understand the critical role played by entrepreneurial individuals as agents of change and creators of profit opportunities for the business. We have not discussed the entrepreneur from the perspective of the government policy maker because such a person is concerned less with the detail of entrepreneurship and more with wider

3.4 **Summary** (continued)

socio-political issues than the typical business person. Examples of questions to which policy makers want answers include: 'How much employment do entrepreneurs create in the economy?'; 'What influence does educational background have on the success of entrepreneurs (typically equated with small business proprietorship)?'; 'Which regions of the country are more entrepreneurial than others?' We do not address these issues here but if you are interested in studying some of the related statistics we can recommend a visit to the website of the UK Department of Trade and Industry. Neither do we explicitly examine typical personality traits of entrepreneurs or motivations for becoming an entrepreneur. A multitude of empirical studies has been directed towards these questions and the consensus of opinion seems to be that no reliable identikit picture has emerged in terms of personality traits and also that entrepreneurs can come from a diverse range of backgrounds in terms of previous experience and education. In the light of these findings we have left the job of inferring likely personal qualities to you the reader; our hope is that the brief overview of Richard Branson's early career may provide some pointers, as may the story of Victor Kiam. Clearly our summary of Casson's theory of the entrepreneur is useful here too.

Another deliberate tactic on our part has been to discuss entrepreneurs without placing them in any particular organizational context in as far as this has been possible. Implicitly we have in mind the notion that entrepreneurs will operate via some kind of commercial organization, although this need not be the case; but we have refrained from specifying whether this organization is small or large, or owned by the entrepreneur or some other party. **Entrepreneurs are found in a variety of business organizations** from sole proprietorships to large corporations. Entrepreneurial executives in large corporations are called intrapreneurs. The practicalities of fostering intrapreneurship in the large organization will be discussed in Chapter 11; for now we will note that most writers on the subject point to an inherent tension between the disruptive change that intrapreneurship implies and the stable routinized environment (bureaucracy) that one normally associates with large established organizations.

Our final point is that the connectionist view offers us the prospect of an economic theory of the entrepreneur/intrapreneur that has the potential to offer practical guidance about the act of new business idea creation because it offers clues about how the seeds of business opportunity, that is newly

3.4 **Summary** (continued)

perceived connections, can be acquired. For example, one might imagine entrepreneurs/intrapreneurs systematically looking at a matrix of all possible combinations of products or components about which they have knowledge to see what new connections might be made in theory and what might be the practical objections to them. The other economic theories on entrepreneurship are less promising in this regard but they offer complementary analysis of other aspects.

3.5 Some questions to consider

1. What qualities did Richard Branson display that helped him create a successful business? Which of these qualities do you think was essential?

2. Can you construct an argument that the owner of a small corner shop that sells sweets, magazines and newspapers is an entrepreneur? Can you construct an argument that suggests the shop owner is not an entrepreneur? How would you reconcile your arguments?

3. Can you explain how trade would be facilitated in the absence of entrepreneurial market-making activity?

4. Does the theory of the entrepreneur as a constructor of connections reinforce or undermine Casson's theory of the entrepreneur as a person who is capable of exercising superior judgement?

5. If someone asked you to define entrepreneurship what would you tell them in the light of this chapter?

6. Using the terminology of the economics of entrepreneurship compare and contrast the Richard Branson story with the Victor Kiam story.

3.6 Recommended additional reading sources

Mark Casson (1982) *The Entrepreneur*, Oxford, Martin Robertson. This is a very clearly written book and, as well as providing a seminal economic analysis of entrepreneurship, a careful reading will provide you with a useful lesson in how to think like an economist.

All of the quotations in our account of the early years of Richard Branson were taken from his autobiography, Richard Branson (2002) *Losing My Virginity: The Autobiography*, London, Virgin Books. This is the updated edition of Richard Branson's original 1998 autobiography. It is an excellent insider perspective on what it takes to be the kind of entrepreneur who creates new companies. The non-business aspects are quite interesting too – especially if you are a fan of adventure sports.

All of the quotations for Box 3.1 were taken from Victor Kiam (1986) *Going for It! How to Succeed as an Entrepreneur*, Glasgow, William Collins. Hidden among the attempts to inspire you lurk interesting biographical details of Kiam's journey to entrepreneurship and some useful practical insights into the entrepreneurial mind. Unlike Richard Branson, Victor Kiam began his career as a corporate executive. Later he became famous for reversing the poor fortunes of Remington Inc. following his buyout of the company; the details on this aspect of his career are a very clear example of how one can reallocate resources.

For a very accessible overview and discussion of the relationship between entrepreneurship and small firms in the UK economy, including a timely discussion of e-business and the small firm, see David Deakins and Mark Freel (2003) *Entrepreneurship and Small Firms* (3rd edn), Maidenhead, McGraw-Hill.

Frédéric Delmar and Per Davidsson (2000) 'Where do they come from? Prevalence and characteristics of nascent entrepreneurs', *Entrepreneurship and Regional Development*, 12, pp. 1–23. A fine example of the practical problems with empirical research in the area of entrepreneurship which, in addition to providing cross-country comparisons of entrepreneurship rates in the population, also highlights typical characteristics of entrepreneurs including an analysis of gender and education.

Richard Swedberg (ed.) (2000) *Entrepreneurship: the Social Science View*, Oxford, Oxford University Press. A collection of important papers including Schumpeter's seminal statement on the entrepreneur as innovator and a useful chronology of theories of entrepreneurship in economics by Mark Blaug. The book goes beyond economic perspectives and the collection taken as a whole provides the reader with a relatively seamless transition from economic perspectives through sociological perspectives, anthropological perspectives and management perspectives.

Israel Kirzner (1979) *Perception, Opportunity, and Profit: Studies in the Theory of Entrepreneurship*, Chicago, University of Chicago Press. A digest of Kirzner's early papers on the role of the entrepreneur. Essential Kirzner.

The 'constructor of connections' view of entrepreneurship is presented at greater length in Peter E. Earl (2003) 'The entrepreneur as a constructor of connections', pp. 113–30 of Roger Koppl (ed.) *Austrian Economics and Entrepreneurial Studies: Advances in Austrian Economics*, Volume 6, Amsterdam, JAI/Elsevier. Many other chapters in that volume will also repay study.

For a recent wide-ranging major contribution that includes psychological perspectives and considers policies for promoting entrepreneurship, see David A. Harper (2003) *Foundations of Entrepreneurship and Economic Development*, London and New York, Routledge. This is a sequel to Harper (1996) *Entrepreneurship and the Market Process*, London and New York, Routledge. In the initial book, Harper focuses on the experimental nature of entrepreneurial activity, emphasizing problems of information and knowledge and likening the entrepreneur's task to that of a scientist.

4

Who wants the product and in what quantity?

Learning outcomes

If you study this chapter carefully, it may help you to understand:

♦ the impact that the context of a purchasing decision has on the problems with which buyers have to deal

♦ why the mix of goods purchased changes as incomes change and as technological progress occurs

♦ how different purchasing decision rules work and why they matter for business policy

♦ the economic significance of both changes in fashion and the 'lifestyle' concept

♦ why there are both similarities and differences in the ways that consumption and business purchasing decisions are made

♦ what is meant by, and what determines, 'brand equity' and 'brand loyalty'.

To the extent that you develop such understanding, you should be better able to:

♦ provide advice on which questions market researchers should ask in a particular context

♦ critically appraise alternative proposals for changes to product designs, prices and methods of promotion and distribution.

4.1 Introduction

In this chapter we assume that the entrepreneur has conceived of an opportunity to make a profit and, as a result, needs to be able to form an idea of exactly what good or service to provide, how to promote and distribute it and how its sales may be affected by its price. In essence, to answer this question requires answering the related question, '**How do buyers choose what to buy?**' This is not easy because each different combination of product specification, promotion campaign and distribution method has its own particular demand curve.

> A demand curve is a graphical representation of the relationship between the prices that might be asked for a product and the quantity that consumers are prepared to buy at each of these possible prices.

Worse still, although economists talk loosely of demand 'curves' and then normally go and represent them as straight lines that slope smoothly down to the right on diagrams that depict price on the vertical axis and quantity on the horizontal axis, **demand curves in reality may have multiple segments with different slopes and breaks between them**, implying very jerky responses of sales to changes in price. Sometimes a demand curve may even slope upwards along part of its length. Figure 4.1 shows examples of both well-behaved and badly-behaved demand curves. Economists normally draw demand curves with respect to sales at the level of the market as a whole, but if a consumer may buy multiple units of a particular product then that consumer's willingness to purchase it at various prices could be depicted as a demand curve. In the latter case, we could then sum individual consumers' demand curves together horizontally (that is, in terms of how much each would buy at a particular price) to get the overall market demand curve.

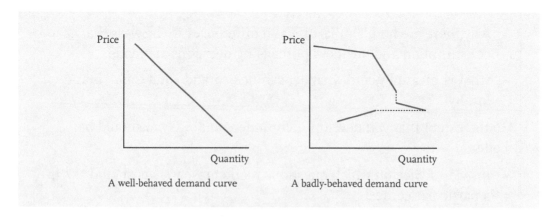

Figure 4.1 Well-behaved and badly-behaved demand curves

Discontinuities in demand curves can arise for **psychological reasons**, such as the consumer's cognitive mechanisms being subject to **threshold effects** (a change may need to be substantial to be noticed), or for **institutional reasons**, such as conventions being used in the setting of budgets. When a price goes above normal ranges of expectations, sales can fall away sharply until customers get used to the idea of that product being *that* expensive. This phenomenon is known as **'sticker shock'** (here, 'sticker' refers to the pricing stickers attached to products). **Kinks in demand curves** can also arise as a consequence of how other firms respond to changes in the price charged for the product, by changing their prices. The seemingly perverse case of higher prices leading to higher sales may arise if, in the face of uncertainty, consumers use price as a proxy for quality (and perhaps do not even look at a product at all if its price is less than the lower end of the budget range in which they have chosen to look), or if a higher price means that the product serves better as a status symbol.

These phenomena might lead one to expect that when economists theorize about the nature of buyer behaviour they would do so in an interdisciplinary manner, bringing in ideas from psychology and sociology. Heterodox economists do precisely this, but mainstream economists over the past century have sought to distance themselves from these disciplines. We explore both perspectives in this chapter, though because our concern is with ideas that have practical implications for business, coverage is skewed in favour of heterodox contributions.

It might be tempting to argue that, if we are so interested in the practical problem of sizing up demand, we should be covering market research here, not theories of choice. An entrepreneur or manager seeking to answer the question that this chapter poses could hand it over to market researchers, without acquiring any theoretical explanations of how buyers reach their decisions. The market researchers could then set to work with their clipboards and telephone-based questionnaires, or by staging consumer clinics to preview new products and have focus group discussions about them. However, there are some problems with this approach:

- The researchers may be prone to ask questions that have little to do with the particular issues that shape respondents' choices, or with how they resolve difficulties in making choices.

- The producer often needs to know what consumer choices will be long before purchases are actually made, but consumers themselves may only make up their minds, or even realize they have a need for a particular product, long after the decision to go ahead with production has been taken.

Given these problems and the costs of doing market research, **theories of buyer behaviour** may be useful to both business economists and market researchers because they may:

- provide a framework that helps in deciding **which questions** to ask during market research;

- help business economists to make better **predictions** about consumer choices in cases where it is not possible, for reasons of timing, secrecy or cost, to gather market intelligence from consumers;

- help business economists to **interpret** past data about changes in patterns of consumption and hence to draw inferences about future behaviour;

- influence the formation of government **policies** that have an impact on market conditions.

Theories of buyer behaviour present simplified pictures of the forces underlying choices in general. They are not intended to provide insights about the distinctive way that a particular consumer chooses, say, which television programme to watch and how such a choice is made in a manner different from a choice of which shampoo to buy, brand of hire car to rent or whatever. Given this, it may seem remarkable that they could be useful for thinking about business policy with respect to specific products. In fact, the mainstream approach is weak in this role precisely because it tries to present all choices as being made in the same way. The frameworks that we find most helpful are those that allow for a variety of approaches to choice and provide a means of assessing **which broad kinds of processes are likely to be operating in particular kinds of contexts**.

Before we examine the diverse ways that economists use to approach the question of how people choose what to buy, one important question must be raised: who is the customer? Most texts focus on consumers, that is to say, individuals who are buying the end products of supply chains to satisfy their personal wants or needs. Yet, in terms of value, the vast majority of transactions are **business-to-business** and concern **intermediate goods** – either things to be used to facilitate production, or components and flows of service inputs for a production process. This means that there is a link between this chapter's concerns and the discussion of make-or-buy decisions in Chapter 9. The relationship between what we say about firms and what we say about consumers also works the other way: consumers also face make-or-buy decisions, and the household is very much a **production system**, just like a factory, except that we call its machines 'domestic appliances' and 'power tools'. To achieve a more powerful perspective on consumer choice it will thus be useful to reflect on Chapters 5, 6 and 9 (once you have read them!) in terms of what household choices have in common with what is being said about the choices that face managers in firms.

Other texts probably do not focus on the purchasing behaviour of firms and organizations because their authors presume that these items all figure in the firms' or organizations' cost structures and hence that the basis for choosing them is simply a matter of how well they serve towards meeting goals such as profitability. If so, the demand for these kinds of products is covered in other chapters where production and cost theory and theories of demand for factors of production are considered.

Such an approach is reasonable if it is possible to work out the different monetary costs and benefits of rival models of an item, say, a photocopier or an office chair. But often it may be very difficult to do such calculations with any degree of precision and reduce everything to numbers representing overall net benefits offered by rival models. In these kinds of situations, the processes underlying purchasing decisions may end up being rather similar to those used by consumers. Hence in this chapter we mix both kinds of examples, though our focus is mainly on decisions made by consumers.

4.2 Mainstream consumer theory

Mainstream economists tend to regard their approach to the theory of choice as one of the major achievements of their way of thinking about economic problems. They have constructed a body of analysis that attempts to pin down the essence of the nature of choice in a manner that lends itself to very elegant formal presentations. They have found it to be useful for reflecting on many problems in areas such as public sector economics and international trade theory, as well as for analysing the conditions that might be required for the economy as a whole to achieve a state of equilibrium in which no one could be made better off without someone else being made worse off. Unfortunately, the mainstream way of looking at choice has little to offer in the context of a practical approach to business economics. It is bereft of testable hypotheses or policy implications that would be of use in designing market research programmes or debates about business policy in respect of pricing, product design, promotion or distribution methods. For this reason, the discussion of mainstream consumer theory presented here is brief and does not focus on the kinds of diagrams that dominate presentations of consumer theory in textbooks on intermediate microeconomics. We will merely concentrate on conveying the essence of the vision of the choice process contained in this body of thought and then see how its restrictive nature opens our eyes to issues that a practically useful approach to consumer theory should be able to address. In this context, then, the theory's usefulness comes, perversely, mainly from its uselessness!

Mainstream economists actually have **two basic approaches to choice: indifference analysis**, which dates from the 1930s, and **marginal utility theory**, which was developed half a century earlier. We will consider indifference analysis first, and only briefly because, while it has advantages for formal theorizing, it was actually a retrograde analysis in terms of its plausibility (as one of its inventors, Sir John Hicks, later conceded). After then considering marginal utility theory, we end this section by introducing a **third mainstream perspective**, the **characteristics approach to demand**, that was introduced in the 1960s to correct some of the deficiencies of the two basic approaches.

4.2.1 Indifference analysis

Central to this perspective is the idea that consumers are forced to choose because though they have **unlimited wants**, they have **limited budgets** to allocate between different types of goods.

The consumer's wants are presumed to take the form of a **preference ordering** that can be specified across all possible combinations of goods and services. The theory gets its name because the consumer is presumed to be able to say, for any pair of rival bundles of goods, whether one is better than the other, or whether he or she is indifferent between them. (This leads to scope for representing preferences graphically in terms of 'indifference curves'. These are rather like contour lines on a relief map except that they have no unit of measurement attached. They show which sets of combinations of goods are ranked equally, with the combinations along each curve all being ranked differently from those shown on other curves.) Only some of these combinations will come within the consumer's budget constraint, which is determined by the consumer's income and price per unit of each product. Indifference analysis portrays consumers as carefully fine-tuning what they purchase – 'Shall I have a bit more of this, versus a bit less of that?' – in order to make the most of their limited spending power.

From this perspective, changes in patterns of spending may be induced either by changes in relative prices or by changes in levels of income. Note, however, that real income (that is to say, purchasing power) may change without a change in money income because the prices of some of the goods that the consumer buys have been reduced. Thus, for example, if the price of mobile phone calls is reduced, the consumer can:

- make the same volume of calls as before and have more money left to spend on other goods and services; or

- spend more time making mobile phone calls without having to give up the consumption of anything extra to do so; or

- opt for a bit more of both mobile phone use and consumption of other goods and services.

How the consumer will choose will depend on the shape of his or her preferences and, according to the theory, **consumers are more willing to give up one thing to get more of something else if they are already consuming a lot of the former relative to the latter**.

The scope for consumption to change as a consequence of changes in real income leads mainstream theorists to **classify goods** into particular categories on the basis of how their sales are affected by income changes rather than according to any intrinsic properties they have. Thus **luxuries** are defined as those products that have **income-elastic demand** in the sense that their sales increase faster than income increases. Products whose sales decline when real incomes rise are known as **inferior goods**. It is important to note here that what is a luxury to some buyers may be an inferior good to other buyers, depending on their preferences and income levels. A rise in real income might thus lead some consumers to switch from hang-gliders to microlight aircraft but others to switch from microlight aircraft to a 'real' aeroplane. As incomes rise in the economy as a whole, the crucial thing for a business is the mix of consumers for whom its product is an inferior good or a luxury.

The basic notion of consumers having preference orderings and limited budgets and switching the mix of what they buy as relative prices and/or their incomes change may seem a reasonable approximation of some kinds of choices, such as how people choose their groceries. As any student would recognize, there is a major difference between being a teenager and being able to raid one's parents' fridge and pantry whenever one feels peckish, and trying to get by on a student allowance or whilst preventing a student loan from ballooning out of control. However, the theory has limited usefulness as a general way of modelling choice:

- The indifference approach to theorizing about choice needs the amounts consumed to be capable of small variations. This is because it focuses on the consumer's willingness to make marginal substitutions in response to changes in price. Although the theory may seem plausible in situations in which the consumer is choosing between goods and services that come in divisible amounts, such as kilos of apples or litres of petrol, it has less success representing **discrete choices**. Discrete choices have an all-or-nothing nature, such as the choice to see a particular movie, to buy a particular mobile phone or to live in a flat rather than a house.

• The theory portrays preferences in terms of a **'field'** in which the consumer thinks in terms of trading off anything against anything else with a view to achieving an improvement in well-being. This presumes that the consumer is not troubled by **bounded rationality**, even though the number of items in each bundle being ranked in a preference ordering might be rather large. In effect, the theory asks us to conceive of consumers beginning their shopping by doing a reconnaissance of the prices of things in a supermarket (or rather, all the nearby supermarkets), working out what is the best bundle to get that week, and then buying the set of goods that makes up the bundle. In reality, of course, we shop sequentially by comparing items grouped in particular categories, as in 'Aisle D: oriental foods, soups and pasta'. The field view also denies that there may be some non-negotiable areas in the consumer's life where the consumer will not be willing to consider trade-offs even in the event of major price changes.

• The theory also presumes that a **lack of experience** is not a problem for the consumer by specifying that preference orderings exist over all possible bundles. We may indeed, as mainstream theorists often put it, 'know what we want and know how to get it' in the sort of financial and environmental circumstances with which we are familiar. However, we would find it difficult to know what to do if suddenly thrust into a new situation due to losing our jobs, winning a lottery, having a major change of family circumstances or finding that what is available has changed dramatically due to technological progress since we were last buying in a particular market. Mainstream economists might defend their position by presuming rapid learning, but they have little to say about how consumers learn or manage to cope whilst in the process of learning.

• It is **weak** as a piece of science **in terms of predictions**. It does not even lead to the prediction entailed in the so-called 'law of demand', namely, that if the price of something goes up, consumers will buy less of it. This arises because, as noted earlier, a price change not only affects the relative attractiveness of rival products but also the overall purchasing power of the consumer's budget. If a price reduction of a good that forms a large part of the consumer's spending is on a big enough scale to have a significant effect on the consumer's real income, the consumer might now switch in favour of luxury items and reduce consumption of the good whose price has fallen.

4.2.2 Marginal utility theory

Indifference analysis emerged with these flaws from attempts by economists to remove from consumer theory any notion that what was being optimized subject to a constraint was a psychological variable that might need to be measured: all that consumers need to be able to do is to say whether rival bundles of goods are worse than, better than or equally valuable to them personally. **Consumers are presumed to be able to rank bundles of goods in order of preference** but they do not have to attach any rating of satisfaction to each of them. By contrast, the earlier approach, marginal utility theory, was based around the notion that consumers compare things in terms of a common unit and choose so as to end up with the most value in terms of that unit. They called the unit of satisfaction '**utility**'. Just as most economists have been prone to assume that the net benefits of anything purchased by firms and other organizations can be reduced to a **common unit** – money – marginal utility theorists assumed that people buy diverse goods and services with a single question in mind. The question is: 'How much utility will I get from buying this product, or combination of products, and could I get more by buying something else instead?' This leads to a question for theorists: 'If the consumer's bottom line is in terms of 'utility', can we measure it and can we compare individuals in terms of the satisfaction they derive from their lives?'

If we wish to avoid some kind of psychological way of measuring how consumers expect alternative consumption choices to affect their well-being (such as, say, trying to measure how different meal prospects provoke different amounts of salivation), the obvious solution is to try to get a monetary measure of utility. Merely to look at the price consumers have paid for something is not good enough for doing this, for some of the consumers might be enjoying **consumer's surplus**. In other words, they might be paying less for some or all the units purchased than the maximum they would be prepared to pay. Hence we might instead ask consumers how much money they would require in order to give up something they had already chosen to consume. Alternatively, we might ask them how much they would be willing to pay for an extra unit of the good in question, in a particular context. This is called their **contingent valuation** of the item. Such questions are often asked of samples of consumers who may be affected by environmentally sensitive projects – for example, how much would you be prepared to pay to preserve an area of forest or a scenic view?

In terms of mainstream theory, the answers that consumers give should be the same regarding **willingness to pay** to get something versus willingness to accept a sum of money in exchange for giving it up. For example, suppose you are offered the chance to buy a mug and are asked what is the maximum you would pay for it. You reply '£2', but are then given the mug and asked what is the lowest price you would accept for it. If your preferences in respect of the mug are consistent, then you ought to be willing to part with the mug for £2.01. When this is tried experimentally, the second figure is typically appreciably larger than the first, implying that perhaps mainstream theory has a problem, for the theory treats choices as straightforwardly reversible.

Aside from expecting consistency in consumer choice, economists who follow the 'money as a proxy for utility' approach would expect consumers sooner or later to display **diminishing marginal utility**.

> Consumers are said to be experiencing diminishing marginal utility if, having already consumed a number of units of a product, the maximum amount that they are prepared to pay for the next unit is less than they were prepared to pay for the last unit they previously consumed.

This seems perfectly plausible in respect of food and drink, where we start getting physically satiated as we consume more and more. It also seems consistent with the tendency of many buyers of recorded music to buy a lot of recordings when they are young, and fewer and fewer the older they get. (Note that each extra recording stands as a potential obstacle to further enjoyment of recordings purchased earlier.) It might also help explain the tendency for recording artists' sales to tail off as they release their successive albums – unless they keep reinventing themselves in a new style.

The diminishing marginal utility idea is, however, at odds with the way that some people become **obsessive collectors** of related items, wanting more of them the more that they have of them because they get more and more fascinated with and appreciative of them. Likewise, the executive who seems to work longer and longer hours with each promotion is hardly displaying diminishing marginal utility in terms of income or job satisfaction, despite the increasing price being paid in terms of foregone leisure or effects on health and family relationships. In defence of the notion, it might be argued that collecting and workaholic behaviour are pathologies rather than normal behaviour, or that it is most unusual for collectors to seek to acquire multiple units of a single item, as opposed to sets of items.

The idea of **diminishing marginal utility implies an inverse price/quantity relationship**, which in turn implies that demand curves are downward sloping to the right if price is shown on the vertical axis and quantity purchased is shown on the horizontal axis. Lower prices are required if more is to be sold, and at some point, which may differ between consumers, even a zero price will not induce extra consumption and it will be necessary to bribe the consumer to accept extra units. The 'I'll only accept more of the good if you pay me to take it off your hands' scenario could result not from physical satiation but due to:

- **costs of disposal** of unwanted items;
- **costs of storage** of, or the impossibility of storing, particular goods to be consumed at a later date when the consumer might value them rather more.

By introducing the **time dimension** into the story, we may become aware that in order to make the theory work we formally need to treat goods consumed on different occasions as if they are different commodities: on any particular day, we may have limits to how many French fries we are willing to consume, but that does not mean we will wish to consume no French fries the next day.

Unlike indifference analysis, this approach to choice does not presume that consumers spend their entire budgets within the period under analysis, or that they necessarily set out to perform incredibly complex comparisons when they go shopping. Rather, consumers are assumed to keep asking themselves: 'Is it worth spending the asking price on a unit of this particular good, or on an *extra unit* of it?' If the consumer considers a particular product on its own, then this is done by **comparing** (a) the **marginal utility of spending on the good in question** with (b) the **marginal utility of holding on to the money** that would have to be given up to purchase it and which might instead be spent on something else that presently is not specified. Thus in terms of marginal utility theory we can indeed imagine shoppers walking up and down the aisles of a supermarket choosing what to add to their shopping trolleys on a **sequential** basis, without being troubled by the scope for trading off any particular item against the thousands of other product lines available in the store.

When consumers do compare rival brands of products, or different types of goods that are substitutes for each other (for example, Red Delicious apples versus Granny Smith's apples, or apples versus oranges), the process can also be seen in terms of the marginal utility of unspent money: for example, the marginal utility of a bag of apples costing £1.70 plus the marginal utility of an unspent £1.05 versus the marginal utility of a bag of oranges costing £2.75. Alternatively, and particularly where the question is 'shall I have a bit more of A and a bit less of B?', the theory sees the consumer as adjusting the relative quantities of the rival products until the **marginal utility of A divided by the unit price of A equals the marginal utility of B divided by the unit price of B**. If the consumer's budget limit is not a binding constraint, as it might not be if marginal utilities for the goods decline sharply, the consumer will purchase more units of each commodity up to the point at which value placed by the consumer on marginal units of both goods is equal to their prices, so both sides of the equation come out as one. Of course, this may not hold exactly if the consumer is choosing between indivisible goods, but the general idea is clear: where a better product may be available if the consumer pays more, then how much the consumer spends will depend on whether he or she judges that the extra value a more expensive product seems to offer is worth the sacrifice in terms of money that might later be used to purchase more of something else.

In terms of indifference analysis a pair of products would be seen as **substitutes** if a rise in the price of one was associated with an increase in sales of the other, and as **complements** if a fall in the price of one led to an increase in the sales of both. From the standpoint of marginal utility theory, we can go a bit further in thinking about substitution and complementarity, focusing not merely on observed price/quantity interactions between products but also on whether or not they have spillover effects in the production of utility for the consumer.

> Two products can be defined as being substitutes when the marginal utilities derived from consuming extra units of either are totally independent and the only relationship between them concerns the consumer's limited budget, such that to get more of one (and thereby getting its associated marginal utility) requires giving up some of the other (and thereby foregoing its marginal utility), and vice versa.

> Products are defined as complementary to each other if the utility derived from one of them depends on how much of the other is being consumed.

Complementarity may be positive or negative. A DVD is of little use without a dedicated DVD player, or some other product that will play it, such as a PC or a PlayStation 2. By contrast, beer and wine often produce negative complementarity – mixing them may have adverse effects on perceived taste or the kind of intoxication they produce. Interactions between products in the production of utility may be quite complex. For example, negative complementarity between beer and wine might not arise at all if the consumer only drinks moderate amounts of both, so they might merely seem to be substitutes. The sequence of mixing one's drinks might also matter: drinking several glasses of wine first and then switching to beer might be far worse than drinking them the other way round or alternating between them. Although marginal utility theory enables us to reflect on the significance of spillover effects between different products, along with indifference analysis, it **lacks any psychological or physiological basis** for explaining why particular goods produce the levels of satisfaction, either in total or at the margin, that affect consumers' decisions about how much of them to purchase. Neither approach is thus particularly helpful for explaining differences in what economists call **price elasticity of demand**, that is to say, the differences in responsiveness of product sales to changes in relative prices.

4.2.3 Demand for product characteristics

Traditional expositions of both marginal utility theory and indifference analysis envisage consumers as having sets of preferences in respect of a pre-specified set of goods. This means they are not well suited for showing how consumers decide whether or not to buy products that are new to the market and which they have not hitherto been imagining. Unimagined new products seem to require the consumer to develop a revised set of preferences and mainstream theory has nothing to say about how that might be done. Reflection on what consumers actually do when faced with unexpected new products has led some economists to realize that consumers may think about their choices in a way that does not require them to come up with new sets of preferences to deal with the new goods: all the consumers seem to need to know is what features these goods have to offer. Recognition of this has led to the reformulation of consumer theory as a theory of the demand for **product characteristics** (known as product 'attributes' in marketing). The **demand for goods and services is thus derived from the demand consumers have for the characteristics they offer**.

The essential idea here is that as the consumer thinks about the merits of rival products, their characteristics get traded off against each other, as in the old saying 'never mind the quality, feel the width'. The **price of the product can be thought of as a negatively rated characteristic to be traded off against the various non-price characteristics**, with a diminishing marginal willingness to substitute between characteristics.

Practical applications of this idea focus on using market research to discover consumers' contingent valuations of particular changes in a product's specification. For example, someone considering the purchase of a microlight aircraft is perhaps interested in price, safety record, flying range, manoeuvrability, ease of transportation on the ground and top speed – a total of six characteristics – and might be looking at, say, four rival models with different ratings in some or all of these dimensions. The manufacturers whose products are not being ranked top thus need to get some idea of how consumers are weighing things up, what their willingness is to pay to get better performance in certain areas to a particular degree or how much their willingness to pay would be reduced by downgrading the product so that it can be offered at a lower price. Once armed with such information, a manufacturer can decide whether it is better to try to increase sales by moving the product up- or downmarket, charging more (less) after improving (downgrading) the performance in particular areas. Clearly, if the vast majority of the potential market puts a smaller value on a particular feature than it costs the firm to add that feature to the product, it would be best to offer the product without it and at a price that reflects the saving in production costs. Likewise, if an extra £50.00 of unit production costs spent could *either* produce a speed increase valued at £70.00 by the typical consumer, *or* an increase in range valued at £55.00, then the manufacturer's first priority should be to increase their microlight's speed.

4.3 Contexts of choice

Though the mainstream models of choice may differ in their plausibility in different contexts (for example, with discrete versus divisible choices), the basic philosophy is that, as far as theorizing is concerned, 'one size fits all'. **Heterodox economists,** by contrast, **view decision making as if context matters for how decisions are reached.** Before we examine how heterodox theories of buyer behaviour differ from mainstream models it is thus useful to set the scene, and do some implicit theorizing, by examining how the context of the buying decision might be expected to affect the verdict that the buyer reaches.

Within the economics of information, and in marketing, it has become common to **classify products** as falling into one of three categories: **search goods, experience goods** and **credence goods.**

> A search good is a product for which prospective buyers can acquire the knowledge they need to have to know whether they really want to buy it before they actually make a commitment to do so.

One way of getting desired information is via in-store demonstrations; another is from consumer magazines.

> An experience good is a product for which buyers can only discover for sure how well the product performs after they have bought it.

Classic examples of experience goods are a used car or a meal in an unfamiliar restaurant. How much a magazine or book is an experience good rather than a search good depends on how long we spend browsing before purchasing it.

> A credence good is a product purchased on the basis of a supplier's recommendation without the buyer knowing for sure whether they really do need to buy it and without subsequently knowing whether they really did need to buy it.

Examples of credence goods include a medical procedure recommended by a doctor, or refurbishment work on a house that one is hoping to sell, as recommended by a real estate agent.

This three-way distinction is a very useful starting point, which has led us to develop a more extensive set of questions that we habitually ask regarding context. These are as follows:

(i) *Is the product technologically complicated?* If so, this may affect:

    (a) its reliability and hence the need for an assured spare parts and service network;

    (b) the risk perceived by potential buyers, unless warranties are offered or it can be demonstrated to buyers that the product can be repaired in a modular manner if anything goes wrong;

    (c) acceptability to users who do their own maintenance and have already incurred the costs of learning how to maintain rival brands, or to users who have already incurred the costs of finding out who can be relied upon to maintain a particular brand at an acceptable price.

Note that the last two points may present a dilemma. An example here is the choice of cars by a police force or aircraft by an airline. A commitment to a particular brand keeps maintenance costs down but opens up a major strategic risk in the event that there is a product recall that grounds the entire fleet.

(ii) *Is the product likely to be perceived as complicated to use by its target market?* If so:

    (a) sales may be affected by buyers' familiarity with products that have similar systems of operation, such as memories, timers and menus (a bread-maker is simpler to use if one already knows how to programme a VCR, or to use a bank auto-teller);

    (b) information overload could prevent buyers from appreciating all the features of the product, so there may be a case for offering a stripped down, cheaper version, or for offering a 'design it yourself' opportunity for the customer to specify a particular configuration of optional features that they know they want;

    (c) sales may be dependent on the provision of satisfactory before- and after-sales support, unless the buyer is part of a network of experienced users of the product.

(iii) *Is there technological uncertainty, or uncertainty about which product standard will prevail in the long run?* If so:

    (a) buyers may hold back until the future becomes clearer;

    (b) buyers may resist products that are incompatible with rival systems;

    (c) buyers who want the product now may adopt whichever product has the biggest market share, on the basis that this one has the biggest chance of success.

Note that this issue arises mainly where products last a long time, or where the user has to invest in learning how to use the product. In the 1980s there were two incompatible standards for quadraphonic hi-fi systems, and three standards for video cassette recording. Both quadraphonic standards failed completely. In the case of video cassettes, the developers of the VHS system opted to license it widely to rival manufacturers, which increased the probability of purchase simply because most models on display were VHS, as were most of the videos that the early video stores offered for rent. Modern-day examples include many computer products: X-Box versus PlayStation 2 versus Nintendo GameCube, and Apple Macintosh versus Windows computers. In the case of computer game consoles, continuation of rival standards may be assisted insofar as consumers are only in the market for a few years, whilst Apple's continuing survival as a minority player has been made possible because the firm ensured that its computers can read files created on DOS and Windows systems.

(iv) *Will an unsatisfactory experience with the product have major implications for the customer?* A consumer's willingness to pay a higher price, if necessary, to guarantee the desired outcome may be easier to anticipate if one can guess the kind of mess the consumer could be in if let down by a product. If a cheap but unknown brand of car polish could do terrible things to our paintwork, we opt for the familiar but more expensive brand. Likewise we steer clear of unknown brands of video cassettes that could damage the heads on our VCR, and of public transport providers whose erratic service could make us late for a job interview. If the consumer knows that a choice that turns out not to meet with social approval may cause great ridicule and embarrassment, then playing safe is likely to be the preferred strategy, even if it is a costly one.

(v) *Is the price of the product a significant issue for the customer?* Where something is a substantial proportion of the customer's budget, we might expect them to take greater care in shopping, both to reduce the chances that they will end up with a needlessly poor product for the price and because of the greater likely payoffs to search for a cheaper price for a given product. If you could earn £100 per hour, it would not make much sense to spend half an hour shopping around to save £20. However, if you could only earn £20 for an hour of overtime, it would pay to forego it if you thought you could save £20 by spending less than an hour shopping around. The rich thus seem likely to shop in a more casual manner than most consumers and to rely more on brands as signs of quality.

In fact, consumers often do not shop with the kind of logic an economist might hope to see. When deciding whether to spend more time on searching or haggling over prices, we tend to make mistakes in the sense that we allow our decisions to be framed in terms of the savings we might make *relative* to the price being asked, not the *absolute* amount that we might save. Thus, for example, we may end up spending ten minutes trying to save £5 on a £100 car radio (a 5 per cent saving) but not bother to haggle for ten minutes more to save £50 more on a £5000 used car (a 1 per cent saving).

(vi) *Is there a well-established second-hand market for the product?* If not, and if there is a serious possibility that the buyer's circumstances could change during the lifetime of the product, then buying it entails a bigger risk. If the product is unusual or unpopular, it may have a very **thin market**.

> A product is said to have a thin market if most of the time there is hardly anybody looking to buy or sell it, even if for the category of products into which it falls there is a well-functioning 'thick' market.

Examples here include unusual, architect-designed homes, properties in out-of-the-way locations and top-of-the-range models of low-prestige brands of cars. If these need to be sold in a hurry, their prices tend to have to be heavily discounted. If in doubt, it pays to conform.

(vii) *Is there difficulty in identifying the quality of the product before buying it?* If so, buyers are more than usually likely to give their custom to those suppliers with reputations for delivering an adequate standard of quality with great reliability. The superstars of popular music are not necessarily vastly more talented than wannabes that are barely scraping a living as recording artists, but they have achieved a great advantage: they are known quantities, and therefore they stand out from the thousands of other artists that have achieved far less exposure. They are safe choices.

This problem of **quality uncertainty** tends to arise in markets that are **easy to enter** and hence prone to **excess capacity** – such as pizza production, taxi services and used-car retailing. If there are too many suppliers, it will be hard to survive and some will cut corners in desperation. The mismatch between the apparent ease of production and the difficulty of survival also means that these lines of business tend to have a continual turnover of suppliers. How, then, are consumers to know if any of the new hopefuls are any good at what they do?

The problem of identifying a satisfactory supplier is particularly acute if the product is one that customers often seek to purchase in a hurry, in diverse locations. If so, the only way their past experience will count is if they can find a familiar brand, such as Pizza Hut, Yellow Cabs or a Hertz car rentals, *and* if the suppliers attached to the brand have managed to ensure that quality is consistent between different locations. A brand shared by businesses that offer it with inconsistent quality is of no use at all to the consumer as a proxy for quality of a known standard.

(viii) *Is the product something that is purchased very infrequently?* If so, and if technological progress occurs in the market, then any expertise the consumer had at the previous time of purchase may be obsolete. This is a major issue for many consumer durables, such as fridges, washing machines, beds, carpets and lounge-suites. To deal with the knowledge gap, the customer can:

(a) incur the costs of acquiring state-of-the-art expertise (unlikely, unless the product is a high value one);

(b) follow the recommendations of trade magazines or peers known for their expertise and willingness to share it;

(c) take seriously the advice of sales personnel, if they seem credible;

(d) copy the behaviour of others;

(e) find something with a timeless-looking design;

(f) stick to a trusted brand in the hope that the brand has kept pace with the rest of the market.

Many household services, such as plumbers and roof-repairers, or funeral services, are also purchased infrequently. These may not present a problem because of technological change, but they are prone to be needed at short notice and knowledge of reliable suppliers may be rendered obsolete because the consumer has moved since last needing them. In such cases, the consumer will rely on the recommendations of others or favour those suppliers who can signal something about their capabilities and integrity – for example, how long have they been in the business? Are they members of the relevant trade association?

(ix) *Is the product an element in a complex system of interrelated products and activities?* If it is, then its ability to match the other elements may be a decisive issue at the time of purchase. Examples here include choices of shoes and clothing in terms of styles and colours, vehicles that have to match up with recreational activities and family sizes (including the pet dog), furniture that has to be compatible with room sizes and existing furniture, and home locations that fit in with jobs, schools and public transport.

(x) *Are substitutes available that, to a greater or lesser extent, offer features offered by the product, or does it have a 'unique selling point' (USP)?* The important thing to recognize here is that the items we buy are collections of features that economists call **characteristics** and marketers call **product attributes**. If differences in price are to lead people to switch from one product or brand to another, then they must be willing, in principle, to give up a lower price in order to get better features and/or more features, or to give up features altogether, or have less of some features, in order to get a lower price and have more money left to spend on other things. Economists have been prone to presume that this willingness *always* exists and hence that it is always possible to generate more sales with a lower price or by offering more of the same in terms of features.

Introspection is likely to make most readers wary of such a *general* presumption. Consider the following questions. Is it simply unacceptably low earnings or the risk of trouble with the police that deters most people from becoming prostitutes or criminals? Will people who can afford to travel on British Airways switch to an airline with a very poor safety record if the latter lowers its price dramatically? Is it really the case that unattractive relative prices stop an opera-lover from buying rap or grunge recordings, or vice versa? For most people, there are certain kinds of substitution that are simply unthinkable, that would not even enter their minds as possibilities.

(xi) *Is the product consumed in a social setting?* If so:

(a) its sales may depend on whether it is acceptable to the entire group – for example, just one vegetarian in a group of diners may mean that the group will not select a restaurant if it cannot meet the vegetarian's requirements, even though everyone else in the group would find it acceptable;

(b) it may be hard to sell if members of the consumer's social group do not know what it is and if it represents a mysterious departure from their normal choices – an odd choice marks the chooser out as a deviant and normally leads to demands for justification;

(c) decisions to buy it might be compromised by previous public statements that the potential buyer has made, which would have to be retracted for its selection to be justified – if people operate in a competitive manner, their peers may seize upon evidence of actions at odds with positions they have previously taken if it offers opportunities for one-upmanship. Fortunately, since the memories of social groups and organizations decay as time passes, past positions will gradually be less significant;

(d) consumers may be concerned about the **signals** that it sends in terms of how much they appear to be able to afford to spend on this kind of product. In a world of incomplete and dispersed information, the appearance of a product or its brand name may be taken as indicators of its likely cost – for example, a finely crafted and well looked after second-hand BMW may appear much more expensive than a new Hyundai of the same price, particularly if the former carries a personalized number plate that disguises its actual age and each generation's design is a gradual evolution from the one before.

Economists would normally call this an example of the economics of **conspicuous consumption**, in which people are trying to stake claims for (or cling to) a higher place on the social ladder than their budgets really justify, or to claim unambiguously that they have 'arrived' at a particular level. If appearances count for signalling the consumer's wealth, the policy implication is that efforts aimed at improving a product may best be aimed at building perceived quality into what is visible, so long as the underpinnings are at least maintaining class standards. This is something that Volkswagen appear to have been doing in their attempts to push their brand upmarket by offering cars with chic, elegant styling, wonderful interiors and doors that feel very solid, but with a fairly ordinary driving experience offered by the engines and chassis.

Three variations on the conspicuous consumption theme should also be added to the checklist. First, in societies where being conspicuously rich is socially frowned upon or likely to invite the attention of criminals, manufacturers of upmarket products need to consider whether or not their products need to have understated outward appearances so that, except in relation to those 'in the know', buyers can engage in **inconspicuous consumption**. Secondly, there are some products that are consumed very privately and yet their act of purchase has major implications regarding the social standing of the consumer. Here we are talking of more than just a situation in which a buyer tries to impress a sales person. Instead, consider the lingerie sold to women via the Ann Summers Party Plan: working-class women are much more likely to try to impress their peers by splashing out on expensive lingerie on such an occasion than are middle-class women who happen to find themselves there. The third point integrates elements of the previous two: consumers are embarrassed to be seen purchasing some products and in these cases mail-order catalogues or Internet retailing may be ideal distribution modes since the customer does not have to face up to a sales person or run the risk of being seen by friends. An Internet pharmacy makes no sense for distributing quick-acting painkillers to those who suddenly find themselves in pain, but it may do wonders as a means of enlarging the market for aphrodisiacs such as horny goat weed tablets.

These 11 questions (which are summarized in Box 4.1) and many of the discussions following them may seem like commonsense. Yet a layperson would be unlikely to be able to articulate them readily if asked, 'In what ways do the contexts of choice differ?' Consumers deal with the problem of choice without necessarily being aware of how they do so. Their task entails dealing with **problems of knowledge, uncertainty and access to information**, associated with the passage of **time** and changes in **location**. If economizing by customers is indeed about substitution in the face of changing market opportunities and personal circumstances, it appears that substitution may actually be going on only amongst things that have not already been ruled out on the basis of undue risk or lack of approval from those in positions of influence. The crucial thing to get right may not be the price of the product but its **reputation**, what its brand signifies.

> ### Box 4.1 Eleven key questions every entrepreneur should ask about their product
>
> 1. Is the product technologically complicated?
>
> 2. Is the product likely to be perceived as complicated to use by its target market?
>
> 3. Is there technological uncertainty, or uncertainty about which product standard will prevail in the long run?
>
> 4. Will an unsatisfactory experience with the product have major implications for the customer?

> ### Box 4.1 (continued)
>
> 5. Is the price of the product a significant issue for the customer?
>
> 6. Is there a well-established second-hand market for the product?
>
> 7. Is there difficulty in identifying the quality of the product before buying it?
>
> 8. Is the product something that is purchased very infrequently?
>
> 9. Is the product an element in a complex system of interrelated products and activities?
>
> 10. Are substitutes available that, to a greater or lesser extent, offer features offered by the product, or does it have a 'unique selling point' (USP)?
>
> 11. Is the product consumed in a social setting?

4.4 Behavioural/evolutionary consumer theory

Within the various branches of heterodox economics, the most comprehensive alternatives to mainstream consumer theory come from the behavioural and evolutionary approaches. **Behavioural economists** use findings from cognitive science and psychology about **how humans actually cope with complex tasks.** **Evolutionary economists** are particularly interested in the ways that **new products** come to be adopted by consumers and the roles that **consumers' capabilities** play in determining which kinds of products they are prepared to try. In this section we try to summarize and synthesize some of the key themes from this wide-ranging literature.

4.4.1 The struggle against increasing entropy

> Entropy is a term from physics that refers to the measurement of the degradation or disorganization of the universe. In heterodox economics the term is used to refer to how far a complex system of connections has unravelled due to a lack of investment in maintaining its structure.

Instead of seeing choice as a utility-maximizing activity, evolutionary thinking sees much of everyday life as concerned with maintaining orderly systems in the face of tendencies towards increasing entropy. These systems include our personal appearances, networks of social relationships, the cars we drive and living environments that come up to our standards of tidiness and cleanliness. Decision making is very difficult in the face of complete chaos and is much easier if there are established **points of reference** (including an established picture of one's self), though sometimes we playfully let our lives get very untidy because this helps throw up scope for building new systems.

Attention to maintaining one system comes at the expense of giving attention to other entropy-prone systems. Because of this, the best that people can hope to achieve is to keep the states of different parts of their lives from falling below targets that they set. If something falls below what they define as an acceptable standard, they set about replacing it or giving it a makeover that takes it, at least for the moment, a good way beyond the minimum level. (The process of choice may thus be likened to the operations of a thermostat that maintains a room's temperature within acceptable bounds.) Then they turn their attention to the most important of whichever other system is falling below their target. Life is thus a matter of muddling through, staying afloat, rather than achieving a state of rest and optimal allocation.

Note here that individuals may not only differ in terms of the standards they set for a given system (tidiness of a teenager's bedroom is an obvious example!), but also in terms of how rigorous the standards they set are for different parts of their lives, and how they rank them in order of importance. Most people are more obsessed with some parts of their lives than others (as in the case of collectors of certain classes of goods), but fortunately few people set such high standards in any area that their behaviour becomes totally dysfunctional in the manner of those afflicted by an obsessive–compulsive disorder. Most consumers who do find life is getting problematic are nonetheless laid back enough about their lives to be able to let entropy mount for a while and then reflect on how things are going before 'getting their priorities right'.

4.4.2 Consumer preferences exist at several levels

The idea that preferences may have a hierarchical form figures in heterodox analysis in a variety of ways. The most basic is the **'hierarchy of needs'** idea borrowed from the work of psychologist Abraham Maslow. Our most **basic need** is to have enough water to stay alive right now. Next comes the need to have enough food to keep going beyond the present moment. If in a desperate situation, we will let nothing get in the way of our physical survival: as Shakespeare's King Richard III pleaded, 'A horse, a horse, my kingdom for a horse.' Maslow suggests that once people have got *enough* food and water on which to live, their attention will shift to obtaining *adequate* clothing and shelter, and once they have achieved this, they begin to worry about their self- and social-esteem, seeking friends, a partner and a position in the social pecking order. If all this is under control, then any spare resources they have may be devoted to 'self-actualization' – in other words, to setting out to make a reality of how they dream of themselves as being. For example, a person might ideally like to be some kind of creative artist and live a life based around laudable environmental principles, but they will not try to live like that if it leads to them being denied friendship or enough of a roof over their heads.

Although Maslow's hierarchy of needs suggests that people may sometimes refuse to substitute in particular directions because this would compromise meeting their basic needs, it does not preclude substitution in general. For example, if people are trying to get a roof over their heads, then it helps to have some skill in assembling cost-effective combinations of food products to liberate funds to pay for housing. Note, too, that some products may assist in meeting several levels of needs. For example, being affluent enough to trade in a rough, old, gas-guzzling saloon car for a new, versatile and fuel-efficient mini-people-mover may make it easier to meet family goals, impress the neighbours and help save the planet. For the business economist, then, the key question to keep in mind is whether the firm's products are a cost-effective means towards helping consumers move to a new level on their hierarchies of needs without getting in the way of meeting their more basic needs.

A more complex hierarchical approach to the mind of the consumer is that which sees our minds rather as if they are like legal or constitutional systems in which there is great freedom for action so long as high-level principles are not compromised, and where conflicting points of view are resolved by appealing to a higher authority. On this view, lower-level mental operations may throw up a variety of perspectives on a particular issue in the consumer's life, including whether the consumer does indeed have a problem to address. The person may thus be 'in several minds' about what to do unless the various possibilities are viewed in terms of more fundamental principles on which the person builds their life.

On this view, the mind is a bit like an onion, with a **core set of beliefs** that can be maintained by adjusting more peripheral beliefs to make them consistent with the core ones and managing subsequent gathering of information to generate evidence consistent with the core. New ideas, which may concern new products to try, will be ruled 'out of order' unless they can somehow be shown to be consistent with the core beliefs. Challenges to a person's core beliefs are likely to generate hostile responses aimed at defending these beliefs. The process envisaged here is rather akin to the way that the idea that the sun revolved around the earth was maintained for many years by the use of ad hoc and increasingly convoluted explanations of anomalous observations and by the political repression of those who proposed that the earth revolved around the sun.

For example, suppose a person is anxious about the possible maintenance costs of their old car and does not see themselves as 'the sort of person who, at my stage in life, will still be running an old bomb', but does not have the ready cash to buy a new one and at the same time does not view themselves as 'the sort of person who relies on debt'. Here is what psychologist Leon Festinger called a state of **'cognitive dissonance'**, since two aspects of the person's view of themselves are at odds with each other. Festinger's theory of how cognitive dissonance is resolved incorporates the everyday notion of 'wishful thinking' and runs against the mainstream economist's tendency to ignore subjective aspects of opportunity costs. It also implies that we should take seriously the idea that consumer choice is open to being manipulated by marketing strategies.

One possibility is that the person ends up buying the new car without being influenced by marketing strategies of car firms and suppliers of finance, after looking at the different patterns of damage to their view of the world that would result from buying a new car versus staying out of debt. For example, the person may find it harder to live with continuing anxiety about repair bills and lifetime achievements than with the implication that they are indeed the kind of person who gets into debt. If so, Festinger's theory of dissonance reduction predicts that they will set about constructing a case – note the parallel with a courtroom process – for why the act of getting into debt is not so bad, after all. For example, they may adjust their estimates of depreciation rates and maintenance costs on the new car so that the choice seems perfectly logical in financial terms and there is no need to admit to themselves that the 'real reason' for their choice is that they are trying to avoid all the scope for embarrassment that seems to be implied by staying with their present vehicle.

Marketing messages can be used to try to ensure that the consumer does achieve such a resolution – for example, 'fear appeals' that emphasize the downside of living with an old car, and by packaging the financing issue in a manner that removes the connotation of being in debt. Personal leasing packages obviously have potential here: they sound like standard business practice and are really (yes, really!) about renting a flow of services, not about being in debt; and, by being based around a sizable 'balloon' payment linked to the value of the car at the end of the lease, the monthly payments can be made very attractive.

Consumers who do not think in an open-minded manner present quite a challenge for marketers and a barrier to the acceptance of novel products, but not an inherently insuperable one. Under certain conditions, people who have long clung to a particular self-image will reinvent themselves, just as countries with repressive regimes can undergo revolutions in which the army that once supported a dictator sees that it is in its interests to switch sides and support a popular uprising. If potential customers see a product as conflicting with how they see themselves and if the product cannot be positioned otherwise by carefully chosen marketing messages, it may nonetheless be possible to expand sales by appealing to a higher-ranking mental notion, or to a more significant aspect of self-identity, such that target consumers decide to change how they see themselves. One might thus seek to sell, say, men's cosmetics to macho customers by (a) portraying them as useful aids to higher-level goals such as the conquest of women, or (b) presenting a case for viewing the essence of being macho in a manner consistent with consumption of men's cosmetics, or (c) presenting a case, in relation to some higher-level notion, that the time has come to move away from being macho.

4.4.3 Rules for closing open minds

The mental processes just outlined may sometimes be quite enough to determine a consumer's choice of brand as well as the bigger decision to buy that kind of product. For example, a consumer who has a strong ethical outlook might reject any food products that carry the 'Kraft' brand since that company is owned by the Philip Morris tobacco company (or Altria, as it has recently re-branded itself), reject a brand of ginger beer that is produced by a firm owned by Coca-Cola and only buy cosmetics at The Body Shop. But often the complex system of beliefs that limits a consumer to particular kinds of activities will leave open the choice of a particular brand or product design in preference to rivals. For example, an ethically motivated consumer might discover that The Body Shop is not the only firm to offer cosmetics products produced without animal testing and with a concern for the environment, or that there are many small, fuel-efficient cars between which to choose.

One way of achieving theoretical closure in such a situation is to go back to the 'demand for product characteristics' view of choice in the mainstream literature and see the consumer as having a set of preferences in which there are trade-offs between product characteristics. Behavioural/evolutionary economists take a rather different approach. They suggest that the consumer brings into play not a set of preferences but an **evolving set of decision rules**. These decision rules may take very different forms not merely between consumers in regard to a given class of products, but between different classes of products chosen by a single consumer. Examples could include the following:

- Rely upon the opinion of a seemingly knowledgeable friend.

- Follow the recommendation of 'best buy in its class' from a consumer magazine.

- Choose the product in the class in question offered by a manufacturer with whom the consumer has previously had a trouble-free consumption experience, and if there are several brands that come into this category, choose the cheapest (or, perhaps, choose the one with the highest social standing, subject to it coming into one's budget range).

- Choose the cheapest of those products that offer enough of all the required features on one's current checklist for this type of product.

- Take one's current checklist of desired product characteristics, rank them in order of priority and then choose the product that gets furthest along the priority listing before it fails to match up to a required standard.

- Choose the product that has the longest list of non-core features, so long as it has all of the core features on one's checklist.

- Form an overall rating of rival products by averaging their performances (say, out of ten) on each dimension of interest, and then choose the one with the highest overall score.

- Choose the product with the best performance in a particular, single dimension.

- Choose the top-selling product in the category.

- Choose the underdog brand on the basis that they must be trying harder and could therefore be under-rated.

This list is by no means exhaustive. Note that several rules may be used in combination, as with rules that are only bought into operation where there is a tie for first place, or where nothing is deemed good enough in terms of an initial rule. Note also that some rules may entail a mixture of intolerance (absolute requirements for particular kinds of performance) and willingness to make trade-offs between other dimensions.

The business economist or marketer obviously cannot hope to know the rules that each potential customer employs. The important thing to do at the very least is to try to become aware of the kinds of rules that are likely to be commonly used in the situation in question and then see how one's product and the products of rivals fare when appraised in terms of these rules.

Knowledge of the different forms that selection rules can take is especially useful in relation to the design of market research questionnaires or data derived from them. For example, if consumers have been asked to 'rank product features in order of priority', a mainstream economist would see their answers as saying something about the relative weights attached to the product's features. On this basis, a particular product may still achieve the highest score even if it performs poorly in a 'high priority' area, because it does really well in 'low priority' areas. However, from the heterodox viewpoint, the consumer may actually be thinking hierarchically, so that if the product fails to pass a high priority test it is out of the running altogether, *regardless of how well it performs in respect of lower priority tests*.

The use of hierarchical decision rules or checklists by customers opens up some interesting marketing dilemmas. Box 4.2 gives an example of one of them.

Box 4.2 Should a car manufacturer fit anti-lock braking systems as a standard feature to all its cars?

Anti-lock braking systems (ABS) were fitted to top-of-the-range Mercedes-Benz cars in the early 1980s and have gradually become available on all types of cars, right down to the humble 2003 Daihatsu Charade. But at the time the new Charade was launched with ABS in the UK, some leading manufacturers such as Ford and Vauxhall were still only fitting ABS as a standard feature on selected models. What advice would you give a car maker about whether to fit ABS on its lower-tier models, either standard or as an option, or whether it should be reserved only for top-tier luxury and sports models?

Standardization of a technologically complex feature such as this will simplify production logistics, so if the feature is made optional for some models and standard for some it will cost more to offer, and the firm could have trouble matching the costs of rivals who keep their production logistics simple by making all the complicated features standard. Those rivals may be more likely to end up with a clear run in terms of consumer checklists, but they will have trouble extracting consumer surplus by using diversity of features as a basis for a bigger range of prices.

Leaving the feature off lower-tier models in terms of standard fitment may reduce production costs enough to enable the manufacturer to cut the price of the product so that it lies just inside the upper budget limits of customers who would otherwise have to choose something from a lower market segment (such as a Korean product or a near-new model). There is also the possibility that such marginal consumers might be persuaded to rethink their budget ranges and settle for something even better, if only they can be enticed into the showroom and shown, in effect, how dealer-arranged finance can help them to avoid compromising their non-price aspirations. When Vauxhall excluded even optional ABS from lower-tier models in its Corsa range, this could have lost the firm sales from consumers who rejected cars that did not have ABS and also rejected the top-tier Corsa GSi sports

Box 4.2 (continued)

models, which did have ABS, because their prices were beyond their budget ranges. Some consumers might not want the sports version even if it came within their price range, because it is more expensive to insure and uses more fuel.

On the other hand, if the product has got a lower priority feature that rivals do not offer but which is standard across the range (such as particularly chic styling), then limiting ABS to top-tier models may be an effective way of forcing some more affluent consumers to pay to the limit of their budgets in order to get it, even though they are not particularly interested in extra features offered by the top-tier model aside from ABS. If ABS were available on lesser models, such consumers would be able to meet their aspiration in terms of styling by buying one of the latter, and would not compromise their safety aspirations.

The basic practical lessons here appear to be as follows:

- Ideally, market research should be aimed at **segmenting** the potential market in terms of the types of decision rules they are likely to use in the context in question.

- To achieve mass-market appeal, a product should **at least meet average standards for the product class in all respects**. This reduces the probability of it being rejected by those who use hierarchical or checklist rules without being likely to cause it to perform poorly with trade-off based rules, even if the resulting product is quite bland and stands out in no particular area.

- Market research efforts should be devoted particularly to finding out which **tiebreak rules** consumers employ when they are trying to apply checklist-based decision rules and judge that several products offer adequate performances in all core respects: do they decide by moving on to peripheral features in respect of which the products differ, or do they, say, ask themselves what is the most basic feature they really want and then see which one performs best in that respect? The product should then be tailored to be consistent with the answer. Matters are rather simpler if the market is one in which consumers tend to compute some kind of overall score for each product. A supplier merely needs to get some idea of the willingness to pay for/sacrifice particular features or degrees of performance and then examine the profitability of making different changes given the costs of implementing them.

- Because of their **bounded rationality**, consumers may need help in working out how to choose even if they have certain non-negotiable requirements. Advertisements can thus be designed to present reasonable-looking decision rules to consumers, or cases for changing to particular decision rules, that imply the firm's product is the best one to choose.

- The closer the match between products in terms of non-price factors, the more problematic it is for firms to allow their prices to diverge from those of their rivals. This is because such a situation will favour the application of 'choose the cheapest' tiebreak rules. Hence firms must instead prompt substitution by making products appear different in non-price terms, which then makes it safer to experiment with different prices.

The discussion above portrays consumers as if they actually bother to think carefully about their choices in terms of product characteristics. Heterodox economists do not presume that this always happens. Many things in life are done on the basis of **habit**, without any thought about alternatives. This is not to say that at some stage in the past the consumer made a decision involving the consideration of alternatives from which the habit evolved as an **institution** in the sense discussed in Chapter 2. Consider, for example, 'See you at the pub on Friday night?', with no mention of which pub, or 'I'll have the usual', with no mention of the brand or type of drink, once at the pub. Both may be habitual forms of behaviour descended from a choice made long ago about what to do on Friday night, and with whom, or what to drink. Even back at that stage, however, the person may not have evaluated alternatives. For example, suppose the habit stems from the first time the person was invited out by colleagues after moving to a new job in a new area: he or she might simply have adopted a 'when in Rome, do as the Romans do' kind of decision rule.

4.4.4 We're all hunter-gatherers, really

One of the most exciting recent developments in economics is an interest in using ideas from evolutionary psychology to make sense of the choices that people make. The essence of this line of thinking is that the human race has not been around for very long in evolutionary terms and, as a result, we are essentially still operating with brains adapted to life in a hunter-gatherer society and programmed to do the best we can to pass on our genes to future generations. Thus the people alive today are descendants of those from the early years of the human race who happened to have modes of behaviour that were suited to enabling them to survive and produce offspring.

One application of this perspective is towards making sense of differences between men and women as consumers and workers. For example, it has been argued that gender differences in pay do not reflect discrimination against women in the labour market. Rather, once they are of child-rearing age, women's minds may be focused on caring activities rather than on pursuing income, even if they are consciously choosing not to have children yet; men, meanwhile, may be preoccupied with their careers and status as means of demonstrating their suitability as mates.

Modern society is, of course, very different from life in a hunter-gatherer society, so how we respond to particular kinds of modern situations may not be particularly ideal if our responses are those of hunter-gatherers. For example, what our bodies do when we feel threatened at work or in a social setting may have been very effective for enabling us to survive threats from lions and other dangerous animals. Unfortunately, having one's body fired up for 'fight or flight' is physiologically unhelpful when we are, so to speak, chained to a desk and a mortgage that goes with attempts to 'keep up appearances' within our tribe. Our need to be on the alert for wild animals is something that may help explain why our attention can temporarily be diverted by displays in modern shopping malls that are designed not to make it easy to find what we want but rather to get us to stop and buy things for which we were not shopping.

4.5 Fads, fashions and product lifecycles

A demand curve is drawn subject to a number of things being taken as given:

◆ Consumer tastes.

◆ Consumer budgets.

◆ Consumer knowledge.

◆ The prices of other goods.

◆ The characteristics offered by other goods and the good in question.

◆ The list of types of goods available.

◆ The product's distribution system (for example, which shops are stocking it) and the means by which it is being promoted.

◆ The way and extent to which the product and its rivals are being advertised.

Changes in any of these factors as time passes can shift a product's demand curve to the right or the left and generate changes in quantities sold without the product's price being changed.

Within traditional consumer theory, it was easy enough to tell stories about how falling prices or rising real incomes might lead to the fading away of some goods and increasing sales of others. However, discussions of inferior goods and luxuries were problematic in cases where the goods whose sales were growing were new types of products. The '**characteristics approach** to demand' offers a way of showing how a new product might be able to win sales and sometimes force existing ones out of the market. Put simply, the idea was that a new product might offer a cheaper way of producing a particular combination of characteristics and/or enable consumers to achieve higher utility by obtaining combinations of characteristics that were not previously available within their budgets. This can be readily appreciated by reflecting on the greater speed and lower price of current computers compared with those of only a few years earlier, or the growing size of television screens that one can get for a particular price. In this approach, nothing has to be changing in terms of consumer preferences over rival combinations of characteristics, or the set of characteristics in terms of which preference orderings were specified. The behavioural/evolutionary approach recognizes that this may not always be the case and it draws attention to the following:

- *Consumers' **aspiration levels** may rise following increases in their incomes (or in the attainments of those whom they use to judge what they should expect to be able to consume).* When consumers find themselves in new territory they do not, in the heterodox perspective, necessarily have a set of preferences applicable to what they can now afford. Rather, they feel their way towards some idea of what is achievable by setting themselves new aspiration levels – **targets for performance** – and then seeing if they can meet them, adjusting up or down, with a lag, in the light of what seems to be possible.

   Here lies a problem. It is easy to be impressed when first in the midst of products that were previously beyond one's budget, but it is also easy to make mistakes due to the lack of experience and end up with choices that deliver well below what would have been possible. This is particularly important if goods are consumed conspicuously and crass or vulgar choices impede entry into new social circles. The newly rich need to be able to crack the consumption codes of those into whose social circles they wish to be accepted. Ostentatious consumption of things that look obviously new and expensive or are on a grand scale might succeed in impressing the social circles they are trying to leave. Unfortunately, such behaviour provides clear signs that they do not have the insight to move into established elites whose confidence is matched by choices that display restraint, subtlety and a penchant for classic designs.

Those who recognize these risks may conclude that what people in similar circumstances appear to be able to achieve is a good place to start when setting targets. An entire bundle of products to target may even be implied and become the norm for those achieving particular kinds of upgrades in their work status: note, for example, the phenomenon of the 'executive home' and 'executive car'. Buyers who have moved into a new consumption league may thus shun goods that they previously saw as perfectly acceptable. Hence, as the population mix changes in terms of career types and value systems, demands for some products will rise spectacularly, while other products will sell less rapidly.

- *A new product may offer new features.* If the product offers new features without offering inadequate performances on established dimensions, then the new features provide a ready basis for consumers to develop a new tiebreak rule or a longer checklist of required features. Note that, if consumers view this class of product in terms of a priority-ranking, there is no necessary reason to assume that the new feature may simply be placed at the bottom of the list; it may seem clearly to be something of great importance. If so, rival brands that hitherto would have beaten earlier versions of the product in terms of lower priority tests may now be sidelined for failing to pass the new test that has been slotted in higher up (for example, the new question, 'Does the computer include a CD burner?', may seem more important than, say, the size of the monitor).

- *New products may 'set new standards' in terms of particular dimensions.* This issue may be related to the previous one insofar as the new feature determines how the product is judged in terms of a high-level criterion, as with the case of an airbag as a safety feature in cars. Again, this may be of major significance in explaining competitive performance of rival brands if consumers are using checklists based around criteria specifying adequate performance. In the mid-1980s, only very expensive brands of motor vehicle could reasonably be expected to offer even a driver's airbag; by the mid-1990s, the ordinary consumer might expect a driver's airbag to be provided, and some might even be expecting one for the passenger too. Now the same consumer's expectation might be to find a car with six airbags, seatbelt pre-tensioners and active headrests.

If consumers use checklists and can find something from another manufacturer that matches their requirements, a firm that fails to keep apace with rising expectations may find its market share severely limited, even if it tries to maintain sales by trimming prices 'to compensate' for its product's shortcomings. This is something that Henry Ford learnt the hard way in the 1920s: the success of the Ford Model T was based on making it progressively more affordable as a good basic car, and it drove out cars that were cheap but nasty.

However, by the late 1920s affluence had increased and customers wanted even better cars and/or variety, not even cheaper examples of the same thing.

◆ *Consumers **learn** what products can do for them.* The properties of a product are not self-evident but have to be learned by trial and error. This fact underlies our earlier remarks about the problem of uncertainty over product quality and how well a product will do a particular job for them. But here we wish to emphasize that sales dynamics are also driven by consumers forming increasingly complex pictures of the purposes for which a product can be used, and with which other products it can be combined to produce a more complex system.

Personal computers and the Internet are obvious exemplars of this phenomenon but it is evident in all manner of product categories, including food items and cleaning products (highly versatile bicarbonate of soda comes into both categories!). Manufacturers that study what consumers do with their products as well as trying to think up uses by themselves, and whose promotion campaigns focus on educating consumers, may be able greatly to extend the lives of their products.

From a complex systems perspective, consumer learning entails the making of new sets of mental connections. The marketing problems or opportunities faced by firms can change drastically if consumers change the mental images that they associate with particular products: for example, many consumers who would have seen smoking as 'cool' a generation ago now see it as inconsistent with a healthy lifestyle, while the modern heterosexual male increasingly does not see the use of cosmetics products as effeminate but as devices for holding back the process of ageing and maintaining sexual attractiveness.

◆ *Consumers learn from opinion leaders and from other members of their **social networks**.* The 'field' approach to economics proceeds with little consideration of the social context of choice, whereas the complex systems approach of heterodox economics ascribes a major role to the sharing of information and imitative behaviour, with some people playing much bigger roles than others as connective nodes. This applies not merely to the 'what' of products (the previous point) but also to 'which' ones should be consumed and in which combinations, to create a particular **style**.

The consumer that is used as a reference point need not actually be part of one's social circle, or even a real person. The television series *Sex and the City* had a major impact on women's fashion, particularly via the novel combinations of items worn by the character played by Sarah Jessica Parker. In other words, capabilities in constructing connections are significant on the demand side, not merely on the supply side considered in Chapter 3.

To be truly 'cool' or 'hip', a consumer needs to stand out from the masses, which entails being innovative, choosing styles of consumption that are not yet popular and having the confidence to display them in public. At the other end of the spectrum is the timid, uninventive, 'sheepish' consumer who fears standing out from the crowd and hence must change in line with changes in popular styles.

The existence of these different approaches to novelty and conspicuousness generates via social competition an endless spiral of changing fashions. The cool are copied by the not quite so cool, forcing the cool to work on new consumption strategies but also forcing the timid to defend their positions by conforming to the emerging – but inherently short-lived – consumption standard. Conventional market research is not going to be particularly effective for anticipating this phenomenon. Instead, firms need to get to know who the trendsetters are and study their behaviour closely.

4.6 Products in the context of lifestyles

Lifestyles are defined as ways of life that 'revolve around' particular bundles of linked consumption choices related to value systems people develop or adopt for making sense of the world and their place in it.

From the standpoint of complex systems theory, the lifestyle notion embodies a far more extensive view of **complementarity** between goods than the typical economist seems to have in mind. Typically, coverage of complementarity runs only as far as a few examples, such as gin and tonic, coffee and cream, or video cassettes and VCRs, followed by a brief discussion of how a fall in the price for one of them shifts to the right the demand curve of its complement.

Within heterodox economics, and in marketing, complementarity means the sets of connections – in terms of particular kinds of goods, habits and modes of conduct – that make up the fabric of everyday lives. People choose a broad strategy for their lives and then set about choosing at a lower level of abstraction a set of connected goods and services consistent with it. Groups with similar incomes may consume systematically different sets of goods depending on the types of consumption 'business' they have chosen to be in, for example:

♦   whether to live in the city centre or suburbs;

♦   whether to have children;

♦   how they see borrowing and the need to save for retirement;

♦   which kinds of ethical systems they use as foundations for their lives.

The lifestyle phenomenon implies that it is important for business economists to understand the fit of their firms' product with particular lifestyles, and their roles in helping people solve the kinds of problems that their lifestyles entail. Box 4.3, on the Atkins diet, gives an example of how a perhaps faddish change in one commonly employed foundation of everyday life can have major implications on a number of fronts.

Box 4.3 Fallout from the popularity of the Atkins diet

The Atkins diet suddenly became very popular in the UK during 2002–3, and the 5 November 2003 edition of BBC2's *The Money Programme* explored how its popularity had been affecting the food and beverages sector. This diet involves taking the radical step of trying to cut out one of the major food groups – carbohydrates. While meat and cheese sales are not threatened by this strategy, sales of potatoes and bread have been dramatically reduced as more people have taken to the diet plan. Both of the trade associations connected with these foods are now on the marketing offensive. Furthermore, the makers of Slim Fast have seen a 30 per cent fall in sales and a big drop in their share price. On the other side of the coin, Michelob low carbohydrate beer (made by Anheuser Busch) had seen a growth in sales in the previous 12 months, and several new 'low carbohydrate' entrepreneurs have emerged running businesses (for example, 'Carbolite') that specialize in offering Atkins-compatible food products. *The Money Programme's* investigator visited a popular City of London wine bar whose manager stated how he had noticed a large drop off in beer consumption and a corresponding increase in wine consumption as the fad-following City clientele followed the diet. Part of the explanation for its popularity is the number of Hollywood stars who have been following the Atkins plan.

Unlike the genteel imagery of gin and tonic and other simple exemplars of complementarity, the sets of connections that make up lifestyle may sometimes entail a tangled mess and place a great burden on the ability of household managers (parents!) to **juggle** time, money and products competently. From this perspective, it appears that many products will be purchased simply to prevent **chaos**: they liberate time and make it possible to make or maintain connections in terms of hopes/expectations about social interaction, images presented to others, the kinds of lives that children will have and how they will develop. If one (or a single) parent is not in paid employment, many of these materialistic hopes will have to be abandoned, yet fitting in with the demands of employers may cause logistical nightmares in terms of looking after children and ferrying them around – hence the demand for multi-purpose vehicles, convenience foods and microwave ovens, reliable washing machines and dishwashers, home security systems and so on. Rising mass consumption permitted by increased productivity levels may entail rising stress levels insofar as aspiration levels are based upon the achievements of somewhat better-off members of society who are themselves also on the treadmill of lifestyle maintenance, basing their aspirations on yet better-off people.

4.7 Purchasing decisions of businesses

Consumers' purchasing decisions are dwarfed in terms of total value by those of business buyers choosing amongst supplies of raw materials, components, services and capital items. Like consumers of end products, those who purchase inputs for businesses will suffer from **bounded rationality**. However, if they specialize in buying particular kinds of products for a living, then it might seem reasonable to expect them to have considerable **expertise** in respect of what rival products and suppliers offer and of the kinds of deals they can reasonably expect to obtain.

The presence of expert business buyers is important in ensuring the ultimate consumer gets a good deal, because such buyers may enable their firms to compete more aggressively with rivals. Particularly important in this process is the retailing stage in the supply chain. Retailers such as major supermarket chains set out to compete for customers by providing a convenient and simplified shopping environment and by using their superior understanding of purchasing behaviour (gathered from checkout scanner information) to lever deals from manufacturers. They can be seen as a kind of information filter, opting to stock some goods on the consumer's behalf but not others that they have judged offer inferior value for money. They enable consumers to assemble their trolleys of weekly groceries cheaply and without fuss, rather as many 'no-name' PC suppliers use their skills in shopping around for computer components as a basis for putting together cheap computer packages, or as package tour companies assemble holidays. Notice, however, that the nature of the consumer's opportunity cost problem means that getting the weekly groceries has a kind of credence to it as far as the choice of supermarket is concerned: consumers using supermarkets as one-stop shops *need to be confident* that the purchasing staff in these firms are good at their jobs and that benefits of the latter's expertise are being passed on to them due to pressure of competition with rival chains. The trouble is, they don't know what they might be getting if they shopped elsewhere. If they start to question whether their habitual supermarket is offering the best value, given the kind of products and standard of service they want, they can only check this by spending a good deal of time in other stores, each of which has thousands of product lines and differs in layout. This is because the supermarkets themselves cannot demonstrate their competitiveness across all of the products they stock; they can merely hint at it by promoting a very limited set of items 'on special' or presenting themselves as offering 'everyday low prices' and illustrating this with a small selection of examples.

There are some grounds for consumers to have such confidence (rather than sticking with a particular retailer merely due to being too busy to check the deals available elsewhere) and for business economists to have a general expectation that purchasing by businesses is based on expertise. Where markets can easily be contested (for example, by established firms from other markets diversifying into them), purchasing officers will be under great pressure from senior managers to perform well so that their firms can keep prices at levels that both keep existing competitors at bay and deter new entrants, as well as delivering an adequate long-run return for shareholders. Moreover, in some cases, well-motivated purchasing officers enjoy particular leverage because they can:

- get to know of or infer something about **rivals' experiences** with particular suppliers by observing who is dealing with whom (if necessary by observing the vans that come and go at a rival's factory gate!), reading reports in the business press or via the grapevine of social interaction and business institutions – for example, when a major firm changes its advertising agency, this is typically announced in advertising journals such as *Campaign*, to the embarrassment of the agency that has been dumped;

- achieve **economies of scale in obtaining redress** through legal channels if suppliers offer products that do not come up to contractual specifications in terms of quality or timely delivery;

- have the power to give **large orders** for a range of inputs, the loss of which would be very significant for the supplier (see further, Section 9.4.4).

Despite this, major problems of information and knowledge stand between professional buyers and the achievement of the best possible choice. Services of advertising agencies, public relations companies, corporate lawyers, accountants, engineering and other consultants are products whose quality is inherently difficult to know or specify in advance. Hence established 'name' brands may seem far safer and more cost-effective choices, despite the premium prices that they charge. The sudden collapse of accounting giant Arthur Andersen following revelations about its role in the failure of Enron is a telling reminder about the value of a good name in the corporate services sector. Fortunately, for those suppliers of corporate services whose name presently signifies nothing good or bad, industrial buyers often experiment with such players by giving them smaller, less sensitive tasks and gradually build up relationships with them. By doing so, they can signal to the major players that they should not be taken for granted. Of course, it helps if staff members of the fledgling businesses have track records as former employees or partners in 'name' businesses.

With more tangible products that are produced by the winner of a tendering process there will still be uncertainty about quality and delivery that severely taxes the industrial buyer's pool of expertise. Choosing the cheapest quotation may not be wise, as it could result from inexperience leading to over-optimistic estimates, or from desperation. Sticking to suppliers of whom one has experience is thus a tempting strategy if they are cheap enough, even if one tries to 'keep them on their toes' by putting things out to tender from time to time, or divides business between several suppliers.

The latter strategies have their own risks, compared with buying from a sole supplier: the more people that have to be brought into the picture about the firm's business, the greater the risk of information seeping out to the advantage of rivals, while firms that are repeatedly given the impression that the customer will switch elsewhere if a better deal seems available in the short run may be loathe to invest in specialized customer-specific equipment that will enable them to offer a superior longer-term deal.

Organizational factors may complicate the industrial buying process. Suppose the buyer is indeed a corporate professional with responsibility for getting a good deal for the employer. If so, the buyer may be at risk of being fired if an adventurous choice turns out badly, with no reward on offer if a risky supplier choice pays off and saves the firm a considerable sum of money or leads to revenue-enhancing improvements in quality of the firm's output. Logic points here towards following the maxim 'Nobody ever got fired for buying IBM' and sticking with an existing supplier who is proving satisfactory. This applies even if the professional buyer is aware that the existing supplier is not currently regarded in the industry as a superior performer: here we have a case of **information impactedness** with the **opportunistic agent** (the buyer) knowing more than the **principal** (the employer) about the situation.

Such a situation is less likely to arise if a would-be supplier can communicate with other interested and potentially influential people within the organization – such as workers who actually have to use the machine in question, or the marketing manager who could benefit from a more consistent standard of manufacturing quality if it were adopted – and seek to demonstrate that the firm risks a mediocre deal if it sticks with its established supplier. This may be no easy task, particularly if they first have to get their personnel or promotional materials past the potential customer's gatekeepers, such as their secretaries or personal assistants.

4.8 Brand loyalty and brand equity

Mainstream theorists have had little place for the concept of a 'brand', tending to construct models of choice in which buyers are choosing between precisely differentiated products and have precise wants.

> A brand is defined as a name or symbol that consumers see as signifying something particular about the nature of a product and those who consume it. Brands serve the role of shorthand product summaries for boundedly rational buyers who are sufficiently knowledgeable to decode them.

Global brands such as McDonald's, Kodak, Nike, Sony or IBM enable internationally mobile consumers immediately to achieve some sense of familiarity, rather than feeling like totally clueless, recently arrived aliens, when they try to make choices in a new location. Such brands are, in short, devices that enable us to simplify the process of choice by generalizing across time, space and (when a 'brand extension' is successful) different types of products. They are like friends to which we turn for assistance in moments of need and, so long as they do not let us down too much, we tolerate their occasional lapses.

> Brand loyalty may range from passionate commitment to particular brands, that buyers are prepared to defend publicly, down to much more common but rather loose polygamous attachments to a number of suppliers of a particular kind of product.

The notion of brand loyalty is clearly at odds with the mainstream 'field' perspective, for it suggests that buyers form relationships of various kinds with particular brands and steer well clear of others. In the case of polygamous brand loyalty, there may be a hierarchy of brands that a consumer is prepared to consider if they are available, based on previous experience with them. But often, any of the consumer's favoured brands is seen as acceptable, with choices between them being triggered by the particular juxtaposition of circumstances, such as whichever happens to be cheapest on the day in question or is most easily noticed and reached on the supermarket shelf.

> Brand equity refers to the extent to which a supplier can earn a premium return via a higher price or larger market share relative to competing products because of the way in which customers view its brand.

This phenomenon can be observed across a diverse array of products, from groceries through to opera singers. A firm whose products lack brand equity may find itself with a much smaller market share than suppliers of products that enjoy considerable brand equity, even if the latter are much more expensive.

Brand equity is easier than the relationship aspect of brand loyalty to bring within the mainstream perspective. Mainstream economists argue that the ability to charge higher prices for similar, but not quite identical, products gives the owners of the brand a big incentive not to tarnish their reputations by letting their standards slip towards those of lesser products. If consumers recognize this, they will continue to be prepared to pay higher prices and in return will indeed receive better quality. The mainstream story makes sense with, say, the food, aviation and automotive sectors, where adverse news reports regarding product safety could tarnish a firm's image overnight, and particularly if the brand name is applied to an entire range of products.

Other cases are less supportive of the mainstream 'markets are efficient' view of brand equity. A striking case concerns model-sharing joint ventures between General Motors and Toyota in both the USA and Australia during the 1990s. Despite differing physically in terms of only minor trimmings and badges, the 'original' products drastically outsold the re-badged models. In the US context, the Toyota Corolla sold spectacularly better than its Geo Metro twin despite the Toyota carrying a substantially higher price. If this was because customers thought that the former came from a Japanese factory and might therefore be of higher quality, then the customers were wrong: both were produced in a General Motors factory in Fremont, California, managed in Toyota's style.

The Australian arms of General Motors and Toyota should both have learnt a lesson from this: do not expect unfamiliar model names to sell even if attached to familiar manufacturer brand names. But they did not, only to discover that Holden Nova and Apollo ('really' Toyota Corolla and Camry) meant nothing to most buyers and neither did a Toyota Lexcen ('really' a Holden Commodore – the late Ben Lexcen had been well known as an Australian yacht designer a decade earlier). Even buyers who knew what they were getting and chose on the basis of the best deal would still have had to contend with the social embarrassment of their peers not being familiar with what they had purchased or suggesting they did not know what they had 'really' bought (as in, 'Geez, mate, I thought you said a Lexus; it's just a Commodore with the wrong badges!'). Not surprisingly, the Toyota/GM–Holden alliance did not last long.

However poorly grounded may be the customer perceptions that give rise to brand equity, careful management of these perceptions may pay off handsomely in terms of profits. Once again, the car market provides excellent lessons. The Volkswagen–Audi Group uses differences in brand image and brand equity to run a sophisticated strategy of charging very different prices for different brands of cars whose underlying designs and components have much in common. This strategy is a form of what economists call **'price discrimination'**. It would collapse rapidly if customers started seeing its models for what they were – shared underpinnings with different clothes and designer badges – and just bought the firm's good-value Skoda or sporty SEAT products instead of some buying premium Volkswagen and prestige Audi products. Differences in the kinds of dealerships through which they are sold further serve to permit differences in price and perception: for example, Skoda dealers in the UK are typically small, independent local businesses without the sophisticated showrooms of Volkswagen or Audi dealers. In the long run, and particularly in an age in which customers can learn the truth about products via reviews in magazines and the Internet, premium prices will tend to be paid only if products are indeed better than their cheaper rivals. However, this may still leave room for manufacturers of highly regarded brands to capture the value they create: the crucial thing is that the customers are prepared to pay, as a premium, more than it costs to add the extra quality that they can only get by paying more.

4.9 Summary

Theories of buyer behaviour can help in designing market research programmes or thinking critically about the results of such programmes, as well as in exploring the possible implications of changes in price, product, distribution method or promotion strategy in situations where no relevant market research data are available. Unfortunately, mainstream economists have provided a theoretical framework that is not particularly helpful in these situations. Their framework certainly provides a way of thinking rigorously about the process of solving a well-defined problem of choosing a mix of goods subject to a budget limit. It also draws to our attention the significance of the benefit the consumer receives from consuming extra units of a particular

4.9 **Summary** (continued)

product. However, it has little to say about what determines the limits to substitution or the extent of complementarity between products.

Heterodox approaches to the theory of choice lack the formal elegance of the mainstream view and its emphasis on the willingness of consumers to make marginal substitutions. Instead, they are built around the idea that consumers make their decisions by using evolving frameworks of hierarchically related decision rules. These rules often entail intolerant checklists and require that products meet target-based performance criteria if they are to get purchased. In the face of problems of information and knowledge much simpler rules are prone to be employed, such as choosing trusted brands or following recommendations or observed behaviour of other buyers. Different forms of decision rules can lead to vastly different policy implications, so the business economist needs to develop skills for analysing which decision rules are likely to be popular in particular contexts and/or should try to ensure that colleagues engaged in market research frame their questions in ways that will accurately identify decision rules that subjects use.

The differences between mainstream and heterodox approaches very much reflect their respective 'field' and 'complex systems' perspectives. The former, in treating everything as directly linked to everything else, provides little basis for understanding the determination of the extent of substitution and complementarity between goods. The systems approach points the business economist towards studying, or getting market researcher colleagues to study, how choices are affected by patterns of linkages in terms of:

- the ideas that make up consumers' views of the world, including how they see patterns of implications of particular acts of behaviour and the symbolic connotations of particular brands;

- the rules that consumers create for specifying acceptable ways of combining products (such as styles of dress, cuisine, décor and so on);

- the match between products and decision rules (whether it 'fits the bill', or is 'a square peg in a round hole') and the strength of connections thus made (that is to say, brand loyalty);

- the social networks of influence within which buyers operate;

- the linked sets of activities that consumers assemble as their 'lifestyles'.

4.10 Some questions to consider

1. Critically evaluate the design of the Amazon.com website in the light of material covered in this chapter.

2. If consumers start buying their groceries on-line and having them delivered to their homes, how might this affect their purchasing behaviour between rival brands and supermarket chains?

3. How can it make sense for a used-car dealer to advertise an ageing Mercedes-Benz or Volvo as providing 'budget-priced prestige'?

4. Globalization does not mean that strong-selling products in global terms necessarily fare well in all their markets. The Toyota Camry sells over 400 000 units a year in the USA, and in the relatively small Australian market it sells over 25 000 units a year. In the UK, however, barely 1000 Camry are sold each year and they depreciate to about 25 per cent of their new price within three years. A similar fate befalls large cars offered in the UK by Hyundai, Kia and Nissan. Depreciation makes these cars very expensive to run in the UK, despite their low purchase prices relative to European 'prestige' brands, so the importers seem to be stuck in a vicious circle: if they cannot increase residual values, only the unwise will buy their cars, and hence the cars will remain relatively unknown and unappreciated by the market at large and will suffer poor residuals. Can you suggest any possible ways out of this, in the light of theory covered so far in this book?

5. Examine any consumer magazines you have to see what kinds of decision rules their journalists use when they reach verdicts in multiple product tests. Examine, too, how the formats used in these tests and the verdicts reached may affect consumer choices.

6. Examine the movie business mindful of material covered in this chapter. For example, can you make sense of the rise of chains of multiplex cinemas, the presence of 'stars' and sequels, different cinemas charging different prices to see a given film, or the exorbitant price of cinema popcorn compared with home-prepared popcorn? How helpful is the theory material for working out how worried cinema companies should be by the advent of DVD and home-theatre technologies?

4.10 Some questions to consider (continued)

7. Examine the likely consequences for Western firms if they adopt the widespread Japanese practice of allowing decisions about the purchase of factory equipment to be taken by the worker who will use what is selected.

8. Examine the problems faced by consumers and retailers of wine when choosing between rival brands to drink or to retail.

9. What lessons does buyer behaviour theory offer to an international textbook publisher considering the publication of a new business economics textbook that will 'break the mould' by covering both mainstream and heterodox economic theory?

4.11 Recommended additional reading sources

The tendencies of economists to ignore similarities between households and firms are explored in Alec Cairncross (1958) 'Economic schizophrenia', *Scottish Journal of Political Economy*, **5**, pp. 15–21.

Mainstream consumer theory was originally set out in J.R. Hicks (1939) *Value and Capital*, Oxford, Oxford University Press. Hicks proceeds with greater caution at times than do subsequent mainstream textbooks. A more useful classic for business economists to read, however, is Book III of Alfred Marshall (1920) *Principles of Economics* (8th edn), London, Macmillan. Here, as in other areas, Marshall's work has a strong evolutionary flavour, with an emphasis on learning by consumers. Marshall even thinks of consumer demand as a demand for the characteristics of products. However, as far as mainstream theorists are concerned, the key references here are two 1966 articles by Kelvin Lancaster: 'A new approach to consumer theory', *Journal of Political Economy*, **74**, April, pp. 132–57; and 'Change and innovation in the technology of consumption', *American Economic Review*, **56**, May, pp. 14–23 (the latter is the more accessible of the two).

For alternative pluralistic treatments of consumer demand in intermediate-level microeconomics texts, see: Susan Himmelweit, Robert Simonetti and Andrew Trigg (2001) *Microeconomics: Neoclassical and Institutional Perspectives on Economic Behaviour*, London, Thomson Learning/Open University (Chapters 2–6); and Peter E. Earl (1995) *Microeconomics for Business and Marketing*, Aldershot, Edward Elgar (Chapters 2–4).

For a mini-encyclopaedia of short guides to over a hundred topics in the consumer behaviour area (including brand loyalty, brand equity, cognitive dissonance, conspicuous consumption, habit and impulse buying), see Peter E. Earl and Simon Kemp (eds) (1999) *The Elgar Companion to Consumer Research and Economics Psychology*, Cheltenham, Edward Elgar.

Edward Fullbrook (ed.) (2002) *Intersubjectivity in Economics: Agents and Structures*, London and New York, Routledge. This collection provides a 'state of the art' guide to thinking in economics about the impact of social interaction on consumer behaviour. A classic earlier contribution on this topic is Harvey Leibenstein (1950) 'Bandwagon, snob and Veblen effects in the theory of consumers' demand', *Quarterly Journal of Economics*, **64**, pp. 183–207.

An interesting set of essays focusing on experimental and innovative aspects of consumer behaviour has been assembled by Marina Bianchi (ed.) (1998) *The Active Consumer: Novelty and Surprise in Consumer Choice*, London, Routledge.

The scope for businesses to manage consumer behaviour via advertising and other promotional ploys has been explored at length by Jon D. Hanson and Douglas A. Kysar, in two articles that both appeared in 1999: 'Taking behavioralism seriously: the problem of market manipulation', *New York University Law Review*, **74**, pp. 630–749; and 'Taking behavioralism seriously: some evidence of market manipulation', *Harvard Law Review*, **112**, pp. 1420–572. These papers make a fascinating and chilling antidote to the 'consumer is king' view expressed by mainstream libertarians such as Milton Friedman and Rose D. Friedman (1980) in *Free to Choose*, Harmondsworth, Penguin Books.

For an intriguing case study of conspicuous consumption, see Merl Storr (2002) 'Classy Lingerie', *Feminist Review*, **71**, No. 1, pp. 18–36. It concerns the Ann Summers Party Plan method of selling lingerie, where display to peers is essentially at the time of purchase rather than at the time of use. The 'classy' aspect includes a social class dimension.

A superb website on evolutionary psychology has been developed by Paul Kenyon at the Department of Psychology, University of Plymouth. See: http://salmon.psy.plym.ac.uk/year3/PSY339EvolutionaryPsychology/Evolutionary Psychology.htm. An evolutionary psychology approach to work and pay is offered by Satoshi Kanazawa (forthcoming) 'Is "discrimination" necessary to explain the sex gap in earnings?', *Journal of Economic Psychology*. This article also refers to most of the previous applications of evolutionary psychology in economics.

The discussion of fashion cycles in this chapter is inspired by yet to be published work by Andreas Chai, which was influenced by the chapter 'I'm hip' in Morris Holbrook (1995) *Consumer Research: Introspective Essays on the Study of Consumption*, Thousand Oaks, CA, Sage. This book provides a fascinating and provocative account of how consumer research within marketing has changed over past decades.

Frederick E. Webster and Yoram Wind (1972) *Organizational Buying Behavior*, Englewood Cliffs, NJ, Prentice-Hall. This is one of the pioneering works on purchasing processes of organizations. For a classic empirical study revealing inertia and limited search by industrial buyers, see M.T. Cunningham and J.G. White (1974) 'The behaviour of industrial buyers in their search for suppliers of machine tools', *Journal of Management Studies*, **11**, pp. 15–28.

The classic mainstream analysis of the economics of brands is Benjamin Klein and Keith Leffler (1981) 'The Role of Market Forces in Assuring Contractual Performance', *Journal of Political Economy*, **89**, pp. 615–41. Klein provides a more user-friendly discussion, with some examples, at http://www.econlib.org/library/Enc/BrandNames.html.

5

How shall the firm produce the product?

Learning outcomes

If you study this chapter carefully, it may help you to understand:

- the law of diminishing marginal returns

- the concept of returns to scale

- what a production function is and what it is not

- different types of knowledge

- the importance of learning-by-doing

- the division of labour.

To the extent that you develop such understanding, you should be better able to:

- appreciate the difference between the mainstream theory of production and the heterodox approach

- identify the different kinds of knowledge needed in order to produce a good or service.

5.1 Introduction

In this chapter we assume that the entrepreneur is confident that consumers will want the product and we direct our attention to the issue of how to produce the good or service in question.

> Production is defined as the process of using materials and factor services, in conjunction with technology, to create new goods and services.

The aim of production is to add value to the chosen inputs. The branch of economics that addresses how best to produce a good or service is called the **theory of production**, but before we discuss the technical details of this theory we will take a look at some of the practical issues that faced the British vacuum cleaner entrepreneur James Dyson in his attempts to get his revolutionary Dual Cyclone technology into production. We will then take a look at the mainstream approach to the theory of production before moving on to look at the modifications and extensions to this framework that have been constructed by heterodox economists.

It is probably fair to say that the mainstream story of production is somewhat easier to understand than the heterodox story by virtue of the fact that it makes several simplifying assumptions that, in turn, make it a good place to start developing your theoretical understanding of production. On the other hand, the heterodox approach tells a more sophisticated story in which many of the simplifying assumptions of the mainstream story are either relaxed or criticized and replaced. Ultimately, we hope that by presenting the Dyson story and then the theoretical stories in sequence you will develop a sound grasp of the issues a real world entrepreneur has to grapple with. One final point before we begin: this chapter is an essential prerequisite to the one that follows where we will be taking a look at the costs a firm incurs as a result of the answers it provides to the production question.

5.2 The story of Dyson vacuum cleaners

In these opening years of the twenty-first century it is probably fair to say that Dyson vacuum cleaners with their distinctive design, colouring and advanced Dual Cyclone technology are a familiar sight in all electrical retailers, department stores and mail order catalogues throughout the UK and, increasingly, the rest of the world.

Given the ubiquity of the marque, it is easy to forget that the 'Dyson phenomenon' is a relatively recent addition to the rather staid world of the vacuum cleaner market. The first model produced by entrepreneur James Dyson's own

UK factory was manufactured on 1 July 1993, but the story of Dyson's struggle to bring his technology to market begins way back in 1978 when he discovered why the dominant vacuuming technology was such a poor performer and arrived at a solution to the performance issue by making connections between domestic vacuum cleaning and the apparently unrelated technology found in a typical sawmill.

In 1978 James Dyson was already a successful designer-engineer-entrepreneur sitting on the board of a company called Kirk-Dyson, which produced and marketed the 'Ballbarrow' (an all terrain wheelbarrow) and other gardening products. One day, while he was vacuuming his house with an old reconditioned upright cleaner, he began to think about why it only seemed capable of pushing dirt and dust around the floor rather than sucking it up as it was supposed to do. He reasoned that it was probably because the dirt-collection bag was full so he replaced it, but performance was little better. Thinking that this was probably because the cleaner was so old he purchased a brand new cylinder cleaner. This worked much more efficiently, but only for a short while. Once again, reasoning that the dirt-collection bag must be full he replaced it and performance was restored. As before, the improvement was only transitory and soon the vacuum cleaner was as ineffective as the old reconditioned upright he had been using. Rather than replacing the bag again he emptied it and reused it. He was intrigued to find out that this did not improve performance, even briefly, in the same way that a brand new bag had done. After conducting a few more experiments Dyson concluded that vacuum cleaners with bags became inefficient very quickly because the pores in the bag were becoming clogged with dust and this was reducing its porosity to the air, which had a knock-on effect of reducing the power of the suck generated by the vacuum cleaner's motor-driven fan. At this juncture he did not have a solution to the problem of diminishing suction power, but then a similar problem involving reduced suction power became apparent at the Ballbarrow factory in its powder coating process and the seeds of an idea began to germinate.

The frame of the Ballbarrow was epoxy-coated for toughness. The first stage of epoxy coating was achieved via the rather messy process of spraying a mist of powder over the Ballbarrow frames with the excess powder (the stuff that missed the frames) being sucked onto a fine gauze mesh for collection and reuse. The suction power was provided by a fan housed behind the mesh, but as more frames were coated the build up of plastic dust on the mesh reduced the efficiency of the suction provided by the fan. This required production to be stopped at regular intervals throughout the day to clean the mesh and collect the excess powder for reuse.

Unhappy with having to stop production at such frequent intervals Dyson inquired of the mesh filter manufacturers if a more efficient technology was available. They informed him that they could supply a cyclonic filter, as supplied to sawmills, which extracted excess dust from the atmosphere without the need for a mesh barrier. Instead it used a large conical funnel (some 30 feet in height) to generate a vortex of high-speed air which spun dust particles to the edges where they lost speed and fell into a collection bag. This technology proved to be too expensive for Kirk-Dyson to purchase so James Dyson visited a nearby sawmill, made some sketches and built a cyclone filter for the Ballbarrow factory. Then he made the important **mental connection** between this relatively large-scale technology and the small-scale technology of the vacuum cleaner – a connection that nobody else had ever made.

Eager to turn the mental connection into a **practical connection** James Dyson returned home and produced a small prototype cardboard cyclonic filter which he attached to his old upright vacuum cleaner (after ripping off its bag). Then he vacuumed his house and discovered that this basic small-scale cyclonic filter worked very satisfactorily in its domestic application, just as he had hoped it would.

Having got the basic idea Dyson threw himself into designing and developing a perfect cyclonic filtration system. He was convinced he had a technology that would take the vacuum cleaner market by storm. However, to his surprise and dismay the road to success was going to prove to be far from smooth.

In early 1979 Dyson left Kirk-Dyson to pursue development of the cyclonic system full-time. In conjunction with an old business associate, Jeremy Fry, he set up the 'Air Power Vacuum Cleaner Company' and commenced the lonely process of technology development in a run-down coach house adjacent to his home in Bath, England. In late 1982, after three years of constant work, the single cyclone idea had been transformed into a more efficient double cyclone (patented as the 'Dual Cyclone'), which was capable of sucking up dirt particles of any size, from the microscopic through to the very large (not to mention items such as coins, etc.). During this period Dyson had constructed more than 1000 working models before he achieved 100 per cent efficiency of the system. The idea of the Air Power Vacuum Cleaner Company manufacturing a product based on the technology was mooted, but the financial position of the company prevented Dyson from following this path. Instead Dyson set up a new company called 'Prototypes Limited' and set out to license the technology to the big players in the UK vacuum cleaner market.

Amazingly, nobody was interested in the new technology except for a small company called Rotork with whom Dyson had been involved several years previously. In 1983 Rotork financed an operation whereby Dyson designed a vacuum cleaner, Zanussi manufactured it and Klene-eze sold it. All in all just 500 units (which they named 'Cyclon') were made and sold. This perhaps was a false start but it was a chance to **learn from experience** and, importantly, to obtain **customer feedback** with respect to function and durability. A picture of the Cyclon found its way into a TWA in-flight magazine, which stimulated international interest and there followed a protracted period of negotiations with a variety of vacuum cleaner manufacturers in the USA. By the middle of 1984 a licensing deal looked to be set with the American company Amway but, after handing over technical drawings and flying out to the USA to sign the final agreement, Amway decided they wanted to **renegotiate** the deal (this is something economists call 'hold up' and we will return to it later in the book). By the start of 1985 the Amway deal had collapsed and Prototypes Limited was getting very short on funds due to the costs of negotiation (mainly the fees of expensive lawyers to oversee the contract) borne to date. Furthermore, Amway had decided to sue for various reasons. Prototypes counter-sued and the legal battle ended in early 1985 when Dyson handed back the front money paid to him by Amway, who had to return his patents and terminate their licence agreement.

Fortunately for Dyson the Cyclon had also stimulated interest in the Dual Cyclone technology in Japan from a company called Apex Ltd. A deal was struck and James Dyson spent much of 1985–6 in Japan designing a vacuum cleaner called the 'G-Force' (which retained many features of the Cyclon) which he saw all the way through to production. Yet again another **learning experience** for Dyson and a much-needed financial lifeline. As he recalls: 'In the year I spent with the Japanese, I learnt an awful lot about design that would stand me in great stead when I set up alone to make the Dyson Dual Cyclone.'

In March 1986 the G-Force hit the Japanese market at a retail price of £1200. Despite this astronomical price it became a hit in Japan and within three years it was making sales of £12 million a year, although thanks to the terms of his licensing agreement Dyson only received £60 000 a year.

The success in Japan paved the way for a renewed assault on the North American market and in July 1986 a deal was reached with a Canadian company called Iona for a dry shampooing machine to be called 'Drytech' (ostensibly a Dual Cyclone vacuum cleaner, but in order to get around certain legal restrictions placed on Iona it had to be redesigned to deliver a powdered carpet shampoo). Back at his coach house, Dyson gathered a small team around him consisting of 'a couple of designers, recent graduates of the RCA, an engineer and a draftsman', in order to design the dry shampooer. This went on sale in June 1987.

In the background negotiations for a 'pure' vacuum cleaner to be called the 'Fantom' were in train, but just as the deal was about to be signed Iona informed Dyson that their buyer, Sears, had already got a dual cyclone vacuum cleaner in their stores which was manufactured by none other than Amway! Unsurprisingly, Amway's cyclonic vacuum cleaner infringed several of Dyson's patents and once again a legal battle followed with the help of Iona, although at a cost to Dyson of a renegotiated (i.e. worse) deal for the Fantom. This legal battle would rumble on for several years at an annual cost of £300 000.

By 1989 the Dual Cyclone technology was becoming well known. In 1990 Dyson signed a worldwide licensing deal with Johnson Wax to apply the technology to a tank vacuum cleaner and a back pack vacuum cleaner for sale to industry and commercial cleaners. Early this same year Vax got in touch with Dyson and asked him to build an upright vacuum cleaner for the UK market and, as Dyson put it: 'My little staff at the coach house and I were designing vacuum cleaners, and other bits and bobs, for our current licensees, and the Vax deal looked like the final piece of the jigsaw.'

It had always been Dyson's intention to produce an upright cleaner for the UK market so the Vax proposal was attractive. After signing the agreement and taking receipt of £75 000 front money Dyson and his team delivered the final design and drawings to Vax at the end of 1990. It soon became clear, however, that Vax were not entirely happy and they asked for a number of redesigns. By July 1991 it didn't look like they were going to commit to production so Dyson parted company with Vax. He was now keen to produce a vacuum cleaner for the UK market himself. The major problem he faced was obtaining finance. The Amway legal battle was still rolling on and it was diverting much-needed funds away from the company, but, just as he was despairing of reaching an agreement with Amway, the case was resolved and the financial burden removed. Dyson and his team launched into designing their first UK upright vacuum cleaner.

The product that was to become the DC01 took as its point of departure the G-Force. The design team worked in the now-refurbished coach house for over nine months. Computer-aided design was carried out upstairs while prototype models were built downstairs. According to Dyson: 'We made hundreds of little technical improvements to the cyclone, and to the cleaner head, and at the same time concentrated on reducing the number of screws, joins, and parts in the finished design – this would concentrate our minds on the essence of the function, and force the form to follow it most efficiently, and also, most importantly since *we never knew how much money we were going to have to put the thing into production, it could keep down the amount of tooling that we needed* (at about £20 000 a

mould, any part we could possibly do without was rejected...).' [emphasis added].
On 2 May 1992, Dyson's 45th birthday, the team delivered 'the first, fully operational, visually perfect, Dyson Dual Cyclone'.

With a fully working demonstrator model in place Dyson now needed to obtain finance so that his newly formed company 'Dyson Appliances' could invest in the required production tooling required to mass produce the Dual Cyclone. Merchant banks proved to be sceptical towards the project and in the end he obtained a loan of £600 000 from the high street lender Lloyds Bank, secured on his London and Bath houses. He raised another £750 000 by selling all rights to Alco (who had taken over the Apex licence) for production of the G-Force in Japan.

Having sorted out the finance, Dyson travelled to Italy where he negotiated directly with 18 toolmakers, whom he had first dealt with via Zanussi when he was involved with the Cyclon project, for the production of 40 large moulding units (some of which weighed up to two tonnes). The tooling, which cost £900 000, was ready by the end of November and it arrived in the UK at the end of December 1992 where it was transported to a newly set up American-owned company called 'Phillips Plastics' who were based in Wrexham, Wales. Dyson had decided to contract out the moulding of the vacuum cleaner's parts and its assembly to Phillips rather than take on direct control of the production process. By the end of January 1993 the first Dyson DC01s rolled off the production line and fulfilled delivery contracts that Dyson had negotiated earlier in 1992 with the catalogue-based mail order shops Great Universal Stores (GUS) and Littlewoods. Orders had also been received from several chains of regional electricity board shops and John Lewis department stores and, in April 1993, a large order from the electrical retail chain Rumbelows was received. Things were looking good, but all was not quite right at Phillips Plastics. The first problem was a very poor system of **quality control**, so Dyson placed five of his own employees in the factory to **monitor** production practices to ensure that substandard cleaners did not find their way to the market. By the end of May about 12 000 vacuum cleaners had been sold when problem number two arrived in the form of a visit from Phillips's senior managers from the USA. They had decided that they wanted to renegotiate the original agreement with Dyson to allow them to double the assembly costs and increase the price of manufacturing the plastic parts (with Dyson's own machines, remember!) by 16 per cent. By this stage Dyson had had enough of such behaviour and he severed the relationship with Phillips after a hasty bout of legal action. What followed was an impressively quick reorganization that saw Dyson contracting out manufacture of the parts of the DC01 to various suppliers around the UK and Europe (which meant relocating his moulds and negotiating new contracts) and setting up his own assembly plant. This plant was located in an old Royal Mail depot in Chippenham, Wiltshire, England. The depot had floor space of 20 000 square feet.

On 1 July 1993 Dyson's efforts were rewarded when his first own-built DC01 rolled off his new Chippenham assembly line. Assembly of the DC01 was carried out entirely by hand and within a fortnight the new production line staff (14 in total) had output up to 100 DC01s a day with excellent quality control. The labour force was not the only thing that was up to speed; demand for the DC01 with its superior vacuuming technology soared so much that by February 1995 the Dyson had overtaken established companies such as Hoover and Electrolux to become the UK's top selling upright vacuum cleaner by volume. In addition, Dyson brought out his first cylindrical vacuum cleaner, the DC02, in 1995. This proved also to be a runaway success with the buying public and is illustrated in Figure 5.1.

In an attempt to keep pace with the rapid increase in demand Dyson expanded his labour force (there was no shortage of willing workers and he offered a good remuneration package) and made the most of the land at his disposal on the Chippenham site by assembling six Portakabins, four containers and a 10 000 square-foot tent to accommodate the goods inwards and higher levels of production called for by the explosion in demand. However, despite these ad hoc arrangements,

Figure 5.1 Earl cleans up with a Dyson
(Photograph by G. Rosales-Martinez)

Dyson hit a constraint in the land he could use and the Chippenham facility proved unable to produce more than 30 000 units per week. This was not enough; Dyson needed to find a new assembly plant.

In August 1995 production was moved to a 90 000 square-foot factory in Malmesbury, Wiltshire (just a few miles away from Chippenham). By 1996 the company's turnover had swollen from £3.5 million in 1993 to £85 million and Dyson Appliances was officially recognized as the fastest-growing manufacturing company in the UK. Again the success continued in the UK market and overseas and despite 12-hour shifts being the norm for the production line workers Dyson hit a constraint in production once more. After utilizing the 20 acres of land at his Malmesbury site as best he could (he opened a £20 million extension to the factory in 1998) Dyson attempted to expand facilities further by buying the field adjacent to the factory. Unfortunately the objections of local residents prevented this and in September 2002 Dyson relocated vacuum cleaner manufacture once again, but this time he left the UK and set up production facilities in Malaysia.

Lessons from the Dyson story

It is clear from this brief history of James Dyson's efforts that turning even the best of ideas into a final good or service requires the entrepreneur to display a dogged determination and a degree of **organizational ability**. It involves the need to **negotiate contracts** with suppliers, the need to **find a suitable production facility** and the need to **identify a suitable production technique**. It also requires the entrepreneur to **monitor** the **quality** of the inputs, the **effort levels** of the factor services used and of course the quality of the final good or service. None of these activities is costless and all of them take place in an environment that displays a fairly high degree of **uncertainty**. Furthermore, the **knowledge** of how to carry out each of these activities is not easily obtained, but it is susceptible to improvement over time as the entrepreneur goes through a **learning process**. In short, the Dyson case illustrates that the answer to the question posed in the title of this chapter is multifaceted and far from straightforward. How then does the economic theory of production approach the topic?

5.3 The mainstream theory of production

5.3.1 Overview

In order to introduce you to the mainstream theory of production we shall tell a simple story that emphasizes its key features. You will notice as our story unfolds that much of the detailed richness of the Dyson tale we have told above seems to be missing. This is not because neoclassical economists walk around with their eyes closed, nor is it because they do not appreciate the complexity of real world production issues! Instead it reflects the mandatory assumption that lies at the heart of all formal neoclassical models that all decision makers (entrepreneurs) are as equally knowledgeable as each other and as equally well informed about relevant issues. In addition, and as we have mentioned before, Ockham's razor has been applied vigorously to formal neoclassical models which has enabled neoclassical economists to develop an elegant body of formal theory which can be expressed concisely in the language of mathematics.

This does not mean that the neoclassical theory of production is incapable of providing some useful practical insights, but it has resulted in a theory of rather limited scope because it concerns itself exclusively with a **quantitative analysis** of the **conversion process** by which various amounts and combinations of inputs are converted into particular quantities of output with the aid of given quantities of labour and capital. In fact, as you will discover, the neoclassical theory of the firm assumes that the entrepreneur has already answered questions about how best to organize labour and capital and it focuses exclusively upon the quantitative input–output relationship that results. The input–output relationship is described by a conceptual tool called a **production function**.

The neoclassical theory of production, and by association the neoclassical theory of the firm, is often called a **black box theory**. This is because it provides no details about 'soft' or qualitative issues that are internal to the firm, such as how the firm is structured (e.g. its hierarchy) and the nature of its culture. In addition, it ignores the role of the entrepreneur and management and as a result it sheds no light upon the nature of knowledge in the firm. You will discover that issues related to the identification of suitable sources of supply, negotiation of contracts and quality control, all of which we have identified as important issues faced by Dyson, are assumed to have been satisfactorily dealt with by the entrepreneur, so they do not feature in the analysis either.

5.3.2 The basic elements of the mainstream story

Given what we have said about the limited scope of the neoclassical theory of production it is useful to begin by extracting the elements of the Dyson story that are reflected in the theory. As you might expect, these elements relate to the quantitative elements of the story so our attention will focus primarily upon the reasons given by neoclassical theory to explain why Dyson Appliances and other firms face restrictions on the quantity of output they are able to produce.

The part of the Dyson story that is most relevant from the perspective of neo-classical production theory occurs from 1993 onward, i.e. after Dyson had set up his own vacuum cleaner assembly plant. During this period the story illustrates that demand for Dual Cyclone vacuum cleaners expanded quite rapidly and in an attempt to ensure that production could keep pace with this exploding demand Dyson expanded production in **two distinct ways**.

The **first** way Dyson found to expand production was by employing increasing numbers of people (labour) who were organized into 12-hour shifts to work within the space available at the given sites. When this happens the firm is trying to make the most of its **fixed factor input** (land in our example, which of course means that factory size – that is capital – is necessarily restricted also). Economists characterize this way of increasing (and decreasing) the firm's output as taking place in a **short-run** decision period. This terminology can be quite confusing when you meet it for the first time because it is not defined in historical units of time (e.g. seconds, minutes, hours, days, etc.).

> The short run is defined as a decision-making period during which the quantity of at least one of the factor inputs to the production process is fixed.

The short-run analysis of Dyson Appliances illustrates one of the most famous 'laws' of economics: the **law of diminishing returns**. For example, at the Chippenham site, James Dyson attempted to increase production by expanding the input of labour and making full use of his other readily available inputs, but eventually he faced a constraint upon further expansion brought about by a physical shortage of land. This meant that even if he had added more people to his labour force he simply would not have been able to build a factory large enough to accommodate them and they would therefore have been able to contribute very little to the firm's output. We will illustrate and define the law of diminishing returns in more detail below.

The **second** way Dyson used to expand output was by changing the quantity used of **all of the factor inputs** into the production of vacuum cleaners, e.g. a bigger plot of land at Malmesbury was obtained, which allowed a bigger factory to be built to accommodate an increased number of workers. If the entrepreneur/management team wishes to avoid diminishing returns but has no access to productivity-enhancing innovation or learning effects, it has no choice but to expand all of its factor inputs, in particular the factor input that is giving rise to the output constraint. This way of expanding output takes place in something that economists call a **long-run** decision period.

> The long run is defined as a decision-making period during which the quantity of *all* of the inputs to the production process can be varied.

The distinction between the long run and the short run is important and it leads to two complementary theories of production: the **short-run theory of production** and the **long-run theory of production**.

The short-run theory of production examines the implications for the quantity of output of combining different quantities of a variable factor input with a given quantity of fixed factor input(s). The long-run theory of production examines the implications for the quantity of output of combining factor inputs when all of them are variable in quantity; in this situation the firm does not face a constraint on output caused by one of the input factors as it does in the short run, so the long-run problem for the entrepreneur is to decide how large the firm's output capacity should be. As you might imagine, it is useful to have some expectation of the likely size of the market for your product when making the long-run decision.

5.3.3 The short-run theory of production

The short-run theory of production revolves around the concept of diminishing returns that we introduced briefly above. It also requires us to assume that production of an output is best carried out by a team of factor inputs rather than by individuals striving to produce a particular output entirely on their own (more on which we will discuss a little later). To illustrate the theory we will use a simple example based upon the decisions a fictional entrepreneur makes when faced with a particular short-run production function.

Art and craft teacher Samantha Pinewood is looking for a new challenge. Despite earning a weekly wage of £150 as a teacher and pleas by the principal of her school to stay on Samantha has decided to change career and try her hand at running a business that manufactures ready-to-assemble coffee tables. With an offer from her former principal of re-employment if the business does not work out Samantha sets up 'Tables 4U', a small firm that will manufacture basic unfinished wooden coffee tables in boxed flat-pack form. Each flat-pack contains a simple (unstained, unvarnished) wooden table top, four wooden legs and a small packet of screws and glue that can be used by the final customer to assemble the table.

Tables 4U's production facilities consist of a small workshop (300 square feet) with enough space to accommodate three workbenches (a lathe, a bandsaw and a packing machine). We say it has **three units of capital (K)**, and we will assume that it cannot change this quantity of capital in the short run. Tables 4U has no problem getting hold of its raw materials from its suppliers who are happy to provide as much wood as it can use. The packets of screws and glue are bought in from an outside supplier also. Once again this supplier is able to provide as many packets as Tables 4U requires. Tables 4U can **easily hire as many units of labour (L)** as it requires at any time. The relationship between the relative quantities of factor inputs (K and L) and the weekly output of coffee tables is described by the **short-run production function** shown in Table 5.1.

> A production function is a way of presenting the quantitative relationship between factor inputs and the *maximum output* attainable given the current state of technological knowledge.

In other words, it shows a list of **'ingredients'** (factors of production) required by the production process and it tells us in what quantities these factors can be combined to produce a maximum output by an entrepreneur who understands the latest techniques of production, i.e. **the state-of-the-art**. The assumption that the entrepreneur is *au fait* with the latest technological understanding might seem like a rather strong assumption to make, but it is of course nothing more than a natural extension of the assumptions made about human decision makers in all neoclassical models. We will return to this point in Section 5.4 below.

Samantha has just won Tables 4U's first contract. This is to supply Pinewørld, a UK-based chain of Swedish furniture stores, with 450 flat-packs a week. The question Samantha faces is, given that capital is fixed in quantity at three units, how many people should she employ to ensure that she can fulfil Pinewørld's order? Inspection of Table 5.1 reveals that Samantha will need to employ three units of labour.

If you examine the information contained in Table 5.1 you will notice that each successive unit of labour added leads to a **change in output** that is **increasing** until we add a fourth unit. For example, when the second person is employed

Table 5.1 The short-run production function for Tables 4U when K=3 units

Quantity of capital (K)	Quantity of labour (L)	Number of flat-packs per week (output, or total product, TP)
3	1	100
3	2	250
3	3	450
3	4	550
3	5	600
3	6	480

output increases from 100 flat-packs per week to 250 flat-packs per week, giving an increase in output *caused by* the introduction of the second person of 250 − 100 = 150 flat-packs. The change in output *caused by* adding the third person to the labour force is 450 − 250 = 200 flat-packs. The name we give to the change in the number of flat-packs that we attribute to each successive unit of labour employed is the **marginal product of labour (MP$_L$)**. So, the MP$_L$ of the second person employed by Samantha Pinewood is 150 flat-packs.

> The marginal product of any input (e.g. labour) is the *addition* to total output that results from employing *one extra unit* of the variable factor input.

If MP$_L$ is increasing then we say that there are **increasing marginal returns** to the variable factor input. That is, every time we make a marginal change in the factor input (i.e. a one unit increase) our total output increases by more than it increased when we added the *previous unit* of the variable factor input. How can we explain this phenomenon? Three potential explanations of increasing marginal returns are possible.

The first explanation is that the second worker is more skilled at using the workbenches than the first worker and the third worker is more skilled than the second worker. The second explanation is that each extra worker added works harder (i.e. puts in more effort) than the previous worker. Both of these explanations are plausible; for example, you probably have friends and colleagues whom you consider to be more skilful and/or harder working relative to yourself when it comes to carrying out various jobs. However, the mainstream theory of production does not resort to either of these reasons to explain increasing marginal returns. In fact the mainstream theory assumes that each unit of labour works equally as hard as the other units of labour and is as equally skilled. The correct terminology here is to say that **labour** is considered to be a **homogeneous** input with respect to its level of effort and skill.

The third explanation of increasing marginal returns revolves around the concept of **team production**. Having a team of labour inputs allows the entrepreneur to **organize** the production process in such a way that each team member does not carry out every single task required to produce the good or service. Instead, the entrepreneur can divide the total number of tasks between the members of the labour force and in this way gain productivity benefits. The benefits arise because each member of the labour force is able to **specialize** in a subset of tasks rather than having to execute all of the tasks associated with the production of the final output. Economists call this concept **the division of labour** and we will explore it in greater detail below.

Increasing marginal returns do not last for long with the production function we have shown here which implies that there are limits to the practice of dividing labour in the short run. We can see that this must be true because Table 5.1 tells us that the marginal product of the fourth unit of labour is only 100 flat-packs compared to the MP_L for the third unit at 200 flat-packs. The MP_L of the fifth unit of labour is just 50 flat-packs. We can say, therefore, that at levels of employment beyond three units of labour **diminishing marginal returns** are present in our short-run production function. The phenomenon of diminishing marginal returns is believed to be present in all short-run production functions so economists have granted it the status of a 'law'.

The *Law of Diminishing Marginal Returns* states that, if successive units of a variable factor input are combined with a given amount of fixed factor inputs then *beyond some point* the addition to output will begin to decline.

The full results of increasing labour by one unit at a time are shown in Table 5.2 where we have recorded the marginal product of labour, MP_L, and average product of labour, AP_L (which is found by dividing the firm's output by the total number of workers employed). Note that we have recorded the marginal product of labour in the table in between the units of labour input and output. This is because **marginal product** is a measure of the **rate of change** of output, that is, it should be recorded at the point of transition between the previous level of output and the next level of output.

Table 5.2 Short-run production function showing increasing marginal returns initially followed by diminishing marginal returns

Quantity of capital (K)	Quantity of labour (L)	Number of flat-packs per week (TP)	Marginal product of labour (MP_L)	Average product of labour (AP_L)
			100	
3	1	100		100
			150	
3	2	250		125
			200	
3	3	450		150
			100	
3	4	550		137.5
			50	
3	5	600		120
			−120	
3	6	480		80

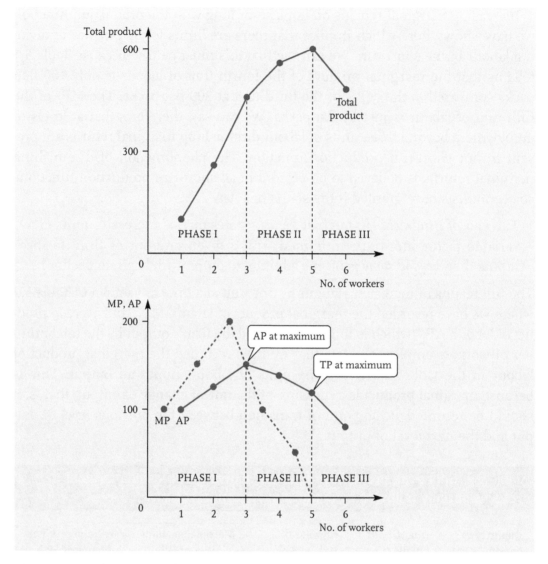

Figure 5.2 Total, average and marginal product at Tables 4U with quantity of capital fixed at three units

As you can see, diminishing marginal returns take a particularly strong hold if we add a sixth worker; in this case total output falls and we discover the **capacity limit** of the flat-pack workshop. This is useful information for Samantha to have, because if her business grows she will know the maximum output she can produce with her current quantity of capital. The MP_L, AP_L and total product (TP) are represented graphically in Figure 5.2.

Of particular interest is the relationship between MP_L and AP_L. You will observe that the plot of AP_L is at its maximum point where it intersects the plot of MP_L. We can use this to help us identify **three phases of production** where each phase represents how effectively the firm is using its fixed factor inputs:

- **Phase I**, which has an upper bound at the intersection of AP_L and MP_L, represents an **underutilization of the fixed factor inputs** in the production process, because increasing total product (output) within this phase leads to an increase in the AP_L and this can be interpreted as an increase in the effectiveness with which the firm is using its resources.

- **Phase II**, which begins at the boundary with phase I and ends where $MP_L = 0$, represents an increase in total product (output) as more labour is employed although now the firm is using its resources less effectively (as measured by the declining AP_L). We can say that compared to phase I, a firm that finds itself in phase II is **using its fixed factor inputs 'properly'** (i.e. it is not underutilizing them).

- The firm will not wish to find itself in **phase III** because here it has gone **beyond the capacity of its fixed inputs.** We can say, therefore, that a rational firm will want to operate somewhere in phase II, although we cannot say precisely where.

If the demand for the firm's product grows and takes the firm to the boundary between phase II and phase III the entrepreneur will need to expand the firm's productive capacity. This requires an understanding of the long-run theory of production.

5.3.4 The long-run theory of production

The long-run theory of production makes use of **two conceptual tools**. The first tool is something called an **isoquant map**. The second tool, which is used in conjunction with the isoquant map, is called an **isocost map**.

You will recall that a short-run production function tells us how output will change if we add successive units of a variable factor input, which in our example was labour, L, to a fixed factor input, which in our example was quantity of capital, K. In principle we could produce a short-run production function for every conceivable value of the fixed factor input and if we assume, for the sake of simplicity, that there are just two inputs, we can present this collection of short-run production functions in tabular format to obtain a **long-run production function**.

> A long-run production function tells us the quantitative relationship between output and factor inputs when the quantities of all of the factor inputs in the production process are variable.

If you look at Table 5.3 you will see that we have produced an example of a long-run production function.

The two axes of Table 5.3 record the quantity of inputs used to produce the output figures contained in the body of the table. For example, the table tells us that 6 units of factor input Y can be combined with 4 units of factor input X to produce 673 units of output. If we fix the quantity of Y at 6 units we can read across this row in the table to find out how output varies in the short run as we add successive units of input X. To maintain consistency with the story of the short-run theory of production we have told in the previous section we will call the factor inputs X and Y labour, L, and capital, K, respectively, but you should note that this is not an essential element of the analysis because the theory of production can be applied to any two things that combine together to produce a good or service. For instance, input Y could be quantity of farmland (measured in hectares) while input X could be quantity of dairy cows and the relevant output quantity of milk (measured in litres). Alternatively, Y could represent the number of telephones in a call centre, X the quantity of telephone operatives (those annoying folk who call you up and try to sell you double glazing/insurance/kitchens, etc. at the most inconvenient of moments) with the relevant output being the total number of calls possible.

If you look carefully at Table 5.3 you will see that some of the output figures recorded in one cell are repeated in other cells. Take 230 units of output as a case

Table 5.3 An example of a long-run production function

Quantity of input Y (e.g. Capital, K)										
10	398	603	770	915	1046	1167	1280	1386	1487	1585
9	374	566	722	859	982	1095	1201	1301	1397	1487
8	348	528	673	800	915	1020	1119	1213	1301	1386
7	321	487	621	738	844	942	1033	1119	1201	1280
6	293	444	566	673	770	859	942	1020	1095	1167
5	263	398	508	603	690	770	844	915	982	1046
4	230	348	444	528	603	673	738	800	859	915
3	193	293	374	444	508	566	621	673	722	770
2	152	230	293	348	398	444	487	528	566	603
1	100	152	193	230	263	293	321	348	374	398
	1	2	3	4	5	6	7	8	9	10

Quantity of input X (e.g. Labour, L)

in point. The production function tells us that **230 units of output** can be produced by combining the inputs in **three alternative ways**. The alternative input pairs that will give us 230 units of output are: (4Y and 1X), (2Y and 2X) and (1Y and 4X). We have highlighted in blue the cells containing 230. We have also highlighted in blue the cells containing 528 units of output. We are now in a position to introduce you to an isoquant map.

> An isoquant is a line plotted on a graph in X,Y space that joins together all points that have the same quantity value.

In Figure 5.3 we have translated the highlighted information contained in the production function table into isoquants; one isoquant represents 230 units of output while the other represents 528 units of output. There are **three main points** you should note about the isoquant map we have drawn:

(i) It tells us that there are three combinations of the inputs X and Y that will enable the firm to produce 230 units of output. It tells us the same thing for 528 units of output. These alternative combinations of the inputs can be described as **alternative techniques of production**. If we let input X denote quantity of labour and input Y quantity of capital then point *a* is an example of a **capital intensive** production technique.

> A capital intensive production technique is one where the quantity of capital used is relatively high per unit of labour employed.

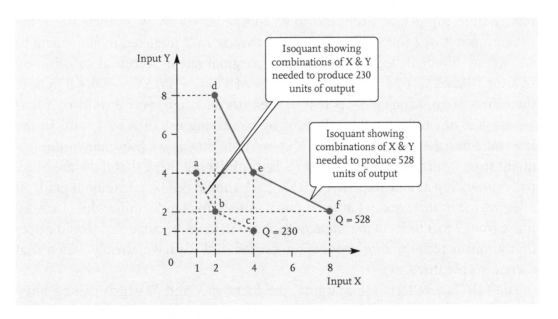

Figure 5.3 An isoquant map showing increasing returns to scale

In contrast, point c is an example of a **labour intensive** production technique.

> A labour intensive production technique is one where the quantity of capital used is relatively low per unit of labour employed.

(ii) It is showing the presence of **increasing returns to scale**. This is easy to see because at a point such as a the firm can produce 230 units of output if it uses 1 unit of input X and 4 units of input Y. If the firm **doubles** the quantity of both inputs (so it uses 2 units of X and 8 units of Y) it moves to point d where output is 528 units, which is **more than double** that at point a. A similar story holds true for the pairs of points (b,e) and (c,f), respectively.

(iii) There is a **trade-off** between the inputs, which simply means that the firm can **substitute** X for Y, and vice versa. However, the **non-linear** shape of the isoquants indicates that the rate at which the firm can substitute one input for the other will vary along their length. In other words, the two inputs are **imperfect substitutes**. The rate of substitution of one input for the other is found by calculating the **slope** of the isoquant in the intervals between the points that denote the different techniques of production. We will use the $Q = 230$ isoquant to demonstrate.

If we move along isoquant $Q = 230$ from point a to point b then in order to **maintain output** at 230 units the reduction in input Y of 2 units has to be compensated for by an increase in the use of input X by 1 unit. However, if we move along isoquant $Q = 230$ from b to c in order to maintain output at 230 units the reduction in input Y of 1 unit has to be compensated for by an increase in the use of input X of 2 units. The ratio of the change in Y (denoted in shorthand as ΔY) to the change in X (ΔX) is called the **marginal rate of technical substitution of X for Y ($MRTS_{XY}$)**. Moving from a to b the $MRTS_{XY} = \Delta Y/\Delta X = -2/1 = 2$ (ignore the minus sign), which tells us that in the interval a to b every 2 units of Y that we use less of can be compensated for by increasing use of X by 1 unit. In the interval b to c the $MRTS_{XY} = 1/2 = \frac{1}{2}$, so we note that as we move down the isoquant from a through b to c the **MRTS is diminishing**. Note that if we are originally producing at b the fact that $MRTS_{XY} = \frac{1}{2}$ should not be taken too literally; it does not mean that we can reduce input Y from 2 units to $1\frac{1}{2}$ units while increasing X from 2 to 3 units to maintain output at 230 units because that would imply that a fourth technique of production existed and we have already stated that there are only three.

The $MRTS_{XY}$ reflects the **marginal products** of X and Y, which can be illustrated by inspection of Table 5.3 and Figure 5.3. Consider the move from a to b on isoquant 230. We can break this move down into two steps: **step 1** is the reduction in input Y while X is left unchanged; and **step 2** is the increase in input X required to compensate for the reduction in the use of input Y.

Step 1: the move from *a* to *b* consists of a reduction in input Y of 2 units. If we do not increase our use of X we will now produce 152 units of output (i.e. cell 1X, 2Y in Table 5.3). Recall that marginal product records the change in output caused by a change in the variable input when other inputs remain fixed in quantity, so if we treat X as a fixed input, then $MP_Y = (152 - 230)/-2 = -78/-2 = 39$. **Step 2**: now if we increase input X from 1 to 2 units while holding Y constant at its reduced level of 2 units we discover that $MP_X = (230 - 152)/1 = 78/1 = 78$.

You will recall from our earlier calculation that between *a* and *b* $MRTS_{XY} = \Delta Y/\Delta X = 2$, and you can now see that $MRTS_{XY}$ is also equal to the ratio $MP_X/MP_Y = 78/39 = 2$. So, more generally we can state that:

$$MRTS_{XY} = \Delta Y/\Delta X = MP_X/MP_Y$$

Now that we have identified an isoquant map and looked at some of its properties we can move on to the next stage of long-run analysis. Imagine you are an entrepreneur and you are confident that demand for your product will be 230 units per week. The long-run production function tells you that there are three techniques of production that will enable you to produce 230 units so **your problem is to choose one of the three techniques**. Note, if input Y is capital as in the Tables 4U example above, then the choice of technique is effectively a choice about the size of your production facility (often called 'plant size'). Clearly you will want to choose the technique that allows you to produce 230 units at the **lowest possible cost**. The total costs you will incur depend on the relative input prices you will have to pay. To illustrate we will assume that the price of one unit of input X, $P_X = £20$ and the price of one unit of input Y, $P_Y = £10$. Given these input prices we can work out total production costs for the three available techniques:

- Technique *a*: total production cost = $1 \times £20 + 4 \times £10 = £60$
- Technique *b*: total production cost = $2 \times £20 + 2 \times £10 = £60$
- Technique *c*: total production cost = $4 \times £20 + 1 \times £10 = £90$

Given these figures, it is rational to choose either technique *a* or technique *b*. However, **if input prices change**, these calculations will have to be repeated to find out if alternative techniques are preferable. For example, if $P_X = £10$ and $P_Y = £20$ the total costs for the three alternative techniques will now be:

- Technique *a*: total production cost = $1 \times £10 + 4 \times £20 = £90$
- Technique *b*: total production cost = $2 \times £10 + 2 \times £20 = £60$
- Technique *c*: total production cost = $4 \times £10 + 1 \times £20 = £60$

Given the new relative prices it is now rational to choose either technique *b* or *c*.

We can represent the relative prices of the two inputs by drawing an isocost line in X,Y space.

> An isocost line plots the combinations of the inputs that can be purchased at current relative prices for a given level of expenditure.

The **slope** of an isocost line is given by the ratio $-P_X/P_Y$. So for our first example above ($P_X = £20$ and $P_Y = £10$) the slope of the isocost line will be -2. In Figure 5.4 we have plotted two isocost lines with this slope. The line closest to the origin of the graph represents a total expenditure of £60 and the line furthest from the origin a total expenditure of £90.

We can superimpose the isocost map of Figure 5.4 onto the isoquant map illustrated in Figure 5.3 to give us Figure 5.5, which shows that the rational entrepreneur will choose either technique *a* or *b* but not *c*. If *c* were chosen it would lie on a higher isocost line than *a* or *b* and as a result the entrepreneur would unnecessarily incur higher costs. If you inspect Figure 5.5 you will notice that between *a* and *b* the slope of the isoquant is identical to the slope of the isocost line. This illustrates a more general rule which states that the **optimal combination of factor inputs** to produce a given level of output is found when $MP_X/MP_Y = P_X/P_Y$, which we can rearrange as:

$$MP_X/P_X = MP_Y/P_Y$$

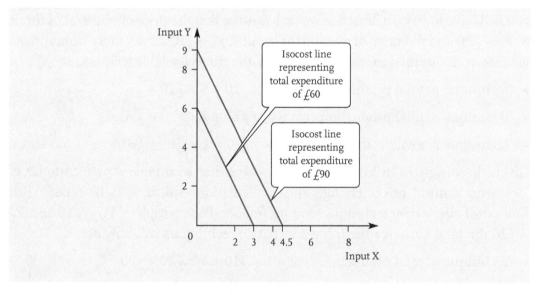

Figure 5.4 An isocost map for $P_x = £20$, $P_Y = £10$

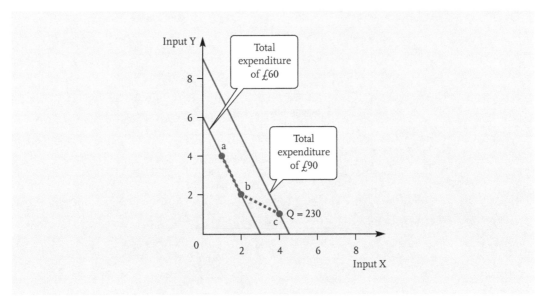

Figure 5.5 The isocost–isoquant map showing least cost techniques of production to produce 230 units of output when P_X = £20, P_Y = £10

In plain English this equation states that two inputs are optimally combined when the marginal product of the one in relation to its price is equal to the marginal product of the other in relation to its price. At point *c* this rule is violated when P_X = £20 and P_Y = £10. However, if the input prices change to P_X = £10 and P_Y = £20 the rule is satisfied at point *c* (and *b*) and diagrammatically we will observe the isocost–isoquant map shown in Figure 5.6.

Isoquants can take on a variety of shapes. We have been using discrete isoquants up to this point. This means they consist of a series of linear segments, which in turn implies that a finite number of production techniques are available. When economists build conceptual models, however, it is more common for them to **assume that isoquants are continuous**. This makes very little difference to the outcome of the analysis but it will enable a single best technique of production to be identified (as opposed to the two we have arrived at in our examples above) because an isocost line will only touch the relevant isoquant at one point. In addition, the assumption of continuous isoquants has the virtue, from the perspective of the economic model builder, of rendering the production problem amenable to the mathematical technique of differential calculus (we will not use calculus here).

We have shown an example of a production function with continuous isoquants in Figure 5.7. In our example, as we move away from the origin the distance between successive isoquants is not constant; initially the **isoquants move**

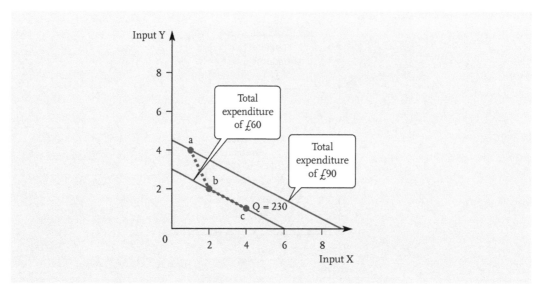

Figure 5.6 The isocost–isoquant map showing least cost techniques of production to produce 230 units of output when P_X = £10, P_Y = £20

closer together, indicating the presence of **increasing returns to scale** in the range 0 to 300 units of output.

> Increasing returns to scale occur when the rate at which the quantity of output increases is *greater than* the rate at which the quantities of factor inputs increase.

In the range 300 to 500 units of output the successive **isoquants are equal distances** apart, indicating the presence of **constant returns to scale**.

> Constant returns to scale occur when the rate at which the quantity of output increases is *equal to* the rate at which the quantities of factor inputs increase.

Finally, beyond 500 units of output the **isoquants spread out**, indicating **decreasing returns to scale**.

> Decreasing returns to scale occur when the rate at which the quantity of output increases is *less than* the rate at which the quantities of factor inputs increase.

With given input prices represented by the isocost lines shown in Figure 5.7 we can identify the least cost technique of production for each level of output. These are represented by the points labelled *a* through *g*, which trace the efficient firm's **expansion path**.

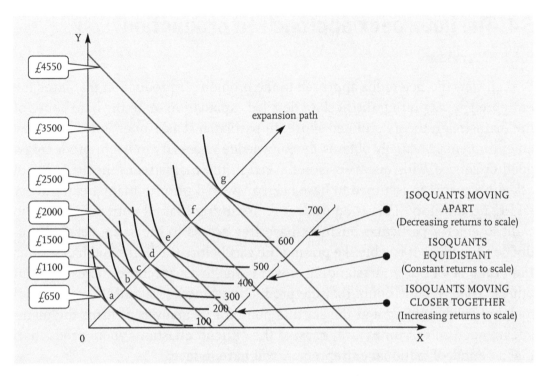

Figure 5.7 Isoquant–isocost map showing expansion path of the efficient firm

An entrepreneur faced with expanding demand for his or her product would be wise to identify the point at which decreasing returns to scale begin to take effect. If demand grows such that successively larger production facilities have to be acquired (as in the Dyson story) there may come a point where **increasing returns to scale** become **exhausted**. If this occurs then the best strategy for the entrepreneur is to build **more than one production facility** so that each facility can enjoy increasing returns to scale.

It should not have escaped your attention that we have introduced the concept of returns to scale without providing an explanation of how increasing, constant and decreasing returns occur in practical terms. Unfortunately, the mainstream approach does not deal with this question in much detail, in fact it tends to conflate it with the concept of **economies of scale** which you will meet in the next chapter. With this in mind we shall explore the theory of production further under the title of the next section in which we will get to grips with the sources of returns to scale and explore the heterodox contributions to the analysis of production.

5.4 The heterodox approach to production

5.4.1 Overview

We can view the heterodox approach to the problem of production that faces the entrepreneur as putting the flesh of detailed explanation on to the bare bones of the mainstream theory outlined above. In particular it asks questions about **how** an entrepreneur actually obtains the knowledge necessary to begin producing a good or service. This question is not asked in the mainstream theory. It is not asked because it is assumed to have been answered prior to mainstream theory taking up the story. This is equivalent to assuming that all entrepreneurs who want to enter a particular business have free access to the same detailed production function. It is a bit like putting the cart before the horse and has serious implications for our understanding of why some firms are more successful than others. There is little doubt that the production function is a useful conceptual tool, but by identifying it as the starting point for its analysis of firms the mainstream approach assumes away most of the difficult questions about production that a boundedly rational entrepreneur will have to face.

In essence, the heterodox approach can be thought of as starting with a **long-run production function** in which the cells are **blank** and asking how the entrepreneur sets about filling in the cells in a world where knowledge is less than perfect, where uncertainty is common and where learning takes place.

5.4.2 Knowledge

Having knowledge of a production function is just like having knowledge of a list of **ingredients** required to bake, say, meringues. If this is the only information you have at your disposal you will find the prospect of producing decent (edible) meringues very challenging indeed. In other words, on its own, this knowledge is of **limited value**. To make use of it you will need **complementary knowledge**. In other words, you will need a **suitable recipe**. A recipe is a set of instructions that tells you the **sequence** in which ingredients from your list are to be mixed, how long the ingredients must be cooked for and what to expect if you follow the prescribed steps. Even if you have a suitable recipe you are still likely to face a series of practical challenges, such as how to obtain usable egg whites, when you attempt to make your meringues. It is also likely that your first attempt will not be as good as your second attempt, in other words the more practice you get at making meringues the more **skilful** you will become. The point we are making here is that possession of a list of ingredients in isolation from other knowledge (i.e. a recipe, skill in applying the recipe, etc.) is not sufficient to enable you to produce successful meringues. More generally, we can say the same thing about any production function – **a production function does not encapsulate all of the knowledge that is necessary to successfully produce a good or service.**

The implication of these observations is that **different types of knowledge** exist in the world. Consequently it is extremely useful to be able to identify and classify the different types, because this will help us to understand the production problem facing an entrepreneur in greater detail. Fortunately heterodox economists have devoted a considerable amount of time to the issue of knowledge and have identified **three broad categories**. We will use the meringue example to introduce each category.

The list of ingredients for meringues is very short:

♦ two large egg whites

♦ 120 grams of caster sugar.

These ingredients are enough to make ten meringues of 6 cm diameter. This is the cook's equivalent of the knowledge imparted by a production function. We have obtained this knowledge from a cookery book. Heterodox economists call this category of knowledge **'know-that'** because it provides a list of **objective data**.

> Know-that is information that can be turned into 'bits' and transmitted from one party to another. It can be further sub-divided into *'know-what'* (knowledge about facts such as the ingredients of a recipe, the population of a country, etc.) and *'know-why'* (knowledge about scientific principles such as how an internal combustion engine functions).

If know-that is the only kind of knowledge we have access to we are unlikely to bake very satisfactory meringues. We need to complement our 'know-that' with a recipe. A recipe is more generally called **'know-how'** by heterodox economists.

> Know-how is the capability to perform a series of actions in order to achieve a desired result.

A recipe provides a set of instructions written by a practised cook which is designed to impart know-how to an aspiring cook.

As you may realize from your own cookery book assisted experiences in the kitchen, it is one thing to follow a recipe and quite another to produce results that look anything like those promised in the book! This is because, unlike know-that, know-how is not always easily transferred from one party to another. In our meringue example this might be because the writer of the cookery book faces difficulties in trying to convey to the reader some of the more subtle elements of their own hard won know-how. For example, meringues require the cook to obtain egg whites. This means that the yolk of the eggs and the white of the eggs have to be separated – this is not a task easily accomplished by the novice cook. However, through a more eloquent command of language some cookery book writers may be able to convey something of the subtlety of their own **experience-based skill (capability)** better than other writers are able to. Compare these two passages:

Tap the egg against the rim of a bowl to crack it around the middle. Holding the egg over the bowl, carefully open the shell with your thumbs, holding the two halves together to let some of the white run out. Gently tip the yolk from one half of the shell to the other, letting the white run into the bowl and taking care not to break the yolk.

(*Cooking Basics*, Hamlyn Publishers, 1999: 22)

Everyone always tells you that the best way to do this [separate egg whites from yolks] is by cracking open the egg and, using the broken half shells to cup the yolk, passing it from one to the other and back again ...I don't think so. All you need is for a little sharp bit of the cracked-open shell to pierce the yolk and the deal's off. It's easier and less fiddly altogether just to crack the egg over a bowl and slip the insides from their shell into the palm of your hand near the bottoms of your fingers. Then splay your fingers a fraction. The egg white will run out and drip through the cracks between your fingers into the bowl...

(*How to Eat*, Nigella Lawson, 1998: 18)

The second passage describes a different method to the generally received wisdom outlined in the first passage. Nigella Lawson has developed her method after obtaining bad results with the first method and by articulating this clearly (she certainly has an above-average dexterity with the written word) has enabled the novice cook to benefit from her own costly experiences. Nonetheless, despite the clarity of Nigella Lawson's exposition it might take a few attempts before aspiring cooks can **develop this capability** themselves, and even then the other elements of the meringue recipe will have to be tackled satisfactorily too if the end product is to be close to that desired. It is no coincidence that trainee-chefs do not learn their craft solely from books but through a series of experience-based apprenticeships under the knowing eye of a seasoned professional chef.

When knowledge is difficult to convey to third parties, either because it is impossible to articulate clearly the steps that give rise to the necessary capabilities or because the owner of the capabilities is simply unaware of the more subtle skills they have developed, it is called **tacit knowledge**.

> Knowledge is tacit when it is difficult or impossible for the person who has it to articulate it clearly to a third party.

Tacit knowledge is acquired and developed entirely from experience or **learning-by-doing**. This does not necessarily mean that it is impossible to gain access to tacit knowledge, or knowledge of any other kind, that you do not possess yourself. If you possess the third category of knowledge called '**know-who**', you may be able to identify and obtain the services of a person who does possess the knowledge that you would like to use.

> Know-who is the possession of information about other people or groups of people (organizations) who have knowledge that you do not possess yourself.

For convenience we have shown the categories of knowledge discussed here in Figure 5.8.

If you take another look at the Dyson story you should be able to recognize the different categories of knowledge at various points. When Dyson first recognized the original filtering problem at the Ballbarrow factory he used his own stock of *know-who* to identify the filter supplier as a possible source of *know-that* (more particularly their *know-what*) with respect to finding a solution. Once they explained to him that sawmills used a cyclonic filter he set about exploiting his own design *know-how* in order to produce a working prototype. Having done this for the Ballbarrow factory, and made the connection between this large-scale version of the technology and the small-scale technology of the vacuum cleaner filter problem, he improved his own *know-that*, in particular his knowledge of the scientific principles behind cyclonic filtration (*know-why*), and through the production of hundreds of model cyclones his *know-how* reached a high level of sophistication.

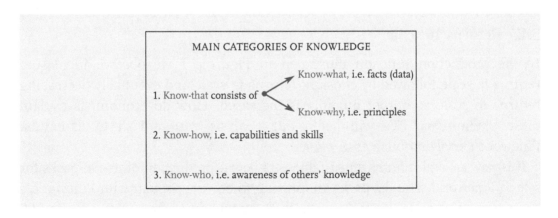

Figure 5.8 Categories of knowledge identified by heterodox economists

When it came to producing commercial products from his original designs (Cyclon and G-Force) Dyson exploited the manufacturing, distribution and marketing *know-how* of other companies through the use of licensing agreements. He learned much from this experience (one could suggest that this was his apprenticeship) and in turn developed his own manufacturing, distribution and marketing *know-how* and *know-who*. He put this to good use when he and his team (who brought in extra design and engineering *know-how*) developed the DC01 so as to minimize the number of components needed to construct it (and therefore the number of stages in the assembly process).

Dyson made use of his manufacturing and distribution *know-how* and *know-who* when he opened his own vacuum cleaner assembly facility (which required him to find reliable suppliers of inputs, to find willing retail stockists and to organize the assembly line). In the original Dyson factory at Chippenham it took a while for the newly created workforce to acquaint themselves with the production facilities but within two weeks they had developed their assembly *know-how* sufficiently to be able to produce 100 vacuum cleaners a day. Before too long Dyson was exploiting his hard won know-how even further when he introduced the DC02 cylinder-style vacuum cleaner.

It should be clear from our discussion here that knowledge comes in various guises and from a variety of sources and that the capability to produce something is not simply a matter of access to *know-that*. It should also be clear that entrepreneurs need to recognize this and **actively develop** their **knowledge** in such a way that they can turn business ideas into practical realities. To be successful this process will require the exploitation and development of all of the categories of knowledge we have identified and it is likely to take a significant amount of **time** during which a lot of **learning** will take place. Bearing these thoughts in mind we will turn our focus of attention to the concept of returns to scale.

5.4.3 Returns to scale

In the production function illustrated in Figure 5.7 we observe increasing returns to scale followed by constant returns to scale and eventually decreasing returns to scale as output quantity is increased. How do economists explain these phenomena? We will begin our analysis with a visit to Samantha Pinewood's evolving business.

It is now several months since Tables 4U began production of its flat-packs for sale to Pineworld. The flat-packs are proving to be very popular with Pineworld's customers so they decide to increase their weekly order from 450 units to 900 units. If Samantha is going to be able to meet this order she will have to expand her production facilities because, as we have seen, with just three units of capital, diminishing returns set in at relatively low levels of output and the capacity of the workshop peaks at 600 flat-packs. The problem Samantha faces is how best to produce 900 flat-packs. In order to get to grips with this long-run problem Samantha draws upon the specialized knowledge of an engineer whom she asks to provide an estimate of how many units of capital she should invest in in order to produce 900 flat-packs. The first thing the engineer does is take a look at the **rate of use** of Tables 4U's current capital equipment. This reveals something interesting; the lathe and the bandsaw have both been used 100 per cent of the time during the last few months of production but the flat-packing machine has been lying idle for 50 per cent of the time. This information indicates that the flat-pack machine is underutilized at the present rate of output; that is, it is capable of easily handling the volume of output provided by the solitary lathe and the solitary bandsaw. Consequently the engineer estimates that Samantha needs to invest in another lathe and another bandsaw but not another packing machine. To accommodate the two extra units of capital will mean extending the workshop to 500 square feet. He provides an estimate of the short-run production function for a 500 square-foot workshop which will apply *if Samantha organizes her capital and labour 'appropriately'*. This is shown in Table 5.4.

Samantha inspects the data gathered from her original workshop (Table 5.1) and compares them with the data provided by the engineer for the larger workshop (Table 5.4). She notes from Table 5.1 that with her current workshop she is able to produce 450 flat-packs by employing three units of capital and three units of labour, while Table 5.4 tells her that she will be able to double this level of output to 900 flat-packs if she increases her factor inputs to five units of capital and five units of labour. In other words, expansion of the production facilities will enable Tables 4U to enjoy **increasing returns to scale** (that is, it can double its output without the need to double its factor inputs). How is this possible? The answer is that at a higher level of output Tables 4U can make much better use of the packing machine which was underutilized in the smaller workshop. Even though the packing machine was underutilized in the smaller workshop, Tables 4U could not dispense with its services altogether. In such a situation capital is said to be **indivisible**.

Capital is indivisible when it cannot be obtained in quantities that provide a rate of service that exactly matches the firm's requirements. This simply means that the firm cannot obtain a fraction, say half, of a packing machine. Instead a whole packing machine has to be acquired and used only half as often as it is capable of being used.

Table 5.4 Weekly production of flat-packs at Tables 4U with varying levels of labour usage (500 sq. ft. workshop housing five units of capital)

Quantity of capital (K)	No. of workers employed (L)	Number of flat-packs per week (TP)	Marginal product of labour (MP$_L$)	Average product of labour (AP$_L$)
5	1	100		100
			150	
5	2	250		125
			200	
5	3	450		150
			200	
5	4	650		163
			250	
5	5	900		180
			250	
5	6	1150		192
			200	
5	7	1350		193
			100	
5	8	1450		181
			−150	
5	9	1300		144

Increasing returns to scale in our example arise because at larger outputs the firm is able to overcome the indivisibility problem. In other words, even though another lathe and another saw have to be obtained to enable Tables 4U to meet the new quantity ordered by Pinewørld the firm does not have to obtain another packing machine.

You should note that our discussion about the sources of increasing returns to scale has assumed that Samantha is capable of organizing the capital and labour at her disposal 'appropriately'. We made the same assumption when we introduced the short-run production function for three units of capital shown in Table 5.1 where we also briefly introduced the related concept of the **division of labour**. We will now examine this concept in greater detail.

The division of labour is the practice of dividing the production process into its component tasks and allocating each one of these tasks to a particular member of the labour force. Such a unit of labour is said to have *specialized* in that specific task.

The division of labour was first introduced to economics by Adam Smith over 200 years ago in his famous book *An Inquiry into the Nature and Causes of the Wealth of Nations*. Mainstream economics has taken Smith's message on board but it does not provide any detail about how the division of labour should be achieved to best exploit its benefits. Instead, as we have seen, a mainstream production function simply relates a quantity of inputs to a quantity of output without saying how the tasks involved should be organized and co-ordinated. The significance of this point is that the successful division of labour requires the entrepreneur to possess some **organizational know-how**. This is for the very simple reason that the division of labour is an **organizational concept** that relies upon the entrepreneur being able to organize the **flow of work** between the different stages of the production process adequately. Furthermore, it provides us with another very important reason for increasing returns to scale.

Adam Smith's original analysis of the division of labour used the example of pin production. He pointed out that pins, or anything else for that matter, can be produced either by a single multi-skilled person (an artisan) who carries out all of the stages of production or, alternatively, each stage of production can be allocated to different members of the labour force. Here's what he said:

> ...a workman not educated to this business [pin manufacture]...nor acquainted with the use of machinery employed in it...could scarce, perhaps, with his utmost industry make one pin a day and certainly could not make twenty. But in the way in which the business is now carried on...it is divided into a number of branches...One man draws out the wire, another straights it, a third cuts it, a fourth points it, a fifth grinds it at the top for receiving the head; to make the head requires two or three distinct operations; to put it on, is a peculiar business, to whiten the pins is another; it is even a trade by itself to put them into the paper; and the important business of making a pin is, in this manner, divided into about eighteen distinct operations, which, in some manufactories, are all performed by distinct hands, though in others the same man will sometimes perform two or three of them. I have seen a small manufactory of this kind where ten men only were employed...they could, when they exerted themselves, make among them...forty-eight thousand pins in a day...if they had all wrought separately and independently...they certainly could not each of them have made twenty...
>
> Adam Smith (1776/1986: 109–10)

The implications of Smith's analysis are far reaching. In simple terms, one major **implication** is that the greater the number of stages a production process contains then the greater the scope for dividing labour becomes. However, it is pointless employing greater quantities of labour and allocating each person to a specific task if there is insufficient **demand for the product** to support larger scale production facilities. So if the size, or **extent**, of the market for the product is **limited** then so is the scope for further division of labour. As Smith put it:

As it is the power of exchanging that gives occasion to the division of labour, so the extent of this division must always be limited by the extent of that power, or in other words, by the extent of the market.

ibid, 121

But why should dividing labour and allocating each unit to a specialized task lead to increasing returns to scale? Smith's answer rests on **three propositions**:

(i)   Workers who specialize in performing only one task on a production line will experience an improvement in their capability to perform that particular job that is greater than if they are expected to perform a multiple set of tasks. Clearly a learning process is implied here:

The different operations into which the making of a pin...is subdivided, are all of them much more simple, and the dexterity of the person, of whose life it has been the sole business to perform them, is usually much greater. The rapidity with which some of the operations of those manufacturers are performed, exceeds what the human hand could, by those who had never seen them, be supposed capable of acquiring.

ibid, 113

(ii) If workers do not have to move from one task to another (e.g. from one workbench to another in the Tables 4U example) then a considerable amount of time will be saved. Smith points out that time is also saved by the fact that workers who do not have to switch between different tasks, each of which requires different skills, will not have to use their brains in order to think about the new task at hand:

It is impossible to pass very quickly from one kind of work to another that is carried on in a different place and with quite different tools...

ibid, 113

(iii) As workers become more practised at specialized tasks they are likely to adapt their tools so they help them to become even more efficient at the task:

Men are much more likely to discover easier and readier methods of attaining any object, when the whole attention of their minds is directed towards that single object, than when it is dissipated among a great variety of things.

ibid, 114

Assumptions:

(1) Production takes place over 5 successive stages.
(2) Each stage uses a specialized piece of capital.
(3) Each piece of capital requires a human operator.
(4) The capital at stages 3 and 4 is capable of operating at a rate that is at least twice that of the capital at the other stages.

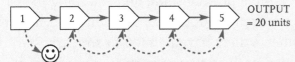

OUTPUT
= 20 units

Case 1: when size of market is 'small' a single unit of labour, who works at his/her own pace, operates capital at all successive stages of production. Labour productivity is very low.

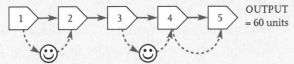

OUTPUT
= 60 units

Case 2: when size of market is slightly bigger than case 1, two units of labour, who adjust their own work rates in order to synchronize the successive stages of production to avoid stockpiling and lags, operate a subset of capital each. This is PARTIAL DIVISION OF LABOUR. Labour productivity is enhanced modestly.

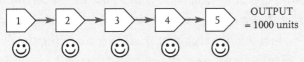

OUTPUT
= 1000 units

Case 3: size of market has grown sufficiently to allow one unit of labour per unit of capital. This is FULL DIVISION OF LABOUR but the labour at stages 3 and 4 are not working at the same rate as the labour at stages 1, 2 and 5 because of the rate at which 'their' respective units of capital are capable of working. Labour productivity is significantly increased.

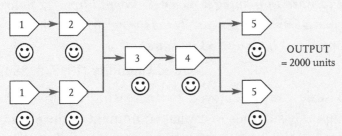

OUTPUT
= 2000 units

Case 4: when size of market is 'large' capital can be duplicated at stages 1, 2 and 5 and at stages 3 and 4. INDIVISIBILITY OF CAPITAL IS OVERCOME and accompanied by FULL DIVISION OF LABOUR. Labour productivity is enhanced once again.

Key:

| A stage of production | A unit of labour | Labour moving from one stage to another | Movement of partially finished product between stages |

Figure 5.9 An example of increasing returns to scale due to exploitation of the division of labour and overcoming capital indivisibility as the extent of the market grows

To help us clarify the reasons for increasing returns to scale Figure 5.9 illustrates a simple example which shows how an entrepreneur can organize the firm's production process in **four different configurations** as the **size of the market** for its product **expands**.

As we have seen, Adam Smith's own estimates of the benefits from the division of labour in the pin factory example provide some quite startling increases in productivity and output (one man can produce 20 pins, while ten men can produce 48 000 pins in a day). Other writers have pointed to similarly startling productivity improvements in studies of their own. A particularly famous example is the evolution of the production line for the Ford Model T as described by Alfred Chandler in his book, *The Visible Hand*:

> *Ford and his colleagues adopted the most advanced machinery,... and followed the 'line production system' of placing machines and their operators in a carefully planned sequence of operations. Ford's factory engineers designed improved conveyors, rollways, and gravity slides to assure a continuing regular flow of materials into the plant. These engineers also began to experiment with the use of conveyor belts to move parts past the worker doing the assembly, with each man assigned a single highly specialized task. The moving line was first tried in assembling the flywheel magneto, then other parts of the engine, next the engine itself, and finally, in October 1913, in assembling the chassis and the completed car. The innovation – the moving assembly line – was an immediate success. The speed of throughput soared. Labor [sic] time expended in making a model T dropped from 12 hours and 8 minutes to 2 hours and 35 minutes per car. By the spring of 1914...the average labor time per car dropped to 1 hour and 33 minutes.*

Alfred Chandler (1977, p. 280)

So, increasing returns to scale can be enjoyed by increasing the division of labour and also overcoming indivisibilities in capital equipment as the extent of the market grows, but there is a third reason too. If you look carefully at Figure 5.9 you will note that we have made the explicit assumption that capital equipment is specialized to the particular task it is assigned in the production sequence. The division of labour therefore involves each unit of labour becoming an expert, that is a specialist, in the use of a particular piece of specialized capital equipment. There is no reason, however, that further increasing returns to scale cannot be enjoyed by the firm if the entrepreneur is able to **automate several specialized tasks** so that they are performed not by a series of separate pieces of capital but instead by one **integrated piece of capital**. If this is possible, the firm can reduce its quantity of capital and, if the integrated piece of capital can be attended by a single human operator, its quantity of labour can be reduced also. Some writers have suggested that this is exactly the process that has occurred in the late twentieth and early twenty-first centuries in the manufacturing sectors of the developed economies of the world, and they have used this argument to explain why a significant proportion of the labour force in these economies is increasingly employed in service industries.

We will finish this section by explaining the reasons we might observe constant returns to scale and decreasing returns to scale. Firstly, **constant returns to scale** will occur when all of the opportunities for further division of labour have been exhausted and when all indivisibilities have been overcome; however, they will only persist as long as the reasons for decreasing returns to scale have not taken hold.

To understand why **decreasing returns to scale** arise we need to raise three points. The first point is that an entrepreneur has to make a conscious effort to organize the factors of production. This is not a trivial task. The second point is that the entrepreneur will have to oversee the production process and manage the people involved (an example of a management task is making sure that all workers are using their best efforts rather than shirking on the job). The third point is that the entrepreneur is, like all human beings, boundedly rational with all that this implies with respect to his or her ability to be able to cope with an increasing workload. The first two points in combination with the third imply that beyond a certain size of organization the entrepreneur will be unable to give the firm the degree of effective management it requires. So, in rather blunt terms, decreasing returns to scale may arise because the entrepreneur **loses effective control** of the firm due to his or her **cognitive limitations** coupled with the increased size and **complexity** of the production process. Given that different entrepreneurs are endowed with different degrees of cognitive ability one may be able to manage effectively a given size of firm where another may experience a degree of control loss. As you will discover later in the book, many firms have discovered ways of overcoming this problem to a greater or lesser extent, but these 'solutions' have brought their own problems.

5.5 Summary

We have covered a lot of ground in this chapter and along the way we have introduced you to a number of fundamentally important concepts. At first reading you may find it difficult to make sense of all of the arguments we have outlined, especially as some of them seem to conflict with each other. Do not worry about this – it is perfectly normal; even professional economists have trouble keeping tabs on all of the strands!

In order to help you make better sense of everything we have discussed you might find it beneficial to re-read the details of the Dyson story in the light of the theoretical discussions that have taken place in the rest of the chapter. Given that the heterodox approach takes as its point of departure a critical look at the mainstream production function approach, in particular the assumptions it makes about knowledge and organization, you may be tempted to think that the mainstream approach is of little practical use to you. This would, however, be a hasty conclusion to jump to. It is very rarely a good idea to ignore the lessons provided by 100 years of theoretical development! Yes, the production function approach does make some rather strong assumptions with respect to the nature and availability of knowledge, but this is simply because the theories of mainstream economics are built upon the assumption that a human decision maker, which in this chapter is the entrepreneur, has full information about all relevant facts and is perfectly capable of processing this information optimally.

While this assumption might not accord with the world we live in, and indeed the world James Dyson occupied, it is nevertheless a useful assumption to make *as a first step* to help us frame some of the issues that are relevant to the problem of production. In particular it helps us to identify easily the concepts of diminishing marginal returns, returns to scale and capital intensive and labour intensive production techniques – all of which are concepts an entrepreneur needs to be aware of. However, if we accepted the mainstream approach unquestioningly we would provide a message for entrepreneurs that runs as follows: you and all other entrepreneurs like you have access to the latest production techniques and full knowledge of them; in addition you are all as equally capable of utilizing these techniques. As a result, if any of you start a business enterprise then you can expect to be no better at carrying out the tasks associated with production in this business than any other entrepreneur – consequently, if you wish to make decent profits you will need to create some kind of barrier to entry into the industry you are a part of. We have already

5.5 **Summary** (continued)

mentioned this in Chapter 3 and we will revisit it again in greater detail in Chapter 7. For now you can note that it is a generally recurring theme in the mainstream approach.

Once we began to look at the production problem through the eyes of a heterodox economist we dispensed with the globally rational, infinitely capable model of the entrepreneur and we started to pose questions that asked how a boundedly rational entrepreneur could obtain the knowledge that is necessary to provide the data that a mainstream production function take as given. This model of the entrepreneur is more 'realistic' in the sense that it is more like the people we see around us every day. The questions we asked led us to distinguish between three broad categories of knowledge and, in turn, these revealed that we need to distinguish between the data recorded in the cells of a production function and the ability to actually turn the relationship between quantity of inputs and quantity of output shown there into a practical reality. This requires the entrepreneur to be able to organize the factors of production appropriately.

A boundedly rational entrepreneur needs to acquire and develop not only *know-that* (which is equivalent to having knowledge of the data recorded in the cells of the production function), but also *know-how* (which is often referred to as capabilities) and in all likelihood *know-who*. Learning was therefore identified as a very important part of the heterodox analysis of the production problem, which also implied that the time taken to achieve successful production is another salient issue that needs to be taken seriously by the entrepreneur.

Finally we used the broader concept of knowledge to help us understand better the concept of returns to scale, and we showed that specialization through the division of labour is absolutely key here, along with the concept of indivisibility of capital. You should note also that, because of the pervasive influence of uncertainty, when an entrepreneur makes the initial decision regarding the scale of production facilities, he or she is unlikely to know with any degree of accuracy the likely extent of the market for the firm's product. Consequently, we might suggest that not only is the division of labour limited by the extent of the market, but it is also limited by the **predictability** of the extent of the market; as we saw, James Dyson grew the scale of his production facilities *organically* as the extent of his market grew and revealed itself to him.

The heterodox message for would-be entrepreneurs is slightly different from the mainstream message; if we accept that entrepreneurs need to

5.5 **Summary** (continued)

develop particular capabilities that are peculiar to their chosen production process, and if such *know-how* has been difficult to develop (and would be equally as difficult to explain to someone else), then maybe different but competing businesses will experience different degrees of success because of their **different levels of capability**. We will return to this point in Chapter 8.

One final point: in emphasizing learning-by-doing, the heterodox approach has some interesting implications for the growing firm's expansion path. If you look at the isoquant–isocost map shown in Figure 5.7, it should be evident to you that the locus of the expansion path followed by the firm illustrated there depends upon the **relative prices** of the factor inputs X and Y, as shown by the slopes of the isocost lines. This implies that **a change in relative prices** at any time will cause the firm to **change its technique of production** (i.e. the relative mix of quantities of X and Y). This analysis does not sit easily with the learning story told by the heterodox approach.

The mainstream approach does not sit well with a learning approach because, if knowledge is not easy to obtain, then once a particular technique has been chosen further expansion and development of the firm's production capability is likely to be based upon **learning** more about **this particular technique**. In other words, while alternative production techniques might well exist (as implied by an isoquant) the fact that the entrepreneur has made an **initial choice** may well mean that he or she devotes all of his or her (scarce) attention, (scarce) energies and (scarce) time in the future to developing the firm's capability at using this particular technique to the **exclusion of all alternatives**. The implication of this is that as time passes the entrepreneur will become more and more knowledgable about the firm's chosen technique and relatively **ignorant of alternatives**. Furthermore, the firm will have developed its capability with the technique to quite a high degree of sophistication (it might even have developed integrated labour-saving capital).

In such a situation it might be very difficult for the firm immediately to change technique in response to factor price changes. This is not to say that a change in technique is entirely out of the question, but it is likely to require the firm to undergo a period of painful and costly learning about the new alternative (and 'un-learning' of the original). These costs, which are over and above the direct costs incurred as a result of hiring the factors of production, are called **switching costs**. If switching costs are considered to be *too high* the firm will carry on with its original technique. If this happens the

5.5 **Summary** (continued)

firm is said to be **locked in** to its original production technique. In other words, the choice made by the entrepreneur at the birth of the firm has determined how it will do things later on in its life.

When the number of options for later decisions about the technique of production is restricted by the decision made in the initial period, economists say that the firm's expansion path exhibits **path dependence**. Put another way, path dependence suggests that if different entrepreneurs in the same line of business make different decisions at the birth of their firms then we might see firms **evolving** along quite different trajectories from each other. This sits in stark contrast to the mainstream analysis of production where it is assumed that firms will be able to jump easily and without cost from one technique to another in response to factor price changes, and that every entrepreneur will make identical decisions in this regard.

5.6 **Some questions to consider**

1. Does the phrase 'a unit of capital' have a precise meaning?

2. If you were asked to define what is meant by the phrase 'technique of production' how would you start? Is the mainstream notion of technique of production as being either capital intensive or labour intensive helpful?

3. Do you think it is likely that the quantities of output recorded in the cells of a production function will stay constant over time? Give reasons for your answer.

4. Think of some of the things you have learned in your life (including skills) and attempt to allocate each to one of the categories of knowledge identified by the heterodox approach. Can you think of any categories of knowledge that are *not* captured by the heterodox classification?

5. Do you think that the process of the division of labour means that we will see firms becoming larger and larger? What role do you see for small firms in the economy?

6. Can you think of any decisions that you have made in your life that have locked you in to a particular set of options at a later date?

5.7 Recommended additional reading sources

For the story of how some of the world's major businesses have coped with the problems of production, see Alfred Chandler (1977) *The Visible Hand: the Managerial Revolution in American Business*, Harvard, Belknap Press.

The Dyson story is told in great detail by Giles Coren (2002) *James Dyson Against the Odds: An Autobiography* (New edition), London, Texere Publishing. All of the Dyson quotations used in this chapter are taken from this book.

For an interesting view of the theory of production, see Nicolai Foss (1997) 'The classical theory of production and the capabilities view of the firm', *Journal of Economic Studies*, **24**, no. 5, pp. 307–23.

A more advanced discussion of some of the topics we have covered in this chapter is provided by Richard Langlois (1999) 'Scale, Scope and the Reuse of Knowledge', in S.C. Dow and P.E. Earl (eds) *Economic Organization and Economic Knowledge: Essays in Honour of Brian J. Loasby*, **1**, Cheltenham, Edward Elgar, pp. 239–54.

Another advanced discussion of the topics we have covered in this chapter, which is complementary to Langlois' article, is given by Axel Leijonhufvud (1986) 'Capitalism and the factory system', in R.N. Langlois (ed.) *Economics as a Process: Essays in the New Institutional Economics*, New York, Cambridge University Press, pp. 203–23.

Our discussion of types of knowledge and the production function was informed by Brian Loasby (1999) *Knowledge, Institutions and Evolution in Economics*, London, Routledge (see Chapter 4, 'Capabilities', pp. 49–68).

The original account of the division of labour can be found in Adam Smith (1776/1986) *An Inquiry into the Nature and Causes of the Wealth of Nations*, London, Penguin Books (see Book 1, Chapters I–III).

6

Where do costs come from and how do they behave?

Learning outcomes

If you study this chapter carefully, it may help you to understand:

- the different types of cost a firm may incur
- the concept of economies of scale
- the concept of economies of scope
- the concept of the learning curve
- the reasons for X-inefficiency.

To the extent that you develop such understanding, you should be better able to:

- explain the distinction between average and marginal cost thinking
- explain how the short-run theory of production relates to the short-run theory of costs and how the long-run theory of production relates to the long-run theory of costs
- work out how the cost curves of a firm will be influenced by a combination of economies of scale, economies of scope, learning effects and X-inefficiency.

6.1 Introduction

In this chapter we draw upon material introduced in the previous chapter, so if you have not yet read it we would suggest that you do so before embarking on the material covered here. The previous chapter focused on how the entrepreneur should organize the firm's productive resources. In this chapter we focus upon the consequences of the decisions made by the entrepreneur for the costs the firm will incur. An effective entrepreneur acquires and uses the firm's assets in such a way that the costs of doing so are kept to a minimum. It is self-evident that a firm which provides a good or service that is identical to that of a rival but which is able to do so at lower cost is more **efficient** and, therefore, has scope to make greater profits than its rival and/or acquire bigger market share by virtue of its cost advantage.

An efficient firm does not incur unnecessary costs, but of course before assessing whether costs are unnecessary the entrepreneur needs to understand in greater detail the **types of cost** that a firm can incur and why they arise. At first sight developing an understanding of costs might appear to be a straightforward task. However, as you work through this chapter you may be surprised to learn that an understanding of costs involves more than simply totting up the numbers and that some costs are **hidden** or not immediately obvious, so they have to be hunted down before they can be taken into account.

6.2 The mainstream approach to the behaviour of costs

The mainstream analysis of the firm's costs draws directly upon the mainstream theory of production. As a result it downplays the costs of things we might call support activities, such as marketing and distribution, while emphasizing the costs of productive activity, that is the activities associated directly with 'making' the good or service sold by the firm. The mainstream analysis of costs, like the mainstream theory of production, is an excellent foundation stone upon which to build your general understanding of costs. To help us illustrate the key concepts involved we will revisit Tables 4U. Just like the theory of production the theory of costs is divided into a short-run analysis and a long-run analysis.

6.2.1 The short-run theory of costs

You will recall from the previous chapter that the short run is defined as being a decision-making period during which the quantity of at least one of the factor inputs to the production process is fixed, and that we can represent the short-run production opportunities open to an entrepreneur in the form of a short-run production function. Consequently it will not surprise you to learn that the short-run theory of costs involves discovering the cost implications associated with a given short-run production function. All that this requires us to do is find out the prices the firm will have to pay in order to obtain the required quantities of labour, capital and material inputs. To illustrate how this is done we will use the production function produced for Tables 4U in Table 5.1 as our starting point and combine this information with additional assumptions about the **prices of inputs** and their **availability**. These additional assumptions are:

♦ Rental of the workshop (300 square feet plus three workbenches inclusive of electricity costs) is £90 per week. In other words, capital costs £30 per unit.

♦ Each unit of labour employed must be paid wages of £100 per week. Tables 4U is located in an area of relatively high unemployment so willing labour is easy to find at this rate of pay.

♦ The cost of raw materials (wood, packets of glue and screws, etc.) amounts to £2 per table. Many alternative raw material suppliers exist and are willing to supply Tables 4U at these prices.

Armed with this information it would be easy to calculate the costs associated with producing a particular volume of output and consider that our job is done. For example, in order to produce 450 flat-packs per week Tables 4U will need to employ three units of labour at a price of £100 each to operate its three units of capital, which cost £90 per week, and buy raw materials at a price of £900. The **total cost** of producing 450 flat-packs per week will therefore be £300 + £90 + £900 = £1,290. If Samantha Pinewood showed these calculations to an accountant the accountant would happily agree that this is how much Samantha has had to pay out in order to produce 450 flat-packs. However, if she showed these figures to an economist the economist would not be very happy! So where's the problem?

The problem an economist has with these figures is that when we calculated them we ignored an important **hidden cost**. As the figures currently stand they record Samantha's **out-of-pocket costs** but they ignore her **opportunity costs**. We mentioned the concept of opportunity cost briefly in Chapter 1, where we introduced it as the idea that anything we do involves the **sacrifice** of something else. In other words, when we choose to undertake a particular activity we must also be choosing not to undertake alternative activities. If you recall the beginning of Samantha Pinewood's story in the previous chapter, you will be aware that in order to become an entrepreneur she gave up her job as a teacher. Put a slightly different way, by choosing to be an entrepreneur Samantha chose not to be a teacher. This is the cost she paid to become an entrepreneur.

Opportunity cost is the (foregone) value of the next best alternative activity to the one you have actually chosen to undertake.

For Samantha the value of being a teacher was the £150 per week she earned, so this is the opportunity cost she has incurred by becoming an entrepreneur. We must add this amount to our cost calculations in order to obtain the **true cost**. The true cost of producing 450 flat-packs is actually £1,290 + £150 = £1,440.

True cost is equal to out-of-pocket costs *plus* opportunity costs.

The true short-run costs of Tables 4U when it has three units of capital are recorded in Table 6.1 and presented graphically as **cost curves** in Figure 6.1. In Table 6.1 we have distinguished between **fixed costs** and **variable costs**.

Fixed costs are costs that are incurred by the firm even if it produces zero units of output.

Fixed costs arise from owning or hiring fixed factors of production such as build-ings, computers, construction machinery/tools, vehicles and the like, all of which cost the firm money even if they are lying idle. In our example the fixed factor is capital, of which Tables 4U has three units at a cost of £30 per unit per week. This fixed factor cost is listed in column 4 of Table 6.1. The opportunity

Table 6.1 Short-run costs of Tables 4U with 300 sq. ft. workshop and three units of capital (£)

1	2	3	4	5	6	7	8	9	10	11	12
			Cost of	Opp cost	Av'ge fixed cost (AFC)	Wage cost	Raw material cost	Av'ge va'ble cost (AVC)	Total costs (TC)	Av'ge total costs (ATC)	Marginal costs (MC)
K	L	Q	K								
											3.00
3	1	100	90	150	2.40	100	200	3.00	540	5.40	
											2.67
3	2	250	90	150	0.96	200	500	2.80	940	3.76	
											2.50
3	3	450	90	150	0.53	300	900	2.67	1440	3.20	
											3.00
3	4	550	90	150	0.43	400	1100	2.73	1740	3.16	
											4.00
3	5	600	90	150	0.40	500	1200	2.83	1940	3.23	

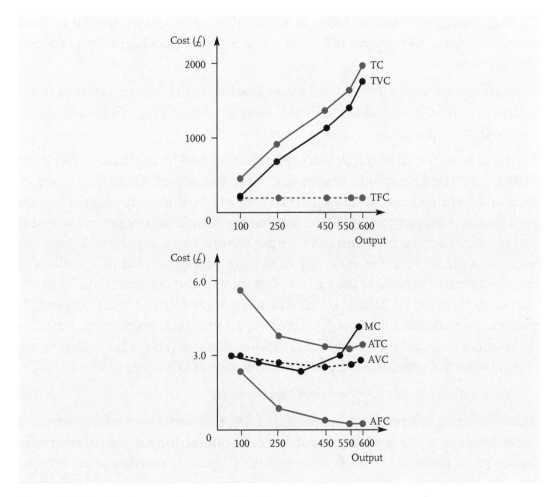

Figure 6.1 The short-run cost curves of the firm

cost of the entrepreneur, which in Samantha's case is £150 per week, is also a fixed cost; this is listed in column 5 of Table 6.1. **Total fixed costs (TFC)** therefore amount to (3 × £30) + £150 = £240.

TFC = fixed factor costs + entrepreneur's opportunity cost.

To prevent cluttering up Table 6.1 we have not recorded TFC, but you will note from the plot in Figure 6.1 that it is a horizontal line which means that TFC remains **constant** as output is increased. If we divide TFC by the number of units of output produced by the firm we will obtain **average fixed cost (AFC)**. This is recorded in column 6 of Table 6.1 and shown graphically in Figure 6.1.

AFC = TFC ÷ Q

Given that TFC is a constant value it follows that the greater the volume of output produced by the firm then the lower AFC will be, because TFC will be divided among a greater number of units. This is known as **spreading fixed costs**. The plot of AFC shown in Figure 6.1 is, therefore, a continually downward sloping curve.

> Variable costs are costs over and above fixed costs that are incurred by the firm as a direct result of the activities associated with producing each unit of output.

Variable costs arise from purchasing raw materials and hiring variable factors of production. The assumption here is that these things will not be purchased or hired if the entrepreneur decides that the firm will produce zero units of output. As a result, if the entrepreneur decides that the firm is to produce no output it will not incur any variable costs. As output volume increases, variable cost will increase also, because the only way to achieve this expansion of output is to employ a greater amount of the variable factor input and raw materials. The variable costs incurred by Tables 4U consist of its wage bill (Table 6.1, column 7) plus its raw material bill (Table 6.1, column 8). Once again to prevent cluttering we have not recorded the sum of these variable costs in Table 6.1; however, these expenditures are reflected in the **total variable cost (TVC)** curve of Figure 6.1.

> TVC = variable factor costs + raw material costs.

The TVC curve is a reverse S-shape, indicating that variable costs increase at a decreasing rate at low levels of output, but once **diminishing marginal returns** to labour set in (beyond 450 units of output) variable costs increase at an increasing rate. If we divide TFC by the number of units of output produced by the firm we will obtain **average variable cost (AVC)**. This is recorded in column 9 of Table 6.1 and shown graphically in Figure 6.1.

> AVC = TVC ÷ Q

Given that TVC is not a constant value at each level of output it follows that the plot of AVC is not a continually falling curve. Instead the AVC curve is U-shaped, indicating that while the firm is enjoying increasing marginal returns to labour this enables it to expand output at decreasing cost per unit, but once diminishing returns have set in (when the fourth unit of labour is employed) the curve begins to turn upwards.

Total costs (TC), which are recorded in column 10 of Table 6.1, are found by adding TFC and TVC together, which means that the TC curve shown in Figure 6.1 is found by displacing the TVC curve vertically by the amount of fixed costs.

> TC = TFC + TVC

Average total costs (ATC), column 11, Table 6.1, can be found either by summing AFC and AVC, or dividing TC by total output.

$$ATC = AFC + AVC = TC \div Q$$

Given that the ATC curve is composed of the continually falling AFC curve and the U-shaped AVC curve it will initially slope downwards and eventually begin to turn upwards. The point at which it begins to slope upwards will be determined by the size of the firm's **fixed costs relative to its variable costs**. If fixed costs account for a large proportion of the firm's total costs the ATC curve will continue to fall, even at high levels of output, because the effect of spreading the fixed costs over larger levels of output will outweigh the strength of influence of the upward sloping portion of the AVC curve. In Figure 6.1 we have shown an ATC curve for which the influence of the falling AFC curve is overcome by the rising portion of the AVC curve at the point where output is increased from 550 units to 600 units (i.e. when the fifth unit of labour is employed). It should be clear that the **ATC** tells the entrepreneur how much **each and every unit** of output has cost the firm to produce on average – for this reason it is often referred to as the **unit cost of production**. For example, when Samantha Pinewood decides to produce 450 units of output to meet Pinewørld's initial order the unit cost of production is £3.20 per flat-pack (see Table 6.1, column 11). You must be careful not to confuse ATC with **marginal costs (MC)**, which are recorded in column 12 of Table 6.1.

You will recall from the previous chapter that we calculated the marginal product of labour and explained that it measures a **rate of change** of output as successive units of labour are employed. Marginal costs are also a measure of a rate of change and this is why they appear in between the other values in Table 6.1.

Marginal cost (MC) is the *addition* to total cost that occurs as a result of producing one more unit of output.

Before we explain how we have arrived at the marginal cost figures in column 12 of Table 6.1 we will consider a somewhat simpler example to illustrate its basic calculation. If it costs a firm a total of £100 to produce 10 units of output and a total of £105 to produce 11 units of output, then the **addition to total cost** as a result of producing the 11th unit of output is £105 – £100 = £5. In other words, the **marginal cost of the 11th unit is £5**. Note that the marginal cost of the 11th unit measures the extra costs generated by production of **this unit only** whereas the ATC, which for 11 units of output is £9.55, by contrast spreads the total costs of production across **all** 11 units of output.

Back to Table 6.1: it should be clear to you now that the marginal costs recorded in column 12 measure how much the production of one additional flat-pack adds to the firm's total costs. However, in the case of Tables 4U the quantity of output (column 3) is not increasing by one unit at a time. Instead it is increasing in 'lumps' as a result of adding successive workers to the labour force. To overcome this problem we arrive at the marginal cost data in column 12 by calculating how much the extra units of output attributable to a new member of the labour force cost the firm *on average*. For example, the second person added to the labour force causes output to increase by a 'lump' equal to 150 units (i.e. this person's marginal product) and the subsequent increase in total cost is £400 (= £940 − £540) so, on average, **each one of the extra 150 units** produced **adds** £400 ÷ 150 = **£2.67** to the firm's total costs. Like the AVC data the behaviour of the marginal cost data is also explained by the presence of increasing and diminishing marginal returns in the production process. In fact **marginal costs** are another class of **variable costs**. You can confirm this for yourself by subtracting TFC (£240) from the TC recorded in column 10, leaving you with TVC. If you now calculate MC (suitably redefined as 'the addition to TVC caused by producing an extra unit of output') you will arrive at figures which are identical to those in column 12. The implication of this is that **fixed costs do not influence marginal costs.**

Even though the behaviour of both AVC (and therefore ATC) and MC as output is varied is explained by increasing and diminishing marginal returns it is very important to understand the fundamental difference between average calculations and marginal calculations. This is because of their implications for business decision making. For example, if we return to our simple example from above, we can consider the case where the firm is already producing 10 units of output for its current customers (giving unit costs of £10) when unexpectedly an 11th customer turns up and demands the firm's good or service but is only willing to pay £6 for it. Assuming the firm has the production capacity available, is it sensible to produce an 11th unit of output to satisfy this extra customer? In order to arrive at an answer to this question many people would calculate ATC for 11 units of output and see that this gives us a figure of £9.55 per unit. As a result they would recommend that the firm should not produce the 11th unit of output because the price the extra customer is willing to pay is less than ATC. However, marginal cost calculations indicate that these people would be wrong! The sensible entrepreneur should ask, 'Can the firm make a profit on the 11th unit of output?' Given that producing an 11th unit of output adds just £5 to the firm's total costs and it can be sold at a price of £6 the answer to the entrepreneur's question is 'yes'. This is because the firm will make a profit of £1 on the sale of this extra unit.

6.2.2 The long-run theory of costs

When we left Samantha Pinewood in Chapter 5 Pinewørld had increased its initial order to 900 units per week and Samantha had made a long-run decision to obtain two extra units of capital and expand her workshop. The production function for the larger workshop was shown in Table 5.4 and we noted that it displayed increasing returns to scale when compared to the production function for the smaller workshop. We can use this information in conjunction with our assumptions about the prices of factor inputs and raw materials that we made in Section 6.2.1 above to calculate the costs of the larger workshop. Recall that the price of capital is £30 per unit (inclusive of electricity costs and building rental), the price of labour is £100 per unit and raw materials cost £2.00 per flat-pack. Using this information we have produced Table 6.2 by following exactly the same procedures that we outlined above for the 300 square-foot workshop. You should note that although we are discussing the long run here, once the decision to invest in a given size of workshop has been made we are interested in the short-run cost information relevant to this particular size of workshop. As a result Table 6.2 records short-run cost data for the 500 square-foot workshop.

Table 6.2 **Short-run costs of Tables 4U with 500 sq. ft. workshop and five units of capital (£)**

1	2	3	4 Cost of K	5 Opp cost	6	7 Wage cost	8 Raw material	9	10	11	12
K	L	Q	K		AFC		cost	AVC	TC	ATC	MC
											3.00
5	1	100	150	150	3.00	100	200	3.00	600	6.00	
											2.67
5	2	250	150	150	1.20	200	500	2.80	1000	4.00	
											2.50
5	3	450	150	150	0.67	300	900	2.67	1500	3.34	
											2.50
5	4	650	150	150	0.46	400	1300	2.62	2000	3.08	
											2.40
5	5	900	150	150	0.33	500	1800	2.56	2600	2.89	
											2.40
5	6	1150	150	150	0.26	600	2300	2.52	3200	2.78	
											2.50
5	7	1350	150	150	0.22	700	2700	2.52	3700	2.74	
											3.00
5	8	1450	150	150	0.21	800	2900	2.55	4000	2.76	

If we plot the ATC data contained in Table 6.2 and compare it with the ATC data from Table 6.1 we obtain Figure 6.2.

Figure 6.2 allows us to compare the unit costs of flat-pack production in the two sizes of workshop at various levels of output. Inspection of Figure 6.2 reveals **two key points:**

(i)   Tables 4U is able to produce 900 tables in the 500 sq. ft. workshop at a unit cost that is less than the unit cost it incurred when it produced 450 tables in its 300 sq. ft. workshop. This means that for a given selling price the firm will be able to make a **higher profit margin on each and every one** of the 900 tables produced by the new larger workshop than it would make on each and every one of the 450 tables produced by the smaller workshop. This is possible because with the new workshop Tables 4U has **translated increasing returns to scale into economies of scale**.

> Economies of scale occur when the *unit cost of production* is lower in a larger sized plant (i.e. one operating at relatively high levels of output) than it is in a smaller sized plant that is operating at its least-cost level of output. Economies of scale are, therefore, a long-run phenomenon.

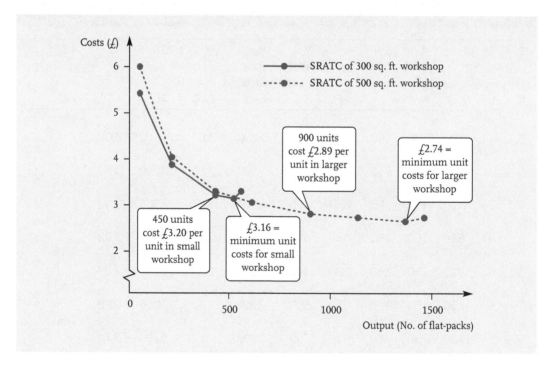

Figure 6.2 Comparison of short-run ATC curves between two different sizes of workshop for Tables 4U

Note that we can only make this point because we have assumed that the input prices paid by Samantha have not changed. Consequently, we observe that the economies of scale Table 4U enjoys at 900 units of output are purely a function of the **organizational relationship** between its inputs that we have described in the previous chapter. Other non-organizational sources of economies of scale do potentially exist, but we will reserve discussion of these until later on.

(ii) At relatively **low levels of output** (e.g. 450 units) the **smaller workshop** has a **cost advantage** over the larger workshop. The evidence for this is the fact that the **short-run average total cost (SRATC)** curve of the larger workshop lies above the SRATC curve of the smaller workshop at low levels of output. This occurs because the higher fixed costs incurred by the larger workshop cannot be spread effectively at low levels of output. At higher levels of output the larger workshop exceeds the capacity of the smaller one and it can spread its fixed costs more thinly, although eventually diminishing marginal returns set in as it approaches its maximum capacity.

In principle we can repeat the cost calculation exercise shown here for any number of different sized workshops (plant) so that we end up with a family of SRATC curves. Figure 6.3 illustrates a situation where the entrepreneur has identified seven potential sizes of plant that could be used to produce various levels of output. Each plant is described by its typically U-shaped SRATC curve (labelled (1) through (7)), indicating that once a particular plant has been chosen

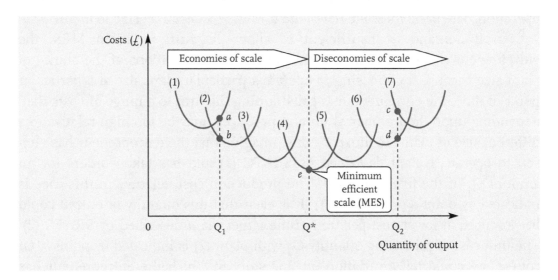

Figure 6.3 A family of SRATC curves indicating economies and diseconomies of scale as output increases

the usual short-run law of diminishing marginal returns will bite at some point. As we move from (1) through to (4) the successive SRATC curves become lower in cost-output space, indicating that in this range **economies of scale** are present. Beyond plant size (4), however, the successive SRATC curves are located higher and higher in cost-output space, indicating that **diseconomies of scale** afflict larger sizes of plant.

> Diseconomies of scale arise when the unit costs of production in larger sizes of plant are higher than the unit costs of production in relatively smaller sizes of plant. Diseconomies of scale occur principally because of the costs associated with control-loss by the entrepreneur.

When economies of scale are followed by diseconomies of scale it is possible to identify an **optimal size of plant**. In Figure 6.3 the optimum occurs on SRATC curve (4) at its minimum point, *e*. Given these cost curves a firm cannot produce its product at a unit cost any lower than this amount. In other words, the size of plant described by SRATC (4) is the most efficient and its minimum point is therefore known as the **minimum efficient scale (MES)**.

> Minimum efficient scale (Q*) is the size of plant at which unit costs of production are minimized *in the long run*.

It should be clear to you that MES is a level of output that can only be achieved by changing the quantity of the factor of production that is fixed in the short run and, therefore, it can only be attained in the long run and on the assumption that there is sufficient demand for the firm's good or service to justify this scale of operation. The basic message here is that MES is a desirable size to attain.

Even if demand is insufficient to allow the firm to attain MES, the entrepreneur must still think carefully about the implications of the choice of plant size because, by choosing to operate a particular plant size at a particular point in time, the entrepreneur is **constraining the firm to a range of costs** that, depending upon the number of units it produces, **may be too high** relative to a different size of plant. To illustrate this, imagine that the entrepreneur has chosen to operate a plant described by SRATC (1) and has taken orders for an amount Q_1 of the firm's product. The production cost per unit in this case is indicated by point *a* on SRATC (1). It is clear that this quantity of output could be produced at lower cost per unit at the larger plant described by SRATC (2). The unit cost of producing quantity Q_1 with plant (2) is indicated by point *b*. Of course, we could tell a variation on this story in which the entrepreneur has decided to carry out production at a very large plant such as that described by SRATC (7). If the firm has received orders amounting to quantity Q_2 it will incur unit costs c and the firm would be better off at the smaller plant described by SRATC (6) where unit costs are lower at d.

By now you have probably worked out that the **long run** is made up of a series of **short-run decision periods** which are **strung together**. Once a (long-run) capacity decision is made the firm operates within the constraints of the (short-run) law of diminishing marginal returns until another (long-run) capacity decision is made. As a result the 'family' of SRATC curves illustrated in Figure 6.3 traces out the **long-run average cost (LRAC)** curve for the firm; or, more accurately, the portion of each successive SRATC curve up to the points at which they overlap their adjacent SRATC curves makes up the LRAC curve. The LRAC curve associated with Figure 6.3 is illustrated in Figure 6.4. If a firm is producing a quantity of output that allows it to operate on its LRAC curve it is producing this quantity of output for the lowest unit cost possible. For example, the firm cannot produce an amount Q_1 at a unit cost lower than b in Figure 6.4 (but as we have seen it could produce the same output for a higher unit cost at point a in Figure 6.3). Ideally then a firm should seek to operate on its LRAC at all times.

> The long-run average cost (LRAC) curve shows the lowest unit costs of production that can be attained in the long run for each quantity of output.

The scenarios we have outlined here indicate the relationship between long-run capacity decisions and short-run and long-run costs. Furthermore, they raise another implication in relation to the point we made in Chapter 5 about the

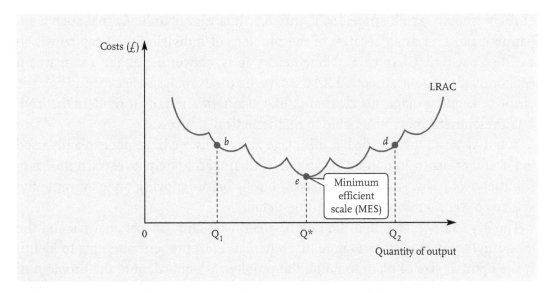

Figure 6.4 The 'composite' long-run average cost curve consists of the family of short-run average total cost curves

difficulty of predicting the extent of the market. It is obvious that a wise entrepreneur would be well advised to undertake some sort of **capacity planning** exercise prior to setting up production facilities, but predicting demand is very likely to be an exercise in guesswork as much as anything else. As a result there is plenty of scope for making some costly mistakes here. For example, if the firm begins its life with a small production facility and the growth in demand for the firm's product rapidly exceeds its productive capacity the entrepreneur may well have to instigate some ad hoc expansion of facilities if an alternative production plant cannot be located immediately (remember Dyson's portakabins, containers and tent?). The speed at which a bigger (or smaller) plant can be acquired is a measure of how long the firm's short-run period actually is. For example, if you are a shipping magnate running a fleet of cargo ships and you decide that you need a brand-new supertanker to add to your fleet, it will take a number of years for a ship-builder to supply you because building new ships takes a significant period of time. On the other hand, if you are a road haulage entrepreneur who runs a fleet of lorries and you decide that you would like to add more lorries to your fleet, these can be supplied to you within a matter of weeks, or even days, so your short-run period, that is the period within which you are capacity-constrained, will be quite a lot shorter than that of the shipping magnate.

The greater the number of different plant sizes that can be identified then the greater the number of SRATC curves that can be plotted and the *smoother* the LRAC curve will be. In fact if we make the rather extreme assumption that an infinite number of plant sizes can be identified then the LRAC curve will be entirely smooth, as illustrated in Figure 6.5. It is highly unlikely that such a situation could ever arise because of the problem of **indivisibility of capital** which we discussed in Chapter 5. Nonetheless it is conventional for mainstream economists to use a smooth LRAC curve in their analyses because it has the virtue of keeping diagrams clear and, like isoquant analysis, it renders theoretical development more amenable to mathematical analysis.

You may be a little puzzled at this stage about why we have not explicitly used the isoquant–isocost analysis discussed in Chapter 5 to help us explain the long-run theory of costs, so we will discuss it briefly before moving on to examine the sources of economies of scale in more detail.

The key to understanding the link between isoquant–isocost analysis and the long-run theory of costs is to note that when an entrepreneur attempts to identify the **optimal size of plant** to build, the problem is equivalent to the problem of identifying the **optimal point on an isoquant map**. Recall that an isoquant represents a particular quantity of output and that it tells us the relative quantities of

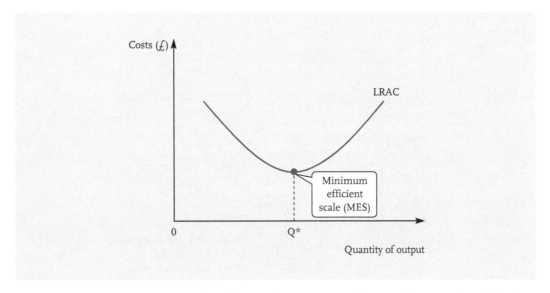

Figure 6.5 A smooth LRAC curve based upon the assumption that an infinite number of plant sizes can be identified

factor inputs that can be used to produce this quantity of output. As we showed in Figure 5.7, if we assume continuous isoquants and given input prices, we can identify a single point on each isoquant which tells us the lowest cost combination of inputs that can be used to produce each quantity of output. Therefore, each of the points *a* through *g* in Figure 5.7 tells us the total cost of producing 100 units of output through to 700 units of output respectively (in increments of 100 units). For example, at point *a* the firm can produce 100 units of output at a total cost of £650. Average total cost, ATC, is therefore £6.50 per unit. At point *b* the firm can produce 200 units of output at a total cost of £1100 which gives us ATC of £5.50 per unit. If we repeat these calculations for the other points on the expansion path we can plot the resulting ATC values and generate the long-run average cost curve depicted in Figure 6.6.

In Figure 6.6 you can see that the curve has a flat-bottomed U-shape reflecting the three types of returns to scale identified in the original isoquant–isocost diagram of Figure 5.7. You should also note here that the flat bottom of the LRAC curve implies that there is **no longer a unique optimum size** for the firm's plant because once MES has been reached, at 300 units of output, the firm will not incur any cost penalties (diseconomies of scale) unless it expands output beyond 500 units. Consequently the entrepreneur will be happy to operate anywhere between 300 and 500 units of output in the long run where ATC = £5.00.

When the LRAC curve has a portion which is **horizontal** then long-run **average cost** and **long-run marginal cost (LRMC)** will be **identical**. To illustrate this

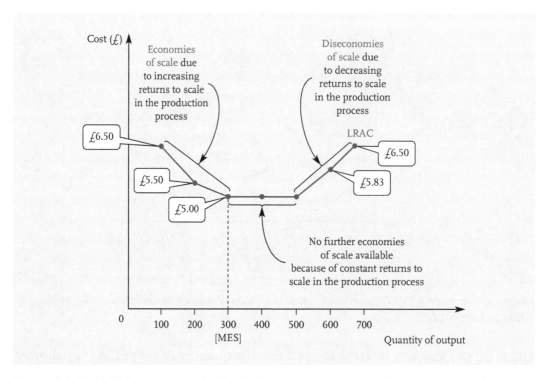

Figure 6.6 The LRAC curve generated by the isoquant–isocost map shown in Fig. 5.7 of Chapter 5

consider the following example. If the size of the market for the firm's product is currently 300 units of output then the total cost of production (shown in Figure 5.7) amounts to £1500 and the ATC is £5.00. Now suppose that the market grows by 100 units. The question the entrepreneur needs to ask here is: 'Will expansion of production facilities to produce the extra 100 units add an amount to total costs that will cause average costs to increase?' At a plant capable of producing 400 units of output total costs amount to £2000, so the addition to total cost as a result of expanding production facilities is £500. This means that each of the extra 100 units has a marginal cost of £500 ÷ 100 = £5.00. The average cost of producing 400 units amounts to £2000 ÷ 400 = £5.00. So the answer to the entrepreneur's question is 'no', and as we have seen this is because LRAC and LRMC are identical in the output range of 300 to 500 units.

6.2.3 Economies of scale – further discussion

In this section we will explore potential sources of economies of scale that may occur for reasons other than the ones we have discussed above. Up to this point we have explained that economies of scale will arise if the firm's production facilities display increasing returns to scale. In this situation the firm is able to produce higher levels of output at lower unit cost simply because of the way in which the entrepreneur is able to organize the inputs to the production process more effectively. Nowhere in this story have the prices of inputs been allowed to change. Consequently the cost savings associated with higher levels of output are purely a result of organizational factors, or more crudely put, the way in which the entrepreneur has decided that the firm's operations will be carried out. We shall call economies that arise from this source **organizational economies of scale**.

> Organizational economies of scale occur when the entrepreneur is able to overcome indivisibilities in the production process, take better advantage of the process of the division of labour and possibly introduce integrated labour-saving machinery at higher levels of output. *Input prices* are assumed to remain *unchanged* at all levels of output so unit costs fall purely as a result of the fact that a proportionate increase in the quantity of output requires a less than proportionate increase in the quantity of inputs.

Other sources of economies of scale can be found if we focus our attention on activities that are not explicitly dealt with in the long-run production function. In particular we should recognize that the firm has to procure material inputs from suppliers, advertise its product and distribute its product. In addition it may carry out research and development (R&D) to improve its product. Each of these activities requires the firm to spend money and each of these activities may be more cost effective at higher levels of output. We shall examine each one in turn.

Procurement of inputs requires the entrepreneur to **negotiate** input prices with suppliers. If the entrepreneur (or the firm's procurement officer) is able to exercise some power over the input supplier then he or she will be able to procure the required inputs at a favourable price. A firm that produces a large output will require a large amount of each input and will therefore buy in **bulk quantities**. Suppliers of inputs usually find such bulk sales an attractive proposition and, because they do not wish to lose such lucrative customers to rival suppliers, will offer a **bulk purchase price discount**. Firms which produce smaller levels of output are less valuable to input suppliers so their input prices are correspondingly higher.

Once the firm has produced its product it needs to **advertise** in order to inform and persuade potential buyers of the product. A given amount of advertising expenditure averaged over a small quantity of output is clearly not as cost effective as the same amount averaged over a larger quantity of output. In other words, if we treat advertising expenditure as a fixed cost it can be **spread more thinly** at larger levels of output. A similar argument holds for R&D expenditure.

Distribution of the firm's product can take a number of forms depending upon the nature of the product. In all cases the basic idea is to physically transfer custody of the product from the producer to the customer. If the product is software then the costs of distributing it will be relatively small because it can be transferred easily and cheaply via the Internet, so the opportunity to enjoy scale economies in distribution seems fairly limited (although not impossible). However, if we consider the **transportation costs** associated with a physical product economies of scale may arise from two potential sources. To illustrate, imagine the case of a book-binding firm which produces books for sale to high-street bookshops. Assume that the firm owns a lorry which is capable of hauling a variety of different sizes of cargo container. If the firm produces only relatively small numbers of books for delivery each week it will probably be unable to fill even the smallest cargo container. In this case the transport costs, which include the fixed cost of owning the lorry and the container plus the variable costs of fuel, will be relatively high per book. However, if the firm can produce larger quantities of books per week so that it is able to fill the cargo container then the transport costs per book should fall (assuming that the distance travelled by the lorry remains unchanged). This potential source of economies of scale is a version of the **indivisibility** story we told in Chapter 5, but here it is applied to transport of the product rather than its production. The second potential source of unit cost savings in transport arises from something that is commonly called **geometric economies**. The basic idea behind geometric economies is to exploit the relationship between the surface area of a structure and the volume of a structure. Consider the book-binding firm again. If its market size expands so that it needs to acquire a cargo container with twice the volume of its original one it is unlikely that this bigger container will cost twice as much as the smaller one. One reason for this is that the volume of its cargo space can be doubled without the need to double the quantity of materials it is constructed from. This geometric fact is illustrated in Figure 6.7. You should note that these kind of economies may also apply in non-transport related areas of the firm's activities, e.g. warehousing.

The sources of economies of scale that we have examined in this section fall into **four broad categories**:

(i) **Organizational economies** arising in the production process (including spreading production related fixed costs).

(ii) Economies that arise as a result of being able to **spread non-production related 'fixed costs'** such as advertising expenditure, R&D expenditure, etc. over larger quantities of output.

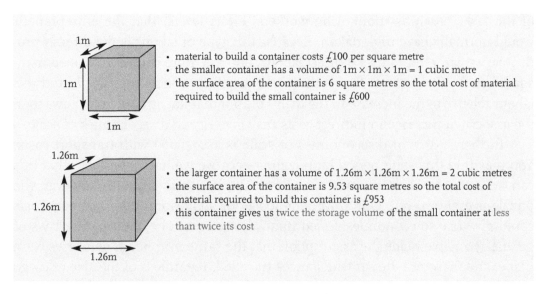

Figure 6.7 The principles behind geometric economies of scale

(iii) Economies that arise from **improved negotiating power** over suppliers.

(iv) Economies that arise from exploitation of the **laws of geometry**.

We can add a fifth potential source of scale economies to our list. Given that every firm borrows money at some time or another and that the rate of interest on these borrowed funds tends to reflect the lender's perception of the risk this money is being exposed to, it might be the case that a firm which produces a relatively large quantity of output is perceived to be a lower risk than a firm which produces a small quantity of output. In this case the 'larger' firm may be able to borrow funds at a preferable rate of interest compared to the 'smaller' one. We can call this a **financial scale economy**.

We have focused our attention in this section upon the potential sources of economies of scale, but we must not forget that at high levels of output there is the potential for diseconomies of scale to arise.

6.2.4 Diseconomies of scale – further discussion

We mentioned briefly above that diseconomies of scale arise principally because of the **control-loss problem** (discussed in Chapter 5) which will occur because of the bounded rationality of the entrepreneur. However, the control-loss problem can be overcome to a certain extent if the **administrative structure** of the firm is changed so that the mental and physical workload of the entrepreneur is lessened. This is achieved by employing non-production line labour to take on some of the tasks (such as monitoring workers' effort levels) that the entrepreneur would normally have undertaken. Because this type of labour is not directly productive we can refer to it as **indirect labour**, but it is more commonly called **managerial staff**. We can note that if there is a disproportionate increase in indirect labour relative to the increase in the firm's output that its introduction allows then the associated increase in indirect costs may give rise to diseconomies of scale.

A further source of diseconomies of scale is associated with **transport costs**. You may find this statement a bit puzzling because we have suggested that this can be a source of economies of scale in the previous section! However, the puzzle is easily solved. Our argument above for suggesting that transport costs could give rise to economies rested upon the concept of exploiting the laws of geometry and we made the assumption that the same number of deliveries were made, and therefore the same distances travelled, regardless of the size of cargo container. If we relax this assumption and postulate instead that the firm's higher level of output is a response not only to a bigger market in terms of customer numbers but also to a **bigger market in terms of geographical area**, then it is possible that the costs associated with the greater distances (e.g. fuel costs) that need to be travelled in order to transport the firm's product may rise sufficiently to create diseconomies of scale.

The final potential source of diseconomies that we will discuss here involves relaxing the assumption about the ready-availability of labour that we made at the start of the chapter. We assumed at the outset that the firm could readily obtain labour for its production line. This can be explained if there is a high level of unemployment in the firm's catchment area (the geographical area from which it obtains its labour), which has the implication that relatively low wages will be sufficient to attract large numbers of applicants. This will mean that the price of labour (wages) will remain constant because there will be an excess of applicants for each vacancy in the firm. If we assume now that there is high employment leading to a **shortage of labour** in the firm's catchment area then when it comes to expanding output to higher levels the firm will have to offer higher wages in order to attract greater numbers of applicants (possibly from outside its catchment area). Consequently the price of labour will no longer remain constant and higher levels of output will only be attainable at higher cost, giving rise to diseconomies of scale. You should note that if the price of labour changes mainstream analysis suggests the firm should substitute capital for labour, but as we have discussed in Chapter 5 this may not be as simple as the mainstream theory implies because of the influence of path dependence.

In our discussions of the long-run theory of costs we have directed your attention exclusively to the influence of scale upon the unit costs incurred by the firm.

However, before we move on to discuss the heterodox approach to costs, we will turn your attention away from scale economies in order to introduce you to the phenomenon of economies of scope.

6.2.5 Economies of scope

In contrast to economies of scale, which arise from spreading costs across increased quantities of output of *the same* product, **economies of scope** arise from sharing costs between *different* products.

> Economies of scope occur when a reduction in average total cost is brought about by producing two or more goods or services which share a common input or set of inputs.

At first sight the concept of economies of scope seems to be simple enough. For example, if factories cost £200 per week to rent then a firm which produces two products in a single factory can share the rental (or 'overhead') cost between both products. If 100 units of product A and 100 units of product B are produced then the rental cost that can be allocated to each unit of A and B will be £200 ÷ 200 = £1.00. Alternatively, if the firm rented two separate factories to produce 100 units of product A and 100 units of product B it would have to pay total rental of £400, giving a rental cost per unit produced of £400 ÷ 200 = £2.00. However, this rather simplified story hides a few practical problems, so we will use a more detailed hypothetical example to illustrate the concept of scope economies more fully. You will discover that it is quite **difficult to disentangle** economies of **scope** from economies of **scale**.

Harry Bryson is an aspiring entrepreneur. Inspired by the success of James Dyson in the vacuum cleaner market he thinks he has the basis of an idea that will enable him to manufacture vacuum cleaners that are even more effective than those based upon Dyson's Dual Cyclone technology. Consequently he sets up a new company, Bryson Vacuum Cleaners Limited, and sets to work developing his idea. After two years of development, at a cost of £1.5 million, he has perfected the technology, which he calls the Triple Vortex Vacuuming System (*TV* for short). He sets up a factory, at a cost of £0.25 million for the building itself and £0.25 million for tooling, to produce his first model, the *TV01* upright vacuum cleaner. Each one that rolls off the production line has variable costs of £100. Harry aims to produce 10 000 *TV01*s. Total costs for this volume of output amount to:

$$£1.5\,m + £0.25\,m + £0.25\,m + (£100 \times 10\,000) = £3.0\,m$$

Before long Harry decides to produce a cylinder vacuum cleaner based upon the *TV* system. He calls this model the *TV02*. He decides to go into production straight away by sharing the facilities in his current factory between the two models. The set-up cost of adding tooling capable of producing the *TV02* is £0.25 million. Each *TV02* incurs variable costs of £75. Harry decides to produce 10 000 *TV02*s. The total costs of production incurred by Bryson Vacuum Cleaners Limited now amount to the costs of producing the *TV01* plus the costs of producing the *TV02*:

$$£1.5\,m + £0.25\,m + £0.25\,m + (£100 \times 10\,000) + £0.25\,m + (£75 \times 10\,000)$$
$$= £4.0\,m$$

The **additional cost** incurred as a result of adding the *TV02* to the production line is, therefore, £1.0 m.

In order to illustrate the presence of economies of scope we need to compare the cost attributable to the addition of the *TV02* to the existing production line with a situation where the *TV01* **does not already exist**. In this state of the world, if Harry decided that he wanted to produce 10 000 *TV02*s, the total costs he would incur would be:

$$£1.5\,m + £0.25\,m + £0.25\,m + (£75 \times 10\,000) = £2.75\,m$$

This means that production of the *TV02* would cost 2.75 times as much if the *TV01* production line did not already exist.

There are **two sources** of economies of scope in the case of both the *TV01* and the *TV02* being produced. The first is the **sharing of the costs of acquiring (common) know-how (the TV technology)** between both products. The second is the **sharing of costs associated with building the factory**.

The presence of economies of scope can be seen more clearly if we look at the impact upon **average total costs** (ATC) in the three alternative scenarios outlined here:

(i)   The ATC of producing just the *TV01* is £3.0 m ÷ 10 000 = £300.

(ii)   The ATC of producing just the *TV02* is £2.75 m ÷ 10 000 = £275.

(iii) If both models are produced and we allocate development costs and the factory building costs evenly between the models then the ATC of the *TV01* is **£212.50** and the ATC of the *TV02* is **£187.50**. Joint production therefore leads to economies of scope.

The problem we have here is that our story has assumed a **given quantity of output**. If we change Harry's output decision to 20 000 units of each type of vacuum cleaner and we recalculate scenario (iii) the ATC figures become: *TV01* = £156.25 and *TV02* = £131.25. It will be clear to you that by letting output quantity vary we have introduced a **scale economy** effect into the analysis. This illustrates that it is actually very difficult in practice to identify a *pure* economy of scope effect. This problem is made worse in the real world by the realities of **cost**

accounting practices which tend to follow rather arbitrary rules for allocating overhead costs to different products in the firm. We have ignored this problem in our example by assuming that each product is produced in the same quantity and we have therefore applied our own arbitrary rule and split the overhead costs equally between them.

6.3 The heterodox approach to the behaviour of costs

In our explanation of the mainstream analysis of short-run and long-run costs above we adopted the mainstream technique of assuming that the entrepreneur has full knowledge of the relevant short-run and long-run production functions. Then we translated the production information into cost data by simply introducing a given set of input prices. The result of this process was the discovery that the size of the firm's **unit costs** of production depend exclusively upon the **scale** at which production is carried out by the firm.

In essence the mainstream story has told us that entrepreneurs who wish to keep costs at a minimum level should choose to build an appropriate size of production facility, and that once it is built the firm will be constrained to work within a given set of unit costs which are defined by its short-run cost curves. In other words, once the entrepreneur has made the size decision the firm will incur a particular unit cost at its chosen level of output and this cost **will not change**. The mainstream analysis of costs is therefore a **static analysis**. Put simply this means that it ignores other **non-size related factors** that might well have an influence on the firm's costs; in particular, it does not explicitly examine the impact of the passage of time.

6.3.1 Time and costs

If we incorporate time into our analysis we open up the possibility that things will not stay constant because everyone associated with the firm will undergo a process of **learning-by-doing**.

> Learning-by-doing describes the *process* where human beings become more skilled at and knowledgeable about an activity as a result of carrying out the activity repeatedly.

If we build learning into the story of costs this means that there is scope for the entrepreneur to become more knowledgeable about the way production is **organized** and how it can be improved, and the way other non-production activities are carried out and can be improved. There is scope for workers to improve the way they perform their tasks and to become more **skilful**, not only in their individual roles but also as a coherent production team. In addition, problems with the original **product design** can be identified and rectified and **quality control** issues can be ironed out. In short, all the types of **knowledge** that we identified in the previous chapter can be **improved and augmented**.

To illustrate the impact of learning-by-doing on costs we shall revisit Tables 4U and turn the clock back to when Samantha conducted production in the small workshop with three units of capital. The original short-run production function associated with the small workshop is shown in Table 5.2, and from this information we derived the firm's costs of production in Table 6.1 and showed the relevant cost curves in Figure 6.1. Now let us suppose that **after three months** of production Samantha and her labour force have learned a lot about how to produce flat-packs and, as a result, Samantha's organizational know-how has increased and allowed her to improve the **flow of parts** between the different stages of production. In addition, the labour force has significantly developed its **skill** at using the capital equipment. The upshot of this learning will be an improvement in labour's **productivity** in each time period.

Table 6.3 compares the short-run production function for the first three months of operation with the short-run production function for the second three-month period of operation (**bold figures**). The **difference** between the figures recorded in the respective production functions is the result of learning-by-doing. You should note that in presenting the impact of learning-by-doing in this way we have assumed that the lessons learned apply to all *potential* quantities of labour that could be employed. However, if you remember the details of Samantha's story you will know that she *actually* chose to employ just three units of labour in her first workshop, so presumably only these three individuals will have an opportunity to learn by doing! For the moment we will ignore this complication, but we will return to it below because it has important implications for the growth of the firm.

In Table 6.3 you can see that labour productivity, which is measured by average product (AP_L) has increased in the second three-month period compared to the first three-month period. This increase is due purely to the influence of learning-by-doing, which can only occur with the passing of time. How does this productivity improvement translate into cost data? This can be seen in Table 6.4, where the figures associated with the impact of learning-by-doing are once again shown in **bold**. In drawing up this table we have assumed that input prices have remained unchanged.

Table 6.3 A comparison of Tables 4U's initial short-run production function (first three months of production) with the production function applicable to the second three months of production after learning-by-doing

K	L	Number of flat-packs per week in first 3 months (TP)	Marginal product of labour in first 3 months (MP$_L$)	Average product of labour in first 3 months (AP$_L$)	Number of flat-packs per week in next 3 months (TP)	Marginal product of labour in next 3 months (MP$_L$)	Average product of labour in next 3 months (AP$_L$)
			100			180	
3	1	100		100	180		180
			150			270	
3	2	250		125	450		225
			200			450	
3	3	450		150	900		300
			100			200	
3	4	550		137.5	1100		275
			50			100	
3	5	600		120	1200		240
			−120			−220	
3	6	480		80	980		163

Table 6.4 Short-run costs of Tables 4U with 300 sq. ft. workshop and three units of capital after three months of learning-by-doing (£)

1	2	3	4	5	6	7	8	9	10	11	12
K	L	Q	Cost of K	Opp cost	Av'ge fixed cost (AFC)	Wage cost	Raw material cost	Av'ge va'ble cost (AVC)	Total costs (TC)	Av'ge total costs (ATC)	Marginal costs (MC)
											2.56
3	1	180	90	150	1.33	100	360	2.56	700	3.89	
											2.37
3	2	450	90	150	0.53	200	900	2.44	1340	2.97	
											2.22
3	3	900	90	150	0.27	300	1800	2.33	2340	2.60	
											2.50
3	4	1100	90	150	0.22	400	2200	2.36	2840	2.58	
											3.00
3	5	1200	90	150	0.20	500	2400	2.42	3140	2.62	

It is easier to see the impact of learning-by-doing on the unit costs of Tables 4U in Figure 6.8, where we have drawn the firm's short-run ATC curves for the two respective periods.

In Figure 6.8 you can see that when learning-by-doing takes place there are **two primary effects**:

(i) The SRATC for the second three months of production lies below the SRATC for the first three months of production. Consequently, in the second three-month period Tables 4U is able to produce **a particular quantity of output for a lower unit cost** than it incurred in the first three-month period. For example, after the benefit of three months of learning the unit cost of producing 450 units of output falls from £3.20 to £2.97.

(ii) The firm is able to produce **a greater quantity of output with the same quantity of factor inputs**. For example, the three original employees working with the original quantity of capital are able to produce a maximum output of 900 units in the second three-month period compared with a maximum of 450 units in the previous three-month period.

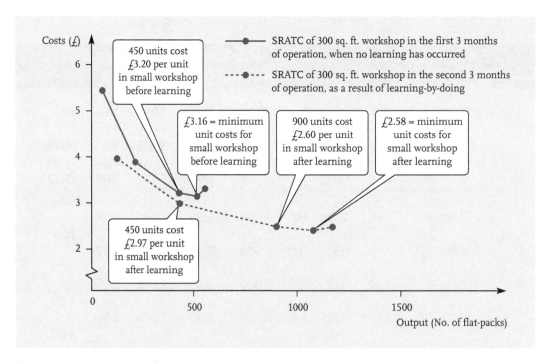

Figure 6.8 Comparison of short-run ATC curves between two different time periods but with no change in quantity of labour and capital for Tables 4U

Now that we have taken learning into account in the Tables 4U story we can see that when Pinewørld increase their order from 450 to 900 flat-packs per week it is no longer necessary for Samantha to expand the firm's productive capacity through the acquisition of extra factors of production. You will recall that the mainstream story we told in Section 6.2.2 required Samantha to obtain two extra units of capital and to employ two extra units of labour in order to produce 900 flat-packs. This is because the mainstream production functions we used in our earlier analysis of costs were based upon the assumption that knowledge (know-that; know-how; know-who) about the production technology and its associated activities is complete. If **knowledge is complete** in this way then **nothing extra can be learned** and the firm will indeed be capacity constrained in the way that mainstream analysis predicts. However, given the boundedly rational nature of the entrepreneur and other human actors associated with the firm the mainstream analysis seems to be a rather strong line to take, at least in the early days of the firm's development.

Learning-by-doing is likely to suffer from a form of **diminishing returns as time passes**; in other words, once the firm has carried out operations with a given technique for a significant period of time possibilities for further learning-by-doing will probably reduce. Once the prospects for further productivity enhancement (and therefore capacity expansion) through learning-by-doing have been exhausted the entrepreneur will have no choice but to expand the firm's facilities and take advantage of economies of scale (assuming a big enough market for the firm's product exists). So, as you can see, there is a place for the mainstream analysis, but it needs to be incorporated into the context of an environment where learning takes place. In particular, once the firm has taken on board extra factors of production a **new learning process** will take place as the entrepreneur learns better how to organize the increased quantity of factors and the new labour intake familiarize themselves with their respective roles. This brings us back to the assumption we made above that learning-by-doing applies to all *potential* quantities of labour employed.

While the short-run production function for Tables 4U tells us that up to five units of labour could be employed (in the 300 sq. ft. workshop) Samantha *actually* employs just three workers. As a result most of the lessons about organization that Samantha will learn as time passes will relate **only to the chosen configuration of capital and labour**; that is three units of capital and three units of labour. In addition, the three units of labour who are actually employed will benefit from their learning-by-doing but the 'other two' who are not actually employed by the firm will not benefit. Of course, once learning benefits have been exhausted and the firm increases its quantity of factor inputs it is possible that some of the lessons about organization will apply to the new configuration and that some of the knowledge gained by the initial members of the labour force could be imparted to the new members; however, this depends upon the extent to which such knowledge is **tacit**. Know-how, in other words skills acquired through experience and practice over time, is likely to be very difficult to teach to the new members of the labour force. You should note also that as the firm's activities increase in scale, it may be necessary to employ professional managers and they, too, will have to learn by doing. The economist Edith Penrose first raised these points in 1959 in what has become a very famous book called *The Theory of the Growth of the Firm*. In this book she made the point that the employment of extra labour (be it production line workers or new managers) will require the current experienced labour force to divert their attention away from their usual tasks into training these newcomers and, consequently, the expanding firm will suffer inefficiencies until the new staff are up to speed. Clearly this is a process which takes time.

A further point you should note about the Tables 4U example is that we have shown the impact of just **one period** of learning-by-doing. While this presentation of learning is fine as a way of getting the basic point across to you, you should note that learning-by-doing is really a **continuous process** and as a result does **not** create a **one-off** fall in unit costs.

The notion that learning-by-doing is a continuous process has been found to exist in many firms and industries and it has been encapsulated in a tool called **the learning curve**.

6.3.2 The learning curve

The learning curve traces the relationship between unit costs and accumulated output. It was first recognized in 1936 by an engineer called Theodore Wright. Wright observed that in aircraft production the average time needed to assemble each additional aircraft produced fell as the accumulated output of aircraft increased. In other words, as time passed labour productivity increased. Table 6.5 provides a simple example of the kind of process Wright discovered. The assumptions we have made to construct Table 6.5 are as follows:

(i)   Capital is fixed in quantity.

(ii) Labour is fixed in quantity.

(iii) Monthly cost of total labour force = £250.

(iv) **Average cost** at any point in time is defined as:

the sum of total labour costs incurred to date ÷ the total quantity of output produced to date.

Table 6.5 A hypothetical example of a learning curve process

Month no.	Output per month (½ means unfinished assembly)	Total quantity of output to date (accumulated output)	Total costs incurred to date (£)	Average labour cost per unit (£)
1	1	1	250	250.00
2	2	3	500	166.67
3	3	6	750	125.00
4	4	10	1000	100.00
5	4½	14½	1250	86.21
6	5½	20	1500	75.00
7	6	26	1750	67.31
8	6½	32½	2000	61.54
9	7½	40	2250	56.25

At first sight you may miss the nature of the relationship between accumulated output and average cost that is present in the data in Table 6.5. However, if you examine these data carefully you will notice that a **consistent rate of cost reduction** occurs every time the total quantity of output produced **doubles**. For example, between months 2 and 3 total output doubles from 3 units to 6 units and the average labour cost per unit falls from £166.67 to £125; this is a 25 per cent reduction. Between months 4 and 6 total output doubles from 10 units to 20 units and the average labour cost per unit falls from £100 to £75 which is another 25 per cent reduction. Similarly, between months 6 and 9 total output doubles from 20 to 40 and average labour cost per unit falls by 25 per cent from £75 to £56.25. Put another way, **as output doubles unit costs fall to 75 per cent of their previous level.** We say, therefore, that we have identified a **75 per cent learning curve**.

Our 75 per cent learning curve is shown in Figure 6.9. Here we have plotted average labour cost per unit against the number of months. Examination of our 75 per cent learning curve reveals that the initial steepness of the early months is followed by a shallowing off in later months, indicating that the rate of productivity increase is **dropping off** with the passage of time.

Learning curves of various rates have been identified in many industries. Wright's original work estimated an 80 per cent learning curve for aircraft production.

A learning curve plots the relationship between the unit costs of production and accumulated output. It is measured as a percentage decrease in average labour cost each time output is doubled.

It should not have escaped your attention that the data presented in Table 6.5 are incomplete. This is because they do not record the addition to total costs

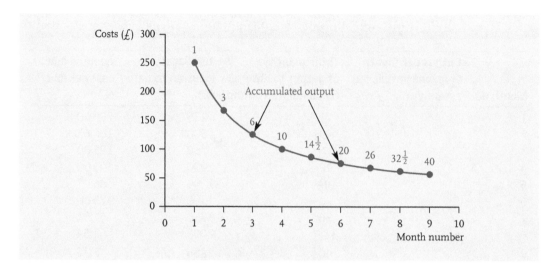

Figure 6.9 An example of a 75 per cent learning curve

incurred to date as a result of the current month's output. In other words, we have not calculated **marginal cost**. You will recall, from the static mainstream analysis, that marginal cost records the addition to total costs that arises as a result of producing an extra unit of output. This definition does not change in the dynamic cost analysis associated with the learning curve, but you should note that there is a subtle and important **difference** between the **source of marginal costs** in the static analysis and the source of marginal costs in the dynamic analysis.

In the **static analysis** of costs it is only possible to increase the firm's output if extra units of labour are employed. In consequence, the firm's total costs increase (because of its higher wage bill) and, as we discovered, the **marginal cost curve** of the firm begins to **slope upwards** once diminishing marginal returns have taken hold (recall from Chapter 5, Figure 5.1 that the firm will want to operate in this zone of diminishing marginal returns or, as we called it, 'phase II'). In contrast, in the **dynamic analysis** of costs that we are examining here the increases in the firm's output that we observe as time passes are not the result of employing extra labour. Instead they are the result of the given quantity of labour improving their productivity as a consequence of learning-by-doing. Consequently we should expect a plot of **marginal cost** to **slope downwards**. Inspection of Table 6.6 and Figure 6.10 confirms this to be the case.

The discovery that marginal costs slope upwards in the static analysis of costs but slope downwards in the dynamic analysis of costs has important ramifications for the firm. In particular it has implications for its supply decisions and the related issue of pricing of outputs.

Month no.	Output per month	Total quantity of output to date (accumulated output)	Total costs incurred to date (£)	Marginal cost of current month's production (£)
1	1	1	250	250.0
2	2	3	500	125.0
3	3	6	750	83.3
4	4	10	1000	62.5
5	$4\frac{1}{2}$	$14\frac{1}{2}$	1250	55.6
6	$5\frac{1}{2}$	20	1500	45.5
7	6	26	1750	41.7
8	$6\frac{1}{2}$	$32\frac{1}{2}$	2000	38.5
9	$7\frac{1}{2}$	40	2250	33.3

Table 6.6 Marginal costs associated with our 75 per cent learning curve

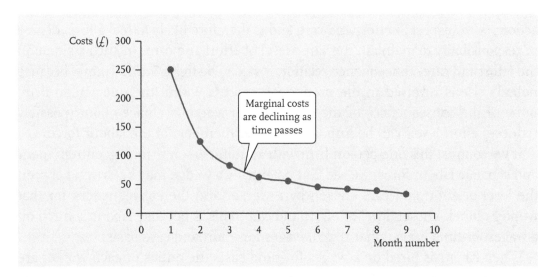

Figure 6.10 Marginal cost curve associated with our 75 per cent learning curve

6.3.3 X-inefficiency and costs

In our discussion of the mainstream theory of production in Chapter 5 we pointed out that a key assumption of the theory is that labour is homogeneous and that each unit of labour puts **maximum effort** into its respective task on the production line. The consequence of this for the mainstream theory of costs is that the firm's chosen level of output in the long run will be produced at the minimum cost that can possibly be attained (in other words, it will be on the LRAC curve). However, Harvey Leibenstein's theory of **X-inefficiency**, which we first introduced in Chapter 3, suggests that this might well be an overly strong assumption to make.

> X-inefficiency refers to the excess of actual costs incurred over the minimum cost that is potentially attainable for a given quantity of output.

The essence of Leibenstein's X-inefficiency theory is most easily seen by contrasting a one-person firm with a multi-person firm. In a **one-person firm** the entrepreneur is also the labour force. The success of the firm will depend upon the quantity and quality of its product which, in turn, depends upon the degree of effort and care that the entrepreneur-worker puts into its production. In the case of the one-person firm this means that the rewards for increased effort and care go directly to the entrepreneur-worker. In other words, there is a **direct link** between the **effort and care** put in by the entrepreneur-worker and the **consequences** of that effort and care. As a result, the entrepreneur-worker will be unable to avoid any of the consequences for costs of production of his or her actions with respect to effort and care and is therefore likely to feel a high degree of **responsibility** to maintain the same level of effort and care. In such a situation the **effort and care–consequence relation** is said to be **tight**. Furthermore, because nobody else is involved in the production process within the one-person firm, none of the consequences of the entrepreneur-worker's choice about (possibly reduced) effort levels can be imposed on other members of the labour force.

If we contrast this one-person firm with a multi-person firm (e.g. entrepreneur and separate labour force) we see that potentially a wedge may be driven between the level of effort and care chosen by a worker and the **consequences for that worker** of their chosen level of effort and care. This is because labour is hired on a **wages-for-time** basis rather than a wages-for-effort and care basis.

When labour is hired on a wages-for-time basis the duties of each worker are usually only loosely specified in the **employment contract**. This is because the entrepreneur may require some flexibility in the use to which the labour force in the firm is put (to enable a quick response to unforeseen circumstances which may arise). In this situation the employment contract is said to be **general and incomplete**. The alternative to a general and incomplete contract is a highly specific one, but this type of contract is extremely rigid and it imposes costs on the firm, not least of which is the cost associated with the need to write a new contract every time unforeseen circumstances arise. With an incomplete employment contract and with wage payments dependent upon hours worked rather than effort expended and care taken, each unit of labour has a degree of **discretion** over the actual amount of effort and care (e.g. attention to detail, speed with which work is carried out, etc.) put into the job. This is because the consequences of the chosen effort and care level will not necessarily be borne by the worker, who gets paid simply for 'putting in the hours' at work.

In his original analysis Leibenstein goes to some trouble to identify the conditions under which a worker will feel the need to increase effort and care levels. In simple terms his argument is that particular individuals will act in such a way that they strike a balance between (a) how they would **like** to behave – which we assume is to put in minimal effort – and (b) how they **ought** to behave – which depends upon the individual's own **personal standards** (for example, taking great pride in their own work) and also upon the degree of **external pressure** to which they are subjected (examples include peer group pressure to perform better and motivational speeches by the entrepreneur). In turn the external pressure that is brought to bear on the workers will be dictated by the pressure the firm is placed under by the actions of its competitors (for example, in the form of superior competing products). If the firm's external **competitive environment** does not provide a particularly rigorous level of threat then its **internal environment** is likely to be more relaxed and consequently its workers will be placed under less pressure. In these circumstances the **effort and care–consequence relation** is said to be **loose**. Furthermore, in a multi-person firm where each stage of production depends on the satisfactory completion of the previous stage, it may take a reduction in effort level on the part of just a single worker to create **knock-on effects** through the production line. So, even if all of the other workers are putting in maximum effort the discretion exercised by the 'lazy' individual may be sufficient to increase costs above their potentially attainable level.

The **fundamental proposition of X-inefficiency** theory is that the weaker the forces in the firm's competitive environment then the less serious will be the consequences of lower effort levels for all members of the firm on average, and so the greater will be the difference between the costs of production actually incurred and the minimum costs of production that are potentially attainable. In terms of the firm's LRAC curve this means that the **actual LRAC curve** will lie **above** the **potentially attainable LRAC curve** specified in the mainstream theory of costs (Figure 6.11).

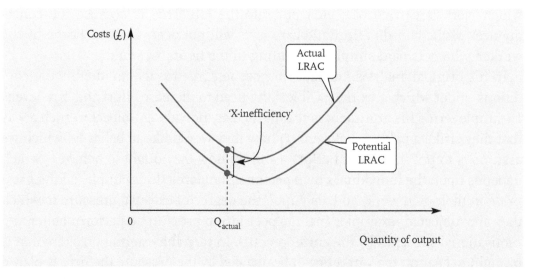

Figure 6.11 LRAC in the presence of X-inefficiency versus LRAC under mainstream assumptions

6.4 **Summary**

In our opening comments to this chapter we stated that understanding costs is a more complex task than simply totting up numbers. Having got to this point you will no doubt have realized that this was something of an understatement! The sources of costs are many and the way they behave is varied depending, as it does, upon the scale of operations, the passage of time and the degree to which labour can exercise discretion over its level of effort and care. In order to explore these concepts we have treated each one individually and along the way we have made extensive use of cost curves of various kinds.

Although we have used cost curves to illustrate the basic concepts behind each approach you should be aware that we are not necessarily suggesting that entrepreneurs will have full knowledge of the cost curves relevant to their firm. You will recall that in Chapter 5 we discussed the nature of knowledge with respect to production functions and we suggested that an entrepreneur was unlikely to have full knowledge of the values in the cells of the production function because of the problem of bounded rationality. Given that we have drawn the cost curves in this chapter by translating production function information into cost information the same points about knowledge that we raised in Chapter 5 apply equally with respect to cost curves. At best an entrepreneur will probably only know costs for a very narrow range of output levels and, as we have seen, the influence of learning will mean that even if a cost curve

6.4 **Summary** (continued)

could be recognized at a given point in time it is unlikely to remain in the same location for long (note that we have only shown the impact of learning upon the SRATC curve of the firm but, given that the LRAC curve is a composite of successive SRATC curves, the LRAC curve will not be stationary either). Furthermore, the potential for the presence of X-inefficiency may mean that the (portions of) cost curves the entrepreneur does have knowledge of do not show the lowest costs attainable for each level of output. None of this means, however, that you should ignore the lessons learned in this chapter. Instead you need to make sense of the different stories we have told and understand what they mean for the practising entrepreneur/manager.

The concepts we have discussed in this chapter are all present in the real world of business, but you must understand that here we have had the luxury of being able to hold complicating factors constant which has allowed us to focus upon the particular concept that we wished to explain. Unfortunately for the practising entrepreneur this luxury is not available in the real world! In the real world the practising entrepreneur needs to develop an awareness of the potential for diminishing marginal returns to bite and push costs upwards and that learning may lessen the upward pressure on costs. But of course learning effects will diminish with time which may necessitate expansion of facilities to enable the firm to exploit economies of scale and scope and further exploit learning effects. On top of all of this any cost data that the entrepreneur is aware of, such as that generated by accountants, need to be treated as providing an imperfect picture only and also need to be adjusted to account for opportunity costs.

The LRAC curve of mainstream analysis can be thought of as a **cost frontier** because it represents the minimum costs potentially attainable by a firm which is operated by a perfectly informed unboundedly rational entrepreneur who has nothing left to learn and who employs an already fully skilled labour force who put in maximum effort and who also have nothing left to learn. As you will have realized the harsh reality of bounded rationality means that knowledge of where the frontier lies is simply not available in the real world. This does not prevent many firms trying to benchmark their costs, but their reference point is not the LRAC curve of mainstream theory. Instead they use their competitors' costs (if they can obtain the information). This is not true benchmarking since it will not tell the firm what potential for cutting costs exists beyond matching the lowest cost rival. Of course matching a lower cost rival's

6.4 Summary (continued)

performance is desirable, but you should realize that the heterogeneity of firm knowledge and capabilities means that one firm's level of costs may quite simply be unattainable by another firm with different capabilities, at least until a significant period of learning has been undertaken by which time the rival may well have improved further.

We will make one final but very important point. In an attempt to minimize complications in this chapter we have assumed that the production plant and the firm are one and the same physical entity. You should be aware, however, that a firm may operate more than one production facility (we mentioned in Chapter 5 that this might be a sensible way of avoiding decreasing returns to scale which may arise in a single production facility). Consequently a further complicating factor will enter the real world entrepreneur's problem set – namely, having to identify when the firm's costs are being influenced by activities that take place in specific individual production facilities and when costs are arising from activities that are shared across all facilities (for example, advertising).

6.5 Some questions to consider

1. If you own a car which you use on just ten days of the year to travel a total distance of 1000 miles and the car costs you £1200 per year in loan repayments, plus £500 per year in tax, insurance and fuel, then what are the true costs of car ownership in any one year if you can hire a car for the ten days at a cost of £25 per day plus fuel costs of £1 per 10 miles travelled?

2. Mr. Jenkins owns a small cake shop. His shelves are full with his current range of cake products and all of them sell well. He has just learned that a new type of cake has been made by one of his suppliers and they are prepared to sell him 20 cakes a week at a wholesale price of £1.00 per cake. In order to display the new cake Mr. Jenkins will have to reduce the number of other cakes on his shelves by 30 units per week. All of his other cakes earn him a profit of £0.50 per cake sold. How much will it cost Mr. Jenkins to stock 20 units of the new type of cake?

3. A shop owner erects another shelf in her shop and uses it to display a new line of products. The new line expands the total number of products she offers for sale. Is the shopkeeper exploiting economies of scale or economies of scope?

6.5 Some questions to consider (continued)

4. Do you think that firms in the real world ever suffer diseconomies of scale? What reasons would you give for your answer?

5. What shape should a learning curve take according to the mainstream analysis of costs?

6. Do you think the emphasis on economies of scale in mainstream theory means that there is no place for small firms in the economy? How might small firms have advantages over large firms? (Hint: learning may be important here.)

7. Given what you have learned about where costs come from in this chapter do you think it is least costly to beat your rivals to the market with a new product that you are not quite 100 per cent sure is ready, or to wait until you are 100 per cent sure that you have developed the product properly?

8. Fixed costs = £1000. At 100 units of output total costs = £1500. At 120 units of output total costs = £1700. What is the average variable cost at each level of output and what is the marginal cost of the 120th unit?

9. The following data have been recorded over a period of time:

Accumulated no. of units of output	Average production costs
1	110
2	85
4	65
8	51
16	39
32	30
64	23

Approximately what per cent value learning curve do these data give rise to?

10. Do you think it is more important to know the costs your firm has incurred in the past, or the costs that your firm will incur in its future activities?

11. What practical measures could an entrepreneur take to encourage faster rates of learning throughout the firm?

6.6 Recommended additional reading sources

For a critical perspective on the development of cost theory in economics, see Chapters 7 and 8 of Peter Earl (1995) *Microeconomics for Business and Marketing*, Cheltenham, Edward Elgar. This can usefully be read in conjunction with Book V of Alfred Marshall (1920/1994) *Principles of Economics* (8th edn), Basingstoke, Macmillan.

For a practical guide to using learning curves in business planning, see P. Ghemawat (1985) 'Building strategy on the experience curve', *Harvard Business Review*, March–April, pp. 143–49.

For an insight into the debate between economists sparked by X-inefficiency and some of its practical implications, see Harvey Leibenstein (1978) 'X-inefficiency Xists – Reply to an Xorcist', *American Economic Review*, **68**, no.1, pp. 203–11.

For an excellent and lucid discussion of learning and skills, see Chapter 4 of Richard Nelson and Sidney Winter (1982) *An Evolutionary Theory of Economic Change*, Harvard, Belknap Press.

For a deeper discussion of the importance of learning curves, see Chapter 16 of M. Rothschild (1990) *Bionomics: Economy as Ecosystem*, New York, Henry Holt.

The single best source for further analysis of economies of scope is David Teece (1980) 'Economies of scope and the scope of the enterprise', *Journal of Economic Behavior and Organization*, **1**, pp. 223–47.

How can the firm set the 'right' price?

Learning outcomes

If you study this chapter carefully, it may help you to understand:

- the nature of the single product firm's pricing problem
- how to define an industry
- the concept of industry structure
- price elasticity of demand
- the concepts of normal and above normal profits
- the conditions necessary for price discrimination
- the problems caused by mutual interdependence
- the concept of mark-up pricing
- the role of reputation in business.

To the extent that you develop such understanding, you should be better able to:

- explain to managers the key questions that they will need to answer in order to arrive at the 'right' price for their firm's products
- analyse a particular firm's actual pricing decision
- appreciate the need for plans, estimates and judgement in the pricing calculation
- draw connections between the pricing problem and the discussions of entrepreneurship, demand and costs that were covered in Chapters 3, 4, 5 and 6 respectively.

7.1 Introduction

Setting the 'right' price for the firm's product is an important determinant of its economic success. Intuitively we know that the firm will lose sales if it charges a price that is *too high* and its profits will suffer. On the other hand, if the firm charges a price which is *too low* it may forego profits that it could have earned, or even fail to cover its costs and make losses.

In this chapter we will draw upon what you have learned so far to discuss the firm's pricing decision. To keep things simple we will assume that the firm produces only one product, so we will not discuss the complicating factors that might enter into the pricing decision of a multi-product firm. Before we proceed we will introduce some basic concepts that will underpin what follows. Specifically, these basics are a **general framework** which can be used to think about the firm's pricing problem and **guidance** on how to identify those competitors who are relevant to the firm's pricing decision.

7.2 A general framework for thinking about pricing decisions

We begin the analysis of pricing decisions by stating formally the relationship between revenues, costs and profits:

$$\text{Profit } (\pi) = \text{Total revenue (TR) } minus \text{ Total costs (TC)} \qquad \text{[i]}$$

If we examine the constituent parts of expression [i] we obtain expressions [ii] and [iii]:

$$TR = P \times Q \qquad \text{[ii]}$$

Expression [ii] states that the total revenue earned by a firm depends upon the price, P, it charges for its good/service and the volume of sales, Q, it can achieve at this price. In other words, it depends upon demand from customers.

$$TC = TFC + (AVC \times Q) = ATC \times Q \qquad \text{[iii]}$$

Expression [iii] states that the total costs incurred by a firm consist of its total fixed costs (TFC), which are independent of the number of units it produces (and which include the entrepreneur's opportunity cost), and its total variable costs (TVC), which depend directly upon the number of units produced.

As a minimum requirement the problem for the entrepreneur is to **choose an asking price** for the firm's product that will generate enough revenue to enable it at least to cover its costs of production. In order to do this the entrepreneur must take account of five important factors:

(i) The **firm's own costs**.

(ii) The likely behaviour of current **competitors**.

(iii) The behaviour of **potential buyers**.

(iv) The **likelihood of new competitors** emerging.

(v) The stance towards pricing adopted by the **regulatory authorities**.

Each of these factors has its own underlying influences.

7.2.1 Underlying influences on the behaviour of the firm's own costs

The firm's costs were the subject of Chapters 5 and 6 where you saw that **economies of scale**, **economies of scope** and **learning curve** effects are important. In addition, the firm can keep costs to a minimum by trying to obtain its inputs (labour, capital and raw materials) on favourable terms. This will depend on the strength of suppliers' bargaining power relative to the firm: if a large number of alternative suppliers exist and the firm is mobile between them then, all other things being equal, the bargaining power of suppliers will be weak because the firm can threaten to take its business to another supplier. Once a firm has obtained its inputs it needs to ensure that it recognizes and eradicates X-inefficiency to the extent that this is possible.

7.2.2 Underlying influences on the behaviour of competitors

The first point to note here is that the firm must be careful to **identify** exactly **who its competitors are**. This will require it to define the **industry** it is operating in (see Section 7.3 for further guidance). It will also require the firm to analyse the **structure of this industry**:

> Industry structure refers to the number of firms in an industry and their relative size distribution.

The presence of a large number of firms in the industry will mean that the firm's competitors are likely to discount their prices heavily in an attempt to attract buyers to their own products. However, the influence of this **numbers effect** is not easy to predict if the number of firms is relatively small: for example, in an industry structure where only four firms compete with each other, and where there is an abundant number of customers who are evenly distributed between the firms, it might be possible for each firm to earn substantial profits without 'poaching' customers from rivals. In this scenario there is little to be gained by being aggressive towards rivals since this may only instigate a harmful price war

– this is known as the problem of **strategic interdependence** and we discuss it further in Section 7.4.5.

The size of a firm is not easy to quantify, but typically it refers to the firm's relative share of total industry output, which is often a function of its cost structure. Generally if firms in the industry are all the same size then no particular firm has an advantage over another. All other things being equal, it is pertinent to ask if competitors have any cost advantage over the firm. The existence of a competitor, or a number of competitors, with lower costs than the firm is capable of achieving puts the firm at a potential disadvantage, and vice versa. In principle, a low-cost competitor that produces an identical product to that produced by the firm can undercut the firm's price but, once again, the ambiguous small numbers effect caused by strategic interdependence may mean that this will not happen in practice.

7.2.3 Underlying influences on the behaviour of potential buyers

Buyers can be individual consumers, government agencies or other firms (Chapter 1). The influences on the behaviour of buyers were the subject of Chapter 4. In essence, an individual buyer's **willingness to pay** will be determined by their **perceived need** for the product which, in turn, will be influenced by a number of factors contingent upon the individual buyer's circumstances. If potential buyers genuinely want the firm's product they will actually buy the product only if, all other things being equal, the price does not exceed their own valuation of the product. From the perspective of the firm then, it is important to have some idea about: (a) the **number** of potential buyers in the market; and (b) the **distribution** of their respective valuations of the product. If the firm's asking price is higher than all potential buyers' respective valuations it will sell zero units of output. On the other hand, it will not be economic to supply the product to potential buyers whose valuation of the product lies below the firm's costs of supplying it.

Just because a potential buyer has placed a valuation on a product does not mean that they will actually *have* to pay the firm this amount. This depends on the bargaining power of buyers relative to the firm. The bargaining power of buyers is strengthened if a significant number of alternative firms exist which are capable of supplying an identical product (perfect substitute) or a near-identical product (a close substitute), and if buyers are **mobile** between these firms. The bargaining power of buyers is also strengthened if they are organized into a collective whole because, in general, we would expect a collective organization to be able to negotiate lower prices for each of its members than an individual buyer negotiating unilaterally would be able to achieve. Another point which might influence the bargaining power of buyers is the **frequency** with which they trade with the firm – in one-off trades the firm has an incentive to try to extract as high a payment as possible from buyers, but if there is the prospect of repeated trading the firm may be more willing to develop a relationship with buyers and offer preferential terms.

From the firm's perspective, a market is more attractive if buyers are **segregated** from each other in some way since this may give it scope to charge the different groups of buyers different prices for the same product: this is called **price discrimination** and we discuss it further in Section 7.4.4 below.

7.2.4 Underlying influences on the likelihood of new competitors emerging

If the firms in an industry are making high levels of profit this will make the industry attractive to **entrepreneurs** who are looking out for profitable opportunities (as discussed in Chapter 3). We are using the term 'entrepreneur' here in its broad sense, which means that potential competition might come from new start-ups and/or firms that are established in other industries whose entrepreneurial managers are looking for opportunities to **diversify**. From the perspective of incumbent firms, all other things being equal, if new firms enter the industry the result will be lower profits for everyone (because they will take a share of the market). The extent to which this **threat of entry** should be a concern to the firm when it sets its prices depends on: (a) the **number of entrepreneurial individuals/firms** that actually exist; and (b) **how easy it is for new competitors to enter the industry**. So, even if a significant number of potential competitors do exist (an assessment of this will require a judgement call by the firm), there is a chance that they may not pose a significant threat to the firm because **barriers to entry** may make it impossible (or at least very difficult) for them to enter the industry.

> Barriers to entry exist when potential competitors find there are obstacles which hinder their proposed entry into an otherwise attractive industry. Typical examples of barriers to entry include: incumbents owning all sources of essential raw materials; incumbents' patents; economies of scale providing incumbents with a cost advantage; and incumbents' past expenditures on advertising (which gives them a higher profile in the minds of buyers relative to newcomers). The important point to note about barriers to entry is that they protect *all* of the industry's incumbent firms from the threat posed by competition from outside of the industry.

7.2.5 Underlying influences on the behaviour of regulatory authorities

In most developed economies competition between firms takes place in an environment that is subject to scrutiny by government-sponsored regulatory agencies. The regulatory agencies primarily exist to ensure that firms do not take advantage of buyers by using 'unfair means'. In simple terms, this means that regulatory authorities exist to prevent firms from using any **market power** they may possess to charge a price for a product which is 'too high' relative to the costs of providing it. Market power arises when firms are able to act as if they were a **monopoly**, so prices that entail inflated profit margins are typically associated with industry structures that contain only a few firms because these present the greatest scope for firms to create monopoly-like structures in which they can manipulate prices. For example, in the UK the utility firms such as British Gas and the telephone operator BT operate under strict regulatory regimes which limit the prices they can charge for core services. Judging whether firms are charging prices that are 'too high' is far from easy, but firms would be well advised to keep the presence of vigilant regulatory authorities in mind when they decide on their price.

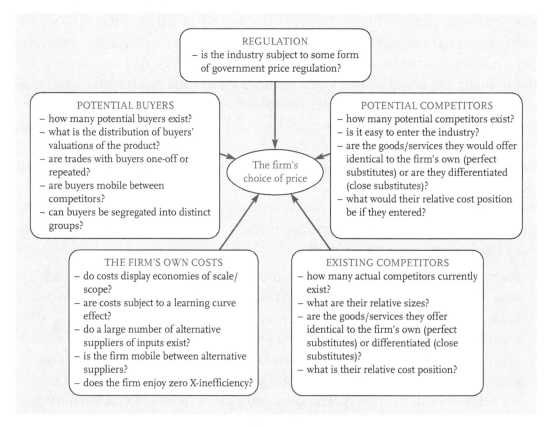

Figure 7.1 A general framework for thinking about the firm's pricing decision

Our discussion in this section is summarized in Figure 7.1, which shows a general framework for thinking about pricing decisions. In this framework we have identified a number of key questions the entrepreneur will need to answer in order to **infer** how each factor will behave. Having done this the entrepreneur will need to appreciate how the various factors identified in the general framework **interact** with each other. In cases where only a few firms occupy the industry this task is less than straightforward because the problem of strategic interdependence means that inferences drawn about each competitor's behaviour might well be incorrect.

7.3 How to define an industry for pricing purposes

Non-economists typically are very sloppy when they refer to an industry: in fact it is not uncommon to see them define an industry simply by grouping together all the producers who use similar materials and production technologies. The problem with this 'definition' for pricing purposes is that it ignores the demand side of the market. Here is a more accurate definition:

> The industry is the group of firms who supply a particular market.

So, for pricing purposes, defining an industry means first identifying and defining the boundaries of a market. This is rarely an exact science so it will call on your **judgement**. For example, consider the group of manufacturers who specialize in the production of steel cans for sale to food producers (note that this is an example of business-to-business trade). We might refer to the group of steel can manufacturers as the *steel can industry*, but this is probably not very helpful because aluminium cans offer food producers an alternative to steel cans. This means that we should include in our analysis the group of manufacturers who make aluminium cans and refer perhaps to the *food-canning industry*. There again, have we identified all possible alternative food storage options? Obviously not – what about cardboard food cartons (which are used to hold foodstuffs like milk and soup), and what about sealed plastic pouches? Perhaps it makes more sense to talk about the *food-packaging industry*?

A useful **rule of thumb** for identifying the industry a particular firm belongs to is to list carefully all of the suppliers of products who offer customers **solutions to their wants** that are **alternatives** to the firm's own solution **regardless of the materials and technologies used** in these alternatives. In other words, it is important to recognize that constraints on a firm's pricing decision can come from a broader group of competitors than may be immediately obvious. For example, if the producers of steel cans propose to increase their prices then their customers, the food producers, may switch to purchasing aluminium cans instead.

7.4 The basic elements of the mainstream analysis of the firm's pricing decision

The mainstream approach to the firm's pricing problem populates the general framework of Figure 7.1 with decision makers (i.e. entrepreneurs, input suppliers and buyers) who are **globally rational** and who have access to **full information and knowledge**. This means the pricing decision made by the entrepreneur is based upon perfect knowledge about the behaviour of the firm's own costs, competitors' and potential competitors' costs, the nature of competitors' and potential competitors' goods/services, and buyers (via knowledge of the demand curve for its product). In particular the mainstream approach focuses our attention on the effects that different types of **industry structure** have on the entrepreneur's choice of price. The usual assumption made in this analysis is that the firm is being run in order to achieve **maximum profits**.[1] As a result, mainstream models of pricing tell us how the decision *should* be carried out in specific industry structures if the firm wants to maximize profits. Finally, mainstream analysis of pricing focuses attention upon **equilibrium** industry structures.

We begin below by identifying two **extreme structural states** of the industry: **perfect competition** and **pure monopoly**. You should note that both of these states of the world are entirely **notional**. They do not exist in reality in the specific form described here. Their chief purpose in business economics is not to describe actual industry structures but to provide us with **reference points** against which we can compare actual industry structures that we see in the real world. In terms of the **number and size distribution of firms** that we observe in the real world, all industry structures lie somewhere in between these two polar cases.

7.4.1 Perfect competition

Perfect competition displays the following properties:

+ **The firm's costs**: the firm's short-run and long-run average costs are U-shaped; no learning curve effects are evident; there are a large number of potential input suppliers and the firm is mobile between them; the firm has zero X-inefficiency.

+ **Current competitors**: there are a very large number of current competitors; all competitors are the same size; each competitor sells a product that is a perfect

---

1   It is possible that the firm may be run to pursue a different goal such as sales volume maximization. If this is the case the same approach is adopted but the price chosen reflects this particular goal rather than profit maximization.

substitute for the firm's product (i.e. the firms in the industry all produce a **homogeneous** good/service); all competitors' cost positions are identical to the firm's cost position.

◆ **Potential buyers**: there are a very large number of potential buyers; the distribution of potential buyers' valuations of the product is represented by a downward sloping market demand curve; trades with actual buyers are treated as one-off events; buyers are mobile between firms; buyers are not segregated into distinct groups.

◆ **Potential competitors**: there are a large number of potential competitors; it is easy to enter and exit the industry; each potential competitor sells a product that is a perfect substitute for the firm's product; all potential competitors' cost positions would be identical to the firm's cost position if they entered.

◆ **Regulation**: the industry is not subject to any price regulation.

The combined effect of these properties is to take the pricing decision out of the hands of the firm. In other words, a firm that competes in a perfectly competitive industry has to be a **price-taker**.

> A price-taking firm is one that has no discretion over the price it charges for its product. Instead it must accept a price that is determined by the interplay of market forces.

The reason why a firm in a perfectly competitive industry is unable to influence the price it receives for its good/service is that the industry is made up of a large number of competitors who sell identical products. In other words, when we aggregate the outputs of all of the firms in the industry a particular firm will contribute a relatively insignificant share to the total. The flipside of this is that the firm can sell as many units as it chooses to produce as long as it charges the market price. This means that it faces a **perfectly elastic demand curve** for its output. If the firm attempted to charge a price higher than the market price it would not sell any output because the **highly mobile, fully informed consumers** would immediately take their custom to the multitude of rival firms. On the other hand, attempting to charge a price lower than the market price would simply not be rational given that it can sell as many units as it is able to produce without having to slash its asking price below the market level. The concept of the **price elasticity of demand** is explained in Box 7.1.

Box 7.1 Price elasticity of demand

The price elasticity of demand is a measure of the **degree of sensitivity** customers display towards changes in the price of a product. It is defined as the ratio of the proportionate change in quantity demanded to a given proportionate change in price. More formally:

$$\text{Price elasticity of demand (P.E.D.)} = \frac{\text{proportionate change in quantity demanded}}{\text{proportionate change in price}}$$

$$\text{P.E.D.} = \frac{\%\text{ change in } Q_d}{\%\text{ change in } P}$$

For example, if a firm faced a normal downward sloping demand curve for its product and a **reduction in price of 5 per cent** led to a **10 per cent increase in quantity of sales** then P.E.D. will be **10% ÷ −5% = −2**. Note here that the elasticity value is a negative number because price and quantity are inversely related for a normal demand curve. In other words, the elasticity value is a **function** of the negative gradient (slope) of the demand curve. But how should you interpret the P.E.D. value obtained here? The following rules apply:

If P.E.D. < −1 demand is said to be 'elastic'

If −1 < P.E.D. < 0 demand is said to be 'inelastic'

If P.E.D. = −1 demand is said to be 'unit elastic'

- If demand is **elastic** this means that a 1 per cent increase (decrease) in price will cause a fall (rise) in quantity of sales greater than 1 per cent.

- If demand is **inelastic** this means that a 1 per cent increase (decrease) in price will cause a fall (rise) in quantity of sales less than 1 per cent.

- If demand is **unit elastic** this means that a 1 per cent increase (decrease) in price will cause a fall (rise) in quantity of sales equal to 1 per cent.

Knowledge of the P.E.D. can be useful for managers because it tells them how **total revenue** will change if they change the price of their product. In general, if demand is **elastic** a **reduction in price** will lead to an **increase in total revenue** because even though each unit of output is sold at a lower price the proportionately greater increase in the number of units sold outweighs the impact of the lower price per unit. However, if demand is **inelastic** the same **reduction in price** will lead to a **fall in total revenue** because the increase in the number of units sold is insufficient to outweigh the impact of the lower price per unit. We can show this in the following diagram where we compare two demand curves:

Box 7.1 (continued)

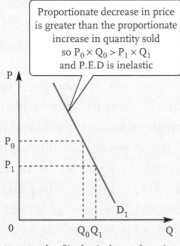

(1) example of inelastic demand – price reduction leads to a fall in TR

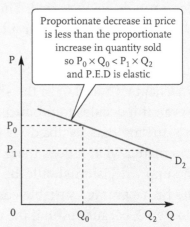

(2) example of elastic demand – price reduction leads to an increase in TR

The diagram shows you that demand curves with different slopes (drawn on the same scale) have different elasticities *within a particular price range*: D_1 is steep *compared* to D_2 so we can say that D_1 is **inelastic relative to D_2**.

Elasticity of demand will be affected by: (a) the price and availability of substitute products (e.g. margarine is a substitute for butter); (b) the price and availability of complements (e.g. software is a complement to computers); (c) whether the product is habit forming (e.g. cigarettes); (d) the proportion of income spent on the product (if expenditure is a major proportion of income the buyer is likely to be quite sensitive to price changes); (e) the time horizon with respect to substitution (e.g. demand for petrol is relatively inelastic in the short to medium term but in the long term alternative fuel technologies may become available and reduce its elasticity).

One final point: a **horizontal demand curve** is **infinitely (or perfectly) elastic**, which means that a price decrease would lead to an infinitely large increase in quantity demanded and a price increase would lead to zero sales. In contrast, a **vertical demand curve** is **perfectly** inelastic, which means that a price decrease will have no effect on the quantity of sales and neither will a price rise.

Exactly how many units a typical firm will decide to produce can be discovered by looking at the relationship between the prevailing market price and the firm's cost curves. Here we need to distinguish between the **short-run decision period** and the **long-run decision period**. The cost curves of a typical firm are shown in Figure 7.2 (these are smoothed or 'idealized' versions of the ones we first introduced in Chapter 6, Figure 6.1).

We will begin by looking at the firm's short-run supply decision. As you learned in Chapters 5 and 6, in the short run the firm is 'stuck' with its current plant, so even if it decides to produce zero units of output it will still incur fixed costs. This means that its fixed costs are **irrelevant** to its short-run decision because no matter what it does these will have to be paid. So the **first step** in its short-run supply decision should be to ask, 'Does the prevailing market price exceed the firm's average variable costs (AVC)?' If the answer is 'yes' it should proceed to step 2, because even if the price it receives is less than its average total costs (ATC), it will at least make a positive contribution to the overall costs of the firm. If the answer is 'no' then it should choose to produce nothing because to do otherwise would just sink the firm further into deficit. Assuming that the answer to this question is 'yes' the **second step** is to identify the level of output that will allow it to maximize profits (or, if the prevailing market price is less than ATC, the level of output that allows it to minimize losses). In order to do this for a particular price level it should ask a more general version of the question we first raised in Chapter 6, Section 6.2.1: 'Will production of one more unit of output add more to the firm's total revenues than it adds to its total costs?'

The addition to total revenue that results from producing and selling one more unit of output is called **marginal revenue (MR)**. In a perfectly competitive industry MR is identical to the price obtained from the sale of the additional unit. This is because each extra unit sold by the firm has to sell for exactly the same price as the previous unit, i.e. the market price. The addition to total costs is found from the **marginal cost curve (MC)**. So, if the answer to the question is 'yes' then the firm should produce the extra unit of output because it will increase its profits. Then it should ask the question once again. It should stop increasing output when the answer to the question is 'no'. The answer to the question will be 'no' at the point where **MR = MC**. To ensure that you understand why this is so, see Box 7.2 later in this chapter.

> As a general rule, the profit-maximizing level of output for a firm can be found at the point where MR = MC.

You can use the profit-maximizing rule to identify the individual firm's short-run supply curve by identifying the firm's profit-maximizing output responses at different prevailing market prices. If you do this you will find that you have traced out the portion of the firm's MC curve that lies above its AVC curve (portion *xz* in Figure 7.2).

The supply decision in the long run is different from the short-run decision because all of the factors of production are variable in quantity and, as a result, the entrepreneur is not 'stuck' with the firm's plant – it can be sold. In the long run the **first step** is to ask, 'Does the prevailing market price exceed the firm's average total costs (ATC)?' If the answer is 'no' then the firm should **exit the industry** because the entrepreneur does not expect the market price to cover *all* of the firm's costs (that is, fixed costs *and* variable costs). If the answer is 'yes' the firm's supply curve is the portion of its MC curve labelled *yz* in Figure 7.2.

It should be clear to you now that the output decision of the firm is dependent upon the market price. In turn market price is dependent upon the interaction of the **market supply curve** and the **market demand curve**. A normal market demand curve slopes downwards from left to right, reflecting the inverse relationship between quantity demanded by customers and the price of the product. In contrast, the market supply curve typically slopes upwards from left to right, indicating that the industry is prepared to supply larger quantities of output at higher prices. The market supply curve is found by adding together the quantities that the individual firms in the industry are prepared to supply at different price levels. Figure 7.3 illustrates a market supply curve for an industry made up of 100 identical firms (note that the individual firms' supply curves are added horizontally).

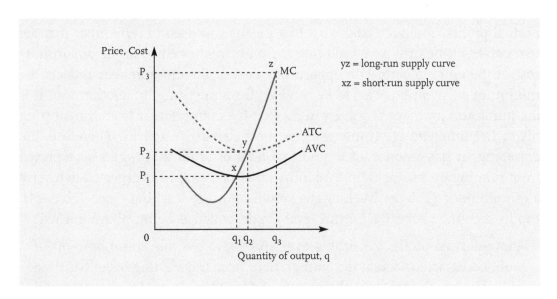

Figure 7.2 The firm's supply decision under perfect competition

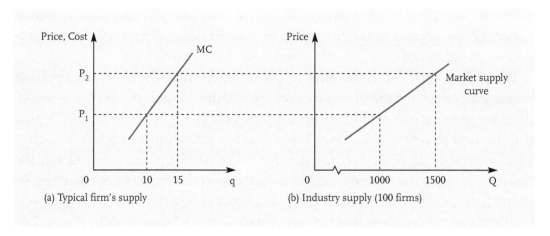

Figure 7.3 The market supply curve is the summation of individual firms' supply decisions

For a given set of market supply and market demand curves we can show the **short-run equilibrium output** of a typical firm. This is illustrated in Figure 7.4, which shows the typical firm choosing an output, q_0, that maximizes its profits given the current market price, P_0, which has been determined by the interaction of market supply, S_0, and market demand, D_0. The important point to note here is that all of the firms in the industry are making healthy profits indicated by the shaded area. (Recall that profit, π, is equal to TR – TC. For our typical firm TR = $P_0 \times q_0$ = the area of the rectangle, $0P_0bq_0$. TC = $C_0 \times q_0$ = the area of the rectangle, $0C_0aq_0$. If we subtract one rectangle from the other we are left with the shaded area, C_0P_0ba.)

The profits being earned by the typical firm in Figure 7.4 are called **above-normal profits**. To understand what this means you need to remember that the cost curves of the firm have built into them an amount equal to the **opportunity cost** of the entrepreneur. The opportunity cost of the entrepreneur reflects the minimum payment expected to be received from the firm. Put another way, it is the minimum payment necessary to prevent the entrepreneur from transferring his or her time and effort into the next best alternative activity. Therefore, the entrepreneur has a notion of the **normal level of profit** that would be expected from running the business (in Samantha Pinewood's case she expected to receive a minimum of £150 per week or she would return to teaching – see Table 6.1). Profits over and above this normal level are described as being 'above normal'.

Above-normal profits are profits over and above the minimum amount of profit necessary to prevent the entrepreneur from transferring his or her time and effort into the next best alternative activity. Other names for above-normal profits are: 'abnormal profits', 'economic profits' and 'supernormal profits'.

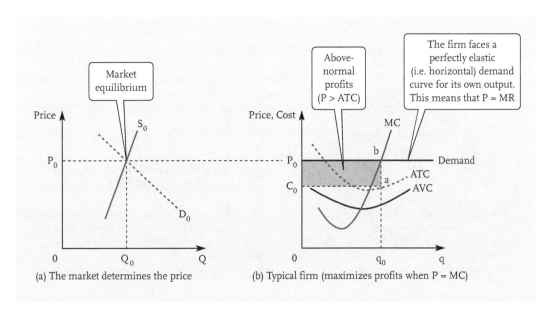

Figure 7.4 Short-run equilibrium under perfect competition

At this point you might be thinking that, despite the fact that the firm has to be a price-taker, the perfectly competitive industry is quite attractive: after all, from the entrepreneur's perspective, what could be better than healthy above-normal profits? Unfortunately for the entrepreneur, this state of affairs is not going to last. This is because the perfectly competitive industry is **easy for potential competitors to enter** and, in addition, there are a large number of **potential competitors** who are able to take advantage of this fact. Furthermore, they can compete with the incumbent firms on equal terms because they have identical cost positions.

Figure 7.5 shows the long-run equilibrium of the typical firm in a perfectly competitive environment. In this situation the typical firm is no longer earning above-normal profits because potential competitors have entered having been attracted into the industry by the large profits that the original (incumbent) firms were enjoying. The effect of their entry, however, is to add their own individual supply curves to the original market supply curve, which causes it to shift rightwards. In turn, this induces a **new equilibrium** market price that is lower than the level you saw in Figure 7.4. As a result the (horizontal) individual demand curve of the typical firm falls. Once the market price is equal to the minimum ATC of the typical firm, entry into the industry ceases. This is because the initial inducement to enter (the above-normal profits) has been competed away as a result of the entry of the newly created firms. The long-run equilibrium therefore looks quite different from the short-run equilibrium and the typical firm earns just sufficient to provide the entrepreneur with **normal profits only**.

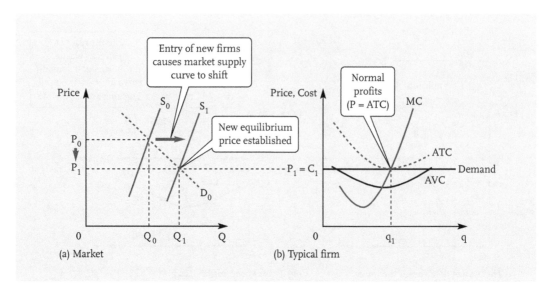

Figure 7.5 Long-run equilibrium under perfect competition

We can use this framework to ask what happens if the industry experiences an increase in market demand (i.e. if the market demand curve shifts rightwards). The short-run response will be an increase in the market price. This will lead to above-normal profits for all firms but, once again, this will induce further entry in the long run and depress the market price back down to the level where the typical firm will earn normal profits only.

We can also use this framework to analyse what equilibrium would look like if the industry was made of two groups of firms: one group with high costs, the other with low costs. In this case, the long-run equilibrium will look exactly like the one depicted in Figure 7.5, but the high-cost firms will have exited the industry in response to the downwards pressure put on price by the entry of more efficient firms.

Box 7.2 **How to choose the price-output combination that maximizes profits**

Assume that the firm faces a fixed market price of £6. Given the following cost and revenue data what level of output should it produce in order to maximize its profits? (MR is the addition to total revenue from the sale of one extra unit of output so, in this example, every extra unit sold will yield a constant MR of £6 because the price is fixed.)

You can see from the table that the maximum profit this firm can earn is £7. It can earn this by producing either four or five units of output. Note that

Box 7.2 (continued)

Output Q	Total revenue TR	Total cost TC	Marginal revenue MR	Marginal cost MC	Profit (TR − TC)
1	6	5			−1
			6	3	
2	12	8			4
			6	4	
3	18	12			6
			6	5	
4	24	17			7
			6	6	
5	30	23			7
			6	7	
6	36	30			6
			6	8	
7	42	38			4
			6	9	
8	48	47			1

the output at which this maximum profit is earned coincides with the equality between marginal revenue (MR) and marginal cost (MC). This will be true for any firm. Why is this true?

It is because at levels of output less than four units increasing output by one extra unit adds more to total revenue than it adds to total cost, so it must be adding a positive amount to profit. However, once the firm produces four units, if it expands output by one more unit it will fail to add anything to total profits. So we can identify a general rule for guiding the firm's decision of whether or not to expand its output:

If MR > MC the firm should *expand* its output up to the point at which MR = MC.

We can approach the problem from the other side too. Imagine the firm is producing eight units of output. At this level of output the firm will earn just £1. It would be better off if it reduced its output. If it cut back to seven units profit would increase to £4, but you can see from the table that it could do better still by cutting output back even further. This gives rise to another general rule:

If MR < MC the firm should *reduce* its output down to the point at which MR = MC.

In summary: in a perfectly competitive industry the powerful forces of competition will work to ensure that no firm has control over its price and that it cannot earn above-normal profits for long. In fact, all firms in the industry will also be operating at peak efficiency. This is indicated by the fact that each surviving firm is producing an output that ensures they are at the minimum point on their long-run average total cost curve. At this point P = MR = MC = ATC. Given the fact that the upshot of perfect competition is a minimum amount of profit, firms in the real world go to great lengths to try to gain a greater degree of control over the price of their goods/services. How do they achieve this? One clue is provided by the model of pure monopoly.

7.4.2 Pure monopoly

Pure monopoly is defined as an industry in which only one firm serves the market. In other words, the pure monopoly firm *is* the industry. It displays the following properties:

- **The firm's costs**: the firm's short-run and long-run average costs are U-shaped; no learning curve effects are evident; there are a large number of potential input suppliers and the firm is mobile between them; the firm has zero X-inefficiency.

- **Current competitors**: there are no current competitors.

- **Potential buyers**: there are a very large number of potential buyers; the distribution of potential buyers' valuations of the product is represented by a downward sloping market demand curve; trades with actual buyers are treated as one-off events; buyers are not segregated into distinct groups.

- **Potential competitors**: there are a large number of potential competitors; it is impossible to enter the industry; each potential competitor sells a product that is a perfect substitute for the firm's product; all potential competitors' cost positions would be identical to the firm's cost position if they could enter.

- **Regulation**: the industry is not subject to any price regulation.

The combined effect of these properties is to grant the pure monopoly firm discretion over the price it charges for its product **subject to its customers' willingness to pay**. In other words, a firm that finds itself in a pure monopoly position will be a **price-maker**.

> A price-making firm is one that has discretion over the price it charges for its product. However, you should note that because it faces a downward sloping demand curve for its product, it can only charge higher prices by selling fewer units of output.

A pure monopoly that wishes to maximize profits will arrive at its price by following the usual MR = MC rule that we introduced in Box 7.2. However, because the firm now faces a downward sloping demand curve marginal revenue and price are not identical (as they were under perfect competition). This means that the firm will charge a price, P_m, that is in excess of MR as depicted in Figure 7.6. To make sure you understand why the marginal revenue curve looks like it does in this figure, take a look at Box 7.3.

In Figure 7.6 you can see that the firm is earning **above-normal profits** indicated by the shaded area $P_m$baC. As you saw in the perfectly competitive model above-normal profits are a great attraction to entrepreneurs, so we might expect entry into the industry to erode these profits in the long run. In a pure monopoly, however, the firm is protected from competition from new competitors by the presence of **barriers to entry**.

Because of the presence of barriers to entry the short-run and long-run equilibrium outcomes of pure monopoly are identical. As you might imagine, real world entrepreneurs seek to create pure monopoly positions by erecting barriers to entry or by attempting to be the first to locate their businesses in industries where naturally occurring barriers to entry exist, because this gives them a degree of discretion over the price of their good/service.

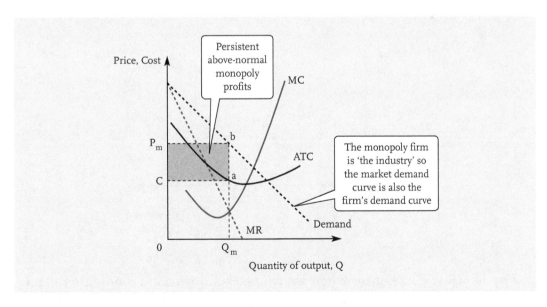

Figure 7.6 Equilibrium under pure monopoly

Box 7.3 Marginal revenue and the downward sloping demand curve

If the firm faces a downward sloping demand curve then marginal revenue, MR, will be less than the price (or average revenue, AR). To see this, consider the following simple data set:

Output Q	Price P	Total revenue TR	Average revenue AR (=TR ÷ Q)	Marginal revenue MR*
1	10	10	10	
				8
2	9	18	9	
				6
3	8	24	8	
				4
4	7	28	7	
				2
5	6	30	6	
				0
6	5	30	5	
				-2
7	4	28	4	
				-4
8	3	24	3	

(* MR is defined as 'the *addition* to total revenue from selling one extra unit of output'.)

If we plot the demand curve and the MR curve we obtain the following graph:

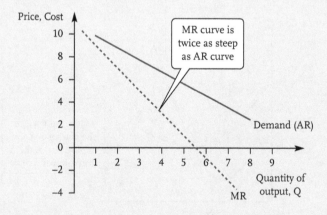

Why is MR < P? Because when a firm faces a downward sloping demand curve higher quantities of output can only be sold if the price of *every unit* is

> ### Box 7.3 (continued)
>
> lowered. Consider a firm which is trying to work out what happens to its revenue if it produces four units rather than three. At three units of output *every unit* would sell at a price of £8. At four units of output *every unit* would sell at a price of £7. This *price effect* of an increase in output is not present if the firm faces a horizontal demand curve (in other words under perfect competition). Because of this price effect the contribution to total revenue of each extra unit sold will be less than the previous unit. For example, to sell three units the firm will charge £8 per unit and total revenue will amount to 3 × £8 = £24. To sell four units the firm will charge £7 per unit and total revenue will amount to 4 × £7 = £28. So, while the fourth unit has sold for a price of £7 its contribution to TR is just £28 − £24 = £4.

We now turn our attention towards models of pricing behaviour in which one or more of the factors in the general framework are altered in some important way. As we have stated, pure monopoly and perfect competition do not exist in the strict forms they are presented above, but they are useful as a basis for understanding more complex pricing problems and practices.

7.4.3 Imperfect competition

The model of an imperfectly competitive industry differs from perfect competition only in that the firms in the industry no longer produce identical products. It is assumed that these **differentiated products** are **close substitutes**. The implication of this modification to the perfectly competitive model is that the firm will face a downward sloping demand curve for its *own* product as opposed to a horizontal demand curve. As a result the firm will now be a **price-maker** subject to the willingness of potential buyers to pay for the bundle of characteristics its product offers them. Imperfect competition is therefore a model of industry structure that shows each one of the many firms that exist in the industry attempting to become more like a monopoly but actually occupying an environment that has much in common with perfect competition. This means that no individual firm has a significant influence on the average industry price.

If you take a walk around your local city centre's shops you will see some good examples of imperfect competition because many retail stores operate in an imperfectly competitive setting. Take clothes shops for example: even the smallest city has a relatively large number of clothes shops and each one differentiates its offerings from rivals by stocking clothes of different styles and from different brand-name manufacturers. Another good example of imperfect competition is the restaurant industry. In any city you will find a multitude of restaurants and each will offer a different menu and ambience to the next. Another example is professional services such as lawyers and accountants. None of these industries is particularly difficult to enter, but typically firms will return quite low profit margins and you will often see quite a high turnover of firms (retail premises vacated by a failed business venture rarely stay empty for long).

The formal model of a firm operating in an imperfectly competitive environment is shown in Figure 7.7 where we have depicted the short-run equilibrium and the long-run equilibrium. One important point to note here is that the costs of a firm in imperfect competition are higher than its perfectly competitive counterpart. This is because product differentiation tends always to be supported by **advertising**, which is designed to reinforce the notion that the firm is offering a unique good or service. Given that consumers are perfectly informed in the world of mainstream economics, the only reason that advertising is undertaken is to **persuade** consumers to buy the firm's offerings rather than to inform them objectively about the features of their goods or services. Advertising is therefore a crucial weapon for firms in their attempts to create **brand loyalty** in consumers. In other words, while firms are trying to create mini-monopoly positions for themselves, they are well aware of the powerful forces of competition, in particular the power of the mobile consumer, so they try to protect themselves by attempting to convince consumers to be less mobile. For this reason we often see a spectrum of different prices persisting in imperfectly competitive industries.

Figure 7.7(a) shows that in the short run the typical competitor in imperfect competition will follow the usual profit-maximizing rule (MR = MC) and produce quantity of output q_{mc} which it sells at a price of P_{mc}. This leads to short-run profits indicated by the shaded area $CabP_{mc}$. These above-normal profits attract new entrants into the industry. Each new entrant sells a product that is differentiated in some (minor) way from the products currently on offer to consumers and, as a result, the typical firm loses some of its customers to these new entrants and its demand curve shifts leftwards. The long-run equilibrium position shown in Figure 7.7(b) shows the firm earning normal profits only. Furthermore, the other effect of entry is to make the firm cut its output back so that it operates with **excess capacity**. This means that firms in the industry will not be operating at the minimum point of their respective long-run average cost curves because the industry as a whole has over-invested in productive capacity relative to the level of long-run demand potential.

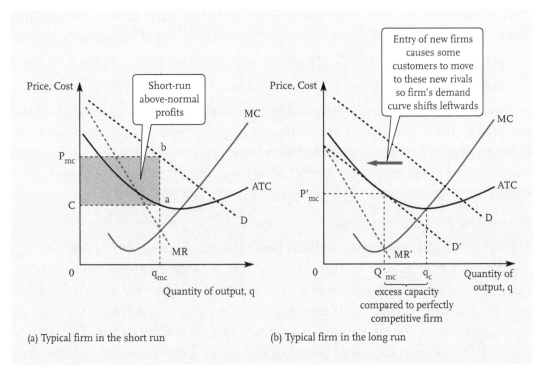

Figure 7.7 Short-run and long-run equilibrium of a typical firm in an imperfectly competitive industry

The basic model shown in Figure 7.7 assumes that the imperfectly competitive industry is easy to enter, but in cases where **strong brand loyalty** (engendered by advertising) exists this may not be true. This is because buyers may have strong preferences for the goods or services of the established firms.

7.4.4 Price discrimination

If a firm sells to buyers who are segregated it might be able to charge different buyers different prices for the same product. The attraction of this for the firm is that it should be able to make higher profits than if it charged every buyer a single uniform price. In order to price discriminate the firm needs to be a price-maker, so it is usual to use the model of pure monopoly to demonstrate how it *should* be done. In terms of the general framework, everything is the same as under pure monopoly except now customers are segregated. In the real world, other factors in the general framework may be different too: for example, the firm might well face competition but, nonetheless, this complicating factor does not prevent many real world firms from practising price discrimination because often they will be selling differentiated products which closely match buyer preferences.

There are three types of price discrimination, but in order to see how each one works it is first important for you to understand the concept of **consumer's surplus**:

> Consumer's surplus is the difference between the amount that a buyer would be willing to pay for a good/service and the price they actually do pay.

A downward sloping market demand curve indicates that as the price of a good or service falls, more buyers are willing to buy the good or service because the lower price brings those consumers who have a relatively low willingness to pay into the market. Buyers in the market whose willingness to pay is over and above the actual price they are asked to pay enjoy consumer's surplus.

First-degree price discrimination

Here the firm charges each individual buyer the maximum amount they are willing to pay for each unit of the product. This is what happens when you are obliged to haggle over the price of a used car, or when you visit a Turkish bazaar and have to agree a price with the seller of a fine rug. In each case the seller is trying to discover the maximum price you would be willing to pay. This type of price discrimination is time-consuming and costly from the seller's perspective, but if each person is charged the maximum amount they are willing to pay the firm will extract all the surplus from consumers. This is illustrated in Figure 7.8 where you can see that the monopolist produces quantity of output 0Q*, which exceeds the quantity it would produce under a single uniform price. Note how the demand curve is also the marginal revenue curve in this case.

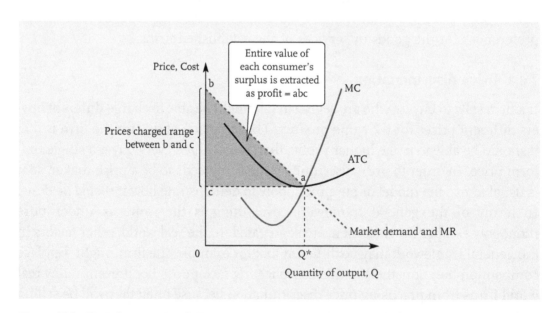

Figure 7.8 First-degree price discrimination under monopoly

Second-degree price discrimination

Here the firm attempts to extract as much of a consumer's surplus as possible by exploiting the notion that an individual buyer's demand curve will typically slope downwards, reflecting a reduction in willingness to pay for successive units of the good or service in question. In order to encourage a buyer to purchase a greater number of units than they would under a single uniform price the firm can adopt a **block pricing** policy. This principle is illustrated in Figure 7.9. Here the firm carries out the usual profit-maximizing calculation (MR = MC), charges a price of £12 per unit and the buyer demands eight units. This is where the story would end if the firm were only able to charge the consumer a single price. However, in this scenario, the firm is able to sell more units to this buyer by reducing the price of the next block of units. In order to find out the profit-maximizing price of the next block, the firm identifies the **residual demand curve**, yz (see Box 7.4), and sets its associated marginal revenue, MR', equal to MC to identify the fact that the buyer will buy four extra units if each of these units is priced at £8.

Box 7.4 Residual demand

Residual demand is the name given to the portion of the market that remains unserved at the current price level. It is represented by the portion of the market demand curve that lies to the right of the current price-output combination. It arises because at a given price level some consumers will be unwilling to purchase the industry's product unless the price is reduced.

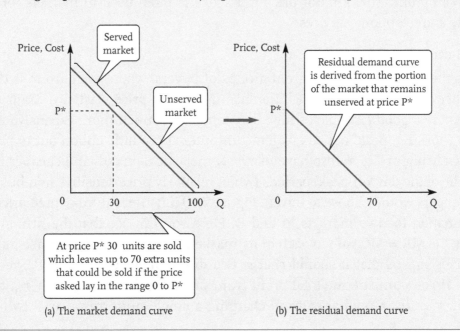

(a) The market demand curve   (b) The residual demand curve

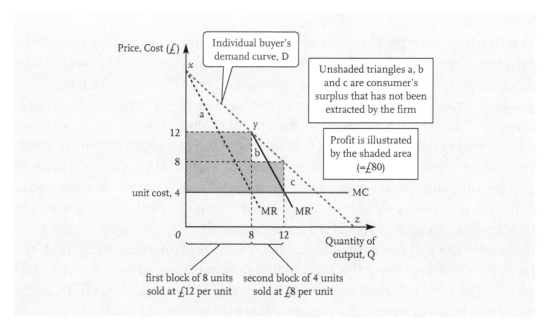

Figure 7.9 Second-degree price discrimination

By adopting the block pricing policy the firm's profits are boosted above that which is possible if each unit were sold at a single uniform price. For example, if the firm asked a single price of £12 per unit the buyer would demand a total quantity of eight units and the firm's profits would be just £64 instead of £80. Likewise, if the firm chose a single price of £8 it would sell 12 units and make just £48 profit. This kind of pricing practice is often used in markets for electricity and telephone services.

Third-degree price discrimination

Here the firm identifies different groups of buyers, where each group is distinguished from the other by a difference in **relative price elasticity**. Train ticket prices are a good example of this: they tend to be much more expensive in the early morning 'peak' periods (when commuters have little option but to pay the relatively high price and so have relatively inelastic demand) and cheaper in the middle of the day 'off-peak' periods (when relatively price-sensitive non-business passengers would choose to travel). Figure 7.10 illustrates third-degree price discrimination for two markets, A and B. Here you can see that the firm should **apply the MR = MC rule in each of its markets** if it wishes to maximize its profits. This means that it should charge **two different prices**, P_A and P_B, respectively. If you compare the total profit from price discriminating, $\pi_A + \pi_B$, to the profit, π_{SP}, that would arise from charging a single uniform price, P (which is

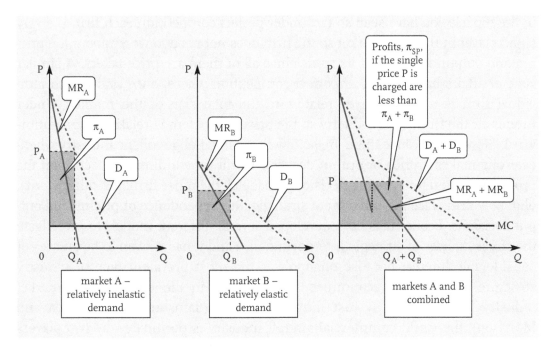

Figure 7.10 Third-degree price discrimination

arrived at by adding together the demand and marginal revenue functions from each market and using the MR = MC rule on the combined functions that result), you will find that this single price generates lower overall profits.

In order successfully to practise each of the different types of price discrimination discussed in this section the firm must ensure that buyers who pay a relatively low price for the product are unable to sell it to buyers who pay a relatively high price. If this kind of **arbitrage** can occur then price discrimination will be unsuccessful. Typically buyers are prevented from engaging in arbitrage by **time** (a person with a low-priced off-peak rail ticket can not re-sell it to a person who wishes to travel at peak time), **geographical location** (a motorist who has bought 200 litres of low-priced petrol in the USA can not sell it to a motorist in the UK where petrol costs more than four times as much) or by the **nature of the product** (typically this applies to services such as doctors and dentists – even if your friend is charged a lower price for her fillings than you are she will be unable to sell them to you!).

7.4.5 Pricing under strategic interdependence

In this section we look at the firm's pricing decision in an environment where the firm faces just a handful of rivals. This type of industry is called an **oligopoly** and in terms of the pricing problem it involves a dimension that has not been present in the models you have seen so far: under perfect competition each firm is a very small player in the total market so the firm does not need to worry about the pricing and output decisions of its rivals since all of them are price-takers. A similar state of affairs holds under imperfect competition where, once again, each individual firm is a small player relative to the total size of the market. Under monopoly the firm *is* the industry so the pricing problem is relatively straightforward. However, because there are so few firms in an oligopolistic industry whenever one makes a price or output decision it will have a direct impact upon the profits (and therefore pricing decisions) made by the other firms. In other words, oligopoly firms face the problem of **strategic interdependence of pricing and output decisions**. Economists have developed several different models to investigate the consequences of strategic interdependence and it has proven to be an area of considerable interest because oligopoly is the most prevalent type of industry structure in developed economies. For example, in the UK the supermarket industry is dominated by just four big players (Sainsbury, Tesco, Asda and Morrison), the world commercial aircraft industry is dominated by two players (Boeing and Airbus), while the world cola market is also dominated by two players (Coca-Cola and Pepsi). Similar stories can be told of the car industry, the computer industry and many more industries that generate billions of dollars' worth of trade both in and between the economies of the world. Arguably, even small convenience stores are members of geographically localized oligopolies.

In this section we will examine three specific models of oligopoly: the Cournot model – named after the French economist Antoine Augustin Cournot (1801–1877); the Bertrand model – named after the French economist Joseph Bertrand (1822–1900); and Chamberlin's 'small numbers' model of monopolistic competition – named after the American economist Edward Chamberlin (1899–1967). In terms of the general framework of Figure 7.1, all of these models share common basic features but differ with respect to some specific details. The problem for an oligopoly firm is to **anticipate how its rivals will react** to its own price-output decision so that it can formulate its own price-output decision in the first place! This means that inferring the behaviour of competitors from answering the questions posed in the general framework is an exercise in choice under uncertainty. To keep things as simple as possible we will specify a 'base model' in which we will assume that all firms are identical in terms of their cost structures. The 'base model' of oligopoly is defined as follows:

♦ **The firm's costs**: the firm's short-run and long-run average costs are U-shaped; no learning curve effects are evident; there are a large number of potential input suppliers and the firm is mobile between them; the firm has zero X-inefficiency.

- **Current competitors**: there are a small number of competitors; all competitors are the same size; each competitor sells a product that is a substitute *to some degree* for the firm's product; all competitors' cost positions are identical to the firm's cost position.

- **Potential buyers**: there are a very large number of potential buyers; trades with actual buyers are treated as one-off events; buyers are mobile between firms; buyers are not segregated into distinct groups (but this factor can be incorporated into oligopoly models).

- **Potential competitors**: there are a large number of potential competitors; it is not easy to enter and exit the industry; each potential competitor sells a product that is a substitute *to some degree* for the firm's product; all potential competitors' cost positions would be identical to the firm's cost position if they entered.

- **Regulation**: the industry is not subject to any price regulation.

The Cournot model of oligopoly

To keep the analysis as simple as possible we will focus attention on a special case of oligopoly called **duopoly**, which is an industry structure where just two firms serve the market, and we will assume that each firm produces a homogeneous product. The analysis focuses on identifying the optimal output necessary to generate a profit-maximizing price.

Cournot set up his analysis of the problem as a series of period-by-period (i.e. sequential) profit-maximizing calculations in which each firm in each period copes with the uncertainty about its rival's output choice by **assuming** that the rival will produce a quantity of output in the current period that is identical to the output it produced in the previous period. This assumption is called the '**Cournot conjecture**'. Cournot told a story where one firm sets up monopoly production in the first period but is joined in the industry in the second period by a rival. In subsequent periods barriers to entry come into effect (although there is no explanation how) and the two rivals follow a path of adjustment to each other before arriving at an equilibrium level of industry output. The series of diagrams shown in Figure 7.11 depicts the adjustment process that the rivals go through. To keep the analysis simple, we have assumed that each firm has constant marginal costs.

In period 1 the first firm to enter the industry maximizes profits by following the familiar profit-maximizing rule (MR = MC) and producing 30 units of output which it sells for £70 per unit. In period 2 the second firm enters the industry and calculates its own profit-maximizing level of output based upon the conjecture that the first firm will produce the same output in this period as it did

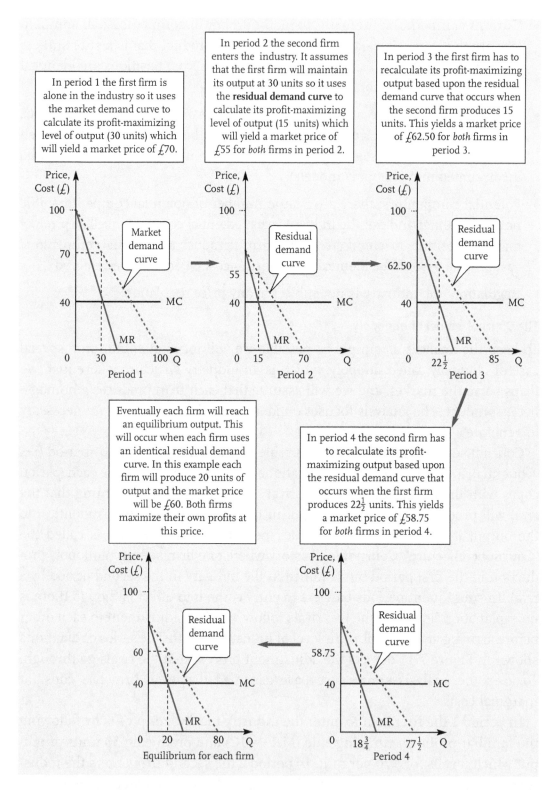

Figure 7.11 Steps towards equilibrium in the Cournot model of duopoly

in period 1. This means using the residual demand curve to identify the residual marginal revenue, which it sets equal to its marginal costs. As you can see, in period 2 the second firm's actions lead it to produce 15 units of output which is added to the first firm's output of 30 units to give a market price of £55 for both firms.

At a market price of £55 the second firm will maximize profits but the first firm will not. This is because the first firm's profit-maximizing output calculation was based upon selling 30 units at a price of £70 per unit. As a result of this mismatch between its output and the market price the first firm will recalculate its profit-maximizing output in the third period. To do this, it will assume that the second firm will maintain its output at 15 units, which will allow it to identify the residual demand curve and its associated marginal revenue from which it can discover its profit-maximizing output (MR = MC) is $22\frac{1}{2}$ units. Total industry output in period 3 will be $37\frac{1}{2}$ units, which gives a market price of £62.50. At this price the first firm will indeed maximize its profits but, because it has reduced its output, it will throw the second firm's profit-maximizing calculations into disarray. This is because the second firm's profit-maximizing output calculation was based upon the assumption that it could sell its 15 units at a price of £55 per unit.

In the fourth period the second firm will recalculate its profit-maximizing level of output based upon the assumption that the first firm will maintain its output at $22\frac{1}{2}$ units. As before it will use the relevant residual demand curve to make its calculations and produce $18\frac{3}{4}$ units of output, which when added to the first firm's output of $22\frac{1}{2}$ units produces a market price of £58.75. Once again this will throw the first firm's calculations out of line and it will react by identifying the new residual demand curve and recalculating its profit-maximizing level of output. This process will continue until an equilibrium outcome is obtained. This is found when both firms find an output level at which their expectations about their rival's output decision are true. This can only occur at a market price that allows both of them to maximize their profits simultaneously. In the example here, this will occur when both firms produce 20 units of output and the market price is £60.

If you look back at the example you will notice that the entry of the second firm into the industry in period 2 causes the market price to fall, which in turn leads the first firm to cut its production back as it attempts to bring market price up again. The response from the second firm is to increase its output further, which brings market price back down again. In response to this the first firm will once again reduce its output and market price will increase. The crucial point to notice about these adjustments in output and market price is that they become smaller with each passing period as both firms **converge** upon the **final equilibrium output**; one from 'above' (the first firm) and one from 'below' (the second firm).

In Figure 7.12 we compare the duopoly equilibrium output and price combination under Cournot competition (P_d = £60 at a total industry output of 40 units) to the pure monopoly outcome (P_m = £70 at an industry output of 30 units) and the perfectly competitive outcome (P_c = £40 at an industry output of 60 units). You will notice that the duopoly outcome lies between the outcomes of the two reference industries. Because the duopoly price exceeds unit costs, **each firm will earn above-normal profits** of £400 (i.e. industry total profit is £800). Remember, however, that like pure monopoly this outcome relies upon the presence of persistent and effective barriers to entry. Furthermore, if the number of firms in the oligopoly industry is greater than two then the outcome of Cournot competition will be a lower price than the one shown in the diagram.

If you think carefully about the situation depicted in Figure 7.12 you might begin to wonder why each firm in the Cournot model goes to all the trouble of **competing** with the other when they could surely agree to **co-operate** with each other instead and act *as if* they were a monopoly – a situation which is called **collusive oligopoly**. If they did co-operate they would increase their profits to £450 each (assuming they split the market equally between them). In order to understand this issue in greater detail economists use **game theory**.

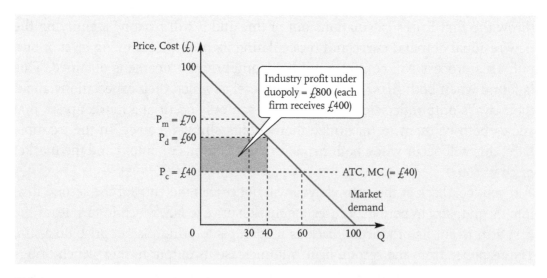

Figure 7.12 A comparison of equilibrium outcomes under Cournot duopoly, pure monopoly and perfect competition

Game theory is a branch of mathematics that is designed to help us understand the nature of the decision problem facing independent rational actors
when outcomes are interdependent.

The game-theoretic presentation of the choice problem for each firm is represented in the matrix shown in Figure 7.13. We will focus on firm 1's problem
(but you should note that firm 2 faces exactly the same problem). The matrix
shows you that the firm must make a choice between one of two output decisions: on the one hand it could produce the equilibrium Cournot level of output,
Q = 20, while on the other hand it could produce its half share of the equilibrium monopoly level of output, Q = 15. The profit it will receive as a result of
making either choice depends upon the choice that firm 2 will make. If firm 1
chooses Q = 20 and so does firm 2 the matrix tells us that each firm will receive
£400 profit. If firm 1 chooses Q = 15 and so does firm 2 the matrix tells us that
each firm will receive £450 profit. The matrix also tells us how much profit each
firm will earn if one chooses Q = 15 and the other chooses Q = 20; here the firm
that chooses the low output will make a profit of £375 while the firm with the
high output will make a profit of £500. (These figures are calculated from the
fact that if a total output of 35 units is put on the market the resulting price will
be £65 – you can work this out from the demand curve shown in Figure 7.12.)
So, what choice should firm 1 make?

We will assume that both firms are fully aware of the payoff structure depicted in the matrix. Firm 1 will realize that co-operating is better than competing
with firm 2 because when each firm produces 15 units each makes £450 profit,
which is better than the £400 profit each would make if they competed. But, at
the same time, firm 1 will realize that if firm 2 actually does produce 15 units it
can make a higher profit for itself by producing 20 units (£500 is better than
£450). In other words, if firm 1 enters a collusive agreement with firm 2 to

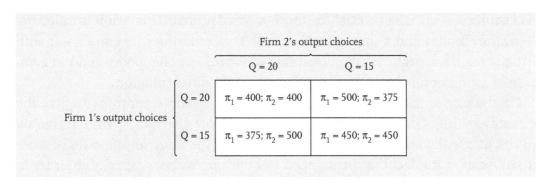

Figure 7.13 The oligopoly problem formulated as a 'game'

produce the co-operative level of output it has an **incentive to cheat** on the agreement and produce the competitive level of output! Furthermore, firm 1's incentive to cheat is reinforced by the fact that firm 2 also has the same incentive to cheat on the agreement. If one of the firms stuck to the agreement and the other cheated on it then the one that stuck would gain a profit of just £375, which is a much worse outcome than it could earn from competing in the first place (£400). This problem is an example of a famous game called the **Prisoner's Dilemma**. On the assumption that the other firm cannot be trusted to carry out its part of a collusive agreement a rational player will always produce the competitive level of output since this will **guarantee** it makes a minimum profit of £400 regardless of what the other firm does.

The Bertrand model of duopoly

In the simplest version of Bertrand's model of duopoly the two firms produce a homogeneous product, but unlike in the Cournot model each firm has to choose its price rather than its output. Each firm announces its chosen price to the market and then produces a quantity of output that is sufficient to satisfy the quantity demanded at this price. Consumers buy the product from the firm with the lowest price. This means that in each period of trading the firm that quotes the lowest price takes all of the buyers for that period. In the subsequent period the firm that quoted the higher price last period will now undercut its rival and take all of the buyers. This undercutting will only stop when both firms are asking a price that is equal to unit cost. For example, if both firms have identical and constant marginal costs of £40 and the first firm asks a price of £70 then the second firm has an incentive to ask a price of £69, which in turn means that the first firm has an incentive to ask £68, and so on and so forth. This process of alternate undercutting leads to an equilibrium where both firms ask a price of £40 and earn normal profits only. Compared to the Cournot model, this result seems to be counter-intuitive because it is unlikely that mutually interdependent firms will compete away the potential for above-normal profits. This result is called the **Bertrand Paradox** and it illustrates the dangers of entering into a **price war** with equally matched rivals. It also illustrates why firms in oligopolies tend to compete by using **non-price** methods such as product differentiation.

On the face of it, the Bertrand model seems to be more appropriate than the quantity-setting Cournot model because we know that real world firms set prices. It actually turns out that the Cournot model is more appropriate because it emphasizes the fact that firms need to build production capacity in order to give them something to sell! As you have seen in Chapter 5, once plant size has been chosen the firm faces a constraint on its output caused by diminishing returns. The Bertrand model ignores this constraint because it assumes that the firm is able to meet any quantity of demand that its chosen price generates. As a result it may be better to think of the price-output decision that faces a firm as a **two-stage decision**: in stage 1 the entrepreneur has to decide how much capacity to build and in stage 2 he or she has to calculate the profit-maximizing price to charge given the capacity decision made at stage 1. In other words, stage 1 is a Cournot decision (an equilibrium output decision) while stage 2 is a Bertrand decision (an equilibrium price decision). Economists have investigated this problem and found that a two-stage approach gives the same price and output results as the Cournot approach.

Chamberlin's 'small numbers' theory of monopolistic competition

Chamberlin published his *Theory of Monopolistic Competition* in 1933 in an attempt to offer economic theory a more general analysis of price competition than the theory of perfect competition with its reliance upon the MR = MC rule. In this theory he examined the pricing problem of the firm under a number of situations. In particular, he distinguished between a situation where the firm faces a large number of rivals (which is very similar to the theory of imperfect competition we looked at in Section 7.4.3) and a situation where the firm faces a small number of rivals (i.e. oligopoly) with each firm producing a differentiated product. In a review of his theory in 1957, Chamberlin stated: 'In the real world the most common case is certainly "differentiated oligopoly", or small numbers *plus* a differentiated product' (Chamberlin, 1957: 33).

Although we are including Chamberlin's theory of oligopoly pricing here, you should be aware that it departs from the other mainstream approaches we have looked at because it does not make use of the MR = MC rule. Instead Chamberlin's theory emphasizes that finding a suitable price for the firm's product might well involve **experimenting** in the market. The theory is based upon the notion that buyers evaluate a differentiated product along two main dimensions: (1) its **price** and (2) the extent to which the **characteristics** of the product match the buyer's list of 'ideal' characteristics. It is assumed that buyers who are confronted with choosing between two differentiated products that have identical prices will buy the one that has characteristics that most closely match their list of ideal characteristics. It is also assumed, however, that buyers are prepared to trade off price against characteristics, which implies that a price reduction in the less-preferred product may induce buyers to switch their custom to this product. In terms of the mass market, if there are say 10 000 potential buyers and their tastes are evenly distributed then ten firms producing appropriately differentiated products will sell $10\,000/10 = 1000$ units each at a given asking price. If all firms cut their asking prices in unison then each firm could expect to sell more units, but if one firm cut its price unilaterally it might expect to increase its share of the market by stealing buyers from its rivals. In essence this means that a firm faces two demand curves, as illustrated in Figure 7.14.

Chamberlin's oligopoly analysis makes use of the idea that buyers will switch between differentiated products in response to a unilateral price decrease. The story is illustrated in the series of diagrams shown in Figure 7.15. The diagrams make use of a 'representative' firm so it is assumed that the cost positions of all firms (both incumbents and potential competitors) are identical and that each firm produces a differentiated product. Beginning at step one, the representative firm is making above-normal profit, so this induces other firms to enter the industry up to the point where above-normal profits are eradicated: in other words, the firm's demand curve shifts leftwards from D to D'. The firm may be tempted now to try to restore its profits to pre-entry levels by encouraging a significant number of buyers to switch from its rivals' products to its own by cutting its asking price from 0M to a price such as 0K (step two). If rivals do not match the price cut the firm will find itself on demand curve d' at point F and it will enjoy above-normal profits once more. Unfortunately for the firm this situation is unlikely to persist, because rivals will want to reacquire the buyers they have lost and they will cut their respective prices also. This means that the firm

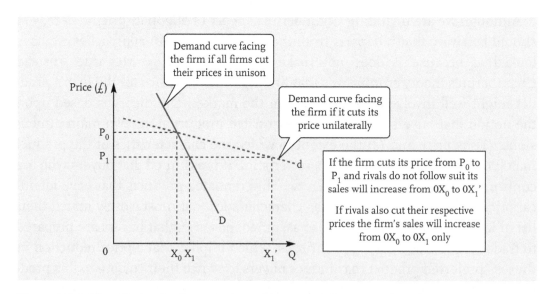

Figure 7.14 The effects of unilateral price cutting with differentiated products

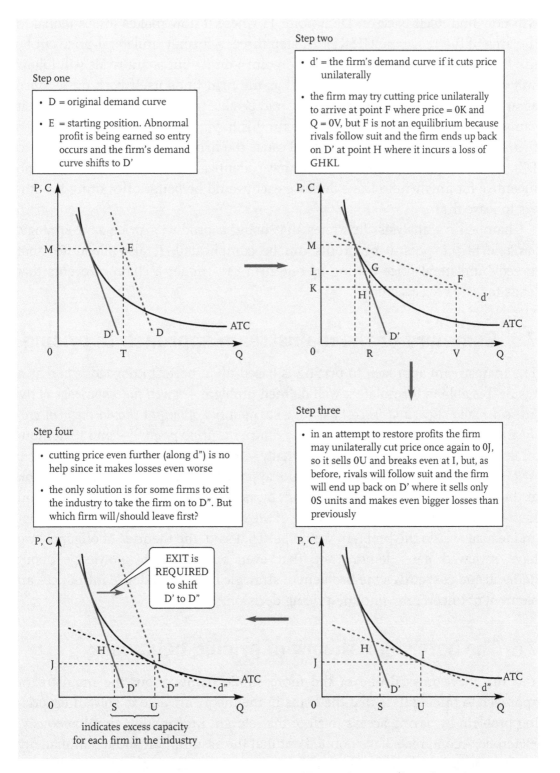

Figure 7.15 Chamberlin's analysis of the pricing problem in the case of 'small numbers' monopolistic competition (oligopoly)

will now find itself back on D' at point H where it now makes losses (equal to the area of the rectangle GHKL). In step three, a further unilateral price cut by the firm to say 0J may take the firm to point I on d'' but again rivals will follow suit and even bigger losses will result as the firm finds itself back on D' once again. Step four shows that the firm would be able to break even at point I but it cannot take any unilateral action to attain this happy state of affairs unless other firms leave the industry (which would cause the firm's demand curve to shift to D''). In an industry where all firms have identical cost positions there is no incentive for any firm to leave because each would be better off waiting for others to leave first.

Chamberlin's analysis illustrates that using a product's price as a strategic variable in the pursuit of profits can be complicated. It also illustrates that 'greedy' unilateral price cutting by one firm can trigger a chain of events that leads to losses for everyone.

7.5 Summary of the mainstream approach to pricing

The mainstream approach to pricing is based upon perfect knowledge and as a result it is able to formulate a **well-defined problem** – *'given full knowledge of the firm's demand curve and its cost curves, what quantity of output should the firm produce in order to yield a price that will maximize the firm's profits?'* – and to demonstrate how this problem is **solved optimally** – *'produce the quantity of output where MR = MC'*. One of the strengths of this approach is that it provides a first look at the problem of choosing a price and, by assuming away the information and knowledge problems that are a feature of the real world, helps us to identify what an ideal answer to the problem would be. That said, the theories of oligopoly we have reviewed here demonstrate that even with perfect knowledge about demand and cost curves the problem of strategic interdependence introduces an element of uncertainty into the pricing decision.

7.6 The heterodox theory of pricing behaviour

You may have missed one of the more subtle points about the mainstream approach to pricing. It is that the firms in the theory are able to solve their pricing problem by having access to all of the relevant information **simultaneously**. Heterodox economists have pointed out that the assumption about simultaneity of demand and cost information does not reflect accurately the situation in which many real world firms find themselves. In the real world, many firms have to make production **plans in advance** of receiving any definitive answers to the questions posed in the general framework of Figure 7.1. For example, as you have seen in Chapter 6, identification of the firm's own costs can be quite complex, so it seems unlikely that competitors' costs will be known with any degree of accuracy at the time when important decisions have to be made about price. Also, information about customers is often based on conjecture rather than fact, so price decisions have to be made without reliable knowledge about the quantity of demand for the firm's product at various price levels. If you think of many of the products that are purchased in developed economies (such as cars, electrical products, computers, bus and rail fares, toll roads, books, Swedish flat-pack furniture, etc.) you will realize that each of these products is **priced in advance** of any customers purchasing them. Furthermore, the prices of these products are in many cases widely advertised and in some cases published in printed catalogues which remain valid for long periods of time (for example, in the UK the retail stores Ikea and Argos produce annual catalogues in which the prices of their products remain fixed for 12 months).

These problems of information and knowledge mean that firms are highly unlikely to have sufficient data to plot reliable marginal revenue and marginal cost curves. In fact, in surveys by economists, many managers have responded that they made no reference to marginal revenue and marginal cost calculations when they decided on the price of their products. How then can firms choose the 'right' price?

For heterodox economists the answer is that firms follow a simple rule of thumb approach called **mark-up pricing**. Several studies of actual business practice with regard to price setting have been carried out over the years and all of them lend empirical support to the idea that in the real world the majority of businesses use some variant of mark-up pricing. The basic idea behind mark-up pricing is a simple one: the seller of a product decides upon a planned or **target margin** of profit **on each unit** sold and proceeds to charge a price which it believes will lead to this outcome. In practice the application of the approach requires the firm to estimate the likely level of demand for its product: this is for the simple reason that the unit costs of production (be they AVC, AFC or ATC) onto which the required margin will be added depend upon the quantity of the product produced. As you can see, without the luxury of simultaneous access to cost and demand information the entrepreneur faces **uncertainty** with respect to important variables that are necessary to carry out the pricing calculation. As a result, he or she is forced into making an educated guess when deciding how much productive capacity to create.

After observing and exploring the behaviour of many businesses (from the late 1940s onwards) the Oxford economist Philip Andrews developed a theory of business behaviour based upon mark-up pricing which offers some useful practical insights into the problems faced by real world decision makers. A striking feature of Andrews's analysis is that it does not make use of demand curves.

Andrews called his approach 'normal cost' analysis. This is because it is based upon unit cost figures that arise from the firm's plan to produce a level of output that the firm considers to be 'normal'. Figure 7.16 illustrates the fundamental features of Andrews's mark-up approach. Here you can see that the firm sets a **sales target**, 0S*, which is equal to the planned normal level of output. The price it decides to charge, 0P, is based upon adding a mark-up to AVC.

Andrews's empirical work led him to believe that the cost curves of the firm sloped downwards in most cases before levelling off and that prudent business managers operated their firms with some **excess capacity** on hand to meet **unforeseen** increases in sales. There is no guarantee that the planned sales target, 0S*, will be met, but if it is then the **planned profit margin** will be the difference between ATC and the price, P. There is also no guarantee that the excess capacity will be utilized, but in an uncertain world it is prudent to have it available.

The important point to note about this analysis is that the **price is fixed regardless of the level of sales (and output)** that the firm actually manages to achieve. This means that the actual or realized profit margin may differ significantly from the one the firm has planned for. For example, consider the case of a firm that estimates AVC = £10 and which employs a simple mark-up rule that price is found by doubling AVC (so the mark-up in Figure 7.16 is £10 and price = £20). If the firm's *achieved sales* are indeed 0S* then, if AFC = £5 at this level of output, the firm's

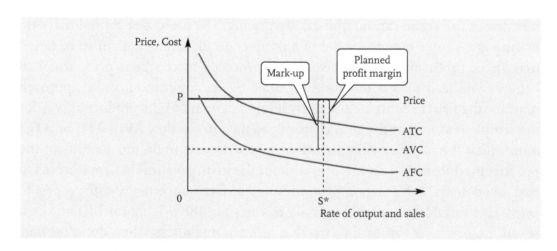

Figure 7.16 Mark-up pricing in Andrews's normal cost analysis

planned *and* realized profit margin will coincide (at 33 per cent on costs, i.e. £5 per unit). However, if realized sales do not reach 0S* and, consequently, AFC = £6 then the firm's realized profit margin will not coincide with its plans (being lower than planned at 25 per cent on costs, i.e. £4 per unit). This approach contrasts sharply with mainstream analysis where, on the one hand, failure to sell sufficient quantities of output results in immediate price reductions and, on the other hand, excess demand leads to immediate price increases to ration this demand. Instead of continually adjusting prices, in Andrews's analysis there is a **key role for marketing and sales efforts** in the firm's attempts to make actual events and its plans coincide.[2] On the one hand, failure to sell sufficient quantities leads to increased effort to meet the sales targets, while on the other hand, in periods of unexpectedly high demand, the firm uses its excess capacity to provide its new customers with its product while continuing to supply its existing customers. It is important to note that if the firm did not have this excess capacity to hand it would face the **dilemma** of whether to meet orders placed by its established customers while ignoring new customers or, alternatively, whether to keep established customers waiting to have their orders fulfilled while it diverted its current output to its new customers. Neither option is attractive because each one leads to disgruntled customers and this, in turn, might cause them to look elsewhere for alternative suppliers who can meet their needs promptly. **Firms with an eye on growth do not ruin their future prospects by turning customers away.** Therefore, the firm's excess capacity is not a waste of resources but is instead a prudent business strategy that helps the firm to generate and maintain **goodwill** and its **reputation** among both established and new customers. This, in turn, helps to further perpetuate future sales growth (see further, Section 9.6).

The question that you should be asking at this point is, 'How does the firm decide what size their profit margin should be?' Several answers have been proposed by heterodox economists, and common to most of them is the notion that the firm's target profit margin should be **fair** to rivals and customers alike. Also, a wise firm will probably not set prices that encourage **new competitors** to enter the industry (for Andrews the threat of entry by **diversifying** firms who are established in other markets/industries was an important consideration). Quite what being 'fair' to rivals means depends upon the particular context within which the firm finds itself but there does seem to be a general consensus that firms try to avoid harmful price competition (to the extent that this behaviour is possible) and prefer instead to pursue apparently non-price strategies such as **product differentiation** and **innovation**.

---

2 Note how there is no obvious role for marketing and sales in the mainstream theory of pricing (cf. our discussion in Chapter 1).

Ultimately, the decision on the size of the margin the firm will aim for requires a **judgement** call on the part of the entrepreneur which must be informed by an understanding of the firm's particular **situation and context**. The size of an established margin will not necessarily be maintained if the firm's costs change, because the firm may well wish to maintain a particular price for long-term strategic reasons. On the other hand, it may not be immediately reactive to changes in demand for the firm's product either. In other words, unlike in the mainstream story of price determination, **prices in the heterodox approach do not respond** *automatically* **to changes in costs and demand**. Instead prices are viewed as being less volatile than in the mainstream story and as having something of the status of an **institution**. This is because their stability helps to provide rivals and customers with a **degree of certainty** in a complex and highly uncertain world. This, in turn, helps all parties to make plans for the future. For example, consider the problem if the entrepreneur's firm operates in an industry which is occupied by several rivals who produce close substitutes for its own product, but where each firm uses a different method of production and possibly different inputs. In this case if the entrepreneur's firm experiences a cost reduction for some reason (say a fall in the price of one or more of its inputs) but its rivals do not, it is not immediately obvious that the entrepreneur should cut the price of the firm's product. This is because such an action may kick off a **price war** and lead to volatility in the industry in the long term, which would of course exacerbate further the inherent uncertainty felt by all competitors and the industry's customers.

When setting prices the wise entrepreneur will try to understand the **psychology** of the consumer. Heterodox economists have suggested that making pricing decisions based on an assumption that consumers' preferences are adequately thought of as if they were described by normal demand curves may not be very wise. This is because of consumers' beliefs about what is considered to be **fair** and **unfair** behaviour by firms. For example, consider your own response to the following question (which was posed by psychologist Daniel Kahneman, one of the 2002 Nobel laureates, and heterodox economists Jack Knetsch and Richard Thaler, 1986: 319):

> *A hardware store has been selling snow shovels for $15. The morning after a large snowstorm, the store raises the price to $20. Please rate this action as:*
>
>
>
> *Completely Fair*   *Acceptable*
> *Unfair*   *Very Unfair.*
>
>

Kahneman et al. asked this question of a group of 107 people and found that 82 per cent of respondents thought that the hardware store was acting unfairly.

Yet mainstream economics tells us that, by taking advantage of the short-run increase in demand caused by the snowstorm, the (fictitious) storeowner is acting rationally. This is because an increase in demand (a rightward shift of the demand curve) *should* be met by a corresponding increase in the asking price of snow shovels. However, from the perspective of the majority of respondents in this experiment the previously established price of the shovels acted as an **anchor** for their expectations of price against which any new price would be judged. The evidence provided by Kahneman and his colleagues suggests that if managers adopt the rational advice of mainstream economics (which may make sense in the immediate term) they may run the risk of damaging the long-term **goodwill** and **reputation** of their businesses.

7.7 Summary

In this chapter we have examined the key factors that entrepreneurs need to take into account when choosing the price of a good or service. We have summarized these in the framework shown in Figure 7.1. You can use this framework to analyse many different pricing scenarios.

We have explored a variety of mainstream models of pricing, designed to apply to different market contexts. The usefulness of the mainstream approach to the pricing problem arises because it illustrates the volume of information that a firm would need to obtain and process in order to choose a **profit-maximizing price** for its product. If it could obtain this information the pricing decision is reduced to a simple algorithm: the optimal price is found at the output where MR = MC but the problem of strategic interdependence in oligopoly industries will complicate matters.

In the real world problems of information and knowledge mean that the MR = MC rule is unlikely to be used by most firms. This is despite the fact that many real world firms have developed sophisticated data gathering processes (particularly with respect to accounting information and marketing surveys). Of course these data *are* useful, but they do not overcome the fundamental problem that they are **historical** in nature while the pricing decision has to be made with reference to the **future**. The future state of the business environment for most real world firms is not easily predicted. Consequently, in the heterodox approach, firms use **mark-up pricing**. The essence of mark-up pricing is to decide what kind of profit margin the firm aspires to and then set about devoting resources to trying to ensure that the

7.7 Summary (continued)

state of the world in which this margin will actually happen is made a reality (to the extent that this is possible). This means keeping a tight control on costs so as to avoid or eradicate X-inefficiency and also being proactive in terms of sales promotion to ensure demand is cultivated and maintained or even grown. Given the uncertainty about the future the wise firm will hold some excess capacity to meet unanticipated booms in sales and to ensure that any positive reputation it might have earned remains intact.

7.8 Some questions to consider

1. On 9 December 2003 Britain's first toll motorway ('turnpike') was opened. The new 27-mile long 'M6 Toll' was built in order to relieve chronic traffic congestion on the stretch of the original M6 motorway which passes through North Birmingham. The original M6 motorway is free to use, but it was originally built to take 72 000 cars a day and now takes about 180 000. The new toll motorway cost £900 million to build and its owners, 'Midlands Expressway', have set peak-use prices at £2 per car, £5 per van and £10 per lorry for the first 10 million users (off-peak prices are lower). Thereafter prices are scheduled to increase. The Transport Secretary Alistair Darling said: 'The M6 Toll gives motorists an important new choice when travelling through Birmingham. They can pay a toll and have a faster journey.' The managers of Midlands Expressway believe that the new road will save drivers an average of 45 minutes per journey. One lorry driver was quoted as saying: 'As a car driver, I would use the M6 Toll. As a lorry driver, not a chance. It's just overpriced.'

   Can you use the general framework of Figure 7.1 to assess whether the owners of the M6 Toll have set the 'right' price?

2. Can you identify any situations in which you think the mainstream approach to pricing might actually be possible?

3. Can you think of any real world industries which are very close to perfect competition and any that are very close to pure monopoly?

7.8 **Some questions to consider** (continued)

4. Make a list of some of the shops you see in your local town/city centre. Which ones are monopolistic competitors and which are oligopolistic competitors?

5. In this chapter we have examined the pricing problem which faces a firm that produces a single product. What complicating factors do you think would enter into the pricing decision of a multi-product firm?

6. Look at the major supermarkets in your local area. Write down a list of the major features of each one (location, range of goods sold, prices of certain goods, frequency of price changes on certain items, etc.). Now try to identify how each one differentiates itself from its rivals.

7. What factors do you think might lead to the collusive outcome being sustainable in the Prisoner's Dilemma game?

7.9 Recommended additional reading sources

For an in-depth look at the evolution of economic models of pricing and a detailed discussion of mark-up pricing in general and Andrews's approach in particular, see Chapters 8 and 9 of Peter E. Earl (1995) *Microeconomics for Business and Marketing*, Aldershot, Edward Elgar.

Daniel Kahneman, Jack Knetsch and Richard Thaler (1986) 'Fairness as a constraint on profit-seeking: entitlements in the market', *American Economic Review*, **76**, pp. 728–41 (reprinted in D. Kahneman and A. Tversky (eds) (2000) *Choices, Values, and Frames*, Cambridge, Cambridge University Press, pp. 317–34). This paper is full of examples of departures from rational economic behaviour which have implications for the pricing decision.

For a non-technical introduction to game theory, see R. McCain (2004) *Game Theory: a Non-Technical Introduction to the Analysis of Strategy*, Mason, OH, Thomson Learning, South-Western. This text discusses the game-theoretic approach to the oligopoly problem in some detail along with other useful applications. The author's explanations are very clear indeed.

For a very clear overview of a number of issues in pricing, see Hugh Stretton (2000) 'How firms price their products', *Economics: a New Introduction*, London, Pluto Press, Chapter 34, pp. 418–29.

8

How can the firm earn persistent above-normal profits?

Learning outcomes

If you study this chapter carefully, it may help you to understand:

- the concept of firm resources
- the concept of firm capabilities
- the concept of routines
- the process of competition between firms
- the fundamental difference between monopoly rent and Ricardian rent
- the importance of entrepreneurial conjectures and experiments
- the stylized pattern of industry evolution.

To the extent that you develop such understanding, you should be better able to:

- advise managers how they might achieve persistent above-normal profits for their firms
- explain the relationship between resources, capabilities and routines
- explain how competition between firms can be seen as an example of evolutionary struggle
- draw connections between the mainstream and heterodox theories of the firm.

8.1 Introduction

The managers of most firms are not content simply to earn normal profits. This can be for any number of reasons, including:

- the desire to keep the firm's employees happy by offering them perks over and above what they would get if they transferred elsewhere;

- the desire to keep shareholders happy by paying bigger dividends;

- the need to generate surplus funds in order to carry out costly research into product improvements/the development of new products;

- the need to have a 'fighting fund' to enable the firm to lobby for its case with respect to government legislators.

In short, if a firm can generate surplus funds these can provide it with the resources it needs to explore future opportunities while maintaining its current line of business and while keeping its various stakeholders happy.

In this chapter we explore how the firm can earn above-normal profits on a persistent basis. If you followed the discussion in Chapter 7 you will realize that the mainstream models of pricing under different industry structures lead to the conclusion that the way to earn persistent above-normal profits is for incumbent firms to shelter behind **barriers to entry** in combination with a policy of **avoiding mutually harmful aggressive price-cutting policies**. On the face of it this is good advice, but it is incomplete in two respects:

(i) It presupposes that competition between firms is exclusively based on prices. Clearly, setting the 'right' price is important, but focusing on price competition alone may be misleading – competition has more than one dimension.

(ii) It only explains that *all* of the firms 'inside' the industry can earn higher profits by keeping other firms 'outside' the industry – it does not explain how *one* incumbent might be able to outperform another incumbent. In other words, it does not provide any clues about how one firm can gain a competitive advantage over another firm when both firms are already inside the industry. This means that the theory cannot easily explain the empirical fact that different firms which occupy the same industry often enjoy different levels of success (for example, in the financial year 1999–2000 the British supermarket chain Tesco reported a 10 per cent increase in pre-tax profits while one of its main rivals, Sainsbury, reported a 23.3 per cent decrease in pre-tax profits).[1]

---

1 Data sourced from company reports.

In this chapter we delve deeper into the ways in which a firm might achieve persistent above-normal profits by introducing the heterodox analysis of the firm. The heterodox analysis of the firm accepts that barriers to entry can be important, but it adds an extra dimension to our understanding of how a firm might achieve persistent above-normal profits based upon its own idiosyncratic resources and capabilities. It also introduces the idea that if we focus our attention exclusively on equilibrium pricing models we run the serious risk of ignoring the essentially dynamic nature of the competitive process that plays out between firms. Consequently, the heterodox theory of the firm is set in the context of an evolving industry.

8.2 The heterodox theory of the profit-seeking firm

In Chapter 5 we introduced you to the idea that a firm produces a good or service by **organizing** its productive **resources** (i.e. labour and capital) in such a way that the **services** provided by these resources (e.g. the work done by labour and capital) convert the firm's material inputs into outputs. What we did not do, however, was explore the implications for firms if they own or hire productive resources that differ in the **quality** of the services they provide. If different firms have access to productive resources that are not uniform in terms of the quality of the services they provide then we might expect to see firms differing from each other in terms of the costs they incur. To illustrate the implications of this point for a firm's profits, consider the following simplified (fictitious) example.

Entrepreneur Barney Marshall thinks that there is potentially a healthy market for ceramic busts of the England football captain David Beckham. He is not certain that this is the case, and he is not aware that anyone else has had a similar idea, but he is an entrepreneur with a high degree of self-belief so he sets up a facility to manufacture the busts. He rents capital equipment (e.g. kilns, workshop, etc.) that is commonly available on the market and can therefore be purchased or rented by anyone who wishes to set up a ceramics business. The total cost of capital equipment is £100 per week. In order to obtain appropriately skilled labour to use the capital equipment he visits his local art college and, after scrutinizing examples of the work of its students, he offers jobs to the five graduates whose sculpture work he considers to be the best. Each graduate is employed on wages of £100 per week. Finally Barney's own opportunity cost is £200 per week.

Unknown to Barney Marshall, a fellow entrepreneur called Kay Montgomery has had the same idea. Kay has set up a workshop facility identical to the one set up by Barney, but she has been less discerning about the quality of her labour force, which she has obtained by advertisement in the small ads of the local newspaper and without close scrutiny of any previous work. Like Barney she employs five people and pays each one £100 per week and her opportunity cost is also £200 per week.

Both Barney's firm and Kay's firm supply retail outlets at a price of £20 per bust. It turns out that there is a massive demand for the busts of Beckham (such is his popularity and celebrity status). It transpires that Barney's firm is able to produce 80 busts per week while Kay's firm is able to produce just 40 busts per week. This is because Barney's sculpture graduates are highly adept and work much more quickly than the rather ordinary sculptors who are employed by Kay. The impact of this difference in output is reflected in each firm's costs of production; for Barney the total cost, TC, of producing 80 Beckham busts per week is labour cost of £500 + capital cost of £100 per week + opportunity cost of £200 per week = £800. This means that **Barney's ATC = £800 ÷ 80 = £10**. In contrast, while **Kay's** total costs also amount to £800, her **ATC = £800 ÷ 40 = £20**. Given the selling price of £20 you can see that Barney's firm enjoys large profits of £10 per bust (£800 per week) while Kay's firm earns normal profits only. This situation is illustrated in Figure 8.1.

It should be clear to you that the **only difference** between Barney's firm and Kay's firm in this example is the **superior** quality of Barney's labour **resources** and it is this fact that has allowed his firm to earn above-normal profits. This is obviously a very nice position for Barney to find himself in, but he should not just sit back and let the good times roll. Instead, he should ask himself the question: 'Will my firm continue to earn above-normal profits as time passes?'

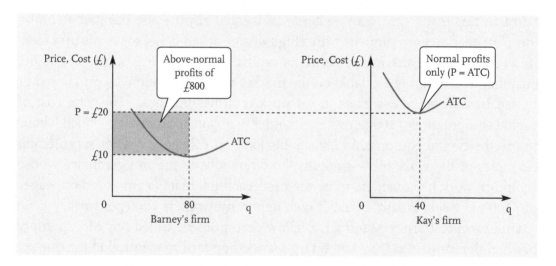

Figure 8.1 Comparing costs and profits between Barney's firm and Kay's firm

In order to find an answer to this overarching question, Barney needs to ask (and answer) two more specific questions:

(i) Can Kay, or any other entrepreneur who wants to enter the industry for Beckham busts, obtain labour resources which produce a service that is at least as good as the service provided by Barney's labour resources? In other words, **are substitute resources available?** If the answer is '**yes**' then Barney cannot expect his position to last for long. This is because other entrepreneurs will enter the market (attracted by the lure of high profits) and the price will fall in a manner similar to that shown in Figure 7.4 (the perfectly competitive industry). On the other hand, if the answer is '**no**' then it would mean that Barney's labour force is a **scarce resource**.

> A productive resource is scarce when it exists in a quantity that is insufficient for it to meet the entire demand for its services.

However, the fact that Barney is employing a scarce resource does not guarantee by itself that his firm will earn persistently high profits. Now Barney needs to consider the second question.

(ii) **Are the labour resources 'tied' to the firm in some way, or are they mobile?** If the labour resources are tied to the firm for some reason then Barney can feel quite good about things. This is because only he will be able to enjoy their stream of services. Alternatively, if the labour force is not tied to the firm then it may be tempted away from the firm by offers of higher pay, or the promise of better working conditions made by rival firms. If this is the case Barney may find himself having to pay higher wages to his scarce labour resources and, as a result, he will see his costs increase significantly. If this happens it may well mean that the scarce labour resources end up taking the lion's share of the profits that were previously accruing to the firm. In other words, the **productivity benefits** of employing the scarce labour resources are **negated** by the high wage demands that have to be met to keep the labour force working for the firm.

In short, Barney's firm's profits will only persist if the scarce labour resources upon which they are based (a) have no substitutes, (b) remain tied to the firm and (c) do not appropriate the profits for themselves in the form of higher wages. If the firm is going to earn above-normal profits then one or more of the resources it commands must be unique to the firm and also must be capable of providing it with an advantage over actual and potential rivals (in our example this means giving the firm lower costs). The firm in heterodox theory is therefore a **heterogeneous organization**. This approach to the firm is subtly different to the approach adopted in mainstream theory. As we have stated in Section 8.1 above, in the mainstream theory the only way to secure large and persistent profits is to locate the firm behind barriers to entry (alongside rivals) and ensure that the firm's choice of output quantity is not so large that it drives prices down to perfectly competitive levels: in other words, incumbents should try to make the industry behave as much like a pure monopoly as possible. In the heterodox case, the firm earns **above-normal profits** not because it is deliberately restricting output but because it has a **limited supply of the scarce resource** (notice how Barney's firm is operating at the minimum point of its ATC curve – i.e. it is operating efficiently). Above-normal profits which are based upon a limited supply of one or more scarce resources are given the special name '**Ricardian rent**' after the British economist David Ricardo (see Box 8.1).

Box 8.1 **Ricardian rent**

David Ricardo (1772–1823) was an early ('Classical') economist. His most famous work is contained in his book *Principles of Political Economy and Taxation* which was originally published in 1817. In this book Ricardo outlined a theory of the size of the rent which would accrue to owners of agricultural land. When Ricardo was writing, the British economy was mainly agrarian with tenant farmers working land that they rented from landowners (the gentry).

Ricardo's theory of rent begins with the observation that agricultural land differs in quality due to differences in its soil; some land has good soil and is therefore very fertile while other land is less fertile due to poorer soil quality. The relatively **fertile land** will be more **productive** and the associated **costs per unit** of output will be **lower**. Ricardo's theory of rent uses these observations to state that the rent which will accrue to the owner of a given parcel of land will be equal to the difference in productivity between this land and the poorest piece of land currently under cultivation for a given crop (e.g. corn). The theory assumes that all land is farmed using identical techniques.

Ricardo's theory is tied in with his analysis of population growth. It works as follows:

(i)   When the population of a country is relatively low only land of the highest quality will be used to produce corn to feed the people. Because this land is highly productive the **cost** per bushel of corn will be relatively **low** (i.e. ATC is low).

Box 8.1 (continued)

(ii) As the **population grows** (which was happening at quite a dramatic rate) there will be pressure on the high quality land to produce increased quantities of corn and this land will begin to suffer from **diminishing returns**. This means that land of a lower quality will be brought into cultivation. Because this lower quality land is less productive its costs (per bushel of corn) are higher than those incurred by the high quality land and, consequently, the **price** of corn to the final consumer will **increase** (think of this as a simple mark-up effect).

(iii) With the higher price of corn prevailing farmers working the low-cost high quality land will earn a **surplus** in excess of their costs, i.e. they will make above-normal profits (see diagram below).

(iv) Ricardo believed that the owners of the high quality land would realize that farmers were earning a surplus so they would **transfer** the farmers' surplus profits to themselves by **increasing the rent** the farmers had to pay to use their land. Given that high quality land was fixed in quantity and demand for corn had a tendency to grow the surplus profits generated by the land were a reward for its **scarcity** relative to the low quality land.

(v) You should note that a resource can only be scarce if there exists a level of demand in excess of the resource's ability to fully meet this demand.

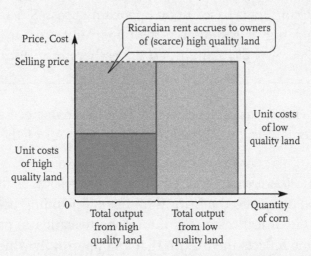

As you can see, in Ricardo's day the term 'rent' really did refer to the rent that farmers had to pay to landowners, but in modern economics it is a **general term** used to signify the surplus of revenues over true costs, i.e. above-normal profits. Rents can arise for two reasons. *Either:*

Box 8.1 (continued)

(i) the firm has a monopoly-like position and is protected by barriers to entry. This gives the firm scope to **deliberately restrict its output** even though it has sufficient quantities of resources to be able to supply a much greater number of customers than it actually chooses to supply.

Or,

(ii) the firm has a limited amount of the resources required to produce the product and as a result it is simply **unable** to meet the current level of demand. In this case firms with inferior resources (which means higher costs) supply the rest of the market.

Economists are keen to distinguish between these two different types of above-normal profits, so they reserve the special terms '**Ricardian rent**' or '**scarcity rent**' exclusively for surpluses generated by scarcity of essential productive resources. The alternative is called '**monopoly rent**'.

An example of Ricardian rent

If there is a shortage of bus drivers the wages offered by bus operators will increase to encourage new bus drivers to take up the job. If bus drivers' wages are £250 per week and taxi driver Joe, who earns £200 per week in his current job, becomes a bus driver his rent (surplus earnings) will be £50. As you can see, the concept is based upon **opportunity cost**. Since Joe's next best alternative occupation is taxi-driving the opportunity cost to Joe of being a bus driver is £200. Any payment over £200 is therefore a Ricardian rent.

Margaret Peteraf (1993) has categorized the requirements necessary for a firm to earn Ricardian rents into four broad '**cornerstones**'. All of these cornerstones must be in place:

- **Cornerstone 1:** *Heterogeneity* – at least one of the resources that the firm possesses must be unique to the firm. If all firms (including potential entrants) have access to identical resources then nobody stands to gain large profits from them. This reflects the maxim that **an opportunity which is available to everyone is unlikely to be profitable for anyone**. In our example it is not clear that Barney had exclusive access to the sculpture graduates from the art college, but it is notable that Kay's approach to recruitment was less successful. If Barney can keep the source of his skilled workforce a secret from Kay and other entrepreneurs he may be able to sustain his firm's heterogeneity (although it seems unlikely that Kay will be unable to 'discover' Barney's secret, so she may well visit the college herself in the near future and recruit her own highly skilled labour force).

- **Cornerstone 2: Ex ante *limits to competition*** – effectively this means that very few entrepreneurs should recognize that an opportunity to make profits potentially exists. In our example, if a multitude of entrepreneurs had recognized that there was a potential market for busts of David Beckham then competition between the start-up firms would lead to low prices and profits would be competed away. Note here that Barney Marshall was uncertain that a profitable opportunity existed but he acted upon his hunch. Uncertainty about whether a market for Beckham busts existed may have prevented other entrepreneurs who had the same idea from starting up a business. You can see from this that there is a very important role for **Schumpeterian entrepreneurs** in the heterodox theory. Kay Montgomery was the only other entrepreneur to act, but she failed to acquire a bundle of resources that could perform as well as the ones acquired by Barney Marshall.

- **Cornerstone 3: *Imperfect mobility of resources*** – this means that the resources which are responsible for the firm's profits cannot be traded for some reason and, as a result, they remain 'tied' to the firm. There are a number of reasons why resources may be tied to the firm. In our example the sculptors employed by Barney Marshall may feel that they should remain loyal to Barney's firm because he was the first person to give them the opportunity to use their skills in a commercial setting. Alternatively they may not feel any loyalty whatsoever and may be keen either to move to another firm or to use the offer of employment from another firm as a bargaining chip to boost their salary at Barney's firm. Another reason why resources may be tied to the firm is something called **asset cospecialization**. This is another way of saying that the firm's assets have a much higher value if they are used in conjunction with each other (e.g. as a production team) than they have as separate individuals. This may prevent Barney's skilled labour from leaving the firm. This is because all members of the labour force would have to agree to move *en masse*. In practical terms this could prove to be a very difficult thing for them to organize successfully (for example, it may only require one member of the team to disagree with a proposed move to unravel the plans of his or her co-workers).

- **Cornerstone 4: Ex post *limits to competition*** – this means that the firm's position as leader in the industry must be protected in some way from **imitation** by others. If rivals can obtain **substitute** resources that can equal or surpass the firm's productivity then its Ricardian rents will not persist. This is because we might expect to see numerous rivals come into existence as more and more entrepreneurs realize that this is a profitable industry to be in. Of course the very act of entry into the industry erodes the profit opportunities that made it attractive in the first place (this is one of the basic lessons of the theory of perfect competition). In our example, if the skilled sculptors obtained by Barney are the best in the land, and no alternative method for producing Beckham busts has been discovered, then it is unlikely that rivals will be able to imitate Barney's superior productivity.

While each of the cornerstones is distinct from the next it should be clear to you from our example that they are not independent of each other. For example, *ex ante* limits to competition imply that the firm formed by the entrepreneur will be heterogeneous, and imperfectly mobile resources help to ensure that this heterogeneity is maintained as long as *ex post* limits to competition (e.g. lack of availability of substitute resources) prevent rivals from imitating the successful firm.

As you will have gathered, our example is highly simplified in a number of details. In particular we have identified just a single scarce resource (skilled labour) and we have assumed that this is the only thing which sets Barney's firm apart from its rivals, but if you recall our discussion in Chapter 5 we introduced the idea that different entrepreneurs possess different abilities and different endowments of **knowledge** (see Figure 5.8). This implies that if two different entrepreneurs have **identical bundles of resources** at their disposal each may well arrive at a different outcome to the other. This is because of differences in the effectiveness with which the respective entrepreneurs **organize these resources** and **use the services** they provide. We can use this idea to develop a more fully specified model of the firm that takes into account its capabilities as well as its resources. The resulting **resources and capabilities perspective** will provide us with a more complete story about how to achieve large and persistent profits. Before we go any further it will be helpful to define the meaning of the two principal terms.

> A resource is an input to the production and selling process. Resources can be tangible (e.g. raw material inputs) or intangible (e.g. the firm's reputation), or they may have both a tangible and an intangible dimension (e.g. a unit of labour is both a tangible resource *and* it provides an intangible resource when it applies its skills for the firm's benefit). In the latter case the intangible resource is a characteristic or quality of the tangible resource.

> A capability is the aptitude a firm has to perform a co-ordinated set of tasks in order to achieve a desired outcome. Capabilities flow from and make use of

the firm's resources. Capabilities are a combinatorial phenomenon. For example, a highly skilled manager/administrator (i.e. one of the firm's managerial resources) may be able to organize labour, capital equipment and raw materials (i.e. yet more of the firm's resources) into a co-ordinated production process to give the firm a capability in the production of a particular output.

In order to produce goods and services firms need to have **both** resources and capabilities. In other words, resources and capabilities are **complementary assets**. Robinson Crusoe may have been a highly skilled survivalist but he would not have survived for long on his desert island if he had not had access to resources (such as a knife, water, wood, gulls' eggs and coconuts) to which he could apply his skills (to build shelter and provide the other basic necessities of life).

In terms of the different types of knowledge that we identified in Chapter 5, a **capability** is most closely associated with **know-how**; that is, the knowledge of how to do something with 'things' and ability to apply it. For an individual, such as Robinson Crusoe, this concept seems straightforward enough because we can recognize that know-how resides in his consciousness or brain and gives rise to the skills he possesses. However, a firm is not a sentient being like a person; a firm is an (often complex) organization and it has no recognizable consciousness or brain. So, what do we mean when we say that a firm has particular capabilities?

This issue has been analysed in detail by the American heterodox economists Richard Nelson and Sidney Winter in their path-breaking book *An Evolutionary Theory of Economic Change* which was first published in 1982. This book has since become a modern classic of economics and it is a key part of the bedrock upon which modern heterodox economics has been developed.

Nelson and Winter make sense of firm capabilities by recognizing that when we say an organization knows how to do something (i.e. has a capability) what we really mean is that the individuals who are members of the organization are organized so that their individual actions **interlock** with the actions of others to produce a **co-ordinated pattern of activity** in the organization. This gives the impression that the firm itself has a capability. For example, recall Samantha Pinewood's flat-pack business from Chapter 5: we can say that her firm, Tables 4U, has the capability to produce flat-packed coffee tables, but this capability really arises from the fact that Samantha has employed a skilled labour force and she has organized them in such a way that the actions of the individuals interlock to form a co-ordinated production team. **The firm's capabilities are therefore derived from the knowledge, experience and skills of the individual members of the organization.**

A notable feature of the flat-pack production capability possessed by Tables 4U (and indeed the capabilities possessed by many real world firms) is that it is **repeated** week in, week out. In other words, the individual members of the labour force repeat the tasks involved in flat-pack production and exercise their skills **in the same way** over and over again. Their responses are therefore pre-learned: in other words, they do not need to work out from scratch how to carry out their respective tasks every time they are faced with the same task. Nelson and Winter call these patterns of repeated interlocking activity **routines**.

> A routine is a pattern of co-ordinated behaviour within an organized group of individuals in which the group follows a pre-learned set of responses to problems/tasks they encounter.

The question you should be asking now is: 'How do routines come into existence?' In order to help us answer this question it is useful to build a model that incorporates key features of the real world. This means that the model is populated by boundedly rational individuals who face uncertainty about the actions and reactions of others, and uncertainty about the future. In this model, each individual begins with an endowment of knowledge and skill, but different individuals possess knowledge and skills which have relevance to different activities. For example, Ella Fitzgerald's endowment of knowledge and skills enabled her to build a career as a world-class singer of jazz, blues, bebop and swing, while Muhammad Ali's endowment enabled him to build a career as an extraordinary world heavyweight boxing champion.

As well as having knowledge and skills that have relevance to different activities, each person is also endowed with a different amount of knowledge and skill to the next person; so some people are simply better than others at executing a particular activity. For example, Madonna has nowhere near the vocal virtuosity that Ella Fitzgerald possessed, and George Foreman was never as skilled a boxer as Muhammad Ali. In short, in this model the world is a place that is occupied by heterogeneous individuals. It is against this background that the 'birth' of routines is best understood. To illustrate we will take another look at Tables 4U.

At the point where Samantha Pinewood decided to turn her dream of running a business into a reality she faced the problem of ignorance. In other words, she had to discover a number of things before she could get her flat-pack coffee table business up and running effectively. Among the things she needed to discover was how to organize her labour force into a co-ordinated working unit. In our original example we assumed that this was easily accomplished because

Samantha was able to call upon the services of an expert who told her the combinations of labour and capital to employ in order to achieve a specific level of output. In this model, by contrast, we have no reason to believe that the advice of experts is infallible. This is because so-called experts are equally as subject to uncertainty as everyone else. This means that their predictions about the outcomes that will actually occur if their advice is followed are at best a rough guide only. (Be wary of anyone who offers to predict the future – especially if they want money in return for performing the service!) In the absence of prior experience in flat-pack production, and because of the inherent uncertainty associated with the advice of experts, the only way to discover what works for the firm is to conduct **experiments** with different configurations of labour and capital.

An experiment is usually conducted with reference to some **desired outcome** so, as a **first step**, Samantha needs to decide what quantity of output is acceptable. This quantity of output is an example of something called an **aspiration level**. (This term is used by the behavioural economists Richard Cyert and James March in their seminal book *A Behavioral Theory of the Firm*, which was first published in 1963. Cyert and March were influenced by Nobel laureate Herbert Simon's research into decision making. Cyert, March and Simon heavily influenced the later work of Nelson and Winter.)

> Aspiration level is the name given to an outcome that is considered by an individual to be 'satisfactory'. What is considered to be satisfactory by an individual will depend upon a number of factors including the individual's past experiences and the context within which the outcome is required. Given their subjective nature it is likely that different individuals will have different aspiration levels.

For the purposes of this example we will assume that Samantha will be satisfied with a total output of 400 flat-packs per week. We will also assume that Samantha decides to hire three workers (Anne, Bill and Charlie) and that she builds a workshop with three workbenches (a bandsaw, a lathe and a flat-packing machine) as in our original analysis. She is now in a position to take the **second step**.

The second step involves trying out **different combinations** of the firm's resources to see what level of output they are capable of producing in these different combinations. Once she discovers a combination that leads to the attainment of her aspiration level she can stop these experiments. However, you should note that experimentation in this model may not be so straightforward because labour is a heterogeneous resource. This implies that the **identity** of labour matters. It matters because the firm's employees may have **different**

aptitudes for the tasks that need to be undertaken at the various stages of the production process. Anne may well be a world-class lathe expert but an average bandsaw operator and a slightly above average flat-pack machine operator. Bill may be a great flat-pack machine operator and an excellent lathe operator but have no aptitude for bandsawing, and Charlie may be average at everything. When she is confronted with this information, it is not immediately obvious to Samantha how she should deploy her labour resources. While this information may make the design of experiments a little trickier than if labour was a homogeneous resource, it also reinforces the need to carry out the experiments. This is because an analytical solution (i.e. a solution arrived at by a *thought experiment* rather than a real experiment) to the problem of identifying an appropriate combination of resources will become even more elusive.

You should note that the process of experimentation will take up Samantha's **time** and use her **scarce cognitive capacity**, but once the experiments have been conducted, and a satisfactory pattern of co-ordinated production activity has been identified, it can be applied automatically and repeatedly, i.e. it can become **routine activity**. This will allow Samantha to **reallocate** her time and cognitive resources into other problems thrown up by her business. These other problems (e.g. how to distribute the product, which raw materials to use, what invoicing practices to adopt, what accounting systems to employ, what quality control procedures to adopt, etc.) will themselves be subject to experimentation. Their respective solutions will eventually become routinized also. **New routines will only be sought out when established routines no longer provide satisfactory outcomes.** This will occur when the entrepreneur's aspiration levels change. This might happen because the context the firm operates in has changed (see Section 8.3 below).

The example we have used here is very simple, but it serves to illustrate the more general point that **routines emerge as a result of experimentation and learning**. Most business organizations in the real world are far more complicated than Tables 4U and, as a result, the emergence of routines is much more complex than in our simple story. That said, the basic principle of learning by trial-and-error experimentation is a key feature of actual business practice. Once satisfactory routines have been discovered, they tend to persist over time and in doing so they **reduce uncertainty** in the organization. For example, a new recruit can be shown 'how we do things around here'. Furthermore, given that different organizations employ individuals with different knowledge, skills and abilities, and that different entrepreneurs may hold different aspiration levels, the results of experiments to discover what 'works' for the organization are likely to lead to organizations developing dissimilar routines to each other. In addition, the routines that do emerge are likely to be based in part upon **tacit knowledge** (see Section 1.4.1 and Chapter 5) that has been acquired as a result of the experience of executing the original experiments and then been augmented by the repetition of the routines. Put another way, repetition of routines leads to them being enhanced because of **learning-by-doing**. For example, do you know how to ride a bike? If so, could you explain it to someone who has never ridden one so that they could immediately attain your level of bicycling skill? Probably not. This is because the skill needed to ride a bike is largely based upon tacit knowledge that has been gained from learning-by-doing.

So, how does an understanding of routines help us to answer the original question of this chapter – 'how can a firm earn persistent above-normal profits?' The answer is that firms that have developed 'superior' routines will benefit from lower costs and/or higher quality output. They will therefore enjoy higher profits than other firms. These superior routines will lead to Ricardian rents, provided that they satisfy the conditions identified in the **four cornerstones** framework. However, this is not the end of the heterodox story.

If industry structures remained stable and unchanging for ever we could stop our analysis here, but industry structures in the real world are rarely, if ever, found in a stable structural state. As a result, heterodox theory places the profit-seeking firm in the **context of a changing industry structure**. This means that in order to understand how a firm can acquire large profits and maintain them it is necessary to understand something about the **evolution of industry structure**.

8.3 The evolution of industry structure

As time passes, industries and markets have an unerring tendency to change. This means that firms that earn high profits today may well be tomorrow's losers. Entrepreneurs need to be aware of this fact of business life and, accordingly, develop an understanding of the forces of change to which their firms will be exposed. These forces operate in a manner that is similar to the biological process of **natural selection** that was explained by Charles Darwin in his famous book *The Origin of Species by Means of Natural Selection* (first published in 1859). The key phrase that most people associate with this great work is '**the survival of the fittest**' and, it turns out, this is not a bad metaphor to adopt in the realm of business too. Before we explain how the process of the survival of the fittest works in business it is helpful to outline the basics of the biological theory because we will be using it to draw parallels.

The process of biological **evolution** is explained by reference to **three basic building blocks:**[2]

- a source of **variation**
- a **selection process**
- a means of **retaining** variations that are selected.

The modern interpretation of the Darwinian account of natural selection explains the evolution of species as a result of random variations (mutations) in the **genes** of some members of the species. If a random genetic mutation gives rise to a **characteristic** that confers some advantage in the **environment** inhabited by the species then the mutants will have a higher probability of survival. Members of the species who do not possess the mutant gene will eventually diminish in number while the mutants will become more numerous and pass their genes, and therefore their advantage, on to their offspring. To illustrate the process at work consider the following stylized story of the evolution of long-necked giraffes.

Assume that giraffes need to eat the leaves of trees in order to maintain their strength and to have sufficient energy to be able to outrun lions (who like to eat giraffes). Assume also that the most nutritious leaves can only be found at the tops of tall trees. Now assume that all giraffes have relatively short necks and are unable to reach the highly nutritious leaves. This will mean that **competition** for the leaves that grow at the lower level will be **intense** and, as a result, most giraffes will be malnourished and unable to outrun hungry lions. Now, if a mutant giraffe with an unusually long neck is born (i.e. the first of the 'building blocks of evolution' is put in place) it will be able to reach the nutritious leaves that are out of reach to the other members of the species. As a result of this advantage the mutant will not have to compete with the other giraffes, so it will become strong and healthy and be able to outrun the lions easily. We can say that this mutant giraffe **fits the environment** better than the other giraffes and, as a result, it has a much better chance of survival. The fact that the mutant fits the environment so well gives the impression that the environment has **selected** it for success (the second 'building block of evolution'). Of course, the environment is not a sentient being that exercises choices, so it has not deliberately selected the mutant giraffe at all, but this is a useful way of describing the process. If we assume now that the mutant giraffe gives birth to baby giraffes, then

---

2   The three building blocks, variety–selection–retention (VSR), are often referred to collectively as 'the evolutionary algorithm'.

the babies will **inherit** the mutant gene and grow up to have similar advantages to their parent. The parent will eventually die of old age but despite this the characteristic of the long neck is **retained** in the species because the gene that causes it has been **replicated** and passed on from parent to child (the third 'building block of evolution'). In time, the offspring of the original mutant will give birth to their own offspring to whom they will pass the mutant gene and, as a result, the proportion of members of the population who possess long necks will increase. You should note that what has actually been retained in this process is the **information** carried by the long-necked gene: in other words, the original long-necked giraffe no longer exists, but the genetic information that led to it having a long neck does. Biological evolution is a story about how 'genotypical' information is retained in a system.

If you have followed this stylized account of giraffe evolution you should now be clear what the phrase 'the survival of the fittest' really means. When evolutionary theorists talk about 'fitness' they are not referring to some abstract notion of good health and athletic ability; instead they are talking about how well the organism they are examining fits the environment it is living in (which means effectively examining how well the genotypical information it carries fits the environment). So, an organism cannot be declared as 'fit' without reference to the context in which it finds itself. For example, a garden sparrow may well be 'fit' in the context of an urban environment, but it is certainly not 'fit' in the context of an underwater environment. Also recall that 'fit' should be seen in **satisficing** terms: it is merely necessary to fit adequately, not to have the best fit possible, though as time passes, what constitutes an adequate standard may keep increasing.

There is an undeniable appeal to seeing business competition as if it were a process of the survival of the fittest (or, rather, the *sufficiently* fit), but exactly what does a theory of industry evolution look like? Do firms have genes? This is precisely the question that Nelson and Winter asked in their book. It was also asked by the heterodox economist Kenneth Boulding in his 1981 book *Evolutionary Economics*. In what follows we will lead you through the basics of the story told by these important writers.

Nelson and Winter begin with the notion that firms operate using routines. They accept also that entrepreneurs, and other decision makers, are boundedly rational and face uncertainty, and that experiments with different combinations of resources have to be carried out if entrepreneurs are going to overcome their ignorance. Finally, they embrace the notion that firms use mark-up pricing (which can itself be the subject of experimentation). In order to understand how these basic foundations fit together to form an evolutionary theory of the firm and industry, Nelson and Winter make an **analogy** between **genes** and **routines**. In the biological story genes display **two key features**:

+ They are subject to random mutation and are therefore the **source of variation** upon which the process of selection operates.

+ Mutations are infrequent, so the genes remain **stable** for significant periods of time. This allows any advantageous mutation (e.g. an unusually long neck in giraffes) that has occurred to diffuse through the population via the mechanism of inheritance.

From what you have learned so far it should be clear to you that the **routines** of the firm **also display these two key features**; they are a source of variation between firms (because, as we have discussed above, no two entrepreneurs are likely to develop the same capabilities within their respective firms) and once satisfactory capabilities have been discovered they become routine which, by definition, means that they persist over time.

The next stage in building an understanding of industry evolution is to identify the selection environment and the nature of the selection process. Identifying the **selection environment** is fairly straightforward – it is the **market** for the firm's good or service. This means that the **selection process** is driven by **buyers' preferences**; if customers like the features of the firm's good or service, and if the firm is asking the 'right price', they will buy it and the firm will prosper. This makes sense, but you may be wondering what the relationship is between the firm's good or service and its routines. Kenneth Boulding was very clear about this: he pointed out that **the features of the goods and services that a firm offers to the selection environment are the product of the routines the firm has established**. For example, if the firm has established a routine for quality control of its good or service, then the quality of the good or service offered to customers will depend crucially on the **effectiveness** of its quality control routine. Rival firms will also have developed quality control routines, but given the heterogeneity of firms these may differ in their effectiveness. If we assume that all other features of the product (e.g. price, number of features, availability, etc.) are identical then customers will select the product of the firm that has the most effective quality control routine. In other words, the most effective quality control routine is the equivalent of the mutant giraffe's long-neck gene and, just like the long-necked giraffe, the firm which possesses it will be more successful (i.e. make higher profits) than its rivals in the selection environment.

The story of economic evolution does not end here, because now we come to the crucial issue of identifying the necessary requirements for high profits to persist.

In other words, what are the requirements for the firm's routines to be **retained** by the selection environment for a significant period of time? At this point you need to be careful not to take the analogy between economic evolution and biological evolution too literally, because while giraffes have offspring firms do not necessarily spawn baby firms (although spin-off firms are quite common, particularly in high technology industries, as are franchise systems, so you should not dismiss the possibility altogether). Here we shall take the term 'retention' to mean that the entrepreneur wants the firm to continue to enjoy a profitable position and recognizes that this will happen if its routines fit the environment.

For the firm to continue to enjoy persistent profits the entrepreneur must ensure that its routines evolve to keep pace with changes in buyers' preferences. As you learned in Chapter 4, consumers' preferences do not remain fixed as time goes by. Consumers are quite sophisticated and as they learn more about the goods and services that are offered to them they become better educated about what is possible in terms of quality and features and, as a result, they become more discerning. This is another way of saying that consumers are just like everyone else; they have **aspiration levels** too. As they get more exposure to particular goods and services they adjust their aspiration levels upwards. For example, when TV sets first became a mass-market product (in the 1950s) they delivered a black-and-white picture, and in order to change channels the user had to get up off the couch and push buttons on the set. The concept of a TV that was capable of providing a colour picture was unknown to consumers, and the idea that a remote control channel changer was possible belonged in the realm of science fiction. Clearly, consumers' preferences have changed considerably since these early days; consumers today regard colour sets and remote controls as basic features. The **implication** of these observations **for profits** is clear. The entrepreneur must continually **monitor the firm's routines** in order to evaluate whether they are capable of delivering a good or service that is compatible with the selection environment, i.e. the current or anticipated state of buyers' preferences. In order to get a feel for the trends in preferences, the wise entrepreneur keeps an eye on the **feedback** coming from the market. An example of feedback that would require action is falling sales volume ('exit'). Another example is an increase in customer complaints ('voice'). If other entrepreneurs are more skilled at interpreting feedback then the firm's high profits will not persist for long.

If you have had trouble following our explanation of evolutionary theory up to this point it would be a good idea to read through it once more. However, before you do that take a look at the schematic diagram in Figure 8.2, which summarizes the principal features discussed so far.

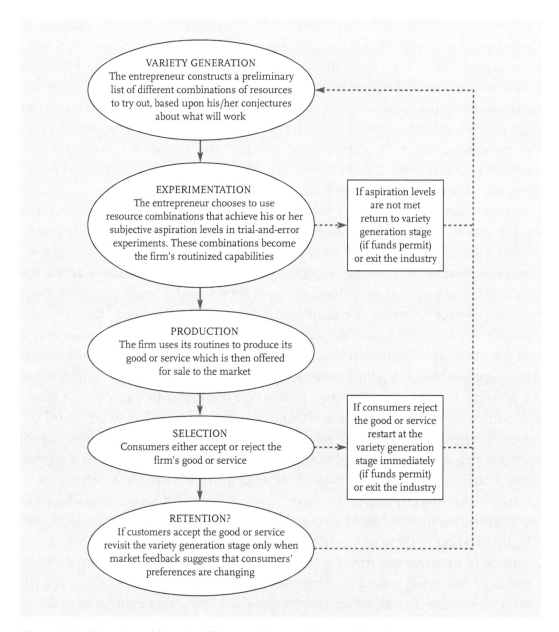

Figure 8.2 The principal features of the evolutionary theory of the firm

As you can see, the evolutionary theory of the firm emphasizes the **dynamic** aspects of competition. While mainstream economics tends to cause us to focus our attention exclusively on price competition, the evolutionary perspective emphasizes that competition between firms in an industry involves much more than setting the 'right price'. It tells us that competition between firms is based upon the **creation of routines** that are distinct from those used by competitors.

Furthermore, it tells us that the entrepreneur has to be ready to **adapt** the firm's routines to a changing environment.

If firms follow the steps outlined in Figure 8.2 some will be successful and others will be less successful in their quest for profits. Typically the process of **dynamic competition** played out between firms in the industry will generate a pattern of **evolving industry structure** that passes through **four distinct phases** (see Figure 8.3):

◆ **Phase 1:** *Emergence* – in the early days of the industry a few pioneering entrepreneurs create the industry by introducing new goods or services (in a variety of substitute forms) that have not been previously available to consumers. The goods or services on offer are usually prototypes or custom made. Pretty soon other entrepreneurs enter the nascent industry and the population of firms grows. This growth can be very rapid as more and more entrepreneurs try their luck in the selection environment with their own innovative version of the goods or services.

◆ **Phase 2:** *Shakeout* – consumers' preferences reveal that the features of some goods or services on offer are favoured over the features of others, so the firms of entrepreneurs who made unsuccessful conjectures about consumers' preferences exit the industry (i.e. they are 'deselected'). Consequently the number of firms in the industry begins to fall. Eventually the number of firms in the industry stabilizes.

◆ **Phase 3:** *Maturity* – a dominant group of firms emerges and the goods and services on offer evolve so that eventually the surviving firms produce fundamentally similar offerings to each other. This is because the opportunities to produce highly differentiated products are now exhausted. Firms now focus on minor incremental improvements and in doing so begin to imitate the goods or services offered by their rivals. In this phase firms tend to focus their efforts on developing and exploiting improvements in production processes as they try to exploit the learning curve and economies of scale and eradicate X-inefficiency. Very often this means that the firm becomes committed to a particular design because economies of large-scale production and the like are based upon the need to produce large volumes of an 'identical' product.

◆ **Phase 4:** *Decline* – depending upon the nature of the goods or services on offer, some industries go into decline as industries which are based on superior and alternative technologies emerge. This phase will not necessarily take place, especially if the product of the industry is a basic necessity such as housing, food or clothing.

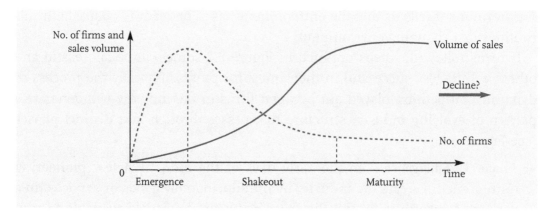

Figure 8.3 The stylized pattern of the evolution of industry structure (and volume of sales)

Empirical research has shown that many industries pass through these phases, although the numbers of firms and the time scales involved differ. For example, in the emergence phase of the US car industry around 250 firms populated the industry at its peak (c.1914) and the shakeout phase lasted for around 40 years to leave just seven firms by the late 1950s. In contrast, US producers of television sets peaked at 89 firms in 1951 when the shakeout phase began, leaving less than 40 producers by 1960, a handful by 1980 and none by 1995.

Just because an industry has reached maturity does not mean that it will not provide an attractive environment for a profit-seeking entrepreneur. In 1993, when James Dyson entered the vacuum cleaner industry, the major players in the industry (particularly Hoover and Electrolux) had been mass producing pretty much identical products for decades (see Chapter 5). Dyson's entry sparked a number of 'me-too' responses from industry incumbents as they tried to copy his Dual Cyclone technology. This goes to show that profitable opportunities can exist for entrepreneurial firms who begin at the variety generation stage (of Figure 8.2) when other firms in the industry have pretty much given up experimenting with new conjectures about consumers' preferences. In a dynamic industry environment the only way to maintain large profits is to keep revisiting the variety generation stage in an attempt to meet consumers' changing preferences.

The case of Dyson and the vacuum cleaner industry illustrates that when a firm has been using established routines its managers may be reluctant to embrace disruption to the way things are done. The fact that Dyson offered to license his Dual Cyclone technology to the industry's major players (prior to setting up his own manufacturing business) and their refusal to take him up on his offer illustrates vividly the dangers of failing to break out of the ingrained behaviour patterns implied by routines; in the period since Dyson entered the industry he has stolen a significant share of their allegedly 'established' markets.

8.4 Summary

The heterodox ideas discussed in this chapter are core to building an understanding of how an entrepreneur can build a successful business. The approach relaxes the strict mainstream assumptions about knowledge and rationality and takes us into a world where time matters in decisions. Here, entrepreneurial conjectures are crucial and they lead to a system where evolution takes place as people (both consumers and entrepreneurs) discover new information about the world. Firms differ from each other because they are constructed from idiosyncratic resources and capabilities and these give them different chances of survival in an evolutionary setting. The above-normal profits earned in the heterodox world arise as a result of the firm owning resources and capabilities that are both scarce and unique to it and of value in the selection environment.

The importance of feedback is emphasized by the heterodox approach since persistent profits can only be earned by those who are prepared to adapt their resources and capabilities to a changing environment. But routines are a double-edged sword: on the one hand, they reduce uncertainty in the firm; on the other hand, they may make the firm less able to adapt to a changing environment.

In the final analysis, both the mainstream and the heterodox analyses recognize the same main point: a firm will not be able to earn large and persistent profits if it does exactly the same thing as everyone else. In mainstream theory the way to avoid being like everyone else is to shelter behind barriers to entry and to exploit your market power by restricting output to drive a wedge between price and unit costs. In the heterodox theory we begin with the assumption that everyone is different in the first place and examine how these differences can be exploited and how others can be prevented from acquiring them if they prove to be useful in the selection environment. Unless at least some of the firm's resources and capabilities meet the criteria identified by the four cornerstones, rivals will soon be able to catch up. This means that the best route to success lies in the development of capabilities rather than resources, because capabilities have a tacit knowledge dimension to them and are more likely to satisfy the four cornerstones' criteria. This raises an interesting point: if a firm possesses a capability for innovation it can obtain patents on its innovations and this will protect it from rivalry in a manner that is similar to barriers to entry.

8.4 **Summary** (continued)

Finally, the heterodox approach draws our attention to the important topic of the relationship between profits and the dynamics of industry structure. This might lead you to wonder about the usefulness of the equilibrium models found in mainstream theory. One way to reconcile the two perspectives is to look at equilibrium models as stationary snapshots of the evolving structure. In particular, if the industry has reached its mature phase the models of oligopoly may be especially useful for helping us to understand the strategic nature of price competition between established incumbents.

8.5 **Some questions to consider**

1. Look at the major supermarkets in your local area. For each supermarket on your list:

   (a) try to identify its resources;

   (b) try to describe its capabilities.

2. Can you name an example of a routine carried out at your college/place of work?

3. On 10 December 2003 the London newspaper *The Times* reported that Benetton had vowed to steer clear of a price war with 'fast fashion' rivals Zara and H&M. Silvano Cassano, Benetton's CEO, unveiled plans to raise profits by 40 per cent over the next four years, but he also said: 'We talked to our customers and found they didn't want us to change. They want a brand they can trust that is young and colourful. We just have to jazz things up a bit.' Furthermore, he described the business plan as a 'Wow! Boom boom! Dring dring! strategy'.

   What do you think Signor Cassano had in mind? Do you think Benetton will achieve the 40 per cent growth in profits that they aspire to? If you were advising Signor Cassano what would you tell him?

4. In the summer of 2001 the footballer Ruud van Nistelrooy was bought by Manchester United Football Club from the Dutch football club PSV Eindhoven for £19.5 million. His contract specified that he would be paid around £35 000–£45 000 per week. To December 2003 van Nistelrooy had

> **8.5 Some questions to consider** (continued)
>
> scored a record-breaking 97 goals in 118 games. In January 2004 the acting chief executive of Chelsea Football Club was reported to have said that Chelsea would be prepared to buy van Nistelrooy for £60 million if they considered him to be a good investment. The Spanish giants Real Madrid also expressed an interest in securing his services. Later that month Manchester United increased van Nistelrooy's weekly wage to around £80 000.
>
> Can you use the resources and capabilities approach to explain Manchester United's decision to double van Nistelrooy's wages?

8.6 Recommended additional reading sources

One of the clearest accounts of the parallels between biological and economic evolution is provided by Kenneth E. Boulding (1981) *Evolutionary Economics*, London, Sage. This book should be read in conjunction with G.M. Hodgson and T. Knudsen (2004) 'The firm as interactor: firms as vehicles for habits and routines', *Journal of Evolutionary Economics*, **14**, no. 3, pp. 281–307.

For a paper that explicitly outlines the things an entrepreneur needs to consider in an evolutionary environment, see P. Cohendet, P. Llerna and L. Marengo (2000) 'Is there a Pilot in the Evolutionary Firm?' in N. Foss and V. Mahnke (eds) *Competence, Governance, and Entrepreneurship*, Oxford, Oxford University Press, pp. 95–115.

The classic account of the internal economics of an organization that is run by boundedly rational decision makers is provided by Richard M Cyert and James G. March (1963) *A Behavioral Theory of the Firm*, Englewood Cliffs, NJ, Prentice-Hall.

Nicolai J. Foss (ed.) (1997) *Resources, Firms, and Strategies: A Reader in the Resource-Based Perspective*, Oxford, Oxford University Press. This is a collection of some of the classic papers on the resources and capabilities perspective on the firm including a copy of Peteraf (1993) (see below). This is the best one-stop source for the basics and it will also give you an appreciation of the historical development of the perspective.

For a highly readable and relatively short book that is packed with stories about the evolution of real world industries, see Paul Geroski (2003) *The Evolution of New Markets*, Oxford, Oxford University Press.

The seminal contribution to the evolutionary theory of the firm is Richard R. Nelson and Sidney G. Winter (1982) *An Evolutionary Theory of Economic Change*, Cambridge, MA, Harvard University Press/Belknap Press. See especially Chapter 2 'The Need for an Evolutionary Theory', Chapter 5 'Organisational Capabilities and Behaviour' and Chapters 6 and 11 on search and selection.

Margaret Peteraf (1993) 'The cornerstones of competitive advantage: a resource-based view', *Strategic Management Journal*, **14**, pp. 179–88.

9

A business enterprise is born

Learning outcomes

If you study this chapter carefully, it may help you to understand why:

- entrepreneurs often have trouble raising money to start a business

- firms need to build relationships with workers, suppliers and customers

- many different types of contracts are used in organizing business transactions

- firms typically outsource some of their inputs but produce others in-house

- many new businesses have a big struggle to achieve long-term viability.

To the extent that you develop such understanding, you should be better able to make critical appraisals of new business plans and of proposed make-or-buy decisions.

9.1 Introduction

So far, we have looked at the origins of ideas for businesses, the problem of sizing up whether there will be a big enough market for the output of a new business, how the product might be made, how much it might cost to make, what determines the price of the product if it is offered for sale to customers and what determines the long-run prospects for production to be profitable. These are some of the key ingredients of a **business plan**. However, even if an entrepreneur is convinced that a product *could* be profitable in the long run if produced in a particular way and sold for a particular price, this does not guarantee that the entrepreneur *will* be able to get it produced and sold in the expected quantities at the planned price. In this chapter we consider some further issues that have to be addressed if business plans are to be turned into companies with some hope of surviving in the long run.

Before you read this chapter you should re-read the case study of the Dyson vacuum cleaner at the start of Chapter 5, as James Dyson's struggles to turn his idea into a profitable business involved many of the things that we explore here. In particular, pay careful attention to how Dyson's efforts were affected by:

- problems in obtaining finance;
- problems in dealing with suppliers and distributors;
- interactions with the surrounding community, both as a pool of labour and as a population worried about the impact of a large factory in a non-industrial area.

This chapter's structure is based on a particular view of the nature of a business enterprise:

> A business enterprise is a pool of resources directed by an entrepreneur and/or by a team of hired managers.

In the previous chapter, we considered what modern business economists mean by a 'resource'. Four main kinds of resources are vital for bringing a business into being and keeping it out of receivership. In listing them, we emphasize the importance of quality, not merely quantity.

1. **Financial resources**, including:
   - loans;
   - capital raised by selling shares;
   - working capital gained by success in getting customers to pay their bills faster than suppliers of inputs require their bills to be paid.

How useful such resources will be depends on the terms under which they are supplied. For example, an overdraft facility may be much more valuable to some firms, if they operate in an unstable environment, than a fixed-term loan with a fixed repayment plan that has a much lower rate of interest. For a small business, a good working relationship with the firm's bank manager may be a major competitive resource if the firm's rivals have to deal with much more rigid and austere bankers.

2. **Complementary businesses** that serve as suppliers of inputs or downstream services such as distribution. These will be more valuable to the enterprise if they are:

   - competent;
   - reliable;
   - trustworthy;
   - flexible;
   - solvent;
   - cost-effective.

   Given the importance of non-price factors in buyers' decision processes (see Chapter 4), it may be unwise for a firm to use the cheapest suppliers. Such suppliers might be cutting corners or be desperate for business. The result could be poor product quality, erratic deliveries or major disruption due to a supplier going out of business altogether.

3. **Human resources**, ideally including:

   - visionary entrepreneur(s);
   - managers who can lead and motivate as well as take decisions;
   - workers with relevant skills. They will be more valuable if committed to the enterprise, open to change, adaptable, attentive and neither tardy nor prone to absenteeism.

4. **Customers**, who are more valuable if they:

   - provide repeat business;
   - are willing to provide feedback;
   - are loyal enough to remain customers after making complaints and offering suggestions, and thereby give the business a better chance to improve what it does.

A firm whose customers are mostly unsophisticated and undemanding in terms of quality and design and who are prone to choose on the basis of price or sheer size is hardly likely to face the kinds of pressures to be innovative and dynamic experienced by rivals whose clientele are knowledgeable and discerning.

As well as needing an ability to assemble a set of resources, the entrepreneur needs to be able to maintain it or be a good judge of people to whom that task may be delegated. As time passes, the set of resources connected together as a particular firm will tend to change: some shareowners, suppliers, workers and customers will sever their links and switch to other firms, or be attracted from them. But the enterprise will retain an identity beyond its legal status insofar as these comings and goings take time and entail similar kinds of players replacing those who leave the scene.

The four main sections of this chapter look, in turn, at some of the economics associated with assembling these four kinds of resources into a viable business. However, before we move to these four sections, a short discussion regarding the nature of capitalist enterprise may help further to set the scene.

9.2 Capitalism and risk

In seeing relationships with suppliers (of finance, goods and services, and skills) and customers as part of the firm's pool of resources we are portraying the firm with three visions in mind:

* The firm as a (sometimes shifting) coalition of groups with different interests.

* The firm as a connective node in the fabric of industrial structure.

* The firm as an evolving institution known, at least to some degree, for doing business in a particular context and manner.

The first of these visions is the most useful to have in mind if one is trying to make sense of the nature of capitalist enterprise.

It may seem odd to portray the firm as a coalition of interest groups that includes customers and complementary businesses. Mainstream economists traditionally emphasize the role of natural resources and capital equipment in production processes. To them, complementary businesses and customers are external, legally separate entities with which transactions may be made. Heterodox economics takes a rather different perspective, despite agreeing that access to natural resources and capital equipment play a major role in shaping a firm's costs and hence its viability. The heterodox viewpoint, beginning with the writings of Karl Marx in the nineteenth century and running into modern writing on the 'resource-based view of the firm', sees capitalism with a focus not on the role of **physical assets** in production processes for **making goods** and delivering services but on what goes on in the process of **making money** in terms of **systems of relationships**.

> Capitalism is a mode of business organization in which those who risk their financial capital seek to increase their wealth by extracting the value that is added when workers produce commodities that are then exchanged for money by being sold in the market.

Capitalist enterprise is not inherently associated with the buildings and machinery that comprise factories and other production systems in which commodities are produced from commodities via a sequence of inputs of labour, assisted by the physical capital. State-owned businesses or worker co-operatives entail exactly the same sort of thing in physical terms. Instead, the distinguishing feature of capitalist enterprise is the **division of risk-taking roles**.

Although employees of a business run the risk of becoming unemployed, their financial risks are otherwise strictly limited, since:

- employees do not buy the inputs to which they add value and then sell their value-added outputs to the colleague that performs the next value-adding activity (note the contrast between this and what happens when the process of adding value involves a number of different firms and a **chain of transactions** between them);

- employees do not typically own/rent the capital items they use in production;

- many employees work for a particular salary, which does not vary as the performance of the business varies.

The owners of the firm thus carry the bulk of the risks associated with being left with un-saleable inventories, being let down or held up by slack or devious employees and suppliers, or being mucked around by customers. In return they get to keep the net revenues of the business; in other words, they are the **residual claimants**. By contrast, in a worker co-operative, the residual claimants are the workers who are members of the co-operative; and with a state-owned enterprise, the residual claimants are, ultimately, voters/taxpayers.

To some extent, the owners of a firm can offload their risks to other parties. Examples of this include:

- waiters who receive a large part of their income from tips;

- sales personnel whose pay includes commission;

- the payment of end-of-year bonuses to employees (which are much more common in Japanese business than in the West);

- payments based on the number of items the worker makes, or hours worked, with no guarantee of a particular output being required;
- managers whose 'remuneration packages' include performance-based pay and/or stock options.

When capitalists share the risks and returns with workers, they do not necessarily end up capturing less value added, for those to whom some of the risks have been shifted may now have bigger incentives to perform in a way that increases the total value added by the business. The crucial thing for the capitalists is that those with whom the risks are being shared do not capture all the extra value that they create when responding to the chance to earn more by foregoing certainty in their incomes.

In short, how much money the owners of a business can make depends on the terms of the deals that are done with the workers, customers and other businesses involved in the supply chain, and on what happens as a consequence of these deals being done.

Unlike the human players in the process of adding value, machines and buildings do not **negotiate terms** or **act strategically**. In any case, the physical resources of a business are really nothing more than financial resources that have been turned into a financially more risky form. The entrepreneur can turn them back into money by selling them, but doing this could entail a loss compared with the original purchase price. The only way they can be strategically valuable to the firm is if rivals cannot obtain them on similar terms. Such a situation might arise if the entrepreneur has had better foresight than the rest of the population about what might be done with particular resources and has purchased them for far less than they later prove to be worth. This would be an instance of '*ex post* limits to competition', the fourth of Margaret Peteraf's 'cornerstones of competitive advantage' discussed in the previous chapter.

9.3 Financing the enterprise

9.3.1 Alternative financing strategies

Many businesses are financed initially from the entrepreneur's own resources, such as a redundancy settlement, a major legacy or by mortgaging the family home. If the business succeeds, the entrepreneur captures all of the residual earnings, but if it fails the entrepreneur may suffer major financial difficulties, even bankruptcy. **Self-financing** is a high-risk strategy for an inexperienced entrepreneur: even if entrepreneurs are able to generate good ideas, their inexperience in terms of marketing, management or dealing with suppliers and distributors may result in poor sales or unexpectedly high costs. The Dyson story illustrates well these difficulties.

Sharing the financial risks with others comes, of course, at a price, namely, that the other parties may capture much of the profits. Profit-sharing can be reduced if finance is raised in the form of a loan rather than by letting others take a share in the business. However, a loan is unlikely to be forthcoming unless collateral is offered, and the lender will be at the front of any queue of creditors and able to call in the receiver if interest obligations are not met. Giving others a share in the business in return for their financial input at least gives the entrepreneur scope for keeping the firm going in difficult times by not paying any dividends to the shareholders. It also opens up scope for what is commonly referred to as the principal–agent problem.

> A principal–agent problem can arise in conditions of imperfect information where a person who is undertaking an activity (the agent) on behalf of someone else (the principal) faces a conflict of interest: what serves the principal best may not be in the best interests of the agent and the state of imperfect information may enable the agent to act in a self-serving manner without this being detected.

Other shareholders run the risk that the entrepreneur may choose not to act in their best interests. This problem arises with loan finance too, but there the incentive to take care and make the business succeed is enhanced by the prospect of losing a major asset such as the family home that has been used as collateral. With share-based finance, an entrepreneur who has not put much into the business may stand to gain a lot if it is profitable, whereas if it fails, most of the losses are borne by the other shareholders. Entrepreneurs in such situations may be tempted to take bigger risks than are prudent, or to try to capture profits by paying themselves fat fees for 'management services'. They will be less likely to do this, however, if they are worried about possible damage to their reputation and their ability to raise money for future enterprises.

Given this, it is not surprising that hybrid forms of financing business start-ups are sometimes used. For example, an entrepreneur starting a publishing business that specializes in economics books might get it started as a joint venture with an established publisher in the social science area. The entrepreneur contributes financially by mortgaging the family home, as well as offering creative insight about which books to commission and relationship management expertise to bring them to fruition. The established publisher provides the rest of the finance, along with, say, warehousing and marketing capabilities.

With such an arrangement, the entrepreneur has a major incentive to make the business succeed and is able to begin operations on a much stronger footing. The other publisher may get better utilization of its assets pending growth in its own catalogue of products and the deal may include an **option** arrangement whereby the entrepreneur can eventually buy this publisher's stake in the firm and then go it alone. Such an entrepreneurial buyout only makes sense if the entrepreneur foresees stronger long-term prospects for the business than the partner firm does, or if the partner firm has an urgent need to put money back into its primary business, either to solve problems or to take advantage of new opportunities to earn higher returns.

There are two main barriers to the greater use of external finance. One is the inability of suppliers of finance to share the entrepreneur's vision of the potential market and ability to implement the project. Too much may depend on a gut instinct in the case of a radical new venture, or there may be disagreements about assumptions underlying the entrepreneur's business plan.

The other problem is that in many economies **venture capital markets** are very poorly developed, both in terms of risk-taking traditions and market institutions that enable entrepreneurs to find suppliers of finance. Venture capital markets in such economies do not operate like that for which Silicon Valley is famous. Its venture capitalists often see past failures as indicators of experience rather than incompetence and focus on the case an entrepreneur is making for his or her latest business. If they do not judge themselves competent to assess the proposal's chances, they will rapidly point the entrepreneur to other venture capitalists who are likely to be better able to make a fair appraisal of it.

Note here that the efficiency of Silicon Valley as a venture capital market depends upon a network of connections for solving problems of knowledge. At the opposite extreme are capital markets in which connections work in a dysfunctional manner, where flows of finance are determined by 'the old boy network' and by rigid checklists regarding how an entrepreneur must operate in order to fit in. In the case of our new publishing firm financed as a joint venture with an established firm, network connections would probably play a major role: without a track record in the industry as, say, a commissioning editor, the entrepreneur's chances of making the deal might be rather limited.

9.3.2 Making a case to suppliers of finance

Raising finance to start a business would be a fairly straightforward activity if entrepreneurs did not have to wrestle with problems of information and knowledge. The entrepreneur would prepare a business plan that sets out expected costs and revenues for as far into the future as possible and hence predicts an **expected rate of return on capital**. If this rate of return were less than the minimum rate required by the market then funding would not be available, but if it were at least as high as the venture capital market's **required rate of return** then funding would be readily available. To determine whether an investment proposal offered a high enough rate of return the entrepreneur might try to calculate the **net present value (NPV)** of the proposed business, or its **internal rate of return (IRR)**. The method for calculating a project's NPV or IRR is explained in Box 9.1.

Box 9.1 Calculating a project's net present value by discounted cash flow analysis

$$NPV = Rev_t - Cost_t + \frac{Rev_{t+1} - Cost_{t+1}}{(1 + r)} + \frac{Rev_{t+2} - Cost_{t+2}}{(1 + r)^2} + \ldots + \frac{Rev_{t+n} - Cost_{t+n}}{(1 + r)^n}$$

(Where: t = in the first year; $t+1$ = in the second year, and so on; and r = the required rate of return.)

The equation converts costs and revenues expected to arise at different points in the future into a common unit, namely, the equivalent in terms of outlays or receipts right now. This enables schemes with very different time profiles of costs and revenues to be placed on a comparable basis. For example, a forestry project may involve major costs at planting and harvesting but nothing much for many years in between, and no revenue at all until harvesting. By contrast, a manufacturing business involving identical total outlays might have major fixed costs at the start but also revenues coming in without much delay and ongoing production outlays for labour and bought-in inputs.

The discounting method of turning these future flows into present values comes from the opportunity cost idea. If investors can get at least, say, 10 per cent by placing their money in another scheme, they will only be prepared to put £100 into the project for a year if, in a year's time, they will receive at least £110. To receive a mere £100 in a year's time is only as good to them right now as receiving £90.91 today, since £90.91 invested elsewhere for a year at 10 per cent would generate £100 a year from now. Likewise, £100 in two years' time is only worth having as much as £82.64 is today, since £82.64 invested at 10 per cent per annum will be worth £90.91 in one year's time and £100 in two years' time. A loss of £100 in a year's time is as bad as a loss of £90.91 right now, since the latter loss would deprive the investor of the

---

Box 9.1 (continued)

opportunity to grow that £90.91 into £100 a year from now by earning 10 per cent elsewhere.

A project's internal rate of return (IRR) is simply the rate of return which, when inserted in a discounted cash flow (DCF) analysis, generates a net present value (NPV) of zero. If the projected IRR is greater than the rate demanded by financial markets, then the scheme should be able to secure finance and leave a profit for the entrepreneur. There is a potential mathematical problem with this method due to the process of compounding, namely, that with some cost and earnings profiles there may be more than one rate of return that will solve the DCF equation. Thus a plan might have an IRR of, say, either 13 per cent or 18 per cent, leaving it unclear whether it would really pass a requirement that it generated, say, a 15 per cent rate of return for suppliers of finance. In such a situation it would be wise to calculate the project's NPV.

Computers make such calculations very easy, but they cannot overcome a common practical difficulty, namely, uncertainty about which numbers should be inserted to denote the projected outlays and revenues at particular points. In the face of these problems, practical decisions about whether a project or new business should go ahead have tended to end up focusing not on the outcome of a discounted cash flow analysis, but on the sales volumes required to break even at the price that is envisaged, and on how long it is likely to take for the scheme to break even, including costs of capital.

A **break-even analysis** begins with the following equation:

$$PQ = F + VQ$$

In this equation, P is the intended price; F is the sum of all the fixed costs; V is the variable costs per unit produced; and Q is the quantity sold. PQ is thus total revenue and F + VQ is total cost. The equation may be rearranged to solve for Q as follows:

$$Q = F/(P- V)$$

Thus if fixed costs are £1 million, the intended price is £11 and the variable cost per unit is £7, then to break even the business must sell at least 250 000 units, generating a total revenue of £2 750 000.

Time does not figure in the break-even equation. It might, for example, be set out on an annual basis, in which case fixed costs would include an allowance for depreciation of assets owned by the firm whose working life is of more than a year. Equally, it might be set out for a longer period, such as the term of a loan used to finance the business, with the interest charges being included amongst the fixed costs. (Note that it is not necessary to include amongst the costs the amount of money borrowed and then paid back during the terms of the loan, since the inflow from and back to the lender sums to zero except for the interest paid.)

Payback period analysis investigates how long it might take to accumulate the level of sales required to break even. This will be sensitive not only to the rate at which sales are assumed to accumulate, but also with respect to the assumptions made about the **scrap value** or **second-hand value** of physical capital as time passes. In markets where technological progress is expected to be rapid on the production side and/or where the capital equipment cannot be used to produce anything else, it may be reasonable to simplify calculations by assuming that these capital items will be of negligible value after only a few years. If the product itself is at risk of suffering a short life due to changing tastes or the advent of technologically superior rivals, then it may seem unwise to proceed with its production if the payback period is more than, say, three years. In the most rapidly changing markets, even shorter payback periods may be used. Even in relatively slow-moving industries, firms that employ payback period investment criteria commonly require a maximum payback period of only five years.

Whilst payback period analysis provides a simple decision-making mechanism that avoids looking far into the future, mainstream economists would generally argue that uncertainty can be handled perfectly well within the framework of discounted cash flow (DCF) analysis, and DCF analysis is preferable since costs and returns further into the future are not ignored. All that is required is that the entrepreneur can work out the probabilities of different possible cost and revenue outcomes and knows how to build them into the calculations. Heterodox economists do not approve of this approach. The issue is not that these probabilities are likely to be subjective in nature (based on guesses by the entrepreneur) rather than objective (based on past statistics), such as those with which insurance actuaries normally hope to work. Rather, the problem is that the entrepreneur may be taking a **crucial decision** in the sense that, if things turn out badly, it might not be possible to raise money again and/or the entrepreneur's own financial situation will be ruined, whereas, if things turn out really well, it may be unnecessary to seek outside finance again.

Although individuals may talk about probabilities when taking big decisions, what they may really be asking themselves are questions related to **possibility**. And if they are not, the heterodox view is that they should be doing so. Thus, in thinking about the scope for making or losing money with a new business or new project, one might ask, for example: 'How surprised would I be if the first year's net revenues were only X? Would I be amazed, because I can see all manner of reasons why they couldn't turn out *that* badly? Or would I regard such an outcome as perfectly possible, because I can't readily imagine possible barriers to it?' Within heterodox economics, this kind of thinking is known as **potential surprise analysis**, on the basis that we can measure how believable a person finds a particular possibility by asking them how surprised they imagine they would be if it actually happened. Thus we might have:

- Only £500 000? I'd be utterly astonished.
- £750 000? I'd be very surprised.
- £900 000? I wouldn't be very surprised if this were the outcome.
- £1 000 000? This would be a bit more surprising than £900 000.
- As much as £1 100 000? I'd be very surprised indeed, astonished, almost!

The potential surprise approach to thinking about uncertain business decisions is particularly useful for discussing whether it might be wise to proceed with a project once a break-even analysis has been done. This is because it encourages one to look out for things that may channel the future down a particular bounded pathway. For example, 'Clearly sales couldn't be greater than Y units a year, given the demographics of this area and its income distribution,' or, 'It is hard to imagine us not picking up at least Z units a year, since the product is no worse than the one launched last year by W and they've been selling that many without any trouble.' However, there is always the risk that dogmatic commitment to a particular course of action will result in the entrepreneur tending to be blind to possibilities that would prove problematic for upside outcomes.

Potential surprise analysis has been influential within the Shell International Petroleum Company in the development of a very different approach to facing up to uncertainty. It is called **scenario planning** and can be employed by firms of any size, despite its origins in a giant multinational business. The planners at Shell realized that many things that we worry about never happen, but many things that we fail to foresee do eventuate and cause great problems. The ability to judge how seriously particular future possibilities should be taken is useful, but first one must generate the possibilities. Shell's planners have found that a powerful way to do this is to create rival stories based on different sets of assumptions. They then see where these lead, whilst using seemingly related examples from history to help judge possible weaknesses in the plot lines.

A good starting point is to uncover sets of assumptions that underpin the continuation of business as it presently operates and then consider what happens if some of them are reversed.

It does not particularly matter if none of the scenarios that are constructed actually happen. Rather, the point is that they force the planners to examine opportunities they might be unable to exploit, or threats to which existing plans might be vulnerable. No one can be prepared for every eventuality, but if it is impossible to foretell the future then it may be wise to develop business plans that can demonstrate to suppliers of finance that what is being proposed is not dependent on one particular set of circumstances coming about. Uncertainty favours the use of **general-purpose machinery** even though it may entail higher production costs than machinery that is specific to the product in question. It also favours production systems that consist of a number of small facilities that can be shut down or fired up as the need arises, rather than single large facilities that are expensive to operate at low rates of output.

There is room for both discounted cash flow approaches and scenario approaches to exploring the case for a particular project in a business plan. For suppliers of finance involved with many clients, the numbers enable comparisons to be made between rival ways of allocating scarce funds, whilst the qualitative story-telling provides a basis for judging the credibility of the numbers that entrepreneurs are presenting.

9.3.3 The Richardson Problem

A key hurdle that an entrepreneur's business plan may need to get over in order to win support from suppliers of finance (possibly including the entrepreneur!) is an issue that is increasingly becoming known as the 'Richardson Problem'.

George Richardson was an Oxford University economist for 20 years and then served as the CEO of Oxford University Press from 1974 to 1988. His academic writings focus on the problem of economic co-ordination and the role of business organization in reducing the practical impact of co-ordination problems.

> The Richardson Problem is the difficulty caused for investment decision making by the dependence of a firm's costs and revenues on the investment decisions taken in other businesses.

Consider the problem of estimating sales for a business plan. It is not simply a matter of working out how many consumers might buy a particular product that is offered as a particular combination of product characteristics and price. Sales will also depend upon the products that other firms choose to offer and the prices at which they try to sell them. This is so even in markets where the product is standardized and where no individual producer's investment decision will, on its own, change the total output sold in a way that affects the market price, and where each supplier can sell as much as they wish at the going price in the market.

For example, a sheep farmer in Australia might have an enormous number of sheep and yet be a tiny player in the global markets for wool and sheep-meat. If this farmer ceases operations or doubles the number of sheep on the farm, there will be a negligible impact on the price of wool of particular grades and on the price of sheep-meat. But if many sheep farmers around the world decide, say, to cease raising sheep and instead turn their land over to forestry operations, then there may be a substantial cut in total supply of sheep products and a rise in their price. Decades later, there may also be a fall in the price of forest products as the trees reach maturity and are harvested.

> Richardson's competitive investment problem: a firm's willingness to supply a product depends on the price it is expected to command as well as on its costs, but that price depends on the investment decisions of competitors, who face exactly the same puzzle.

It is a paradox that this problem is at its most acute in markets that approximate the mainstream economist's ideal of a perfect market: a profit opportunity that is widely perceived and which many businesses can pursue is a profit opportunity for no one in particular. Hence, for a business plan to be able to make a credible claim for funds it needs to explain on what basis the product market in question is judged sufficiently imperfect to leave the entrepreneur with scope for capturing a viable level of revenue. In other words, the entrepreneur should be able to demonstrate that the venture has a sustainable competitive advantage in the sense explored in the previous chapter.

It will be possible to form guesses about the possible volume and nature of competitors' supplies of products *if*:

- there is good reason to believe that the potential market will not be widely perceived by others;

- there is good reason to believe that those who *do* perceive the potential market will have trouble acting upon their perceptions, owing to a lack of access to funds, production knowledge or other inputs, or because they are tied up with other activities that are even more profitable;

- the firm has enforceable **patents** over key aspects of the production of the product, or in respect of the product itself, so rivals can only copy what it does after engaging in a licensing agreement;

- **intelligence** can be gathered by observing the investment activities of potential rivals (such as the construction of factories and delivery of equipment), by mingling with their personnel at professional conferences, trade fairs and trade associations, or even by industrial espionage;

- rivals make credible **announcements** about their plans in order to pre-empt the decisions of others.

The further into the future the entrepreneur's business plan goes, the harder it will be to maintain that competitive threats are limited, for other firms may be able to develop necessary capabilities. Also, any success achieved by the entrepreneur may give the game away to potential producers who had not previously entertained the idea of supplying the product.

Being able to address the competitive investment problem is not the end of the difficulties that Richardson raises. There is also uncertainty about the firm's cost situation. If few workers have acquired the skills needed by the entrepreneur, it may be necessary to offer very lucrative deals to entice them from other employers. These workers will thus capture some of the entrepreneur's potential profits. Likewise, if suppliers of intermediate goods and services have underestimated the demand for them (or have taken an overly pessimistic stance in relation to *their* competitive investment problem), then the entrepreneur may find these goods unexpectedly expensive or their production plans disrupted due to being put on a waiting list for them. In Richardson's terms, there is an issue with **complementary investment** by other parties as well as with competitive investment.

> Richardson's complementary investment problem: the profitability of a business venture will depend not just on how much revenue can be captured but also on how well costs can be contained, which in turn depends on investment decisions made by suppliers of inputs.

The complementary investment problem was one that afflicted many enterprise managers in Eastern bloc countries during the communist era, despite central planning supposedly being a device for preventing failures of market co-ordination. Attempts to run these economies with minimal slack often meant that managers would find their bonuses for meeting or over-fulfilling production targets were being jeopardized by failure of inputs to be delivered on time. They soon developed a solution to this: if supplies are unreliable, ignore directives about specialization and make them oneself. Capitalist firms may do likewise, assuring supplies at the cost of having to develop new **capabilities** and acquire additional equipment.

Richardson suggests that firms can often avoid many of the anxieties about the adequacy of complementary investment *and* the costs of do-it-yourself if they develop connections with suppliers to assure their supplies of inputs. These connections include:

- Establishing informal/implicit **relational contracts** by generating track records as **regular customers**, who pay their bills on time, thereby creating obligations for priority service when they next need it.

- Negotiating long-term forward purchase contracts (formal, **classical contracts**).

- Taking **partial shareholdings** in suppliers to gain influence, possibly via board membership.

- Overcoming a supplier's nervousness about purchasing **specialized machinery** to make outputs to the customer's particular specifications by purchasing it on behalf of the supplier.

- Working closely with **preferred suppliers** at the development stage, rather than developing a design first and then calling for tenders to make particular components to particular specifications.

Such sets of relationships between a firm and its input suppliers are increasingly known as a firm's **architecture**. With increasing awareness amongst the business community of the importance of **supply-chain management**, any entrepreneur is wise to include an analysis of the firm's extant and envisaged architecture in business plans aimed at raising finance. Let us now, therefore, explore in some detail how economists have tried to make sense of decisions affecting the division of stages in a supply chain between different businesses.

9.4 To make or to buy?

The extent to which a new enterprise will need to grapple with the tasks of raising funds and hiring personnel depends not merely on the number of units of the product that are going to be produced but also on how much of the total value of each unit is to be produced in-house and how much is to be produced by other businesses. In other words, an activity may be **internalized**, in the sense of being undertaken by the staff hired by the organization in question, or **outsourced**, in the sense of being undertaken by staff in another organization with the resulting products being purchased through a market contract.

Different entrepreneurs in the same industry may reach different conclusions about which activities to internalize. For example, in the market for sports cars in the 1960s, Colin Chapman built up Lotus by making extensive use of other car firms' components. This strategy was copied by many other players, including TVR, and is still employed by many enterprising 'kit car' businesses. By contrast, in reviving TVR in the 1990s, Peter Wheeler went in the opposite direction, even going so far as to have the firm make its own engines. In this section we explore some of the economics that have been developed for analysing such choices.

Although we are going to focus mainly on **activities**, much the same kind of analysis can be applied to the question of whether a firm should **own** the physical **assets** that it employs in those activities that it does undertake, or whether it should **rent or lease** them from other businesses. As with an individual facing the choice between renting a house or renting money (in other words, borrowing) to buy a house, so firms can rent or lease buildings, office equipment, company cars and machinery, rather than raising more money upfront and buying them outright. The range of capital goods that firms can lease is now very wide indeed: for example, many large airlines lease their jets from specialist finance companies, while a boutique brewery may lease its beer kegs.

Similar choices arise in respect of goods that are held in stock by retailers. A retailer may take title to the items that it stocks, or it may sell them for commission on a sale-or-return, consignment basis, shifting back to the supplier the risk that they might not get sold. The theoretical analysis can also be used for analysing different kinds of employment arrangements. Some staff working in a business may be employees on contracts of unspecified duration with particular arrangements for termination, while other employees may be working on contracts for particular periods that offer no guarantee of being rolled over upon expiry. In some cases, workers may be working on secondment, or under some kind of leasing arrangement with another firm, such as a management consulting business or a business owned by the person in question. In yet more complicated arrangements, people may be working for a succession of firms that pay fees to temporary-employment agencies, and the agencies, in turn, pass the pay on to the workers, less commission charges.

9.4.1 Alternative ways of organizing value chains

Back in Chapter 2, and particularly with Figures 2.1 and 2.2, production was characterized as a sequence of operations, each of which adds some value to a good or service, *en route* to the ultimate consumer. Figure 9.1 presents a simplified value-adding chain for the bread industry and indicates a variety of different ways in which the value-adding process might be divided up between different businesses. Note that this diagram focuses on the grain inputs alone, ignoring other elements such as yeast, flour improvers, packaging and advertising, or the production of capital items used at any of the production stages, such as farm or milling equipment, or ovens.

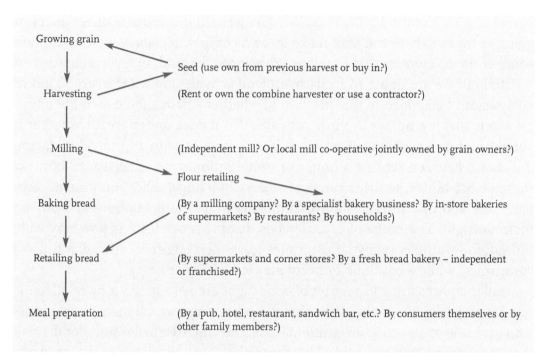

Figure 9.1 Alternative divisions of labour in the production and consumption of bread

If a firm is engaged in more than one of the stages in a value chain, then we say that it is to some extent **vertically integrated**. Full vertical integration is most unusual. In the making and marketing of bread, it is hard to think of any business that comes close to full vertical integration. Some oil companies appear to come close to being fully vertically integrated, if they own mineral rights, ship crude oil in their own tankers (sometimes, to great corporate embarrassment, as with the wreck of the EXXON Valdez), operate oil refineries and distribute their products through their own chains of petrol stations. However, they are unlikely to make, say, their own petrol pumps or petrol tankers; they often participate in joint ventures and partially outsource some activities; and they tend to have a mix of company-owned and franchised petrol stations.

Before we explore economists' attempts to understand how supply chains are organized, it is useful to note some variations on the basic vertical integration theme:

♦ **Taper integration** is where a firm involved in more than one stage of the value-adding process uses *both* contractors *and* internal supply sources in one or more of these stages and does so to different degrees at different stages. There is a taper in the sense that its width of involvement varies as one moves down the value chain. For example, a firm might divide the production process up as follows: Design: 60 per cent in-house; Components: 40 per cent in-house; Final assembly: 90 per cent in-house; Distribution: 10 per cent in company shops, 90 per cent in authorized dealerships. This mixed strategy provides flexibility as well as points of comparison that it can use to try to get better performance out of its internal staff or from outside contractors ('If you don't raise your game, we will change the sourcing mix').

◆ **Quasi-integration** ('almost integration') is where a firm develops close links with firms contributing to upstream or downstream stages in the value chain without actually taking full control of them. It does this via strategies such as taking out minority shareholdings, interlocking directorships and the provision of trade credit, training or particular assets. All of these give the firm leverage over the actions of the other firms and yet it is still able to switch to alternative suppliers without having to make its own staff redundant.

◆ **Relational contracting** is a variation on the quasi-integration theme that is rather like a *de facto* marriage. The firm builds up relationships of trust by making repeated use of particular suppliers. Close relationships between customers and suppliers also facilitate the two-way transfer of knowledge about issues such as customer needs and technological possibilities. This strategy was an ingredient in the long-standing success of retailer Marks and Spencer prior to its recent troubles. The firm specialized in retailing but did not ruthlessly switch between suppliers on the basis of minute differences in the prices they quoted. Being a favoured supplier of Marks and Spencer made it much easier for these firms to have the confidence to invest in assets that were specific to what they were making for Marks and Spencer, and easier for them to raise finance.

◆ **Long-term contracts** between legally separate companies are tantamount to vertical integration in that the buyer of the inputs does not keep returning to the market and the buyer or supplier may be able to vary rates of delivery so long as a total particular volume is delivered by the end of the period covered by the contract. These are used, for example, with human assets who cannot actually be owned, such as movie stars and recording artists signed to a particular company. By having a long-term contract with singer George Michael, Sony could invest in developing him as a star performer without the risk that after only a couple of hits he might switch to another record company. Such a company would be able to offer him a better deal and still make a profit, having not had to make the investment that Sony had done but still benefiting from it. Not surprisingly, Sony fought hard to enforce its contract in 1993 when

George Michael tried to escape, claiming that it amounted to 'professional slavery'. (Sony won the three-month court case, but Virgin Records subsequently bought out Michael's contract from Sony. In 2003, George Michael surprised many when he signed a new contract with, of all firms, Sony. This was rumoured to cover both new albums and his extensive back catalogue.)

♦ **Franchising and licensing** enable the firm that develops a product to limit its involvement in production and distribution whilst still maintaining some control of how its ideas are used and earning money from them. The originating firm receives a **royalty fee** from firms that it allows to use its product or process and/or brand name. It may also do **bulk purchasing** and advertising on their behalf, as well as **monitoring** them to ensure that standards are being maintained (see further, Section 10.3).

♦ **A virtual firm** is a method of arranging production that makes extensive use of contractors and subcontractors, and yet it has much in common with the way that the hierarchical management system of a firm gets things done. Co-ordination is undertaken by an outsourced management company and is also achieved via hierarchical relationships between contractors and subcontractors.

Strictly speaking, a virtual firm is the complete opposite of vertical integration, for it is a method of adding value that involves all parties in the value chain specializing in one particular activity and selling their outputs to other businesses. However, it also resembles a firm that has a lot of employees working for it on short-term contracts. The difference is that the virtual firm's 'employees' are other companies.

A classic example of this is the construction industry, where entrepreneurs from a property company may hire a construction management company to get a building erected, and the latter then hires specialist contractors and tries to make sure they do their work on time. Major contractors, in turn, may hire more finely specialized subcontractors in their broad areas and oversee their operations.

A particular firm may be using a combination of these strategies.

9.4.2 The case against vertical integration

Involvement in multiple stages in a value chain does not seem at first sight to be a particularly natural strategy for a firm to choose:

♦ *Multiple capabilities are required.* Vertical integration goes against the idea of specializing according to one's comparative advantage, of developing capabilities for doing one thing really well and thereby having a better chance of surviving in a competitive market. The kinds of capabilities required at the different levels of a vertical supply chain may be very different indeed, so a firm that adopts a vertical integration strategy has to learn much more and risks ending up a 'Jack of all trades and master of none'. The case of the TVR sports car company in recent years gives a sense of this: by making most of the parts for its cars in-house the firm has been able to shake off its earlier 'kit car' image, but its target image as a producer of powerful, upmarket sports cars is hampered by their reputation for unreliability and having parts fall off.

- *Minimum efficient scale of production may differ at different stages in the value chain.* Even if capabilities are not an issue, costs may still be problematic for a vertically integrated firm if its needs for a particular input are significantly below the volume rate required to get unit costs down to a level that can be achieved by a specialist provider of that input.

- *Strategic risks.* In producing an input for itself, a firm is committing to something that could be rendered obsolete by technological change. For example, the firm might invest in making particular parts by metal fabrication only to discover that it becomes possible to make them more cheaply, or with greater functionality, from plastic or carbon fibre.

- *Foregoing advantages of 'divide and rule' in the market.* Vertical integration goes against the idea that the best way to get things done is via competitive markets. Co-ordination in a vertically integrated production system is done by managers **directing** an established team of workers to change what they are doing as internal circumstances and/or the market prices of inputs and outputs change.

  The **visible hand of management** co-ordination is quite different from the 'invisible hand' of the price mechanism. With the latter, the entrepreneur would look at changes in input and output prices and make new contracts with suppliers of inputs as circumstances changed. The entrepreneur can change not merely what or how much the organization is producing, but also from whom inputs are purchased. Being able to play one supplier off against another sounds like a recipe for getting a better deal than engaging in do-it-yourself and being stuck with a particular team of workers and machinery – but relational contracting might be better still.

Why, then, do firms engage in do-it-yourself rather than specializing on the basis of their existing capabilities, and using the market to obtain inputs and distribute their output to the next stage in the supply chain?

9.4.3 The transaction cost analysis of vertical integration/internalization

If a firm chooses do-it-yourself rather than using a market to obtain inputs of goods or services, there must be something problematic about the market in question. As we noted in Chapter 2, the institutions that make up a market help buyers and sellers to deal with problems of information and knowledge but they do not eliminate them entirely. In respect of make-or-buy decisions, there are several types of situation in which outsourcing could prove problematic:

+ *Where a firm fears that a supplier or distributor could seek to hold it to ransom by refusing to fulfil existing contracts unless better terms were offered.* James Dyson's experiences in the development of his revolutionary vacuum cleaner, discussed in Section 5.2, provide some telling examples of the **hold-up problem**.

+ *Where an organization needs to handle emergencies immediately* and there is no time to arrange an outside contractor, let alone shop around to find the best deal from alternative suppliers. This is particularly likely to be an issue in businesses that deal with intrinsically dangerous systems involving hazardous chemicals, or that are based on integrated production systems in which a hold-up can be problematic all the way along the line (as with a steelworks). With other production systems, breakdowns can be handled in a more routine manner via formal **maintenance contracts** (for example, with photocopier servicing companies, rather than having office staff dealing with major photocopier problems themselves), by **relational contracting** (returning to the same maintenance firm each time, despite having no formal obligation to do so) or by dealing with unprecedented problems via traditional one-off deals with the right kind of specialist. This basis for vertical integration needs, however, to be viewed with some caution. For example, note that even though airports come into this category and often have their own fire-emergency crews, they could instead quite rationally choose to arrange a contract with another organization that specialized in providing on-site emergency crews on permanent stand-by. Such a supplier would suffer major damage to its reputation with other airports if it attempted to abuse its position by demanding a better deal, or else threatened a hold-up in service at the time an emergency arose.

+ *Where a firm fears that, despite what a contract specifies, a supplier will provide inputs that are of inadequate quality or a distributor will not market its output properly.* This is a more general example of the **principal–agent problem**: as the layperson often says: 'If you want to get something done properly, do it yourself.' If the supplier has a conflict of interest and if the activity in question is a core one as regards demand for the firm's product, then it may pay to internalize the activity even if the in-house expense of undertaking it is somewhat higher than the price being quoted by outside suppliers that specialize in the activity in question.

This issue can also arise due to **tacit knowledge** problems. A firm may have trouble pinning down in a contract exactly what it wants from a supplier, unless it makes an investment on such a scale as to be able to demonstrate this – by which stage it has then acquired the capability itself. Similarly, a firm may opt to sell its own products because it believes it knows more about them than a distributor could know, or to ensure that messages from customers about what they want do not get 'lost in translation' or suffer from the 'Chinese whispers' effect whilst passing through an intermediary.

◆ *Where novelty makes other businesses nervous about getting involved.* Once an entrepreneur has had an idea, the tacit knowledge problem may also stand in the way of convincing other businesses to get involved in the supply chain. Hence the firm may experience difficulties in finding suppliers of components or in arranging the distribution of the product. The only way to turn the vision into reality may be via vertical integration. This also has the advantage of making it easier to incorporate running changes as scope for improvement is discovered.

Such a situation is particularly likely to arise when the firm is a new one without a track record of success, and/or where the prospects for the business are clouded by uncertainty about which product standard will dominate in the market. For example, a century ago it was far from clear that petrol-fuelled cars were going to dominate, given that an electric car had already reached over 100 miles an hour in 1904 (see http://www.speedace.info/statistics.htm) and steam cars could match petrol cars in performance and were not dependent on a new infrastructure for refuelling. The diesel engine had only recently been patented (in 1893) and made to work as a functioning prototype (in 1897), so its potential was similarly uncertain. The risks that fledgling car makers might back the wrong technology or lack business skills were good grounds for potential suppliers and distributors to be hesitant about getting involved with them. If electricity companies had sought seriously to market off-peak electricity for charging up electric car batteries at this time, things might have turned out very differently.

An implication of this line of thinking is that as time passes and such markets become institutionalized in terms of product standards and business reputations, the surviving firms may seek to concentrate in their strongest areas and outsource things that they find it harder to do well. This is particularly likely if the product that becomes the norm can be broken down into modules with standard interfaces that enable elements supplied by different businesses to be joined together easily – the PC is an obvious example.

Instead of being content with listing such specific kinds of cases, economists have taken a rather more general view of how problems with markets may lead buyers to become their own suppliers, and sellers to become their own customers, by integrating forward towards the ultimate buyers. The central focus of this analysis is on the **transaction costs** of getting things done in the market. These comprise:

- costs of finding potential trading partners;
- costs of appraising deals that are offered and of haggling over terms of contracts;
- costs of monitoring what is being delivered;
- costs of ensuring that suppliers deliver what they have been contracted to deliver;
- costs of obtaining redress in the event of failure to deliver as per contract.

These costs may, but need not, include fees paid to lawyers and brokers. They may also entail means to induce parties to have confidence that those with whom they deal will actually deliver the goods as specified, such as:

- **Hostages**. In other words, a firm allows its client a claim on it that will only be relinquished once the task has been performed.

- **Instalment payments**. As work progresses, these act as a means of spreading the risks associated with a contract.

- **Warranty provisions**. These are variations on the 'hostage' theme. If a firm offers a very extensive warranty that would be costly to honour if a product is full of defects, then customers may infer that the firm has really taken great trouble to ensure that the product is defect-free (unless they infer, on the basis of other cues, that it is a 'fly-by-night' operator that will not be around to honour the warranty claims).

- **Marketing expenses more generally**. Major investments in marketing may help not merely to make clear what the firm does, or grab the attention of customers, but may also signal that its operations are being taken seriously by those who are financing it.

If markets are expensive to use, firms have an incentive to do business via open-ended employment contracts and relational contracting. Repeated dealings between particular businesses enable the firms to:

- eliminate the costs of shopping around;

- develop pro-forma ways of documenting what they do;

- become better able to deal with changes as the need arises, because of familiarity with each other's modes of thinking and operations (nowadays the management information systems of firms engaging in relational contracting may be wired together).

Given this, and given the other advantages of relational contracting in terms of enabling firms to concentrate in areas where they have a comparative advantage, the implication seems to be that vertical integration is something that we might expect in situations that are conducive to suspicion and fear, rather than the kind of trust and give-and-take that is essential to good relationships.

Precisely such a perspective is central to the work of Oliver Williamson, the leading American writer on this topic. He argues that contracting between businesses is likely to be unworkable if *all* of the following *four* conditions prevail:

(i)   The situation is complex and hence the decision makers are likely to suffer from **bounded rationality**. If so, states of the world will be hard to anticipate, describe and even identify if they materialize.

(ii) The people involved are seen as prone to act with **opportunism** – in other words, tending to pursue their self-interest guilefully by exploiting contractual ambiguities and information advantages that they have over those with whom they are dealing.

(iii) There are only **small numbers** of suppliers from whom to buy, or small numbers of customers for one's product.

(iv) The production process entails **asset specificity** – in other words, investments in skills or equipment that cannot be used for any other purpose and which cannot be recovered easily because the asset has a second-hand market that is thinly populated with buyers.

If only some of these conditions prevail, transaction cost theorists argue that contracts should suffice to guarantee that parties to outsourcing transactions do not get less than that for which they bargained: asset specificity is not a worry if opportunism can be ruled out and with it the risk of a hold-up situation, and neither should small numbers be problematic if opportunism is absent, while opportunism would not be a problem if situations were sufficiently simple as to be transparent. If *all* these conditions prevail, however, customers may fear being let down, or taken advantage of, by their suppliers, or vice versa: the contracts cannot cover everything. One cannot be sure what the other party is really up to, and one cannot force the other party to deliver the required outcome by making a credible threat to do business elsewhere or to switch to an alternative line of business.

Transaction cost theorists have offered two main reasons why internalization may be more likely to deliver a better outcome when the four conditions for market failure are present:

(i) If producers with competing interests are 'all in the same boat', it makes little sense to try to serve their own interests in a devious manner at the risk of sinking the entire operation. The incentive is to 'all pull together'.

(ii) Monitoring and quality control may be easier inside an organization, where managers can walk around freely and to some degree observe what is going on.

9.4.4 Critique of the transaction cost perspective

Despite its prominence in the literature in this area, the transaction cost analysis of vertical integration is questionable. One major issue is that it seems implicitly to presume that there is no problem in obtaining **capabilities** to perform an upstream or downstream activity in-house. Contracts are discussed as if they refer to end results, not processes of production. However, even checking on what is being delivered may be impossible to do successfully without having the capacity to perform the task oneself; it often entails not merely observing people at work, but also knowing what they are supposed to be doing and being able to see that they are doing precisely that. Where there are differences between external and internal capabilities, it may be better to allow oneself to be held to ransom (at least for the moment) because do-it-yourself would cause even more damage to one's business. This can be appreciated readily if applied to the household context: consumers may feel they are being overcharged and given poor quality service when they pay to have their cars serviced by a factory-authorized dealership that has a local monopoly; yet they continue to suffer this, knowing that they could make a mess of the job if they did it themselves and that, without a service record stamped by an authorized dealer, the value of their car could suffer.

Even aside from the capabilities issue, the argument that it is easier to monitor internalized activities seems flimsy once we recognize that a clause enabling on-site representation may dispel customer unease. For example, airlines such as Qantas and Singapore Airlines are allowed by Boeing to have their own quality inspectors present whilst their aircraft are being assembled. You may have noticed in Section 5.2 that James Dyson did exactly the same thing to deal with poor quality work by his contractor, Phillips Plastics.

As for the 'all in the same boat' argument, it neglects the following:

◆ The **principal–agent** problem arises *within* firms between managers and workers, as well as when one firm deals with another. Hence, even if know-how is not an issue for a firm that opts to internalize to avoid dealing with opportunistic businesses, the firm that internalizes a particular activity may find that it has 'jumped out of the frying pan and into the fire'. Employees may conclude that, as long as they do not carry shirking so far as to jeopardize the viability of the vertically integrated operation, they have a captive internal market for what they produce. This may lead them to take it easier than otherwise would be the case, especially if the capital assets that they use have poor second-hand values due to their specificity.

◆ If two firms in a buyer–seller relationship depend on each other in the long run, it makes little sense to try to jeopardize the viability of the other through opportunistic behaviour aimed at extracting disproportionate returns from a transaction. This line of thinking has an important strategic implication. A firm should limit the number of suppliers it uses, rather than giving small chunks of business to lots of suppliers, none of whose viability will be jeopardized by losing repeat business as a result of being caught acting against the firm's interest. A firm will be able to exert considerable leverage over its suppliers in terms of quality requirements and in capturing rents from them if the suppliers know that the loss of repeat business from it would be enough to threaten their own viability. This was a lesson that the Jaguar car company was taught by Ford, who took Jaguar over after its customer base withered due to persistent problems of unreliability. These problems arose mainly from failures of minor electrical components supplied cheaply by an army of different suppliers, none of which saw Jaguar as a major client. A slightly more expensive but much more reliable BMW or Mercedes-Benz was a far more cost-effective tool for executives, for they might miss vital meetings whilst waiting for breakdown assistance on a Jaguar.

◆ Managers that hope to be running particular firms in the longer term have an interest in cultivating the **reputations** of their firms as potential trading partners with whom business can be done without the deal turning sour in the execution via post-contracting hold-ups and haggling.

Aside from the capabilities issue, the criticisms raised so far are essentially about how well the case has been made for the potential for internalization to result in less opportunism than one might expect from outsourcing. They do not deny that prospects of opportunism may lead some firms in some contexts to prefer a do-it-yourself strategy for a particular activity. Nor do they deny that in complex and fast-moving situations the visible hand of internal management might be a better means than market contracting as a way of avoiding the waste of resources: bounded rationality seems a perfectly credible ingredient in an analysis of make-or-buy decisions.

If we are looking for a major problem of logic in the transaction cost approach, we find it in the necessary role it gives to asset specificity. This was not an ingredient in early versions of the theory and seems to be a device for showing why difficulties with a transaction could prove expensive. Logic actually favours the reverse of the idea that asset specificity drives the internalization of activities. A firm is at much greater risk if its suppliers (including suppliers of downstream services such as distribution) have invested in assets that are *not specific to serving its needs and its needs alone*. This is because the owner of the non-specific asset may decide to use it to serve another business. The defection of suppliers could be catastrophic if replacement supplies cannot be found, as might be the case if vertically integrated rivals control the assets required for this kind of production. Just as a long-term contract with George Michael was Sony's means of protecting its investment in developing him as a pop star, so vertical integration may be a firm's method of ensuring that its investments can make money.

As an example, consider the position of a new airline in respect of its terminal facilities at particular airports. An air-bridge is certainly a specific asset in that it is not much use for anything except for enabling passengers to get from an aircraft into the terminal. But it is an asset that could be used by other airlines for the same purpose. If the new airline can only get a short lease on terminal facilities it risks losing terminal rights to a rival when the contract comes up for renewal. If it builds its own terminal, it avoids this risk. It then has a different risk: the risk that it will have trouble selling the terminal to anyone else if its assessment of the size of the market is wrong and it has to abandon services to that airport in the face of competition from other airlines.

This line of thinking leads to a simple but powerful question and a strategic implication. The question is: 'Can the firm easily find alternative sources of supply of key strategic inputs?' If the answer is 'No', and if it is difficult to arrange guaranteed but flexible flows of supplies via long-term contracts or other market-based methods, then vertical integration may make sense, despite the problems that it may entail. For example, the brewing industry displays a good deal of vertical integration between production and distribution, despite the lack of similarity between the two activities, and some brewers also integrate backwards into hop production. Strains of hops that have been carefully bred and cultivated may be vital ingredients in giving a brewing enterprise's beer its winning taste; internalization of their production is a way of keeping them out of the beers of rivals. Likewise, pubs and hotels could easily switch from distributing one brewery's beers to distributing those of rivals. There is a good reason to consider owning one's own distribution outlets if the supply of available sites is limited in each local market. And the more one's rivals are pursuing this strategy, the more it makes sense to pursue it too – unless, of course, the regulatory authorities start objecting. In the case of the UK, the Monopolies and Mergers Commission eventually cracked down on this strategy with its 'Beer Orders' following an inquiry into the beer industry initiated by the government in 1989. The Beer Orders were aimed at ensuring beer drinkers would be able to purchase beers from a wide range of breweries rather than a few giants. They have forced large firms such as Scottish and Newcastle Breweries to sell off hundreds of pubs over the past decade.

None of this is to say that asset specificity should not give entrepreneurs pause for thought when they are taking make-or-buy decisions. A firm is certainly very vulnerable if it has invested in assets that are specific to what it makes and then discovers that it cannot find alternative customers if its existing customer causes problems. But the customer is in the same boat, too. Here, our car-servicing example is again instructive. It may well be that a lack of access to tools and know-how specific to his or her car is one of the things that stands in the way of do-it-yourself service. Without a local dealership, things could be even more inconvenient for the car owner. But if the car owner becomes so fed up with the dealership that he or she decides to switch to a different brand, then the dealer will make less money out of investing in these tools and training the mechanics. The car owner and the dealership both need each other; both will incur significant costs if the owner switches to another brand.

The crucial thing when setting up an outsourcing arrangement is for the balance of risks not to be skewed in one party's favour. Note in Section 5.2 what happened when James Dyson bought the specific tooling of his vacuum cleaners outright for use by his contractor, Phillips Plastics. He was in a position to change suppliers and his suppliers were not so dependent on him as they would have been had they made the investment in tooling. Even so, he was then faced with 'hold-up' problems once things were going well for his business. In this case, the supplier's opportunism was mistaken: Dyson sacked the supplier and incurred the costs of disruption, moving the tooling and getting to grips with making the vacuum cleaners in-house. Here, the signs are that Phillips Plastics judged that the disruption costs to Dyson were more substantial than Dyson saw them to be, relative to the costs of handing over future profits to Phillips Plastics.

If the distribution of risks is unequal, the 'both in the same boat' argument might be insufficient to allay fears of a buyer and/or seller regarding investment in specific assets. If so, the solution is not necessarily to internalize the activity. If the supplier feels that the risks are skewed in the customer's favour, one option is for the customer to buy some of the specific assets and let the supplier use them (note 'some' here, in contrast to the Dyson case). Alternatively, the customer could buy a partial shareholding in the supplier itself. This should remove the supplier's worries about asset specificity since the customer will be harming its own interests if it presents the supplier with a hold-up problem. By the same token, because the supplier still has some investment in the specific assets, or runs the risk of the customer selling the partial shareholding to a potential takeover raider, there is an incentive for the supplier to behave without opportunism and not inflict a hold-up problem on the customer at a crucial moment.

One further point needs to be emphasized before we close this discussion of make-or-buy decisions. Despite what a focus on scope for opportunism might lead one to expect, firms in some markets are often quite comfortable about using their rivals as suppliers. Such arrangements are especially useful for dealing with the mismatch between minimum efficient scales of production at different stages in a value chain, even though they superficially sound like a recipe for serious principal–agent problems. If a firm invests in more capacity than it needs for a particular stage of production, it may only be able to use this capacity at the efficient rate of output if it can get business as a supplier to some of its rivals. This opens up a potential conflict of interest. For example, if a small publisher lets another publisher act as its distribution agent, how can it know whether poor sales are due to the quality of its books or due to the distributor deliberately underselling them in favour of its own ones? However, if firms in the same industry differ in which parts of their value chains they internalize, potential for opportunistic behaviour is likely to be held in check by a set of reciprocal dealing arrangements, as well as by scope for switching to other supply sources. For example, suppose firms A and B both undertake activity X in-house at an efficient scale of production, but firm A also integrates into activity Y on a bigger scale than its own needs and uses its spare capacity to serve firm B. Firm B, meanwhile, has internalized activity Z at the minimum efficient scale of production, which is more than its own needs, and it uses its spare capacity to provide Z to firm A. They are rivals but by 'taking in each other's washing', so to speak, they can help each other to be stronger competitors against third parties. If the market is big enough for there to be a number of producers operating at each stage in the value chain, small players may be able to obtain inputs with confidence from larger rivals even without having anything to offer by way of reciprocity, for their large rivals run the risk of losing them as customers if thought to be behaving opportunistically or charging an excessive price.

This mixture of competition and co-operation is precisely what George Richardson found in the publishing sector during his time as CEO at Oxford University Press. The passenger aviation sector provides another example of this phenomenon, with airlines often running their own check-in or aircraft maintenance facilities in their main 'hub' airports, using these to serve those of other airlines based at other airports, and using the latter's facilities at their respective 'hub' airports.

9.5 Recruiting and retaining staff

Within mainstream economics, the business of hiring staff reduces to the following simple proposition: the number of workers that it is profitable to hire is that at which the nth worker's wage is equal to their **marginal revenue product**, in other words, the extra revenue that the firm generates by selling what they make. A firm that has to pay £15 an hour for an extra worker of a particular grade should hire more staff if the output produced by an extra worker per hour can be sold for a gain in revenue of £16, since this will add £1 to profits, whereas if cutting an hour of work would only reduce revenue by £14 the firm should cut employment, because it will be reducing its costs by £1 more than it reduces its revenue.

This 'marginal revenue product' view of pay is a powerful starting point for analysing the economics of hiring staff. However, we will now use some real world puzzles to demonstrate that it needs to be applied mindful of the complications associated with problems of information and knowledge, as well as systems-based issues.

9.5.1 Why do firms often make it quite difficult to apply for the jobs they offer?

Modern information technology, in principle, makes it very easy for people to find the best employer to work for or for employers to hire the best available worker for a particular job. Prospective applicants can find vacancies via the Internet and then fire off email applications immediately, with their resumés being sent as attachments. Since the Internet works globally, a firm can expect a global pool of applications. As in the 'field' view of economics, everyone can connect readily with everyone else and then decide with whom it is best to make a deal. This seems to contrast with societies in which job-hunting and job-offering is very selective and based on networks of connections (including 'the old school tie' and 'jobs for the boys') as one might expect from a complex systems perspective on labour markets.

In practice, the labour market still operates as a complex system rather than a field. Although applications can now be made on-line, the present-day job applicant still finds the task very time-consuming. There is often a major need to cut and paste existing resumé materials into a required format and add supporting arguments to demonstrate competence in respect of long lists of 'essential' and 'desirable' selection criteria. Moreover, despite the scope for doing job interviews by video-conferencing, whether a candidate will be able physically to attend an interview is often an issue. As a consequence, job seekers make applications to far fewer employers than they might otherwise do, and many of the applications they trouble to make only occur as a consequence of having some prior connection with the employer.

All this is readily understandable in terms of the economics of information and knowledge and the related idea of transaction costs:

- *There are major costs entailed in **screening** large numbers of job applications.* Until software is developed for screening electronic job applications to separate potentially hireable applicants from those who are marginally qualified or woefully unsuited to the job, then it may make sense to impose a hurdle for potential applicants in order to cut down the number of applications received. Although this may put off some applicants who would have been well suited to the job, it should increase the average quality of applicants and reduce the time it takes to decide on a shortlist.

- *Uniform styles of applications are easier to process without errors due to **information overload** and cognitive biasing.* If people making selection decisions can only keep in mind a limited number of pieces of information at any one time, more information about a candidate is not necessarily preferable if it is not relevant to the job in question. As with the wearing of business suits as a kind of uniform at the interview stage, a standardized format for job applications makes it easier to compare applicants without being distracted by irrelevant information or problems of finding required information in the text supplied by the candidate.

- *Highly specific selection criteria enable candidates to use their self-knowledge in judging whether or not to apply. They are also necessary insofar as the employer works with production systems that do not permit particular trade-offs.* Although it would be possible to obtain knowledge of how well candidates match up to selection criteria at the interview stage, after widening the field by specifying the job quite vaguely, this is clearly costly if many apply. Moreover, in contrast to the presumption in mainstream economics that trade-offs are always possible, real world production systems may only work with specific kinds of inputs, including specific kinds of worker capabilities (for example, a plumber cannot do the job of an air traffic controller, and vice versa, without expensive retraining and particular innate capabilities). This is particularly to be expected where the customer at the end of the value chain tends also to choose on the basis of very specific product requirements. Hiring someone who cannot deliver a particular standard of work, on the basis that they are cheaper, makes little sense if their failure to meet the particular standard results in the customer being lost, even if the product is offered at a lower price (see Chapter 4). And, if there is good reason to believe that someone can be hired who has exactly the skills required, why should the prospective employer even think of wording the job specification more vaguely if this will create a veritable haystack of applications within which to find the right person for the job?

Where specific skills are required, the supply side of the labour market tends to develop signalling devices in the form of professional accreditation and membership of professional bodies to separate those who have particular skill bundles from those who do not. Employers, in turn, can then simplify their search processes by specifying such credentials.

9.5.2 Why don't job contracts spell out more precisely the tasks they entail?

Despite the long lists of performance criteria often spelt out in modern 'further particulars' packages, the actual contracts agreed with workers are typically very fuzzy and open-ended. They do not tend to specify exactly what a worker will be doing at any particular point in time. This appears to open the way for a **principal–agent problem**: the worker might exercise discretion, at the employer's expense, in terms of the tasks undertaken and the volume of output achieved. If pay is not performance related, this sounds like a recipe for disaster unless workers are **intrinsically motivated** – that is to say, unless they are driven to do their jobs well for reasons that have nothing to do with pay, such as pride in their work – or unless the employer incurs the costs of having **supervisors** to watch what they are doing all the time and cajole them into doing things that are in the interests of the business.

Concerns with the prospect of **shirking** by workers and a lack of connection between pay and outputs have led many large organizations to try to tighten up their employment relationships, with much more detailed job specifications, performance reviews, performance-related pay and a rising ratio of supervisors to line workers. But these measures often seem to have been implemented without regard to the possible benefits of vague employment contracts:

- *Avoid the costs of spelling the job out in detail.* Highly specific job descriptions are difficult to prepare if supervisors do not know exactly how workers produce the output, or where the output involves generating new knowledge, as with scientists in a university or corporate laboratory. Another problem area is where workers operate as **teams**, their efforts interacting to produce a particular rate and quality of output. Here, it may be much easier to **monitor** the cost of the team as a whole, and the value of its output, than to pin down individual contributions, particularly if there is a good deal of 'give and take' amongst team members – which leads to the next point.

- *Avoid the costs of locking the worker into doing something that turns out to be impossible or unprofitable as events unfold.* Sometimes, tasks are specified in an adaptable manner via **contingent contracts** that contain many 'if this is the situation, then you will do the following' kinds of clauses. Insurance contracts are typically of this form, but not employment contracts. The trouble is, contingent contracts are very costly to draw up, tend to contain many redundant clauses and could in any case founder due to a failure to anticipate events that actually happened or disagreements about what actually had happened. Nor would it make much sense for firms and workers to keep arranging one very short-term contract after another, with particular prices being negotiated for the delivery of particular outcomes. Instead, it seems that the flexibility provided by partially incomplete contracts is an essential aspect of the nature of a firm as an organization which tries to deal with variability in its environment by having **managers** to decide what to do as and when the need arises and reallocate workers accordingly.

  To some extent, of course, workers themselves can be left to do this, but some inputs from managers are often needed to ensure that their behaviour is properly **co-ordinated**. Whilst managers may also monitor what the workers are doing, in keeping with recent policy thinking, their skills in making judgements, co-ordinating and allocating tasks can still be worth paying for even if workers can be relied upon not to shirk and to do exactly what they are asked to do.

- *Obtain scope for using uncertainty about acceptable rates of output as a means of* ***motivating*** *promotion-hungry workers to work harder.* For many workers, the route to higher pay in a firm entails working their way up a promotion pyramid.

In effect, they are players in a **tournament**, competing mostly against fellow employees, in an **internal labour market**. Those who do not win promotion to a higher league within the firm may have to leave if they are to get positions of greater pay and responsibility. If internal competition takes this form, rather than workers being promoted purely according to years of service or actually meeting specific performance levels, then the productivity of the workers will depend on just how strongly each cohort sets about competing with each other. This sort of workplace competition *requires* that job contracts do not specify *exactly* what the basis for promotion will be, even if the job specification seems quite detailed at the time of the application.

The existence of tournament systems for promotion and worker motivation makes it difficult to attach the pay of particular job slots to worker productivity in those jobs. Rather, the division of tasks and remuneration packages need to be worked out mindful of the complex system comprising the whole promotion pyramid. For example, it may be perfectly rational to offer senior jobs with pay in excess of the marginal revenue products of workers in those jobs if the prospect of being promoted into them leads workers in lower-level positions to work at a level that generates output that is worth more in net revenue than the pay that they receive. In short, output today may depend not on the pay offered today but on the perceived scope for achieving a particular level of pay via a future promotion that is somewhat dependent on how the worker works today.

9.5.3 Why do 'leading-edge' employers sometimes pay less than their rivals?

In many parts of the labour market, there is a definite pecking order in terms of places where qualified people would like to work, just as in a typical product market there will be differences in brand equity across rival products. This enables the employers to capture more of the value added by being able to get away with paying lower wages than their rivals find it necessary to pay to attract people to similar kinds of jobs. Superficially, this may seem like the workers are making a simple trade-off between pay and working conditions or prestige. But there is more to it than that.

Take the case of Ericsson, a leading telecommunications company and one of Sweden's most highly regarded employers. Ericsson can pick and choose from the cream of electrical engineering graduates. The tapering hierarchy of positions means that, as with other organizations, many of its lower-level employees will eventually have to leave in order to advance their careers. In the meantime, they tolerate pay levels below those offered by less significant local firms in this sector. As they do so, they **learn** how the firm works as a superior device for generating and applying new knowledge, and thus they enhance their own capabilities. This learning is of a quality that they would not hope to achieve whilst working in lesser organizations. It makes them keenly sought after by such organizations. In turn, they learn to some extent in intermediate roles in second-tier firms, making them sought after by third-tier firms in the industry in the event that they are willing to move on if they fail to win further advancement in the second-tier firms. In short, it is the quality of the on-the-job learning in a first-tier firm, and scope for transferring the knowledge to a lower-level firm, that makes the latter willing to pay a premium for workers who are willing to defect to them.

9.5.4 Why do some 'talking heads' and bosses earn so much?

A new television station could doubtless find itself swamped with applications for a newsreader job from people keen to demonstrate that they look attractive, can read an autocue, do some story editing and interviewing, work unsociable hours and keep cool both physically and mentally whilst on air. Many people could doubtless do this job, particularly if the role is restricted to reading the news as opposed to managing the content of the programme. And yet those who hold such positions typically command salaries vastly in excess of those that would be demanded by aspiring newsreaders as compensation for leaving their existing jobs and for the higher stresses and problematic working times, insofar as these were not offset by the benefits of becoming well known. The job is not rocket science, but those lucky enough to do it often earn more than the senior politicians about whom they report, and way more than rocket scientists.

Much the same kind of puzzle arises in respect of pay levels of senior managers, which do not necessarily reflect a principal–agent problem in which managers are setting their own pay to the detriment of shareholders. If business economics students and their teachers can mount withering critiques of the strategies implemented by managers in companies that they study, then how is it that such executives earn millions and that competition for senior staff often resembles a game of musical chairs to which access is granted only to the select few, despite their inconsistent performances?

Joe or Joanna Public might well be very happy to read the news for, say, £30 000 a year, but if an established newsreader such as Sir Trevor McDonald can add £1 million *more* per year in revenue to the enterprise in question, then it could be worth paying him almost £1 million a year more than the television company would need to pay to get Joanna Public to do the job. If Sir Trevor McDonald earns so much that his employers are only £1 better off than they would be by having Joe Public read the news, they should still hire him, since that extra £1 is worth having. If so, Sir Trevor McDonald would capture almost the entire Ricardian rent that he generates.

The same goes for managers who can make a major difference to their employers' earnings through their skill or their connections. Because these are in short supply, they are in a position to capture much of the extra net revenue – the Ricardian rents – that they enable their employers to earn.

What stops exceptional performers from capturing *all* the extra revenue they generate is the presence of rivals who are prepared to do the job for less. Suppose Peter Sissons is the next best newsreader and adds only an extra £750000 in revenue but is willing to read the news for £200000. This would leave £550000 in profits. If so, Sir Trevor McDonald, despite his superior productivity, is now worth paying only £450000, not £1 million, for he must offer the TV channel at least as good a net profit. If, however, the third-best newsreader could generate £725 000 in extra revenue and was prepared to read the news for a mere £150000, both McDonald and Sissons would have to lower their demands.

A major problem here is that those who hire the big revenue generators cannot be sure how far they can limit their offers without losing the desired employee. Even if (a big 'if') the person's likely impact on revenue can be identified with confidence, it may be very difficult to guess the total worth of the job to the person in question – reading the news may open up opportunities for earnings from other sources, either now or in the future. There is also the problem of guessing the person's opportunity cost, the next best alternative that they believe they might be able to get. Suppose Sir Trevor McDonald guesses that his best earnings elsewhere would be £280000 and that, for simplicity, reading the news does not bring other earnings possibilities. If, in ignorance of this, the TV station only offers him £250000 and he rejects the offer and the TV station then (just!) succeeds in hiring Peter Sissons for £200 000, a very expensive mistake has been made. If McDonald had been offered, say, £300000, profits would have been increased by £700 000, whereas hiring Sissons now only adds £550 000 to profits. Cautious managers, worried about profits and wary of such risks, could well end up offering more than they need to, leading to escalating pay for the superstars.

Executive remuneration packages are often inflated in part by the precariousness of such careers. If an executive is fired after making a spectacularly unsuccessful business decision, it might be very difficult to find a similar kind of job ever again. Since the person would seem over-qualified for lesser jobs, the result may be a forced early retirement. Given this risk, one would only step up into such a job with a very major increase in salary that will cushion the costs of retirement if one ends up 'carrying the can'.

A basic problem here is that high-level decisions are often taken in the face of uncertainty and ambiguity, and it would be very difficult to demonstrate what would have happened if a different choice had been taken. It takes time to demonstrate how often one's judgement is good in a particular decision-making role. Consequently, the market has a huge problem in separating bad luck from bad judgement when it appraises decisions taken by an executive who has not been working at that level for very long. If the present-day demands for accountability lead to the likelihood that senior staff will not be given a second chance, then they will demand much higher remuneration than under a system that is prepared to judge them over the long term. Likewise, those with good track records will seem less risky to hire and if in short supply will be able to bid for high pay even though they have their track records to fall back on if a decision goes wrong.

The talking heads may not run such risks associated with the complexity of the business environment, but they do run risks of falling out of fashion and getting into a downward earnings spiral as they are demoted to lower-profile jobs.

Problems of information are at least as important in the story as the competence of those who receive high pay. A veteran newsreader such as Sir Trevor McDonald has an air of authority and credibility that comes from being etched in viewers' minds over many years, right from his early days as a reporter. He can be relied upon even if there are many people who could do likewise, given the chance, but who presently are unknown quantities. The point is much the same as that which explains the mass consumption of McDonald's hamburgers (Big Macs, not ones made by Sir Trevor!): they may not be the pinnacle of hamburger cuisine in terms of taste but you know where you are with them. It might well be the case that many professors of business subjects could take business decisions every bit as good as big-league executives and would be prepared to do so for a fraction of the cost. But since they are unknown quantities in this context and mistakes could be very expensive, they are not asked to demonstrate their expertise. Hence they never build up a track record and never get asked. Meanwhile, the same, safe 'high-profile' names figure time and again in announcements of new appointments. Like some products, some people have **brand equity**.

The brand equity of personnel may be an issue in another way when a new enterprise is trying to build up a team of staff. This way relates to the Ericsson example from the previous subsection. For a new organization to seem worth working in, it may be necessary to demonstrate that people of note, with whom it would be good to be associated in terms of subsequent career advancement, have already signed up to work there and are going to be key players in the team that is being assembled. The signing up of these key players is a signal that the new enterprise is being taken seriously by people who ought to be able to make good judgements in this respect and who will be able to contribute to its success as well as enhance the capabilities of those working alongside them. Paying these key players somewhat over the norm for the job in question may enable other staff of quality to be hired for rather less than they would demand to work in similar enterprises. Once again, then, we may not expect a well-defined link between each employee's pay and the marginal revenue they generate for their employer by the actual work that they undertake.

9.6 The vulnerability of a new business and the importance of goodwill

It is not surprising that many new businesses fail. Even if the entrepreneur's idea is well conceived, the enterprise may founder if costs turn out to be unexpectedly high, owing to insufficient experience in doing deals with outside contractors, in hiring workers or in internal management. Even if costs turn out according to plan, it may take an unexpectedly long time to attract enough customers to break even. A century ago, all this was recognized in the leading British economics text of the time. This text was written by Cambridge economist Alfred Marshall and reflected both his own extensive knowledge of the world of business and Charles Darwin's then recently published work on biological evolution.

Marshall likened industries to forests and firms to trees and other forest plants, competing for space, light and nutrients. The population of firms in an industry was likely to be continually changing, even if the total output and revenue of the industry and its broad character did not change much. The restaurant sector illustrates this phenomenon very well. There is a tremendous turnover of restaurants, often within the same buildings as used by previously hopeful restaurant owners. What failed as, say, a Thai restaurant might get refitted under new ownership as, say, a steakhouse. Some restaurants last for many years and become local '**institutions**', returning healthy profits, but many make little or no money.

Firms that manage to survive the initial period of teething troubles will emerge stronger, with lower costs and an ability to sell more at a given price.

They will **learn** how to do things better and become better at **anticipating** the requirements of their customers, and more of the pool of potential customers will learn of their existence, the kinds of deals they offer and the quality of services and product they deliver. Their costs of management, marketing and production will thus fall, increasing their profitability.

A puzzle here is how the new players get established at all in the face of competition from more experienced firms, whose **reputations** give them **brand equity** and/or **brand loyalty**. Surely, these firms ought to be making bigger profits, enabling them to invest in yet better products and production processes. The puzzle can be resolved by recognizing the following possibilities:

+ Staff in well-established firms may no longer be strongly motivated to chase sales or productivity improvements. In terms of everyday expressions, they may 'rest on their laurels', whilst for the new enterprises 'the fear of being hanged concentrates the mind wonderfully'.

+ New enterprises may begin with the latest technology, unencumbered by past investments in production methods that are now outmoded but not yet fully written off.

+ New enterprises may be based around a novel approach to the product, that established firms cannot rapidly copy, or do not immediately see as a threat.

+ Established businesses may have underestimated the growth of demand in the market, leaving space for new entrants to pluck customers from their waiting lists.

+ Even in well-motivated established businesses, errors will be made from time to time that alienate customers and lead them to investigate alternative suppliers and see if the latter can do any better.

+ New enterprises may be less bureaucratic than established, major players in the market, with decision makers closer to customers. Hence their decision makers may be better able to sense how customer requirements are changing and ensure that the firm rapidly adapts to meet them. In large organizations, relevant information may get filtered out long before it reaches the decision maker who is in a position to do something about it.

+ Major buyers of a product may try to keep their established major suppliers from taking them for granted by giving smaller jobs to untried firms that beat a path to their door. If these crumbs of work are handled well, they may eventually lead to substantial slices of business being offered to the new firms in the future.

These lines of thinking are much in evidence in Marshall's evolutionary view of the firm, but they were largely forgotten when mainstream theorists tried to frame the theory of the firm in terms of equilibrium situations represented in graphical terms. A century later, they are once again taken seriously, at least within evolutionary/behavioural versions of heterodox economics.

Modern Marshallians take a very different view from the mainstream economists regarding the determination of a firm's market share. The mainstream argument is that if products and their prices are basically identical, then market shares are determined probabilistically. The more brands of a product that a firm offers, and the greater the number of retailers that stock these brands, then the bigger its chances of getting sales. New producers are only disadvantaged on the demand side if they are operating fewer branches or offering fewer brands in the product category. This argument starts looking questionable as soon as we recognize that buyers and sellers in the market have problems in assessing each other as potential trading partners. This may result in some buyers being disappointed. The quality or price might be worse than they expected at the time of agreeing to do the transaction, or it might turn out that they were unable to implement an expected transaction with a particular supplier because the latter was too busy dealing with other clients or did not have the item of interest in stock. Some sellers may be disappointed too, because the interaction with the customer was a lot more time-consuming and/or earned less revenue than they had expected.

In such situations, customer **goodwill** can play a major role in determining a firm's share of a market. This is a key theme underlying the theory of mark-up pricing proposed by Philip Andrews. His work, introduced in Chapter 7, was greatly influenced by Marshall's approach. Instead of pricing with a view to making the most of a short-run demand curve and its associated marginal revenue curve, a firm is portrayed in Andrews's analysis as being concerned about avoiding eroding its goodwill. This is why it keeps its mark up down to a level that enables it to compete with established players without encouraging new ones into the market. It is also the key reason for planning to have capacity growing slightly faster than sales targets.

From the Marshall/Andrews standpoint, the crucial theme is that customers often form relationships with suppliers rather than normally engaging in transactions that are the economic equivalent of a 'one-night stand'. Buyers give a business their goodwill when they return to buy from it from time to time, even though they believe there exist other suppliers who may be capable of serving them just as well. So long as the firm does not disappoint them unduly in terms of quality or timely delivery and they do not have reason to believe that its prices are significantly out of line with those of its rivals, they remain loyal to the business even though its performance may fluctuate somewhat.

Goodwill-based choices are **satisficing** in their nature, but economic logic underpins them, even for customers who are fussy in their requirements:

◆ *Sticking with a particular supplier reduces* **search costs**, along with any need to learn new **routines** to fit alternative suppliers into an established **lifestyle** or way of doing business.

◆ *There is a reduced risk of an unsatisfactory outcome if you 'stick with the devil you know'* and that supplier has a record of a low variance in quality. However, there is a potential **lock-in effect** here, for the only way to get a better idea of the average standards of deal offered by rivals, and of their variability, is to try them repeatedly too. To Marshallian economists this is less of a problem than it might seem to mainstream ones, since the former recognize that buyers operate in a social world, exchanging information and observing each other's behaviour and the consequences of the choices made by others. We also know that consumers often give their goodwill to several firms within any one market – in the language of marketing, their brand loyalty is polygamous – so while they do not have complete information regarding probable outcomes of dealing with all possible suppliers, they are sending a signal that they cannot be taken for granted. (Note the similarity in logic here with the thinking underpinning **taper integration**.)

◆ *The quality of service that customers receive may depend on how well they are known by a supplier*, both in terms of their needs and their track records as customers with that business – the latter giving some indication of their probability of being a worthwhile customer now and in the future. Underlying this point is the fact that it is costly for firms to give **attention** to customers and not all interactions actually result in profitable deals being struck. This will be particularly important in markets where the flow of customers is sufficiently erratic for it not to be viable to carry enough capacity to serve immediately everybody who shows up as a potential customer in the busiest periods. In such situations customers can reasonably expect to be prioritized on the basis of how valuable they are expected to be for the business in question. If so, it pays to be easy to evaluate and likely to return with substantial orders.

Where customer needs are complex, the scope for lock-in is much greater. If the customer deals with several preferred suppliers for a series of interrelated purchases, it will be harder for any of the suppliers to know the full picture of the customer's situation. The consequences of this may not merely entail the need to spend time bringing a different supplier back up to date but also unexpected problems or over-servicing because it cannot, at the start of the new transaction, even be established what the previous supplier did (as in, 'Oh XXXX! *That's* where they laid the cable/pipe!'). Such experiences may lead the customer in future to stick with a single supplier.

At any moment, the population of buyers in a market will be divided between those who have goodwill relationships with particular businesses and those who are ripe for forming new relationships, either as first-time buyers or as experienced buyers who have decided to sever their previous goodwill links with particular firms. If this market is characterized by problems of information and knowledge, the new business could actually stand a worse-than-random chance of picking custom from the floating part of the population. Buyers in such a market will not simply choose randomly when faced with a large number of would-be suppliers listed in Yellow Pages. Rather, they will look for reasons to take some more seriously than others, such as how long they have been in business, their membership of trade associations or ISO accreditation, as signalled in their advertisements. The new firm can copy some of these signals, at a price, but otherwise it faces bigger marketing costs to start a snowballing effect of word-of-mouth recommendations.

Whether a new supplier will have much hope of picking up customers without throwing a lot of money at marketing will depend on how questions such as the following can be answered:

◆ *Should it try to compete by offering lower prices?* Conceding its lack of brand equity will increase its required break-even sales volume and may backfire if buyers judge likely quality via price or use decision rules that rarely give a deciding role to price.

◆ *Should it buy instant brand loyalty by joining an established franchise scheme?* Two crucial issues here are whether the entry fee and ongoing royalty payments seem likely to capture most/all of the extra profits, and whether the prospect of having to operate according to the strictures of the franchise's manual does not clash too much with hopes the entrepreneur might have had of being his or her own boss. In a well-conceived franchise system, both the brand owner and the franchisees should end up winners, since the brand owner gets a bigger market presence without having to find so much financial capital, while the franchisees benefit from advertising economies as a given advertisement can promote many franchises simultaneously. However, opportunistic franchisers sometimes wreck the long-run prospects of their systems by allowing too many businesses to join (franchise systems are discussed further in Section 10.3).

♦ *To what extent can the business profit from pre-existing relationships between its staff and potential customers?* Employees who decide to jump ship and set up as rivals to their employers may be able to take their established clients with them if the latter's goodwill is towards the person, not the company for whom they have been working. The advertising industry and in particular the careers of the brothers Charles and Maurice Saatchi provide excellent case study material in relation to this, but it is a widespread phenomenon, evident in markets as diverse as legal services, hairdressing, publishing and estate agencies. Employers who anticipate this 'biting the hand that feeds them' kind of competition may try to prevent it via restrictive covenants in the employment contracts that they offer, which prevent employees from setting up as rivals within a year or more of quitting. Even if they do so, defectors might judge that the costs of taking them to court to enforce the contract might be greater than the perceived present value of the profits associated with the stolen clients. (Note that the enforcement costs include not merely legal fees but also the effects of management time being diverted from running the business to fight the court case.)

♦ *Does the entrepreneur's name count for something, even if the new business is unrelated to that for which the entrepreneur is known?* Former television personalities, movie stars, supermodels, sporting heroes and popular musicians have a much bigger chance of getting established as business people than do the rest of the population. Their names suggest commitments to certain kinds of standards and values, or at least provoke curiosity and invite potential customers to experiment if the downside risks seem low. Moreover, since their names have brand equity, they have an incentive to be careful about only associating it with products that will not damage their reputation and prevent them from attaching it to other products in the future. The potential customer should thus take them seriously, unless their glory is widely known to be fading and they seem unduly likely to be trying to milk it for all it is worth before it ceases to count for anything at all. These entrepreneurs will also find it easier than the rest of the population to get production and distribution done by experienced and reliable businesses. All they may need to do is retain ownership of their name and the product design/recipe, which they allow to be used under licence.

9.7 Summary

This chapter has examined the economics of building a business with a view to generating value and capturing it within a particular value chain. We explored the economics that make it possible to understand some of the difficulties that new enterprises have in getting started and obtaining a secure foothold in their chosen markets. The difficulties arise from problems of information and knowledge, which are more acute the more that the enterprise lacks track records that provide evidence of competence and trustworthiness. In extreme cases, it may be possible to get a business started only on the basis of an extreme do-it-yourself strategy. In the long run, however, firms may be expected to specialize in areas where they have superior capabilities and to outsource complementary activities, unless there are strategic risks of being dependent on other businesses.

We have portrayed the process of building a viable firm as one that entails the construction of connections/relationships with suppliers of finance, complementary businesses in the firm's supply chain, employees and customers. Success in building such connections results in reduced costs of using markets to ensure reliable streams of costs and revenues. Rather than seeing the new firm as if it faces a 'given' demand curve for what it is trying to sell, we have argued that the firm's sales are constrained by the amount of goodwill that it has been able to build up through its own efforts, the shortcomings of rivals and the word-of-mouth recommendations of previous customers, as well as on purely random or contingent factors that led particular customers to try that business rather than a rival.

9.8 Some questions to consider

1. Examine the difficulties that the manager of a new rock band will face in devising a credible business plan to win a major recording deal with an established record company, even if familiar with financial techniques such as discounted cash flow analysis. Given these difficulties, how can record company executives decide whom to sign to their recording labels?

2. Compare and contrast a pine plantation, a suburban shopping centre project and a project involving the development of a new kind of vacuum

9.8　Some questions to consider (continued)

cleaner, in terms of the ease with which they can be appraised in relation to prospective cost and revenue streams by venture capitalists.

3. Attempt both of the following questions on the legal services industry, the first of which should be treated as a short-answer problem and the second as a more extensive essay.

   (a) Normally, bosses hire workers rather than workers getting together to hire someone to assign tasks to them and check on what they are doing. Criminal law practices, by contrast, seem to be driven by legal clerks paid by the lawyers that own their firm as a partnership (or who work independently 'in chambers' as members of a kind of miniature business district) and handle the cases that the clerks take on and assign to them. How do you make sense of this situation, in which the law professionals willingly get bossed around by relatively poorly educated clerks (though often well-paid ones) of lower social standing than themselves?

   (b) National and local government departments in many countries are major purchasers of legal services: for example, in respect of the sale of buildings, car leasing arrangements, employee relations, contracting with suppliers of military and other equipment, the interpretation of competition law, and so on. In the past, they used their own legal staff to undertake most of this work, but such work is increasingly being handled by private law companies in return for substantial fees. Discuss the costs and benefits of outsourcing these kinds of legal services by government departments.

4. In typical remote-area mining operations, mining companies engage in very little outsourcing. Indeed, internalization often goes so far as to include the provision of housing and infrastructure services such as roads and railways, and settlements are basically 'one company towns'. The Western Australian gold-mining town of Kalgoorlie stands in sharp contrast to this, and has done so for many years. In the Kalgoorlie area, just about everything can be outsourced so long as the mining company retains title to the particular ore deposit. This includes the planning and operation of mines, processing the ore and producing the gold metal. Most of the mine owners in Kalgoorlie make extensive use of these outsourcing opportunities, though often via some kind of quasi-integration/relational

contracting. Using economic theory covered so far in this book, discuss the likely reasons for this contrast between Kalgoorlie and the organization of business in other remote mining districts.

5. Discuss the economics of reorganizing car production along the lines of the virtual firm/network arrangements that are common in the construction industry.

6. Discuss the economics of vertical integration in the case of an airline, given that the airline business involves leasing or buying aircraft and airport facilities, training aircrews, aircraft maintenance, catering and ticket sales, and that sometimes airlines have owned holiday resorts to which their aircraft fly.

7. Discuss the relevance of theories of buyer behaviour for understanding hiring decisions in labour markets and for the design of job advertisements.

8. Why are car mechanics often expected to have their own tools and university lecturing staff expected to buy their own books for their office libraries?

9. How can multi-million-pound severance packages for executives ever make economic sense for employers?

10. Examine the options open to a new publisher of economics books who wishes to ensure that academics and libraries in universities all over the world purchase these books. Discuss the pros and cons of each strategy you suggest.

11. Production in Australia's wine industry has grown rapidly in the last decade and is continuing to grow, with a new wine producer starting up every 61 hours. Because of this, some analysts predict an overcapacity problem. If you had been analysing this industry a decade ago, would economic theory have led you to predict it to be particularly prone to suffer from investment co-ordination problems? Explain your reasoning. If a problem of overcapacity arises in this industry, does economic theory lead you to expect major changes in its organization in terms of the role of small wineries and interactions between wine producers and retailers?

9.9 Recommended additional reading sources

The view of the firm as a growing pool of resources and capabilities co-ordinated by entrepreneurs and managers was developed at length by Edith Penrose (1959) *The Theory of the Growth of the Firm*, Oxford, Basil Blackwell, and by business historian Alfred Chandler (1977) *The Visible Hand: The Managerial Revolution in American Business*, Cambridge, MA, Belknap/Harvard University Press.

For an entire and substantial text that deals with many of the issues raised in this chapter, see Paul Milgrom and John Roberts (1992) *Economics, Organization and Management*, Englewood Cliffs, NJ, Prentice-Hall.

The non-probabilistic, potential surprise approach to uncertainty was developed by George Shackle and presented in many of his books and articles, such as his 1979 book *Imagination and the Nature of Choice*, Edinburgh, Edinburgh University Press.

An account of Shell's experience with scenario planning has been provided by one of its senior staff, Michael Jefferson (1983) 'Economic uncertainty and business decision making', pp. 122–59 in Jack Wiseman (ed.) *Beyond Positive Economics?*, London, Macmillan. Another useful work, linking scenario planning with Shackle's approach to uncertainty, is Brian J. Loasby (1990) 'The use of scenarios in business planning', pp. 46–63 in Stephen F. Frowen (ed.) *Unknowledge and Choice in Economics*, London, Macmillan. For a recent text devoted entirely to this topic, see Mats Lindgren and Hans Bandhold (2003) *Scenario Planning: The Link Between Future and Strategy*, Basingstoke, Palgrave Macmillan.

George Richardson's key contributions are his 1960/1990 book *Information and Investment*, Oxford, Oxford University Press, his 1972 article 'The organisation of industry', *Economic Journal*, **82**, pp. 883–96, and two more recent book chapters: 'Some principles of economic organisation', pp. 44–62 in Nicolai Foss and Brian Loasby (eds) (1998) *Economic Organization, Capabilities and Co-ordination: Essays in Honour of G.B. Richardson*, London, Routledge; and 'What can an economist learn from managing a business?', pp. 1–13 in Sheila Dow and Peter Earl (eds) (1999) *Contingency, Complexity and the Theory of the Firm: Essays in Honour of Brian J. Loasby, Volume II*, Cheltenham, Edward Elgar.

The importance of relationships for business success is explored by John Kay (1993) *Foundation of Corporate Success: How Business Strategies Add Value*, Oxford, Oxford University Press (see especially Chapters 3–6).

Economists owe the 'quasi-integration' term to Keith Blois (1972) 'Vertical quasi-integration', *Journal of Industrial Economics*, **20**, pp. 253–72. The view presented by Blois has much in common with that in Richardson's article of the same year but his contribution is particularly useful on the significance of being a major customer. Also recommended is Blois (2003) 'B2B "relationships" – a social construction or reality? A study of Marks and Spencer and one of its major suppliers', *Marketing Theory*, **3**, March, pp. 79–95.

The key articles on internalization decisions and transaction costs are collected, with an excellent introduction, in Peter Buckley and Jonathan Michie (eds) (1997) *Firms, Organizations and Contracts: A Reader in Industrial Organization*, Oxford, Oxford University Press. It includes the 1972 articles by Richardson and Blois referred to above, and the seminal early paper by 1991 Nobel Prize winner Ronald Coase (1937) 'The nature of the firm', *Economica*, **4**, pp. 386–405. A more extensive set of reprinted major articles in this area is the two-volume set edited by Oliver Williamson and Scott Masten (1995) *Transaction Cost Economics*, Aldershot, Edward Elgar. An exhaustive and excellent textbook in this area is Martin Ricketts (2002) *The Economics of Business Enterprise* (3rd edn), Cheltenham, Edward Elgar. The critique of the role of asset specificity and the case for replaceability being the key issue driving vertical integration comes from Chapter 3 of Neil Kay (1997) *Pattern in Corporate Evolution*, Oxford, Oxford University Press. Kay discusses this in relation to oil companies as well as with respect to long-term contracts such as those between musicians and record companies.

For a readable analysis of how the problems of using markets change over product lifecycles, see Richard Langlois and Paul Robertson (1995) *Firms, Markets and Economic Change*, London, Routledge. This book has some excellent case studies, including the hi-fi audio market and microelectronics.

The kinds of issues considered in this chapter in respect of human resources are part of a rapidly growing literature on 'personnel economics'. The standard text here, by one of the pioneers of the workplace 'tournament' idea, is Edward P. Lazear (1998) *Personnel Economics for Managers*, New York, Wiley.

The evolutionary analysis of the firm appeared originally in Alfred Marshall (1890) *Principles of Economics*, London, Macmillan. A perceptive discussion of Marshall's way of thinking is provided in Chapter 4 of Brian Loasby (1989) *The Mind and Method of the Economist*, Aldershot, Edward Elgar. A classic Marshall-inspired portrait of the firm that is unusual in its avoidance of economic jargon and its focus on the problem of building goodwill is provided by Philip Andrews (1949) *Manufacturing Business*, London, Macmillan. For discussions of the Marshallian/evolutionary view of business, and a case study of a virtual firm in the context of the construction industry, see Chapters 2 and 7, respectively, in Peter Earl (ed.) (1996) *Management, Marketing and the Competitive Process*, Cheltenham, Edward Elgar.

10

How can the firm grow?

Learning outcomes

If you study this chapter carefully, it may help you to understand:

- why managers are motivated to make their firms bigger

- the limits to the rate of growth of a firm

- the kinds of contexts in which licensing and franchising can be used as the basis for a growth strategy

- how firms choose whether and how to take on new kinds of activities and the impact of their actions on the behaviour of their rivals

- the circumstances in which firms will try to enhance their growth through collaborative agreements with other firms

- how to analyse the problem of designing an organizational structure for a growing firm in economic terms.

To the extent that you develop such understanding, you should be better able to:

- make critical appraisals of strategies chosen by firms

- contribute to policy discussions about how, and how fast, a particular firm might seek to grow.

10.1 Introduction

It tends to take an average entrepreneur several attempts to succeed in assembling a business that consistently generates a profit. Those who manage to establish a profitable firm then face choices about whether they should try to turn it into a larger enterprise and, if so, how best to do so. This is what we explore in the present chapter, with the aid of economic theory that has been developed quite recently to help understand the kind of thinking that has led today's giant firms to be put together.

Mainstream economics has a low profile in this chapter, for aside from an interest in the impact of mergers and takeovers or vertical integration on competitive conditions, mainstream economists have had rather little to say about how firms grow. The approach taken in this chapter is particularly influenced by the work of Neil Kay, a Scottish economist who pioneered a **complex systems** approach for analysing corporate growth in his books *The Evolving Firm* (1982) and *Pattern in Corporate Evolution* (1997). What we are going to do is explore the growth of firms as a process of building complex systems of linkages that produce and distribute products that are themselves complex systems and that do so in the context of complex sets of relationships with other businesses. The bulk of the chapter is organized around discussions of the economics associated with the following kinds of linkages involved in the growth process:

- Contractual linkages, such as licensing and franchise networks.

- Vertical linkages: in other words, the supply chain of a product.

- Horizontal linkages: shared or complementary aspects of research and development, production and marketing among different products.

- Ownership linkages with other firms, involving complete or partial ownership.

- Directorship linkages: interlocking board memberships between firms.

- Joint ventures with other firms.

- Strategic alliances with other firms.

- Clubs/networks consisting of a number of firms with overlapping linkage interests.

- Internal organizational structure.

Before we consider them, however, we must examine the limits to the growth of the firm, and whether growth seems likely to be a steady, well-ordered process or one prone to be erratic and sometimes chaotic.

10.2 How rapidly will a firm grow?

10.2.1 The motivation to grow

At the outset it is important not to take for granted an enduring drive for expansion in businesses. The empire-building aspirations of some entrepreneurs may be quite limited, as may be their willingness to place their assets at risk. Some may be perfectly happy only to employ a few people, be their own boss, generate enough income for a comfortable living and retire the mortgage against the family home that was used to provide the initial finance for the firm. Making the business larger may entail raising more money on the basis of one's track record and being willing to delegate more. Growth requires an urge to make more money, and sometimes that may come from someone outside the business. For example, the McDonald's empire would not exist today if matters had been left purely in the hands of the founding McDonald brothers: it all depended on the drive of Ray Kroc, a passing kitchen equipment salesman who saw in their business potential for something much bigger.

Even if founding entrepreneurs are keen to grow their businesses, their successors are not guaranteed to have the same drive or skills. Alfred Marshall recognized this problem over a century ago and he made it part of his 'trees of the forest' evolutionary model of the firm. Having emphasized the difficulties firms have in finding a foothold (see Section 9.6), Marshall next suggested that many family-dominated businesses would fail within a few generations, owing to the founding entrepreneur's descendants tending to consume much of the profits themselves rather than ploughing them back into the business and losing interest in the running of the business. Ongoing profits seem unlikely if the entrepreneur's heir siphons off the firm's profits to pay for a country estate and rarely visits the business.

Even as Marshall put forward this analysis, other economists noticed that some firms were surviving this succession problem because the owners took a longer-term view and hired salaried managers to act on their behalf. This failed to persuade Marshall that it would be wise to see firms as always trying to grow as fast as their resources would permit. He pointed out that large businesses might suffer from bureaucratic problems that hinder their performance and help more nimble, smaller firms to steal some of their market share; firms might not die after a few generations – indeed, as Neil Kay emphasizes, 97 per cent of the US manufacturing firms with assets of over $20 million in 1917 (the largest 236 enterprises at the time) were still in business 80 years later – but from time to time they could appear to lack energy and go through periods when they were, so to speak, slipping down the competitive league tables and even in danger of being relegated to a more minor league.

If we are not troubled by Marshall's warnings about forces of inertia in large organizations, should we expect senior decision makers to be interested in making their firms bigger? The answer appears to be 'yes' if we note the following:

- Managerial pay and feelings of power are likely to increase with the number of layers of staff working below the manager, and/or with the total number of staff subordinate to the manager.

- The larger the organization, the more scope there may be for managers to enjoy lavish perks (expense accounts, corporate jets, etc.) and to be able to dabble with 'pet projects' that interest them but whose likely contribution to the firm's earnings is at best debatable.

- Managers in larger companies may feel greater job security insofar as larger companies are less likely to get taken over – it is rare that a takeover raider is smaller than its victim, so the bigger the firm, the fewer the potential raiders with which it must contend – and hence there is less risk of their posts being axed in a post-takeover reorganization.

- How managers feel about their achievements in life may depend upon their firm's relative standing in corporate league tables: the bigger their firm's market valuation and/or annual sales revenue, the better it is for their status.

There is a potential **principal–agent problem** here if growing the firm in terms of number of employees, value of assets or turnover is at odds with maximizing the rate of return on shareholders' funds. Should we expect there to be a conflict between growth and profitability, and are managers likely to be able to get away with acting against shareholder interests?

10.2.2 The relationship between growth and profitability

If we draw a diagram such as Figure 10.1 (p. 347), plotting the rate of growth of a firm's assets on the horizontal axis and its rate of profit on the vertical axis, then we can look at the relationship between growth and profitability in two ways:

1. *Growth may affect profitability and hence how fast managers **want** to grow the firm.* This is because they may jeopardize their jobs if they generate a stream of profits that is frowned upon by shareholders. If managers prefer their firm to be as big as possible, the way that the growth rate affects the profit rate serves as a constraint on their demand for finance.

Slow growth is bad for profitability if it is a symptom of a firm that:

- has not been buying the equipment that is necessary for upgrading its products so that they match **standards** offered by rivals in markets where rising real incomes result in consumers demanding better products even if these cost more;
- has not been increasing the **scale** of its production facilities in order to get lower unit costs by taking a bigger share of an existing market or maintaining its position in an expanding market in which other firms are getting economies of scale;
- has not been investing in the production of related products that will enable it to achieve **economies of scope** (see further, Section 10.5).

In short, if it operates in markets where technical progress and economies of scale and scope are significant, a firm that stands still may be driven into losses by rivals that are growing faster.

Very rapid growth of a firm can produce problems of indigestion, rather as when we eat a lot of food in a short space of time. There are a number of reasons why these problems arise:

- It takes time for new staff to work effectively together as **teams** and pick up unwritten knowledge within the firm about the ways that things are routinely done and what kinds of actions are valued highly (the firm's **corporate culture**), as well as to get to know the distinctive **capabilities** of those with whom they are working. These problems are variations on the **tacit knowledge** theme from earlier chapters.
- Managerial time and **attention** taken up in hiring and inducting new staff is time taken from dealing with strategic and operational problems. To hire yet more managers to deal with such issues runs back into the same problem: these managers have themselves to be hired and to learn how the firm ticks.
- Rapid growth may be more likely to cause problems if it involves debugging new technologies and if insufficient attention to detail results in poor quality products or **co-ordination failures**. It is rather like the difference between juggling five balls compared with juggling just three.

These kinds of problems were emphasized by Edith Penrose in her classic 1959 book *The Theory of the Growth of the Firm*, in which she argued that whilst there may be little to limit the absolute size of the firm in the long run, there are limits to the rate of growth that can be sustained.

In the light of this analysis of the impact of growth on profitability, the managers' **demand for finance constraint** is drawn in Figure 10.1 as an upside-down U-shaped curve. If the managers are forced to maximize profits to avoid losing their jobs, then they will only grow the firm's assets at the rate G_{pmax}, at which this curve peaks. However, if they believe they can get away with a somewhat faster rate of growth, they will choose a point on the curve to the right of G_{pmax}. For example, if they think that P_{req} is the minimum rate of profit they must deliver to avoid jeopardizing their jobs, then they can aim to grow at $G`$, but no faster than this.

2. *Profits achieved from past choices regarding the pace and direction of growth will affect how much growth managers can finance right now.* For example, an after-tax profit rate of 10 per cent could be used to finance growth of assets of 10 per cent without any need for external finance if no dividends were paid to shareholders (see line 0A on Figure 10.1, which has a 45° slope). If a 4 per cent dividend were paid, then the firm could grow by only 6 per cent in the absence of new external funds. (We show the firm's internal supply of funds constraint to the left of 0A as the line 0B, which is steeper the higher the rate of profits tax and the dividend rate.) However, the higher the rates of past profit and dividend payments, the easier it ought to be for the managers to raise new external funding for growth. Hence the **overall supply of finance constraint**, 0C, is to the right of 0B. We have drawn 0C as initially following 0B (on the basis that unless dividends and retained profits have reached a particular threshold level, external funds are unlikely to be forthcoming). It is also drawn with a slope that eventually increases to the right, on the basis that suppliers of external finance may get increasingly nervous about financing a very fast rate of growth, even if the firm's past profitability has been very strong. How steep 0C becomes depends on shareholders' concerns about:

- being asked to provide further funds via a rights issue;
- dilution of their control over the firm if additional shares are sold to new shareholders or used as a means of financing a takeover via a share exchange;
- greater financial risk being imposed on them if external finance is raised in the form of borrowing (since an inability to pay interest could force the firm into liquidation, whereas dividend payments on shares can be suspended in difficult times).

The picture of the constraints faced by growth-oriented managers that is presented in Figure 10.1 is highly stylized and it would be unwise to presume that the two constraints maintained the same position from year to year. (For example,

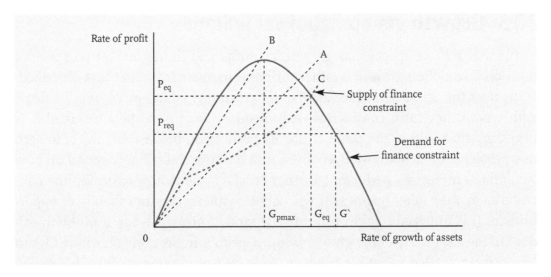

Figure 10.1 The relationship between the growth rate of a firm's assets and its profitability

occasionally, in times of crisis, managers may be able to raise finance from share-holders with a 'rights issue', even though the firm is currently losing money, because the shareholders judge that this will help prevent the value of their shares from falling in future if the funds are spent effectively.) However, it is a useful tool for appreciating the difficulties faced by managers if they try to grow their firm at a steady pace with a constant rate of profit. The point at which the demand for finance function and the supply of finance function intersect (P_{eq}, G_{eq}) shows the profit rate/growth rate combination that is sustainable as a steady state, equilibrium growth path for the firm. Any other combination will cause oscillations in the way that the firm expands. For example, suppose that in 2004 the managers maximized the rate of return and only grew at G_{pmax}. If so, the high rate of profit would enable them to generate the funds to grow at a rate faster than G_{eq} in 2005. However, such a rapid rate of growth would cause a collapse in the rate of profit in 2005, which would limit the rate of growth achievable in 2006, leading to a recovery in the rate of profit in 2006, which would permit faster growth in 2007, and so on. What appears likely to happen to a firm depends on how one sets up the positions of the two constraints: either the oscillation of growth and profits may continue, or it may converge to the steady state combination; or the firm may find itself in a fatal downward spiral. In a downward spiral wild growth leads to such a bad collapse of profits that further growth is not possible and profits turn to losses, so even worn-out equipment cannot be replaced, which leads to a further decline in performance.

10.3 Growth via contractual linkages

Firms that achieve spectacular growth in profits and in the market presence of their products often grow in a rather different manner from that just described. It involves the actual growth of assets and personnel taking place in *other* firms with whom they form contractual relationships. For this to be successful it is necessary that neither the product nor its production process is subject to serious problems of **tacit knowledge**. Given that the firm's earnings depend on how well other enterprises perform, a further crucial issue is how to design the contracts so that the other businesses will act in its interests rather than with **opportunism**. It is important not to run into the kind of **principal–agent problem** evident in the case study of the Dyson vacuum cleaner in Section 5.2, where Dyson (the principal) tried to get his product made by Amway (his agent). This ended up with Amway producing a very similar device of their own after opportunism on their part caused the collapse of the contract.

The question of how far the firm's activities are affected by tacit knowledge problems is a major one for firms whose products have to be close to their markets, for any attempt to reach a wider market will necessitate opening new production sites. This applies to services, such as hotels and restaurants, and to bulky products, such as bottles of soft drinks, that are expensive to transport relative to their market value. If tacit knowledge is not a serious problem, all that needs to be known about the product can be written down in a contract that can then be used as a basis for, in effect, cloning the firm's operations. In this situation, the firm may be able to use a **licensing** or **franchising** arrangement to increase its earnings and the geographical reach of its product.

> In a licensing arrangement, the licensor firm provides to another firm (the licensee) comprehensive details of the nature of its product and, often, details of how to make it. In return the licensee pays a flat fee and/or a per-unit royalty for the right to make and sell the product in question.

There are many variations on the licensing theme. At one extreme, all that might be involved is the right of the licensee to use a particular brand name and/or trademark. At the other extreme, the licensor may provide complete kits of parts for the licensee to assemble, along with technical assistance to help get the licensee's factory producing them to the desired standard (in other words, to bridge the tacit knowledge gap). The latter is common in the process of **technology transfer** from rich nations to developing ones. Much of the production of Coca-Cola around the world is undertaken via licensing arrangements somewhere between these two extremes. Being mostly water and low in value relative to its bulk, Coca-Cola needs to be made near its customers (unlike, say, premium bottled beers). Its ingredients and production process can be expressed readily as a recipe, and its commercially sensitive ingredients (the legendary syrup) and global advertising campaigns come from the parent firm. There may also be quality control visits from time to time by representatives of the parent firm to ensure that there are no breaches of contract (for example, that the finished product is technically up to specification or that Coca-Cola logos have been reproduced correctly on delivery trucks and signs).

The term **franchising** is quite hard to separate from licensing, but tends to be applied where firms expand the geographical reach of their product via the creation of contractual networks for cloning their activities in services and the retail sector, as with Avis and Budget car rentals, Wimpy and McDonald's in the fast food sector, The Body Shop and even parts of Virgin Airlines. Whereas licensing agreements are often between well-established firms, franchise systems often entail a thriving business helping in the establishment of brand new franchisee firms: it has the know-how and brand recognition in the market, and they provide the capital. Franchising and licensing arrangements enable the firm that shares its entrepreneurial success with others to benefit in a variety of ways compared with setting up more branch operations of its own:

♦ It reduces the amount of capital the firm has to raise and hence reduces the amount it stands to lose in the event that the product's lifecycle goes into decline. For example, consider the recent troubles at McDonald's, which have led to some outlets being closed: to the extent that these were franchised rather than company-owned, the firm loses royalty earnings but does not have to write off capital.

♦ The firm's managers do not have to get to know the peculiarities of the particular locations into which the network expands. For example, they provide the technology that workers use but they do not have to get to grips with local employment relations legislation.

♦ When franchises are run by the franchisees personally, there may be a much better motivation, compared with salaried managers of company-owned branch operations, to make the most of their local opportunities, since the owner-operator gets to keep the residual earnings. (Note, however, that performance-related contracts for managers of firm-owned branches might reduce the significance of this point. Recognize, too, that some franchise systems involve a large number of outlets being in the control of a single franchisee, with each outlet having a hired manager.)

The franchisees/licensees also benefit compared with a do-it-yourself strategy:

◆ The costs of developing the product, management systems and brand presence that the franchiser/licensor firm has already incurred can be spread across a large number of operators. This enables all of them to buy into it for a lower average cost than if they tried to develop and market a competing product themselves.

◆ Sharing a brand name and product may generate spillover effects between the sales enjoyed by members of the network. This comes via the familiar brand being used by consumers as a means of avoiding **search costs** or, in the case of **experience goods** and **credence goods**, for resolving the question of supplier credibility as they move around, whether as tourists, on business or in changing their place of residence. McDonald's hamburgers may not be the best ones available but if you are in a hurry for food they are an easily found source of known quality. In other words, fast food is not just about the food being served up and consumed rapidly, it is partly about finding it rapidly. It is important also to note the possibility of negative spillover effects: substandard output/service from a single member of a franchise network could tarnish the image of other members (for example, via exposure on national television, rather than merely due to disgruntled customers of that franchisee subsequently avoiding other members of the network) and wreck the flow of royalty earnings. Hence the franchiser has a major incentive to police the degree to which franchisees adhere to the instructions in the franchise manual. The more the franchiser has at stake, the more confident the customer should be about the reliability of its franchisees.

◆ The buying power of a franchiser may enable franchisees to obtain inputs far more cheaply than if they were purchasing them as individual businesses, or with smaller **transaction costs** than if they formed a buying consortium with similar businesses to get bulk-buying power.

If these kinds of network arrangements are to endure, the distribution of benefits needs to be such that both sides earn acceptable returns. Franchise schemes that involve a large upfront entry fee and small royalty rates on turnover are prone to encourage the franchiser to sell more franchises than will be viable in the market area in question. It appears that a major contributing factor to the initial success of the McDonald's empire was Ray Kroc's innovative combination of entry fees *and* royalty rates that were both lower than those of rival systems: the only way for McDonald's to make a lot of money was to ensure that its franchisees could make a lot of money. The other crucial ingredient for success, at least from the franchiser's point of view, is that the costs of establishing and maintaining a competing brand name should be high enough to deter franchisees from breaking away and setting up rival businesses on the basis of the knowledge they have acquired from operating the franchise.

10.4 Growth via vertical linkages

When we first discussed the process of production and the role played in it by specialization, we did so with the aid of diagrams of multi-stage craft-based and factory-based production processes in which, as time passed, increasingly valuable products moved from the left to the right of the diagrams (see Figures 2.1 and 2.2). In the previous chapter, however, when considering the process of setting up a firm to produce a particular product, we rotated the diagrammatic treatment by 90 degrees and looked at the process of adding value in terms of a stack of vertically linked stages (see the bread production example in Figure 9.1, where value is added as inputs move downwards on the diagram). The latter is the more common approach when discussing the evolution of large firms, and the 'vertical' terminology is typically used when discussing the linkages that make up a **supply/value chain** and the extent to which a variety of activities are integrated in the operations of individual firms.

Now, since we have provided a theoretical discussion of the economics of vertical integration in Section 9.4, we will not be focusing in this chapter on potential to grow a firm by increasing the extent of its vertical integration. Even so, we urge you to keep in mind that it may be undertaken in place of other growth strategies if managers are having problems with suppliers or customers that might be addressed via vertical integration, or if they fear that they *could* have problems because of their dependence on other firms involved in a production system in which they are participating. The crucial question is whether it would be better to use scarce corporate growth resources on tackling such problems rather than leaving them be and growing the firm in other directions, or changing how the firm makes the product so that it is less dependent on how other firms in the production system perform (for example, by redesigning it to use alternative materials for which it is easier to obtain reliable supplies).

There are, however, a couple of major points to reiterate regarding vertical linkages before we move on to look at other linkages that managers make in the process of growing their businesses. First, it is important to note that the conventional 'chain' idea can be misleading with regard to the various stages of adding value that culminate in the ultimate user purchasing a product and doing something with it. We noted this briefly when introducing our bread example in Figure 9.1. For many products, a technically more appropriate analogy would be with the various streams that flow together to make up a particular river that eventually reaches the sea. In other words, at each node in the production chain where something further is done, a number of components from different manufacturing systems may be brought together.

The engine of a car, for example, contains many components, some made of steel, others of aluminium, plastic or rubber, some made by machining, others made by casting, forging, stamping, extruding or moulding. In turn, the engine may be bolted to transmission components before being mated up with the car body, cooling system and wiring loom, and so on. Even something as simple-looking as a car seat is a complex, multi-technology system. It comprises steel tubing, springs, foam, cloth/leather and various metal and plastic components that permit its adjustment. The seats of many upmarket vehicles are even more complex and include heating elements, side airbags and motors for electrical adjustment. The finished car may consist of several thousand different components, but clearly it is mainly a modular product made up of identifiable sub- systems. This enables its design to be improved in a piecemeal manner via upgrades to particular modules.

In terms of the river analogy, what is also clear is that in many cases the value-adding process should be likened to a river basin such as that of the Nile, at whose mouth there is a delta, rather than one such as that of the Thames that enters the sea as a single channel. The delta is the equivalent of the distribution network for the product – that is, the specific set of channels by which it can reach the customer. This may entail the progressive dividing up of the flow of physical output into smaller and smaller streams, as it passes through regional distribution centres or wholesalers and on to the retailers, some of which may themselves be multi-branch operations with centralized buying followed by the allocation of the product to particular retail outlets.

The second key point to keep in mind regarding vertical linkages was originally raised in Section 9.4.2, namely, that the capabilities required at successive stages in the production process may be very different. For example, the business of making an airliner is most unlike that of running an airline, as is the business of making aluminium from which an airline's fuselage is made. Vertical integration may thus not be a particularly obvious basis for growing a firm, though firms often do expand via vertical integration because bitter experience in dealing with upstream suppliers or downstream customers leads them to judge that strategic considerations outweigh the problems associated with the need to develop new capabilities. (Recall the experience of James Dyson, outlined in Section 5.2: in order to make his vacuum cleaner venture work profitably, he had to take on far more of the production process than he originally intended.) In the absence of such problems, firms are more likely to try to grow not by vertical integration but in directions that make more use of existing capabilities and investments. The latter kind of growth is discussed in the next section.

10.5 Growth via diversification

A firm is said to be diversifying if it increases the number of supply chains in which it is involved. Some writers also include growth by vertical integration in the category of diversification but the term is primarily used in discussions of growth that involves firms increasing the variety of product markets in which they participate.

10.5.1 An example and a tool for mapping the strategy of a diversified firm

Before we look at how economists make sense of firms' diversification choices it is useful to have in mind an example of the kind of complex firm that can result from a long-term strategy of diversification. It is also useful to have a means of summarizing in graphical form a firm's range of interests and how they interrelate. To this end, we offer first a vignette describing a fictitious company, Dunsell Ltd. We then draw a picture of the firm using a technique developed by leading diversification theorist Neil Kay, which he calls a **synergy map**. The name Kay gives these diagrams comes from the term that management theorists began to employ during the 1960s to discuss what economists came to think of as **economies of scope** after about 1980. (As you will shortly see, economies of scope figure strongly in the theoretical analysis of diversification.) Dunsell Ltd is actually inspired by a real company, Ansell, formerly known as Pacific Dunlop, which began as a tyre company a century ago and went through almost 20 diversification moves before opting recently to focus on becoming one of the world's largest manufacturers of rubber gloves and condoms. Later in this chapter, when discussing the role of takeovers in the growth process, we will present a map of Pacific Dunlop's complex diversification history but for the moment its simpler fictitious counterpart Dunsell has all the ingredients we need to get started:

Dunsell was first set up a century ago as a maker of bicycle tyres and it soon adapted this technology to making tyres for cars, trucks and aircraft as these markets took off. Its expertise with rubber took it during ensuing decades into a number of industrial product areas that involve rubber mouldings and to products based on rubber sheeting, such as cable manufacture, industrial conveyor belts and roofing materials. Meanwhile, the tyres operations were integrated forward into tyre retailing, which led in turn to further automotive retailing in the areas of discount spare parts and car batteries, which also led to car battery manufacture. The firm also became increasingly involved in the sporting goods sector, initially via Dunsell golf balls and tennis balls. The sporting goods market was extended via the development of skills in making racquets and sporting footwear, the latter also to some degree being based around rubber. The firm further developed its expertise with rubber into mass production of products made from thin, high strength rubber, namely condoms and rubber gloves, the latter for both surgical and domestic use. (Dunsell's condoms and domestic rubber gloves are both sold through pharmacies and supermarkets.) Dunsell also developed expertise in foam rubber manufacture, which led to the establishment of a bedding and soft furnishings division, with some foam rubber also going into its sporting footwear. A fresh departure has been the takeover of ice cream and snack foods producer ICSF Holdings.

The portfolio of product areas in which Dunsell has become involved is summarized as a synergy map in Figure 10.2.

The idea here is very simple: each distinct area of the firm's business is represented by a blob whose size represents the revenue associated with that area of business relative to the firm's other areas of activity. In contrast to the vignette, many actual firms' websites provide figures of the relative importance of their different activities that can be used for this purpose or provide text that one can use to make rough guesses. The blobs are then linked together by lines wherever we can identify likely economies of scope, though we must keep in mind that this is a subjective assessment and the firm's managers may see things differently and may not be achieving some synergies in practice even if they see the same potential as we do. Vertically related activities can also be marked even though they typically entail very different sets of capabilities. (Note: the synergy maps in Neil Kay's books do not normally do this.) To the extent that we can make guesses about how much synergy/economies of scope the firm is achieving from a particular linkage, we can indicate this by the thickness of the link. If we wish we can also number the blobs or use arrows to show the sequence of acts of diversification undertaken by the firm, though the arrows method is problematic with complex companies that expand on a number of different fronts.

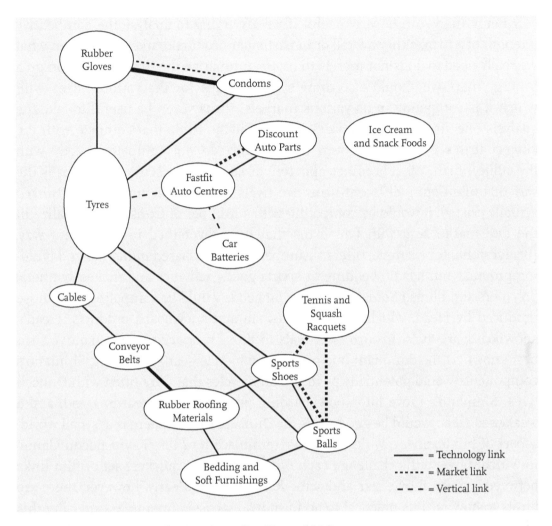

Figure 10.2 Synergy map for imaginary firm 'Dunsell Ltd'

When a company is represented as a synergy map it tends to have more than a passing resemblance to the kinds of diagrams of molecular structures that chemists draw. As with any map, synergy maps can be generated at various scales. At one extreme, we can draw broad-brush maps that lump together similar kinds of products as if they were a single product market, and which only show linkages at a high level of abstraction, such as 'technology links' and 'market links'. A much more fine-grained synergy map can specify individual products and break linkages into quite precisely defined areas. For example, instead of simply looking for 'manufacturing links' we might look for overlap in terms of 'shared equipment', 'logistical similarities', 'materials handling capabilities' and so on.

Synergy maps can be very useful if we are trying to analyse the competitive strength of a firm, either overall or in particular product markets. However, what we really need to do is not merely to try to summarize the firm in question on a synergy map; we should also draw synergy maps for the various firms with which it is competing in its various markets. It may even be useful to take the analysis one stage further and draw maps for the firms that compete with the subject firm's competitors, even though they do not compete directly with the subject firm. What becomes apparent as soon as one starts doing this is the way that often quite different firms are rivals in particular markets. If Dunsell actually existed, it would be competing with a number of firms that specialize in the tyre market and with tyre firms that have diversified in a different way. (Bridgestone, for example, offers a number of rubber-based industrial and building products but has no bedding or sports goods activities and makes synthetic polymers and fibres.) Some of its sporting goods would be competing with those produced by Head, which also produces ski and snowboard products. Head's snowboard products, in turn, are rivals to those produced by Shimano, a firm best known as the dominant business in the bicycle gear-set market. Shimano's components would potentially be found on bicycles that were fitted with Dunsell tyres. Shimano's move into snowboarding products is a threat to Head, and a weakened Head would be good news for Dunsell. Implied here is a 'small world' aspect of big business, which is rather reminiscent of the 'Kevin Bacon Game' in which movie buffs challenge each other to find the quickest set of film links between a given movie star and actor Kevin Bacon. Clearly, however, there are limits to how far it is practical to go in individual assignments in exploring this rich tapestry of overlapping areas of corporate interest.

10.5.2   Diversification and economies of scope

In trying to make sense of the kinds of diversified firms that managers create, the first thing to understand is why firms opt to grow by venturing into somewhat unfamiliar territory rather than doing more of what they know about already and trying to obtain larger economies of scale. A 'more of the same' strategy may be possible in a market that is growing or where there are weak competitors from whom one can steal market share without reducing one's own profit margins: ideally, a small price reduction may force the weaker firms out of the market and give a volume increase which lowers average costs by enough to leave one's profit margin no worse than before and hence give a rise in total profits. Even if a firm can grow in this manner, however, its managers may have good reason to consider a strategy of diversification, for they can reduce the risks that go with 'having all their eggs in the one basket'. Their positions are vulnerable:

+ *A temporary downturn in their market may leave them having to face the wrath of shareholders,* even though shareholders can insure against individual markets doing badly by buying shares in companies in a variety of different sectors. If the managers diversify, they may be able to achieve a smoother earnings profile with fewer questions being raised about their competence. They may also make their firm more attractive to small shareholders who do not enjoy economies of scale in trading shares and who prefer therefore to limit the number of companies whose shares they own. (The latter point is perhaps less significant in an age of unit trusts and Internet share trading.)

+ *Product lifecycles can sometimes come to a sudden end, as opposed to a temporary downturn, due to changes in technology, government regulations or fashion, or the discovery of product safety issues.* The invention of the scientific pocket calculator wiped out the market for slide rules in 1975 and a decade later the rapid take-off of the compact disc wiped out most of the market for firms that specialized in pressing vinyl long-playing records or making record turntables. Similarly, it is little use being the most competitive producer of asbestos-based insulation and building products if they are suddenly banned by government regulations. So, whilst shareholders can diversify against such threats by buying shares in firms in many different sectors, managers may judge that their jobs will be safer if they hedge their bets by diversifying the operations of their firms. Moving into unfamiliar territory may seem to carry smaller risks than those associated with having all their eggs in the one basket.

+ *In the case of the owner-managed business, much the same logic applies except that the pressure tends to come instead from the firm's bankers,* who may not always be very accommodating in the event of a temporary problem. In the event of a catastrophic change in the firm's environment, the entrepreneur may stand to lose not merely the ability to run the company but also most of his or her personal wealth.

The simplest way of trying to limit the firm's vulnerability in these respects without unduly taking risks associated with venturing into new market territories and acquiring new technical capabilities is to **make variations on existing products**. The strategies of car makers illustrate this very well. We can see how they have diversified either into different market segments (as when Mercedes-Benz introduced smaller cars or Toyota added its upmarket Lexus range of cars), or attempted to satisfy different customer requirements (as when car makers began to introduce a wide range of four-wheel-drive recreational vehicles and multi-purpose 'people movers'). The new products are of course not *exactly* the same as existing ones but they nonetheless may immunize the firm against some threats. For example, having expanded its product line into the luxury four-wheel-drive segment with its M-class products and into the small car market via its A-class products, Mercedes-Benz is less vulnerable if the fashion for four-wheel-drive vehicles continues to take customers away from large saloon cars and station wagons, or if rising petrol prices and increasingly 'green' attitudes lead customers to opt for smaller vehicles that manage to combine its prestigious brand name with political correctness. Note, though, that this particular example also indicates the hazards of moving into a new part of the market: Mercedes-Benz came up with a radical design for the small A-class vehicle in order that it would match the crash safety standards of its larger cars and offer a large interior despite a short length. The resulting tall A-class hatchback then spectacularly fell over in a simulated 'elk avoidance'/emergency lane changing exercise whilst being tested by a Scandinavian motoring journalist. The 'elk test' debacle caused major public relations damage and production of the car was suspended whilst new technological fixes were developed to make it more stable.

The relationships that a firm seeks to create between its products may result in economies of scope in a variety of ways. Most obviously, there may be opportunities to produce new products using **spare capacity** in existing production facilities and then to market them using established brand names and distribution channels. Another way of spreading investment more widely and getting reduced average costs is to make extensive use of parts from elsewhere in the firm's product range. By combining parts from different products, a 'new' product can be offered with relatively limited investment having to be made in new components. This is an extension of the idea of the entrepreneur as a constructor of connections, from Section 3.3.7. It can be labelled **'parts bin enterprise'**. This form of diversification has potential to be cumulating: parts from product A are used in product B along with new parts created for product B; parts from products A and B are then used in product C along with some newly designed ones; parts from products A, B and C may then be used, in different combinations, along with some new ones, to create products D and E, and so on.

A classic example is the Toyota RAV4, which pioneered the 'soft roader' class of light four-wheel-drive vehicles. This was essentially a jacked-up, re-skinned Toyota Corolla station wagon with the engine, gearbox and drivetrain of a Toyota Camry 4WD saloon. So, while the early 1990s fad for 4WD saloons fizzled out before the Camry 4WD achieved many sales, the investment in its drivetrain paid off via its use in the RAV4. Many of the other car makers that copied Toyota's soft roader concept did so in much the same way: Subaru, for example, had specialized in producing saloons and station wagons for the on-road 4WD niche and came up with the Forester as a rebodied, higher-riding version of its Impreza model, which was in turn essentially a shortened version of its Legacy.

When management writers call these benefits 'synergy effects', rather than economies of scope, they often try to get the message across by saying that 'the whole is greater than the sum of the parts', or that there is a '2 + 2 = 5 effect'. As might be expected with any case of '2 + 2 = 5', these kinds of economies pose major problems for deciding precisely what the cost of a product is or, if there are economies of scope in marketing, what a product's demand is. Box 10.1 provides an example of this.

Box 10.1 The problem of separating joint costs

Economies of scope/synergy effects may seem ripe for discussion in terms of cost curve/demand curve diagrams. We could first draw a pair of diagrams for two distinct products to show what their costs and revenues would each be if they were developed, produced and marketed entirely separately. If economies of scope exist in terms of development or production, total fixed costs are reduced if the two products are developed and/or produced to some extent jointly, so their cost curves move to the left to some degree. If there are economies of scope in marketing, then marketing the products together pushes their demand curves out to the right and/or pushes their cost curves to the left (as marketing expenses in total are reduced). So far so good, but we are then presented with a puzzle that makes decisions about the viability of any of the related products difficult to resolve: how do we separate any shared costs and allocate them to each of the products?

If the products are developed sequentially, as with the original Toyota and Subaru soft roaders, then any sunk costs in terms of technology used from the earlier donor product should not, in economic terms, be included in the costs of the later one. In other words, the development of the original Subaru Forester did not reduce the fixed costs of developing the Subaru Impreza, since the Impreza had already been developed before the Forester concept had been dreamt up, but the pre-existence of the Impreza certainly lowered the fixed costs of the Forester compared with what they would have been if Subaru had started designing it from scratch. Matters are different, however,

> **Box 10.1 (continued)**
>
> regarding the development of the second generation Impreza and Forester products, and here the problem of allocating shared costs is much as it would be where two products are developed jointly at the same time. Although once again the Impreza came out first, Subaru's engineers would have been incurring development costs on it mindful of which parts of the design would be incorporated into the next Forester. They could consider rather more expensive engineering options than with the original car. As far as variable costs are concerned, we can say that if the use of particular components in both the Impreza and the Forester enabled Subaru to get these components supplied in a larger volume at a cheaper unit price, then producing both the Impreza and the Forester enables the variable cost curves of both cars to be lower than they would if only one of the two were produced.

Economies of scope/synergy effects may also be achieved in terms of the firm's pool of expertise, so that learning how to do particular new things has payoffs for the firm's pre-existing lines of business, whether in the form of improved systems of production or distribution, or in improvements to product quality. For example, Toyota had to learn how to make a better finished, much quieter, more refined car when it set out to compete with Mercedes-Benz, BMW and Cadillac with its Lexus range. Many of the lessons it learnt are now incorporated in lesser Toyotas, one example being sound-deadening steel made from a steel/asphalt sandwich that is used in the firewall between the engine and passenger compartments.

To the extent that we have information about shared components and expertise, we can use this as a basis for deciding on the relative thickness of the links we draw on synergy maps. Figure 10.3 attempts to capture the essence of the 'same broad technology, same broad market' strategy of Mercedes-Benz, though for simplicity we have not tried to show the coupe, convertible or sports versions that are part of some of its model lines. The marketing link is shared by all – same brand name, same distribution network – whereas in terms of parts the A-class rather stands alone, despite embodying the firm's engineering expertise, compared with the larger products, which draw from a shared set of engines. Note that this diagram applies to the firm's car products prior to the Daimler–Chrysler merger and the merged firm's purchase of about 40 per cent of Mitsubishi Motors, which have bought further opportunities for synergy.

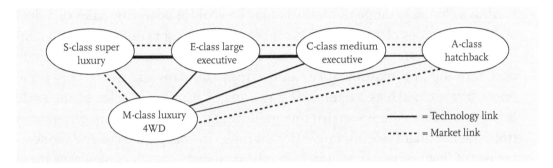

Figure 10.3 Simplified synergy map for Mercedes-Benz cars

On the marketing side, economies of scope may be achieved in a variety of ways:

◆ A bigger product range enables more effective use of investments in advertising – for example, being able to show more products in a full-page newspaper advertisement or getting a particular image attached to multiple products (such as the range-embracing 'Bloody Volvo Drivers' campaign, rather than just a 'Bloody Volvo XC90 drivers' campaign).

◆ There may be 'halo effects' from a new top-range model that will enhance the brand equity of cheaper models – for example, Volkswagen's venture into the super-luxury car segment with its Phaeton product may pay off not so much from Phaeton sales being profitable in their own right but by adding to perceptions of status and quality associated with owning a more mundane VW Golf or Passat, thereby reducing their price elasticities of demand and/or making customers more willing to purchase their more expensive variants. In other words, much of the profit generated by the Phaeton is expected to come from an increased willingness of buyers to see a top-end Golf as a substitute for a BMW. (As it happens, the Phaeton also has a good deal of engineering overlap with new Bentley products being developed since VW took over that firm, and with the luxury VW Touareg and Porsche Cayenne four-wheel-drives.) Related to this is what we might call **aspirational brand loyalty**, in the sense that young, relatively poor customers who have dreams of one day owning the top-end model may get a taste of the brand by buying the cheapest model offered under the brand, and then progressively trade up as their incomes increase. A crucial ingredient here is that the low-end products do give a taste of the top end in terms of, say, the way that the components fit together, their perceived quality and overall finish, even if the product's price is kept down by offering rather little as standard by way of features and performance. If the customers' dreams are not shattered, there is a chance of keeping them loyal for the rest of their lives.

- Having a complete range of products may be vital for achieving sales of a fleet of different grades of a product. This is because sticking to one brand with similar parts and systems reduces the buyers' **transaction costs** and may simplify user training and maintenance. Aside from company car fleets, this issue arises in areas such as aviation. It was a major hurdle for sales of the early European Airbus: there was just one product and it had significant differences from the dominant Boeing range (for example, in cockpit design and pioneering use of fly-by-wire rather than hydraulic systems); nowadays, however, there are Airbus products for many different parts of the air transport market.

- Faced with a choice between stocking products from a multitude of manufacturers and offering extensive product lines from just a few, retailers may prefer the latter strategy if it is seen as reducing their transaction costs and giving them, as more substantial customers, greater bargaining leverage – the manufacturers with which they deal have much more to lose if the relationship goes sour.

Note here that firms have to consider very carefully the perceptions of different customer groups when diversifying into new market segments. Sometimes it pays *not* to use an established brand in a new setting, even if the product has technological linkages with existing ones. A case in point is the Lexus luxury car. In Japan, Toyota is the dominant car maker and is highly regarded, so what was sold in the rest of the world as the first Lexus was branded in Japan as a Toyota Celsior, with scope for halo effects on lesser models as per the Volkswagen Phaeton strategy. However, for export markets, the firm opted to invest in creating the Lexus brand from scratch because outside Japan Toyota was not recognized as a maker of premium quality, standard-setting vehicles in lower market segments.

Now, suppose that in a particular market niche the competing firms are pursuing very different strategies in terms of scale and scope. Some might be specializing in that niche (for example, as Daihatsu does with small cars, or Subaru does with its all-wheel-drive vehicles), but others might offer a much more comprehensive range of products in an attempt to achieve wide-ranging economies of scope. Unless the specialists are able to come up with better product designs in their chosen niche or better ways of making their particular kind of product, or achieve marketing economies because they become known as the specialists who offer better value for money in that area, their ability to survive against the firms with broader product ranges may be in doubt. (Note here that in recent years Daihatsu and Subaru have become associates of Toyota and General Motors, respectively.) Unless specialization has these kinds of advantages, the message is loud and clear:

Attempts by one firm to achieve economies of scope by extending its product range are prone to be contagious, since they increase the competitive pressure on rival firms that have smaller product ranges.

For example, the expansion of the Mercedes-Benz product range into smaller cars and luxury four-wheel-drive vehicles enabled the firm to offer a better deal (or achieve higher profit margins and, with them, stronger potential for research and development) on its traditional products. Hence the firm was able to steal sales from rivals such as BMW, Saab and Jaguar that had narrower product ranges. BMW soon followed with its own four-wheel-drive vehicles and began developing a smaller, entry-level range. Meanwhile, both firms were facing stronger competition from Toyota as the latter expanded its Lexus range. For Saab and Jaguar, already struggling with smaller product ranges and ageing designs, there would have been little hope had they not been taken over by, respectively, General Motors and Ford. They were then able to share components or the costs of developing new models with other product lines in their new owners' empires. In the case of Saab, the situation was sufficiently desperate in North America for a complete car to be borrowed from elsewhere in the GM family: with minor reworking of body panels, Subaru's Impreza has thus been reborn for the North American market as the Saab 9-2X. The hope is that this will help North American Saab dealers achieve enough business to stop them from defecting to rivals. It also assists Subaru to fill its production lines and spread its engineering costs across a larger volume of output. Such strategies are risky expedients: what is gained in terms of economies of scope on the production side may be offset by damage to brand equity if customers, assisted by the reports of motoring journalists, realize how much the prestige brand's product shares with products that have far less cachet.

10.5.3 Synergy and hedging

The kinds of strategies just considered increase the competitive strength of firms within a particular sector and reduce their vulnerability to shifts of demand between different parts of that sector. Such strategies do, however, leave firms that implement them vulnerable to disturbances that affect the sector as a whole. For the managers of the car firms it is probably unthinkable that the market for cars could vanish overnight, but even so we can find some car makers involved in other sectors. Their component manufacturers may have a much more obvious need to hedge their bets: they have to worry about the risk of losing a major customer or that a particular kind of component will no longer be required. For example, carburettors have been replaced in most vehicles by electronic fuel injection (EFI) systems due to a combination of stiffer emissions controls and learning effects in the production of EFI systems.

Even if managers are not nervous about the prospects for the kinds of products they presently make, all of the previous arguments about the case for diversification apply if they expand into new areas that at least have (or seem potentially to have) some things in common with what they are already doing. So long as the managers' attention is not unduly diverted from their existing operations, any economies of scope they achieve by growing their business into new markets may help their strength in the existing ones, in whose markets further growth may in any case be difficult.

A more radical approach to linkage-based diversification is thus where the new products that the firm takes on are based on **transferring knowledge and capabilities amongst different kinds of products** rather than variations on the same basic idea. For example:

- Canon makes still and video cameras, fax machines, printers, scanners and photocopiers.

- Shimano, famous as the most successful supplier of gear-sets and other parts for bicycles, has expanded its operations to include fishing tackle, golf clubs and, as mentioned earlier, snowboarding products.

- Within a few decades of its formation, General Motors' activities expanded beyond cars to include railway locomotives and the Frigidaire range of 'white goods' (stoves, refrigerators, washing machines and air-conditioning systems). Likewise, half a century later, Daimler-Benz, the makers of Mercedes-Benz cars and trucks, came to have interests in aircraft production and control of the A.E.G. brand of electrical appliances.

If we reflect on the kinds of capabilities/strategic assets likely to be required for success in the areas that these firms have linked together, the strategies all seem to have a logical basis:

- All of the Canon products listed capture images (whether on film, on paper, on tape or in an electronic memory). The quality of their performance depends on optics, ability to process images into digitized dots, capacity to be programmed in a user-friendly manner and ability to move a complementary product (paper, film or tape) in a precise and reliable manner.

- Shimano's products all involve outdoor recreation in areas where sudden lapses in performance could prove very costly to the user. Bicycle gear-sets and fishing reels use similar kinds of components (gears, bearings, mounting assemblies, control grips); the main difference is simply that one handles a chain and the other handles a line. Like bicycle components, golf clubs have cold-forged metal parts. Golf clubs also have handgrips, as do fishing rods. Snowboards need to be able to grip the user's feet but in a way that enables the user to disengage from them without difficulty, just as with racing-style bicycle pedals (otherwise, though, links between snowboarding products and other Shimano products are harder to see).

♦ White goods have a surprising amount in common with cars: they are essentially assemblages of coated steel pressings, plastic and electrical components, with doors that open. General Motors has even been able to use the same trademarked model name on both kinds of products: 'Caprice' has been applied to mundane Chevrolets in the USA and both top-of-the-line GM–Holden Statesman cars (which are also sold in the Middle East as Chevrolet Caprices) and, in the 1970s, Frigidaire ovens in Australia. (Given the iconic role of the Holden brand in Australian culture, it is perhaps no surprise that the ovens also had badges proclaiming 'Frigidaire by General Motors–Holden.) Modern electrical appliances increasingly depend on complex electronic control systems and in some countries A.E.G. appliances have been advertised as being produced by the company that makes Mercedes-Benz cars. Expertise in the design of upmarket cars has, if one thinks about it, quite a lot in common with the design of aircraft, in areas such as expertise with aerodynamics, control systems, design of seating and so on. We might also note that A.E.G.'s expertise with electric motors for washing machines could prove valuable in upcoming Mercedes-Benz hybrid petrol-/electric-powered vehicles.

Given this, we should not be surprised to find automotive parts manufacturers also having associations with white goods production: Bendix may be best known in the UK for washing machines and driers, but in the USA the firm nowadays specializes in automotive parts (even including an air drier system for truck trailers). Similarly, we find that German domestic appliance maker Bosch is also one of the world's leading manufacturers of automotive technology systems (there is even a Porsche-designed coffee maker in the Bosch range of appliances!).

From a synergy map standpoint, we can see that strategies that involve a firm trying to link activities together whilst branching into new areas can take two main forms. One is where there is a consistent thread, either in marketing or on the production side, running through the firm's activities; this is known as a

related-constrained strategy (see Figure 10.4). The other is where there are a variety of marketing and technology threads linking different elements of the firm's set of production activities; this is known as a **related-linked strategy** (see Figure 10.5).

Our fictitious firm Dunsell initially had a related-constrained strategy, since everything it did in its early years was related to rubber but for an increasingly diverse set of markets. Even its initial diversification in the tyre market might be said to be related-constrained rather than variations on its original theme, since the distribution channels for bicycle and car tyres are different, even if there are marketing synergies in terms of the brand name being associated in people's minds with tyres in general. Gradually, however, its strategy became related-linked, since it began to develop products with different kinds of production technologies (car batteries and sports racquets) according to choices of markets it had already made in order to exploit its expertise in rubber. Overall, though, Dunsell still has the flavour of an essentially related-constrained business: it is a rubber-based company by and large and it would have very major problems in the event of something catastrophic happening to the supply of rubber. For hedging against nasty shocks it is wiser to choose a related-linked strategy in which the firm's viability does not depend crucially on the continued viability of any particular market or technology. The crucial thing to do before making such

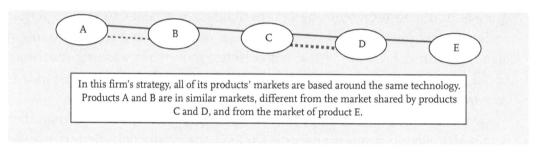

In this firm's strategy, all of its products' markets are based around the same technology. Products A and B are in similar markets, different from the market shared by products C and D, and from the market of product E.

Figure 10.4 Synergy map of related-constrained diversification

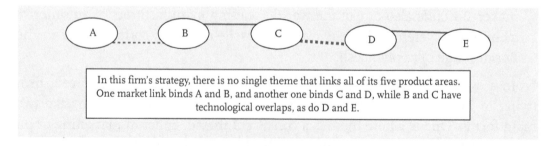

In this firm's strategy, there is no single theme that links all of its five product areas. One market link binds A and B, and another one binds C and D, while B and C have technological overlaps, as do D and E.

Figure 10.5 Synergy map of related-linked diversification

choices is to explore **scenarios** regarding such catastrophes and consider how much paranoia is justified.

10.5.4 Synergy links are subjective and in need of management

The strength or even the existence of particular links in a synergy map may be highly debatable. Consider once again the case of Dunsell in Figure 10.2. We might argue that since the three categories of sports goods that Dunsell makes may sell through the same stores and carry the same brand name as a symbol of the kind of performance they offer for a particular price, it is appropriate to indicate strong marketing links between these areas of the firm's business. A much weaker marketing link, but still probably a link of some kind, seems likely between condoms and domestic rubber gloves because they are both distributed via supermarkets and pharmacies and carry the same brand name, which may signify something about their strength despite the thinness of the rubber from which they are made. (Links in terms of production technology seem to be very strong indeed here.) But is the significance more to purchasing officers in supermarkets, rather than customers who might come from quite different age and demographic groups? Moreover, these products also sell through other distribution channels: hospitals and medical practices do not buy their surgical gloves from supermarkets. It would be yet more tenuous to draw a link between the ice cream and snack food operations and anything else in Dunsell's portfolio of activities. Even so, we might argue that it is possible that there is a little scope for transfer of expertise between this sector and the condoms/gloves sector in terms of production line management. There might also be a synergy effect on the distribution side in terms of bargaining leverage with supermarket chains. However, although it may be possible to buy the firm's sporting products and refresh oneself with its ice cream and snack foods at some sporting clubs, it seems unlikely that there is any marketing synergy here since the products carry different brand names and are delivered from different sites.

Though the strengths of links may remain uncertain, a willingness to debate the likely strengths of synergy linkages in a firm whose strategy is being mapped should help you develop skills in doing a finer-grained analysis of economies of scope and in knowing the kinds of questions it would be fruitful to ask when visiting firms or talking with managers to whom you are going to be providing advice.

The subjective element in mapping synergy from the outside applies on the inside of the firm too, implying a vital role for management in ensuring that synergy potential is recognized and realized in highly diversified businesses. Once we move beyond a focus on products sharing production lines and parts towards the idea that much of a firm's pool of strategic assets consists of expertise, the potential for economies of scope seems far greater in a firm with a related-linked strategy than it otherwise might do. In other words, there may be potential for synergy between products that are *not* developed in the same laboratories, are *not* made using some in-common parts on a shared assembly line and are *not* sold through the same distribution channels. In such cases, it is necessary to focus on the firm's ability to use its **human resources** to spread their special knowledge around inside the firm to improve other parts of its business and in the process to generate new capabilities. This is particularly likely to happen if fostered by a management team who know where expertise lies within their firm and can combine it in new teams to produce cumulating benefits from related diversification. Without management actively seeking to co-ordinate the use of their firm's capabilities, or without active networking by staff with key forms of expertise, potential for achieving the various forms of economies of scope/synergy may be wasted. Some knowledge of the track record of a firm's management style and internal operational culture may be very useful in assessing whether or not knowledge that a firm possesses is likely to be mobilized to achieve synergy, or whether it will be prone to be akin to **tacit knowledge** – not tacit knowledge in the usual sense that people with expertise couldn't articulate it, but in the sense that, because they weren't asked, they didn't voice it to people in the firm who might have found it useful.

The role of management in realizing this potential becomes more significant the larger the business. Universities provide a good example of this: in a small university, interdisciplinary collaboration is likely to thrive because specialists in particular disciplines have a bigger chance of meeting staff from other fields in central refreshment and dining areas, and people who have been around for a while may know quite a high percentage of staff in the university as a whole. In a large institution, by contrast, it may be hard enough even to get to know well all of one's colleagues in a large specialized department (perhaps with its own tearoom and localized dining area), let alone to mingle with staff from other departments, even those in the same faculty.

Some indication that, in practice, economies of scope are far from easy to achieve in large, highly diversified organizations comes in what financial economists know as the '**diversification discount**': stock markets seem to value diversified firms less than diversified portfolios made up of shares in specialized firms. This phenomenon may not be due merely to capabilities being harder to co-ordinate in highly diversified, sprawling businesses whose scope breaches Miller's Rule in terms of the demands they place on the limited attention of boundedly rational managers. It may also be a consequence of the tendency for them to be put together via mergers (see Section 10.6) or the internal politics of large firms and how they are structured (see Section 10.8).

10.5.5 Can we make sense of conglomerate firms?

A conglomerate business is one whose activities are largely or entirely unrelated to each other in terms of either shared technologies or shared markets.

Less than 5 per cent of the world's largest companies are conglomerates but, despite the competitive strengths offered by strategies based around the pursuit of economies of scale and scope, the conglomerate firm shows little sign of being a dying breed. To be sure, some famous conglomerates have reinvented themselves as far more focused businesses: for example, Hanson, now a leading UK supplier of heavy construction materials, was previously a successful conglomerate which also manufactured products as diverse as Smith's potato crisps and Ever-Ready batteries. However, new conglomerates continue to be assembled: one recent success story is the Australian firm Wesfarmers, which claims to achieve 'strength through diversity' from a portfolio of activities that includes hardware retailing, rail transport, forest products, energy, industrial and safety products, chemicals and fertilizers, and insurance (though no longer does its portfolio include the network of rural agencies on which the firm was originally based).

Such firms remain rather mysterious to business economists, for they ought to have trouble surviving in the face of competition with firms that benefit from specialization or economies of scope. Even if we see them as miniature capital markets in which top managers are milking some divisions of funds to provide investment resources for other divisions that they judge to have better prospects, we need to ask why the managers can generate better results for shareholders than the latter could get by holding diversified share portfolios. Some plausible explanations for the enduring phenomenon of the conglomerate are as follows:

◆ What managers of conglomerates lack in terms of expertise about the specific operations of their firms' various divisions they might more than make up for in terms of ability to make credible threats to sell off or close down areas of poor performance, since this can be done without harming other parts of their businesses. Divisional managers with a lot of autonomy thus have a strong motivation to get the best out of their parts of the business, to avoid being fired or ending up in less powerful positions if their part of the firm is sold off and merged into a division of a more focused business. Note that this argument presumes that the external capital market is somewhat inefficient, for otherwise the various divisions would perform just as well if they were stand-alone businesses.

- Some conglomerates might result from the operations of entrepreneurs who are particularly adept at spotting companies that are well run but undervalued by the stock market. Such entrepreneurs may be rather like used-car dealers or antiques dealers: they keep churning over their portfolios of companies, buying them cheaply and then selling them for much more after finding businesses for which they fulfil a strategic need.

- Some conglomerates may emerge as a result of firms with related-linked strategies having experienced difficulties that led to the demise of particular divisions and hence the breaking of the chain of linkages (in Figure 10.5, for example, the demise of divisions B and D would leave a much reduced firm with no links between the remaining divisions).

- The top managers of some conglomerates may function like a team of superior management consultants with generic skills in improving performance of particular kinds of ailing businesses that they have taken over. (Hanson seemed to fit this characterization when it revived the faded glory of Smith's and Ever-Ready after taking control of these firms.) This line of argument also implies weaknesses in capital markets such that the ailing businesses were not sufficiently under pressure to hire consultants themselves and to take their advice. However, it does not imply that the management team will have a need to keep control of the divisions that they revive. In the absence of further firms to buy and, so to speak, to 'renovate', they would tend to be driven to focus, as Hanson did, on developing a particular area after divesting the revived businesses.

- Some firms that superficially seem to be conglomerates may on closer examination be quite closely integrated structures. In the case of Wesfarmers, for example, it is conceivable that the rail division handles movements of timber, coal and liquefied gas, that its timber and fertilizer products are sold through its hardware stores, that its industrial/safety products are used extensively in its primary industry activities and that their retailing to other users has much in common with hardware retailing. At the very least, such a firm could be said to be mainly involved in primary industries, all of which have some things in common in terms of safety and logistical issues as well as involving products that are low in value relative to their bulk.

- Some conglomerates might be temporary devices created by managers who cannot see a long-term future for their firm's core operations and who are trying to get a sense of what business they might be suited to managing instead. The ones with which they do not feel comfortable will then be sold off.

◆ Some conglomerates might result from managers having foresight regarding the potential growth of entirely new businesses and using earnings from older businesses to develop unrelated new activities one after another. The history of Nokia has some similarities with this scenario: the firm began as a forestry company and branched into rubber products and cables, and then into information technology activities before setting out to become a major player in the mobile phone market. After divesting its earlier activities, Nokia now specializes in mobile phones.

These lines of thinking all entail an attempt to see economic logic for the conglomerate form of business in a world of problems of information and knowledge. But we should not discount the possibility that some conglomerates are assembled by entrepreneurs who have some kind of personality disorder, such as a desire for grandiosity in the things that they do, and a sociopathic disregard for those whose money they lose when their empires collapse due to an inability to service the debts incurred to put them together.

10.6 Growth via mergers and takeovers

As far as the economic well-being of the population at large is concerned, it is often preferable that firms grow in size by building new factories, filling them with new equipment and training up new teams of workers. In this way, corporate growth is associated with growth in output and employment, though of course in some cases the social outcomes may not be improved if extra industrial activity adds to pollution and the new factories simply drive existing ones out of business. Much of the corporate growth that has taken place over the last century has, however, been based not on creating new productive assets but on changing the ownership of existing firms. Sceptics might see this as mere paper-shuffling that mainly benefits the merchant bankers who help firms to put together takeover or merger deals.

As an example of how a firm can use the acquisitions approach to growth to assemble a complex business over the long term, consider the history of Pacific Dunlop, the inspiration for our fictitious Dunsell case. Figure 10.6 comes from an ingenious attempt by one of our MBA students, Mark Grimmer, to save several thousand words by charting the firm's growth diagrammatically both in terms of synergy linkages and acquisitions. This corporate empire is now gradually being

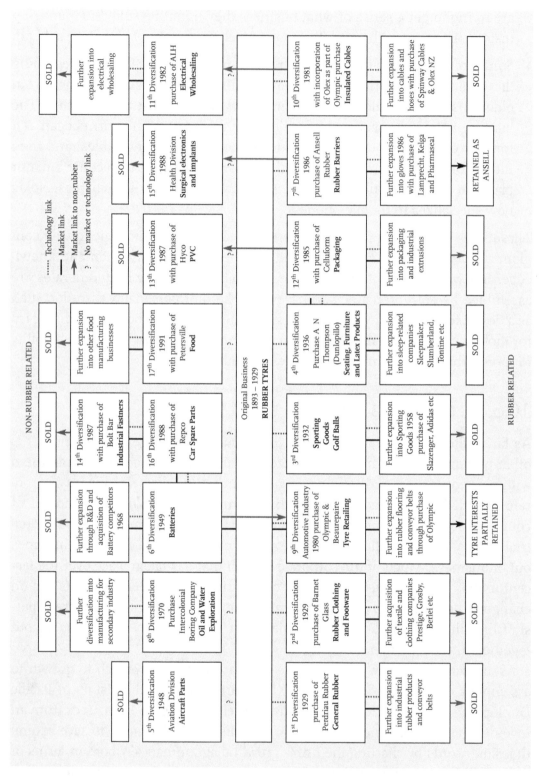

Figure 10.6 Diversification and acquisitions in the history of Pacific Dunlop

unravelled via a series of divestments as the firm recasts itself simply as Ansell, a world leader in rubber barrier healthcare products.

From the standpoint of managers, acquisition-based growth such as this has a number of advantages over internal growth based on investment in new assets:

- Aside from fees to merchant bankers, it may be possible to 'pay' for the firm that is being acquired purely by a share issue in which new shares in one's company are offered in exchange for shares in the company that is being taken over. This may be rather more straightforward than an attempt to float new shares on the stock market, given that one is dealing with a particular group of shareholders, not the market at large.

- The purchase of an existing company removes the need to incur transaction costs in hiring new workers or in buying buildings, plant and machinery.

- The firm obtains instant access to an existing share of the market, rather than having to compete for it.

- The 'Penrose problem' of having to assemble a new management team and overcome problems of tacit knowledge is largely avoided if a going concern is purchased.

Despite these apparent advantages compared with internal growth, studies of pre- and post-merger performance often find that the combined business turns out to be less profitable than the parts from which it was formed; it is as though there is a kind of **negative synergy**, a '2 + 2 = 3 effect', hence the **diversification discount** observed in terms of stock market valuations of such firms.

This should not be very surprising, since:

- If existing shareholders and other potential shareholders are aware of the attractions of the taken-over firm, the acquirer may have to pay a premium price to win control and gain little compared with starting from scratch in the market in question. Worse still, if the acquirer gets involved in a bidding war it may end up paying more than the assets are worth, a problem known as the **winner's curse**. In some cases the rival bidder may have a clearer idea of the worth of the firm (for example, because it is an existing rival, whereas the winner is entering new territory) and may be deliberately trying to weaken the acquirer.

- Mergers and takeovers are often done in a hurried manner, to try to prevent other bidders from entering the battle for control. This may result in a failure to see problems with the target company due to an insufficiently diligent investigation of its situation. As with used cars or houses that are bought in a hurry, a pre-owned company can often be a major source of disappointment to its new owners.

- Once the ownership of two companies is combined, performance improvements will only occur if there is **integration** and **rationalization** of operations to achieve economies of scale and scope. This may be difficult if the **operating cultures** of the two organizations are very different and if managers concentrate their efforts on protecting their existing empires and status. While top management are trying to assess what can really be done to achieve economies in the face of such 'turf guarding' behaviour, other areas of the firm's operations may suffer due to a lack of **attention** from them.

- Any competitive advantage that a firm does get from rapid, merger-based growth is prone to be eroded rapidly by rivals in the same market engaging in copycat mergers. Of course, if the copycat mergers are done in a hurry, whilst there are still potential corporate 'marriage' partners available, then the latter may be similarly prone to deliver poor performance.

A consequence of the frequency of disappointing corporate marriages is further corporate marriages that rewire the pattern of ownership links in the economy: one firm divests a company that it had previously purchased, which is then acquired by another company as part of the latter's growth process. Acquirers face further risks in such cases, for a firm that is being sold supposedly on the basis that it did not fit properly with its owner's strategy might well have been subject to a process of **asset stripping**, in which key equipment and personnel that were indeed useful to the initial acquirer's other lines of business are transferred to it.

10.7 Inter-firm linkages

Business economists nowadays need to make sense of forms of corporate growth involving various forms of **quasi-integration**. Firms are increasingly expanding their spheres of influence or achieving greater economies of scope in ways that make it hard to consider their situations in isolation from other firms with whom they have some kind of connection. For example, it often turns out that a takeover raider does not bother to obtain all the shares in its target company and then have it de-listed from the stock market. It may simply rest content with a 51 per cent shareholding or even a significant minority shareholding. Such strategies may enable the management team to extend its domain far wider than it could by always taking 100 per cent control. Minority shareholdings elsewhere in the firm's supply chains, combined with interlocking directorships, provide opportunities to improve the co-ordination of complementary investment and to assure supply. If necessary, a minority shareholder can seek to influence the company's behaviour by threatening to sell its shareholding to another player who might thereby gain control and replace the management team. In short, such shareholdings can have major **strategic value** even if it is difficult to see how they are likely to be conducive to economies of scope.

Another kind of inter-firm linkage arises when a firm seeks to limit its need to acquire new capabilities when diversifying and does this by trading economies of scope/synergy with other firms. Firms can get involved with new products by combining untapped potential of their own resources with resources from other firms that specialize in doing different things that are not specific to the latter's product lines. For example, another business might be able to use a brand name under licence, or a business with a valuable brand name might purchase output from another and then resell under that brand name. These trades are common. (The Saab 9-2X could have been created in this way even if Saab and Subaru were not both under the wing of General Motors.) Sometimes they can even be win–win ways of dealing with actual or potential producers of pirated versions of one's products. Common, too, is the practice of letting other companies have access to technical expertise or production capacity, for a fee. Classic examples of the latter are Lotus and Porsche, whose expertise in the design of sports cars has led them to be sought after as consultants by manufacturers of more mundane vehicles who want better suspension systems for their products. Lotus has also allowed a somewhat reworked, Vauxhall-engined version of its Elise to be sold by Vauxhall (as the VX220) as part of the latter's efforts to 'sex up' its product range.

These kinds of synergy trading arrangements are far less of a challenge for managers than **joint ventures** and **strategic alliances** in which two or more companies pool some of their resources to work together on new projects. The original European Airbus project was an early example of this that straddled several borders and resulted in Boeing having to compete with a product that none of the consortium members was big enough to handle on their own.

Economists initially tended to view **joint ventures as *single* collaborative projects**. Their rationale was not obvious, since co-ordination of such projects is inherently costly when the management teams know little about each other's operations. Worse still, there is the problem that when a definite end point is looming, such ventures would be vulnerable to **opportunistic behaviour**: each player would start trying to milk the arrangement in their best interests, particularly if, at the end of it, they would be seeing each other only as rivals.

Given these difficulties, it might be tempting to see a single joint venture as a prelude to merger activity between the venture partners, rather like seeing living together as a prelude to marriage: the firms can treat the costs of the joint venture as an investment in getting to know each other. This is a perspective that Neil Kay challenges. He argues that joint ventures are undertaken between firms that do not have enough in common to make a merger worthwhile or feasible, but where there is a *temporary* 'hot spot' of mutual interest whose scale is pretty small compared with each of the players' overall operations. To merge, as a means of both getting benefit from the opportunity, would be like 'taking a sledgehammer to crack a walnut'. Co-ordination costs may be high in a joint venture but the costs of product development, say, may be far less than if each firm tried to go it alone and acquire missing know-how by themselves rather than by sharing their distinctive capabilities: if firms A and B developed new products independently the cost might be, say, $100 million each, whereas if they developed them together, the total cost of both might be only $150 million, despite all the difficulties involved in managing the process. If it were expected that the joint development cost could be reduced to $120 million by a merger between A and B but that negative synergies in respect of other areas of the merged firm would lead to a reduction in profits in these other areas by more than $30 million, the joint venture would be the preferred strategy.

Strategic alliances involve *multiple collaborative arrangements* between a pair of firms, rather like twinning arrangements between pairs of towns or universities. Each individual arrangement thus needs to be understood in its broader strategic context: sometimes it may entail one firm getting a better return than the other, on the expectation of doing better on another act of collaboration later on, possibly by tapping into the growing strength and expertise of its partner in a particular area. Frequent interaction reduces the costs of managing interactions between the firms: managers get to know each other personally and to know the cultures of their respective organizations. The longer-term focus discourages opportunistic behaviour towards the end of any single project, since it might jeopardize the continuation of the relationship.

As with mergers, where one major marriage in an industry may spark off a wave of counter-mergers, the formation of one strategic alliance in an industry may increase the competitive pressure on other firms who, in turn, pair up in search of ways of innovating or reducing their costs. This, in turn, may lead to the formation of corporate *networks* or *clubs*, **in which firms form alliances with multiple firms, but tend to choose as their new partners firms that are already collaborating with their existing partners**. It is only recently that business economists have started to recognize and try to make sense of how these networks provide benefits for members. One emerging theme is that alliances that are formed in these contexts have much better potential for not being marred by opportunistic behaviour, including leaks of sensitive knowledge to firms in rival networks. Networks help to deter opportunism by providing extra channels of influence: if you can't influence a partner directly, you might be able to get some leverage via another member of the same network. The network may also lead to more rapid spread of information about opportunism, hence deterring it, and about the location of people with particular capabilities within other firms in the network, hence facilitating synergies.

10.8 Intra-firm linkages: economics of organizational structure

A firm's organizational structure is the set of connections by which employees are linked to each other in the process of decision making.

10.8.1 The organization problem

A small firm, such as a partnership, may get by without a formal organizational structure, with all members being able to interact directly with each other, in effect operating as a **field** rather than a **complex system**. As a firm grows, however, the problem of **bounded rationality** forces its managers to divide it up into specific departments and limit communications to particular channels. Some kind of tree-like management hierarchy is a typical solution to the bounded rationality problem: overload is limited because the number of other members of the firm with which any one member normally communicates is limited to a specific set of connections.

In large firms, top-level managers may thus have little interaction with line workers, or with middle managers from other divisions, except on specific committees. From the standpoint of the line worker, it may be frustrating to be unable to 'take it to the top' when there is a problem that an immediate manager is not addressing, but without the requirement to communicate through particular channels, senior decision makers would get overloaded. It may also be frustrating if the firm's structure limits scope for direct sideways communication between people on the same level and instead requires that their messages are passed up the management hierarchy to a person who has links back down to the person with whom they need to communicate. However, if people at low levels can freely interact with others on similar levels, their particular managers may have difficulty knowing what their subordinates are doing.

The problem of organizational design is thus to come up with a structure that limits information overload by limiting connections (along with the associated costs of arranging and attending meetings) and at the same time does not promote **opportunism** by subordinates whose bosses cannot **monitor** all that they do.

The solution in large organizations often involves in part the creation of markets inside the firm:

(i) **An internal product market.** Divisions of a firm will trade goods and services with each other at internal 'transfer prices' that are the result of negotiation between divisions and may even be the subjects of contested bidding processes.

(ii) **An internal capital market.** Like bankers and buyers and sellers of shares, managers at various levels make decisions on the relative merits of competing proposals for the allocation of funds to the various activities in which the firm has, or might have, an interest.

(iii) **An internal labour market.** Decisions are taken about whom to promote, demote or move sideways on the basis of how well workers compete with their fellow employees.

Collusion may be a problem in internal markets, just as in external ones. The internal politics of a firm may thus affect its performance.

The impact of internal politics on the process of organizational change is very evident in the pioneering work of Alfred Chandler (1962) on the relationshp between corporate strategy and organizational structure. Chandler's picture of the process of organizational change sees the process as often driven by management problems due to increasing size, which force the management team to slow down growth temporarily and come up with a more effective structure. He identifies four 'chapters' of evolution:

1. The initial growth and accumulation of resources.

2. Rationalization of the use of resources and the development of an integrated, *function*-based organizational structure. Because this way of organizing things lumps all of the firm's products together, it is commonly known as a **U-form structure**, where the 'U' stands for 'unitary'.

3. Expansion into new markets in an attempt to ensure the continuing full employment of corporate resources.

4. The development of a new structure based on *product* or *regional* divisions. This arrangement, known as a multi-divisional (**M-form**) structure, recasts the firm as a set of **profit centres** as a way of trying to make it easier for top

managers to make effective use of the firm's resources in the face of both short-term changes in market demands and long-term trends.

10.8.2 The U-form structure and its problems

Our fictional firm Dunsell Ltd provides a useful vehicle for exploring the costs and benefits of the two kinds of organizational structure that Chandler highlighted. According to Chandler's thesis, we would expect Dunsell to have a U-form structure in its early days as an expanding company yet to diversify beyond the markets for tyres. This is illustrated in Figure 10.7.

Insofar as a firm's growth has been based around the pursuit of economies of scope, this sort of structure seems to make perfect sense: each department can concentrate on achieving a particular synergy effect. Hence, in Dunsell Tyres Ltd, all the different kinds of tyres would be made in the same factory and improvements would be devised in the same laboratory, ensuring that what benefited one type of tyre could be readily used to improve other types of tyre and so on.

Unfortunately, the lack of separation of products under the U-form structure means it is difficult for the chief executive to decide which products and departments are performing well. If overall performance is not looking good, the chief executive officer (CEO) may have a hard time getting to the bottom of the problem at meetings of the executive committee. On such occasions, the heads of each functional division may seek to shift the blame to each other or promise that it can be sorted out if their own division is given more resources. Lobbying may continue outside of these formal meetings, making it hard for the CEO to get decisions made in a detached manner. CEOs can also become decision-making bottlenecks within their firms if they try to keep an eye on what is going on in

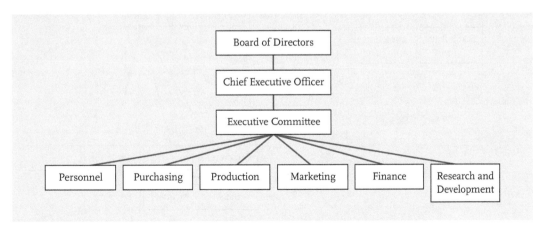

Figure 10.7 U-form (function-based) structure for Dunsell Tyres Ltd

each department by requiring that any expenditure of significance must be signed off by themselves.

10.8.3 The M-form structure

Figure 10.8 presents a plausible M-form structure for the grown-up version of Dunsell. Though we have not indicated any low-level structure for any of the divisions except for sporting products, the structure is fleshed out a bit more than a typical textbook example of an M-form firm. Mindful of Miller's 7 ± 2 Rule (see Section 1.4.1), we have added an extra layer – of divisions within divisions – to keep to a cognitively manageable seven the number of profit centres about which head office has to worry. To judge from the similarly limited number of divisions typically in evidence on corporate websites, and their tendency to have lower-level sub-divisions, actual management teams are devising structures that fit in with Miller's 'magic number' 7 ± 2.

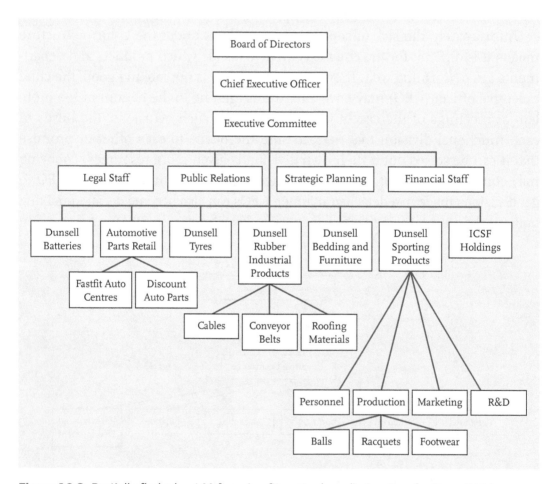

Figure 10.8 Partially fleshed-out M-form (profit centre based) structure for Dunsell Ltd

An M-form structure is supposed to simplify the strategic decision-making task whilst providing incentives for employees to perform in the interests of shareholders. The CEO can readily compare the performance of each division of the firm in terms of profitability, because the firm is divided up into a series of miniature U-form companies (as fleshed out on the diagram for Dunsell's sporting goods division), each of which handles a particular product area or is responsible for a particular geographic territory in which the firm operates, and each of which has its own specialized divisions for production, marketing, research and development, and so on. A head office of strategic planners advises the CEO on the merits of claims for resources and new projects to be signed off by the CEO. In theory, the CEO and colleagues at head office should be able to operate dispassionately when deciding where to expand or contract the firm, since the empires that are being expanded or contracted are those of the divisional heads and hence they do not have a conflict of interest. (It should also be noted that there is an 'out of sight, out of mind' issue here: head offices are often a long way away from operating divisions that might sometimes have to be closed down and whose workers might have to be made redundant.) Better still, the 'divide and rule' aspect of such a system of resource allocation should concentrate profit-centre managers and subordinates on delivering the best performance from their division to ensure a better chance of survival and growth for that division. In addition to providing performance data on their existing operations, divisions may be required to submit major proposals for approval by head office. Once some firms successfully adopted this structure, competitive pressures became greater still for other firms whose strategic expansion plans ran ahead of their awareness of the limitations of a U-form structure.

Based on these lines of thinking, M-form organizational structures have been employed in many recent attempts to restructure public service organizations, with efficiency advantages being expected due to a 'funder/provider' split. (The strategists decide who gets the funds; the operating divisions use their funds allocations to provide the outputs.) The 'Research Assessment Exercise' (RAE) that dominates the lives of many British academics is an example of this philosophy. However, M-form structures are by no means free of problems, and these provide further insight into the **diversification discount** phenomenon:

- There is an additional layer of highly paid senior managers and advisory staff, the price of getting lower-level personnel to behave in the interests of the company as a whole.

- ◆ The profit centres/'divide and rule' philosophy on which the M-form system is based may promote an obsession in the divisions with delivering results that can be measured immediately in terms of the indicators used by head office for deciding on funding allocations between the divisions.

- ◆ Strategic decision makers may not really be as coolly detached as all that from the interests of particular divisions if they have been promoted to head office from a particular division or if they have mixed head office/operational roles in order to save management costs. (This may not be so foolish as it sounds, for though divisional heads may naturally be inclined to try to defend and extend their empires, they have a much clearer idea of the resources they are working with and may be much closer to their customers. The arguments they put forward *may* be entirely sincere, not opportunistic.)

- ◆ There is a fundamental conflict between building a strategy around economies of scope and implementing it with the aid of a structure that works on a 'divide and rule' philosophy. A firm that adopts an M-form structure may unwittingly sacrifice synergy and actually promote non-co-operative behaviour between divisions that damages its overall long-run performance. This difficulty is particularly prone to arise for companies whose operations are both multinational and multi-product. Vertical links present similar problems: for example, Dunsell's tyre and battery divisions may hope to achieve much of their sales via the firm's automotive parts retailing division, while the latter's interests might be better served by being able to stock products by a range of manufacturers.

From the standpoint of this chapter, the threat to the realization of economies of scope is a major concern. Some firms have tried to deal with it by a matrix structure, in which middle managers are subordinate to several senior managers, but this often turns out to be too complicated as well as enabling subordinates to play off their superiors against each other. A more practical solution is for divisions to trade with each other, with the division having the biggest commitment to a particular shared function being the one that acts as a supplier to the others. Many firms end up employing mixed structures in which some departments offer centralized functions (for example, marketing or the services of a central research facility) to other divisions that are product-based.

10.9 Summary

The paths that firms take as they grow are shaped by problems of information and knowledge. Where tacit knowledge is not a problem, and where contracts can be designed to limit the use that other businesses make of knowledge that is made available by a contract, a firm can use licensing and franchising methods to capture profits whilst letting other businesses shoulder some of the burden of bringing its ideas, brand symbols and/or products to a wider market. Limits to the use of contracts in these ways force managers to develop bigger management teams and acquire new assets or take over existing businesses in order to expand both profits and the sizes of the empires that they administer. Such growth can only occur at a limited pace, both because of the time it takes to make bigger management teams function effectively and because new activities require new capabilities to be acquired. Management play a major role in the development of capabilities, both in terms of constructing alliances with other firms to develop new skills and in mobilizing their existing and newly hired resources in ways that foster the creative sharing of expertise.

Firms that grow by trying to exploit economies of scale reduce their need to develop new skills and complex organizational structures, but they make themselves strategically vulnerable by 'having all their eggs in the one basket'. Since cost advantages can come from economies of scope as well as of scale, there are competitive pressures to diversify into related activities. This also helps firms to hedge their bets against risks of sudden market- or technology-specific changes in their environments. Were it not for the limitations of management in a world of bounded rationality, it would be hard to see any limit to the size a firm might achieve by creating an intricate, multinational network of directly and indirectly connected activities to maximize economies of scope. Though some of today's firms are indeed sprawling diversified giants, there do indeed seem to be limits to the range of activities with which managers feel comfortable, and the linking threads between a typical corporation's activities can normally be inferred without great difficulty when one visits its website.

The emphasis on the role of economies of scope in the growth of the firm is problematic for traditional approaches to economics based on the presumption of separate cost and revenue curves for each product. Linkages between products markets served by a firm make the appraisal of the contribution of any particular product hard to assess. Dividing a firm up into profit centres runs the risk of solving this appraisal problem at the cost of losing potential economies of scope.

10.10　Some questions to consider

1. In contrast to the UK and northern Europe, domestic swimming pool maintenance is a sizable industry in Australia. Residents of a typical Australian suburb can normally choose between several specialist shops to buy equipment and pool chemicals, as well as being able to purchase some pool chemicals from supermarkets and hardware stores. If you had just arrived in Australia with no previous experience of this sector, would you be surprised to discover that franchise networks such as Poolwerx (see www.poolwerx.com.au) and Swimart (see www.swimart.com.au) dominate the market? Explain your economic reasoning.

2. The phrase 'McDonaldization' was coined by sociologist George Ritzer (2000) (in *The McDonaldization of Society*, Thousand Oaks, CA, Pine Forge Press) to denote the application of McDonald's-style business practices to a wide range of products beyond just hamburgers. These processes involve the use of highly programmed production methods to simplify production tasks for staff and bring calculability and predictability to production processes. Ritzer sees the higher education sector as one that is succumbing to this process. What limits the extent to which the principles of the fast-food restaurant can be applied to the supply of higher education services, particularly in the case of universities seeking to have their programmes offered at sites in other countries?

3. Imagine you are on the board of a tyre company and your fellow board members are debating whether or not the next phase of the firm's expansion should be (a) to integrate backwards into rubber plantations; (b) to diversify into producing rubber belts and hoses for the automotive sector; or (c) to diversify into the production of chemicals for use in solvent-based adhesives. Explain how you would use your training in business economics to contribute to this debate.

4. Nokia's pre-eminent position in the mobile phone handset market may seem remarkable given the firm's earlier history in the forest products, rubber and cable industries (see www.nokia.com). One of its major competitors, Ericsson, gave up producing mobile phone handsets to concentrate on telephone systems but has recently formed a 50:50 joint venture company with Sony, called Sony Ericsson Mobile Communications AB (SEMC), and both firms are investing heavily in it. In the light of material

10.10 **Some questions to consider** (continued)

on these firms' websites and at websites on the history of the telephone (for example, http://www.abc.net.au/rn/science/ss/stories/s871809.htm), discuss how much of a threat this alliance poses to Nokia's dominance of the mobile phone handset market. You are encouraged to try to identify key capabilities possessed by the firms as a result of their past evolution.

5. US-based tobacco and food giant Philip Morris changed its name to Altria on 27 January 2003. In the light of material available at Altria's website (www.altria.com), examine the firm's long-run prospects and its strategies for surviving in the face of anti-smoking legislation, litigation and changing tastes.

6. Compare and contrast Shimano (www.shimano.com) and Wesfarmers (www.wesfarmers.com.au) in terms of the challenges they would have faced in designing effective organizational structures as they expanded.

7. Is it at all surprising to find that giant firms in the media and entertainment sector are often both multi-product and multinational businesses?

8. In the 1980s, Charles and Maurice Saatchi set about trying to apply Levitt's ideas about global business to the advertising and management consulting sectors. They engaged in a series of takeovers to create a global Saatchi and Saatchi operation that was intended to be a one-stop shop for such businesses services and as global as its customers. If you had been their economic adviser at the time, would you have encouraged them or tried to deter them from doing this?

9. Firms in the Korean car industry have gained considerable expertise from close relationships with Western and Japanese car makers. Given the rapid advances in the quality of Korean cars and the productivity of their factories, do you regard these close relationships as mistakes on the part of Western and Japanese car makers? Explain your reasoning.

10.11 Recommended additional reading sources

Many of the themes in this chapter are explored at greater length in Neil M. Kay's books: (1982) *The Evolving Firm*, London, Macmillan; and (1997) *Pattern in Corporate Evolution*, Oxford, Oxford University Press. Kay's interest in diversification and synergy was inspired by H. Igor Ansoff's 1965 management classic *Corporate Strategy*, New York, McGraw-Hill (1968, Harmondsworth, Penguin).

For a historical perspective on the origins of the modern large firm, see the following trio of major works by Alfred D. Chandler, Jr: (1962) *Strategy and Structure*, Cambridge, MA, MIT Press; (1977) *The Visible Hand*, Cambridge, MA and London, Belknap/Harvard University Press; and (1990) *Scale and Scope*, Cambridge, MA and London, Belknap/Harvard University Press. The last two of these are enormous but contain very useful summary/conclusion material.

The relationship between profitability and growth is explored in more detail by Robin L. Marris (1964) *An Economic Theory of 'Managerial' Capitalism*, London, Macmillan. Marris in turn drew on the work of Edith T. Penrose (1959) *The Theory of the Growth of the Firm*, Oxford, Blackwell (3rd edn, 1995, Oxford, Oxford University Press), which is very strongly recommended also for its analysis of diversification and the process of developing capabilities.

A very useful set of case studies on franchise networks has been provided by Antony W. Dnes (1992) *Franchising: A Case Study Approach*, Aldershot, Avebury.

The idea that corporate growth patterns are the outcome of problem-solving activities drives much of the analysis in Scott Moss (1981) *An Economic Theory of Business Strategy*, Oxford, Martin Robertson. This work is much inspired by Chandler and Penrose and has received less attention than it deserves in economics.

For an excellent collection of classic contributions on the diversification of firms and the development of firm capabilities, see Nicolai J. Foss (ed.) (1997) *Resources, Firms and Strategies: A Reader in the Resource-Based Perspective*, Oxford, Oxford University Press.

The limitations of M-form approaches to internal organization come under scrutiny in two useful contributions from Robert F. Freeland: 'The Myth of the M-Form? Governance, Consent, and Organizational Change', *American Journal of Sociology*, 102(2), September 1996, pp. 483–526; and (2001) *The Struggle for Control of the Modern Corporation: Organizational Change at General Motors, 1924–1970*, Cambridge and New York, Cambridge University Press.

11

What can an established firm do when its sales volume stagnates or declines?

Learning outcomes

If you study this chapter carefully, it may help you to:

- understand that business competition is a never-ending struggle for survival

- understand how firms may be able to improve their performance without offering better products and services

- identify the main types of innovation that take place in firms

- appreciate the economic impact that past decisions have on an established firm's current set of choices

- appreciate the role of organizational capabilities in the innovation process

- understand more about the concept and role of routines in the firm

- understand the determinants of competition in a market which is in terminal decline.

To the extent that you develop such understanding, you should be better able to:

- appraise critically explanations that are offered of why particular firms or industrial sectors are in difficulties

- contribute to discussions about strategies for revitalizing firms or particular industrial sectors.

11.1 Introduction

In this chapter we examine the options open to a mature firm that has enjoyed considerable success to date but which now faces a crisis in one or more of its markets. All firms, both old and new, face the same basic problem of trying to acquire and maintain economic rents, but the mature firm differs from the newly founded enterprise because it carries the legacy of its previous decisions. Even if it has been successful, this legacy may hinder its chances of continued success in a changing selection environment.

A slip into serious decline or commercial oblivion can be the fate not merely of firms that have never really delivered strong commercial performances but also of well-established firms that are household names. For example, in the 1960s the British motorcycle industry was enjoying great success: the machines from Norton, BSA and Triumph were the UK's third-largest export dollar earner, but by the mid-1970s the British manufacturers had been decimated by the Japanese motorcycle manufacturers Honda, Suzuki, Yamaha and Kawasaki, and UK production of motorcycles all but ceased. Similarly, in the early 1990s Sainsbury were the undisputed leaders of the UK supermarket industry, but by 1996 they were overtaken by Tesco who have since gone from strength to strength as Sainsbury have struggled in vain to regain their old position of dominance.

The lesson to be learned from these and many other examples is that **competition is a never-ending struggle for survival**. This means it is **inevitable** that, sooner or later, every firm, no matter how successful it has been in the past, will be faced with the prospect of **stagnant** or **declining demand** in one or more of the markets that it serves. To help us understand why this is the case we can draw upon the **evolutionary theory of the firm**. You will recall from Chapter 8 that market competition is an example of the process of the survival of the fittest. Core to the evolutionary theory of the firm is the notion of **routines**. These routines serve two basic functions:

- They determine the nature of the firm's product offering to the *outside* selection environment (market).

- They provide the degree of stability *inside* the firm that is necessary for it to function effectively as a **co-ordinated organizational unit** (including its relationships with suppliers and distributors).

When the routines developed by the firm enable it to produce goods and services that are favoured in the selection environment *and*, at the same time, enable it to achieve smooth internal co-ordination of its resources, the firm will become an industry leader. Unfortunately, however, the changing nature of the selection environment means that such periods of perfect **congruence** between the firm and the selection environment may not last for long unless they are managed very carefully indeed. In essence, this means that the firm's management team must be prepared to foster the development of the firm's routines and products in order to maintain its competitive position. In other words, the management team needs to ensure that the firm has the capacity to **innovate**. By definition, innovation is a force for **disruption** in the firm, which means that the process is fraught with difficulties. In the middle part of this chapter we will examine the innovation process and the problems it causes for mature firms.

Despite what we have said about innovation as the route to continued prosperity, the markets for some of the goods and services produced by the firm may have reached the end of their lifecycle for one reason or another. In these situations, the firm will have to formulate and execute a sensible **exit plan** or **end-game strategy**. End-game strategies and their problems will be examined in the final part of this chapter. Before we consider innovation and end-game strategies, however, we consider scope for firms to restore their profitability by cutting their costs and raising their productivity without necessarily investing in new equipment.

11.2 The role of slack in the competitive process

From the standpoint of mainstream economic theory, firms that start to have trouble making money in a market that is not suffering from collapsing demand must be doing so because they have been less successful than the market leaders at achieving economies of scale and scope. The market leaders must be using their superior unit cost positions to buy market share by lowering their prices, thereby squeezing the profit margins of their smaller rivals. The mainstream view leaves no room for declining businesses to restore their profits by cutting their costs: it presumes that managers have access to state-of-the-art knowledge about technology and use whatever technology they have efficiently. If anything, a firm that gets behind is likely to suffer rising relative costs since smaller profit margins leave it less able to purchase the latest technology or the size of plant necessary to achieve economies of scale. A firm that puts a foot wrong and starts falling behind its rivals appears to be doomed to be squeezed out of existence. Unless economies of scale level off at only a small share of the market and economies of scope are limited, the mainstream view points deterministically towards market shares being concentrated in the hands of fewer and fewer firms.

In the late 1950s, Jack Downie, one of the pioneers of the evolutionary approach to competition, labelled the scenario just outlined as the **transfer process**. It looks rather like what has been going on over the past decade or so in the market for personal computer operating systems with the growing domination of Microsoft. However, Downie saw a way out of this gloomy prognosis and he called it the **innovation process**: under pressure, firms may either come up with new products and production processes (which we focus on in Section 11.3) or they may work out ways of increasing the productivity of their existing investments. (As the saying goes: 'The fear of being hanged concentrates the mind wonderfully.') In the latter case, we need a non-mainstream view of costs, for the firm has previously been failing to maximize its profits and searches for ways of doing better when its profit levels are inadequate. In a world of **satisficing** decisions, there is potential for a firm to recover from decline and claw its way back up the competitive league tables.

Downie's perspective is entirely consistent with a key theme in the behavioural theory of the firm that Richard Cyert and James March were developing around the same time, namely, that firms operate with **organizational slack**. In their analysis, the firm is seen as a **coalition** of groups with different interests who continue to interact so long as they judge that they cannot get a better deal by joining a different coalition. This implies a rather fuzzy view of the firm's boundaries, for such coalitions include not merely shareholders, bosses and workers, but also (as in the analysis in Chapter 9 of this book) bankers, suppliers of inputs and customers. Organizational slack arises because coalition members do not know how far they can push their demands without causing the coalition to fall apart, and they are reluctant to risk this unless they can see a better deal elsewhere. Hence as long as coalition members are meeting their **aspirations** they do not try, as the expressions go, to 'push their luck' or 'rock the boat'.

In good times, many members of the coalition that comprise a particular firm may be enjoying payoffs that are greater than the minimum they are prepared to tolerate:

- Some consumers may be enjoying a **consumer's surplus**, paying lower prices than they are willing to pay and/or getting better quality than they require.

- Shareholders may be receiving bigger dividends than the minimum they are prepared to tolerate.

- Bankers may be receiving loan repayments sooner than the latest date they would accept or with more collateral than the minimum they require.

- Workers may be working more slowly and/or less carefully than they would be prepared to do.

- Managers may be engaging in more pet projects and making more use of opportunities to take advantage of perks than is enough to make them feel happy about staying with the firm.

Each group is getting away with enjoying a surplus because the others are holding back from making more aggressive demands for fear this will backfire. For example, if everyone is doing all right, why jeopardize things by putting up prices or presenting increasing demands on workers? If customers went elsewhere, or the workers went on strike, managers could find it harder to meet their own demands and might even be placing the firm at risk of a takeover raid.

When the going gets tough, things are different: adverse reactions to changes are worth risking if the alternative for managers is the demise of the company. They may thus try to get away with cutting dividends, going slow on loan repayments, raising production line speeds and reducing staffing levels, and/or raising prices or downgrading the quality of the product. To the extent that these kinds of measures do not backfire, they will increase the funds available to managers for investment in better products and production methods or, at the very least, ensure that a big enough cash flow is generated to keep shareholders and bankers at bay.

A related way of understanding how productivity improvements are possible when a firm is under pressure is via the notion of **X-inefficiency** proposed by Harvey Leibenstein in 1966. We introduced this in Chapter 3, when considering a variety of perspectives on the role of the entrepreneur, and in Chapter 6, when we looked at costs. According to Leibenstein, X-inefficiency arises because:

◆ *Knowledge of the production function is imperfect.* For example, few computer users know all the things they might do about Microsoft Word or PowerPoint, even if they have these programmes installed on their computers and do make some use of them.

◆ *Employment contracts are incomplete*, leaving workers with some discretion over how much effort they put in, when they work and the quality of the work that they do. Because of this, workers may be enjoying a quiet life, without pressures to perform at a high pace or concentrate on the details of what they do; hence output and quality may be far lower than they could be. Such workers might be acting with **opportunism**, claiming to their bosses that they are working as hard as they can.

◆ *The market for managers is not perfect*, so the needs of businesses may not be properly matched with the skills that managers have to offer (this is why a turnaround in profits performance sometimes only comes if a firm is taken over by someone who recognizes scope for better use of its assets and has the capacity to bring it about).

The policy measures that managers or shareholders might choose to try as means for reducing X-inefficiency include the following:

* Hire new managers with better track records.

* Call in management consultants, since they may be able to see scope for improvements that cannot be seen by regular staff members.

* Engage in benchmarking. This involves studying closely how strong performing organizations with similar kinds of business activities address their tasks. If competitors cannot be studied, firms may instead try to glean insights from other organizations: for example, Formula One racing teams have been known to allow their operations to be studied by manufacturers that need to be adept at making very quick changes in their production tools to deal with variations in demand across their product ranges.

* Put staff on performance-related pay and make their contracts subject to periodic review with no guarantee of renewal.

* Tighten up job contracts in terms of their content.

* Reorganize the firm on a 'divide and rule' basis, by creating a structure based on 'profit centres' – this might mean going from a U-form to M-form structure.

These kinds of policies have often enabled organizations to emerge 'leaner and fitter' from periods of crisis. However, they need to be applied with awareness of their possible downsides. In Chapter 10, for example, we noted some of the limitations of the M-form approach to internal organization, while from Chapter 9 you should recognize that employing people on more detailed and shorter-term contracts may greatly increase transaction costs and reduce organizational flexibility (something that militant trade union leaders have long known: a 'work to rule' can be almost as bad as a strike in some cases), and they may result in the loss of valuable staff to rivals whose contracts are less stringent. Those who stay may opt to fit in with new contracts in a perfunctory manner, rather than co-operating with enthusiasm and helping their bosses find further productivity improvements. More generally, it should be noted that a work environment that is overshadowed by a management obsession with cost-cutting and fear for one's job might be counter-productive in the long run because it interferes with creative thinking and the innovation process.

11.3 Innovation and the competitive process

The study of innovation in economics is associated most closely with the writings of Joseph Schumpeter. Schumpeter placed innovation (along with entrepreneurship) at the heart of his theory about how a capitalist economy works, and for this reason the process whereby firms attempt to outdo each other through innovation is often called '**Schumpeterian Competition**'.

11.3.1 Schumpeter and innovation

Schumpeter agreed with the earlier writings of Marshall in recognizing that improvements in society's welfare are derived largely from improvements in firms' bundles of **knowledge** that make it possible to use scarce resources in new and improved ways. He saw this process of knowledge growth as passing through three phases: **invention – innovation – imitation**. Each of these phases is given a strict definition to distinguish it from the next:

Invention occurs when someone has an idea and demonstrates that this idea will work in practice. For example, the Wright brothers had an idea that it was possible for man to be able to fly in a heavier-than-air machine, but until they turned their idea into a working flying machine ('the Wright Flyer') in 1903 their idea could not be called an invention.

Innovation occurs when somebody perceives that there is a commercial use for an invention. Usually the first person/firm to use the invention to make money is called the innovator. You should note that the inventor and the innovator will not necessarily be the same person/firm.

Imitation occurs when the (successful) innovation is copied by other people or firms who wish to share in the commercial success it has brought the original innovator. Imitation causes the innovation to 'diffuse' through the economy.

While Schumpeter's definitional trilogy is useful, it is usual nowadays to use the term 'innovation' as a catch-all term to describe all three phases. Indeed, in practice it is often hard to distinguish where one phase ends and the next begins.

Economists who have studied the economics of innovation have taken a rather narrow view of the process by focusing their attention almost exclusively upon **technological innovation**. Technological innovation can be divided into two categories: **technological product innovation** and **technological process innovation**.

Technological product innovation occurs when new technologies lead to the creation of previously non-existent goods (e.g. desktop PCs and new pharmaceutical products), or when established products embody new technologies as components in place of components based on older technologies (e.g. electronic fuel-injection systems have replaced mechanical carburettors in most petrol-powered vehicles).

Technological process innovation occurs when new technologies are embodied in the manufacturing process in order to enhance productivity and reduce unit costs (e.g. replacing manually operated machine tools with computer controlled robotic systems).

Technological innovation arises from formal **research and development (R&D)** activity, which is aimed primarily at improving **scientific** and **engineering knowledge** in order to create innovative products and processes. Firms in many industries have entire divisions dedicated to R&D activity: for example, R&D-driven technological innovation is an especially important activity in industries such as pharmaceuticals, automotive and electronics, but it is much less important in industries such as food and clothes retailing. This difference in emphasis on R&D is usually reflected in the fact that technologically based firms have specialized R&D divisions which consume significant proportions of their overall budgets, while non-technologically based firms typically do not have specialized R&D divisions. Table 11.1 lists the top 12 R&D investors in the world in 2003.

While there can be no doubt that technological innovation has been, and still is, a very important part of the process of wealth creation and improved living standards that have been experienced in all of the major economies of the world, it is not the only type of innovation that we should be paying attention to: in fact Schumpeter, in his discussion of the types of innovation, identified **five categories**:

Table 11.1 **The top 12 R&D-investing companies in the world in 2003**
Company name (Sector)
Ford (Automotive)
DaimlerChrysler (Automotive)
Siemens (Electronics & Electricals)
General Motors (Automotive)
Pfizer (Pharmaceuticals & Biotechnology)
Toyota Motor (Automotive)
IBM (Software & IT services)
GlaxoSmithKline (Pharmaceuticals & Biotechnology)
Matsushita Electric (Electronics & Electricals)
Volkswagen (Automotive)
Microsoft (Software & IT services)
Intel (Software & IT services)

(Source: UK DTI R&D Scoreboard 2003)

(i) **The introduction of new goods and services** (product innovation) – this includes the introduction of brand-new products and changes in the features, functionality and quality of existing products or services offered by the firm.

(ii) **The introduction of new methods of production** – this includes such things as employing robots (rather than manually operated machines) in the production process and replacing paper-based administrative systems with computer-based systems.

(iii) **The opening up of new markets** – this includes diversification into new geographical territories (such as the current ongoing expansion of Western firms into the growing Chinese market).

(iv) **The opening up of new sources of supply** – this includes the discovery of new raw material deposits and the strategic outsourcing of components and services (for example, many UK insurance companies have relocated their telephone inquiry services to India where costs are much lower).

(v) **Improving the organization of current resources** – this includes the adoption of new practices, such as Just-in-Time manufacturing principles, and pursuing further the benefits of the division of labour.

If you examine the annual accounts of many non-technology companies you will find that some funds have been allotted to R&D activity; but R&D here is more to do with the generation of new knowledge about how to run and organize the business (which may entail using new technologies 'off-the-shelf' rather than developing these technologies). You should be careful, then, not to view innovation solely as a technology-based activity. It is more appropriate to think of it as an activity that encompasses *both* technological and organizational activities. Indeed, technological innovation nearly always has significant organizational implications.

11.3.2 Innovation, technology and organization – some stylized facts

Following Schumpeter's writings on innovation, many economists and other management scholars have investigated the process of innovation and a significant body of empirical work has emerged. Of particular interest to us in this chapter is the work which has asked the question: **'Who has the advantage when the need to innovate arises – do mature firms with their wealth of experience and resources behind them have advantages over new firms, or do new firms have the edge?'** In seeking to answer this question researchers have identified some interesting patterns which seem to be consistent across several industries and which explicitly demonstrate the relationship between technological and organizational innovation.

You will recall from Chapter 8 that the evolution of industry structure passes through several stages and that firms which make erroneous conjectures about consumers' wants are deselected from the industry. The firms that survive this shake-out go on to become the established heart of the industry: that is, the mature firms which are the focus of this chapter. In Chapters 5 and 6 we explored the decisions that firms must make when they choose how to produce their products and we introduced the concepts of the **division of labour**, **economies of scale** and the **learning curve**. In this section we bring the discussions of Chapters 5, 6 and 8 together in order to draw the relationship between industry evolution and production decisions more clearly and derive the implications for innovation in the mature firm.

A new industry is 'born' when someone introduces **new knowledge** in the form of a product that has not been seen before. The introduction of this brand new product is an example of **radical (or drastic) innovation**. For example, the construction of the world's first roadworthy motor car by Gottlieb Daimler in 1889 was a radical innovation which heralded the birth of the car industry.

In the emergent years of an industry it is common to see many radical innovations, based upon a multitude of designs and different technologies, being offered to the market. For example, if you had been around during the emergent years of the car industry (1889–1920) you would have seen some weird and wonderful contraptions being offered for sale: some cars were steam-powered, some had tillers rather than steering wheels, engines were mounted at the rear on some cars and at the front on others, and a whole host of differences in body design, transmission and braking systems was evident. In other words, manufacturers were busy creating a large **variety** of **product innovations**. Eventually, however, the variety of product innovations diminished as consumers made their preferences known by choosing to purchase some designs instead of others and Ford's Model T became the car of choice. The Model T was an example of the emergence of something that modern day scholars call a **dominant design**.

> A dominant design is a product which embodies a particular combination of features and technologies in such a way that it meets consumer wants/needs in a relatively complete manner.

The Model T emerged from the initial pot-pourri of product innovations with a front-mounted water-cooled petrol-driven engine with rear-wheel-drive, a gearbox and a wet clutch. Over the next 40 years or so this basic design configuration was **imitated** by all of the surviving car manufacturers and the high frequency of radical product innovation that was observed in the emerging years of the industry diminished significantly as the dominant design became the accepted

template of design features and technologies. When this happens in an industry the product is said to have become **standardized.**

Once a dominant design has been identified product innovation will still take place, but it will tend to involve less radical change to the standard design configuration. In other words, the emergence of the dominant design is accompanied by a reduction in the number of radical product innovations in the industry in favour of performance-enhancing **incremental product innovations.** This has important ramifications for the methods adopted by firms in their **production processes:** once a product has become fairly standardized there is scope for the **focus of competition** between firms to move away from the introduction of drastic product innovations towards innovations in the **methods of production** (with the aim of reducing unit costs). Typically, in the emergent years of an industry (i.e. pre-dominant design) firms employ production practices and processes that do not require specialized equipment. This gives them the freedom to **experiment** in the **selection environment** with several innovative designs without having to commit to any particular one. At this stage, therefore, the **organization** of the firm's productive resources is deliberately **flexible** and the firm cannot pursue the full potential advantages conferred by specialization and the adoption of automated production processes. This is because the **extent of the market** for any given radically innovative product is **highly uncertain.**

In terms of resource allocation issues in the firm, in the emergent years of the industry the major **investments** being made by entrepreneurs are directed towards reducing the uncertainty about the extent of the market by obtaining and developing knowledge about **consumers' preferences**, rather than knowledge about the most efficient production methods. Once the dominant design has emerged, however, the uncertainty over the extent of the market is reduced sufficiently so that many entrepreneurs will take the **strategic decision** to shift their investments into developing efficient production processes. In other words, the focus of attention within a firm where this decision has been made will turn to **process innovation** and the pursuit of the advantages associated with economies of scale and moving down the **learning curve.** The aim of this strategy is to bring production costs down dramatically and offer the product at a more competitive price than rivals. Thanks to the exploitation of the division of labour and new ways of organizing the production process (as detailed in Chapter 5) the average price of a Ford Model T dropped from $3 500 to $900 in the period 1909–1923.[1]

---

1 Data sourced from Abernathy, W.J. & Wayne, K. (1974) 'Limits of the Learning Curve', *Harvard Business Review*, Sept.–Oct., pp. 109–119. Prices are adjusted to 1958 dollar values.

If you recall our analysis of production in Chapter 5 you will realize that productivity gains in production processes are 'unlocked' as a result of the choices the entrepreneur makes about how to **organize** the firm's productive resources (including management) which, in turn, entails exploiting the division of labour and the development of specialized machinery. This means that the pursuit of ever-decreasing unit costs in the period following the emergence of a dominant design brings into existence an **extensive and complex organization**. For a large organization to work effectively as a coherent system, **routinized behaviour** must evolve (as discussed in Chapter 8) and disruptive change in any of its subsystems must be minimized. The implication of this analysis is that as long as the selection environment remains relatively stable the organization will become an established incumbent and enjoy a profitable existence.

The analysis of the preceding section not only helps to explain how mature firms evolve, but also hints at the reason why mature firms may find further product innovation difficult to embrace and, subsequently, may find themselves in trouble. As William Abernathy and Kenneth Wayne (1974: 109) put it:

> ...*management cannot expect to receive the benefits of cost reduction provided by a steep learning-curve projection and at the same time expect to accomplish rapid rates of product innovation and improvement in product performance. Managers should realize that the two achievements are the fruits of different strategies.*

Abernathy and Wayne's detailed analysis of Ford's history reveals that the company pursued a single-minded policy of continued cost reduction with its Model T production process. At the same time, rival manufacturers (in particular General Motors) adopted a strategy of producing cars which more closely followed **evolving consumer tastes**, which were calling for higher engine performance and heavier enclosed-body designs. Ford had invested heavily in specialized capital so it was **committed** to volume production of the basic open-bodied Model T design. This meant that it responded to changing consumer tastes as best it could within the **constraints** placed upon it by its commitment to specialized large-scale manufacture of the basic dominant design. Unfortunately for Ford the engine and chassis were simply not designed to cope well with the extra weight introduced by the addition of an enclosed body, so performance of the Model T suffered. Ford's market share, which had grown rapidly from 10.7 per cent in 1910 to 55.4 per cent by 1921, began to drop off in the middle of the 1920s as a result of the **inflexibility** of its production systems in the face of GM's policy of competing on superior vehicle performance. With the writing on the wall, in 1927 Ford developed a new car, the Model A, and built up suitable production capability, but thanks to its previous policy of specialization in Model T production, the change was costly and painful:

> *[Ford] had...so specialized its workforce, process technology, and management that it consumed nearly a year in model development and changeover. As an illustration of its specialization, in the course of the model change Ford lost $200 million, replaced 15,000 machine tools and rebuilt 25,000 more, and laid off 60,000 workers in Detroit alone.*
>
> Abernathy and Wayne (1974: 115)

The stylized general relationship between the relative levels of investment committed to product and process innovation as time passes is reflected in Figure 11.1. Here you can see that the rate of product innovation is high in the early days of the new product, but it diminishes in the later days as firms concentrate their resources on cost-reducing process innovations.

As the story of the car industry told here illustrates, the extent to which any given firm commits to a policy of process innovation can have serious implications for its **adaptability** to a changing selection environment. This poses something of a **dilemma** for firms: on the one hand, once a successful product innovation has been discovered, the firm will be tempted to **exploit** it to its maximum by channelling its scarce resources into creating an integrated productive and administrative system that is capable of unlocking the potential economies of learning and scale that can be achieved by producing a standardized product in large volume. On the other hand, future success depends on channelling scarce resources into continued **exploration** of the selection environment in order to

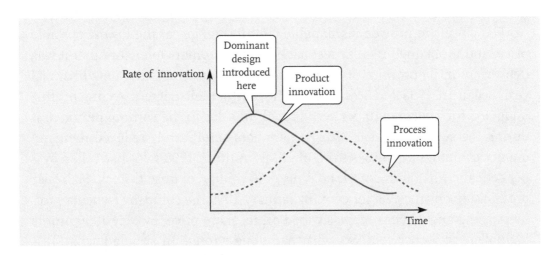

Figure 11.1 Stylized representation of the resources devoted to product and process innovation by the firm as time passes

anticipate changes in selection criteria, and it is important to complement this activity by retaining a significant degree of **adaptive capability** in the firm's productive and administrative systems.

The **trade-off** between exploitation and exploration is often managed poorly in established firms: in fact, some researchers have noted that the longer the period the successful exploitation of an innovation lasts, the lower the adaptive capability of an organization. In an ideal world managers will anticipate change rather than wait for it to hit their firm, but business history suggests that firms which operate in this ideal way are few and far between: for most firms change only occurs after the crisis has begun. The attitude of managers in charge of successful firms is summed up as, 'we're making healthy profits today, what more can we do?', and in taking this view the seeds of future trouble are sown. According to Judi Bevan (2001) this particular problem afflicted the 100-year-old British retail giant Marks and Spencer in 1998 (see Box 11.1).

Box 11.1 The 1998/9 downfall of Marks and Spencer

For the year to March 1998 Marks and Spencer (M&S) reported pre-tax profits of £1.2 billion. This incredible figure reflected unprecedented growth in the company which, since its inception over 110 years earlier, had prided itself on living up to its widely publicized claim of providing 'value, quality and service' to its customers. In order to achieve its aims M&S had introduced several innovations into the world of retailing, including the use of modern fabrics in its clothing ranges and the introduction of chilled ready-meals. It had also developed a dedicated network of suppliers with whom it worked closely to provide fashionable clothing ranges at the lowest possible price, and it obtained regular feedback from customers to ensure that it was delivering on its promise of value, quality and service. As the new financial year began in 1998 M&S directors, buoyed by their current record profits, budgeted for a further 10 per cent growth in sales in the coming period, but during the summer period British customers significantly reduced their frequency of clothes purchases from M&S. By autumn 1998 sales had fallen by 2 per cent and M&S found itself holding £150 million of unsold stock. Half-year profits were down by 23 per cent. By January 1999 the company issued a profits warning and 23 per cent was wiped off its share price. By May 1999 profits had fallen by 50 per cent. So, what had gone wrong? In simple terms M&S directors had taken their eye off the ball and failed to respond to changing

Box 11.1 (continued)

customer feedback. Most of M&S's expansion in the 1990s was into out-of-town stores, which crowded out investment in its established high street stores. These high street stores began to look run down and shabby, which severely harmed the company's reputation with its customers. Furthermore, the expansion had been accompanied by a reduction in staff numbers per square foot of store from one employee per 165 square feet in 1991 to one employee per 265 square feet in 1998. This resulted in a reduction in the quality of service that M&S customers had come to expect. On top of these damaging changes, clothing rivals Next and the Gap were proliferating in many high streets with bright stores and modern product ranges. Even as the 1998 results were announced several of the directors had perceived that customer feedback was becoming less favourable and that the tide seemed to be turning against the company, but when they raised the issue in board meetings the chairman, Sir Richard Greenbury, dismissed their views with the question, 'If we are getting it so wrong, why are we making £1 billion a year?' (Bevan, 2001: 3). Consequently the company persisted with more of the same approach and the crisis hit. As Bevan puts it:

> *Marks & Spencer, 114 years old and the second most profitable retailer in the world, the subject of three Harvard Business School case studies, five times winner of the Queen's Award for Export Achievement and with cupboards groaning with trophies for managerial excellence, steamed on full-throttle towards the iceberg.*

> Bevan (2001: 5)

The story we have told so far makes a distinction between radical and incremental product innovation, but we have not defined the meaning of these terms. This apparent omission has been deliberate on our part. In essence the stories told by many scholars of innovation run as follows: an industry is born when a radical innovation emerges. In this story a radical innovation is defined as something that is so new to the world that it is based upon a new set of scientific and engineering principles and, as a result, it causes problems for established firms who have based their products (and associated processes) on different knowledge. In contrast, an incremental innovation is defined as something that introduces relatively minor changes to an existing product and, as a result, it is much easier for established firms to assimilate this type of knowledge. The trouble with these stylized stories is that in reality the distinction made between radical and incremental innovation is largely a matter of **degree** (so innovations should be thought of as lying along a spectrum rather than slotting neatly into one of these two categories) and **perspective**. For example, one firm may take a view that an innovation is more incremental than it is radical while another firm might take the opposite view: ultimately, it depends upon the knowledge and capabilities owned by the respective firms. For Ford, the introduction of the enclosed-body design represented a fairly radical innovation in terms of the disruption it caused in its extant routines, while for GM it was much less disruptive.

From what we have said up to this point you might think that the only real concern for a mature firm is the potential threat that an established rival or a new entrant might introduce a radical innovation which either diminishes or destroys the usefulness of its current knowledge and routinized capabilities. However, studies of the innovation process have revealed that even the introduction of innovations based upon similar or identical technological knowledge can cause serious problems for established firms. A particularly well-documented example is that of the Xerox Corporation.

In 1938 Chester Carlson, a physicist, invented a basic system of electrostatic copying of images on to plain paper (plain paper copying, PPC). In 1948 Carlson licensed his invention to the Xerox Corporation, which proceeded to refine the technology (which it protected with over 500 patents). The resulting Xerox photocopier machine was a big hit with many large corporations worldwide and by 1970 Xerox had a 93 per cent share of the world market. The Xerox business model was based upon leasing machines to firms and supporting them with an extensive network of technicians. The machines were physically large, which meant that they needed to be placed centrally in offices where large numbers of users could access them. As time passed, Xerox focused its development efforts on increasing the speed of the photocopying process and it was able to replace older, slower machines with its faster models with minimal disruption to its customers (mainly large firms that were attracted by the economies associated with large-volume copying). Over the years, Xerox refined its knowledge of PPC technology (it spent over $100 million per year on R&D[2]) but, despite the speed improvements, the physical size of the machines remained unchanged and, in addition, Xerox stuck to its policy of leasing its copiers rather than selling them. In the mid-1970s Xerox's patents began to expire which opened the door to new entry into the industry. Among the new entrants was Canon who had spent the latter part of the 1960s developing its own capabilities with PPC technology.

---

2   Data sourced from Ackenhusen, M. (1992) 'Canon: Competing on Capabilities', INSEAD case study.

However, Canon's approach to the market was different because it innovated with the basic technology and this enabled it to produce small desktop photo-copiers that were extremely reliable (reducing the need for technical support) and much cheaper than the large Xerox machines. Essentially, Canon's innova-tion was based upon reconfiguring the same PPC technology that lay at the heart of Xerox's copiers. As a result of Canon's innovation, the market was trans-formed and, despite its abundance of knowledge about the PPC technology, it took Xerox eight years to produce a competitive innovative product of its own. During this period Xerox lost half of its market share.

The important point to note about the Xerox story is that the product innova-tion introduced by Canon was not radical (i.e. it was not based on new scientific knowledge) yet it had a devastating impact upon Xerox, despite the fact that its knowledge of PPC technology was in many ways superior to Canon's. In fact the case of Xerox is by no means an isolated one: the story of a dominant firm being devastated by a rival which uses the same basic technological knowledge in an innovative way is repeated in many diverse industries. Scholars who have stud-ied this phenomenon have come to realize that the simple distinction between radical and incremental innovation is insufficient to understand such cases and they have added a third category, called **architectural innovation**.

In order to understand the concept of architectural innovation we begin by rec-ognizing that many products are constructed from separate component parts. Each component is based upon its own distinct body of knowledge: for example, a simple microlight aircraft, such as that shown in Figure 11.2, is constructed from metal tubing, fibreglass bodywork, a hi-tech cloth wing, a petrol engine and a propeller. Each of these component parts requires the developer of microlight aircraft to **learn** something about metallurgy, the behaviour of composites, the aerodynamics of cloth wings, the power-to-weight characteristics of petrol engines and the design of propellers, respectively. Note, however, that having knowledge about individual components is only part of the story: in order to pro-duce a microlight with acceptable performance characteristics (such as adequate airframe strength, decent airspeed, easy handling, good fuel economy and so on), the developer must **combine** the component parts in such a way that they work as a coherent **system**. The particular system of components present in a given product constitutes that product's **architecture**. This means that a given product's architecture will be based upon a particular collection of knowledge about how its components work in combination with each other.

It may well be possible to **recombine** the same or similar components in dif-ferent ways to achieve improved/different product performance. It is this **new**

Figure 11.2 A modern microlight aircraft

combination of familiar component technologies (a phrase popularized by Schumpeter) that is called an **architectural innovation**. So, an architectural innovation makes use of existing component knowledge but it links the components in a new way (e.g. by reducing their size).

The three types of product innovation we have identified in this section differ from each other in terms of the **impact** they have upon a firm's **existing capabilities**. Radical product innovations tend to **destroy** the usefulness of a firm's current capabilities because they are based upon entirely new knowledge (e.g. in watches quartz movements replaced mechanical movements and the craft-based Swiss watch industry collapsed as a result), while incremental product innovations tend to **enhance** the firm's current capabilities because they are based upon improving individual components of the current product's stable architecture (e.g. microlight manufacturers switched from wooden propellers to composite propellers to reduce both noise and vibration in their aircraft). In contrast, architectural innovations have an **unsettling** impact on the firm's capabilities because the recombination of components means that some of the firm's established knowledge and capabilities will still be useful while others will not.

When it became clear that Canon's small desktop photocopiers were the key to future success, Xerox's knowledge of PPC technology remained useful, but its architectural knowledge was geared towards the development of large photo-copiers and it took many years for Xerox to adjust its architectural knowledge appropriately (i.e. to develop its own desktop-sized copier). Of course, the concept of architectural innovation can seem clear-cut in the pages of a textbook, but in the turbulent environment of the real world, when confronted by an innovating rival, it may not be very clear to a firm which parts of its portfolio of knowledge are still useful and which need to be replaced or improved. This uncertainty may partly explain Xerox's lengthy reaction time.

Getting the balance right between allocating resources to exploiting current success and creating the capabilities that will be the basis of future success is a major challenge for the firm's senior management team. The innovation experts Michael Tushman and Philip Anderson (1997) point out that entrepreneurs and managers must build **ambidextrous organizations** which are capable of coping with the tension between the need for **experimental entrepreneurial** units in the firm and the maintenance of a **well ordered set of routinized capabilities** that are the basis of current success.

While innovation is necessary if the mature firm is going to be able to rejuve-nate itself in the face of inevitably declining demand, it is not necessarily the case that a firm that manages to create innovations will actually benefit from them. Just as there are numerous cases of established firms failing to innovate until it is too late, there are also numerous cases of established firms that innovated in a timely manner but then failed to enjoy fully the fruits of their own innovative efforts as they watched **imitating** rivals take their markets away from them. This is known as the **appropriability problem** and a classic example is provided by the British company Electrical Musical Industries (EMI) Ltd in the 1970s.

> The *appropriability problem* refers to a situation where the originator of an innovation is unable to enjoy fully the rewards of its costly development efforts because it is unable to protect its innovation from being copied by rivals. In other words, other firms who did not contribute to the costly devel-opment efforts appropriate some or all of the rewards that the innovator is expecting to receive.

In the late 1960s Godfrey Hounsfield, a senior research engineer for EMI Ltd, developed a device called a **computerized axial tomographic scanner (CAT scan-ner)** which was capable of displaying three-dimensional images of human organs such as the brain. This was a massive breakthrough in the field of medi-cal diagnostic equipment and, in the hope of rejuvenating the company's for-tunes (which had been severely hit by their failure to find a replacement for their main cash-cow, the Beatles, in the record publishing side of their activities), EMI decided to invest in further development of the CAT scanner. EMI launched the world's first commercially available CAT scanner in 1973 to an eager medical community in both the UK and North America. Despite its high price tag, the product was an immediate success for EMI and profits came rolling in. Unfortunately for EMI their success stimulated two American rivals, General Electric (GE) and Technicare, to bring their considerable technical resources to bear on the development of their own CAT scanners. It was easy enough for both of these companies to benefit from the fruits of EMI's pioneering research with the technology through the simple expedient of **reverse engineering** (i.e. dismantling and examining components) EMI's own product. Armed with this knowledge they then set about developing CAT scanners of their own (while trying to skirt around EMI's patents). By 1978 both Technicare and GE had stolen most of the market from EMI, and by 1981 EMI exited from the very market they had created in the first place. Today both Technicare and GE are still enjoying considerable success with their CAT scanner businesses. So, what went wrong for EMI? It had innovated and brought an excellent product to the market, but it proved incapable of holding on to the lead it had created. Part of the answer lies in the fact that their product was fairly easy for rivals to emulate with their own versions of the CAT technology, but another part of the answer lies in EMI's lack of suitable capabilities with which to support their innovative product appropriately.

When an innovative product is introduced to the market the firm needs to ensure that it has created or obtained a set of business capabilities that are able to support the new product adequately. EMI demonstrated great technical capability with the product itself but ended up being beaten by rivals who had superior overall business capability which they used to great effect. Both GE and Technicare possessed the necessary technical capabilities to develop their own CAT scanners, but they were also capable of providing the high level of end-user training that a technically sophisticated product like a CAT scanner needed – EMI did not possess this capability. In addition, both of EMI's rivals had significant experience in marketing medical equipment where EMI had little, and both rivals enjoyed good reputations for quality, reliability and after-sales service and maintenance while EMI had no similar track record. So, the basic lesson from the EMI story is that, in order to appropriate in full the potential returns from an innovation, the firm needs to possess more than the capability to innovate; it also needs to possess or obtain fundamental **complementary capabilities**.

11.3.3 Routines and innovation

In general terms innovation is a process that requires the firm to replace or modify some or all of its routines. As Nelson and Winter (1982: 128) put it, 'innovation involves change in routine'. They go on to argue that firms need to develop routines which are explicitly designed to interrogate and if necessary overhaul the current routines. This can be very confusing. This is because our discussion of routines up to this point has been based upon the contention that the term 'routine' is shorthand notation for an **established and repeated pattern of activity** of the firm rather than a description of a force for change. In order to overcome this confusion Nelson and Winter introduced the notion that **three kinds of routine** should be developed in the firm:

(i) **short-run routines** – that is, routines which guide the firm's operations with its current set of resources;

(ii) **long-run routines** – these are routines which guide the acquisition of new productive capacity to enhance/expand the usual activities carried out by the firm;

(iii) **modifying routines** – these are routines which lead to scrutiny of what the firm is doing and a reassessment of why it is doing it that particular way.

David Teece, Gary Pisano and Amy Shuen (1997) bring greater clarity to the issue by re-labelling Nelson and Winter's 'modifying routines' as **dynamic capabilities** (cf. routinized capabilities).

11.4 Coping with a market in terminal decline

As you have seen, innovation is the route to future success for a mature firm. However, some firms are active in markets that are not susceptible to innovation because they have entered a phase of terminal decline. One reason for market decline is a sea change in consumer tastes (e.g. firms in the gentleman's hat-making industry suffered greatly when the fashion for wearing hats and caps ended, and British tobacco companies are currently facing a decline in domestic demand for their cigarettes in an environment where advertising is banned). Another reason for market decline is the introduction of radical technological change which supersedes the technology embedded in the firm's current products (e.g. pocket calculators replaced slide rules). Whatever the reason for decline, it is unlikely that the market will disappear immediately, so the firm faces the problem of how best to manage its resources and capabilities with respect to its declining markets in order to extricate itself from these activities with minimal financial impact. Management consultants traditionally advised companies to adopt a 'harvest' strategy in situations of terminal decline. However, according to Kathryn Harrigan and Michael Porter (1983), this advice (which entails stopping all investment immediately upon recognizing the problem, generating maximum cash flow and eventual divestment) ignores the fact that the pattern of decline in markets differs from one case to the next and, as a result, such a 'one-size fits all' strategy may be unsuitable.

11.4.1 The nature of the decision problem in a terminal market

On the face of it, dealing appropriately with a terminally declining market is simply a question of calculating **opportunity costs**. The management teams of each firm which serves the declining market should be asking themselves if the prospective return on spending additional money in this market is better or worse than using the same money elsewhere *plus* the net proceeds (e.g. from selling off capital equipment) after exiting the market. This decision will have to be made against a background in which the firms in the industry need to deal with the legacy of investments that were made in the market's boom years. These investments mean that the industry will probably be characterized by **excess productive capacity** which, in turn, means that every firm would be better off if one or more of its rivals left the market to allow the remaining firms to exploit more fully their own underutilized production capacity. The problem is like sharing out a shrinking cake: if some people decide they do not want a slice then, despite the fact that the cake is shrinking, having a slice of the diminished cake might still be worthwhile. Alternatively, if everyone decides that they would be happy with a smaller slice, rather than none at all, then it might still be worthwhile to have some. Trouble starts when one or more of the people decide, despite the fact that the cake is shrinking, they still want just as big a slice as they were getting previously: in this case the cake may end up not worth having at all.

The shrinking nature of the market makes the competitive environment potentially volatile for all of the players in the market, but the actual impact on profits will depend upon two things: (i) how orderly the retreat of firms from the market will be; and (ii) how fiercely remaining firms are prepared to fight for their piece of the shrinking market. As with most business decisions, the presence of **uncertainty** about these two factors makes an accurate opportunity cost calculation all but impossible. Part of the uncertainty problem lies with potential differences in **managers' perceptions** of the nature of the declining market. If the managers of all firms perceive that the market will decline slowly they are less likely to take drastic action which would destabilize the market for all.

We can obtain some insights into the destabilizing potential of different managerial perceptions by using the framework of analysis first proposed by the Australian economist Wilfred Salter (1960) in his classic work *Productivity and Technical Change*. Salter pointed out that any firm that has been operating for a significant period of time is probably making use of capital equipment that varies in age (or 'vintage'). In other words, as firms grow they expand their productive capacity either by adding new capital equipment to existing capital in their current plants, or by opening entirely new plant. Depending on when they entered the market and how they expanded, firms may differ in the sets of equipment vintages that they possess.

Now, if we make the assumption that the youngest equipment is more productively efficient than the older equipment (because of technical advances) and that both old and new capital is operated simultaneously, it follows that the state of the industry as a whole will be as shown in Figure 11.3.

In Figure 11.3 you can see that the younger the capital equipment in use the lower the **average variable costs** associated with it. If market demand is D_1 and firms are trying to match each other's price quotations, the forces of competition will yield a market price of P_1. At this price, the owner of the oldest vintage of capital (block 1) will let it lie idle because it represents excess capacity and it cannot cover its average variable costs (AVC_1) (which we have assumed are constant over the range of output to keep things simple – the horizontal width of each block in the diagram represents the capacity of output that each vintage of

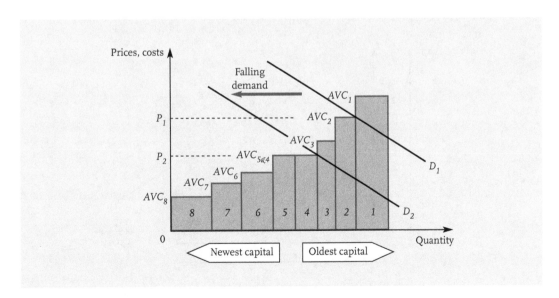

Figure 11.3 An industry with different vintages of capital operating simultaneously under conditions of declining demand

capital can produce). This does not necessarily mean that the owner of block 1 will leave the industry, because it may also own one or more of the other blocks (2–8) which are still capable of making a profit. If demand begins to fall (so the demand curve D_1 shifts leftwards to, say, D_2) competitive forces will drive the market price down to P_2 and yet more capital will become uneconomical to run.

The key point to note here is that the firms in this declining market **should** be able to **retreat** from it in a relatively **orderly manner**. This is because older vintages of capital will usually have already covered their **payback** costs and, as a result, fixed costs associated with them will be negligible. This relatively painless retreat for the firms in the industry will only be possible if managers all share a similar perception that the market is in terminal decline (i.e. the demand curve will continue to migrate leftwards) and that it therefore makes sense to shut down capital in an orderly manner (i.e. in order of relative efficiency) to extract the maximum returns possible in the declining years of the market.

The chances of the scenario of orderly retreat depicted in Figure 11.3 happening may not be high. Here we have a variation on the **Richardson Problem** (see Section 9.3.3) due to **uncertainty** and **bounded rationality**. These two factors mean there is plenty of scope for the managers of different firms to form **different expectations** about the likely future state of the market. As a result, they may be tempted to try to **maintain** their market share by investing in the latest capital equipment: a practice called **defensive investment**. If they do this they may start a chain of events that leads to turmoil in the declining market.

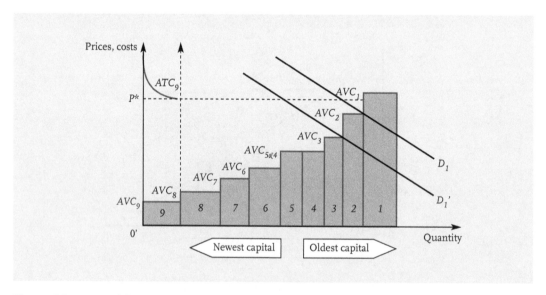

Figure 11.4 Destabilizing aggressive investment in a declining industry with capital of different vintages

Consider the scenario depicted in Figure 11.4. Here, a firm has invested in new capital equipment (block 9) and, as a result, it has caused the origin of the diagram to shift leftwards (from 0 to 0') along with the demand curve (D_1 has shifted to D_1' but *not* because of declining demand at this stage of the analysis). This investment has created **extra excess capacity** above and beyond that represented by block 1. However, it is no longer obvious which plant should be shut down: the average variable costs of the new vintage are AVC_9, which is lower than any other vintage, but because the capital is new the firm will have to take account of its associated **fixed costs** also. The diagram shows the **average total cost curve** associated with block 9 (ATC_9). This implies that the owner of block 9 requires a price of at least P* in order to make a profit. On the assumption that vintages 1 through 8 have already paid back their upfront costs, this puts the owner of block 9 at something of a disadvantage and a price war may result (especially if the owner of block 2 tries to defend its position). If we now add declining demand to the story then the owner of block 9 may find itself in so much trouble that it ends up in receivership. The receivers may well sell the capital at well below book value to a third party who continues to run it but at a much lower cost than the original owner and, as a result, causes further chaos for the other firms left in the industry.

A further variation on the theme of different vintages of capital is called the **sequential wear-out trap**. Firms can find themselves caught in the sequential wear-out trap if their production system is built from parts that wear out at different rates. If the firm replaces these worn out parts as and when they occur, it will be continually renewing subsystems so that the overall system continues to function (one is reminded of the old joke about the broom which, after seven years of use, was still as good as the day it was made – it had only had three new handles and four new heads since then). The issue raised by the trap is that a rational assessment of the overall production system in the face of a declining market might well reveal that it is not worth replacing it in its entirety. As a result, replacing parts as they wear out is an example of throwing funds away that could have been used more productively in an alternative investment. If you have ever owned an old car you will probably be familiar with the workings of the sequential wear-out trap because you will have had to weigh up whether it is worth spending money on replacing worn out tyres one month when you are not sure if the engine will still be in working order the next month, etc. If a firm gets caught in the sequential wear-out trap it may find itself inadvertently committing to a declining market.

11.4.2 Exit barriers

Deciding what the firm should do and how rivals are likely to act in a declining market is further complicated by the potential presence of a set of phenomena that are collectively called **exit barriers**. As the name implies, exit barriers make it difficult for firms to leave the declining market, so their presence is likely to lead to firms fighting to maintain their positions for as long as possible. Exit barriers include the following:

* The extent to which production relies upon **durable or specialized assets** – if assets are highly specialized (i.e. they have no alternative use) this will mean that they have negligible liquidation value because nobody will want to buy into the declining market. As a result, if the firm keeps these assets working it might be able to earn a stream of returns that exceeds the price they would fetch if they were sold.

* The size of the **exit costs** associated with the firm's **obligations** – it is very rare for a firm simply to be able to shut down its production facilities and sack its employees without some form of **compensation or redundancy package** being offered to its employees. The size of this compensation bill may act as a deterrent to exit. In addition, in some industries the firm will have an obligation to **dismantle** its facilities and this can be extremely costly. For example, the nuclear power generator British Energy faces a dismantling cost for its nuclear reactors that runs into tens of millions of pounds.

* The presence of **managers' emotional attachments** to the company – very often a rational approach to the exit decision may not be possible because managers take pride in their achievements to date and hang on too long in the declining market. This problem may be especially acute if the firm runs a single market business, because managers may not have an alternative job to go to and may think that their options in the job market will be limited by the stigma of having run their current company into crisis (even if the crisis was the result of unstoppable terminal decline).

* The degree of corporate **interrelatedness** – if the firm is a multi-product company which enjoys economies of scope it may be reluctant to leave the declining market since to do so may hurt its competitiveness in its other markets.

11.5 Summary

Our discussion in this chapter has briefly examined the array of problems that confront an established firm and can cause its sales and profits to fall. Sometimes it is possible to restore profitability by cutting production costs but at other times innovation or exit is necessary.

The overarching lesson you should take from this chapter is that business success will not automatically perpetuate: it needs very careful management. This is because consumers' tastes will change and rivals will be attempting to make their own products number one in the market. In other words, the selection environment in which the firm operates will rarely, if ever, be stationary. This being the case, the firm must be prepared to innovate but, as we have discussed, innovation creates tensions within the firm as it tries to bring something new to the market while trying to maintain its internal organizational coherence.

The lessons from Chapters 3 through 10 (where our emphasis was on how a new business could grow and become successful) are just as relevant in this chapter: in particular, an established firm needs to adopt an entrepreneurial outlook if it is to continue to prosper. However, unlike a young entrepreneurial venture, the managers of an established firm have to contend with an extra complicating factor: their own history of success. Having a history means that routines will be ingrained and this will make the changes that are necessary for the future prosperity of the firm more difficult both to recognize and to implement.

In the final part of the chapter we examined another side of the problem of maturity: the economics of competing in declining markets. Just because a market is in decline does not mean that the firm should immediately exit, since its own profits will depend upon how the other players in the market respond. Here uncertainty and bounded rationality play an important part via managers' perceptions about the likely future pattern of falling demand. The presence of potential exit barriers adds a further complicating factor. Furthermore, the firm's capabilities will have evolved to enable it to make the most of its current lines of activity, so if it is to do something else its managers will need time to develop new capabilities in the firm.

11.6　Some questions to consider

1.　After several years of success a mature firm usually has an abundance of resources at its disposal, so how would you explain the failure of Hoover to innovate with its vacuum cleaner technology when Dyson first appeared on the scene in the early 1990s?

2.　'[C]reating a "learning organization" is only half the solution. Just as important is creating an "unlearning" organization' (Hamel and Prahalad, 1994: 65). In the light of our discussion in this chapter what do you think Hamel and Prahalad mean by this statement?

3.　Why is it so difficult to appropriate the rewards from innovation? Are product innovations or process innovations more likely to be imitated or emulated by rivals?

4.　What complementary capabilities do you think are the most important for supporting innovation?

5.　Most firms reward their employees for undertaking activities that make an immediate contribution to profits (e.g. making sales of existing products to new customers). In contrast to 'doing more of the same', the outcome of innovative activity is uncertain with respect to its contribution to profits and, as a result, employees who try to innovate may make costly mistakes. Given this, is there any incentive for career-minded employees to be innovative? If you were an entrepreneur or a senior board member what would you do to encourage innovation in your company?

11.7　Recommended additional reading sources

The interplay between the transfer process and the innovation process is discussed in Jack Downie (1958) *The Competitive Process*, London, Duckworth. For an examination of Downie's work in relation to the subsequent literature, see John Nightingale (1997) 'Anticipating Nelson and Winter: Jack Downie's theory of evolutionary economic change', *Journal of Evolutionary Economics*, 7, pp. 147–67.

The classic source on organizational slack is Richard M. Cyert and James G. March (1963) *A Behavioral Theory of the Firm*, Englewood Cliffs, NJ, Prentice-Hall.

For an analysis of some of the cognitive processes that lead firms into difficulties from which they find it hard to escape, see Peter E. Earl (1984) *The Corporate*

Imagination: How Big Companies Make Mistakes, Brighton, Wheatsheaf (see especially Chapter 5).

Two useful analyses of the emergence of standardized product designs and the effects this has on the competitive process are: Burton H. Klein (1977) *Dynamic Economics*, Cambridge, MA, Harvard University Press; and Richard N. Langlois and Paul L. Robertson (1995) *Firms, Markets and Economic Change*, London, Routledge.

William J. Abernathy and Kenneth Wayne (1974) 'Limits of the learning curve', *Harvard Business Review*, Sept.–Oct., pp. 109–19. An excellent account of the tension between the desire to specialize in production processes and the need to retain flexibility in the face of changing selection criteria.

C. Baden-Fuller and J.M. Stopford (1994) *Rejuvenating the Mature Business* (2nd edn), London, International Thomson Business Press. This is a very clear account of how a mature firm can take action to turn around its dwindling fortunes. The authors take a resources and capabilities perspective on the firm and build up their analysis in easy stages. This book was an international best-seller.

A frank account of the rise to success of the British retail giant Marks and Spencer and its subsequent rapid decline is provided by Judi Bevan (2001) *The Rise and Fall of Marks & Spencer*, London, Profile Books. The success story is a tale of innovation in retailing. The story of decline is one of the dominance of routine behaviour and inertia which led management to ignore the changing nature of the selection environment in the late 1990s.

Gary Hamel and C.K. Prahalad (1994) *Competing for the Future*, Boston, Harvard Business School Press. This is another international best-seller in which the authors adopt a similar stance to Baden-Fuller and Stopford and provide a wealth of examples of companies which have successfully reversed their ailing fortunes alongside many examples of failure.

For a very readable analysis of the factors which influence a firm's strategy in a declining market, see Kathryn Harrigan and Michael Porter (1983) 'End-game strategies for declining industries', *Harvard Business Review*, July–Aug., pp. 113–19. For a more extensive treatment with excellent case studies, see Harrigan (1980) *Strategies for Declining Businesses*, Lexington, MA, Lexington Books.

The original analysis of the implications of employing capital of different vintages is from W.E.G. Salter (1960) *Productivity and Technical Change*, Cambridge, Cambridge University Press. Although here we have used it in the context of a declining market Salter's framework has a much wider field of application. In particular you might wish to revisit the material on costs in Chapter 6 and think about the complications added to the problem of identifying and calculating costs if a firm employs capital of different vintages.

David Teece, Gary Pisano and Amy Shuen (1997) 'Dynamic capabilities and strategic management', *Strategic Management Journal*, **18**, pp. 509–33. An influential paper in which the distinction between the capabilities required for current success ('routinized capabilities') are distinguished from the capabilities required for future success in a changing environment ('dynamic capabilities'). The paper has an evolutionary theme.

For probably the most comprehensive collection of readings on the subject of innovation, see P. Tushman and M. Anderson (eds) (1997) *Managing Strategic Innovation and Change: a Collection of Readings*, Oxford: Oxford University Press. The evolutionary perspective is a recurring theme throughout this collection and equal weight is given to both technological and organizational issues. Papers by most of the major contributors on the subject of innovation can be found in this volume.

Fundamentals of macroeconomics

Learning outcomes

If you study this chapter carefully, it may help you to understand:

- the concept of real gross domestic product (real GDP)

- the nature of the components of real GDP

- how real GDP behaves over time

- the concept of the business cycle

- the concept of economic growth

- the Keynesian cross model of the economy

- the Aggregate Demand–Aggregate Supply (AD–AS) model of the economy.

To the extent that you develop such understanding, you should be better able to:

- use the models developed here to explain why the economy behaves in the way it does

- work out the likely consequences for a firm of changes in the different components of GDP.

12.1 Introduction

In this chapter we are going to turn our attention to economy-wide issues. This branch of economics is called **macroeconomics** (from the Greek word *makros*, which means 'large'). Macroeconomics is concerned with analysing the forces which drive the aggregate output being generated by the productive resources of a country. Aggregate output generated per period of time is measured by something called **gross domestic product (GDP)**. Ultimately macroeconomics is used to inform government policy makers (via advisers whom it is to be hoped are decent economists), who are concerned with ensuring that the value of a country's aggregate output continues to grow in a stable and sustainable manner. However, obtaining stable economic growth is far from easily achieved because the problems of inflation (a general and persistent rise in prices across the economy) and unemployment (the proportion of the labour force unable to find a job) are constantly lurking around the corner. This is all very interesting, but why should a business economist be concerned with these things?

So far in this book we have analysed firms as if the major threat to their sales revenues comes from changes in fashion and regulations and, most of all, from rival businesses attempting to offer improved products and/or better value for money. In shifting our focus to the firm's macroeconomic environment we add a new set of threats and opportunities to the picture. Even if a firm is not falling behind relative to its competitors, it may find its sales falling due to falling demand in the economy as a whole. Conversely, even if its relative competitive strength is falling away, its sales might be buoyed up by a rapid expansion of demand in the economy at large, or in overseas markets. The ways in which changes in macroeconomic conditions impinge on a firm will vary depending on the kinds of products that it offers. Tough times in the economy at large will be especially problematic if the firm produces luxury goods and services for which demand is discretionary in nature and highly income-elastic. By contrast, such an environment might be a boon to firms whose products are inferior goods, that buyers would be switching away from if their incomes were rising, and vice versa. In addition it is a very good idea for you to have some understanding of macroeconomic issues because government policies designed to tackle inflation and unemployment (such as changing tax rates and interest rates) will impact upon your business directly, as well as influencing the level and composition of consumer demand.

On the face of it a country's economy is such a complex system of relationships between different firms, individuals and government that the macroeconomist's job might seem an almost impossible task. However, by operating at a highly abstract and aggregated level of analysis macroeconomists have been able to build simplified models of the economy. Of course simplification brings with it some costs, and you should bear in mind that there is no single definitive model of how an economy works. In fact, macroeconomics is a hotbed of argument between economists and we discuss some of the main issues in Chapter 13.

Macroeconomics really took off when one of the most influential men of his generation, the Cambridge economist John Maynard Keynes, published *The General Theory of Employment, Interest and Money* in 1936. Since Keynes's day (he died in 1946) macroeconomic theory has evolved in a manner that is similar to the way a (lengthy) criminal investigation by the police might proceed: that is, the police detective (the macroeconomist) gathers and analyses evidence (the data recorded in the national accounts of a country and by the government statistical services) and uses this to formulate a plausible story about what happened (the macroeconomist formulates a theory). The stories told by both the detective and the macroeconomist are designed to explain the patterns, correlations and trade-offs revealed by the evidence/data. The problem here is that two or more different stories may be quite capable of explaining the same patterns in the data. In short, it is often difficult to pin down accurately exactly what caused a particular effect to happen in the economy. Consequently, different economists base their respective stories on different core beliefs about how people make decisions and about how markets work.

In this chapter our aim is to provide you with a **baseline model** for thinking about macroeconomic issues. After you have read this chapter you should at least be able to read the 'economy' section of a newspaper and understand the rationale behind government policy decisions and formulate your own ideas about why the economy's latest figures for unemployment, inflation and growth are at their current levels. You should also be able to work out the likely impact of macroeconomic changes on the firm.

12.2 What does GDP consist of?

As we have mentioned above, GDP is a measure of the value of aggregate output generated in the economy in a specific period of time (in the UK GDP figures are reported quarterly and yearly). Put another way, it is a measure of total economic activity in a country in a given period of time.

> GDP measures the value of an economy's aggregate output of goods and services in a given period of time.

But how is GDP calculated? We should warn you at this point that what you are about to read is a brief overview of the **accounting definitions** and principles used when statistical agencies calculate a country's GDP: as a result you should not look for economic theory in this section because there isn't any! In order to convey the basic elements of GDP calculation we will begin our analysis by making **two simplifying assumptions**:

(i)   The economy consists of just two types of institution: private individuals who live in **households**, and the productive institutions – **firms**. In other words, there are no government institutions which means we do not have to worry about taxation.

(ii)   The economy is not open to foreign trade so there are no exports and imports to worry about.

After we have explained GDP calculation in this simple economy we will relax our simplifying assumptions and make the analysis more realistic by including both government and foreign trade. For the time being, however, you should concentrate on understanding the calculations relevant to this simple economy because it is an essential foundation for a deeper understanding of the more complex economy to come.

In a capitalist economy **households** are the **ultimate owners** of the factors of production (labour, land, capital and entrepreneurship). Firms need to use the factors of production in order to produce goods and services: they do this by paying wages, rent, interest and residual profits, respectively, to households in return for the services of the factors of production. Payments to the owners of the factors of production constitute household income. Firms, then, do not operate for their own benefit but for the benefit of the owners of the factors of production who live in private households. You should **remember this point.**

Our observations so far imply that GDP can be calculated in three different ways and that each method should give us the same answer:

(i)   By adding up the total value of **output** of goods and services produced by firms in the economy.

(ii)   By adding up the total amount of **income** generated from the sale of this output.

(ii)   By adding up the total amount of **expenditure** on this output.

12.2.1 The output measure of GDP

The output measure of GDP, which we will label GDP_O, is called **national output** and it is calculated by measuring directly the value of final output generated by firms in the economy. Direct calculation of GDP_O reflects the fact that firms are the economic engine of the economy. In order to measure GDP_O it is important to note that we cannot simply calculate the sum of the total value of each and every firm's output. This is because some firms produce **intermediate goods** which are used by other firms as **inputs** in the production of **final goods** (e.g. an Intel Pentium processor chip is an input into Sony PCs). Consequently, if we added up the value of intermediate goods and added them to the value of final goods we would be guilty of double counting and would therefore overestimate the total value of GDP_O. Instead we have to focus on the **value added** at each stage of the **supply chain** for any good or service.

> Value added measures each firm's contribution to the economy's total output. It is the increase in the value of goods as they move along the stages of the supply chain towards their final consumer.

To help you understand how GDP_O is calculated, take a look at Figure 12.1 which shows a simplified supply chain for wooden tables.

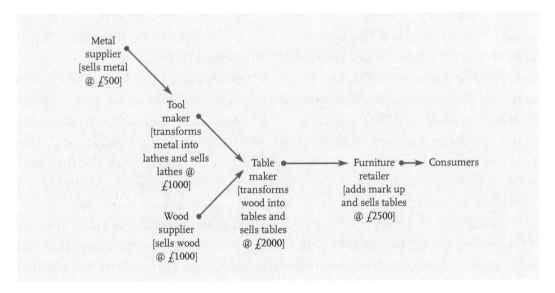

Figure 12.1 The supply chain for wooden tables

Clearly an economy contains thousands upon thousands of supply chains for various goods and services and all of them need to be taken into account to find the economy's GDP_O. Our more modest aim at this stage is not to calculate the whole economy's GDP_O but is instead to find out how much value the specific supply chain for wooden tables contributes to GDP_O in the period under discussion.

In the supply chain shown in Figure 12.1 there are two raw material suppliers: a metal supplier and a wood supplier. To keep things simple we will assume that the metal supplier mines the ore from which the metal is made and the wood supplier cuts down the forests from which the wood is obtained, so each of these suppliers is at the very start of the supply chain. The metal supplier sells metal at £500 to a tool maker. Given that the metal supplier extracted the ore from which the metal was made the value added by the metal supplier is £500. The tool maker transforms the metal into a lathe via the production process and sells this to the table maker for £1000, so the value added by the tool maker is £1000 − £500 = £500. You should note here that the lathe will go no further along the supply chain: this means that the lathe is a **final good**. To be more specific the lathe is an example of **investment** in capital equipment by the table-making firm: this means that it will not be consumed (transformed) in the table production process, instead it will be used over and over again (we will return to this point below). Meanwhile, the wood supplier creates value added of £1000 by selling wood to the table maker. The table maker transforms the wood into tables that it sells on to a furniture retailer for £2000. Value added by the table maker is therefore £2000 − £1000 = £1000. The furniture retailer adds a mark up to the tables and sells them to consumers to generate revenue of £2500. Value added by the furniture retailer is £2500 − £2000 = £500. Note here that although the table maker produces finished tables they are not counted as final goods until they find their way to consumers via the furniture retailer. So although the furniture retailer does not transform the tables in any way it does contribute to value added by adding a retail mark up. These calculations are summarized in Table 12.1.

If we add together the prices charged by each seller (recorded in column 4) the total amount comes to £7000 but, as you can see, this figure overstates the total value of output because it does not take account of input prices. The value added at each stage of the supply chain is recorded in column 5 (the price charged to the next stage in the supply chain minus the price paid to the previous stage in the supply chain). By summing the figures in column 5 we end up with a figure that avoids the double counting problem and which can therefore be used in the calculation of GDP_O.

Table 12.1 An example of how to calculate the supply chain's contribution to GDP_O

(1) Good	(2) Seller	(3) Buyer	(4) Price of seller's output	(5) Value added by seller
Metal	Metal supplier	Tool maker	£500	£500
Lathe	Tool maker	Table maker	£1000	£1000 – £500 = £500
Wood	Wood supplier	Table maker	£1000	£1000
Tables	Table maker	Furniture retailer	£2000	£2000 – £1000 = £1000
Tables	Furniture retailer	Consumers	£2500	£2500 – £2000 = £500
Total of all transactions			**£7000**	
Contribution to GDP_O				**£3500**

12.2.2 The income measure of GDP

We will denote the income measure of GDP as GDP_Y. This measure is known as **national income**. You know from our earlier discussion that households are the ultimate owners of the factors of production, so all of the benefits that accrue to firms will in fact be routed back to households in one form or another. Consider the wood supplier illustrated in Figure 12.1 and Table 12.1. The wood supplier sold wood to the table maker for a total of £1000, so how does this £1000 find its way back to households?

   If we assume that the wood supplying firm is an owner-operated sole trader and that the owner has opportunity costs of £300 then £300 will find its way back to households in the form of the owner's wages. If we assume further that the forests from which the wood supplier cuts its timber are rented from a farmer for £500 then this rent payment will count towards the farmer's income. Where do farmers live? In households. This leaves £200 as a residual. This £200 is economic profit which means it is a reward to risk-taking entrepreneurship. Where do entrepreneurs live? In households. So the economic profit of £200 will also find its way back to households. (Note that in this example the owner-operator is both the workforce and the entrepreneur rolled into one, but this need not be the case.) A similar story can be told for every other firm along the supply chain. The calculation for the wooden table supply chain's contribution to economy-wide GDP_Y is summarized in Table 12.2. There you will see that column 5, *contribution to household incomes*, contains exactly the same figures as column 5 of Table 12.1, so contribution to GDP_Y = contribution to GDP_O.

Table 12.2 An example of how to calculate the supply chain's contribution to GDP$_Y$

(1) Good	(2) Seller	(3) Buyer	(4) Price of seller's output	(5) Contribution to household incomes
Metal	Metal supplier	Tool maker	£500	£500
Lathe	Tool maker	Table maker	£1000	£1000 – £500 = £500
Wood	Wood supplier	Table maker	£1000	£1000
Tables	Table maker	Furniture retailer	£2000	£2000 – £1000 = £1000
Tables	Furniture retailer	Consumers	£2500	£2500 – £2000 = £500
Total of all transactions			**£7000**	
Contribution to GDP$_Y$				**£3500**

12.2.3 The expenditure measure of GDP

We will label the expenditure measure of GDP as GDP$_E$. This is often referred to as **aggregate expenditure**. GDP$_E$ is calculated by adding together the total amount of expenditure on final goods and services produced in the economy. As you will have gathered from our earlier discussion, final goods and services are those which have arrived at the end of their journey along the supply chain, i.e. they are goods which have arrived in the hands of the final user. In our wooden table supply chain there were two final goods: the tables which were sold to consumers by the furniture retailer and the lathe which was sold to the table maker by the tool maker. The retail price of tables sold by the furniture retailer was £2500 and the price paid by the table maker for the lathe was £1000. If we add these two values together we arrive at a contribution to GDP$_E$ of £3500 which is, of course, exactly the same figure we arrived at when we used both the output and income methods of calculating the contribution to GDP from this particular supply chain. So, now we know that contribution to GDP$_E$ = contribution to GDP$_Y$ = contribution to GDP$_O$.

The three methods for measuring the contribution of the supply chain for wooden tables to GDP can be replicated across the entire economy for all other supply chains. To illustrate this, imagine that our simple economy consists of just ten supply chains which are all identical to the one depicted in Figure 12.1. The GDP calculations for our entire economy are represented in Table 12.3.

Table 12.3 GDP for the whole economy

(1) Type of good	(2) Economy-wide household income	(3) Account and type of expenditure in the economy
Intermediate (metal)	£5000	
Final (lathes)	£5000	£10 000 (Investment, I)
Intermediate (wood)	£10 000	
Intermediate (tables for wholesale)	£10 000	
Final (tables for retail)	£5000	£25 000 (Consumption, C)
Total GDP (GDP$_Y$ = GDP$_E$)	**£35 000**	**£35 000**

If you inspect Table 12.3 you will notice that we have identified two types of expenditure which take place in the economy: household expenditure on final goods – which economists call **consumption expenditure (C)** – and firm expenditure on final goods – which economists call **investment expenditure (I)**. (Investment expenditure occurs when firms buy capital equipment from other firms, e.g. when table makers buy lathes from tool makers.) In our example C = £25 000 while GDP$_Y$ = £35 000, which raises the question: what are households doing with the other £10 000 of their income? The answer is that they are **saving (S)** it. But total expenditure in the economy, GDP$_E$, is £35 000 because I = £10 000, so the question you should now be asking is: if firms are only receiving £25 000 from household consumption expenditure how do they get their hands on the £10 000 that households are not spending in order to invest it in new equipment? The answer is that they **borrow** it from households via the financial system. All of this means that we can write the following simple accounting identities:

$$GDP_Y \equiv GDP_E$$
$$\text{where, } GDP_Y \equiv C + S$$
$$\text{and, } GDP_E \equiv C + I$$
$$\text{therefore, } S \equiv I$$

(Note: the symbol '≡' is shorthand for 'is identical to'.)

You should note that saving and investment must always be equal as a matter of definition in our simple economy.

If you have had trouble following our explanation up to this point, take a look at Figure 12.2. There we have shown a diagram called the **circular flow of income**

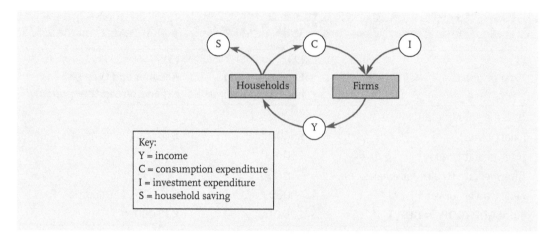

Figure 12.2 The circular flow of income for a simple economy

which tracks how money flows around our simple economy in a given time period. Households supply factor services (labour, land, capital and entrepreneurship) to firms in return for various forms of payment (wages, rent, etc.) which constitute household income, Y. Households use part of their income, C, to buy goods and services from firms and they save, S, the remaining part. Savings therefore represent a **leakage** of money from the system, but firms borrow households' savings (via the financial system) in order to invest, I, in new capital equipment. Investment expenditure by firms therefore represents an **injection** of money into the system. By definition, leakages ≡ injections.

Now we are ready to add government to our model of the economy.

12.2.4 Adding government to the simple economy

The government of a country is an important economic actor. Through various agencies the government has three broad economic roles:

(i) It raises tax revenue from the country's citizens.

(ii) It buys goods and services.

(ii) It redistributes some of its tax revenues.

Taxes are a legally required payment to a government agency for which no good or service is directly received. Taxes come in various forms and have various names, but each one falls into one of two broad categories: they are either **direct taxes (T_d)** or **indirect taxes (T_e)**. Direct taxes (e.g. income tax and National Insurance) are levied on the basis of a household's income while indirect taxes (e.g. excise duty on fuel and cigarettes, and value-added tax (VAT) on many other goods and services) are levied on a household's expenditure. If a household earns a specific level of income (and remember that household income includes the profits made by firms) then it cannot legally avoid paying direct taxes to the government. In contrast, the total amount paid as indirect tax can be reduced if the household decides to consume lower quantities of the products which are taxed in this way. If you think in terms of the circular flow of income, taxes represent a leakage from the system, but this money finds its way back into the system via two routes: the first is **government expenditure (G)** on goods and services (e.g. the police, the armed forces, nurses, etc.) and the second is in the form of **welfare payments (W)**. Welfare payments are more generally called **transfer payments**: this is because the government does not spend this part of its tax revenues itself, but instead it redistributes it to households which add it back to their income and spend it according to their own needs. The income households have to spend on goods and services – their **disposable income (Y_d)** – is therefore equal to **gross income (Y) + transfer payments (W) – direct taxes (T_d)**. Figure 12.3 shows the circular flow of income amended for the inclusion of government.

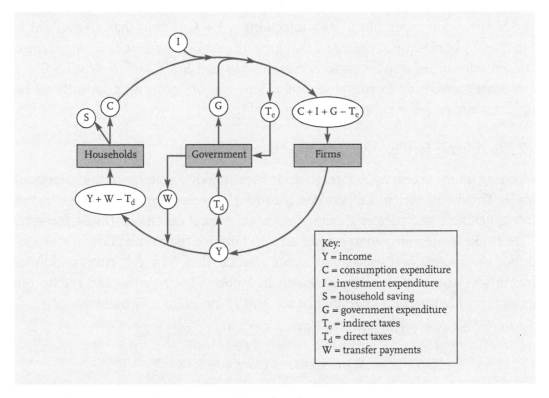

Figure 12.3 The circular flow of income for a closed economy

If you inspect Figure 12.3 you should be able to see that it is easy to calculate GDP by the expenditure method. This is because we simply have to add government spending on goods and services, G, to the other two categories of expenditure (C and I) that we identified in our previous calculations. However, we need also to take account of the impact of indirect taxes because these drive a wedge between the prices that customers pay and the prices that firms receive for their output. Consequently we can identify two values for GDP: GDP at market prices (i.e. prices paid by customers) and GDP at basic prices (i.e. prices received by firms).

$$\text{GDP @market prices} \equiv C + I + G$$

$$\text{GDP @basic prices} \equiv Y \equiv C + I + G - T_e$$

You will recall that we ended our discussion of the simple economy above by pointing out that as a matter of definition leakages $\equiv$ injections. This identity still holds true for the economy with a government sector. Inspection of the circular flow in Figure 12.3 will reveal that leakages from the system occur when households save some of their income (as before) and when taxes (of both types) are levied on households. Some of these leakages are fed back into the system in the form of transfer payments. So, **leakages = S + T$_d$ + T$_e$ – W**. Injections of income back into the system come from two sources – investment expenditure (as before) and government expenditure – so **injections = I + G**. Given that investment is financed by borrowing savings and that government expenditure is financed from tax revenues net of transfer payments, it follows that **S + T$_d$ + T$_e$ – W $\equiv$ I + G**.

We are now ready to complete our discussion of accounting definitions by opening our closed economy to foreign trade.

12.2.5 Adding foreign trade to the closed economy

Opening up the economy to foreign trade means taking account of the balance of trade. This is the difference between incoming revenue from **export sales (X)** to foreign citizens and outgoing income spent on **import purchases (Z)** by domestic citizens. Revenue from export sales is an injection into the circular flow and expenditure on imports is a leakage from the circular flow. The full circular flow of income for an open economy is shown in Figure 12.4. Now we can restate the accounting identities for GDP to take account of the balance of trade (X – Z):

$$\text{GDP @market prices} \equiv C + I + G + (X - Z)$$

$$\text{GDP @basic prices} \equiv Y \equiv C + I + G + (X - Z) - T_e$$

Once again leakages $\equiv$ injections: $S + T_d + T_e - W + Z \equiv I + G + X$; and this concludes our discussion of GDP accounting.

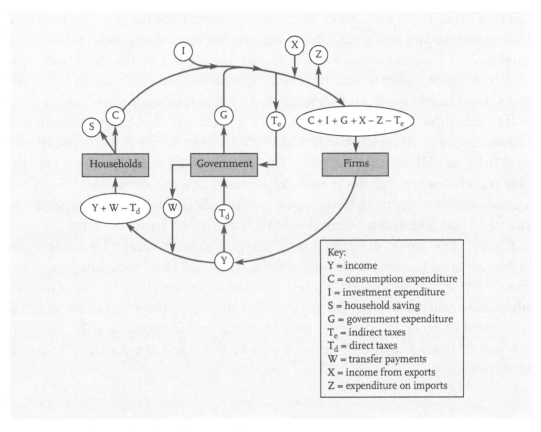

Figure 12.4 The circular flow of income for an open economy

12.3 The behaviour of GDP over time

In this section we will take a brief look at how GDP behaves over time. We will use UK data to reveal that the value of GDP tends to grow over time but that its growth path is often cyclical, passing through phases around a central trend. The cycles tend to bring with them varying levels of unemployment and inflation. This behaviour has been repeated in other developed economies around the world, so we can recognize it as a stylized fact.

Figure 12.5 shows the time path of **real GDP** (at market prices) for the UK from 1970 to 2003.

> Real GDP is the money (or 'nominal') value of GDP recorded in each period adjusted for changes in the general level of prices over time.

We use real GDP in order to be able to compare the **volume of production** in one year with another and to help us identify periods of growth and periods of decline. For example, imagine that nominal GDP in year one is £1 billion and in year two is £1.1 billion. We need to know the general level of prices in each year in order to see if the increase of 10 per cent in nominal GDP (i.e. the extra £0.1 billion) in year two represents an increase in the volume of goods and services produced, or if part or even all of it is simply due to price increases. If prices are also 10 per cent higher in year two then there has been no increase in real GDP (i.e. the volume of goods and services produced) compared to year one.[1]

If you examine Figure 12.5 you will quickly see that the UK enjoyed significant growth in real GDP during the period 1970–2003; in fact in 2003 real GDP was over twice as high as it was in 1970. This is called **long-term economic growth**. You will also notice that the growth in the country's wealth has not followed a steady path. Instead, there have been some significant swings above and below the trend line. These **short-term fluctuations** are called **business cycles**.

Figure 12.6 shows the anatomy of the UK's most recent business cycle (1987–1994). A business cycle begins when real GDP rises above the long-term trend line and continues its above-trend trajectory, creating an **expansionary phase** (also called a 'boom'). During an expansion unemployment falls and inflationary pressure builds so prices start to rise at an increasing rate. In addition, interest rates tend to rise. Eventually a **peak** is hit and the economy enters a

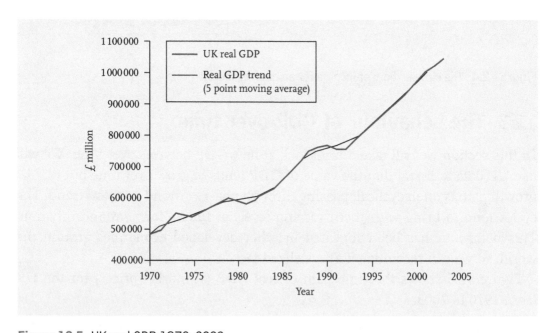

Figure 12.5 UK real GDP 1970–2003

(Original data sourced from Office for National Statistics downloadable chained volume series – 'base' year 2001)

---

[1]   In the UK, the Office for National Statistics uses a technique called 'annual chain-linking' to arrive at a value of real GDP called 'chained volume'.

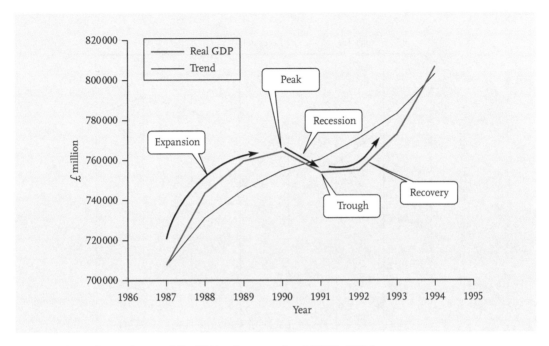

Figure 12.6 The anatomy of the UK business cycle of 1987–1994

recession as real GDP turns downwards and passes below the long-term trend line. Now unemployment increases and deflationary pressure comes to bear so inflation begins to fall. Interest rates also fall. Eventually real GDP bottoms out at the **trough**, turns the corner, and begins the **recovery phase** as it heads back towards the long-term trend line. During the recovery period employment rises only slowly, so the recession creates a 'hangover' that lasts beyond its own duration. For example, from the point at which the recession started to bite in 1990 unemployment increased all the way into 1993, where it peaked at 10.5 per cent of the labour force (that's almost 3 million people out of work), despite the fact that real GDP had begun to increase steadily from the end of 1992. By way of comparison, the unemployment figure for 2003 was 5 per cent (which is just under 1.5 million people). The inflation and unemployment rates that occurred during the phases of the 1987–1994 business cycle are plotted in Figure 12.7.

If you cast your mind back to Section 12.1 you will recall we stated that macroeconomists are a bit like detectives because they look at the evidence and then try to formulate theories to explain the patterns revealed by the evidence. Our key piece of evidence is, of course, the real GDP data from Figure 12.5. Our task is to get to the bottom of the two key features it has revealed: namely, (1) what causes short-term fluctuations?, and (2) what leads to long-term growth? To help us begin to answer these questions we will build some economic models.

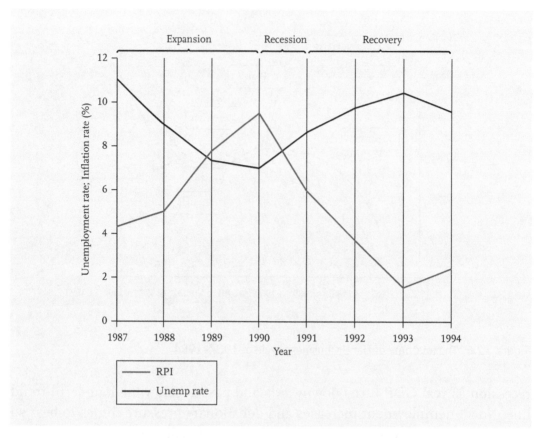

Figure 12.7 Inflation and unemployment rates over the UK business cycle of 1987–1994 (Data sourced from Office for National Statistics downloadable data sets)

The first model we introduce below is called the **Keynesian cross model**. Keynes himself did not use this model but it has become a standard tool for expressing the most basic of his ideas. You will be familiar with its components because the model takes as its point of departure the accounting identities that we introduced in Section 12.2. The second model we introduce is called the **Aggregate Demand–Aggregate Supply (AD–AS) model**. The AD–AS model builds upon the knowledge you will gain from understanding the basic Keynesian cross model and provides you with a very useful framework for thinking about a whole variety of macroeconomic issues. This will be your baseline model.

12.4 The Keynesian cross model of the economy

You know from Section 12.2 that GDP at market prices is defined as GDP ≡ C + I + G + (X − Z). This is a simple accounting identity. It is devoid of any economic theory: in other words, it does not explain why a particular value of GDP will arise. In order to construct an economic theory about why GDP attains a particular value we need to construct stories about each of its component parts, i.e. C, I, G,

X and Z. When we put the individual stories together we will have the makings of a theory of what determines GDP.

12.4.1 A story about consumption expenditure

Households receive disposable income which is equal to their gross income minus any direct taxes they are liable to pay. In any given period they will make plans about how much of their disposable income to spend on consumption, C, and how much to save, S (these plans are sometimes called **desired consumption and desired saving**). These two decisions are different sides of the same coin, because any disposable income that is not allocated to C is, by definition, allocated to S. As a general empirical observation, a relatively low income household will plan to allocate all of its income to consumption while a household which enjoys a very high income will plan to allocate a relatively high proportion of its income to saving. A middle income household, that is the 'average' household in an economy, will lie somewhere in between these two extremes. Given that macroeconomics is concerned with studying **aggregate variables** we can state that in the aggregate, that is taking all households together, the low income and the high income households will cancel each other out and, for any given level of aggregate household disposable income, we can expect a **proportion to be consumed** (retained in the circular flow of income) and a **proportion to be saved** (withdrawn from the circular flow of income). Furthermore, we can add another fact to our theory: empirical studies of the relationship between the levels of real aggregate household disposable income and real aggregate consumption over time have shown that higher levels of real disposable income go hand in hand with higher levels of real consumption spending. In other words, there is a positive relationship between the level of household disposable income and the level of planned consumption in the economy. Economists call the relationship between income and planned consumption expenditure the **consumption function.**

> The consumption function shows a positive relationship between the level of planned aggregate consumption expenditure and aggregate household disposable income. So, if aggregate disposable income increases we would expect to see planned consumption expenditure increase also.

The idea of the consumption function is based on the assumption that other potential influences on the amount of consumption spending are held constant. These other determinants include:

- the **rate of interest** at which households can **borrow** money (if this increases then repayments out of future disposable income will increase and planned consumption may fall);

- the **rate of interest** that can be earned on **savings** (if the savings rate is relatively high then consumption of income in the current period represents an opportunity cost in terms of interest that could have been earned for future consumption);

- how **wealthy** households are (the bigger their stock of wealth the less likely households are to feel they need to save, so their consumption might increase);

- the **general price level** (if households expect the rate of inflation to increase this will both erode the value of savings and make purchases today cheaper than purchases in the future).

The simplest consumption function takes the form of the equation of a straight line: $C = a + bY_d$, where: a is the intercept term, b is the gradient (slope) of the line, and Y_d is disposable income. It is more usual for economists to try and give their algebraic notation some semblance of meaning so the standard notation for a consumption function is:

$$C = \bar{C} + cY_d \qquad [1]$$

Here, $\bar{C}$ is called **autonomous consumption expenditure**, and c is called the **marginal propensity to consume**.

Autonomous consumption expenditure is a level of expenditure that is independent of the level of disposable income.

The marginal propensity to consume (mpc) is the proportion of any addition to disposable income that is allocated to consumption. For example, if disposable income increases by £1 and the consumer plans to spend 90 pence of this increase then the marginal propensity to consume is 0.9. Conversely the marginal propensity to save (mps) is 0.1 or, more generally, (1–mpc).

We can illustrate the nature of the consumption function with a simple numerical example. Imagine the following data are true for a fictional economy:

autonomous consumption, $\bar{C} = £10$ million

marginal propensity to consume, c = 0.8

direct tax rate, t = 0.25

With a direct tax rate of 25 per cent every single £1 earned as household income (Y) will be reduced by 25 pence. This means that disposable income, $Y_d = Y - tY = (1 - t)Y$. If we substitute this into our original equation for the consumption function from above we obtain:

$$C = \bar{C} + c(1 - t)Y \qquad [2]$$

Substituting the numbers from our fictional data set into equation [2] we end up with:

$$C = \text{\pounds}10 \text{ million} + 0.6Y \qquad [3]$$

We can use expression [3] to discover the level of planned consumption spending at various levels of income. See Table 12.4.

Table 12.4 **A consumption function**	
National income, Y (£ million)	**Planned consumption expenditure (£ million)**
0	10
20	22
40	34
60	46
80	58
100	70
120	82
140	94

If we plot the data contained in Table 12.4 we obtain a picture of the consumption function given in expression [3]. See Figure 12.8.

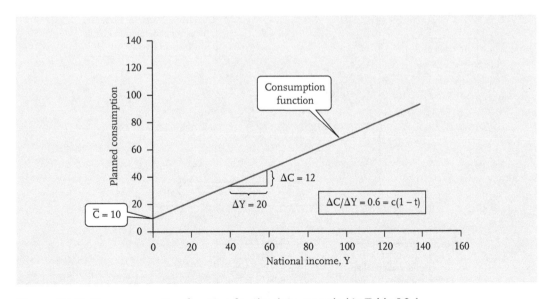

Figure 12.8 The consumption function for the data recorded in Table 12.4

12.4.2 A story about investment expenditure

You will be well aware from our discussions in earlier chapters that investment (I) by a specific firm in new capital equipment will depend upon how confident the entrepreneur/management team is about the future sales prospects for the firm's products. We can postulate, therefore, that planned aggregate investment expenditure will in part be determined by how confident and optimistic entrepreneurs in general are feeling about the future state of demand for goods and services in the economy. In other words, their **expectations** about the future state of the economy will be an important determining factor of the level of desired aggregate investment expenditure. In addition, the level of the interest rate will have some degree of bearing on the level of investment that takes place in the economy because higher interest rates increase the cost of borrowing to fund investment plans. In other words, higher interest rates increase the cost of capital and, as a result, they render marginal investment projects unattractive. For example, imagine that a firm is considering investing in two projects, A and B. A is expected to yield a rate of return of 15 per cent per year while B's expected rate of return is 10 per cent per year. If the interest rate is, say, 7 per cent per year then both projects can be expected to be profitable, but if the interest rate increases to, say, 12 per cent then project B, the **marginal project,** will no longer be profitable. As a result, we can imagine plotting an **investment demand schedule** like the one depicted in Figure 12.9.

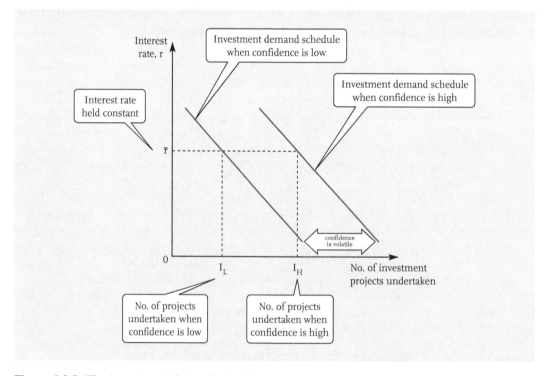

Figure 12.9 The investment demand schedule

As you can see, the investment demand schedule slopes downwards, depicting an inverse relationship between interest rates and the amount of investment spending. Its location is determined by the level of confidence entrepreneurs have in the future state of the economy. If confidence is high then aggregate investment, I_H, at a given interest rate, $\bar{r}$, will be higher than it would be if confidence was low, I_L. This is because high levels of confidence imply that investment projects are expected to yield higher returns than when confidence is low. For example, in our example above, when the interest rate increases to 12 per cent per year it is quite possible that a sudden increase in confidence about the future state of demand for goods and services will cause the entrepreneur to re-evaluate the original expected rate of return on project B and change it upwards from 10 per cent to, say, 14 per cent.

Pinning down the causes of entrepreneurial optimism and gloom about the future is notoriously difficult and in practice confidence can be quite volatile. Keynes himself used the phrase 'animal spirits' to describe the attitudes of entrepreneurs and business people. In the simple Keynesian cross model we assume that the interest rate is fixed, so the primary driver of investment is the state of entrepreneurial confidence. We treat investment in the model as a constant value which will only change if general confidence changes, so our theory of investment can be stated formally as:

$$I = \bar{I} \tag{4}$$

Plotting this investment function in expenditure–national income space gives us Figure 12.10.

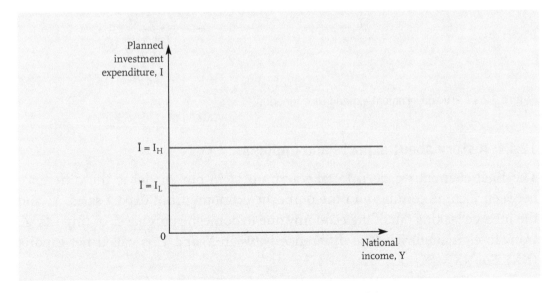

Figure 12.10 The investment function at different levels of confidence

12.4.3 A story about government expenditure

In the UK the government's spending plans are formulated by the Chancellor of the Exchequer, typically in a three-yearly spending review which is tweaked annually when the Chancellor announces the budget for the year ahead. In other words, government expenditure, G, is **discretionary expenditure determined by social and political expediency.** These plans are made well in advance so they are fairly long range and they tend to remain fairly stable over time. For example, real government expenditure between 1999 and 2001 stayed at between £180 000 million and £190 000 million. For the purposes of the simple Keynesian cross model we shall treat government expenditure as a constant value. So:

$$G = \bar{G} \tag{5}$$

If we plot G in expenditure–national income space we obtain Figure 12.11.

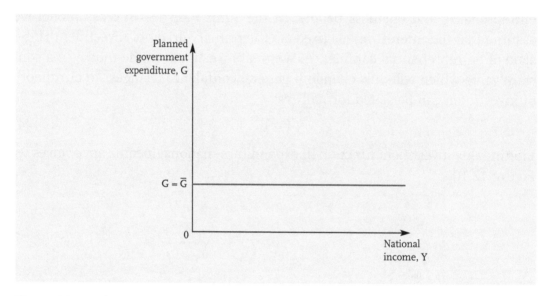

Figure 12.11 The government expenditure function

12.4.4 A story about exports and imports

The final element we need to take account of in our model is the difference between income coming into the domestic economy from export sales, X, and the income leaking out of the economy due to domestic purchases of imports, Z, from foreign countries. The difference between X and Z is called **net exports (NX).** So, NX = (X – Z).

The domestic economy's export sales will depend on:

- the level of **national income in overseas economies** with whom trade is carried out (the higher their income the greater will be their demand for domestic exports);

- the **price level in the domestic economy** relative to the rest of the world (if domestic prices are relatively low we would expect, all other things being equal, demand for domestic exports to increase overseas);

- the **exchange rate** (if the domestic currency appreciates – that is, if its price increases in the market for foreign exchange[2] – then, all other things being equal, foreign demand for exports will fall).

In the simple Keynesian cross model we assume that all of these factors are held constant, so a plot of export income in expenditure–income space will reveal a horizontal line. Formally:

$$X = \bar{X} \tag{6}$$

Import purchases, like export sales, will be determined by:

- the **relative prices of goods and services** on international markets;

- the **exchange rate**;

- the **level of income**, Y, in the domestic economy.

The simplest theory of import spending holds relative prices and the exchange rate constant and relates it positively to the level of income in the domestic economy. A plot of the import function would reveal a positively sloped function in expenditure–income space. Formally:

$$Z = zY \tag{7}$$

where z represents the **marginal propensity to import (mpz)**. In other words, the mpz tells us how much of each extra £1 of national income will be spent on imported goods and services.

In order to obtain the net exports function we subtract equation [7] from equation [6]:

$$NX = \bar{X} - zY \tag{8}$$

Imagine the following data are true for a fictional economy:

$$\text{export sales, } \bar{X} = £10 \text{ million}$$

$$\text{marginal propensity to import, } z = 0.1$$

---

2   We discuss exchange rates further in Chapter 14.

These figures will generate the export and import data shown in Table 12.5. Here you can see that when relative prices and exchange rates are held constant the domestic economy has positive net exports at low levels of income and negative net exports at higher levels of income. When $Y = £100$ million net exports are zero.

Table 12.5 A net exports function

National income, Y (£ million)	Export sales, X (£ million)	Import purchases, Z (£ million)	Net exports, NX (£ million)
0	10	0	10
20	10	2	8
40	10	4	6
60	10	6	4
80	10	8	2
100	10	10	0
120	10	12	-2
140	10	14	-4

Plotting the data in Table 12.5 generates the net exports function shown in Figure 12.12.

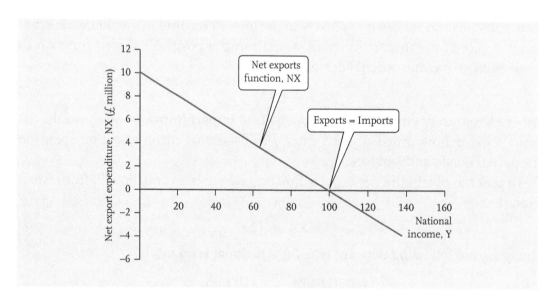

Figure 12.12 The net exports function

12.4.5 Putting the stories together to obtain a model of the economy

We are now in a position to put together all of the stories told above to form our first basic model of the economy. This involves adding all of the various elements of GDP together. So, **planned aggregate expenditure (AE)** is found by adding equations [2], [4], [5] and [8] together:

$$AE = \bar{C} + c(1 - t)Y + \bar{I} + \bar{G} + \bar{X} - zY \qquad [9]$$

We can tidy up equation [9] to gather the Y terms together:

$$AE = \bar{C} + \bar{I} + \bar{G} + \bar{X} + (c - ct - z)Y \qquad [9a]$$

Equation [9a] might look a bit complicated at first sight, but closer inspection will reveal that it is nothing more than the equation of a straight line. On its own this equation does not tell us what the level of GDP in the economy will be. This is because it only tells us one half of the story: it tells us what planned or *desired* aggregate expenditure on goods and services in the economy will be. It does not say anything about the supply of goods and services. As a result, equation [9a] does not tell us whether expenditure plans will be thwarted by a shortage of goods and services from sellers. So, to complete the model we assume that **firms respond to any given level of desired aggregate expenditure by supplying sufficient quantities of goods and services to meet the demand implied by this expenditure.** This means that if AE exceeds the total supply of goods and services currently being produced firms will expand their production, and vice versa. This is a **crucial assumption** in the model, because it implies that real GDP is determined solely by the demand side of the economy. We will return to this point when we introduce the AD–AS model a little later.

In order to illustrate the model of the economy in something that is a little more accessible than an equation, we will breathe life into equation [9a] by postulating the following values for all of the variables:

autonomous consumption, $\bar{C} = £10$ million

marginal propensity to consume, $c = 0.8$

direct tax rate, $t = 0.25$

planned investment spending, $\bar{I} = £10$ million

planned government spending, $\bar{G} = £30$ million

planned export spending, $\bar{X} = £10$ million

marginal propensity to import, $mpz = 0.1$

Using these values we can construct Table 12.6 and derive the aggregate expenditure function, AE, for the economy.

Table 12.6 **The derivation of the aggregate expenditure function (£m)**						
Y	C	I	G	X	Z	AE
0	10	10	30	10	0	60
20	22	10	30	10	2	70
40	34	10	30	10	4	80
60	46	10	30	10	6	90
80	58	10	30	10	8	100
100	70	10	30	10	10	110
120	82	10	30	10	12	120
140	94	10	30	10	14	130

The AE function in the final column of Table 12.6 is plotted in Figure 12.13. As you can see, given our choice of numbers, it is a straight line. (An alternative way of deriving the AE line is simply to add together vertically the lines plotted in Figures 12.8, 12.10, 12.11 and 12.12.) You can also see that we have plotted a dashed line that extends at 45 degrees from the origin. This line is simply an aid to help us identify points of equality between aggregate output as measured by Y (recall from Section 12.2 that $GDP_O \equiv GDP_Y$) and AE. This means that the point

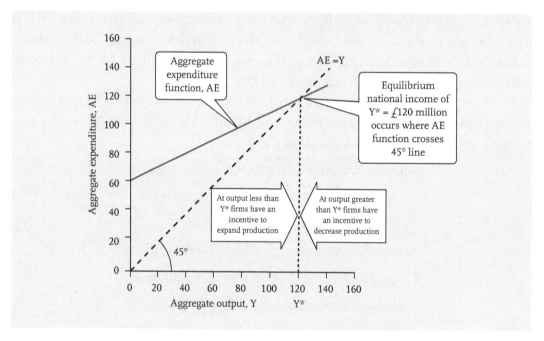

Figure 12.13 The Keynesian cross model of the determination of GDP (£m)

where the AE function crosses the 45° line[3] defines the economy's **equilibrium level of national income, Y***. So, we have a model where the equilibrium level of GDP, Y*, is determined by the level of aggregate expenditure, AE. Y* is an equilibrium because at this point AE is exactly matched by aggregate output. At points to the left of Y* firms have an incentive to increase production in order to meet unmet demand, while at points to the right of Y* firms have an incentive to cut back production because AE is insufficient to justify this volume of output.

Now that you know the workings of the Keynesian cross model you can use it to explore the implications for equilibrium GDP of changing the value of any of the variables in the model. For example, if the government increases the direct tax rate to, say, 50 per cent (t = 0.5) and everything else in the model remains unchanged, the AE function will become flatter and cross the 45° line at a lower level of equilibrium GDP (in this case Y* = £85.7 million – see Figure 12.14). To prove this to yourself take another look at equation [9a]. The term in brackets, (c – ct – z), is the gradient of the AE function. Given that the direct tax rate, t, is a part of the expression in the brackets it follows that a change in the value of t will cause the gradient of the AE function to change. In the example here the gradient changes from 0.5 to 0.3 as a result of increasing the direct tax rate from 25 per cent to 50 per cent. Intuitively the reduction in GDP as a result of a direct tax increase makes sense: an increase in the direct tax rate will reduce disposable income available to households and this will, in turn, reduce the level of consumption spending, C, in the economy.

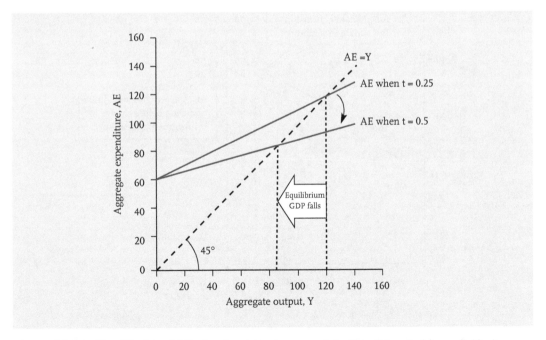

Figure 12.14 The effect on GDP of a direct tax increase (all other things held equal) (£m)

---

[3] This is the 'cross' referred to in the title of the model.

A change in the direct tax rate is part of government's fiscal policy (more on which later). But what happens to GDP if, independent of government policies, entrepreneurs suddenly feel optimistic about the future prospects of the economy and decide to increase their investment expenditure? Consider the situation depicted in Figure 12.15.

Here, investment expenditure in the economy has increased by £10 million (from an initial level of £10 million to a new level of £20 million) and, as a result, the original aggregate expenditure function, AE_0, has shifted vertically by this amount to AE_1. The interesting thing you should notice about this diagram is that although the **change in investment expenditure ($\Delta \bar{I}$)** is £10 million, the **change in equilibrium GDP (ΔY)** that it brings about is twice this amount at £20 million. This is an example of the **multiplier effect** of a change in autonomous expenditure. The £10 million boost in spending has led to a chain of subsequent increases in spending elsewhere. The chain of spending works like this: the increase in investment boosts GDP initially by £10 million. This £10 million ultimately finds its way back to households (remember that all income finds its way back to households in one form or another) where 25 per cent is paid to the government as direct tax. Of the remaining £7.5 million, £1.5 million is saved and £6 million is put back into the circular flow of income where £1 million leaks

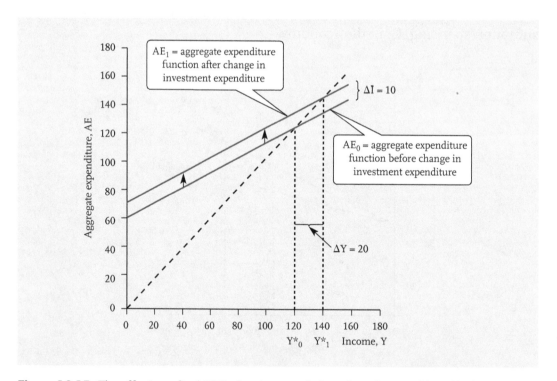

Figure 12.15 The effects on final GDP of an increase in investment expenditure (£m)

out thanks to spending on imports. This leaves £5 million which is spent on domestic goods and services as C. Now the process happens once again: the extra £5 million received by domestic firms finds its way back to households where 25 per cent is paid in direct tax. Of the remaining £3.75 million, £0.75 million is saved and £3 million is spent, but £0.5 million leaks out of the economy because of spending on imports, so domestic firms receive just £2.5 million. Once again this income to firms ends up in the hands of households and the process continues. As you can see, with each successive cycle around the circular flow the addition to GDP diminishes because of the leakages in the system (i.e. direct taxes, savings and import spending). In this example it does not take too many cycles before the successive additions to GDP taper off. Figure 12.16 shows the additions to GDP for the first nine periods of the process. If you add up the successive additions to GDP you will find that they sum to almost £20 million.

Not only will the multiplier process work for increases in investment expenditure but it will also kick in if any of the other autonomous elements of AE changes, that is if any one of $\bar{C}$, $\bar{G}$ or $\bar{X}$ changes. Changes in $\bar{G}$ are made at the discretion of the government, while changes in $\bar{C}$ will be caused by changes in the things we held constant when we plotted the consumption function shown in equation [2] above. For example, if consumption spending increases suddenly and everything else, including income, remains equal, this implies that the consumption function (and therefore the AE function) has shifted upwards. You should note that the multiplier works in reverse too, so if any of the autonomous elements of expenditure falls the ultimate reduction in the size of equilibrium

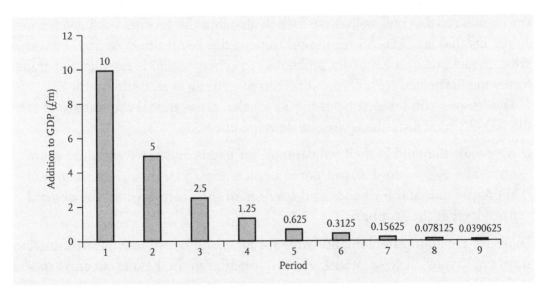

Figure 12.16 The multiplier effect in action

GDP will be greater than the size of the reduction in autonomous expenditure.

For the economy shown in Figure 12.15 the value of the multiplier, k, is found by the equation:

$$k = \frac{\Delta Y}{\Delta I} = \frac{20}{10} = 2 \qquad [10]$$

More generally the formula for the value of the multiplier is:

$$k = \frac{1}{(1 - c + ct + z)} \qquad [11]$$

So, the overall change in GDP will be equal to the change in autonomous expenditure multiplied by the value of the multiplier. Don't worry about the maths – it's the principle of the multiplier that matters. You are now ready to move on to the AD–AS model.

12.5 The Aggregate Demand–Aggregate Supply model

The Keynesian cross model is an excellent foundation for getting you to think about macroeconomic issues, but it is based on the assumption that the general level of prices is fixed. This means that it is cumbersome to use the model to analyse inflation and changes in the price level that might be induced by changes in aggregate expenditure as the economy moves from one equilibrium level of GDP to another. It also means that the model may well overstate the multiplier's impact on real GDP. In addition the Keynesian cross model does not allow us to analyse the supply side of the economy in anything but a rudimentary manner. Don't worry, none of this means that we have to abandon the lessons you have learned so far, because the AD–AS framework retains the key features of the Keynesian cross model but overcomes its problems. In other words, it extends and transforms the Keynesian cross framework into something even more useful.

The lessons you learned from the Keynesian cross model are translated into the AD–AS model via the aggregate demand curve.

Aggregate demand is the total demand for goods and services in the economy. The aggregate demand curve depicts the relationship between real aggregate demand for goods and services in the economy and the general price level in the economy.

To derive the aggregate demand curve for an economy we use the AE function from the Keynesian cross model. The AE function in the Keynesian cross model is drawn on the assumption that the price level is fixed. As a result the equilibrium level of national income found from its intersection with the 45° line represents real GDP at this fixed price level. For example, if equilibrium real GDP is £10 million at one price level and then the price level is doubled, this will halve the value of real GDP to £5 million. So, generally, if the price level is increased the real value of a given nominal GDP will fall, and vice versa. If we apply this insight in the Keynesian cross model it means that the position of the AE function will change if we change the price level: more specifically, if the price level increases the AE function will move vertically downwards and, consequently, it will cross the 45° line at a lower point (so equilibrium real GDP will be lower). If we hold all of the other variables in the Keynesian cross model constant the aggregate demand curve is derived by simply plotting the relationship between equilibrium real GDP and different price levels. This is shown in Figure 12.17.

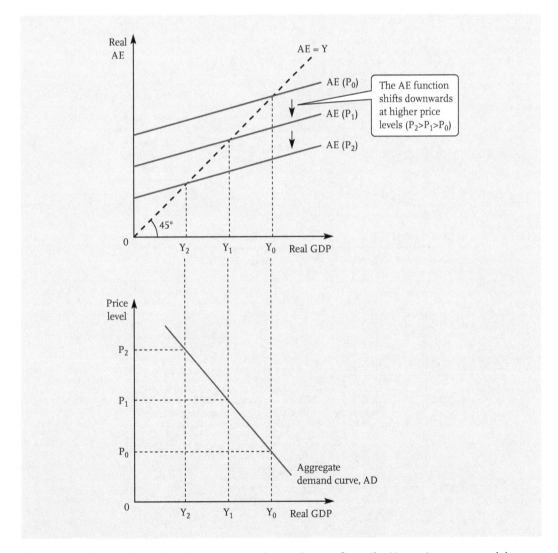

Figure 12.17 How to derive the aggregate demand curve from the Keynesian cross model

If we change anything other than the price level in the Keynesian cross model this will shift the position of the AD curve. If you look at Figure 12.18 you will see how an increase in aggregate expenditure in the Keynesian cross model due to, say, a rise in autonomous consumption spending, $\bar{C}$, is translated into a rightward shift in the AD curve.

Now we introduce the aggregate supply curve, AS. This element was glossed over in the Keynesian cross model so we need to develop a theory of aggregate supply before we can draw the curve. In fact we are going to draw two AS curves: one for the short run (SRAS) and one for the long run (LRAS). In general, an aggregate supply curve shows the output (real GDP) that all firms in the economy will be willing to produce at each prevailing price level.

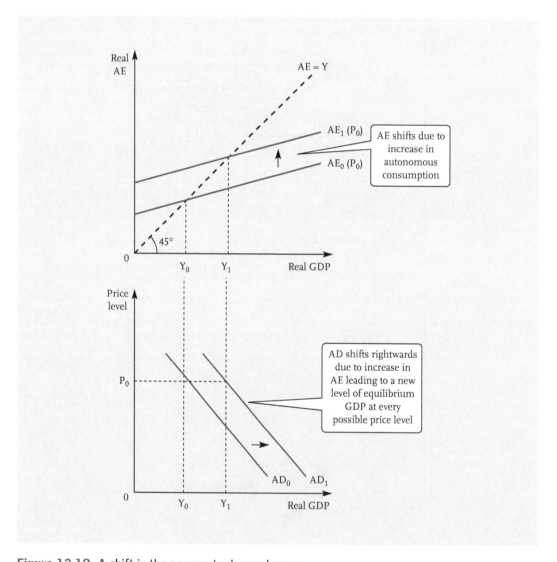

Figure 12.18 A shift in the aggregate demand curve

The short-run aggregate supply curve, SRAS, shows how much real GDP firms will be willing to produce at each prevailing price level on the assumption that their input prices (e.g. wages and raw material costs) remain fixed.

The SRAS curve is generally portrayed as having a positive slope, indicating that firms will only be willing to supply higher levels of national output (real GDP) if the price level increases. The explanation behind the positive slope of the SRAS curve revolves around the assertion that the unit costs of production incurred by firms rise as they increase their volume of output so, as a result, they will only be prepared to meet increased demand for their goods and services if the price level rises. Note here that input prices have *not* changed (so, for example, wages remain fixed). One justification for the assertion that the unit costs of production increase with output is provided by our explanation of Ricardian rents back in Chapter 8, Box 8.1. There we showed that unit production costs will increase if the marginal inputs to the production process that are required to meet higher demand for output are of lower quality than the inputs currently being employed. To the extent that this is true for aggregate production in the economy the SRAS curve will indeed have a positive slope. It is unlikely, however, that the SRAS curve will have a constant positive slope because demand for ever higher levels of output will make the shortage of high quality inputs (particularly labour) even more acute, and the SRAS curve will look like the one depicted in Figure 12.19.

A change in input costs will cause the SRAS curve to shift its position. In Figure 12.20 we have shown how a general increase in wages (which is one of the most important input costs for most firms) will shift the SRAS curve to the

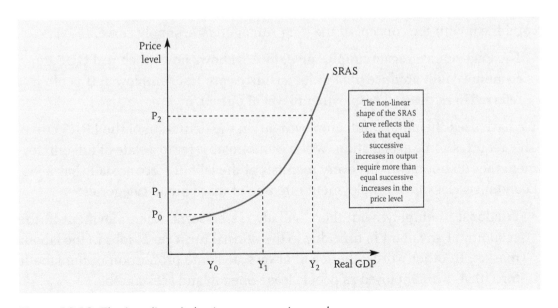

Figure 12.19 The (non-linear) short-run aggregate supply curve

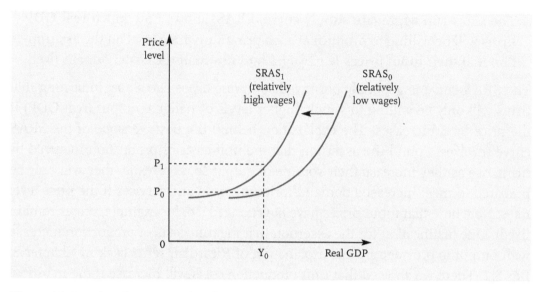

Figure 12.20 The effect on the SRAS curve of increasing input costs

left. This reflects the fact that any given quantity of output (real GDP), say, Y_0, will require the price level to be higher in order to persuade firms to deliver it if their input costs have increased.

The position of the SRAS curve will also be changed if technological change increases labour productivity (the SRAS curve will move rightwards) or if greater quantities of labour and capital become available over time. The second point tells us that the bigger an economy becomes (as measured by its supplies of labour and capital) then the more it will be capable of producing.

In order to use the SRAS curve to help us analyse the economy we need to combine it with the concept of the long-run aggregate supply curve, LRAS.

> The long-run aggregate supply curve, LRAS, shows how much real GDP the economy could produce if all of its resources are fully employed. It is often referred to as the 'full employment level of output, Y_{fe}'.

We have used the phrase 'full employment' in the definition of the LRAS curve. This requires some explanation. When economists refer to a state of full employment they do not mean that every member of the labour force actually has a job. Economists classify unemployment into one of three broad categories:

- **Frictional unemployment:** there will always be some unemployment in the economy at any point in time due to the normal turnover of jobs in the labour market. In other words, there will always be some proportion of the labour force that is unemployed as people leave one job and seek another.

- **Structural unemployment:** people who find themselves structurally unemployed are not really between jobs in the same way frictionally unemployed workers are. Instead they are unemployed because they possess skills which are no longer marketable (possibly due to technological advances in production techniques leading to more automation). Workers who fall into this category face the prospect of long periods of unemployment and they will find it necessary to acquire new skills. This is not always easy for older members of the labour force.

- **Cyclical unemployment:** this occurs when the economy enters a recession. In a recession aggregate demand in the economy falls, so firms contract their output and as a result require lower quantities of labour. In this situation there are plenty of people who have relevant skills and who are willing to work but there is insufficient demand for their services by firms.

So, when economists refer to full employment they mean a state of the economy where cyclical unemployment has been eradicated but where frictional and structural unemployment still exist. The combination of frictional and structural unemployment is sometimes referred to as the **natural rate of unemployment**.

In order to understand the LRAS curve it is helpful to think of the economy as a system of production where labour, capital and technology are combined to produce output. On the assumptions that all three elements of the system are fixed in quantity and that they can be combined in an optimal manner, theoretically we can identify the amount of real GDP the economy is capable of producing. In other words, we can identify its **potential real GDP**. In practice it is difficult, if not impossible, to calculate an economy's potential real GDP but this does not diminish the value of potential real GDP as a theoretical concept. The LRAS curve is simply a vertical line drawn at the economy's potential GDP. It will only shift if the quantities of any of the three variables (labour, capital, technology) in the production system change.

We are now ready to put all of the elements of the AD–AS framework together to help us tell a story about the behaviour of real GDP in the short term (fluctuations above and below the trend line, i.e. business cycles) and the long term (growth in real GDP). You should note that the story we are going to tell here is 'pure' in the sense that it does not involve government intervention. In other words, it is a story about what might happen to GDP if the economy was left to its own devices. It is important that you remember this, because the actual UK business cycle shown in Figure 12.6 was not pure (the UK government actively tried to manage the economy). In short then, the pure story told here is the **baseline model** we promised to deliver at the outset of this chapter.

We will begin with an analysis of above-trend swings in GDP. The explanation for these features is provided in Figure 12.21.

We assume that the economy starts off in equilibrium at the point where AD_0, $SRAS_0$ and LRAS intersect (point a). At this point the economy is trundling along nicely but then, for some reason (maybe an upward surge of confidence by entrepreneurs or an increase in autonomous consumption by households), the economy is hit with a **positive shock** which causes aggregate demand to increase. Thus AD_0 shifts to AD_1 moving the economy off the LRAS curve along $SRAS_0$ to a new point of intersection at b. At point b firms will be producing **beyond** their **normal capacity**, so real GDP will be Y_1 and the price level will increase to P_1. At this point the economy is said to experiencing an **inflationary output gap**. In general, an output gap is a situation where the actual output produced by the economy is different from its potential output.

An inflationary output gap occurs when the actual output of the economy exceeds its potential output.

The question you should be asking at this point is whether the level of real GDP associated with point b is sustainable. The answer is 'no'. This is because the labour market will be 'tight' (meaning that there is a shortage of labour inputs relative to the level of aggregate output that firms want to produce) and workers

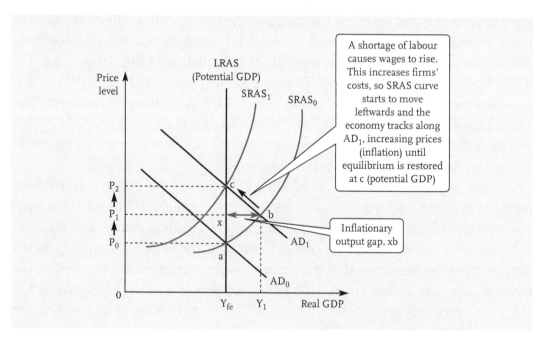

Figure 12.21 The economy in the above-trend phase of the business cycle showing an inflationary output gap

will be demanding wage increases in order to maintain their standard of living in the face of higher prices for goods and services. With wages increasing, firms' costs will begin to rise and, consequently, $SRAS_0$ will begin to move leftwards. The economy will track along AD_1 as firms contract their outputs until (in theory at least) a new equilibrium is achieved where AD_1, $SRAS_1$ and LRAS intersect at point *c*. The price level is now higher at P_2, but further inflationary pressure has been removed and real GDP is back to its potential level. In terms of the time path of changes we have just described, the economy has passed through the above-trend phase of a stylized business cycle, as depicted in Figure 12.22.

The story behind the below-trend swing in GDP is shown in Figure 12.23. Here the economy begins in equilibrium at point *c*. Then it is hit with a negative shock for some reason (such as a negative sea change in entrepreneurial confidence, which reduces the investment component of aggregate demand, or a drop in autonomous consumption) and AD_1 shifts leftwards to AD_2. A new point of intersection between the original short-run aggregate supply curve $SRAS_1$ and AD_2 is achieved at point *d*. The price level falls and real GDP contracts to Y_2, resulting in high levels of unemployment. In this situation the economy is suffering from a **recessionary output gap**.

> A recessionary output gap occurs when the actual output of the economy falls below its potential output.

Once again we ask if this state of affairs is likely to persist. In our theoretical baseline model here the answer is 'no' – but you should note that in the real world the answer may well be 'yes'. See if you can spot the reason why the theoretical model

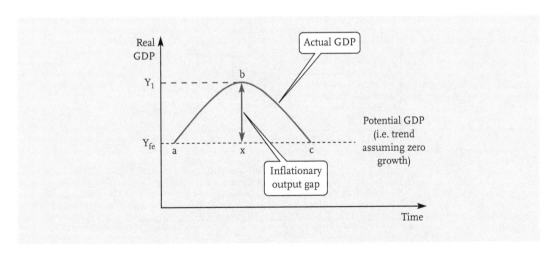

Figure 12.22 Stylized representation of the above-trend time path of GDP corresponding to the story told in Figure 12.21

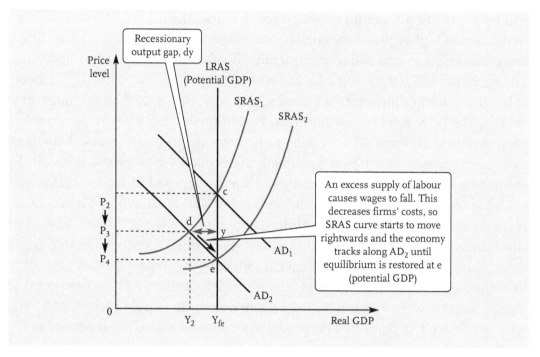

Figure 12.23 The economy in the below-trend phase of the business cycle showing a recessionary output gap

might be overly optimistic. When the economy is at point *d* there will be excess supply in the labour market which means that the price of labour (wages) should fall. If wages do fall then the costs incurred by firms will fall and $SRAS_1$ will track along AD_2 to a new long-run equilibrium position at point *e*, where $AD_2 = SRAS_2$ = LRAS. The time path of actual real GDP is shown in Figure 12.24.

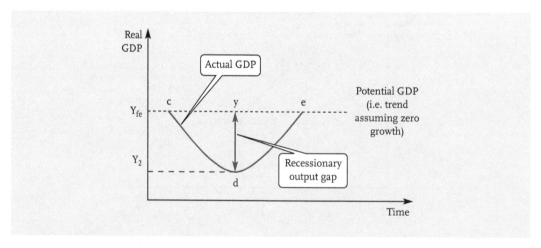

Figure 12.24 Stylized representation of the below-trend time path of GDP corresponding to the story told in Figure 12.23

Have you worked out why the economy might not be able to work its way out of a recession in the self-correcting manner told in our story? The reason is that workers may not be willing to accept reduced wages: a phenomenon called 'sticky wages'. The working of the labour market has been a source of great controversy between economists and we will discuss it further in the next chapter. For now we will note that the potential for prolonged periods of recession and economic hardship to occur if the economy was left alone has provided governments with an incentive and a rationale to intervene and practise macroeconomic demand management, i.e. to attempt to manipulate the level of aggregate demand in the economy by some means.

We have not yet explained how economic growth occurs and in the space available here we can only touch upon an answer. It should be clear to you from our discussion of the LRAS curve that economic growth can only occur if the quantity and/or quality of labour, capital and technology increase. Of these three elements perhaps the most important determinant of economic growth has been the rate of technological change. This rather brief statement brings forth a host of issues, one of which is the need to ensure that the labour force acquire and maintain relevant skills as the pace of technological change increases. If there is a rationale for government intervention on the demand side of the economy to reduce short-term fluctuations then there is also a role on the supply side to ensure long-term objectives such as the availability of a suitably educated labour force.

12.6 The basics of government policy intervention

In this section it is not our intention to provide you with an exhaustive guide to government policy. Instead we will give you a short overview.

As you have seen, fluctuations in real GDP below potential GDP cause unemployment while fluctuations above potential GDP cause inflation. Higher levels of unemployment are undesirable because unemployment represents a waste of productive resources in the economy and, on a more human level, it causes untold misery. Inflation is not an attractive proposition either; this is because if it persists it distorts expectations about the future level of prices held by households and firms alike, so it gets built into wage demands which itself might cause yet more inflationary pressure and cause the economy to career off its long-term trend growth path. Consequently governments try to dampen down the short-term fluctuations that might occur if the economy was left to its own devices. They do this by identifying suitable **policy instruments** that they can manipulate to achieve desired targets. Typically, policy instruments designed to manipulate the level of aggregate demand are classified into two categories: **fiscal policy** and **monetary policy**.

Fiscal policy involves the government manipulating its own budget to influence the level of aggregate demand in the economy. The two primary policy instruments are taxes (which influence the level of disposable income in households) and the level of the government's own expenditure (which is, of course, a component of aggregate demand).

Monetary policy involves influencing aggregate demand indirectly, primarily by altering the official interest rate.

You can discover for yourself how a change in any of direct tax rates, government expenditure and the interest rate will influence real GDP by playing around with different values for these parameters in the baseline model above. If you do this, however, you will probably wonder what all the fuss is about when it comes to government policy! This is because you are working with a simple model in which it is relatively easy to trace through the effect of a change in one variable. This means it is also easy to calculate by exactly how much things have to change in order to achieve a specific value of GDP. In reality things are not so clear cut. While the general nature of the relationships between instruments and targets is understood, the specific changes in the magnitudes of instruments required to achieve a desired target are less clear. The problem is made even more acute by the fact that the full effect of policy instruments takes time to work through the system. In a worst-case scenario this might mean that policy intervention kicks in too late and causes the economy to overshoot the target level of GDP.

At present the current consensus of opinion among policy makers in the UK seems to be to keep major interventions to a minimum (so we don't see big changes in government expenditure) and to undertake small interventions often in order to 'fine-tune' the economy. This fine-tuning is primarily carried out by the Bank of England, which reviews the official rate of interest on a monthly basis. The Bank raises the interest rate if the latest GDP data indicate that the economy is growing 'too fast' and it lowers it if the economy is growing 'too slowly'. The primary aim is to keep consumer spending at an acceptable level. This is because C is by far the largest component of aggregate demand in the economy (see Figure 12.25). In this way inflation is kept in check and, while the process has proved to be largely successful in terms of keeping inflation at a low and stable level, there is an element of hit-and-miss about the process by which interest rates are changed because the transmission mechanism from interest rates to consumer spending is difficult to predict. For example, a small increase of, say, 0.25 per cent in the interest rate that is designed to dampen the level of consumer spending (by making the use of credit cards less attractive, for example) in one month might be revealed to be less effective than hoped and require a further increase (or further increases) in the following month(s).

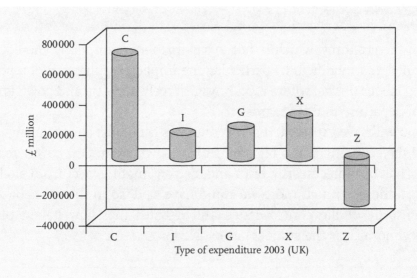

Figure 12.25 The value of the components of aggregate demand in the UK in 2003

(Original data sourced from Office for National Statistics downloadable chained volume series – 'base' year 2001)

12.7 **Summary**

We began this chapter by suggesting that it is wise for the business person to have some knowledge of the macroeconomic environment for a number of practical reasons. In order to help you understand the nature of the macroeconomic environment we then set about identifying the component parts of GDP. We followed this with a review of real GDP data from recent UK history and we identified two major points of interest:

(i)   real GDP has grown over time; and

(ii) the growth path of actual real GDP has a tendency to fluctuate in the short term.

We then set about building a baseline model of the economy that you can use to help you understand what is going on in the macroeconomic environment. In order to build this model we went through a number of stages in which the complexity of the model increased. The final AD–AS model is useful and, despite what you might think at this point, is really not all that complicated, but it does provide us with some valuable insights into the mechanisms at

12.7 Summary (continued)

work in the economy, which is not to say that its assumptions should not be questioned and modified. In particular, the implicit assumption of a perfectly working labour market where money wages freely move up and down is a good point of departure in this regard.

As you will have gathered, macroeconomics is not just about the big picture view of the economy; it is a big subject in its own right. Our coverage in this chapter has been necessarily brief and, as you might expect from such brief coverage, there is much more we could have said, so in the next chapter we look at some of the controversies and debates that have taken place in macroeconomics as the subject has evolved.

12.8 Some questions to consider

1. In the Keynesian cross model what are the consequences for equilibrium GDP of an increase in government expenditure that is accompanied by an increase in the tax rate?

2. Explain why the multiplier in the Keynesian cross model overstates the effect on equilibrium GDP of an increase in investment expenditure. (Hint: use the AD–AS model to derive your answer.)

3. What conditions in the labour market would have to be met for the automatic recovery mechanism of the baseline AD–AS model to work when the economy was in recession?

4. In the baseline AD–AS model the automatic recovery mechanism that kicks in when the economy goes into recession brings GDP back to equilibrium at its potential level. What factors might cause the economy to overshoot this new equilibrium?

5. What's so bad about inflation?

6. Use the Keynesian cross model to trace through the impact of a fall in the interest rate.

7. Would you be worried for your firm if the Bank of England announced an increase in the rate of interest?

12.9 Recommended additional reading sources

There are literally hundreds of textbooks that teach introductory macroeconomic principles, but one of the best with an emphasis on the UK is David Begg, Stanley Fischer and Rudiger Dornbusch (2003) *Economics* (7th edn), Maidenhead, McGraw-Hill. A very well written and accessible North American text is William Baumol and Alan Blinder (2000) *Economics: principles and policy* (8th edn), Orlando, FL, The Dryden Press.

For a very user-friendly layperson's guide to macroeconomics in the context of the UK, David Smith (2003) *Free Lunch*, London, Profile Books, is highly recommended. Another layperson's guide but with a critical edge and with a main emphasis on the USA is Paul Krugman (1994) *Peddling Prosperity*, London, W.W.Norton & Company.

As well as books a number of useful websites exist. Three that we particularly recommend are:

The Bank of England: www.bankofengland.co.uk. This site contains exceptionally clear guidance on the workings of monetary policy in the UK.

The Office for National Statistics: www.statistics.gov.uk. This site is crammed full of GDP statistics (current and historical) for the UK. It can be quite tricky to navigate, so begin your search by looking for the annual report on the state of the UK's national accounts called 'The Blue Book'.

The Organisation for Economic Cooperation and Development (OECD): www.oecd.org. A great source for international GDP data.

13

What are the main sources of controversy in macroeconomics?

Learning outcomes

If you study this chapter carefully, it may help you to understand:

- the relationship between flows of spending and the level of debt in the economy

- how and why economists' opinions differ over the origins of unemployment and methods for reducing it

- how and why economists' opinions differ over the causes, control and costs of inflation

- what makes the total level of demand prone to short-term fluctuations

- the routes by which expectations about future economic conditions shape the current level of economic activity

- the processes that shape business cycles.

To the extent that you develop such understanding, you should be able to understand and critically assess media reports on changing macroeconomic conditions and consider their likely implications for businesses.

13.1 Introduction

In this chapter we go beyond the analysis of Chapter 12 and examine main-stream and heterodox perspectives on macroeconomics. As with our discussion of microeconomics, we emphasize the impact of problems of information and knowledge on macroeconomic outcomes. These problems were central to the pioneering contribution of Keynes in his *General Theory* but in recent decades they have been given a smaller role in macroeconomic theory. Keynes argued that the economy as a whole works rather differently from the pure baseline model introduced in the previous chapter, where markets were assumed to work perfectly. In fact he saw considerable potential for unemployment to emerge due to **co-ordination failures**. He also saw a role for government in stopping economic depressions from lingering or booms from getting out of control, though he was less inclined to argue that government should try to 'fine-tune' the economy if it did not seem to be in, or heading towards, a crisis.

In the seven decades since Keynes proposed his analysis, macroeconomic theory has fragmented into at least eight different perspectives. This presents a major problem for any attempt to provide a pluralistic coverage of macroeconomics in the limited space available here. Rather than risk causing confusion by attempting to sketch briefly a large number of rival perspectives, we have decided to distil them into just two, which we shall as usual characterize as 'mainstream' and 'heterodox'. With the former, we try to encapsulate the kind of thinking that has greatly influenced macroeconomic policy making over the past 30 years. This kind of thinking is critical of Keynes and appears not to accept his claim that macroeconomics is profoundly different from the microeconomics of markets. It also tends to presume that decision makers (households and firms) have no trouble forming **rational expectations**, meaning that they are able to predict, on average, how events in the economy will unfold. (Note that having rational expectations does not mean one always forecasts the future accurately but, rather, that one is not systematically wrong in predictions on average.) Hence mainstream economists end up seeing major macroeconomic disturbances as being caused by unexpected government intervention rather than as occasions requiring such intervention. The 'heterodox' perspective, by contrast, is a modern version of Keynesian thinking.

13.2 The mainstream perspective on macroeconomics

From the mainstream standpoint, the way that the economy as a whole works is pretty much the same as the pure baseline model of Chapter 12 works. In other words, the forces of supply and demand operate freely in all markets, including the labour market.

13.2.1 Mainstream analysis of unemployment

Mainstream economists view the causes of unemployment in five main ways (which go beyond the simple categorization we used in Chapter 12):

- **Frictional unemployment** is of a very short-term nature due to changes in the relative competitive strength of firms and churning of the labour force: some firms may be firing workers and others hiring them but the transfer of workers is not entirely seamless. Similarly, some workers may be retiring and others will be coming into the labour force, and there will be a certain amount of 'musical chairs'-style movement between jobs before the right set of vacancies emerges to soak up the new arrivals in the labour market.

- **Structural unemployment** arises due to changes in the pattern of demand and state of technology. For example, bank tellers may lose their jobs as banks succeed in encouraging their customers to make more use of auto-tellers and on-line banking services. Meanwhile, there might be a shortage of nurses in aged care facilities. Like its even more temporary counterpart, frictional unemployment, structural unemployment is not a matter of insufficient overall demand for workers but is due to a mismatch between the demand and supply of workers in different parts of the labour market. In time, as people respond to market incentives and switch between jobs or attend training programmes to acquire the skills that are in demand, this kind of unemployment will fade away. Note that, in terms of our example, there is no presumption that former bank tellers will retrain as geriatric nurses. Rather, the process is once again more like a game of musical chairs in which, say, former nurses who had been working in some other areas get back into nursing, thereby creating vacancies elsewhere that others may fill, leaving yet other vacancies, and so on, until the former bank tellers are offered jobs.

- **Voluntary unemployment** may arise due to **poor incentives to work**. People may be better off on the dole than if they take up a job and then lose social welfare entitlements and have to pay transport and childcare costs as well as losing some of the pay to taxation and national insurance contributions.

- Some people may opt not to take up readily available jobs after becoming unemployed, because they judge that if they spend some time searching they will be able to get better jobs. This line of thinking presumes that **full-time job search** whilst unemployed is more efficient than searching part-time whilst employed in a lower-grade job than one expects to get. However, if prospective employers have trouble judging rival applicants for jobs they might use current employment status as a signal for the quality of the worker. If so, it might be better to accept a low-grade job and spend one's spare time searching for something better. Note also that employers may be loathe to hire conspicuously over-qualified workers because they suspect these workers would move on the moment their target job came up. If their suspicions were correct, they would have to incur costs of hiring and inducting replacement staff into their workforces.

- **Distortions in the labour market** associated with minimum wage legislation or over-aggressive bargaining by trade unions may cause **involuntary unemployment** because they prevent wage levels from dropping to the equilibrium that would prevail in a free-market setting. Higher wages lead more people to want to participate in the labour force but such wages make it less attractive for firms and other organizations to offer employment. This is shown in Figure 13.1, where there are OL workers employed and LN workers unable to find jobs. The market clearing level of employment is OM jobs.

The overall message here is that when we observe unemployment we should not see it as a consequence of insufficient spending in the economy leading to a low demand for labour. Rather, the economy tends to gravitate towards a **natural rate of unemployment** that reflects the pace of structural change, the tax and welfare system, and the behaviour of trade unions and other social institutions that affect the efficiency with which the labour market works.

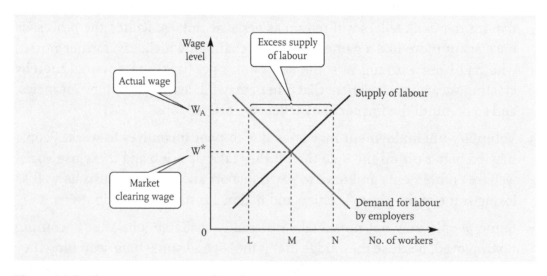

Figure 13.1 The mainstream view of involuntary unemployment

If the observed rate of unemployment is higher than the government's target, then the policy measures recommended by mainstream economists would be as follows:

- **Reform the labour market** (via limits on closed shop union membership arrangements and on the right to strike, etc.).

- **Cut unemployment benefits** in terms of both levels and entitlements.

- **Privatize** public housing or introduce market-based rents for public housing, to ensure that labour mobility is not hindered by the reluctance of workers to part with existing state housing provided at sub-market rental rates.

- **Change the structure of taxation away from direct taxes towards indirect taxes on spending** to provide a bigger incentive to find a job.

- **Provide cheaper childcare** and thereby reduce the cost of having a job.

The mainstream policy instruments all work on the supply side of the economy. They do not include measures to try to promote more spending in the economy as a whole, from which a higher demand for labour might follow.

13.2.2 The mainstream perspective on output and inflation

The supply-side focus of mainstream policies for dealing with unemployment comes very much from their view that inflation is a very bad thing and that attempts to reduce unemployment by trying to stimulate demand in the economy are, sooner or later, likely to result in a rising price level. Inflation, it is commonly said, is the result of 'too much money chasing too few goods'.

Mainstream economists view inflation as a cause for concern for a number of reasons:

- It erodes **real wages (W/P)**. In other words, £1 earned today will buy more today than it will tomorrow and more than £1 earned tomorrow will buy.

- It erodes the **real rate of interest**. For example, if the rate of interest is 5 per cent per annum and the inflation rate is 7 per cent, the real rate of interest is −2 per cent per annum. This may encourage people to borrow recklessly, further fuelling inflation.

- It changes the distribution of wealth away from savers and in favour of debtors because it **erodes the real value of both savings and debt obligations**. For example, if inflation is zero a loan of £1000 taken out today to be repaid after ten years will have a real value of £1000 at that time. If inflation is 10 per cent the real value of £1000 in ten years' time is only £385.55.

- Because prices do not all adjust simultaneously to inflationary pressures, **the invisible hand of the price mechanism works less effectively**: entrepreneurs find it harder to work out which markets to enter or exit.

- Rampant inflation may lead to **speculative behaviour taking the place of genuine enterprise**. This is because it may be easier to increase the value of one's wealth by buying and selling existing assets (for example, by putting money into real estate, antiques, rare postage stamps, etc.) rather than increasing the output of newly produced goods and services (for example, by setting up a new business).

- Increased **transaction costs** due to more frequent wage negotiations, changing prices in catalogues and negotiating over prices, and because buyers have to search more thoroughly to discover where the best deals are to be had.

- When inflation is running at very high rates, some **markets may cease to function altogether** as entrepreneurs start hoarding goods because these serve better than money as a store of value. This tends to be observed during the kind of **hyperinflation** experienced in Russia after the collapse of communism or in many Latin American economies where governments have sought to pay their bills by printing money rather than by engaging in structural reforms of their economies to generate a larger tax base. This phenomenon tends to be limited if customers are prepared to obtain an alternative 'hard' currency, such as US dollars, and offer that in payment.

According to mainstream approaches the overall volume of spending in the economy is not prone to major short-term fluctuations because decision makers take a long-term view of their needs and ability to spend. This is not to say that no one expects that his or her income will fluctuate in the short run. Some workers may lose their jobs, be put on short time because their employers are facing poor sales, or may receive poor performance-based pay such as sales commissions because demand is low. Other workers, by contrast, may find themselves with new jobs, scope for overtime work and earning bonuses. Farm incomes may be prone to variation due to climate fluctuations. Despite these fluctuations in ability to spend, the mainstream view is that spending depends on **permanent income** – income-earning capacity seen from a long-term perspective – because workers in particular areas of the labour market will have a good idea of the risks of income fluctuations that they face and prefer to **smooth out their consumption through time** because of diminishing marginal utility of extra consumption at any point in time. A particular event will only affect their spending via its impact on their long-term assessments of their income-earning power and their wealth. In that case, it should result not in a 'blip' in their spending but in a shift in the amount they will normally be observed to spend. So, from this perspective, we would not expect to see a person who receives a major legacy immediately rushing out and spending spectacularly on holidays and the consumption of non-durable goods and services, though we might expect a 'step' increase in the level of such spending observed thereafter. We might, however, expect to see such a person spending heavily on consumer durables such as houses, cars, electrical appliances and so on, since these will yield a flow of extra consumption over a long period.

Given this 'permanent income' view of what determines people's spending, the **aggregate demand curve** is presumed to slope downwards because:

- a lower price level increases the value of money that people hold as part of their wealth – this leads to what is known as a **real balance effect**: people only want to hold a particular amount of purchasing power in reserve, so when they discover they have more than they want, they will tend to use the excess to buy products and services;

- for a given level of money wages, people will tend to spend more if the price level is lower so long as the price level is not seen merely as a temporary aberration – this is because it implies that their permanent income has gone up.

To put this slightly differently, the mainstream view sees total spending primarily as a function of the value of human capital (the worker's real income-earning powers) and purchasing power of wealth held as money. Other things being equal, the lower the price level, the higher the value of human capital and the higher the purchasing power of money balances that people are holding.

In the long run, improvements on the supply side of the economy can move the aggregate supply curve to the right and permit a higher rate of output without a rise in the price level. In the short run, however, the output level will gravitate to that implied by the intersection of AD and SRAS. As you have seen in the baseline model of Chapter 12, for output to expand beyond this level in the short run the price level would need to be higher and real wages lower, but this is incompatible with a rise in the volume of output being demanded. By contrast, if firms produced a volume of output below the equilibrium level, there would be an excess of aggregate demand. Though fewer workers would be hired, consumer spending would be kept up so long as expectations of permanent income were not revised.

Mainstream macroeconomists use the AD–AS framework to analyse how inflation can be going on with considerable unemployment and spare capacity in the economy. The latter situation, known as **stagflation**, prevailed from the late 1960s to the 1980s. On this analysis, inflation comes about because the government tries to run the economy at an output level that requires unemployment to be lower than its natural rate. Part of the problem with stagflation in the late 1960s/1970s was due to governments not being aware that the natural rate of unemployment had increased due to a more rapid pace of structural change and more generous welfare payments. This led them to try to maintain employment at previous post-War levels by pumping demand into the economy, rather than trying to reform the supply side of the economy to enable output to grow more rap-idly and to increase the flexibility of the labour market. They did this with policies that expanded the volume of money in circulation faster than the rate at which the demand for money was growing. The money supply increased either because governments financed some of their expenditure by borrowing from their central banks, or via policies of low interest rates that encourage more demand for borrowing, which the banks accommodated. This led to a growth in expenditure.

In such a situation, mainstream analysis leads one to expect the following:

◆ When faced with an increased demand for their services, workers who have been used to low rates of inflation interpret offers of higher money wages as implying higher real wages. Some move to jobs whose rates of pay have risen more rapidly, while others give up searching for better paying jobs, believing they have now found them.

◆ As far as employers are concerned, however, this is not a situation in which real wages will be rising, since underlying supply conditions have not changed. The only way the employers will be willing to expand output is by moving along their upward-sloping supply curves and putting up their prices faster than they are having to put up wages to attract additional workers and maintain their existing workforces.

◆ Sooner or later, the workers will discover that they have been duped and their real wages have fallen, not risen. They will then get more aggressive with their wage demands and more thorough with their job searches and, with this left-ward shift of the aggregate supply curve, the level of employment would then fall back to its previous level.

Figure 13.2 illustrates this process. Here, Y_T is the government's target level of employment, while Y_N is volume of output consistent with the 'nat-ural' level of employment. We start with aggregate demand curve AD_1 and aggregate supply curve $SRAS_1$ and a price level/output combination a. Expansion of aggregate demand to AD_2 initially takes the economy to b, with

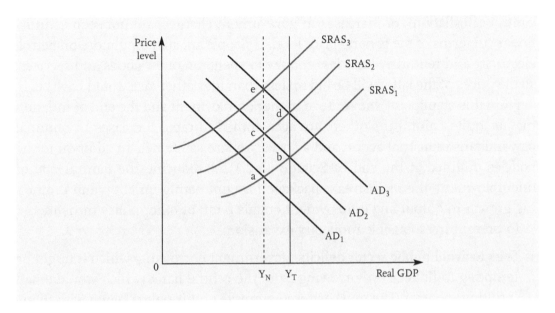

Figure 13.2 Stagflation based on misperceptions

a higher-than-expected price level, so the aggregate supply curve shifts left to $SRAS_2$, with higher wage costs pushing output back down at point c. The government pumps up demand yet more, moving the aggregate demand curve to AD_3, and workers, who do not foresee the extra hike in prices, once again come forward in larger numbers for the higher pay entailed by the move rightwards along $SRAS_2$ to d. On discovering that prices have again gone up, they revise their supply behaviour and the aggregate supply curve moves to $SRAS_3$, taking the price level/output combination to e; and so on.

• The experience of inflation will lead workers to start anticipating that rising wages will be accompanied by rising prices, so the only way that governments will be able to push unemployment below its natural rate is by pumping unexpectedly large increases in the money supply into the economy, with the result that prices rise even faster than expected. Sooner or later the workers will start to anticipate not merely higher prices but also an **accelerating rate of inflation**. As the workers increasingly understand what is going on, the government will have to lower its unemployment target to the natural rate, for otherwise the only way it will be able to maintain it will be via generating ever-accelerating rates of inflation, leading ultimately to a collapse of confidence in the currency.

This view of inflation has no place for the idea that particular supply-side shocks can exert a 'cost-push' impact on the rate of inflation. Sharp increases in oil prices (as OPEC instigated in 1973 and 1979, at the height of debates about the control of inflation), or increases in government charges, are not seen as inflationary in terms of the general price level. If people are spending more on petrol, electricity and rent, they have less money to spend on other goods and services, so the prices of the latter will be bid up less than they otherwise would have been.

From this standpoint, the route to higher employment and the end of inflation may be quite painful if workers are accustomed to rapid increases in nominal pay, militant industrial action and a social welfare safety net. In addition to the policies outlined at the end of Section 13.2.1 for reducing the natural rate of unemployment, the mainstream package for eliminating inflation and promoting growth in output and employment entails a raft of other policy measures.

To prevent irresponsible monetary expansion:

- Seek to **avoid public sector deficits** (government borrowing) which it might be tempting to finance by borrowing from the central bank (which would entail 'printing money'). The most extreme example of this policy (along with many of the others listed) was in New Zealand, where a Fiscal Responsibility Act was passed.

- **Separate the central bank from central government influence**, and make the tenure of the central bank's governor a function merely of success in keeping inflation within a narrow, near-zero target range.

To lower supply-side costs and increase potential output per head:

- **Deregulate** markets (for example, aviation, telecommunications, media and higher education) to allow more suppliers to compete in them.

- **Privatize** nationalized industries, or at the very least turn them into publicly owned corporations run by managers on performance-based remuneration packages.

- Cut costs of providing public services by **outsourcing** them to private providers on the basis of competitive tendering processes.

- Reduce the costs of remaining public provision of goods and services by **introducing user charges**, removing subsidies and introducing performance audits.

- Use savings in government expenditure costs to pay for **reduced rates of income taxation**, to reduce costs of employing workers and to encourage risk-taking behaviour.

Such policy packages tended to be accompanied initially by sharp increases in unemployment wherever they were introduced. This was due both to a shake-out of surplus workers as firms and public sector organizations sought to improve their productivity levels and to the failure of workers and managers to adjust their inflationary expectations downwards as the central bank imposed an unexpectedly tough monetary regime. Typically, initial attempts to cut the growth of the money supply (measured, for example, by the growth of total deposits of the major banks) led to sharp rises in interest rates, substantially reducing the purchasing power of debtors. The adaptability of modern financial systems tended to result in finance being provided to a larger extent by institutions whose balance sheets did not figure in the definition of the money supply being targeted by the central bank. So, despite the mainstream view that inflation results from 'too much money chasing too few goods', monetary targeting has increasingly faded from the policy agenda in favour of tough talking by central bank governors and threats to raise interest rates the moment that the economy shows any sign of tendencies towards higher rates of inflation.

13.3 A roadmap for a journey into heterodox macroeconomics

The heterodox approach to macroeconomics brings up-to-date Keynes's analysis from the 1930s. Here, we present a sketch of its main ingredients before exploring its logic more thoroughly in remaining sections of the chapter.

♦ *Rejection of the 'real balance effect'.* In a modern economy, the 'money balances' part of wealth is likely to be insignificant in determining total spending. This is because most money actually exists inside the balance sheets of financial institutions in the form of deposits, not outside as notes and coins. The deposits that make up the liabilities side of a financial institution's balance sheet are matched on the assets side by loans. A fall in the price level that increases the purchasing power of bank deposits also reduces the value of assets that have been purchased with the aid of loans: a depositor may feel better off, but a borrower now owes more in real terms. (Indeed, the value of the asset financed by the loan may now be even less in nominal terms than the amount of money still owed.) Whether there is any net effect on the volume of goods demanded when a change in the price level changes the value of non-human wealth may thus depend rather a lot on which prices have changed and hence whose wealth is affected: it is not obvious that we should presume the reactions of winners are exactly offset by those of losers, for the socio-economic and demographic status of the different groups may be very different.

- *Attention might be better focused on financial stability rather than price stability.* An economy based around 'inside' money may not work in exactly the same way as one based on notes and coins. Modern economies are intensely financial systems and anything that causes banks to fail may have disastrous implications because bank failures wipe out the financial wealth of those who hold deposits in the banks that fail. Thus, while heterodox economists agree with mainstream economists that inflation can have significant costs, they are much more worried than mainstream economists about situations in which asset prices and wages start falling. Falling asset prices encourage borrowers to default on loans raised against such assets, and falling wages make it harder for people to service loans; either way, the risk of bank failures is increased.

- *Attempts by people to save more will tend to depress aggregate demand because they do not automatically make funds available for firms or other people to use to increase their spending.* Money that is saved may simply be held as an already-existing bank deposit rather than moving around the economy from bank deposit to bank deposit.

- *Keynes's emphasis on the role of confidence in determining investment needs to be extended to recognize that consumer confidence is an important determinant of expenditure in affluent economies.* Through its focus on the role of permanent income as a determinant of spending, mainstream analysis seems blind to the **extent to which consumption expenditure is discretionary** in affluent economies. People in wealthy economies often replace their consumer durables that are not yet completely worn out or beyond repair, and they can choose to postpone expensive holidays, home renovations and so on. Couple this with increased uncertainty in recent decades about employment (associated with the growing need for many to work on temporary contracts or with several part-time jobs) and we have a recipe for consumer spending to be inherently jittery, based on what is known in the media as the **'feel good' factor**, rather than on some objective notion of ability to spend. When people have the urge to spend more and can make a case to lenders, huge overdraft facilities (such as credit-line mortgages) and credit card spending limits may be available to them, but when they feel nervous about spending, there is nothing in the system, except for pressures to 'keep up with the Joneses' and persuasive advertising, to force them to use all this potential spending power.

  These features of the modern economy reinforce the fundamental message of Keynes that the volume of demand in the economy depends on confidence, and on the willingness of people to part with their spending power and commit themselves to goods that it may be rather difficult to turn back into the amount of money used to pay for them. If people decide to hold their wealth as money, or to speculate in things that cannot be produced (such as land and existing real estate or antiques), then they make it harder for firms to make money by employing people to make new things.

- *Changes in spending can have multiplier effects in the same direction that the price mechanism may fail to correct swiftly.* When people are laid off from their jobs, they may cut their spending, in sharp contrast to the 'permanent income' view, because they (or their suppliers of finance) are nervous about increasing their indebtedness. To the extent that they cut back on spending, others may be placed in the same position, and so on. Not only can there be such tendencies for economic disturbances to be amplified, but the normal corrective methods assumed by mainstream economists do not guarantee a swift return to high levels of employment and stable prices. Modern heterodox economists do not deny the existence of the various kinds of unemployment identified in mainstream analysis. However, following Keynes, they see scope for unemployment to arise due to insufficient spending in the economy, whose elimination requires an increase in spending, not a cut in wages. They see no guarantee that wage cuts would produce more jobs, since they do not see the macroeconomic system as working like a market at the microeconomic level. To understand how they reach this conclusion requires a careful examination of how the different parts of the economy fit together.

- *Output is often constrained by a lack of demand, not by a lack of spare capacity.* Heterodox price theory sees firms as typically maintaining some spare capacity in order to be able to build up goodwill if new customers try them out as suppliers. It also sees considerable potential for costs to reflect economies of scale and scope and for investment to depend on the availability of profits to plough back into expenditure on new equipment. This means that higher levels of demand are conducive to achieving lower average costs via higher productivity; they do not necessarily lead to inflation. On the contrary, prolonged periods of low aggregate demand are likely to make inflation more likely, since business closures and the scrapping of equipment will make it hard to restore output levels when demand eventually recovers.

- *Wage cuts may fail to make it viable for employers to offer more jobs.* It will only be viable to employ more workers if all the extra costs incurred for making a bigger volume of output (including wages paid out to newly employed workers) come back to employers as spending. If the expected extra revenues from selling more output are less than the expected costs of producing it, the economy suffers from a **deflationary gap**. A cut in money wages (or their rate of increase) will reduce demand by workers who would have had jobs anyway, and is thus likely to result in a fall in the price level (or its rate of increase) without doing anything in terms of eliminating a deflationary gap and making extra output viable.

This approach to macroeconomics is based on an understanding of the economic system as a complex arrangement of linkages between the various sectors of the economy, both in terms of flows of spending and contractual obligations. It is to this that we now turn our attention.

13.4 Flows of funds between sectors

Because of their focus on financial underpinnings of macroeconomic behaviour, heterodox economists pay careful attention to flows of funds between different sectors of the economy – not just in terms of income and expenditure flows (in the manner outlined in the previous chapter) but also in terms of changes in the amount that one sector owes another. Imbalances between different sectors' income receipts and expenditures during the accounting period can occur *if* (note: *if*) sectors spending in excess of their current incomes can raise money by selling financial claims – that is to say, increasing their net indebtedness – to sectors that are running surpluses. A sector in deficit (surplus) has a negative (positive) **net acquisition of financial assets (NAFA)**. For example, if the household sector spends more than its income in a particular period, its dis-saving is recorded as a negative NAFA. Overall, though, the following NAFA identity must hold:

> Private sector net acquisition of financial assets + corporate sector net acquisition of financial assets + public sector net acquisition of financial assets + foreign sector net acquisition of financial assets ≡ 0.

It is worthwhile to reflect for a moment on how banks fit into the picture here, and what happens when a new loan is made. When a bank makes a loan, it creates simultaneously a new asset (its claim on the borrower) and a new liability of an identical amount (the money it credits to the borrower's account, which the borrower can now withdraw). There is no overall NAFA by the bank. When the borrower spends the money, the recipient's bank deposit rises, and if the recipient does not increase spending, the level of saving increases by the amount of the debt-financed increase in spending. The borrower's dis-saving and decrease in NAFA equals the expenditure recipient's extra saving and increase in NAFA.

The same story applies in the case of the economy's reserve bank (in the case of the UK, the Bank of England), which acts as banker to the main banks and the government. If the Bank of England acquires government bonds from the rest of the economy, these represent an increase in its assets, but the cheques that it issues to pay for them increase its liabilities and result in the major banks increasing their deposits with it when the cheques are paid into their accounts. Table 13.1 shows how changes in holdings of the major classes of financial assets affect the NAFAs of the various sectors. As you study Table 13.1 keep in mind that it only represents changes in holdings of the various kinds of financial assets, not the total worth or earning potential of all the assets of these kinds held by the various sectors.

Table 13.1 A flow of funds matrix for a hypothetical economy

Sector	Advances	Equities	Bonds	Bank deposits	Deposits at Reserve Bank	NAFA ($ million)
Personal	−1300	+400	+400	+1050	0	+550
Corporate	−100	−1000	+500	+950	0	+350
Banks	+1400	0	+200	−2000	+400	0
Government	0	0	−2500	0	0	−2500
Reserve Bank	0	0	+400	0	−400	0
Overseas	0	+600	+1000	0	0	+1600

Note: + indicates an increase in net holdings of these assets by the sector in question; − indicates a decrease in net holdings of these assets by the sector in question or an increase in liabilities of this kind.

Take a moment to reflect on Table 13.1 in the light of the discussion in the previous chapter, where we showed how the total revenue received by businesses during the accounting period can be pulled down by an increase of **leakages** in the form of increased saving (including paying off loans), taxation and imports, or pushed up by **injections** in the form of additional investment spending, government expenditure and exports. Now, the question you might be left asking is whether a leakage from the circular flow of income is associated with a corresponding injection of spending by someone else, given that the various NAFAs shown in Table 13.1 add up to zero. To put it another way, if consumers decide to spend less and make a net increase in their NAFAs, might this mean that firms reduce their NAFAs by borrowing what is being saved and spend more on investment?

The answer is 'not necessarily', and the ability to understand why this is so is central to appreciating the heterodox view of how the macroeconomic system works. Since the reasoning behind it can be bewildering on a first encounter, we devote the next section to exploring it in some detail. Our vehicle for getting the message across is a contemporary one of considerable policy significance, namely, an exploration of the macroeconomic consequences of an **ageing population**. It also helps to bring out the importance of distinguishing between the 'real', productive side of the economy and its financial side.

13.5 Saving, investment and an ageing population

In the decade and a half after the end of World War II, birth rates in advanced industrial countries increased temporarily. The oldest of the 'baby-boomers' born during this period (1945–1960) are now approaching retirement. Millions more will follow during the next two decades. The proportion of the population in retirement will grow, while overall populations in these countries will stagnate or even decline due to much reduced birth rates in recent decades. To many observers, this change in the structure of the population is problematic: we have a rising ratio of dependants to producers in the economy. If the retirees are to enjoy comfortable living standards, the living standards of those who remain in the workforce must fall unless there is a rapid rise in *per capita* productivity levels. If the living standards of those in the workforce are compressed, the prospects for sales by firms involved in production of goods typically consumed by them do not look promising.

This gloomy scenario presumes that the baby boomers do not attempt to fund their retirements themselves by accumulating savings during their years in the workforce. Instead, their retirement spending depends on transfers from younger people who are still in the workforce: for example, in the form of state pensions paid for by higher taxes on income. In short, we might call it a 'pay as you go' scenario: there is no private or public savings fund to draw down over the period of the baby boomers' retirements. The baby boomers do not bother to save up for their retirements and are then bailed out by sacrifices from the rest of the population.

Worried by this prospect, governments in many countries have tried to promote the accumulation of retirement funds by workers. They have done this via alarmist advertising regarding the limitations of future state pensions, by providing tax incentives to increase saving rates and/or by introducing compulsory saving schemes. The hope is that the baby boomers will accumulate assets such as bank deposits, shares and real estate investments during their working lives. When they retire, they will live off the income generated by these assets and from money they raise by gradually selling off their financial assets and running down their capital, to the extent that they do not intend to bequeath their wealth to others. Those who are worried about the prospect of living an unexpectedly long time and running down their wealth too far, too soon, may insure themselves against this by using their wealth to purchase an annuity that guarantees a particular income for as long as they remain alive. Clearly, if the accumulation of a retirement fund is a matter of individual choice, it presents a major puzzle to the baby boomers: how little dare they save at any point while they are working?

The mainstream 'permanent income' view of saving and spending is complemented by a theory of long-run savings behaviour known as the **'lifecycle savings hypothesis'**. This portrays household decision makers as spreading their consumption out optimally over their lives. When they are young, people are often well short of their peak earning power (particularly in white collar jobs within a promotion hierarchy) and can also expect their incomes to rise as part of the rise in general living standards as time passes. Hence they borrow to set up home and finance the rearing of their children. In middle age, they succeed in paying off their debts and then set about accumulating their retirement funds. Over the course of their working lives, their consumption may vary far less than their income does. Figure 13.3 gives an example of this, in which a worker's income rises both gradually with the general increase in living standards and discontinuously via a couple of promotions. The worker starts repaying debt around the time of the second promotion (where the income and spending lines cross), retires in his mid-60s and lives from a retirement pension and savings with a gradually reducing level of consumption until death at age 80. The diagram could, of course, be further complicated to show a period of saving early

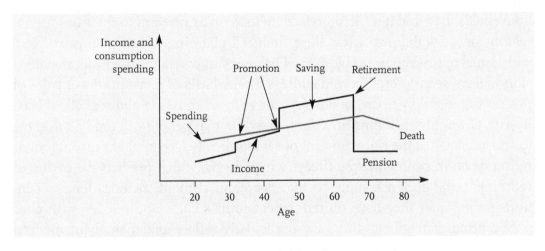

Figure 13.3 Income and spending over a person's lifecycle

on to accumulate a house deposit, the receipt of sums of money via inheritance and so on.

Attempts to work out an optimal borrowing/repayment/saving strategy are clouded, however, not merely by the computational issues associated with their complexity but also by uncertainty regarding:

- careers (including those associated with career disruptions occasioned by the birth of children);

- family size;

- education costs;

- the duration of personal relationships, the break-up of which is both common in modern society and very disruptive financially;

- health costs, particularly as one gets older and insurance cover becomes harder to obtain;

- preferences later in life, which might be affected by one's state of health;

- government policies regarding state-provided pensions and rates of taxation;

- nominal rates of return on assets;

- the rate of inflation;

- the implications of technological progress;

- the rate of economic growth.

Although investment advisers may be able to assist with calculations and strategic advice, many of these uncertainties cannot be reduced to **probabilistic risks**. Even where statistics are easily found, such as the incidence of marital break-up, households may find it difficult to face up to them as relevant to their unique situations or allow them to affect their financial planning. What is in principle a substantial optimization problem thus becomes in practice something that decision makers seem more likely to address on the basis of conventions or rules of thumb suggested by financial advisers, or to avoid thinking about at all, at least in part. Given this, it seems unwise to presume that people will tend on average to accumulate just the right amount of savings needed to see them through their retirements. In contrast to the lifecycle hypothesis, which predicts dis-saving in retirement, the evidence suggests that people in affluent societies tend to continue saving after they have retired. In economies such as the USA, with poor public health safety nets, this may particularly reflect anxieties about medical expenses, but many people in retirement may find less of an urge to spend than they had anticipated, opting for simple, low-stress retirements rather than using their new-found leisure time to immerse themselves in expensive new activities.

In the 'pay as you go' scenario there is a pretty clear connection between the financial side of the economy and the 'real', productive side: there is a limited cake to go round, being produced by those not in retirement; and those who retire get to buy some of it, at the expense of those who are producing it, to the extent that the government makes transfer payments in their favour. The connections between the financial and production dimensions are far fuzzier in the superannuation fund scenario, and an understanding of why this is so takes us to the heart of Keynes's vision of the macroeconomic problem.

The superannuation fund scenario, like the 'pay as you go' scenario, is only consistent with both the maintenance of average real income levels and a rising dependency ratio if there is sufficient investment to raise the productivity of the post-baby boomer workforce to levels that offset the falling number of workers. According to anti-Keynesian thinking, this is something that should occur automatically so long as people make their own retirement provisions by not consuming all their income during the years they are in the workforce.

The anti-Keynesian logic is as follows. When people save up for their retirements, they restrain their claims for consumption goods, making it possible for some of the economy's current output to be used in investment schemes that will raise output in later periods. At the same time, they accumulate funds that can be used to pay for extra investment goods. Banks can lend their deposits to businesses, or the savers may make them available directly by purchasing shares. The investment schemes will generate returns that will enable the future retirees to accumulate substantial funds via compound interest and then enjoy a stream of earnings after their retirements. A society of people who do not discount future consumption highly will have low rates of interest (since only a small reward is required for patience) and a low cost of capital, and will have high rates of saving and investment, with rapid growth in output per head.

According to the anti-Keynesian perspective, we only land up in a painful version of the 'pay as you go' scenario if people consume excessively during their working years because they do not believe government proclamations about the diminished scope for letting everyone enjoy a decent retirement based on state-provided pensions. There would be a scarcity of investment resources and funds in the years before the baby boomers retired and, after retirement, either the baby boomers would have to be bailed out directly by their families, if the government cut pensions, or the government would find it impossible to ignore their voting power and would raise taxes to keep pensions going at acceptable levels despite their growing total cost. From an anti-Keynesian perspective, the issue is essentially one of government credibility and the ability of the government to enable the workforce to form 'rational expectations' about the nature of the economy in which they participate.

This analysis ignores two crucial problems emphasized by Keynes. The first is that an increase in saving decreases demand for current outputs of goods and services without providing clear signals as to when and where the savers will become dis-savers and return their money to the system. For example, if people raise their savings rates, are they doing so because they are planning to retire earlier or because they expect to live longer? And when they retire, will they wish to 'see the world', live quietly in a retirement village or indulge their pent-up passions for particular recreational activities? Acts of saving may precede by many decades the consumption that they make possible, but they are not usually accompanied by advance purchase orders of any kind. Given this, it is possible that firms may react to lower levels of current demand by reducing investment until they have a clearer sense of where demand will come from in the future. This is the opposite of what they should be doing in order to prevent a rise in savings rates from leading to unemployment and to increase the capacity of the economy to deliver consumption goods in the future. An economy in which people stepped up their savings rates to assure their retirement lifestyles could, paradoxically, be less able to deliver a particular level of output in the future than it would have been had the population tried to save less. The sustained stagnation of the Japanese economy, once lauded for its high savings ratio, is worth reflecting on from this standpoint.

The second problem identified by Keynes is that the funds that a person chooses to accumulate by refraining from spending today do not necessarily get used to purchase new financial assets associated with a rise in investment spending. In terms of traditional analysis, one could play down the co-ordination problem by saying that a rise in savings would increase the supply of investment funds and push down the rate of interest. As the interest rate fell, it would deter some people from saving and the market would find an equilibrium that balanced the willingness to defer consumption with the willingness to invest. Keynes challenged this view by pointing out that people might simply hoard the money they were saving, rather than lending it out or buying a financial asset with it. From his standpoint, the interest return received by savers is not a reward for waiting to consume at a later date, but simply a reward for parting with liquidity – in other words, a reward for giving up the ability to spend their savings without first exchanging an asset for money.

In some cultures people do indeed tend to hoard their savings as cash, outside of the banking system. In a modern economy, however, money largely exists only in notional form, in the balance sheets of the financial system. Indeed, with almost all payments now capable of being made electronically, most of us barely need to hold any notes and coins at all. We also have good reason not to hold cash, as banks often pay interest on current accounts. In today's 'inside money' economy, Keynes's argument about the significance of hoarding can be harder to see: if a bank has a deposit on the liabilities side of its balance sheet (a deposit is a liability, since the deposit may be withdrawn), it will have a corresponding claim on a borrower on the assets side of its balance sheet, so how can extra savings not result in extra lending?

The answer is actually quite simple. If a person receives income, money is transferred from their employer's bank account to their own account. If they spend it, it passes to the account of the firm whose product they purchased, but if they do not spend it, the money simply stays in their bank account unless they choose to buy a financial asset with it. In other words, when people increase their savings by doing nothing more than leaving money in their bank accounts this does not increase the ability of the banking system to lend. Such an act of saving does not increase total bank deposits. Rather, it simply slows down the pace at which money moves around in the economy – what monetary economists call the **velocity of circulation** – and it thereby reduces the overall level of demand in the economy below what it would have been had they spent the money instead.

If – note, *if* – the saver opts to try to get a higher return by parting with liquidity and exchanges the bank deposit for some shares, the money certainly moves between bank accounts, but this does not guarantee that any extra non-consumption spending occurs as a consequence of the act of saving. Several scenarios are possible:

(i)   The seller of the shares is simply trying to go liquid, trying to move into cash on anticipating a fall in the price of the shares.

(ii) The seller of the shares is temporarily moving into cash *en route* to buying shares in a different business – in which case, the question to focus on is what the seller of shares in the latter firm intends to do. The more that people pause between one financial manoeuvre and another, the more the flow of spending on newly produced output is likely to be held up.

(iii) The seller of the shares is selling new shares to finance the purchase of new plant and machinery, or new buildings, and/or for working capital to get new production capacity operating.

Only in the third of these scenarios does the increase in saving enable extra planned investment to occur, which might otherwise not have gone ahead owing to money being harder to raise. In the other two scenarios, an unexpected increase in saving will only generate a matching increase in investment in the form of unplanned investment in stocks, which sooner or later will lead to a reduction in production.

This crucial point may be appreciated further if approached from a couple of other angles. One is to note that the great majority of shares being traded at any moment are existing assets, not new ones being issued to raise finance for new investment schemes. Hence, if the retirement savings of baby boomers end up in equity-based superannuation funds, all that may happen is that prices of existing shares *might* be higher than otherwise, which *might* then lead some businesses to issue more new shares. But this result is by no means guaranteed since, at the same time as the superannuation funds are adding to the demand for shares, the fact that money is being channelled into savings instead of consumption is reducing the revenue of businesses, which will tend to depress share prices.

Another way to look at how attempts to save more can fail to generate more investment demand in the economy is to consider the case where savers decide to buy existing assets, such as real estate, works of art or collectibles, on the anticipation of a good yield due to appreciation in their resale values. Just as an increase in a person's demand for money to hoard in bank deposits or piggy-banks does nothing to generate demand to offset the fall in the person's consumption, so purchase of these kinds of assets has a limited impact on current output. These assets are in essence **non-reproducible**, whereas employment comes from people engaging in production. Demand for non-reproducible goods may lead to some subsequent growth in demand and employment – for example, via redevelopment of real estate in higher density forms, or reproduction artworks and collectibles – but the extent of such offsetting expansions is by no means guaranteed to match the initial withdrawal from current demand or to occur immediately.

From a Keynesian standpoint, then, increasing attempts by baby boomers to accumulate funds for retirement manifest themselves as reductions in current revenue and make it harder to sustain investment demand rather than being seen as opportunities to do more investment to satisfy a future flood of demand when the baby boomers retire. Attempts to save more may simply result in demand being depressed and a higher savings ratio being achieved at the cost of a slower growth of income and output. Given the scope for slippage in turning savings into higher investment when savings are made decades before they get spent, governments that take a 'we'll cross that bridge when we come to it' attitude and adopt a 'pay as you go' philosophy to retirement incomes may not be behaving as recklessly as anti-Keynesians would tend to see them. A booming economy in which labour tends to be in rather short supply is probably more likely to be one in which ways of increasing productivity are discovered than one in which business is stagnant much of the time and extra workers can readily be hired.

13.6 Short-term fluctuations in aggregate demand

The Keynes-inspired heterodox perspective does not deny that the 'permanent income' view may apply to some extent to stabilize aggregate demand, but it still sees scope for fluctuations in consumption spending due to a variety of recent disturbances in the economy. A similar contrast in perspectives can be found in respect of spending by firms. The mainstream approach portrays investment decision making as based on rational calculation by people with a good grasp of how the future is likely to unfold over the long term, while the Keynesian approach sees investment behaviour as tending to be based on intuition due to problems of knowledge and uncertainty, and therefore to be inherently jittery. The essence of Keynesian thinking is summarized below.

13.6.1 Demand is likely to be a function of current income

Keynesians see current income as likely to be a significant determinant of spending by many consumers since **credit markets are imperfect**: someone who has lost their job and asks for a bank loan to enable them to keep up their spending until they find a new one may not be seen as a safe prospect by a loan manager, even if their skills have not just been rendered obsolete by a change of technology. Where consumers have pre-arranged access to credit, such as credit-line mortgages, overdraft facilities and credit cards, their fears about how long it might take before their circumstances improve may lead them to be reluctant to make greater use of them when their current income flows are reduced.

13.6.2 The 'feel good factor'

The modern consumer can choose to eat cheaply at home rather than going out to restaurants, can watch television at home rather than going out to see a film or live entertainment, and can choose a cheap, local holiday rather than splashing out on something expensive in an exotic location. Likewise, purchases of new consumer durables can be postponed in many cases, since some are prone to be replaced long before they are worn out beyond repair (as with furnishings, cars and electrical appliances), while others have no urgent need relating to them (the purchase of one's first DVD player, for example). In such a situation, demand can become very loosely related to both current and permanent income in the short run: in essence, spending depends on **confidence** and on the willingness to spend rather than the ability to do so. To the extent that spending is discretionary, it can ebb and flow with shifts in confidence that arise from changes in the 'state of the news', such as terrorist events, election results, expectations of capital losses or gains due to expected changes in property or financial asset prices, rumours about job losses, the latest economic indicators and so on.

Swings in confidence need not result in changes in total spending as opposed to changes in its composition. For example, fears about terrorism that lead people to abandon plans for overseas travel may also lead them to bring forward plans to upgrade things around the house, with no change in their total spending. To the extent that changes in confidence do result in shifts in overall spending, it is useful to see this as reflecting shifts in liquidity preference.

> Liquidity preference is defined as a reluctance to shift one's portfolio of assets away from cash and into physical and financial assets, or non-durable consumption expenditure. This is due to concerns about potential for capital losses or potential dislocation costs arising from changes in the market environment or from changes in one's personal circumstances that would result in a need to trade in some assets in order to purchase others that were more appropriate for the new circumstances.

People who are worried about the possibility of losing their jobs could still go ahead and buy new cars and then sell them if their pessimism is justified. The trouble is, this is a recipe for making a major trade-in loss due to imperfections in the used-car market, a loss far greater than one that merely reflects the physical depreciation of the car. Hence it pays to wait and see, holding on to purchasing power and avoiding making a commitment. By contrast, if the economy seems to be booming and property prices are on the rise, it will be tempting to borrow heavily to bring forward one's plans to enter the property market or move to something bigger: someone who waits may forego the chance of a capital gain that vastly exceeds the interest cost associated with bringing the plan forward. Insofar as consumption depends on willingness to spend rather than being tightly constrained by access to finance, it may be difficult for governments to use small changes in interest rates to manipulate spending in either direction: what they need to be able to shape is confidence, not the price of funds.

Much the same may be said regarding interest rates and the investment spending of firms. Back in Chapter 9 we emphasized the difficulties that firms have in doing formal discounted cash flow appraisals of investment projects due to uncertainty. As a consequence, they may resort to payback period criteria that imply very high internal rates of return, or may essentially end up choosing with a view to broader strategic considerations. In any case, during the life of a project, interest rates could change many times.

13.6.3 Wealth effects

A wealth effect is a change in spending that occurs as a result of changes in relative prices that change the value of a person's wealth in terms of what it could buy if it were exchanged for money.

Whether or not they have been the subjects of speculative choices, changes in relative prices that actually occur can have major impacts on the spending power of people and businesses. In trying to assess how the level of demand in the economy might be affected by wealth effects, it is important to keep in mind the possibility that what is good news for one person may be bad news for another. If wealth effects are 'back-to-back', their overall impact will depend upon differences in the responses of gainers and losers.

For example, when property prices rise, home owners may increase their current spending by increasing their overdrafts or credit card purchases, in effect consuming some of their capital gains. Home owners who need to mortgage their homes to raise finance to start a small business will find it easier to do so, since the rise in house prices will enable them to offer more collateral. Real estate companies may be able to commence new development projects by refinancing loans secured against existing real estate assets, without pushing their debt–equity ratios beyond the levels they were at prior to the rise in real estate prices. Rising property prices are bad news, however, for those who are trying to get a foot on the property ladder, since the value of what they have so far accumulated towards a deposit has been reduced. They may also face rising rental costs. They will need to increase their savings rates to meet their deposit targets.

In principle, changes in monetary policy can have major impacts on purchasing power by changing the price of lending or borrowing. A rise in interest rates may remove a considerable part of a debtor's discretionary purchasing power (as with young couples who have recently taken out a variable-rate mortgage). On the other hand, it will increase the purchasing power of those with bank deposits. As noted above, however, the impact will also depend upon the state of confidence:

confident debtors may react to a rise in interest rates simply by slowing down their repayments, whilst cautious lenders (those in retirement, for example) may adopt a wait-and-see approach rather than increasing their consumption, fearing that before long interest rates could move in the other direction.

At the level of the firm, changes in interest rates may affect investment behaviour via their impact on cash flows and corporate portfolios, even if they do not play a major role in determining whether or not decision makers wish to go ahead with particular projects. For example, if interest rates rise, a small business may remain keen to make a particular investment but be faced with the question of whether or not to delay it due to the drain on its cash flow imposed by higher interest rates on its existing loans. By contrast, if share prices rise, corporate treasurers who have been holding some of their firms' reserves in shares will be able to raise more money for investment than before by selling the shares. On the other hand, firms that had been hoping to expand by taking over existing firms through cash purchases of the latter's shares will find it more expensive to do so. While this might limit their expansionary activities, it might actually help aggregate demand, since increases in the cost of existing shares make it more attractive to expand internally instead by purchasing brand-new buildings, plant and machinery: takeover is no longer such a cheap way of diversifying.

The extent of wealth effects associated with rising or falling share prices may depend considerably on whether or not asset owners have actually realized their capital gains or losses by switching into cash. Until this has been done or until 'paper' profits or losses have be maintained for some considerable period of time, their cognitive processes may get in the way of the gains or losses being viewed as permanent. Instead, they may see them as a transitory aspect of the inherent 'easy come, easy go', 'you win some, you lose some' aspect of involvement with the share market. Investors who do not need to turn shares into cash right now to finance current spending may shrug off a major fall in share values pretty much as mainstream theorists would predict, on the basis that asset values will recover sooner or later and maintain their long-term upward trend.

13.6.4 Crowd behaviour

From the Keynesian perspective, scope for macroeconomic instability is enhanced by the social nature of human action and tendencies for people to cope with uncertainty by following the behaviour of others on the basis that the latter must be better informed or are following someone else who is better informed. The situation is further complicated to the extent that people engage in **conspicuous consumption**, trying to 'keep up with the Joneses', as there is likely then to be a bunching of expenditure on luxury items when confidence is on the rise. When confidence and/or incomes fall, however, status-driven behaviour may help maintain demand, for people will be reluctant to reduce their spending on conspicuous forms of consumption for fear of slipping down the status ladder.

13.7 Effective demand, unemployment and inflation

13.7.1 Expectations and employment

When managers in firms and government agencies decide to hire workers, and when the self-employed decide to make themselves available as suppliers of goods and services, they do so on the basis of their expectations about how much of their output will be demanded at the prices at which they intend to make it available. These expectations may be right or wrong, but regardless of this they are the key element in determining the amount of employment currently offered; together, they constitute the aggregate level of effective demand.

> The amount of effective demand in the economy in a particular planning period is defined as the sum of the streams of revenues *expected* by managers and the self-employed in that planning period. (We highlight 'expected' because this is central to Keynes's original use of the term 'effective demand'. Many mainstream writers, who do not emphasize the role of guesswork in the employment/output choice, use the term to apply to actual demand.)

Corresponding to the level of effective demand will be their intended aggregate expenditure and income payments during the period. An individual firm, for example, will have an expected volume of turnover during the period equal to its expected outgoings on raw materials, wages, rent, tax obligations, interest payments, retained profits and dividends. The sum of such micro-level estimates of revenue and expenditure determines the level of national income and expenditure.

The level of effective demand in an economy could be very different from the sum of notional demands of income recipients in the economy.

> A person's notional demand is defined as the spending they would generate if they could find employment offering levels of income that they could reasonably expect to achieve given their qualifications and experience.

If people had no fears about failing to meet their income aspirations and if suppliers of finance were similarly confident and gave them suitably large credit limits, then everyone could signal their notional demands to businesses in the form of advance purchase orders. Firms could confidently go ahead and hire workers to produce the pre-ordered goods and services and people could use the result-ing income flows to pay off their credit cards and other sources of finance. In reality, we have a macroeconomic co-ordination problem because many business commitments have to be made without definite purchase orders. Co-ordination is a problem for a number of reasons:

- A vicious circle is at work here: without definite sales, firms may be reluctant to hire as many workers as would like to work at current rates of pay, and the experience/observations of involuntary unemployment may make people hold back from spending in case they end up being unable to get jobs and pay off their debts.

- Even if workers are confident about their income-earning abilities, they typi-cally do not place orders for things a long way in advance of taking delivery of them. (Obvious exceptions include some airline tickets, holiday accommoda-tion and places for children in certain private schools, where discounts are available on early bookings and/or there are risks of not being able to obtain supplies if one leaves ordering until nearer the date of consumption.) Although they may be confident about their incomes and ability to obtain credit on particular terms, they may prefer to hold back their purchasing power in case their preferences/circumstances change, or the set of available goods changes, or simply because they cannot think months or years ahead.

The broader significance of the discussion of the ageing population issue in Section 13.5 should now be apparent. Whether people save up for retirement or merely towards something they hope to buy fairly soon, they decrease the flow of spending today and leave resources available for firms to use to expand out-put in future periods when they run down their savings. However, if they send no signals about when and where they will unleash their spending power, firms are taking a leap in the dark if they use the resources liberated by saving to cre-ate capacity to produce particular things and come on stream at particular points in the future.

Unless market researchers happen to ask the right questions, workers have no way of communicating their notional demands to business unless firms are producing less than people are trying to buy and waiting lists start to develop. A low level of effective demand compared with the economy's potential output could leave many people unemployed. In turn, the unemployed workers will not be able to spend as much as they would have done had they received income. Had their hopes of employment been fulfilled, they might have spent more not merely because of their take-home pay being higher than unemployment benefits, but also because they would have had easier access to credit. If they cannot achieve employment, they cannot back their notional demands with purchasing power and make businesses aware of their notional demands by purchasing as much as they would like. Weak levels of actual demand in one planning period may in turn lead businesses to anticipate lacklustre sales in the next period.

Stability in the level of employment and output depends upon the stability of employers' expectations and the expectations of the self-employed. If actual aggregate revenue falls short of the level of effective demand in the previous period, this could lead to a downward revision of sales expectations for the next period and hence a reduction in the amount of employment offered and output planned for production. Since disappointingly low profit levels may have adverse impacts on spending by businesses, and a reduction in wage payments may lead to a reduction in spending, disappointing sales in one period could, on the face of it, open up a downward spiral in economic activity. On the other hand, a surprisingly good level of aggregate demand could produce a self-fuelling upturn in economic activity in subsequent periods. Clearly, we need to delve deeper to find out whether there is anything in the workings of the economy as a whole to prevent small divergences between expected and actual levels of spending from being amplified in a destabilizing manner.

13.7.2 The importance of a fractional marginal propensity to spend from marginal income

Suppose that the level of employment offered in the previous planning period was based on aggregate expected revenue of £100 billion but actual spending in the economy was only £99 billion; in other words, there is a deflationary gap of 1 per cent of GDP. For simplicity, also suppose that the supply curve for aggregate output is horizontal. If so, an attempt to cut output by 1 per cent would involve a 1 per cent cut in employment and a £1 billion reduction in factor payments in the next planning period. Evidently, if the £1 billion reduction in factor payments were fully matched by a £1 billion reduction in spending, there would still be a shortfall of £1 billion in aggregate spending at the end of the next planning period, despite the reduction in output. Cutting output and employment yet further would fail to bring about any convergence of expected and actual levels of demand for the economy as a whole: the deflationary gap remains £1 billion.

Matters would be rather different with a fractional relationship between changes in income and changes in expenditure. For example, suppose that, of a £1 billion cut in income payments, £0.25 billion would have been collected as income tax had it been paid out, whilst of the remaining £0.75 billion,

£0.05 billion would have been saved, £0.13 billion would have been collected in VAT and excise duties, and £0.1 billion would have ended up as payments overseas to suppliers of imported goods. If so, the reduction of £1 billion in outlays would only result in a loss in spending of £0.47 billion on domestic output. In this case, we would say that the economy had a **marginal propensity to spend on domestic output** of 0.47. If aggregate demand had been £1 billion greater than expected and employers had responded by producing £1 billion more output and paying out £1 billion to factors of production, then they would still have found demand unexpectedly high, but only by £0.47 billion. In either case, a further adjustment of output and outlays in the direction of the previous period's level of actual demand will produce a reduction in the gap between expected and actual revenue: a change of output and outlays by £0.47 billion would result in a change of spending in the same direction of £0.22 billion. A further change in output and outlays of £0.22 billion would result in a change in aggregate expenditure in the same direction of £0.10 billion and so on. Eventually, expected and actual levels of aggregate demand would converge.

The smaller the marginal propensity to spend from marginal income, the smaller the multiplier – that is, the smaller the ripple effect of any change in spending. A much bigger multiplier value would arise if the government were trying to balance its budget and adjusted its expenditure up or down as tax receipts went up or down. It would also have a larger value if the leakage of spending overseas went mainly to a very close trading partner: a rise in domestic income would in part leak out to the trading partner, raising that nation's domestic income and leading to a rise in demand for exports from the country that had experienced the original increase in income.

13.7.3 The heterodox perspective on unemployment

Although the multiplier idea shows why economic downturns tend not to result in unemployment rising without limit, mainstream economists see it as begging a major question: why don't market forces eliminate unemployment by driving down wages so that it becomes viable to hire more workers, produce more output and generally smooth out the business cycle? It was in answering this question that Keynes tried to demonstrate that supply and demand logic at the microeconomic level does not translate well to the macroeconomic level.

Keynes agreed that much of the unemployment that we observe when economies are in deep recessions is involuntary. However, unlike mainstream economists he did not see '**involuntary unemployment**' as meaning that some workers could not get jobs because unions were keeping wages too high. Rather, he saw it as something that **workers are powerless to eliminate** *even if* they could get cuts in their money wages. From his standpoint, it is not the wage level that is the problem in such a situation; rather the problem is that potential employers do not expect enough demand to warrant hiring any more workers at existing rates of pay. In other words, **involuntary unemployment is a consequence of inadequate effective demand**, so its reduction requires an increase in effective demand, not a cut in wages. Stated thus, Keynes's perspective is baffling to a mainstream economist: why not make it more attractive to hire workers by cutting pay? The key to his answer takes some time to get one's head around: at the macroeconomic level, **aggregate supply curves and aggregate demand curves are interdependent.**

According to Keynes, a situation of involuntary unemployment prevails when more workers than are presently employed would be willing to work even if this required them all to accept a cut in real wages, that is, a wage deal that would buy less than can be bought at current money wage levels. Workers may be perfectly willing to tolerate less purchasing power than they currently have, or used to have, if that is what it takes to keep their jobs or obtain employment and yet, from Keynes's perspective, they may be powerless to change their real wages to make themselves more attractive to employers.

The difficulty here is not that they are unable or may be unwilling to change their money wages. Rather, the problem is that a change in money wages may not produce a change in real wages if the price level falls by the same amount.

At the level of the individual firm, such an outcome seems unlikely: a reduction in wages lowers the firm's cost curves but should have no significant effect on the firm's demand curve since the firm's employees, who now earn less, will not be its major customers. The same is not true at the level of the economy as a whole, for spending by workers in general is a major source of aggregate demand, so cutting their pay will reduce the amount of revenue received by firms.

The simplest way to see the power of Keynes's view that aggregate supply and aggregate demand curves are interdependent is to take the case where **supply curves are horizontal**, as in the normal cost analysis of the firm. Suppose firms have been employing everyone who wants to work but now have found that demand is 5 per cent less, at the prices they are charging, than is necessary to make it viable to employ all the workers. Then suppose that, as an alternative to a 5 per cent cut in output and jobs, everyone – workers, managers and shareholders – agrees to take a 5 per cent cut in income. The firms mark their prices down by 5 per cent and continue to produce at full employment rates of output. Once again, they are disappointed, for if nothing has happened to change the willingness to spend, then all that has happened is that wages and prices have been scaled down by 5 per cent and there is no increase in the number of units of output being demanded. Better strategies would have been for the government to engineer a reduction in interest rates to encourage the firms to increase their investment spending and income recipients to cut their rates of saving, or for the government to make cuts in taxes or increase its expenditure if interest rate reductions were difficult to achieve or judged to be unlikely to have much of an impact on spending.

Keynes's argument initially looks less powerful in the case of a small open economy that might be able to enjoy a cut in its real wages relative to its trading partners – but then it would be exporting unemployment to its trading partners, and if they follow similar strategies no one may achieve a lasting cost advantage. Keynes himself discussed 'beggar my neighbour remedies for unemployment' and, having questioned them, he looked around for possible indirect ways in which the conventional wage cuts remedy for unemployment might produce the desired result. Unfortunately for the pro-market view, he could find no sure-fire mechanisms.

The indirect mechanisms that have been most used in defences of the orthodox position arise via the monetary side of the economy. First, a cut in money wages, and hence in prices, increases the real value of money that people hold. It will thus produce a particular kind of wealth effect, known as the **'real balance effect'**: people will increase their real spending, to remove their excess holdings of purchasing power. Unfortunately, this is most unlikely to be significant in a modern economy where most money consists of bank deposits. Secondly, the fall in prices reduces the nominal value of the cash 'float' that businesses need in their tills and consumers need in their pockets to finance daily transactions, so demand for bank deposits and other financial assets should rise, interest rates should fall and spending should thus increase. However, even if the volume of new loans were, in principle, capable of being increased, this does not mean that potential lenders would judge it wise to make loans to those who want to increase their indebtedness and feel it is safe to do so. Finally, note that if the price level is falling, it pays to wait until it has reached its floor level before lending (since otherwise collateral values will fall) or borrowing (since it will be possible to buy more cheaply and borrow less in future).

13.7.4 Heterodox perspectives on inflation

When stagflation appeared in the late 1960s, Keynesian economists were not particularly bemused by it. Their analysis of downward wage/price spiralling being capable of taking place without making it viable to employ more workers could simply be reversed. If workers somehow push up wages at any level of employment and their employers mark up prices accordingly, then, for the economy as a whole, revenues will tend to rise in line with costs without there being any change in the number of workers it seems viable to employ. All of the other caveats from the story of why wage cuts may not reduce unemployment – such as open economy considerations and the real balance effect – apply, to the extent that they exert any power, in reverse in cases where wages are being pushed up.

From this standpoint, it appears that inflation need not reflect the strength of aggregate demand in the economy. Rather, it may simply reflect competition between different groups of workers (trying to realign or preserve their wage relativities) and/or between workers and employers (trying to maintain their aspirations for income growth when real output is growing more slowly than their target rates of income growth). If so, the control of inflation might require the use of some kind of **prices and incomes policy**, or some kind of tripartite negotiations between government, employer representatives and trade unions to agree upon the appropriate relative division of income between different worker groups and between workers and capitalists. Such policies proved increasingly unworkable in the UK during the 1970s, but in some other parts of the world – for example, Australia – they continued to be employed into the late 1980s without resulting in a wave of strikes followed by the election of Conservative governments and the introduction of anti-union legislation.

It cannot be denied that, compared with 20 or 30 years ago, we now live in an environment of very low rates of inflation. However, modern-day Keynesians seriously question whether the orthodox analysis of the relationship between inflation and unemployment and its associated policy package was, or remains, an appropriate way of viewing the workings of the macro-economy. The mainstream analysis looks less convincing if one thinks about the following issues:

- **Mainstream theorists presume all supply curves are upward sloping**, so an increase in employment necessarily entails a rise in the price level relative to money wages. By contrast, an eclectic view of pricing and supply issues does not lead to a natural presumption that, on average, supply curves slope upwards. Certainly, in some sectors they might do so – for example, where natural resources have to be extracted from increasingly difficult locations, or where industries contain many different vintages of production technology with differing operating costs. Elsewhere, however, supply curves may be horizontal (as presumed in the **normal cost analysis of pricing**, where excess capacity is held for strategic, goodwill-related reasons) or downward sloping (as is implied in learning curve analysis, or in industries where expansion leads to economies of scale). If supply curves, on average, are not upward sloping, then to make sense of the inflationary process it may be more appropriate to focus on the processes of interaction between employers and workers.

+ The presumption of a **natural rate of unemployment** seems to sweep aside all of Keynes's thinking about the possibility of an economy operating with substantial involuntary unemployment. If the economy did not have involuntary unemployment, then Keynesians would be perfectly willing to see inflation control as a matter of containing tendencies towards excessive growth in nominal aggregate demand. (Keynes himself was a pioneer in the analysis of such a situation, exemplified by the early 1940s UK wartime economy in which the supply of output available for consumption was much reduced and where the government was reluctant to increase taxes by a huge amount to remove consumption demand and pay for the military spending.) If the economy actually has involuntary unemployment, an increase in aggregate demand may cause a one-off rise in the price level *if supply curves on average are indeed upward sloping*. But the labour force in general will be willing to tolerate that price rise relative to wages. If, by contrast, their union representatives are not prepared to allow their members' real wages to fall and try to use actual or threatened strike action to achieve this end, then this may imply a need for reform of the workings of labour markets to remove pressure for a wage-price spiral. But it does not follow that aggregate demand should be clamped down to beat the rank and file into accepting smaller wage increases.

+ It may be counter-productive to use very high real interest rates as a way of frightening people into moderating their pay demands. If the cost of business finance is very high, this is hardly going to promote investment and increase the potential real output per head, even if entrepreneurs find it easier to figure out relative costs and returns of operating in various markets.

13.8 Speculation and business cycles

Economists were writing about business cycles many decades before Keynes presented his theory of effective demand and employment in 1936. His work led to further contributions to the genre, which incorporated the income multiplier concept developed in his book. The discussion in this section is strongly influenced by extensions of Keynes's perspective by an American heterodox economist, the late Hyman Minsky (1919–1996), whose view of the disruptive power of business cycles involves an implicit **complex systems perspective on the macro-economy**.

There are two things that make Keynes's perspective on business cycles different from much of the literature in this area. One is that his view emphasizes the shifting **psychology** that underpins investment spending. It does not focus on mechanistic relationships between the adjustments in the economy's capital stock and the volume of investment as a cause of upswings and downswings in economic activity. The other difference is his attempt to show how it is possible for an economy to become characterized by seemingly chronic high levels of unemployment because of shortcomings in market mechanisms for automatically generating a recovery, even if workers try to price themselves into jobs by offering to work for less. Keynes conceded that if one waited a long time a severely depressed economy might eventually recover by itself, for example, via an increase in investment spending as machinery and consumer durables wore out and had to be replaced. But, as he famously commented, 'In the long run we're all dead,' so it might be rather more sensible for the government to pump up spending and speed up the recovery process in cases where recessions were showing no signs of going away.

Compared with their predecessors in the grim 1980s, modern-day central bankers seem much more inclined to use changes in interest rates to try to keep the pressure of aggregate demand fairly steady, and to keep employment rates high, though not so high as to lead to workers getting more pushy with their pay demands. Their task becomes difficult, however, if expansionary pressures in an economy produce an increasingly precarious set of **interconnected financial obligations.** (Their development might be mapped via more complex versions of the flow of fund analysis illustrated with Table 13.1.) In such a situation, attempts to dampen down demand are at risk of bringing about a widespread collapse of both asset values and financial solvency, rather like what happens when a 'house of cards' is disturbed. It was this prospect that particularly concerned Minsky. Matters are particularly difficult when the web of interconnected fortunes is spread across many countries, and this is very much to be expected in today's age of **globalization** of financial and product markets. The Asian economic crisis of 1997 is a telling example of this: failures of banks in Thailand led to problems for firms in Korea, and the slowdown in construction in Korea led to a major downturn in the New Zealand forest products sector, loss of revenue from Asian tourists visiting Australia and many other ripple effects spreading as far as the United States and even Brazil.

Spectacular boom–bust episodes with complex international ramifications are not, however, a product of globalization; they have been occurring for centuries. Many business decision makers and participants in financial markets unfortunately lack this historical perspective or suffer from short memories. History is therefore prone to repeat itself every 10 to 15 years or so. The timing and magnitudes of cycles of financial instability are inherently hard to predict precisely, owing to their complex nature. Despite this, we hope that, by outlining how they seem to work, we shall at least enable readers to be alert to them as possibilities and to know when caution might be wise.

13.8.1 Classical speculation versus movement trading

Speculation plays a crucial role in our version of the Keynes/Minsky analysis, but not in the way that one might expect from the classical theory of speculation. Speculators used to be stereotyped as professional traders in organized commodity markets, who had great knowledge of underlying supply and demand conditions in the markets in which they specialized (such as gold, grain, tin and cocoa). They would buy up stocks when supply was high relative to demand, with a view to selling them at a profit at a later date. Their actions would thus smooth out price fluctuations and help make the economic environment more stable. Today, however, speculators may not focus on the 'fundamentals' of one or a handful of markets. Rather, they try to profit by 'movement trading'.

> Movement traders are defined speculators who buy assets that they expect will go up in price relative to other assets with the intention of selling them in favour of whichever asset displaces them as the asset whose price is expected to rise relative to all other assets. They may even engage in short selling, which is defined as borrowing assets (sometimes without the permission of the owners) that they expect to go down in value, selling them, waiting for their prices to fall and then buying them back and returning them to their original owners after pocketing the profit from the price movement.

Movement traders hold whatever asset seems to offer the best opportunity for capital gain. The more cautious amongst them will hedge their bets on a mix of assets that seem to be good prospects. They are inherently prone to switch between markets as their perceptions of opportunities change. Since their choices of assets are so promiscuous and not based on in-depth knowledge of particular markets, they may be prone to error. Indeed, **when different speculators are holding different assets, they cannot all be right in their guesses about which way relative prices are going to move** (in principle, they might *all* be wrong, for relative prices might not move at all!). These mistakes could prove problematic if the assets are being purchased with borrowed money or by committing one's life-savings, or if the assets belong to someone else and are being used opportunistically in a short-selling deal. (A widely reported recent example of opportunistic speculation is the National

Australia Bank in 2004, where a small number of staff engaging in unauthorized foreign exchange speculation ran up losses of hundreds of millions of dollars. Evidently, they had learned little from the case of the original 'rogue trader', Nick Leeson, whose activities caused the collapse of Barings Bank in 1995.)

13.8.2 The propensity to speculate is not fixed, nor is the population of speculators

One sign that speculation may be getting out of hand is when professional speculators are increasingly competing for assets against inexperienced players, as word gets round about where money can easily be made. If share prices or real estate prices are rising rapidly, and this is widely discussed in the media, then those who have not hitherto been 'investing' in these areas are prone to get sucked into the frenzy, with growing feelings of euphoria. Box 13.1 gives an illustration of how ordinary households can get on a property speculation bandwagon by buying an investment property. (Media companies have an interest in promoting this, since they stand to obtain more customers in search of information, and to sell more advertising space regarding investment opportunities.) With a perceived need to acquire assets before they become even more expensive, people may give inadequate attention to the underlying soundness of the prospectuses of new firms (as with the dot-com boom) and property companies. In such an environment, some of these prospectuses are likely to be downright opportunistic, owing to the reduced risk of detection.

Box 13.1 The economics of buying an investment property in a rising market

In a property boom, the stream of rental income from a property, less upkeep and other outgoings such as rates and fees to letting agents, is often less than the stream of interest payments on the money that has been borrowed to pay for it. Despite this, banks may be perfectly happy to let a household have such a loan even if they do not have any savings to make a deposit. It all comes down to the way the loan is packaged so as to ensure that the bank's asset is secure unless there is a spectacular downturn in property prices. The package involves both the investment property and the household's place of residence. (For simplicity, we leave out any income tax aspects of the investment.)

The property boom means that the household's residence has gone up in value greatly relative to the mortgage on it. For example, suppose the owners

Box 13.1 (continued)

bought it for £200 000 with a credit-line mortgage of £120 000 on which they have simply been paying interest rather than trying to reduce the amount outstanding. Suppose further that the house is now worth £300 000. If they increase their mortgage credit line to £160 000, they can make a £30 000 deposit on an investment property costing, say £150 000 and still have £10 000 unused credit, yet the ratio of their credit limit to the value of their home is less (0.53) than it was at the time they bought it (0.6). The bank is very happy with this increase in lending, as it would take a totally unprecedented fall in house values to prevent them from getting their money back by selling the house if the owner failed to service the mortgage. The bank is also happy to let the household have a mortgage of £120 000 on the investment property, as the 20 per cent deposit provides the bank with a cushion in the event that it has to foreclose on the loan and sell the investment property in a declining market. In effect, borrowing finances the entire cost of the investment property, but the bank feels perfectly safe because it is dealing with two mortgages that are both less than the value of the respective properties.

For the deal to be a success for the household, their investment property must rise in value at a rate faster than the difference between its net rental yield and the rate of interest. The required rate of price increase may actually be quite modest. For example, if the cost of finance is 6 per cent, the annual interest charge is £9000. If the net proceeds from renting are £7500 per year, the property only has to rise by 1 per cent for them to break even. If it goes up in value in a year by 10 per cent, then they make a profit that year of £13 500. After a few more years of growth at that sort of rate, they could be thinking of increasing the mortgage on the investment property to provide a deposit for a further investment property. If the property market continues to rise, they may succeed in amassing considerable wealth by leveraging a series of loans on their home, rather than by doing any further saving.

Note, however, that until the capital gain is realized, their investment property does entail a negative cash flow, which could be met either by cutting consumption or by increasing borrowing against their home and using up the slack in their credit line. The latter is potentially a slippery slope, for they are, in part, borrowing to service interest on another loan, which means that each year they will owe more until they eventually come to sell the property and realize the capital gain. If the capital gain turns out not to materialize and, worse still, if interest rates rise and rents fall, they could find themselves

Box 13.1 (continued)

in a situation where property prices are falling and they are having major problems servicing their debts. If they are forced to sell the investment property for less than they paid for it, the bank will not be troubled by their capital loss so long as the property sells for at least £120 000 and they can continue to meet interest charges on the mortgage against their home.

13.8.3 Increased risk-taking leads to financial fragility

Growing confidence leads to reductions in perceived **borrower's risk** (the risk of insolvency seen by a borrower falls, leading to the borrower being willing to take on a rising ratio of debt to equity) and in perceived **lender's risk** (the lender is less worried about the prospect of losing the money and becomes willing to allow higher debt/equity ratios). One way to increase indebtedness is to use as collateral paper capital gains that have already been achieved. So, for example, a property company whose office and apartment blocks have risen in value may borrow against these unrealized gains and buy more such properties, thereby tending to fuel further the increase in real estate values.

In such a situation, the volume of finance provided to businesses may grow much faster than the rate of growth of bank deposits. Those who might otherwise have been holding money in relatively secure bank deposits increasingly invest it directly (in which case it moves to the bank accounts of the firms whose financial assets they buy), or they seek to get higher rates of return by placing their funds with non-bank financial intermediaries (NBFIs), such as property trusts, or by buying debentures issued by finance companies. The major banks themselves may acquire interests in some of the NBFIs, either as shareholders or by lending money to them on the basis that the NBFIs have stronger capabilities in the areas in which they operate and hence a bigger chance of making successful loans and generating higher returns.

The upshot of all this is that balance sheets become interconnected in complex ways and additional layers of lending are created. The system increasingly becomes financially fragile as participants operate with smaller safety margins, and their ability to service debts depends on their optimistic expectations proving correct. Borrowers may be assembling 'cocktails' of funds from many lenders and several NBFIs may stand between banks and the assets at the end of a chain of loans. In such a situation, the banks are far less able to form a clear picture of the quality of the assets on which the viability of the chain of loans depends than would be the case if they lent the money directly. Banks also may be living dangerously to the extent that they have **diversified** into new markets.

Once events have moved in this direction, it does not take much to throw everything into reverse. If some borrowers have over-extended themselves and end up engaging in forced sales of assets, this may lead to collapses in asset values upon which other borrowers' balance sheets were predicated. Similar kinds of institutions may be 'tarred with the same brush' and find it hard to refinance loans. Further financial failures could then lead to yet more forced sales and a general flight into liquid assets. The trouble is, such a flight into cash is not possible for the system as a whole, since someone else must buy every asset that is sold. Prices will fall until other speculators judge that they are unlikely to fall further. Major **wealth effects** may be associated with such a financial meltdown; a general fall in share prices discourages investment in brand-new assets, both because funds may be harder to raise and because relatively it has become cheaper to grow via takeover.

13.8.4 Triggers for upswings and collapses

Changes in interest rates are one possible cause of turning points in the unfolding history of the macro-economy, but there are many others.

In the property market, upswings in asset prices can be affected by public policies involving:

- assistance to first-time buyers;
- changes in tax treatment of property;
- changes in lending policies of banks, etc.;
- changes in urban/rural zoning;
- construction associated with major events.

A property market downturn might be triggered by:

- difficulties caused for developers by the exhaustion of supplies of land and other inputs and/or delays in planning approvals;
- wages ceasing to grow or the exhaustion of borrowing potential;
- disruptions to completion of new projects (for example, due to strikes or bad weather);
- failure of a major developer/construction company, leading to failure of subcontractors who were owed money.

Elsewhere in the economy, upswings could be triggered by:

+ technological change;
+ natural resource discovery or a rise in the price of a natural resource which suddenly makes its extraction viable in a particular region;
+ impact of climatic events on commodity prices;
+ changes in the regulatory environment;
+ merger waves initiated by fee-hungry merchant banks.

By contrast, downswings could arise owing to:

+ financial failure due to losses in foreign exchange or property speculation;
+ firms needing to pause in growth activities to consolidate recent achievements;
+ impact of climate on harvests and hence on commodity prices;
+ impact of a health alert on consumer confidence or mobility (for example, the SARS scare of 2003 had major consequences for airline and tourism profitability and could have led to collapses of major businesses had it persisted);
+ discovery of fraudulent behaviour;
+ significant financial ratios (such as price/earnings ratios) passing psychologically significant thresholds and beginning to seem implausible;
+ political events.

These by no means comprise a complete list of potential turning-point triggers.

13.8.5 Limits to the fallout when a speculative bubble bursts

Episodes of financial instability do not always have major impacts upon the state of the macro-economy and the business environment in general. Much will depend on just how interconnected different parts of the economy become during an upswing and the extent to which players jump to the conclusion that gains or losses should be seen as permanent. If a collapse is that of a speculative bubble that has grown up with few links to the 'real' economy, then there may be relatively little damage to confidence overall and investors might simply try their luck, and remaining funds, in another area (as with the 1988 UK property boom that followed the 1987 collapse of share prices). Swift action by central banks, in conjunction with swift recognition by major banks that their interests lie in preventing financial failures from multiplying, may result in money being pumped into the system to allow failing NBFIs to be taken over by major banks, or to allow existing loans to be rescheduled without the supply of new loans being disrupted. However, central banks face a dilemma when trying to limit the fallout from a speculative bubble: there may be an undesirable long-run impact on prudential behaviour if it becomes too obviously clear that debt does not carry responsibilities and repayments can be pushed further and further into the future. They may also experience problems in co-ordinating their policies in a hurry on a global basis.

13.9 Summary

In this chapter we have considered two sharply contrasting perspectives on macroeconomics.

From the perspective of mainstream economics, the macro-economy is really nothing more than an aggregation of individual markets with the added complication of the government being able to affect total spending via its policy interventions. If there is unemployment, it is the result of wages failing to fall when the overall volume of spending falls, and if the general price level is increasing this is due to excess demand, itself a consequence of too much credit being made available.

The heterodox perspective takes the view that, 70 years on, there is still much of relevance in John Maynard Keynes's theory of employment. Keynes emphasizes the extent of scope for co-ordination failures due to savers not signalling to firms what they will eventually want to buy when they spend their savings, and money that is saved not necessarily generating more lending to businesses. Firms have to guess how much to invest to expand output in the future, and how much will be demanded from their current outputs. These guesses determine how many workers they want to hire. If they are pessimistic, they will limit their production and their capacity expansion, and fewer workers will be hired. If fewer workers are hired, consumption demand will be reduced, though not by as much as income, so an initial contraction of activity does not typically turn into a macroeconomic implosion. Bubbles of speculative activity compound swings in output and employment from time to time, but since speculators tend to focus on assets whose supply cannot easily be expanded, these bubbles tend to affect production levels indirectly to the extent that they change speculators' perceptions of how wealthy they are. Heterodox economists do not regard 'labour market reforms' aimed at producing softer wage bargains as an effective means of

13.9 **Summary** (continued)

dealing with unemployment that has come about because of a decline in overall spending. They also worry that if inflation is largely due to attempts by bosses and workers to make irreconcilable claims for shares in national output, rather than due to excess aggregate demand, attempts to squeeze it out of the system via a very tight monetary policy and cuts in government spending may be a needlessly costly way of tackling the problem in terms of unemployment and a slowdown in capacity growth.

13.10 Some questions to consider

1. In some economies, young people may be prone to extend themselves financially in order to engage in conspicuous consumption as an investment in enhancing their marital and career prospects. Consider whether such tendencies are likely to help or hinder the performance of these economies in the long run, compared with economies where consumers are less inclined to engage in impression management.

2. Examine the pathways by which the end of a boom in domestic property prices could affect the sales revenue of an airline that operates in the same country.

3. Why are financial markets so keen to guess what each new announcement by the Bank of England and other central banks will be regarding interest rates? Which economic indicators would you look at if you were trying to predict changes in the rate of interest? Explain your reasoning.

4. Can you suggest any scenarios under which 'stagflation' might return to advanced industrial economies?

5. Suppose that it is reported that the household sector as a whole is currently spending 5 per cent more than its income each month. How might this be possible in financial terms and what factors are likely to bring such a situation to an end?

6. To what extent can a government use changes in the composition of its taxes and expenditures, rather than simply changes in their overall levels, as part of its macroeconomic policy toolkit?

> ### 13.10 Some questions to consider (continued)
>
> 7. To what extent would you characterize current approaches to macroeco-
>   nomic policy as 'Keynesian'?
>
> 8. Suppose that the UK next winter suffers from weather that breaks previ-
>   ous records in terms of low temperatures and the amount and persis-
>   tence of snow and ice. What effect would this have on the country's
>   macroeconomic performance?

13.11 Recommended additional reading sources

More detailed presentations of mainstream perspectives can be found in a vast
array of standard macroeconomics texts, but they rarely cover Keynesian perspectives very well. A good starting point for an introduction to macroeconomics
as seen from a Keynesian perspective is the work of Michael Stewart, from his
(1986) *Keynes and After* (3rd edn), Harmondsworth, Penguin, to his (1993) *Keynes
in the 1990s: A Return to Economic Sanity*, London, Penguin. Those who relish a
challenge should take a look at John Maynard Keynes (1936) *The General Theory
of Employment, Interest and Money*, London, Macmillan and Hyman P. Minsky
(1976) *John Maynard Keynes*, London, Macmillan.

A wide range of variations on mainstream thinking, as well as heterodox macroeconomics, is presented, including interviews with leading figures from each
school, in Brian Snowdon, Howard Vane and Peter Wynarczyk (1994) *A Modern
Guide to Macroeconomics: An Introduction to Competing Schools of Thought*,
Aldershot, Edward Elgar.

A very useful survey of the saving literature with an emphasis on its psychological aspects is offered by Karl-Erik Wärneryd (1999) *The Psychology of Saving: A
Study on Economic Psychology*, Cheltenham, Edward Elgar.

For a thought-provoking view of the supply side of the economy in relation to
macroeconomic policy that challenges both orthodox and Keynesian perspectives,
see Tim Hazledine (1984) *Full Employment Without Inflation*, London Macmillan.

Andrew Tylecote (1981) *The Causes of the Present Inflation*, London, Macmillan,
provides a very readable and thoughtfully argued heterodox analysis of the inflationary process that includes both cross-cultural and organizational perspectives
on how inflationary pressures vary through business cycles and between countries. Also useful and readable is James A. Trevithick (1982) *Inflation: A Guide to
the Crisis in Economics* (2nd edn), Harmondsworth, Penguin.

An entertaining account of speculative bubbles is to be found in Charles Kindleberger (2000) *Manias, Panics and Crashes: A History of Financial Crashes* (4th edn), New York, Wiley. The global dimension is explored in Thomas Friedman (1999) *The Lexus and the Olive Tree*, London, HarperCollins. Also recommended is Karl-Erik Wärneryd (2001) *Stock-Market Psychology: How People Value and Trade Stocks*, Cheltenham, Edward Elgar. A very useful guide to the work of Minsky on financial instability is provided by Perry Merhling (1999) 'The vision of Hyman P. Minsky', *Journal of Economic Behavior and Organization*, **39**, June, pp. 129–58.

14

The international environment

Learning outcomes

If you study this chapter carefully, it may help you to understand:

- what is meant by the 'balance of payments' and what determines the sizes of its main components

- what foreign exchange rates are and how they are determined

- the problems that exchange rate fluctuations cause for firms and measures firms can use to reduce these problems

- why some firms become multinational enterprises

- why firms charge different prices for the same product in different markets

- why firms may opt to change the specifications of their products rather than their export prices when exchange rates change

- the dilemmas a government faces when formulating policies aimed at changing the structure of the country's balance of payments

- why a country's foreign indebtedness can be a problem for its businesses and consumers

- why some economists believe that even unilateral moves towards free trade can improve a country's welfare.

To the extent that you develop such understanding, you should be better able to:

- interpret reports in the financial press on events in the international economic environment

- discuss policy options when working for a firm involved in international business either as a producer or as a purchaser of inputs.

14.1 Introduction

Many firms are driven to seek export sales by limits to the size of their domestic markets relative to the sales required to achieve economies of scale. This is particularly the case for firms that make new kinds of products that offer new levels of performance in some areas but are as yet unable to match older technologies in other respects. (Recent examples include digital cameras and petrol-electric hybrid-powered cars.) These kinds of products initially appeal only to a tiny minority of consumers with particular requirements for, or curiosity about, the area in which progress has been made. In the absence of domestic buyers prepared to pay regardless of the price (as the US defence forces often have been, to get the latest US-developed technologies), such products really have to be launched to the world as a whole. With the rise of electronic commerce and widespread use of credit cards as a means of on-line payment, firms may find themselves operating as international businesses without actively seeking to find customers overseas, because the overseas customers find them on the World Wide Web.

International business activities are also a consequence of competitive pressures that force firms to look for inputs from the cheapest source, wherever that happens to be. Consequently, many firms' customers in export markets are not the consumers of finished products but other firms, or international divisions of the same firm. Indeed, the components of a modern, multi-technology product such as a car or a computer, like the products that make up an individual's lifestyle, could come from many different countries.

International business environments pose many hazards for buyers and sellers, and not just because of scope for co-ordination failures due to language, legal and cultural differences, or delays in delivery over great distances. In this chapter we explore ways in which businesses may be affected by issues in their international environments related to changes in the relative macroeconomic states of different countries. Having explored the nature of a country's balance of payments with the rest of the world, and the economics of exchange rates, we then explore how firms can try to limit the disruptive effects of exchange rate instability and choose appropriate pricing strategies when selling to multiple markets and facing changes in exchange rates. We also examine the reasons why firms set up foreign subsidiaries. The final parts of the chapter then explore policy options for governments seeking to change the structure of the balance of payments and how these impinge on businesses. We also examine whether businesses should worry about involvement in economies with growing foreign indebtedness.

14.2 What do we mean by the 'balance of payments'?

Balance of payments statistics measure the difference between inflows and outflows of funds between the domestic economy and the rest of the world. They are divided up broadly into the **current account,** the **capital/financial account** and **official financing.** They are defined so that they sum to zero: if there is no official financing, then a current account deficit will be matched by a capital/financial account surplus. If the current account has been in deficit by an amount greater than the capital/financial account, then the excess must have been funded either by the government borrowing from overseas – including borrowing from the International Monetary Fund (IMF), if things are desperate – or by its central bank running down reserves of gold and foreign currency/deposits at other central banks.

The balance of payments on the **current account** includes net earnings from trade in goods and services, as well as income from overseas and current transfers, such as payments to and from the European Union by its member nations. The UK has long been running a substantial current account deficit. So, too, for example, have the USA, Australia and New Zealand, unlike Japan, which has long been running a current account surplus. For 2003, the current account deficit for the UK was £18.8 billion, with deficits of about £46.2 billion on trade in goods and £9.7 billion on current transfers being partly offset by surpluses of £13.8 billion on services such as banking and tourism, and £25.5 billion on income from investments overseas. Earnings remitted by UK nationals working overseas were roughly in balance with those remitted from the UK by overseas nationals working in the UK.

The **capital account** in the UK nowadays merely refers to debits and credits associated with EU development funds, debt write-offs and capital transfers by migrants. This was in surplus by £1.2 billion in 2003. The term is often used elsewhere to include what the UK statisticians now call the **financial account.** The financial account nets out the foreign exchange payments associated with:

- the buying and selling of entire companies across national boundaries;
- portfolio investment, where investors buy or sell shares across international borders;
- changes in foreign-owned or foreign currency deposits held by banks;
- net earnings from financial derivatives such as interest rate swaps.

The net figures for 'portfolio investment abroad' and 'portfolio investment in the UK' result from very substantial gross sums, the result of securities dealers switching their portfolios between equities and long-term debt securities and changing the mix of their holdings between domestic and foreign assets.

It is important to be aware of how the current and capital/financial accounts are related in ways other than via the basic balance of payments identity for a particular point in time. If the UK increases its imports of capital goods this year, that will make the current account deficit this year even bigger than otherwise. But if the new equipment enables British firms to expand their output or the quality of their products then in the future exports may be bigger and imports smaller, so the current account deficit will be reduced. Similarly, if British firms put more money into developing their overseas subsidiaries this year, it will reduce the size of the financial account surplus this year, but in the future a consequent increase in the flow of profits into the UK from these subsidiaries will reduce the current account deficit. If the increased profits of the overseas subsidiaries are simply ploughed back into further investment in these businesses, then that is recorded as an increase in direct investment abroad. Some purchases may even affect both the current and capital/financial accounts at the same time. An example of this would be where a UK executive leased an imported luxury car (worsening the current account deficit) and the leasing company was raising its funds from overseas (increasing the financial account surplus).

The balance of payments identity has considerable overlap with the **net acquisition of financial assets (NAFA)** identity introduced in the previous chapter. To illustrate this, consider the consequences of the US public sector deficit rising as a consequence of George W. Bush's decision to invade Iraq in 2003 and the huge military expenditure that followed. If US consumers and firms do not increase their saving and buy the bonds being sold by the US government to pay for its war, then these bonds must somehow end up being absorbed by the overseas sector. In other words, the US government NAFA takes on a larger negative value and the foreign sector NAFA is correspondingly a larger surplus. In terms of the US balance of payments, what this means is that the capital account surplus of the USA increases by the same amount as the increase in the overseas NAFA. It also means, in the absence of any official financing, that the US current account deficit must somehow get even bigger by the same amount.

It may seem fairly obvious from the previous chapter that the US current account deficit will worsen to some degree if the US government steps up its spending and the Federal Reserve does not use higher interest rates to encourage US consumers and firms to cut back their own levels of demand. This policy involves a fiscal expansion and, because incomes are higher than they would have been, some extra spending will leak out of the economy into imports. However, to understand how the increase in the US balance of payments deficit ends up corresponding to the amount of the increase in the US public sector deficit that is funded by overseas investors, we need to understand where foreign exchange rates fit into the story. This we will now do.

14.3 What are exchange rates and how are they determined?

The exchange rate between a domestic currency and a foreign currency is defined as the price of one unit of a foreign currency in terms of the domestic currency. If the domestic currency is described as having fallen (risen) in value, this means that it now takes more (fewer) units of the domestic currency to buy one unit of the foreign currency.

As far as the determination of exchange rates is concerned, the period since the end of World War II can be divided roughly in half. Up until the early 1970s, there was a system of fixed exchange rates in which devaluations or revaluations were politically significant and infrequent events. Such changes in currency values were made reluctantly in the face of a growing need to engage in official financing to make balance of payments figures sum to zero. (Sterling was only devalued twice under this system, in 1949 and 1967.) When, in 1971, it was evident that the US dollar was overvalued, the fixed exchange rate system began to crumble and within two years most of the major currencies had been allowed to have their values determined mainly by the forces of supply and demand. This was facilitated by a growing relaxation of foreign exchange controls that had previously been used by governments as a non-price means of managing currency flows.

Had it not been for this freeing up of access to foreign currency markets, the international use of credit cards and the globalization of commerce and financial markets would have been hindered greatly. Even now, we have some way to go in freeing up international currency flows: whilst domestic electronic banking enables us to move money between domestic bank accounts with ease, moving funds between one's domestic bank account and a foreign one still requires paperwork. This might actually be a good thing, because otherwise it would be very tempting for many individuals, not merely expatriates, to have bank accounts in a variety of currencies and to make speculative switches between them, exacerbating the swings that are a common feature of the current system.

The supply of foreign currency available to the domestic economy depends on the foreign demand for the domestic currency. It will depend on the following factors:

- *The domestic rate of interest.* A rise in the domestic rate of interest relative to rates available overseas will make foreign asset holders more willing to place their financial capital in the domestic economy.

- *The perceived likelihood that the domestic exchange rate will appreciate in value.* If foreign asset holders turn their money into the domestic currency and the latter does indeed appreciate in value, they can then buy back more units of their own currency.

- *Overseas levels of income and the general state of business activity overseas.* A rise in income overseas will increase the demand for domestic exports, except where the domestic products are inferior goods.

- *The relative competitive strength of domestic and overseas producers.* If there is faster technological progress overseas than in the UK, then there will, other things being equal, be a decrease in the demand for sterling from overseas.

Domestic demand for foreign currencies will conversely depend on the following:

- *The difference in domestic interest rates and those available overseas.* Other things being equal, a rise in domestic rates of interest reduces domestic demand for overseas financial assets.

- *Domestic perceptions about the likelihood of the domestic currency falling in value relative to overseas currencies.*

- *The level of domestic income.* For example, a rise in income in Britain may lead to a rise in demand for luxury German cars and hence for Germany's currency, the euro, whereas demand for cheap Malaysian Proton cars and hence for the Malaysian currency, the ringgit, may fall.

- *Relative competitive strength of domestic and foreign firms.*

Figure 14.1 gives a simple illustration of how an increase in the supply of US dollars relative to sterling (an increase in US demand for sterling) will result in the appreciation of sterling: initially it takes £1 to buy $1, but after the shift in the supply of US dollars/increase in demand for sterling, it only takes £0.60 to buy $1. We can also express the exchange rate the other way round and say that it has gone from £1 = $1 to £1 = $1.67. Many economists habitually talk about exchange rates in this inverted manner, in terms of how many units of an overseas currency can be bought with one unit of the domestic currency. However, as you should see from inspecting Figure 14.1, this way of thinking about them is less straightforward to show on a supply and demand diagram.

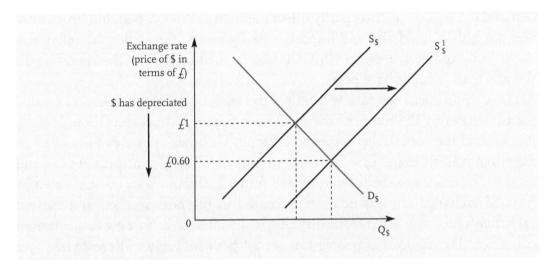

Figure 14.1 A rise in sterling due to an increase in the supply of US dollars

Let us keep this in mind and return to our illustration of the relationship between the current account and capital/financial accounts via the example of George W. Bush's Iraq war deficit. The injection of public sector spending led to a rise in US GDP, which led to a rise in demand for imports. If foreign wealth holders had been unwilling to place more funds in the USA, and if there was no official financing, then the rise in demand for currencies other than the US dollar would have caused its value to fall to a level such that there was no increase in the US current account deficit. The fall in the dollar would have made US goods more attractive relative to imported ones, so the growth in imports would have been reduced, while US goods would have looked more attractive to overseas customers, leading to a rise in exports. In this case, the increase in the US government's deficit would end up being funded domestically as personal and corporate incomes rose and, with them, saving. The less willing the US personal and corporate sectors were to save and acquire US government debt securities, the more US GDP would have risen and the further the US dollar would have fallen.

What actually happened was that the US dollar fell substantially but by less than in the scenario just outlined. Speculators judged that it was likely to recover from the levels to which it seemed to be falling and therefore they placed funds in US assets. Either they bought US government debt directly or, by buying other US assets, pushing up the latter's prices and depressing their effective yields, they induced the sellers of these assets to switch their portfolios into US government debt. If the speculators' hunches were correct, they would get both income from their holdings of US assets and a capital gain. The speculative demand for US dollars thus partly offset the increase in US demand for currencies other than the dollar. US imports rose by more than under the other scenario, and exports by less, so US GDP was pushed up less by the spending on the war than it might have been.

The current exchange rate will reflect the current wisdom of market participants concerning the future of the economy. If an export boom is thought to be just around the corner, the domestic currency becomes attractive to hold as an asset that is likely to increase in value, so people will seek to acquire it now, and vice versa. Differences between expected future exchange rates (as measured by forward exchange rates, which are discussed in the next section) and current exchange rates only arise from differences in interest rates between different countries. (For example, if people can get a 1 per cent higher interest yield over the next year by holding a particular currency now rather than by holding other currencies, then they will be willing to bid the price of that currency up 1 per cent higher today than they expect its value to be a year from now.) In other words, the current exchange rate is determined by the expected future rate, not the other way round.

Those who speculate in foreign currency markets take considerable risks and many corporate failures come from speculative guesses turning out wrong. The big problem for corporate treasurers is in judging how safe it is to switch funds into offshore assets that offer higher rates of return than appear to be available at home. Countries with weak balance of payments positions and poor international credit ratings often offer rates of interest higher than those with better financial credentials. But a few per cent extra in interest payments can be swamped by depreciation in the exchange rate by a greater amount within the same time period.

14.4 How can firms deal with exchange rate variability?

Exchange rate changes are not merely a potential hazard for international fund managers and speculators. They also greatly complicate the environments of producers of goods and services that are internationally traded and which use internationally traded inputs. If you visit websites that specialize in providing exchange rate data (such as www.oanda.com) and explore exchange rate movements over several years, it rapidly becomes apparent that businesses nowadays have to contend with considerable exchange rate variability. For example, consider Table 14.1, which summarizes currency movements of selected currencies against sterling for

	30/03/02	30/02/03	30/03/04	Average	Highest (732 days)	Lowest
Argentine Peso	0.2386	0.2215	0.1905	0.1996	0.2559	0.1699
Australian Dollar	0.3744	0.3819	0.4113	0.3872	0.4298	0.3382
Euro	0.6116	0.6853	0.6684	0.6686	0.7253	0.6098
Japanese Yen	0.00529	0.00530	0.00522	0.00528	0.00558	0.00481
Malaysian Ringgit	0.1847	0.1674	0.1449	0.1634	0.1848	0.1360
New Zealand Dollar	0.3092	0.3532	0.3580	0.3411	0.3775	0.2938
US Dollar	0.7015	0.6357	0.5304	0.6203	0.7018	0.5223

Table 14.1 **The exchange rate of selected currencies against sterling, 30 March 2002 to 30 March 2004**

the two-year period 30 March 2002 to 30 March 2004. The magnitude of these movements is such that the profitability of a particular product could depend much more on luck in the choice of where to make it, or from which countries to source inputs, rather than on its design and other aspects of quality.

One way of dealing with this issue is to hedge one's bets by dividing up manufacturing or input sourcing among a variety of locations. This strategy has scope for promoting high productivity levels via its 'divide and rule' potential but, like adverse exchange rate movements, it could also threaten profit margins by precluding the achievement of economies of scale (see further Section 14.5).

A second strategy for firms is to try to guarantee that exchange rate movements do not interfere with their costs and revenues. To this end, they may consider making use of **forward currency markets** and **currency options**. Suppose a firm expects that its export sales in the USA over a particular time period will yield $10 million but that it does not know what $10 million will be in terms of sterling by the time it has been received. If the current exchange rate is $1 = £0.60, the US revenue would be worth £6 million if received today. To guarantee that the firm will receive £6 million at a specific future date, it can agree today to sell $10 million to be delivered by it on that date in return for £6 million to be delivered on that date. (Alternatively, it might agree to provide a smaller sum in US dollars delivered today, in return for £6 million to be delivered on the particular date. It would get the $10 million today by borrowing this sum, or by foregoing interest on the equivalent sum in sterling and turning it into US dollars at the current exchange rate. The difference between the two deals reflects the cost of borrowing or foregone interest during the period of the contract.) So long as its revenue projections are correct in US dollars, it will have the required number of US dollars needed to honour the contract and receive the £6 million on the day in question. It has shifted the currency risk to the supplier of sterling, who will have to find that amount by the day in question. If the US dollar falls against sterling to $1 = £0.50, the firm will still receive its £6 million so long as the other party does not default, but the $10 million that the latter receives will only be worth £5 million. If the US dollar rises against sterling to $1 = £0.70, then the firm will still get its £6 million but the other party will be able to turn the $10 million that it receives into £7 million.

From the standpoint of the firm trying to guarantee its position in terms of foreign currency, the ideal arrangement would be one which precluded it from losing out due to a currency depreciation and at the same time allowed it to benefit from that currency appreciating instead. This is where it may be attractive to make a deal in terms of **currency options**. If the firm buys an option to sell $10 million for £6 million on a particular date and the exchange rate of the dollar falls to $1 = £0.50, it can exercise its option and still receive £6 million on that date. However, if the exchange rate moves in the opposite direction, to $1 = £0.70, then it can forget about the option and simply turn the $10 million export revenue into £7 million. The other party to the option thus ends up having to find an extra £1 million unless they have covered themselves by buying an option to buy £7 million for $10 million on the particular date, thereby passing the uncertainty on to someone else. The prices of these option contracts will depend upon the mix of market expectations about the future directions of exchange rates. If a particular change is widely seen as unlikely, then options may be a very cheap way of guarding against it.

Forward and options contracts for foreign currencies seem to offer means whereby entrepreneurs and corporations seeking to make money by producing and marketing goods and services can separate themselves from speculators who seek to make money by placing bets with contracts in foreign currency markets. They are essentially **insurance** devices; one group insures and the other does not, just as some people pay to insure their cars, whereas others do not pay such premiums and in some years have accidents that are very expensive. If everyone used the same currency, there would be no need to get involved in such deals. The creation of the euro has thus given firms in member countries a cheaper way of doing international business within the euro area. Everything comes at a cost, however, and if real wages grow at different rates amongst euro currency area members, then no longer can exchange rate adjustments offset tendencies towards differences in unemployment rates in different regions of the euro area.

Forward and option contracts are typically for short periods, such as three months. This is far shorter than the planning horizons of firms, even if they are using simplified decision criteria that do not attempt to incorporate the entire duration of their projects' revenue streams, such as requiring projects to have no more than a three-year payback period. One way of making three-month contracts safeguard a project against exchange rate fluctuations over a three-year period is to have a succession of forward or option contracts that cover all of the expected foreign revenue/cost stream that is still awaited. Thus the first contract would insure the entire three-year stream; the second, three months later, would insure the remaining two years and nine months, and so on.

14.5 Why do some firms become multinational enterprises?

The international business strategies that firms use will affect the structure of a country's balance of payments. For example, if Honda, Nissan and Toyota had not set up manufacturing operations in the UK, the UK's trade deficit would be even bigger due to more cars being imported and fewer cars being exported. The UK would also have experienced a smaller inflow of foreign investment funds on its capital account and would not be so prone to suffer outflows of dividend payments to Japan. These firms are examples of multinational enterprises.

> A multinational enterprise is a firm that has grown by setting up subsidiary businesses in nations other than that in which it was founded. These subsidiaries (i) may supply the parent company with raw materials or components, (ii) may manufacture entire products for the local market or for export, or (iii) may mainly be involved with distributing products supplied as exports from the parent firm's manufacturing operations.

Before we try to understand why many firms choose growth strategies that involve setting up foreign subsidiaries, it is important to make clear that, in this age of so-called globalization, a firm can be a global player without being a multinational, and a multinational enterprise need not operate as if it is in a single, global market. Our definition of a global business is based on the perspective advocated in an influential article written by marketing guru Theodore Levitt in 1983:

> A global business is a firm that seeks to achieve economies of scale and learning curve advantages by offering the same product specification and branding strategy regardless of the country in which it is selling the product; it does not vary the product to make it fit better with local tastes and instead designs it to be functionally adequate whilst offering good value for money.

In these terms a very small firm that sells its products over the Internet could be a global business. Very few large firms actually follow this strategy in its pure form. For example, though McDonald's hamburgers and Honda Accord cars are available on a global basis, it turns out that McDonald's menus are not quite as standardized as legend would have it, whilst a US-market Accord is a bigger, softer-handling car than its European counterpart. Honda is clearly a multinational – the larger, more laid-back US Accord is made in the USA and in Thailand, and the sharp-driving European model is produced in the UK and Japan. But Honda equally clearly is not a global business in Levitt's sense. In a few markets (for example, Australia), Honda even offers customers both types of Accord. A much better example of a large global business would be Nike, yet Nike is not really a multinational manufacturer but rather a US firm that outsources its production to small contractors in low-wage economies around the Pacific Rim.

Of the three kinds of multinational subsidiaries referred to in our definition, it is the second that is the challenging one for economists to explain. The first and third kinds of subsidiaries are essentially examples of the parent firm engaging in vertical integration and should therefore be amenable to explanation in terms of theories covered under that heading in Chapter 9. Amongst the lines of thinking we might employ are thus the following:

- **A firm may invest in a foreign subsidiary to obtain strategic control over supplies of raw materials** whose cost-effective extraction is location-specific but whose delivery cannot be assured via contracts with firms in the overseas economy. Contracts might be problematic if potential suppliers could not be trusted to act in good faith and if the foreign country's legal environment was poorly developed (a common problem for Western firms dealing with the Chinese economy). It might even be the case that there would otherwise be market failure since the economy as a whole was poorly developed and no local suppliers of the product existed at all, or with capabilities on the scale required.

- **Worries about principal–agent problems may deter firms from getting their distribution done by local firms in their foreign markets.** Local firms may lack a long-run commitment to the firm's products if they are involved in distributing those of many businesses. In some cases, they may market them in ways at odds with the firm's long-run plans, or commission pirated versions. They may also be inferior as sources of market intelligence than a subsidiary might be.

- **Multinational vertical integration may be necessary if the firm is to be able to make credible claims about the quality of its products** in the face of difficulties

in doing this via contracts. For example, if fruit comes from your own plantations and is transported in your own ships, you have a bigger chance of ensuring that it is harvested at the best time and not mishandled in transit. Given
the difficulty customers may face in judging the quality of a piece of fruit prior
to peeling it, an international business that controls the production and delivery process may be able to command a premium price for branded fruit and
do major deals with supermarkets for its distribution (as with bananas and
other fresh produce handled by a firm such as Chiquita).

If these kinds of issues do not arise, it is hard to see why a firm would wish to
integrate vertically by setting up a foreign subsidiary, rather than obtaining
inputs from, or exporting with the aid of, established businesses in that country.
The latter have obvious knowledge advantages in respect of language, the legal
system and local culture.

The reason that an overseas manufacturing subsidiary is not an obvious part
of a firm's growth strategy is not merely that it, too, runs into all the local knowledge issues just mentioned. More importantly, it begs a question: why not produce on a large scale from one's home base and export to foreign markets, thereby obtaining a superior cost position in both domestic and foreign markets?
Seemingly obvious answers to this turn out to have problems:

- **Fallacy 1: Foreign subsidiaries are necessary as a means of avoiding uneco-
  nomic transport costs to export markets**. If the product needs to be produced
  close to its customers, having it produced under licence by a local firm in the
  foreign market is a way of achieving this without having to deal with all the
  local knowledge problems (as is done with, say, Coca-Cola).

- **Fallacy 2: Foreign subsidiaries are necessary to get around trade barriers**, such
  as import duties and quota restrictions imposed by governments in foreign
  markets. Here too licensing is a possible alternative strategy, but note that the
  cost disadvantages of licensing need to be compared with the strategy of
  exporting and paying the import duties. One way of mitigating the cost disadvantages of foreign production by a local company is if that firm has spare
  production capacity that can be used, hence achieving economies of scope.
  The 'local' firm in such a position might even be a subsidiary of another
  multinational: for example, during the early 1980s, Nissan Australia had a
  contract to assemble imported kits of Volvo cars for the Australian market.
  (Nowadays, with smaller Australian import duties to contend with, both firms
  simply export to that market, with Nissan sourcing some of its vehicles from
  its UK subsidiary.)

- **Fallacy 3: Foreign subsidiaries are necessary in order to tap into cheap supplies of labour.** This argument might seem particularly important when a product has become commonplace, its technology is widely known and competition is increasingly based on price. Once again, however, an alternative strategy is to involve a producer in the foreign country and contract them to produce it to a particular specification. This is essentially what Nike does: the firm concentrates on design and marketing and has its footwear and apparel products made by a large number of offshore contractors.

- **Fallacy 4: Foreign subsidiaries are necessary in order to hedge or gain leverage against risks associated with changing exchange rates, relative labour costs or political conditions.** Although a firm that has subsidiaries in a number of countries can play them off against each other to gain docile workers or government assistance, a firm that contracts its output out to firms in a number of countries can also make credible threats to change its sourcing policies. If exchange rates move against it, the latter firm can cease sourcing from particular countries when existing contracts come to an end; it has no need to close factories in countries whose exchange rates have risen.

If contractual relationships with foreign firms can be set up to overcome transport cost, trade barrier and cheap labour issues, we should expect to see firms preferring to grow by expanding their domestic production to gain a larger share of their local markets or to obtain economies of scope.

This line of thinking leads us only to expect firms to set up foreign manufacturing subsidiaries when they anticipate or have experienced problems with the contracting alternatives for getting output made in other countries. Such problems mainly relate to the nature of the technology:

- **Quality control issues.** Contractual arrangements may founder if it is difficult to ensure that the contractor produces output of the same quality as the firm can make in its domestic plant. If quality problems arise because of poor management or because the technology is in part subject to tacit knowledge, then it might be easier to set up a foreign subsidiary, run by staff from the parent company, than to change the way a contractor operates. (Note that Honda originally tried to get benefits of having its cars made within what was then the European Community by having some of them made by Rover. By setting up its own UK factory, Honda not only reduced its strategic dependence on the financially fragile Rover company but also achieved superior assembly quality and reduced warranty claims.)

♦ **Leaky technologies.** There may be risks that the technology will leak into the hands of the firm that is granted a licence to use it under its own brand or contracted as a supplier. If the expertise picked up in the life of the contract can be transferred to other products that are not specified in the contract, then the firm whose technology is being used may not only fail to capture revenue from later applications of its knowledge. It may also find itself doing battle with the contractor, who is now using that knowledge to make rival products. The history of British carmaker Austin (latterly Rover) is a chilling example of this. During the 1930s, the Austin Seven small car was made under licence by the firms we now know as BMW and Nissan. After World War II, Austin's cars were made in Japan using its state-of-the-art methods as part of Japan's reconstruction programme. As is shown in an excellent video called 'Japan takes on Detroit', Japanese content was progressively increased as visiting engineers from Austin acted as tutors in technology and signed off the Japanese input as having reached a sufficiently high standard. In the long run, the German and Japanese firms improved upon their automotive industry knowledge faster than the British one did, and their relative fortunes reversed accordingly. A somewhat less risky strategy is to restrict technology transfer contracts to superseded products and tooling/production methods that would otherwise have simply been scrapped.

In the light of this, it is not surprising that multinational manufacturing is particularly common with high technology products. Nor is it surprising that such multinationals tend (particularly in developing countries) to limit the number of foreign workers they hire in senior positions and rotate their own expatriate staff from country to country before they get too comfortable in any particular location: this reduces the risks of local rivals commencing operations, or of losses of key personnel to foreign firms.

14.6 Why do firms charge different prices in different countries?

International price theory is dominated by the theory of purchasing power parity (PPP). Contrary to what many laypeople who have been overseas commonly report as a rough rule of thumb on returning home, the PPP theory does *not* assert that, because of differences in the cost of living, something that costs £1 in London will tend to cost $1 in New York, A$1 in Sydney and NZ$1 in Auckland, etc., or that someone who earns £40 000 a year in London could live just as well on NZ$40 000 in Auckland, etc. Rather, the theory of PPP asserts that if we have free trade and freely floating exchange rates, then when we take a bundle of goods that is internationally traded and compare its price in different countries by using the current exchange rates to convert the prices in different countries into an equivalent price in any one of the countries being compared, the prices should come out pretty much the same for all countries. This prediction is based on the idea that if PPP does not hold then entrepreneurs will buy internationally tradable goods from countries with undervalued currencies and sell them for a profit in countries with overvalued countries. This will put upward pressure on wage rates in the countries with undervalued currencies and the improvement in their balance of trade positions will generate upward pressure on their exchange rates, and vice versa, for the countries with overvalued exchange rates, until PPP is established.

The Economist magazine has been using a simplified way of assessing whether exchange rates are over- or undervalued, which works surprisingly well. Instead of focusing on a basket of goods, *The Economist's* Big Mac index focuses on the international price for a single product, the McDonald's Big Mac, which is available in about 120 countries.

> The Big Mac PPP is defined as the exchange rate that would mean hamburgers cost the same in America as abroad. Comparing actual exchange rates with PPPs indicates whether a currency is under- or overvalued.

Hence, in its 15 January 2004 issue, *The Economist* observed that 'the cheapest burger is in China, at $1.23, compared with an average American price of $2.80. This implies the yuan is 56 per cent undervalued. Relative to its Big Mac PPP the euro is 24 per cent overvalued against the dollar. In contrast, the yen is 12 per cent undervalued.' In the same issue, it was noted that the average US price of a Starbuck's tall latte was also $2.80 and that, in much of the world (Asia is the exception), a Starbuck's latte PPP implies very similar conclusions about which are the over- and undervalued exchange rates. It may seem puzzling that these two simplified ways of looking at PPP approximate the formal approach based on a bundle of goods. After all, both hamburgers and lattes are produced at the point of consumption and are not themselves traded internationally except insofar as international visitors purchase them. However, the important thing to notice is that McDonald's and Starbuck's both have to compete for their labour and other inputs with local firms that do produce internationally tradable products.

Despite the enthusiasm of economists and *The Economist* for the PPP idea, it is often the case that firms charge very different prices in different markets when they export their products. For example, Toyota produces a small car branded as a

Toyota Echo in Australia, New Zealand and the USA, as a Toyota Yaris in Europe and a Toyota Vitz in Japan. The recommended retail prices of a 1.3-litre manual 3-door model of this car differ greatly across markets, as Table 14.2 demonstrates.

Table 14.2 **Prices for a Toyota Echo/Yaris 1.3-litre 3-door manual in selected markets, April 2003**		
Australia	A$14490	(about £5660)
France	€11750	(about £8040)
Ireland	€15575	(about £10660)
New Zealand	NZ$22500	(about £7990)
United Kingdom	£8570	
USA	US$10730	(about £6650)

Note: US figures are for 1.5-litre manual 2-door, the nearest comparable model.

(Source: Toyota websites for the countries in question)

To make sense of this price dispersion requires a more complex analysis than was offered with our first price dispersion example, back in Chapter 2 (Tables 2.2 and 2.3 in Section 2.7). Let us consider critically some potential causes.

Shipping cost differences

These seem unlikely to be significant in this case. The cars are made in France for the European market and in Japan for the rest of the world. It is unlikely that getting a Yaris from France to Ireland costs dramatically more than from France to England. Likewise, New Zealand and Australia do not differ that much in shipping distance from Japan.

Production cost differences

This might be a better candidate as a contributing factor since the three most expensive of the markets sampled are the ones supplied by the Toyota's French factory, which might have lower productivity or higher hourly wage rates than the one in Japan. (The French factory has the advantage of being located in the European Union though, whereas vehicles imported from Japan might be subject to import duties.)

Tax differences

Indirect taxes such as VAT (in Europe) and Goods and Services Tax (in Australasia) do differ but appear unable to explain the width of differences in price in this case. Ireland has 21 per cent VAT, the UK 17.5 per cent and France 19 per cent, whereas GST rates are only 10 per cent in Australia and 12.5 per cent in New Zealand.

Differences in import duties

This explanation is problematic here. There are no duties applicable on French-made Toyotas within the European Union member countries in our sample. New Zealand has abolished import duties on imported motor vehicles and Toyotas imported into Australia are likely to be exempt from import duty because of credits earned by Toyota Australia on its exports of Toyota Camry sedans to the Middle East and New Zealand.

Differences between markets regarding the inclusion of delivery fees and statutory charges in listed prices

It is conceivable that the 'on the road' prices that consumers have to pay are actually less dispersed, because prices in seemingly cheaper countries do not include dealer delivery charges: for example, the Australian price does not include delivery charges of around 6–10 per cent of the list price depending on the dealer.

Differences in product specifications between markets

Since the product is not even a global one in Levitt's sense in terms of its model name, it seems quite likely that price differences to some extent are a reflection of cost differences arising because consumers in different countries are not being offered a globally standardized product. The Australian model is far less well equipped than, say, its UK counterpart, having only a driver's airbag instead of driver, passenger and side airbags, and no anti-lock brake system, with a more Spartan interior that does not even include a clock.

Differences in the product's rivals between markets

Manufacturers may choose their products' specifications partly in order to put them in a price range where they will compete against particular models offered by rivals. In the Australian market, for example, the Toyota Echo's price reflects unique local conditions. It is not priced to compete against better-specified European super-minis, such as the Renault Clio and Peugeot 206, which typically cost at least a third more. Rather, it is pitted against bottom-range Korean cars that have less of a stigma with buyers than they do in European markets and which are similarly poorly equipped with safety features. If the Australian price were higher, not only would this mean that Toyota abandoned that segment to the Korean products but also the Echo would then have trouble winning customers. This is because Toyota Australia's larger cars are also much cheaper than in Europe – again in stripped down form – in order to be priced below the even bigger, locally designed Ford Falcon and Holden Commodore products that dominate this market. The US market is likely to be similarly affected by the relative cheapness of large cars compared with those in European markets. For New Zealand, by contrast, the problem at the lower end of the market is not so much one of fending off Korean cars but of keeping buyers interested in buying a cheap new car at all in a market flooded with low-mileage used cars imported from Japan.

Customers differ between countries in their willingness to pay

Even if none of the factors already considered had a role to play, differences in price between markets could simply represent an example of **third-degree price discrimination** (see Section 7.4.4). In other words, Toyota could be making the most of differences in willingness to pay for its cars in these different markets. Price discrimination of this kind will be unworkable if other entrepreneurs can engage in **arbitrage** between cheap and expensive markets, or if consumers from expensive markets can visit (in person, or 'virtually' as Internet shoppers) cheaper markets at low cost. With products such as cars, manufacturers can discriminate against British and Irish consumers relatively easily because the rest of Europe drives left-hand-drive vehicles and firms can limit the supply of right-hand-drive ones to dealers on mainland Europe. Manufacturers may also discourage personal imports by limiting warranty rights of consumers in such cases. In many countries manufacturers have lobbied governments to make entrepreneurs' arbitrage activities problematic with laws against this practice, which is known as **parallel importing**.

Such lobbying tends to be couched in terms of the long-run interests of consumers, who might find it difficult to get adequate after-sales service on foreign-specification products for which the manufacturers' official dealer networks do not carry spare parts, particularly if the dealer network shrinks due to reduced sales of new products. This argument is far from convincing. It certainly would not convince economists with first-hand experience of New Zealand, the country that pioneered an import free-for-all including both outright parallel importing (for example, of televisions) and the importation of near-new products as diverse as cars and skiing equipment. As one might expect in the age of email, fax machines and airfreight, specialist spare parts importers soon filled voids that manufacturers' official distribution networks failed to fill. Within a few years, car insurance no longer carried penalty rates for used imports and manufacturers' official dealers had become willing and able to maintain vehicles that had never been sold brand-new in New Zealand. Lessons learned in this context seem to have been applied in the UK, albeit on a smaller scale relative to the size of the new vehicle market, with the rise of a so-called 'grey market' for used imports in the late 1990s.

14.7 What should a firm do when exchange rates change?

Consider the plight of a British firm whose products have marginal costs of £100. It had been basing its pricing decisions in March 2002 in its US export market on marginal costs of $100/0.70 = $142.85. If this firm had constant marginal costs they would equal average variable costs, and if the US price that had been chosen were, say, $199.95 per unit, then the firm's gross margin on its US sales would be $57.10. Two years later, with the US dollar only buying £0.53, its revenue per unit would only be £105.81, leaving a gross margin of only £5.81. What should the firm do next if it has not insured its expected revenue in the manner described in Section 14.4? Clearly, the firm should not abandon its US market, for at its established US price sales still make a contribution to covering fixed costs. But should it change its price to try to wring more profit out of the US market?

If you reflect on this question in the light of the theories covered in Chapter 7, it should be clear that its answer depends not just on the price elasticity of demand for its product but also on how the firm expects its competitors to behave. It could well be the case that the least bad solution is to take a reduction in profit margins and leave the US price as it is. For example, from the standpoint of the heterodox **mark-up analysis of pricing**, the firm's choice of a price of $199.95 in the US market might not have been made on the basis of marginal revenue = marginal cost calculations, but rather on the basis that this is the price that US firms are charging for this kind of product because it fits in well with simple customer decision rules ('no more than $200') whilst not generating a rate of return so large as to attract entry. On this way of thinking, $199.95 is the highest price the firm should charge, both before and after the fall in the value of the dollar.

If the value of sterling instead falls against the US dollar, the firm will not wish to spark off a price war unless the rise in its profit margin seems likely to attract others to try to make a profit by exporting to the US market. There might also be the strategic risk of US producers lobbying for protection if they were no longer able to compete against imports, so the UK exporter would have a further reason simply to take a higher profit margin rather than cut prices.

A different way for firms to react when exchange rates affect the profitability of their export markets is in terms of their strategy of **non-price competition**. A price increase to restore profit margins in an export market whose currency has depreciated might attract the attention of customers there and lose sales in cases where it would take a firm's product outside customer budget ranges. However, the firm might get away with a downgrading of the product's specification if customers either do not notice or still judge the product as adequate in terms of their decision rules because previously it was in some ways offering more than their minimum requirements. Conversely, when the domestic currency falls relative to currencies of export markets, exporters may opt to make life difficult for the local opposition in those markets not by cutting prices but by offering more features as standard or by upgrading performance on particular dimensions. Notice here that the marginal cost of doing this is not merely the cost of adding the features to each extra unit sold due to the rightward shift of the product's demand curve as it fits better into customer decision rules in the export market. It also includes the cost of providing these features to customers in the export market who would have bought the product anyway at the existing price. Figure 14.2 illustrates this for the simple case of constant marginal costs, where marginal cost = average variable costs. For a specification upgrade to be profitable in the export market, price unchanged, as sales expand from Q to Q`, the blue shaded area must be bigger than the black shaded area.

Opportunity costs of exports to one market rather than another, and the likely permanence of exchange rate changes, need to be considered very carefully in situations such as our hypothetical example of the falling US dollar greatly squeezing a British firm's profit margins on exports to the USA. Like any market for a firm's products, export markets cannot be tapped into instantaneously and without marketing costs being incurred. Instead, they have to be fought for

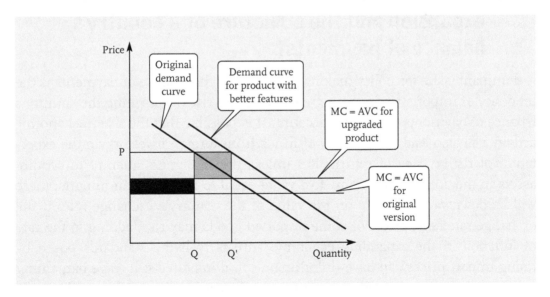

Figure 14.2 Profitability of a product upgrade

and goodwill ties developed with overseas customers and distributors. A decision to pull out of a market on the basis that the firm's marketing efforts could yield higher returns elsewhere (for example, by trying to increase market share in a country whose currency has not fallen sharply against one's domestic currency) may be difficult to reverse because of the damage it would do to customer and distributor goodwill. If the firm has long-term intentions to sell in the country whose exchange rate has depreciated sharply, it may be a wise investment to keep offering its products there despite meagre profit margins (or possibly even with prices less than average variable costs if the country's exchange rate is expected to recover); in this way, the firm trades off poor current profits against the costs of having to invest in a re-launch of its products in future to recover goodwill.

The same Marshallian line of thinking applies when there are shifts in the pressure of demand between different countries' markets: a firm should not abandon one market simply because it has become temporarily easier to sell in another. Unexpectedly rapid growth of demand in any of the markets in which a firm sells its products can be problematic if it causes' the firm to run out of spare capacity and put customers on waiting lists. This may give rivals from other countries the chance to get a foothold much more easily than they otherwise might have done. When demand later dampens down, the new competitors are unlikely to withdraw, so the firm will suffer a loss of sales rather than a recovery of its market share.

14.8 What is the relationship between economic expansion and the structure of a country's balance of payments?

A dominant issue for policy making in respect of the balance of payments is the tendency of imports to rise as aggregate demand rises, worsening the country's balance of payments on current account. It is possible that the rise in economic activity will also lead to an inflow of funds from foreign investors on the expectation of rising rates of return. But unless the foreigners attempt to acquire assets in the domestic economy to a value equal to its growth in imports, there will be downward pressure on the value of the country's exchange rate. If the exchange rate falls, prices of some imported goods may rise, adding to the rate of inflation in the expanding economy. Threats to living standards posed by rising import prices can have unfortunate spiralling effects: if wage bargaining processes increasingly turn sour, strike action may disrupt the flow of domestic output, leading to lost imports and substitution in favour of even more imports.

If the government wishes to prevent rising imports from having an inflationary impact it can increase official interest rates and thereby increase the capital inflow and reduce downward pressure on the exchange rate. Such a rise in the rate of interest may also dampen aggregate demand and may even add to cost-push inflationary pressures to the extent that borrowing costs figure in firms' cost structures. With or without an interest rate rise, the expansion of activity will increase the country's foreign indebtedness by the amount of the net expansion of imports.

One way of preventing increased aggregate demand from sucking in imports would be for the government to introduce **import controls**, such as import licences, quotas or foreign exchange controls, which would only allow imports to increase if exports rose and made more foreign exchange available. This kind of heterodox strategy was long advocated by members of the Cambridge Economic Policy Group in the 1970s and 1980s, but there seems to be little chance of it being selected as a policy in today's environment, where membership of the World Trade Organization carries obligations to dismantle any barriers to trade (see also Section 14.11).

14.8.1 Export-led growth

Implied in what we have just said is a rather happier story of the relationship between economic expansion and the balance of payments, namely, that of those countries whose exports boom because they produce goods with highly income-elastic demands from other nations. Nations such as Japan that produce such goods will have rising GDPs when the rest of the world is expanding, but since their increases in GDP are driven by the injection of export demand they enjoy an improvement in their current account balances. Their imports will indeed increase but not by as much as their exports, since there will also be leakages from the expanded circular flow of income into saving and taxation.

Countries enjoying export-led growth will experience rising exchange rates unless their consumers and businesses tend to increase their acquisition of foreign assets at the same rate as the net increase in export demand. This makes it much easier to manage inflation compared with the situation in trading partners whose exchange rates are falling. Although the profit margins on exports by domestic firms appear to be threatened by increases in the value of the domestic currency compared with currencies of export markets, learning effects in production processes that raise their productivity should mitigate this. Probably of more importance for profits is the ability of governments of nations enjoying export-led growth to avoid having to step on the economic brakes with higher interest rates, in contrast to their counterparts in nations suffering unduly from growth-led imports. A combination of learning effects and the reinvestment of healthy levels of profits contributes to a virtuous circle of export-led growth based on the continual development of leading-edge products. Firms producing goods that have highly income-elastic export demands may also be enjoying rising brand equity to the extent that their products come to symbolize economic success and may thus be able to increase their prices in export markets whose currency values have fallen. By contrast, production capacity may grow falteringly in countries suffering from growth-led imports and stop/go macroeconomic management, with innovation trailing, so that any expansion of demand is prone to give rise to waiting lists locally and suck in more imports. The latter was essentially the fate of the British economy during much of the second half of the last century.

14.8.2 Export-led unemployment – 'the Dutch disease'

A different kind of export-based expansion in wealth is where a country discovers it has a natural resource that is internationally valuable, such as oil or natural gas. This can be a mixed blessing if macroeconomic policies are not adapted accordingly. Economists have coined the term 'the Dutch disease' to indicate the downside of booming resource exports for domestic manufacturing enterprises. The term is a reminder of what happened in the Netherlands in the 1970s when exports of North Sea gas boomed and the country's exchange rate appreciated. Oil and gas extraction can generate enormous export earnings without employing many people, but if they push the exchange rate up, firms in the rest of the economy that produce internationally tradable products may be driven out of business unless their output consists of leading-edge products with income-elastic demands. Local industry will have a better chance of surviving if the government creams off much of the export revenue from the resource via a **resource-rent tax** and then invests the proceeds overseas. This is essentially what the Norwegian government is doing with that country's North Sea oil revenue. Such a combination of policies limits the appreciation of the exchange rate whilst providing a source of investment income for the future when the natural resource is depleted.

14.8.3 Spiralling foreign debt

A country that persistently runs a current account deficit will be building up its foreign indebtedness via the offsetting capital/financial account surplus. It is the latter surplus that prevents its exchange rate from falling further and inducing changes in relative prices of imports and exports to eliminate the current account deficit. The situation is rather like that of a household that keeps spending more than it earns and is able to keep paying its bills because its bank keeps giving it a vote of confidence by upping its spending limit on its credit cards and/or granting a credit-line mortgage that enables consumption to be paid for by running down equity in the house (recall Box 13.1 in Chapter 13). If the bank were not so keen to make money by encouraging such borrowing, the household would have to rein in its consumption.

As we shall see in the next section, economists are divided about whether alarm bells should be sounded when a country is seen to keep piling up foreign debt year after year: should the exemplar be Argentina's recent economic crisis, or the apparently unending ability of the USA to keep writing out IOUs to the rest of the world? Something that might make us particularly nervous is the possibility that a country may start borrowing more and more from overseas each year to meet interest obligations incurred in previous years. Such a ploy is known in monetary economics as **Ponzi financing**, after Charles Ponzi, a Boston (US) 'financial wizard'. For a time Ponzi succeeded in attracting investors by his ability to honour his promises of spectacularly high returns. The trouble was, he did so by using deposits received from new investors to pay interest to existing ones. Eventually, of course, it all fell down like a house of cards when he was unable to attract enough new deposits to pay the interest due on existing ones. This was very like what happens when people start using cash advances on one credit card to make minimum payments on other credit cards and eventually find it hard to get any more credit cards to keep the process going.

At the macroeconomic level, Ponzi financing might generate the following kind of spiral. Suppose the level of GDP in 2005 is £1000 billion and that inflows in the balance of payments current account are £260 billion and outflows are £300 billion. If so, the country must make net borrowing of £40 billion from overseas this year to make the balance of payments balance. If the rate of interest is 5 per cent, then in 2006 the current account will tend to worsen by £2 billion as interest is paid on the money borrowed this year. In 2006, therefore, foreign debt will have to grow by a further £42 billion unless the current account balance improves. The extra borrowing will lead to an outflow in 2007 that is £2.1 billion higher, in other words, £44.1 billion. If things continue at this rate, by 2010 the current account deficit will be £51 billion and rising. The obvious question is, should this be a cause for concern, given that at the micro-level Ponzi financing tends to end in disaster sooner or later? (In the case of credit cards being used to pay interest on other credit cards, rates of interest in the vicinity of 20 per cent can cause payment problems to escalate very quickly.)

14.9 Can market forces stop growing foreign indebtedness from becoming a problem?

If a county's entrepreneurs are not seen to be increasing net exports rapidly enough to prevent the current account deficit from rising as a percentage of GDP, players in financial markets ought to be extrapolating to see where things might be heading. With the kind of figures in the scenario just outlined, it would take only a couple of decades, starting from a position of zero net foreign indebtedness, for the country's net foreign debt to equal its GDP. At that stage, and with interest rates at 5 per cent, to stop debt from growing further next year would require an expansion in net exports of 5 per cent of GDP. Economic growth of 5 per cent might do the trick, provided that export markets could be found on such a scale. Otherwise, a cut in imports would be necessary. Given a fractional **marginal propensity to import**, this would require a multiple cut in domestic income and consumption. (For, example, if a quarter of marginal income ends up leaking out in imports, then it would be necessary to cut income by four times the desired reduction in imports.) Even more dramatic expansions of net exports or cuts in consumption would be required in future years if, for the moment, the economy simply carried on its trajectory and world financial markets poured in more money, like Ponzi's depositors initially did.

Such a scenario implies a question for practising business economists: at what stage should they start worrying that the foreign debt of a country in which their firms operate, or in whose market their firms sell, is reaching levels that pose some kind of threat to their business? In terms of analogies with household debt, no particular answer is obvious. After all, banks used to be willing to let households borrow two-and-a-half times the primary earner's salary to buy a property, but nowadays loans of three times the joint household income may be granted, along with credit cards. If households could have intergenerational mortgages, even bigger income/debt ratios might be perfectly possible. From this standpoint, our 1:1 GDP/net foreign debt scenario starts looking less worrying.

Mainstream economists tend to believe that if market forces are left to function without being distorted by government controls then relative price adjustments will ensure that economies that build up substantial foreign debts do not end up in states of crisis due to an inability to generate enough foreign exchange to meet interest and repayment obligations. They would thus take a relaxed view of countries such as the USA, UK, Australia and New Zealand with both ongoing current account deficits and policies aimed at improving market efficiency.

The key elements in the relaxed mainstream perspective seem to be as follows:

+ While an economy as a whole may appear to be indulging in Ponzi financing, the loans that comprise the capital inflow from overseas are not being drawn in by Ponzi-style ploys; rather, they largely involve regular cases of credit-worthy private sector clients raising money from willing lenders.

+ If some countries are running current account deficits and needing to borrow from overseas, then other countries must be running current account surpluses and have funds that they will want to lend out.

+ A country whose net international indebtedness grows each year by a larger amount might have, or soon expect to have, a GDP that on average is rising even more rapidly. Indeed, the borrowing from the rest of the world may be funding investment activity that produces precisely this expansion of output. If so, current generations of spenders may well be giving their descendants the equivalent of an intergenerational mortgage, but they are also putting them in a position where they will be able both to service the debt and to consume more than they could otherwise have done.

+ As emphasized at the end of Section 14.3, capital flows depend on what investors and speculators expect earnings in overseas currency to be *and* on their expected gains/losses from currency movements. Given this incentive to assess the risk of exchange rate changes, they will be motivated to examine how rapidly firms in the debtor economy are increasing net exports. If their investigations make them nervous, they will cease to make their funds available to the economy and there will be downward pressure on the exchange rate. This will reduce real wages in the debtor economy and bring about the adjustment of relative prices of imports and exports such that the current account deficit decreases or turns into a surplus. Although individual lenders may not have the time or expertise to make such assessments themselves, they can call upon the expertise of international credit rating agencies such as Moody's or Standard & Poor's. That they do so is evident in the impact that changes in international credit ratings by such agencies have on exchange rates. All in all, it seems easier for lenders to get a good idea of the overall debt position of an economy than it is for them to know for sure just how many sources of finance an opportunistic problem debtor has already tapped. This should enable them to avoid losses due to lending on projects that would come out fine so long as current exchange rates persisted but which would be untenable in the event of a major collapse in the exchange rate.

- Rational overseas lenders will recognize that the future course of the exchange rate is crucial to determining whether or not a micro-level loan arrangement is going to work out happily. For example, someone overseas who buys shares in a formerly state-owned enterprise in the domestic economy ought to be aware that the dividend streams and share values in terms of the overseas currency could be harmed if the value of the domestic currency fell. Fears that they have about the possibility of a fall in the currency should lead them to reduce the amount that they are prepared to pay for such shares and to build risk premiums into the interest rates they charge on any loans to that country.

- Prudent borrowers will likewise steer clear of overseas sources of funds if there is the risk of a fall in their country's exchange rate. Borrowing overseas may seem much cheaper in terms of interest rates but could prove very expensive if a fall in the value of the domestic currency increases the cost of both principal and interest payments in terms of domestic currency.

- Governments will be wary of stepping up their foreign borrowing even if they know they can, in effect, always 'print' domestic currency to pay for their debts. Their problem is that they cannot print foreign currency. Attempts to fund overseas debts via credit creation may produce a collapse in the exchange rate when they try to buy foreign currency, thereby ruining their attempts to keep inflation under control and generally jeopardizing their prospects of being re-elected.

In sum, this view of foreign debt adopts what is called a **rational expectations** perspective in that it presumes that decision making is based on assessments of credit risks and of the national economy's prospects that are on average correct. If these sorts of conditions hold, the main role for government involvement seems to be in terms of making it easier for the economy to expand exports in response to changing incentives. It will not be necessary for governments to seek to shape the foreign debt trajectories of their economies.

Heterodox economists, on the other hand, suggest that attention needs to be given to the following areas, which should make managers wary about the foreign indebtedness of the countries in whose markets their firms operate:

- Debts denominated in overseas currencies may prove very hard to service if there is speculation against the domestic currency, leading to a fall in its value. Inability to repay foreign loans may then lead to bankruptcies of domestic firms and falling demand. This is essentially how the Asian economic crisis of 1997 started: borrowers in Thailand were unable to pay back loans denominated in US dollars owing to the appreciation of the value of the dollar against the local currency.

- For errors not to be made, borrowers and lenders need to have a good idea of the likely responses of imports and exports to changes in the exchange rate. If economists do not agree about adjustment speeds or the ways in which processes of resource allocation are likely to operate in response to changing exchange rates, it is difficult to see how rational expectations can be formed about the outlook for net export earnings. If the financial community is unduly optimistic, lending could carry on too far, with too high an exchange rate to encourage domestic capacity expansion rather than debt-financed consumption, until there was a major loss of nerve and a fall in the currency.

- It is by no means clear that borrowers and lenders are as canny as the mainstream analysis seems to require. Given that the use of offshore sources of funds and offshore customers for credit is a rather new activity for many, we may expect people to make errors due to inexperience and a lack of workable decision rules.

- The strength of aggregate demand and the viability of the banking system in a country with mounting foreign debts also depend on how well ordinary consumers appreciate what is going on. If the country's exchange rate collapses in a way that comes as a major surprise to its population, severe **wealth effects** could ensue. Rising prices on essential items that have to be imported (for example, oil) could leave heavily indebted consumers unable keep up the repayments on their mortgages, car loans, hire purchase and so on. Defaults in turn would generate falling asset prices and banks could find their reserve positions being wiped out. More generally, a reduction in real wages caused by a rise in import prices could generate unemployment due to a reduction in demand for local output ahead of any turn around in export demand.

- If debtor nations are to repay their foreign debts they must do more than achieve current account balance; they must actually achieve current account surpluses. This means that their improvements must come at the expense of other debtor nations falling even further into debt or nations with current account surpluses beginning to run deficits. So long as the international financial system does not punish nations that persistently run current account surpluses, such nations may be reluctant to do anything that will help the debtor nations achieve surpluses.

- Psychology is relevant too: awareness that one has a problem tends to come only suddenly, possibly after years of ignoring warnings, and then produces a major reaction, such as panic. People today may be kidding themselves that their country does not need major currency depreciation because it is too troubling to face up to the consequences. Particular pieces of news can serve as a wake-up call, at least to the international currency traders, producing a major jolt. A case in point is Australia in 1986 when the then Treasurer, Paul Keating, captured international attention with a speech saying that the country was no longer the 'lucky country' it presumed itself to be, but rather a nation well on the way to becoming something akin to a Latin American 'banana republic' due to its escalating overseas debts (between 1978 and 1986 net foreign indebtedness as a percentage of GDP had rocketed from about 6 per cent to 32 per cent). The Australian dollar promptly fell in value by about a third. This caused major problems for some firms and public utilities that had borrowed overseas and suddenly found they owed much more in terms of Australian dollars. Note here the role of **attention**: currency traders, like the rest of us, suffer from **bounded rationality** and tend to focus on particular economies more than others at any moment, shifting their focus around the world depending on which news stories stand out.

Heterodox pessimism about the rationality of processes that determine exchange rates and international indebtedness may well seem justified in the light of the way that exchange rates move around (recall Table 14.1). Such volatility hardly seems consistent with foreign exchange traders taking a firmly grounded view of relative national 'economic fundamentals' rather than engaging in casino-style movement trading.

14.10 Why do current account deficits persist even after currency depreciations?

Even if heterodox economists put aside their worries about the speculative aspect of exchange rate determination, they have another reason for worrying about reliance on exchange rate movements for correcting dangerous current account deficits. Exchange rate depreciations have a poor record as devices for reducing balance of payments deficits and countries whose exchange rates appreciate because of strong export performances often continue to enjoy balance of payments surpluses. This should not be surprising if exporters do not change their export prices in terms of foreign currency (see Section 14.7). It is even less surprising from the standpoint of heterodox perspectives on decision making. From that perspective, a country that is losing net exports could be doing so because the products that its manufacturers offer are increasingly failing to match up to the standards required by the decision rules of buyers at home and overseas. If so, making the products cheaper will not solve the problem. For example, if consumers are specifying longer checklists of requirements after seeing what they can now reasonably expect to get from modern products, the firms that are falling behind need to recognize this and find ways of adding the extra features to their products. Making them cheaper without adding the extra features will not win sales if decision rules are rejecting them on non-price grounds, unless price reductions are so great as to make the outdated products available to customers who previously could not afford them and who still cannot afford the 'state-of-the art' products. The same arguments hold in respect of non-price dimensions where customers have noticed that they can now reasonably expect to find higher levels of performance without failing to meet their other aspirations.

The kind of scenario just outlined provides a plausible way of explaining the dismal slide in the UK's international competitiveness against countries such as Germany and Japan during the 1970s and 1980s. This loss of international market share by the UK was sufficiently bad to provoke suggestions that a process of **'de-industrialization'** was under way despite sterling falling in value. **'Non-price factors'** came into the trade literature around that time, but they were raised in terms of a trade-off approach to choices between the bundles of characteristics of which products were comprised, not in terms of intolerant checklists and priority rankings. Because of this, the remedy seemed to be a larger depreciation of sterling on the basis that 'if you can't sell good goods, sell cheap goods'. A strategy of encouraging currency depreciation and helping firms to retreat down-market does not seem particularly wise, however, if the market for 'cheap goods' is growing much less rapidly than the income-elastic market for 'good goods'. It could also founder due to the country's firms facing competition from newly industrializing countries whose products are even cheaper and whose standards are improving rapidly.

If a widespread use of checklist-style decision rules is indeed causing a country's loss of net exports, the depreciation of its currency can still help local producers recover their position and help to prevent further deterioration of the country's balance of payments. The mechanism is more tenuous, however, and works via the currency depreciation providing firms with larger profit margins on sales achieved from *existing* customers with less demanding non-price requirements. The profits can then be used to fund investment in product upgrades or they can be spent, so to speak, on bolting extra features on to the product as standard fittings to win more customers. However, to the extent that a product is out of date in some core senses and the former route has to be used to restore sales, the results will take some time to occur, particularly if the firms in question have to develop new capabilities in research and development. (For example, extra airbags may be easy to add to a car and may win those customers whose decision rules involve a count of airbags as a test for safety. But if the underlying structure of the car is out of date, the airbags may do very little to improve its safety rating in a New Car Assessment Programme (NCAP). If it still only has, say, a three-star NCAP rating, it will fail to win customers whose checklists nowadays require it to have a minimum four- or five-star NCAP rating.) There is also no guarantee that firms will actually use the revived profitability as a basis for rejuvenation rather than as a cushion against change.

The heterodox approach to the decision making leads its adherents to the view that if a government wishes to change the structure of its country's balance of payments away from a current account deficit, then it may be better to look to other policies rather than relying on exchange rate changes – particularly policies that will help local firms develop new capabilities. The trick is to come up with a policy package that gives firms a chance to develop better products and production methods by offering them protection from currently stronger rivals, but to do so without making their environments so cosy that they take it easy. Thus if a government offers a policy package based on import controls, industrial subsidies, improved export credit guarantee provisions, tariffs, quotas and bureaucratic barriers to imports, then it must also ensure there is strong rivalry between the local firms that the package is designed to assist. For example, consider a strat-egy that allows a local manufacturer to source some of its product range overseas without paying import duties so long as it earns offsetting export credits. This gives local firms an incentive to produce world-class export products in order to try to get a competitive edge in the local market – not merely against foreign rivals that have to pay import duties on all their products, but also against local rivals. (This kind of strategy was a major element in the transformation of the Australian car industry into a major export earner during the past decade.) Many developing countries got into a mess in the past because their protectionist policies isolated local firms from international competition without forcing them to compete strongly amongst themselves. But lessons can be learnt from Japan and Korea, whose growth was based on interventionist policies that did not stifle local competition.

14.11 What is the orthodox medicine for countries facing a balance of payments crisis?

An inescapable factor in the current international business environment is the push by the World Trade Organization (WTO) towards global free trade, unhindered by import duties, quotas, licensing requirements and so-called 'non-tariff trade barriers' such as nationally distinctive product safety and environmental standards or agricultural quarantine rules. The WTO's perspective on the merits of free trade is similar to thinking at the International Monetary Fund and the World Bank that shapes the kinds of policy packages imposed upon governments seeking to borrow money while they deal with balance of payments problems. That these countries might find themselves in a mess is not seen as a sign that there is something wrong with the view that rational economic actors in freely functioning markets will prevent foreign debt problems from getting out of control. Rather, their problems are seen as symptoms of markets that have not been allowed to work properly over long periods.

Rescue packages designed by mainstream economists at the IMF and World Bank typically entail the following measures as a precondition for funds:

- Removal/reduction of export subsidies, import controls and tariff barriers.
- Removal/reduction of controls over investment by foreign firms.
- Cuts in public expenditure.
- Privatization of state enterprises and public utilities.
- Removal/reduction of industrial regulations (for example, limits to entry).
- 'Reform' of the labour market.
- A 'tight money' policy to squeeze inflation out of the economy, which both forces firms to find more efficient ways of doing things and enables price signals to work more effectively.

The stringency of such packages sometimes results in would-be borrowers implementing their own reform packages and trying to raise funds from the international capital market with fewer strings attached.

The freeing up of international trade involved in these policy packages is unilateral. This is the case even if a poor country has previously erected import controls to try to deal with balance of payments problems that its government saw as being due largely to import barriers against its products imposed by rich countries. According to the orthodox view, the poor country is supposed to be able to make itself better off by removing the protection.

To see how this line of argument works, consider the case of a small economy that has excellent natural resources and skills in producing primary products but whose government has been trying to develop a manufacturing sector by a variety of import control measures. In the case of its motor vehicles sector, punitive tariffs and quotas can be avoided so long as a vehicle's import content is no more than 60 per cent of what its price would be if it were fully imported. As a result, a number of manufacturers have set up small assembly plants and are trying to contain production costs by making some parts locally and importing the rest. At current exchange rates, a car that would have a total foreign exchange cost (including transport charges and insurance whilst in transit) of $20 000 can only be delivered in locally assembled form if the manufacturers receive $32 000. The 60 per cent difference in local price is, however, only the nominal excess cost. The saving on imports from assembling the car locally is 40 per cent of $20 000, in other words, $8000, but the import bill is still $12 000. If it costs $20 000 in domestic resources (i.e. $32 000 – $12 000) to save $8000 of imports, the ratio of domestic to international costs is 250 per cent on a net basis. If the country were not tying its resources up inefficiently in small-scale local manufacturing/ assembly operations, they could be used to produce for export the kinds of goods and services that it is relatively good at producing.

The WTO/World Bank/IMF approach is very much an application of the **comparative advantage theory** of the gains from specialization and trade. Its basic message is that even if a country is incompetent/disadvantaged or otherwise of low productivity in every sector, it is still worth specializing in doing the things it is best at doing in terms of relative opportunity cost. Consider the following highly simplified case, in which there are only two sectors and Country A has lower productivity than Country B in both of them, and where per unit labour costs are the only production costs:

	Shirts	Kiwifruit
	Labour units per unit of output (dollar cost of labour)	
Country A	10 (100)	2.5 (25)
Country B	1 (7)	2.0 (14)

If Country A gives up one domestic shirt it can produce an extra four trays of kiwifruit and if Country B gives up one domestically grown tray of kiwifruit it can produce an extra two shirts. Scope for both countries to improve their positions seems obvious. However, if relative wages are not right, we may have a problem due to Country B's absolute advantage in both sectors. If Country A's hourly wage rate is $10 per hour and workers in Country B, at current exchange rates, receive $7 per hour, then Country A would be comprehensively undercut in both markets, as the bracketed figures show. (It is interesting to reflect on this in relation to the emergence of China as a rapidly growing exporter of industrial products: see Box 14.1.) The attractions of producing in Country B would mean that it would then run into a labour shortage. This would push up wage rates and/or produce a trade surplus which would push up its exchange rate, and vice versa, for Country A.

Box 14.1 The China question

In the past decade, China has become a force to be reckoned with in international trade in manufactured goods. If China continues on its present growth path it could become the world's largest economy within two decades. Its success is partly due to the increased liberalization of world trade, fostered by the WTO. But its increasing economic power may turn out to be a test case for the theory of comparative advantage and its assumption that free trade is mutually beneficial to those that engage in it. With a population of 1.2 billion, most of whom still live in the countryside, China has a huge reserve of labour that could be redeployed into manufacturing if its agricultural sector were modernized. Its workers are educated and keenly motivated. They are also poorly paid and under the tight discipline of the authorities. All this sounds like a recipe for China's growth to be based on absolute advantage, not comparative advantage, in international trade. To be sure, upward pressures on the value of its currency is coming from a huge export surplus and inflowing capital from Western firms that are eager to make use of its pool of cheap labour and growing domestic market. But so long as the government can restrain domestic consumption growth and so long as the export earnings are fed back to the rest of the world through the purchase of overseas assets, the currency could be held down and China's current account surplus could persist just as Japan's has done. What might then emerge is a situation in which countries with higher wages suffer from de-industrialization, because their factories cannot compete with products produced in China and their firms increasingly locate production in China. In turn, social security payments to unemployed workers could force governments to run up deficits that China then financed by purchasing of their bonds.

For example, if Country B's wages rise to $20 and Country A's wages stay at $10 per hour, the trade-offs become as follows:

| | Shirts | Kiwifruit |
	Labour units per unit of output (dollar cost of labour)	
Country A	10 (100)	2.5 (25)
Country B	1 (20)	2.0 (40)

If the world price of both products is $30, then firms in Country A would not produce shirts unless these had a tariff of at least $90 when imported from overseas, for a $120 price per shirt is needed in Country A to cover production costs and generate a profit at least as good as can be obtained on kiwifruit production for export (i.e. a profit of $20, which is what the four trays that have to be foregone would have generated on the basis of $5 profits (i.e. $30 − $25) per tray). With no tariff on shirts, Country A will concentrate on producing kiwifruit for the export market and be far better off in terms of foreign exchange: each shirt it refrains from producing enables it to earn $120 in foreign exchange from kiwifruit exports, enough to import four shirts. Likewise, Country B will not produce kiwifruit unless there is a tariff on imported kiwifruit of $30 per tray. Kiwifruit grown in Country B must give $20 per tray profit to be attractive to produce in Country B when its shirts sold for export yield $10 profit (i.e. $30 − $20), since each tray involves the sacrifice of two shirts and two lots of $10 shirt profits through the use of $40 of Country B's labour. If kiwifruit sells in Country B for $60 per tray including the tariff, producers in Country B will be indifferent about selling it there or to the rest of the world since either way they receive $30 in foreign exchange. If Country B removes such a tariff on imported kiwifruit, each tray of kiwifruit that its firms refrain from producing enables two more shirts to be exported, generating enough foreign exchange to pay for two trays of imported kiwifruit.

From this line of argument, in terms of the theory of comparative advantage, we can see that unilateral moves towards free trade can make sense in a world that still has many tariffs. Though such moves may wipe out some domestic industries, they may liberate resources that could be used to generate more foreign exchange by being switched to other lines of production. The crucial external requirement appears to be that overseas tariffs are low enough and overseas demand high enough to permit sales that produce such net increases in foreign currency earnings.

New Zealand provides the most striking example of a country following this line of thinking. The change to free-trade policies from 1984 onwards led to the demise of New Zealand's car and television assembly industries and the relocation of much production offshore by its manufacturers of clothing and footwear. The benefits were less immediately obvious in this case, for New Zealand's balance of payments remained strongly in deficit and its economic growth was sluggish.

Such an outcome is of little surprise to heterodox economists, for they see the WTO/World Bank/IMF perspective and policy package as flawed:

- Comparative advantage theory assumes full employment before and after the removal of tariffs. If there is substantial unemployment before tariffs are removed, it is not obvious that import substitution activities are hampering the expansion of attempts to increase production for export unless both areas involve a similar set of skills not possessed by the unemployed. If the resources 'inefficiently' used in import substitution industries end up being unemployed when tariffs are removed, there may be considerable social costs. There may also be a net loss in foreign exchange revenue if export activities fail to expand and thereby absorb the displaced workers, unless the inefficiency had been so perverse as to entail imported kits for local assembly being more expensive than fully finished products in terms of foreign exchange costs. (This perverse case is said to have applied sometimes in New Zealand before 1984, for example, in the television market.) Perverse cases aside, employing workers 'inefficiently' may be far more efficient in terms of national well-being than not employing them at all. It should not be surprising that the reallocation of workers between sectors may be painfully slow. For example, people who have been assembling cars or making, say, wiring looms as part of local content of cars may have skills that are very distant from those in areas where natural resources seem to indicate a comparative advantage, such as primary production or tourism.

- Comparative advantage theory is static in the sense that it focuses on current differences in opportunity costs, not potential ones. As we have been emphasizing when talking about the evolution of firms, new **capabilities** can be developed. Indeed, as the economic histories of Japan and Korea illustrate, if virtuous circle processes of cumulative causation are at work there may be strategic advantages to be had from choosing to cultivate particular industries where potential to achieve dynamic economies of scale is considerable. To protect an industry now may indeed involve a net cost in terms of current foreign exchange at the start, but in future it may be the means to achieving higher earnings.

- Privatization and tight money policies hinder the absorption of labour displaced from the import substitution activities when they are closed down and exacerbate the current account deficit by generating capital inflows and push up the value of the domestic currency. The inflows come to the extent that foreign parties purchase assets of newly privatized enterprises and/or because the tight money policy pulls domestic interest rates above real rates of interest elsewhere, leading foreigners to place money in domestic banks or to buy domestic securities. Local firms and other borrowers will be induced to seek cheaper sources of finance offshore and when they try to turn their foreign exchange loans into domestic currency they too will be pushing up demand for it. The rise in the value of the domestic currency will make it less attractive for domestic firms to supply exports and more attractive to import overseas items, increasing supplies of domestic currency and demands for overseas currencies until the market balances.

- If public expenditure cuts include reduced education and infrastructure spending, this may harm productivity growth.

- Government will no longer receive surpluses generated by state assets and, if these assets become foreign-owned, they will eventually impose a net foreign exchange cost on the economy due to interest/dividend payments. (For example, if they pay dividends of 10 per cent, then after ten years the inflow of currency achieved in the course of privatizing them will have been completely reversed.)

- Freeing up markets in economies with little tradition of free market activity may fail to produce markets that operate much like those in advanced industrial economies. As we saw in Chapter 2, well-functioning markets are complex sets of institutions and thus are unlikely to appear overnight, particularly if property rights are poorly defined and/or there are long traditions of resource allocation being affected by corruption and nepotism.

14.12 Summary

If a country receives less from exporting and from overseas income than it pays out on imports and as income to foreign workers and shareholders, then it needs an offsetting surplus of inflowing overseas funds to domestic bank accounts as deposits or payments for purchases of domestic assets. If the country's current account deficit is tending to exceed its capital/financial surplus, then the value of its currency will fall relative to other currencies due

14.12 **Summary** (continued)

to it being in excess supply relative to foreign demands for it. Although one country's current account surplus implies that it must have foreign exchange to lend to, or to buy assets from, another country that has a current account deficit, capital flows will depend on how borrowers and lenders see exchange risks and credit risks. If overseas lenders or potential borrowers are worried about growing indebtedness and exchange rate risks, capital flows may fail to occur, forcing debtor countries to reduce their imports and/or expand their exports. If they are unwilling to let this be induced by falls in their exchange rates, they will have to engineer reduced imports by cutting aggregate demand via fiscal or monetary policies.

Mainstream thinking opposes the use of import controls for reducing trade deficits and believes that microeconomic processes will sort them out if markets are allowed to work properly and exchange rates are allowed to adjust freely to bring about relative price adjustments that properly reflect differences in underlying cost conditions. The extent to which the fall in the country's exchange rate helps its trade balance by making exports more profitable and imports more expensive will depend on the importance of non-price factors in purchasing decisions. Countries whose firms are producing leading-edge products may continue to enjoy trade surpluses despite their exchange rates rising because their products dominate in non-price terms and are of a kind for which demand is highly income-elastic. In economies where firms have been falling behind in terms of innovation and other non-price dimensions, government will find it difficult to allow aggregate demand to rise steadily as this will tend to suck in imports and push down the exchange rate, adding to inflationary pressures. However, if international investors and speculators judge that the long-term prospects for such countries to improve their trade positions are promising, then inflows of funds from overseas may help these countries to keep up aggregate demand and profits without the exchange rate collapsing and industrial relations problems arising due to the impact of higher import prices on real wages.

Patterns of trade depend increasingly on sourcing decisions of multinational firms. The more mobile production is, the more that exchange rates, inflation control policies and government inducements will determine the profitability of international sourcing decisions. However, exchange rates depend not merely on trade and investment flows but also on massive speculative flows of money around the world as speculators chase prospects of

14.12 **Summary** (continued)

capital gain from currency appreciations. Firms can insure their cost and revenue streams against changes in exchange rates but from time to time speculators may run up enormous losses due to placing their bets on the wrong currencies. Defaults consequent on this may have adverse implications for the level of aggregate demand.

14.13 Some questions to consider

1. Do you think that British business would be better or worse off if the UK abandoned sterling and joined the euro currency area?

2. Examine the implications of the depletion of the UK's reserves of North Sea oil and gas over the next two decades for British firms and their international rivals.

3. Some of the cars made by Vauxhall and Opel, the European affiliates of General Motors, are exported to Australia carrying the badge of Holden, the Australian affiliate of General Motors. Examine the causal chains by which a drought of record-breaking duration in rural Australia could affect the volume of exports of these cars to Australia and employment in Europe.

4. Should European firms exporting to Australia be worried that the Australian balance of trade deficit is running at about 5 per cent of GDP? Should Australian firms exporting to the UK be worried that the UK's current account deficit has recently been around 2 per cent of GDP and reached as much as 4 per cent of GDP in 1999? Explain your reasoning.

5. Firms from developed countries that have won the right to operate privatized enterprises in developing countries have often made spectacular losses on these investments due to subsequent falls in the developing countries' exchange rates. If you had been advising a company that was thinking of bidding to run, say, water supply services in Argentina, what advice would you have given regarding how it might have grappled with this risk?

14.13 **Some questions to consider** (continued)

6. Imagine that New Zealand white goods manufacturer Fisher & Paykel has hired you as a consultant. Your brief is to help the firm resolve questions about when to enter or exit export markets whose profitability is greatly affected by exchange rate movements. What advice would you give? (Note: Fisher & Paykel makes technologically advanced refrigerators, washing machines, dishwashers, ovens and hobs in both New Zealand and Australia and exports to a number of markets, including the USA, the UK (beginning in 1999 with its top-end Quantum range, which is even sold in Harrods) and Singapore. It has also engaged in licensing its flexible manufacturing systems, for example to Costa Rica.)

14.14 Recommended additional reading sources

A very useful general text in this area (especially for UK readers) is Anthony P. Thirlwall and Heather D. Gibson (1991) *Balance of Payments Theory and the UK Experience,* London and Basingstoke, Palgrave Macmillan. Also useful is Part II of Nadia Tempini Macdonald (1999) *Macroeconomics and Business: An Interactive Approach,* London, Thomson Learning.

For a behavioural/evolutionary case study approach to understanding how firms adapt to exchange rate changes, see Peter M. Holmes (1978) *Industrial Pricing Behaviour and Devaluation,* London, Macmillan.

The classic reference on global business is Theodore Levitt's provocative 1983 article 'The globalization of markets', *Harvard Business Review*, May–June, pp. 92–102.

Leading contributors to the theory of the multinational enterprise share their perspectives in Christos N. Pitelis and Roger Sugden (eds) (1991) *The Nature of the Transnational Firm,* London, Routledge.

For macroeconomic examination of the declining relative efficiency of the UK economy during the 1970s, see Ajit Singh (1977) 'UK industry and the world economy: A case of de-industrialization?', *Cambridge Journal of Economics*, **1**, June, pp. 113–36.

A lucid case for using import controls to contain expansions of aggregate demand is made in Francis Cripps and Wynne Godley (1978) 'Control of imports as a means to full employment and the expansion of world trade: the UK's case', *Cambridge Journal of Economics*, **2**, September, pp. 327–34. See also Wynne Godley (1979) 'Britain's chronic recession: Can anything be done?', in Wilfred Beckerman (ed.) *Slow Growth in Britain*, Oxford, Oxford University Press.

The leading heterodox writers on the problems caused for countries by an inability to achieve export-led growth are Nicholas Kaldor and John Cornwall. An essential source is Nicholas Kaldor (1971) 'Conflicts in national economic objectives', *Economic Journal*, **81**, March, pp. 1–16. Kaldor exposed the limitations of currency depreciations as a tool for affecting trade in manufactured goods in Chapter 7 of his 1978 book *Further Essays on Applied Economics,* London, Duckworth. See also John Cornwall (1972) *Growth and Stability in a Mature Economy*, Oxford, Martin Robertson.

The problems and opportunities that rapid growth in hydrocarbon exports present for policy makers are discussed with a number of case studies in Terry Barker and Vladimir Brailovsky (eds) (1981) *Oil or Industry?* London, Academic Press.

For an optimistic view of the market's ability to prevent foreign debt from getting out of hand (in respect of a developed economy), see John D. Pitchford (1990) *Australia's Foreign Debt: Myths and Realities,* Sydney, Allen & Unwin. A much more pessimistic view (in respect of developing economies) is presented by Susan George (1989) *A Fate Worse than Debt* (rev. edn), London, Penguin. More generally on this topic, see Paul R. Krugman (1992) *Currencies and Crises,* Cambridge, MA, MIT Press.

For orthodox and dissenting perspectives on globalization and the impact of the WTO, IMF and World Bank, see, respectively, a best-seller by two of *The Economist's* writers, John Micklethwait and Adrian Wooldridge (2000) *A Future Perfect: The Challenge and Hidden Promise of Globalization,* New York, Crown Business, and Nobel Laureate Joseph E. Stiglitz (2002) *Globalization and its Discontents,* London, Allen Lane.

The China question (Box 14.1) is inspired by pp. 211–12 of Mark Lutz (1999) *Economics for the Common Good: Two Centuries of Social Economic Thought in the Humanistic Tradition*, London and New York, Routledge.

Index